파고다 토익 RC

실전 1000제

파고다 토익 RC 실전 1000제 개정판

초판　1쇄 발행　2020년　1월　2일
개정판 1쇄 인쇄　2023년　2월　3일
개정판 1쇄 발행　2023년　2월　3일
개정판 2쇄 발행　2024년　1월　19일

지 은 이 ｜ 파고다교육그룹 언어교육연구소
펴 낸 이 ｜ 박경실
펴 낸 곳 ｜ **PAGODA Books** 파고다북스
출판등록 ｜ 2005년 5월 27일 제 300-2005-90호
주　　소 ｜ 06614 서울특별시 서초구 강남대로 419, 19층(서초동, 파고다타워)
전　　화 ｜ (02) 6940-4070
팩　　스 ｜ (02) 536-0660
홈페이지 ｜ www.pagodabook.com

저작권자 ｜ ⓒ 2023 파고다아카데미

ISBN 978-89-6281-894-9 (13740)

파고다북스　　　www.pagodabook.com
파고다 어학원　　www.pagoda21.com
파고다 인강　　　www.pagodastar.com
테스트 클리닉　　www.testclinic.com

▎낙장 및 파본은 구매처에서 교환해 드립니다.

파고다 토익

실전 1000제

PAGODA Books

파고다 토익 프로그램

독학자를 위한 다양하고 풍부한 학습 자료

세상 간편한 등업 신청으로 각종 학습 자료가 쏟아지는

파고다 토익 공식 온라인 카페
http://cafe.naver.com/pagodatoeicbooks

교재 Q&A
교재 학습 자료
나의 학습 코칭
정기 토익 분석 자료
기출 분석 자료
예상 적중 특강
논란 종결 총평

- 온라인 모의고사 2회분
- 받아쓰기 훈련 자료
- 단어 암기장
- 단어 시험지
- MP3 기본 버전
- MP3 추가 버전(1.2배속 등)
- 추가 연습 문제 등 각종 추가 자료

매회 업데이트! 토익 학습 센터

시험 전 적중 문제, 특강 제공
시험 직후 실시간 정답, 총평 특강, 분석 자료집 제공

토익에 푿! 빠져 푿TV

파고다 대표 강사진과 전문 연구원들의 다양한 무료 강의를 들으실 수 있습니다.

파고다 토익 기본 완성 LC/RC
토익 기초 입문서
토익 초보 학습자들이 단기간에 쉽게 접근할 수 있도록 토익의 필수 개념을 집약한 입문서

600+

파고다 토익 실력 완성 LC/RC
토익 개념&실전 종합서
토익의 기본 개념을 확실히 다질 수 있는 풍부한 문제 유형과 실전형 연습 문제를 담은 훈련서

700+

파고다 토익 고득점 완성 LC/RC
최상위권 토익 만점 전략서
기본기를 충분히 다진 토익 중상위권들의 고득점 완성을 위해 핵심 스킬만을 뽑아낸 토익 전략서

800+

파고다 토익 입문서 LC/RC
기초와 최신 경향 문제 완벽 적응 입문서
개념-집중 훈련-실전 훈련의 반복을 통해 기초와 실전에서 유용한 전략을 동시에 익히는 입문서

파고다 토익 종합서 LC/RC
중상위권이 고득점으로 가는 도움 닫기 종합서
고득점 도약을 향한 한 끗 차이의 간격을 좁히는 종합서

목차

이 책의 구성과 특징

깜짝 놀랄 정도로 실제 시험과 똑같은 10회분 모의고사 문제집

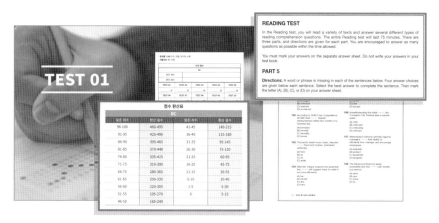

실제 정기 토익 시험과 100% 유사한 형태의 실전 모의고사

RC 100문항 10회분으로 토익 시험에 대비할 수 있도록 구성하였습니다. 각 TEST를 끝마치고 점수 환산표를 통해 자신의 점수를 파악하고 목표 점수를 설정할 수 있습니다.

두꺼운 해설서는 이제 No! 온라인 해설서 + 모바일 해설서 동시 제공!

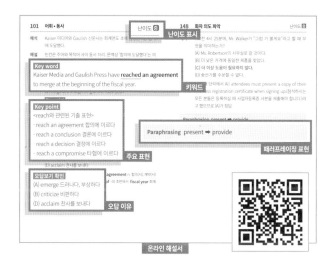

이해력을 200% 상승시키는 온라인 해설서

www.pagodabook.com

교재에 수록된 모든 문제의 답의 근거가 되는 문장을 함께 정리하였고, 정답과 오답의 근거를 쉽고 명확하게 파악하여 똑같은 실수를 반복하지 않도록 구성하였습니다. 또한, 문제 풀이에 필요한 어휘와 키워드 및 패러프레이징 표현 등을 제시하여 정답 적중률을 한층 더 높일 수 있습니다.

언제 어디서나 쉽게 확인이 가능한 모바일 해설서

이동하면서 언제 어디서나 쉽게 궁금한 문제의 해설을 찾아볼 수 있도록 모바일 해설서를 제공해 드립니다. 모바일 해설서 QR코드를 인식하여 접속하면 별도의 로그인이나 회원 가입 없이 바로 해설을 확인하실 수 있습니다.

토익이란?

TOEIC(Test of English for International Communication)은 영어가 모국어가 아닌 사람들을 대상으로 일상생활 또는 국제 업무 등에 필요한 실용 영어 능력을 평가하는 시험입니다.

상대방과 '의사소통할 수 있는 능력(Communication ability)'을 평가하는 데 중점을 두고 있으므로 영어에 대한 '지식'이 아니라 영어의 실용적이고 기능적인 '사용법'을 묻는 문항들이 출제됩니다.

TOEIC은 1979년 미국 ETS(Educational Testing Service)에 의해 개발된 이래 전 세계 160개 이상의 국가 14,000여 개의 기관에서 승진 또는 해외 파견 인원 선발 등의 목적으로 널리 활용하고 있으며 우리나라에는 1982년 도입되었습니다. 해마다 전 세계적으로 약 700만 명 이상이 응시하고 있습니다.

▶ 토익 시험의 구성

	파트	시험 형태		문항 수	시간	배점
듣기 (LC)	1	사진 묘사		6	45분	495점
	2	질의응답		25		
	3	짧은 대화		39	100	
	4	짧은 담화		30		
읽기 (RC)	5	단문 공란 메우기 (문법/어휘)		30	75분	495점
	6	장문 공란 메우기		16		
	7	독해	단일 지문	29	100	
			이중 지문	10		
			삼중 지문	15		
계	7 Parts			200문항	120분	990점

1979	첫 토익
2006	NEW 토익
2016	신 토익

Present

토익 시험 접수와 성적 확인

토익 시험은 TOEIC 위원회 웹사이트(www.toeic.co.kr)에서 접수할 수 있습니다. 본인이 원하는 날짜와 장소를 지정하고 필수 기재 항목을 기재한 후 본인 사진을 업로드하면 간단하게 끝납니다.

보통은 두 달 후에 있는 시험일까지 접수 가능합니다. 각 시험일의 정기 접수는 시험일로부터 2주 전에 마감되지만, 시험일의 3일 전까지 추가 접수할 수 있는 특별 접수 기간이 있습니다. 그러나 특별 추가 접수 기간에는 응시료가 4,800원 더 비싸며, 희망하는 시험장을 선택할 수 없는 경우도 발생할 수 있습니다.

성적은 시험일로부터 12~15일 후에 인터넷이나 ARS(060-800-0515)를 통해 확인할 수 있습니다.

성적표는 우편이나 온라인으로 발급받을 수 있습니다. 우편으로 발급 받을 경우는 성적 발표 후 대략 일주일이 소요되며, 온라인 발급을 선택 하면 유효 기간 내에 홈페이지에서 본인이 직접 1회에 한해 무료 출력할 수 있습니다.

시험 당일 준비물

시험 당일 준비물은 규정 신분증, 연필, 지우개입니다. 허용되는 규정 신분증은 토익 공식 웹사이트에서 확인하시기 바랍니다. 필기구는 연필 이나 샤프펜만 가능하고 볼펜이나 컴퓨터용 사인펜은 사용할 수 없습니다. 수험표는 출력해 가지 않아도 됩니다.

시험 진행 안내

시험 진행 일정은 시험 당일 고사장 사정에 따라 약간씩 다를 수 있지만 대부분 아래와 같이 진행됩니다.

▶ 시험 시간이 오전일 경우

AM 9:30~9:45	AM 9:45~9:50	AM 9:50~10:05	AM 10:05~10:10	AM 10:10~10:55	AM 10:55~12:10
15분	5분	15분	5분	45분	75분
답안지 작성에 관한 Orientation	수험자 휴식 시간	신분증 확인 (감독 교사)	문제지 배부, 파본 확인	듣기 평가(LC)	읽기 평가(RC) 2차 신분증 확인

* 주의: 오전 9시 50분 입실 통제

▶ 시험 시간이 오후일 경우

PM 2:30~2:45	PM 2:45~2:50	PM 2:50~3:05	PM 3:05~3:10	PM 3:10~3:55	PM 3:55~5:10
15분	5분	15분	5분	45분	75분
답안지 작성에 관한 Orientation	수험자 휴식 시간	신분증 확인 (감독 교사)	문제지 배부, 파본 확인	듣기 평가(LC)	읽기 평가(RC) 2차 신분증 확인

* 주의: 오후 2시 50분 입실 통제

파트별 토익 소개

PART 5

INCOMPLETE SENTENCES
단문 공란 메우기

PART 5는 빈칸이 포함된 짧은 문장과 4개의 보기를 주고 빈칸에 들어갈 가장 알맞은 보기를 고르는 문제로, 총 30문제가 출제된다. 크게 문장 구조/문법 문제와 어휘 문제로 문제 유형이 나뉜다.

문항 수	30개 문장, 30문항(101~130번에 해당합니다.)
문제 유형	- 문장 구조 / 문법 문제: 빈칸의 자리를 파악하여 보기 중 알맞은 품사나 형태를 고르는 문제와 문장의 구조를 파악하고 구와 절을 구분하여 빈칸에 알맞은 접속사나 전치사, 또는 부사 등을 고르는 문제 - 어휘 문제: 같은 품사의 4개 어휘 중에서 정확한 용례를 파악하여 빈칸에 알맞은 단어를 고르는 문제
보기 구성	4개의 보기

▶ 시험지에 인쇄되어 있는 모양

어형 문제
>>

101. If our request for new computer equipment receives ------, we are going to purchase 10 extra monitors.

(A) approval   (B) approved
(C) approve   (D) approves

어휘 문제
>>

102. After being employed at a Tokyo-based technology firm for two decades, Ms. Mayne ------ to Vancouver to start her own IT company.

(A) visited   (B) returned
(C) happened   (D) compared

문법 문제
>>

103. ------ the demand for the PFS-2x smartphone, production will be tripled next quarter.

(A) Even if   (B) Just as
(C) As a result of   (D) Moreover

정답 **101.**(A) **102.**(B) **103.**(C)

PART 6

TEXT COMPLETION
장문 공란 메우기

PART 6는 4개의 지문에 각각 4개의 문항이 나와 총 16문제가 출제되며, PART 5와 같은 문제이나, 문맥을 파악해 정답을 골라야 한다. 편지, 이메일 등의 다양한 지문이 출제되며, 크게 문장 구조/문법을 묻는 문제, 어휘 문제, 문장 선택 문제로 문제 유형이 나뉜다.

문항 수	4개 지문, 16문항(131~146번에 해당합니다.)
지문 유형	설명서, 편지, 이메일, 기사, 공지, 지시문, 광고, 회람, 발표문, 정보문 등
문제 유형	- 문장 구조 / 문법 문제: 문장 구조, 문맥상 어울리는 시제 등을 고르는 문제 - 어휘 문제: 같은 품사의 4개 어휘 중에서 문맥상 알맞은 단어를 고르는 문제 - 문장 선택 문제: 앞뒤 문맥을 파악하여 4개의 문장 중에서 알맞은 문장을 고르는 문제
보기 구성	4개의 보기

▶ 시험지에 인쇄되어 있는 모양

Questions 131-134 refer to the following e-mail.

To: sford@etnnet.com
From: customersupport@interhosptimes.ca
Date: July 1
Subject: Re: Your Subscription

Congratulations on becoming a reader of *International Hospitality Times*. ------- the plan you have subscribed to,
131.
you will not only have unlimited access to our online content, but you will also receive our hard copy edition each month. If you wish to ------- your subscription preferences, contact our Customer Support Center at +28 07896
132.
325422. Most ------- may also make updates to their accounts on our Web site at www.interhosptimes.ca. Please
133.
note that due to compatibility issues, it may not be possible for customers in certain countries to access their accounts online. -------. Your business is greatly appreciated.
134.

International Hospitality Times

문법 문제 >>	131. (A) Besides (B) As if (C) Under (D) Prior to	어형 문제 >>	133. (A) subscribe (B) subscriptions (C) subscribers (D) subscribing
어휘 문제 >>	132. (A) purchase (B) modify (C) collect (D) inform	문장 삽입 문제 >>	134. (A) We have branches in over 30 countries around the globe. (B) We provide online content that includes Web extras and archives. (C) We are working to make this service available to all readers soon. (D) We would like to remind you that your contract expires this month.

정답 **131.**(C) **132.**(B) **133.**(C) **134.**(C)

PART 7

READING COMPREHENSION
독해

PART 7은 단일·이중·삼중 지문을 읽고 그에 딸린 2~5문제를 푸는 형태로, 총 15개 지문, 54문제가 출제되어 RC 전체 문항의 절반 이상을 차지한다. 같은 의미의 패러프레이징된 표현에 주의하고, 문맥을 파악하는 연습을 한다. 키워드 파악은 문제 해결의 기본이다.

문항 수	15개 지문, 54문항 (147~200번에 해당합니다.)
지문 유형	- 단일 지문: 이메일, 편지, 문자 메시지, 온라인 채팅, 광고, 기사, 양식, 회람, 공지, 웹 페이지 등 - 이중 지문: 이메일/이메일, 기사/이메일, 웹 페이지/이메일 등 - 삼중 지문: 다양한 세 지문들의 조합
문제 유형	- 핵심 정보: 주제 또는 제목과 같이 가장 핵심적인 내용을 파악하는 문제 - 특정 정보: 세부 사항을 묻는 문제로, 모든 질문이 의문사로 시작하며 지문에서 질문의 키워드와 관련된 부분을 읽고 정답을 찾는 문제 - NOT: 지문을 읽는 동안 보기 중에서 지문의 내용과 일치하는 보기를 대조해서 소거하는 문제 - 추론: 지문의 내용을 바탕으로 전체 흐름을 이해하며 지문에 직접 언급되지 않은 사항을 추론하는 문제 - 화자 의도 파악: 화자의 의도를 묻는 문제로, 문자 메시지나 2인 형태의 대화로 출제되며 온라인 채팅은 3인 이상의 대화 형태로 출제 - 동의어: 주어진 단어의 사전적 의미가 아니라 문맥상의 의미와 가장 가까운 단어를 고르는 문제 - 문장 삽입: 지문의 흐름상 주어진 문장이 들어갈 적절한 위치를 고르는 문제로, 세부적인 정보보다 전체적인 문맥 파악이 중요한 문제
보기 구성	4개의 보기

▶ 시험지에 인쇄되어 있는 모양

Questions 151-152 refer to the following text message chain.

Naijia Kuti 12:02 P.M.	
My bus to Ibadan was canceled due to engine problems, and all other buses to that city are full. I don't know if I can give my presentation at the history conference. What should I do?	
	Adebiyi Achebe 12:04 P.M.
	Not to worry. I'll come pick you up in my car.
Naijia Kuti 12:05 P.M.	
I appreciate it! My seminar starts at 5 P.M. As long as we depart from Lagos by 1:30, I'll be able to make it on time.	
	Adebiyi Achebe 12:07 P.M.
	Where should I go?
Naijia Kuti 12:08 P.M.	
In front of La Pointe Restaurant, near Terminal Rodoviario. Call me when you're getting close.	

화자 의도 파악 문제 ≫

151. At 12:04 P.M., what does Mr. Achebe most likely mean when he writes, "Not to worry"?
(A) He has a solution to Ms. Kuti's problem.
(B) He can reschedule a presentation.
(C) He knows another bus will arrive soon.
(D) He is happy to cover Ms. Kuti's shift.

세부 사항 문제 ≫

152. What is implied about Ms. Kuti?
(A) She has a meeting at a restaurant.
(B) She is going to be late for a seminar.
(C) She plans to pick up a client at 1:30 P.M.
(D) She is within driving distance of a conference.

정답 **151.**(A) **152.**(D)

Questions 158-160 refer to the following Web page.

http://www.sdayrealestate.com/listing18293

Looking for a new home for your family? This house, located on 18293 Winding Grove, was remodeled last month. It features 2,500 square feet of floor space, with 5,000 square feet devoted to a gorgeous backyard. Also included is a 625 square feet garage that can comfortably fit two mid-sized vehicles. —[1]—. Located just a five-minute drive from the Fairweather Metro Station, this property allows for easy access to the downtown area, while providing plenty of room for you and your family. —[2]—. A serene lake is just 100-feet walk away from the house. —[3]—. A 15 percent down payment is required to secure the property. —[4]—. For more detailed information or to arrange a showing, please email Jerry@sdayrealestate.com.

세부 사항 문제 ≫

158. How large is the parking space?
(A) 100 square feet
(B) 625 square feet
(C) 2,500 square feet
(D) 5,000 square feet

사실 확인 문제 ≫

159. What is NOT stated as an advantage of the property?
(A) It has a spacious design.
(B) It has been recently renovated.
(C) It is in a quiet neighborhood.
(D) It is near public transportation.

문장 삽입 문제 ≫

160. In which of the positions marked [1], [2], [3], and [4] does the following sentence best belong?

"A smaller amount may be accepted, depending on the buyer's financial circumstances."

(A) [1]
(B) [2]
(C) [3]
(D) [4]

정답 **158.**(B) **159.**(C) **160.**(D)

TEST 01

준비물: OMR 카드, 연필, 지우개, 시계
시험시간: RC 75분

<table>
<tr><th colspan="2">나의 점수</th></tr>
<tr><td colspan="2" align="center">RC</td></tr>
<tr><td align="center">맞은 개수</td><td></td></tr>
<tr><td align="center">환산 점수</td><td></td></tr>
</table>

TEST 01	TEST 02	TEST 03	TEST 04	TEST 05
_____점	_____점	_____점	_____점	_____점
TEST 06	**TEST 07**	**TEST 08**	**TEST 09**	**TEST 10**
_____점	_____점	_____점	_____점	_____점

점수 환산표

RC			
맞은 개수	환산 점수	맞은 개수	환산 점수
96-100	460-495	41-45	140-215
91-95	425-490	36-40	115-180
86-90	395-465	31-35	95-145
81-85	370-440	26-30	75-120
76-80	335-415	21-25	60-95
71-75	310-390	16-20	45-75
66-70	280-365	11-15	30-55
61-65	250-335	6-10	10-40
56-60	220-305	1-5	5-30
51-55	195-270	0	5-15
46-50	165-240		

READING TEST

In the Reading test, you will read a variety of texts and answer several different types of reading comprehension questions. The entire Reading test will last 75 minutes. There are three parts, and directions are given for each part. You are encouraged to answer as many questions as possible within the time allowed.

You must mark your answers on the separate answer sheet. Do not write your answers in your test book.

PART 5

Directions: A word or phrase is missing in each of the sentences below. Four answer choices are given below each sentence. Select the best answer to complete the sentence. Then mark the letter (A), (B), (C), or (D) on your answer sheet.

101. Kaiser Media and Gaulish Press have ------- an agreement to merge at the beginning of the fiscal year.

(A) emerged
(B) criticized
(C) reached
(D) acclaimed

102. According to GHM Corp.'s regulations, all staff must ------- request reimbursement within two months of a business trip.

(A) formalize
(B) formally
(C) formality
(D) formal

103. The band's latest music video, directed ------- Raymond Howles, premiered yesterday.

(A) from
(B) up
(C) by
(D) aside

104. After Ms. Kitigoe inspects the assembly line, ------- will suggest ways to make it run more efficiently.

(A) her
(B) herself
(C) she
(D) hers

105. The elevators may be used at all times, ------- in the case of an emergency.

(A) and
(B) when
(C) few
(D) except

106. Notwithstanding the initial -------, the Covington City Festival was a popular event.

(A) critic
(B) criticized
(C) criticizing
(D) criticism

107. Wednesday's seminar will help regional managers ------- their ability to efficiently hire, manage, and encourage employees.

(A) evaluate
(B) protect
(C) assemble
(D) progress

108. The Silvercove Resort is easily accessible and has ------- own shuttle bus service.

(A) each
(B) one
(C) other
(D) its

109. The owner of the Mountaindell Bed and Breakfast ------- responds to all reviews that visitors post on the Internet.

(A) slightly
(B) personally
(C) approximately
(D) recklessly

110. The Van Tassel Media is rather small in comparison to other production companies, but its documentary films are ------- among the best in the country.

(A) argued
(B) arguable
(C) argument
(D) arguably

111. You are welcome to catch us at this spring's West Music Festival, ------- our newest song will be performed for the first time.

(A) thus
(B) together
(C) where
(D) resulting

112. Somoza Ltd.'s marketing department will implement new digital strategies to increase the ------- of our online presence.

(A) impact
(B) impacted
(C) impactful
(D) impactive

113. The president of Rocket Bikes sent an e-mail to his factory workers ------- them for the rapid production run.

(A) advancing
(B) substituting
(C) distributing
(D) complimenting

114. Because of missing permits, Ms. Cheung ------- the application to construct a new building on the property.

(A) rejected
(B) reject
(C) was rejected
(D) will be rejected

115. It is helpful to track ------- employee's days off on the same calendar.

(A) when
(B) each
(C) which
(D) anyone

116. No one at Shackleton Incorporated lobbied ------- for the construction of the company parking lot than Garrett Nguyen.

(A) eagerly
(B) more eagerly
(C) more eager
(D) eager

117. Because the Internet connection at the office was not fast -------, employees could not watch the live video feed of the CEO's speech.

(A) either
(B) enough
(C) around
(D) almost

118. ------- predicting what your sales demand will be, remember to include a margin of error.

(A) When
(B) Since
(C) During
(D) Either

119. As our local supplier did not have the raw materials we required on site, we ordered them from a larger provider -------.

(A) alike
(B) rather
(C) though
(D) instead

120. Over the next few months, the company executive ------- to see the profits predicted by the Corporate Strategy Department.

(A) hoping
(B) hopefully
(C) hopes
(D) hoped

GO ON TO THE NEXT PAGE

121. Students are required to check in with their guidance counselors on a monthly -------.

(A) basis
(B) conference
(C) announcement
(D) length

122. After a careful probe of the artist's replica alongside the original, the critic was able to classify the ------- attributes of both.

(A) distinguish
(B) distinguished
(C) distinguishes
(D) distinguishing

123. Signs for the promotion may start being displayed this week, but they must be ------- on the last day of the sale.

(A) broken off
(B) wiped out
(C) used up
(D) taken down

124. Regardless of ------- a proposal is selected for a project, all submissions are kept in the database for two years.

(A) which
(B) even
(C) any
(D) whether

125. Please keep this file securely stored because ------- sensitive personal data about our clients.

(A) one containing
(B) a container of
(C) it contains
(D) to contain

126. Epperson Photo Library ------- features more than ten thousand photographs, and it will keep on growing as new ones are uploaded.

(A) least
(B) plenty
(C) already
(D) alike

127. ------- the Tyson Center for Business Research, allowing employees to choose a flexible schedule improves work performance.

(A) Except for
(B) According to
(C) In regard to
(D) Because of

128. Barnum F&B's mission is to produce the highest quality food products yet ------- them affordable.

(A) keeping
(B) kept
(C) keeps
(D) keep

129. The Saturday broadcast of the local news channel will include an ------- interview with the sports star Steffanie Grove.

(A) indifferent
(B) assertive
(C) exclusive
(D) intermittent

130. Interest rates have dropped, leading to a sudden ------- in the number of people seeking to purchase a property.

(A) objective
(B) unrest
(C) surge
(D) referral

PART 6

Directions: Read the texts that follow. A word, phrase, or sentence is missing in parts of each text. Four answer choices for each question are given below the text. Select the best answer to complete the text. Then mark the letter (A), (B), (C), or (D) on your answer sheet.

Questions 131-134 refer to the following notice.

Dear Valued Customers,

We regretfully announce that this Sunday, July 12, will be your last opportunity ------- a
                                                                                    131.
cup of coffee at Fresh 'n Fragrant's Gardner location. We would like to extend our
deepest gratitude for your business over the years. We will ------- being a spot for
                                                             132.
Gardner residents to recharge during busy workdays. However, we will continue to
operate out of our Lake Shore and Mahwah locations. --------.
                                                     133.

Thank you once again for your continued ------- during our time here. It has truly been
                                         134.
an incredible journey, and we could not have done it without you.

Fresh 'n Fragrant Management

131. (A) enjoy
(B) to enjoy
(C) enjoyed
(D) enjoying

132. (A) miss
(B) explore
(C) initiate
(D) respect

133. (A) Application forms can be
downloaded from our website.
(B) A new menu will be unveiled once
the renovations are done.
(C) We hope to continue serving you all
at our remaining locations.
(D) Please notify our team immediately if
your order is incorrect.

134. (A) supported
(B) supportive
(C) support
(D) supporting

GO ON TO THE NEXT PAGE

Questions 135-138 refer to the following e-mail.

To: vasquez@watertown.gov
From: shenderson@bryantconsulting.com
Date: December 3
Subject: website feedback
Attachment: Analysis

Ms. Vasquez,

I have compiled a summary of my colleagues' thoughts on your city's municipal website in the space below.

Overall, they thought it was not as ------- as it could be. It would be helpful to
          135.
streamline the design, simplifying its appearance for ease of use. They also noticed some bugs appearing persistently ------- the site, causing pages to load very slowly.
                                          136.

They also recommended supplementing the photos used on the front page. -------.
                                                                              137.
Accordingly, it would be a good use of resources to post some brief, professional looking videos that guide users on how to use the website. -------, they have
                                                                  138.
recommended adding a live chat feature that allows users to ask for help in real-time.

Let me know if you have any questions.

Sincerely,

Spencer Henderson

---

135. (A) effectively
(B) effective
(C) effecting
(D) effectiveness

136. (A) throughout
(B) forward
(C) over
(D) against

137. (A) These photos need to be posted in higher resolution.
(B) Without a proper file-naming protocol, the image files become disorganized.
(C) The photos don't look like they were taken by a professional photographer.
(D) It is difficult to keep users engaged with images alone.

138. (A) To be clear
(B) As a result
(C) Nonetheless
(D) In addition

July 16

Derek Hunter
Personnel Department
Milltek Systems, Inc.

Dear Mr. Hunter,

I would like to inquire about the engineering manager opening recently posted on your website. I am confident that I would be a valuable addition to Milltek Systems' engineering ------- as a supervisor.
139.

-------. I am presently employed as a project manager at Tappco Machinery, and I have
140.
designed agricultural and industrial sorting machinery for nearly a decade. ------- to
141.
this, I worked at AgroTec Engineering, where I developed computerized processes for milling and baking applications.

I have attached a copy of my CV, which ------- more information about my experience
142.
and qualifications. If you agree that these are a good match for your organization, I would love to meet and discuss them further.

Best Regards,

Edwin Dearing
Enclosure

---

139. (A) design
(B) quality
(C) proposal
(D) team

140. (A) I have many years of experience in relevant industries.
(B) You mentioned that an engineering degree is required for this job.
(C) You should have received several e-mails from my former coworkers.
(D) Please let me know if a more suitable position becomes available.

141. (A) Following
(B) Prior
(C) Similar
(D) Considering

142. (A) provide
(B) provides
(C) provided
(D) is providing

GO ON TO THE NEXT PAGE

Questions 143-146 refer to the following article.

Celtzer Goods Surpasses Optimistic Goal

CHASTANG (19 March) — Celtzer Goods has secured space to open its fiftieth location on 26 March. Its newest ------- is opposite New Lynn Mall on Southgate Grove. To
                               143.
commemorate passing a historic milestone, events, including live music and other entertainment, are scheduled. No need to worry for residents outside of Chastang. All Celtzer locations ------- the country will be holding their own celebration event. At every
                        144.
location, there will also be a range of prizes, including gift cards and goodie bags.

Celtzer Goods was founded 50 years ago by Simon Celtzer with a simple mission to start his own store in Australia. ------- aim has now expanded to cover New Zealand as
                                145.
well as Britain. -------.
         146.

---

143. (A) state
(B) factory
(C) resource
(D) store

144. (A) throughout
(B) into
(C) toward
(D) before

145. (A) What
(B) They
(C) That
(D) When

146. (A) For an application form, ask any of our employees.
(B) Celtzer Goods is looking to enter new markets soon.
(C) Early entrances may be possible with advance notice.
(D) The cost of exports has risen over the years.

PART 7

Directions: In this part you will read a selection of texts, such as magazine and newspaper articles, e-mails, and instant messages. Each text or set of texts is followed by several questions. Select the best answer for each question and mark the letter (A), (B), (C), or (D) on your answer sheet.

Questions 147-148 refer to the following online chat discussion.

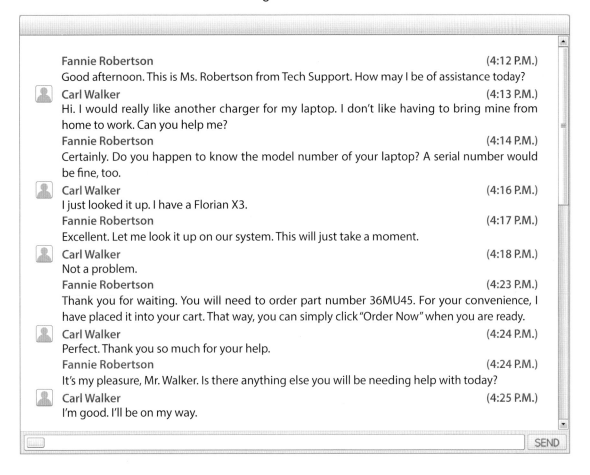

Fannie Robertson (4:12 P.M.)
Good afternoon. This is Ms. Robertson from Tech Support. How may I be of assistance today?

Carl Walker (4:13 P.M.)
Hi. I would really like another charger for my laptop. I don't like having to bring mine from home to work. Can you help me?

Fannie Robertson (4:14 P.M.)
Certainly. Do you happen to know the model number of your laptop? A serial number would be fine, too.

Carl Walker (4:16 P.M.)
I just looked it up. I have a Florian X3.

Fannie Robertson (4:17 P.M.)
Excellent. Let me look it up on our system. This will just take a moment.

Carl Walker (4:18 P.M.)
Not a problem.

Fannie Robertson (4:23 P.M.)
Thank you for waiting. You will need to order part number 36MU45. For your convenience, I have placed it into your cart. That way, you can simply click "Order Now" when you are ready.

Carl Walker (4:24 P.M.)
Perfect. Thank you so much for your help.

Fannie Robertson (4:24 P.M.)
It's my pleasure, Mr. Walker. Is there anything else you will be needing help with today?

Carl Walker (4:25 P.M.)
I'm good. I'll be on my way.

SEND

147. Why does Mr. Walker want to order a laptop charger?

(A) He has misplaced his charger.
(B) He will need one for an upcoming business trip.
(C) He intends to gift it to a colleague.
(D) He would like to leave one at his office.

148. At 4:25 P.M., what does Mr. Walker mean when he writes, "I'll be on my way"?

(A) He will be heading into Ms. Robertson's office.
(B) He has found the same product at a lower price.
(C) He does not require assistance anymore.
(D) He is unable to order the charger.

GO ON TO THE NEXT PAGE

Max Ortiz, Freelance Photographer

· Award-winning photographer for Ashford magazine
· Specializing in immortalizing life's most special personal or professional moments
· Expert at most commonly-used photo-editing software

For any questions or inquiries, call 715-555-4896
or send an e-mail to me@ortizservices.com.
View my complete career history as well as the awards I have received
at www.ortizservices.com/biography.

---

149. What does Mr. Ortiz most likely photograph?

(A) Restaurant food
(B) Historic landmarks
(C) Corporate events
(D) Wild animals

150. According to the business card, what can be found on Mr. Ortiz's website?

(A) An interview
(B) Software manuals
(C) A detailed schedule
(D) His work history

Questions 151-153 refer to the following e-mail.

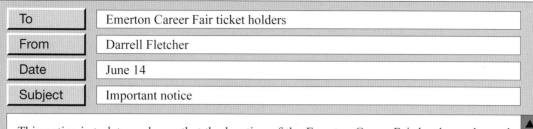

To	Emerton Career Fair ticket holders
From	Darrell Fletcher
Date	June 14
Subject	Important notice

This notice is to let you know that the location of the Emerton Career Fair has been changed due to the sudden spike in attendance. The new venue will now be at the convention hall located next to the train station. We apologize for any inconvenience caused.

Emerton Career Fair, which takes place on July 5, is a great opportunity for students and adults alike to meet recruiters and business owners. Leading companies will all be in attendance. It is a great way to build your professional network while also learning about new, emerging roles at companies.

There will be buses that will transport attendants from certain neighboring suburbs to the venue. To see if your suburb is included, go to www.emertoncity.gov/careerfair and download the bus route. Tickets are still on sale for $25 on our website. If you would like to pay with cash, you will need to come to Emerton Town Hall. Refunds for purchased tickets are subject to conditions.

Sincerely,

Darrell Fletcher
Events Coordinator

151. What is the purpose of the e-mail?

(A) To announce a change in location
(B) To conduct an informal survey
(C) To inform people of a rule change
(D) To advertise a new business

152. According to the e-mail, who should go to Emerton Town Hall?

(A) People who run their own businesses
(B) People who have experience in event planning
(C) People who want to purchase a ticket with cash
(D) People who would like to bring an acquaintance

153. The phrase "subject to" in paragraph 3, line 4, is closest in meaning to

(A) considered as
(B) exclusive of
(C) distinct from
(D) dependent on

GO ON TO THE NEXT PAGE

Questions 154-155 refer to the following advertisement.

Bee Knee Music School
2/30 Jellicoe Lane, Causeway Street
Rutherford, NC 28018

It is never too late to learn a new instrument. Bee Knee Music School welcomes learners of all ages to its offering of piano, violin, and guitar lessons. You don't need to own an instrument—simply come to our studio and borrow one of ours. Our current package provides workshops, lessons, and some studio time in our practice rooms for you to hone your skills.

Children twelve and under:
· Group lessons for the piano or violin at the beginner level. Each lesson lasts 30 minutes and group sizes are capped at six children.

Teenagers and adults:
· One-on-one lessons for beginners to the piano, violin, or guitar. Each lesson lasts 45 minutes.
· For advanced students, please contact us, and we can find an appropriate tutor for you.

Visit www.beekneeschool.com to start your music journey today.

154. What is indicated about Bee Knee Music School?

(A) It uses a new teaching method.
(B) It provides instruments to its students.
(C) It also offers lessons through its online platform.
(D) It specializes in preparing students for competitions.

155. What is offered to adult learners at the beginner level?

(A) A lesson at their residence
(B) A series of books for adult learners
(C) A credentialed mentor
(D) A 45-minute one-to-one lesson

Questions 156-158 refer to the following notice.

NOTICE: SPRING CONCERT UPDATE

With the additional promotions we have done for the concert this year, we are expecting a turnout of nearly 1,200 people. Based on this, our conductor has made the decision to change venues as the current venue can only seat 1,000. We will be providing details on the new location as soon as we receive confirmation. Also, there will be some new faces joining us for the performance. We are cooperating with Chatham City Orchestra, and they would like some of their members to be part of the performance. They are all very experienced, so we are looking forward to seeing what they can bring to the table. Additionally, we will be sending out the official program shortly. If you have not received it by the end of the week, please e-mail kbazemore@ popilorc.com. Finally, we have a staff meeting coming up on Friday. We'd like everyone to come to the meeting with a list of preferred dates they would like to practice on. That way, we can save a lot of time during the meeting.

---

156. For whom is the notice written?

(A) Orchestra members
(B) Government employees
(C) Performance attendees
(D) Event coordinators

157. What is indicated in the notice?

(A) The price of the event has been lowered this year.
(B) The original venue is too small for the expected crowd.
(C) The proposed program has been performed before.
(D) The performance is part of a charity event.

158. What topic will likely be discussed at the meeting on Friday?

(A) Volunteers to set up the stage
(B) Potential practice dates
(C) Nominations for a venue
(D) Event catering arrangements

GO ON TO THE NEXT PAGE

Questions 159-160 refer to the following Web page.

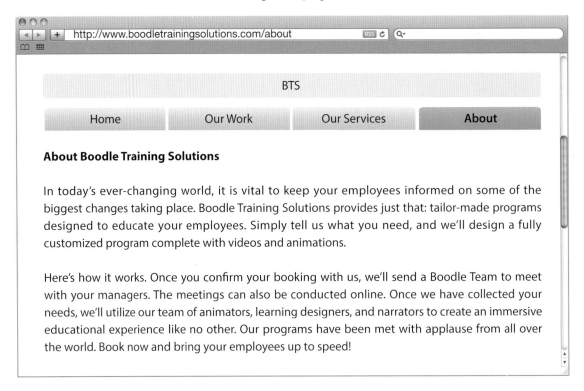

In today's ever-changing world, it is vital to keep your employees informed on some of the biggest changes taking place. Boodle Training Solutions provides just that: tailor-made programs designed to educate your employees. Simply tell us what you need, and we'll design a fully customized program complete with videos and animations.

Here's how it works. Once you confirm your booking with us, we'll send a Boodle Team to meet with your managers. The meetings can also be conducted online. Once we have collected your needs, we'll utilize our team of animators, learning designers, and narrators to create an immersive educational experience like no other. Our programs have been met with applause from all over the world. Book now and bring your employees up to speed!

159. According to the Web page, why should a company use BTS's programs?

(A) To improve employee morale in the workplace
(B) To increase profitability by increasing prices
(C) To keep employees informed on changes
(D) To understand the process of decision-making

160. What is NOT suggested about BTS?

(A) It has had international clients in the past.
(B) It is a relatively new company.
(C) It sends a team to its clients to determine needs.
(D) It provides its services in a digital format.

Questions 161-163 refer to the following e-mail.

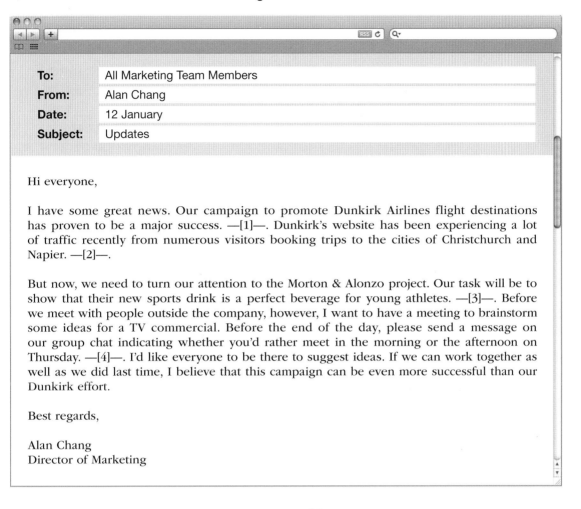

To: All Marketing Team Members
From: Alan Chang
Date: 12 January
Subject: Updates

Hi everyone,

I have some great news. Our campaign to promote Dunkirk Airlines flight destinations has proven to be a major success. —[1]—. Dunkirk's website has been experiencing a lot of traffic recently from numerous visitors booking trips to the cities of Christchurch and Napier. —[2]—.

But now, we need to turn our attention to the Morton & Alonzo project. Our task will be to show that their new sports drink is a perfect beverage for young athletes. —[3]—. Before we meet with people outside the company, however, I want to have a meeting to brainstorm some ideas for a TV commercial. Before the end of the day, please send a message on our group chat indicating whether you'd rather meet in the morning or the afternoon on Thursday. —[4]—. I'd like everyone to be there to suggest ideas. If we can work together as well as we did last time, I believe that this campaign can be even more successful than our Dunkirk effort.

Best regards,

Alan Chang
Director of Marketing

161. What is indicated as evidence that the Dunkirk Airline campaign was a success?

(A) An increase in membership subscriptions
(B) The number of positive customer testimonials
(C) The volume of vacation bookings
(D) A decrease in airline fares

162. What does Mr. Chang request that the marketing employees do?

(A) Develop a survey
(B) Confirm their availability
(C) Contact a travel agency
(D) Read a consumer report

163. In which of the positions marked [1], [2], [3], and [4] does the following sentence best belong?

"For this purpose, we plan to interview both athletes and nutritional consultants."

(A) [1]
(B) [2]
(C) [3]
(D) [4]

GO ON TO THE NEXT PAGE

Questions 164-167 refer to the following online chat discussion.

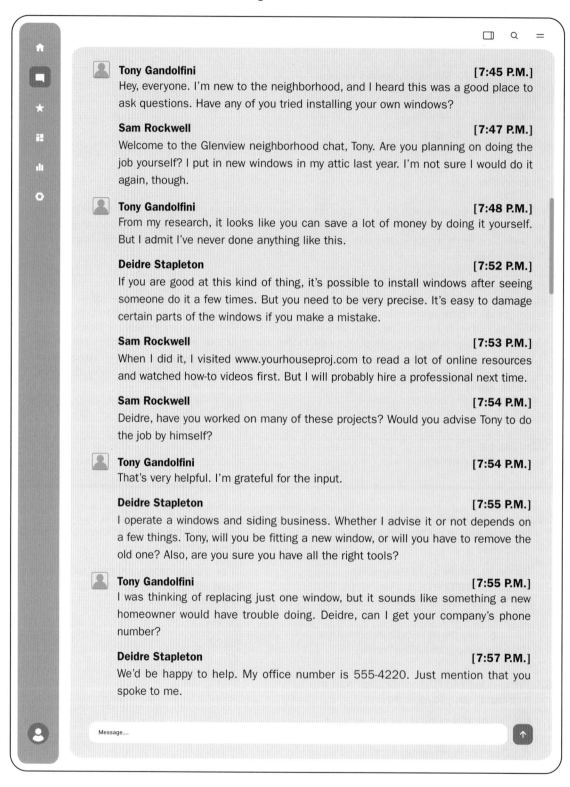

Tony Gandolfini [7:45 P.M.]

Hey, everyone. I'm new to the neighborhood, and I heard this was a good place to ask questions. Have any of you tried installing your own windows?

Sam Rockwell [7:47 P.M.]

Welcome to the Glenview neighborhood chat, Tony. Are you planning on doing the job yourself? I put in new windows in my attic last year. I'm not sure I would do it again, though.

Tony Gandolfini [7:48 P.M.]

From my research, it looks like you can save a lot of money by doing it yourself. But I admit I've never done anything like this.

Deidre Stapleton [7:52 P.M.]

If you are good at this kind of thing, it's possible to install windows after seeing someone do it a few times. But you need to be very precise. It's easy to damage certain parts of the windows if you make a mistake.

Sam Rockwell [7:53 P.M.]

When I did it, I visited www.yourhouseproj.com to read a lot of online resources and watched how-to videos first. But I will probably hire a professional next time.

Sam Rockwell [7:54 P.M.]

Deidre, have you worked on many of these projects? Would you advise Tony to do the job by himself?

Tony Gandolfini [7:54 P.M.]

That's very helpful. I'm grateful for the input.

Deidre Stapleton [7:55 P.M.]

I operate a windows and siding business. Whether I advise it or not depends on a few things. Tony, will you be fitting a new window, or will you have to remove the old one? Also, are you sure you have all the right tools?

Tony Gandolfini [7:55 P.M.]

I was thinking of replacing just one window, but it sounds like something a new homeowner would have trouble doing. Deidre, can I get your company's phone number?

Deidre Stapleton [7:57 P.M.]

We'd be happy to help. My office number is 555-4220. Just mention that you spoke to me.

Message....

164. For whom is the chat room intended?

(A) People who will go on vacation together
(B) People who work in the same office
(C) People who take the same course
(D) People who live in the same area

165. At 7:47 P.M., what does Mr. Rockwell most likely mean when he writes, "I'm not sure I would do it again, though"?

(A) He regrets not hiring a professional.
(B) He thought a project cost too much money.
(C) He purchased some unreliable materials.
(D) He needs to redecorate his home.

166. What is most likely true about Ms. Stapleton?

(A) She works with Mr. Gandolfini.
(B) She is experienced with window installations.
(C) She regularly uploads videos to www.yourhouseproj.com.
(D) She is a new homeowner.

167. What will Mr. Gandolfini probably do next?

(A) Exchange a damaged window
(B) Watch an instructional video
(C) Call a business
(D) Review a price estimate

GO ON TO THE NEXT PAGE

Questions 168-171 refer to the following article.

Compared to other music instructors, Herbert McGraw is truly unique. After spending most of his career as a successful attorney with Roth & Stein Associates, he suddenly turned his attention to music. —[1]—. McGraw struggled to keep up as an elementary school student. But starting in middle school, his school's music program caught his interest. His passion for music also helped him improve his focus on academic studies. So, when he learned that the school district from his hometown had cut all of the music programs from its budget, he knew he had to do something. —[2]—. That "something" became his music studio, To the Beat.

The music studio is located in the heart of the city, making it easily accessible to students in the area. Best of all, McGraw provides everything to the students for free.

—[3]—. McGraw's studio is stocked with instruments of nearly every kind imaginable, and students are encouraged to pick them up and play. Every day, To the Beat offers kids the opportunity to discover their talents and express themselves through music. "I was upset when I heard that the schools in my hometown were getting rid of their music programs," said McGraw. "I know from experience that music teaches important skills for school and for life. I just hope that I can find a way to finance this for the long term—that part won't be easy." —[4]—.

The award-winning band, The Jamming Camels, heard about McGraw's efforts to help these kids. To show their support, they have donated an undisclosed amount to McGraw and To the Beat music studio.

168. Where did Herbert McGraw start his professional life?

(A) In the advertising business
(B) In the legal field
(C) In the music industry
(D) In the education sector

169. What has changed in Herbert McGraw's hometown?

(A) The number of tourists
(B) The number of school programs
(C) The costs of some properties
(D) The size of the community's population

170. What is true about To the Beat?

(A) It recently hired Roth & Stein Associates.
(B) It has received some funding from The Jamming Camels.
(C) It will donate supplies to a local school district.
(D) It will record an album with an award-winning band.

171. In which of the marked [1], [2], [3], and [4] does the following sentence best belong?

"Now, however, help has arrived from an unexpected source."

(A) [1]
(B) [2]
(C) [3]
(D) [4]

GO ON TO THE NEXT PAGE

Questions 172-175 refer to the following job advertisement.

Bekai Boutique is Hiring

Bekai Boutique offers much more than just a job. As the state's most trusted supplier of high-end clothes, a job with us means a fulfilling career. Find out why we are consistently awarded prizes for upholding the highest standards of employee care. We are hiring for the following positions:

Store Manager: Responsibilities include overseeing general operations of the store, planning and executing promotions and events, listening to and dealing with customer complaints, liaising with headquarters, and training staff. Full-time, Tuesday-Saturday.

Inventory Specialist: Responsibilities include recording inventory levels, ordering supplies as required, unpacking orders on a per-need basis, and general warehouse-cleaning duties. Part-time, weekends required.

Interior Designer: Responsibilities include decorating the store to fit monthly themes and changing up the displays every week. Prior experience at a clothing store is preferred. Requirement: must have own car and driver's license. Some overtime may be required during seasonal promotions.

Sales Clerk: Responsibilities include interacting with customers, assisting customers with finding and purchasing products, and working with the cashiers. Part-time, Monday-Friday.

All of our positions offer competitive salaries as well as flexibility in scheduling. If interested, please send a resume and cover letter to Jim Richardson at jrichardson@bekai.com.

172. What does the advertisement mention about Bekai Boutique?

(A) It has been recognized as a good employer.
(B) It intends to expand its product line.
(C) It recently changed its management team.
(D) It has operations in other countries.

173. What is NOT listed as a responsibility of a store manager?

(A) Resolving customer issues
(B) Ordering new inventory
(C) Running special events
(D) Communicating with other employees

174. What is suggested about interior designers at Bekai Boutique?

(A) They take suggestions from customers.
(B) They must learn to use special software.
(C) They may have to travel often.
(D) They work shorter hours than other positions.

175. What is indicated about all the advertised positions?

(A) They can cater to different schedules.
(B) They are entitled to holiday bonuses.
(C) They are full-time positions.
(D) They receive paid time off.

GO ON TO THE NEXT PAGE

Questions 176-180 refer to the following Web page and e-mail.

Huntsdale Botanical Garden Guide

Thanks for visiting! Just a short walk from Grand Central Station and our city's most popular hotels and restaurants, the Huntsdale Botanical Garden offers guests a great way to relax and explore the beauty of nature without having to leave the city. Tours are also available for those who would like to get the most from their visit. There's plenty of onsite parking for both cars and bicycles. And why not stay for lunch at our own Garden Buffet salad bar?

Prices:

Admission Level	Price	Access
General	$5	Main Garden and Greenhouse
Deluxe	$10	General Admission + Japanese Garden Tour
Executive	$15	Deluxe Admission + Organic Farm Tour
VIP	$25	Executive Admission + Wildlife Show

Wildlife Shows:
Meet a Cheetah: Big Cats in the Big City (January – March)
Coyote Beautiful: Coyotes, Foxes, and Wolves (April – June)
The Great Escape: Gorillas, Chimpanzees, and the Orlando Orangutan (July – September)
The Park After Dark: Nocturnal Animals of the Desert (October – December)

To: HPers@huntsdalegarden.org
From: Damian@indioschools.edu
Date: November 6
Subject: Planned visit

Dear Mr. Pers,

I am Leticia Damian, organizer of the Indio Middle School Nature Club (IMSNC). As you might guess from the name, our club seeks to increase young students' awareness of the natural world and ecological issues that face it.

We plan to visit your botanical garden on November 22. At this time, we know that at least 20 members plan to attend, and those individuals have expressed interest in touring the Japanese Garden and the on-site Organic Farm.

I wanted to confirm that we would have access to these areas as part of the tour we arranged. We also hope to see the current wildlife show, if one is scheduled. Please advise which type of ticket we should purchase to ensure that these conditions are met.

Best Regards,

Leticia Damian
Faculty Mentor, IMSNC

176. What is implied about the Huntsdale Botanical Garden?

(A) It has recently opened a restaurant.
(B) It offers discounts for large groups.
(C) It is in a convenient location.
(D) It allows bicycle tours.

177. What is the purpose of the e-mail?

(A) To inquire about tour options
(B) To announce the founding of a club
(C) To reschedule a visit
(D) To explain Ms. Damian's role as a faculty mentor

178. According to Ms. Damian, what is IMSNC?

(A) An entertainment program
(B) A government department
(C) A student exchange agency
(D) An environmental education group

179. Which type of admission will IMSNC most likely choose?

(A) General
(B) Deluxe
(C) Executive
(D) VIP

180. Which show will the IMSNC members most likely see?

(A) Meet a Cheetah
(B) Coyote Beautiful
(C) The Great Escape
(D) The Park After Dark

GO ON TO THE NEXT PAGE

Ratdom Limited

PURCHASING PROCESS

The following steps must be followed in order when placing orders on behalf of Ratdom Limited.

Step 1: Scope out needs, including specifications, quantity, frequency of orders, and required delivery date.

Step 2: Liaise with the finance team to set an available budget.

Step 3: Refer to the approved supplier list and select the best fit.

Step 4: Negotiate with the preferred supplier on terms and conditions.

Step 5: Send confirmed order details to purchasing officer and receive an approved purchase order.

Step 6: Submit the approved order to the supplier.

Step 7: Upon receiving a receipt from the supplier, process the payment.

To	oliver_shelton@ratdom.com
From	alison_holloway@ratdom.com
Date	August 19
Subject	Update

Dear Mr. Shelton,

Thank you for looking into some much-needed server upgrades. It has been years since we updated our hardware, and it has been an area I've felt we were relatively weak in. Our chief strategy officer, Ms. Cruz, shared the opinion that she would prefer a vendor that is known for high-quality equipment. In that regard, I believe she will be happy about our selection of Fieldtron. I am very familiar with the company, and I am comfortable signing off on the purchase order. It helps that Fieldtron's products are within our budget. I have attached the order form with my signature with this e-mail.

I am also advising we also consider upgrading some of our machinery. Therefore, I am sending you a list of manufacturers we have used in the past. Please contact them and inquire about what they can offer us based on our needs.

Thank you.

Alison Holloway

181. What does NOT need to be done in step 1 of the instructions?

(A) Choosing how often orders will be placed
(B) Determining a delivery date for orders
(C) Calculating the amount of money required
(D) Recording how many items are needed

182. What does Fieldtron most likely produce?

(A) Protective gear
(B) Server hardware
(C) Vehicle components
(D) Factory parts

183. What is suggested about Ms. Cruz?

(A) She will consider Fieldtron equipment to be of high quality.
(B) She will be leaving on a business trip.
(C) She was recently promoted to her position.
(D) She must give her approval on any orders.

184. In working with Fieldtron, what will be Mr. Shelton's next step?

(A) Step 4
(B) Step 5
(C) Step 6
(D) Step 7

185. What will Ms. Holloway be providing to Mr. Shelton?

(A) The names of known manufacturers
(B) An organizational chart
(C) An updated price list
(D) Some survey results

GO ON TO THE NEXT PAGE

Questions 186-190 refer to the following planning guide, information, and comment card.

San Lorenzo: Getting the Most Out of Your Visit

Drop in for a couple of hours or stay a while. Either way, you'll fall in love with the city of San Lorenzo. Here are our recommendations for planning your stay.

Partial Day
Go to the San Lorenzo Visitor Center at 113 Main Street for a brief lecture on the city's history. Then, hop on the tour bus that picks up and drops off visitors at landmarks around the city.

Complete Day
On top of all the partial-day activities, check out Phoenix Palace, right across from the Visitor Center. Guided tours of the palace and its botanical garden are available from noon to sundown daily. Be sure to visit the gift shop for some beautiful souvenirs.

Multi-Day (More than one day)
After doing all the activities listed above, discover more of San Lorenzo by taking a walking tour around the city and its surrounding area.

San Lorenzo Walking Trails

Rainbow Ridge (10.3km)
This 10.3-kilometer, mostly uphill hike takes you from the harbor, through downtown, to all the way up to the scenic bluffs of Rainbow Ridge Park. Perfect for the best views of the city, but demanding for novice hikers.

Borges Peninsula (6.1km)
This 6.1-kilometer trail takes you through the rolling hills near Borges Wildlife Reserve. The thick foliage means that the trail doesn't get much light, so head back before sundown.

The Old Church Route (1.7km)
Stroll the cobbled streets from St. Catherine's to St. Jessica's Churches, admiring the sights along the way. A flat, easygoing 1.7 kilometers.

Brilliant Boulevard (2.1km)
A popular route from the Museum District to Crimson Tower. Enjoy great shopping and dining options along the way. This 2.1-kilometer route can be a little hectic at night.

San Lorenzo Visitor Center
Comment Card

Name: Scottie Fitzgerald
Date(s) of Visit: August 1-2

Message:
My family loved our visit to San Lorenzo. Since we'd never visited the city, we followed the recommendations in the Visitor Center's planning guide exactly, and it really helped. We spent both Saturday and Sunday in town, and we saw a lot. The tour bus was well-worth the price. The only walking trail we didn't try out was the longest and most difficult one. Our children are still too young for something like that. However, I wish to try it soon — hopefully, before my San Lorenzo transit card I bought on my first day expires on the last day of August.

186. What does the planning guide indicate about Phoenix Palace?

(A) It offers discounts to residents.
(B) It does not charge an admission fee.
(C) It is located on Main Street.
(D) It is the oldest site in San Lorenzo.

187. According to the walking trail information, what is true about the Borges Peninsula trail?

(A) It provides views of the city.
(B) It is in a shaded area.
(C) It is very beautiful at night.
(D) It should not be used by beginners.

188. What did Mr. Fitzgerald probably do first when he visited the city?

(A) Board a tour bus
(B) Visit a palace
(C) Listen to a lecture
(D) Go on a hike

189. Which trail does Mr. Fitzgerald plan to hike in the future?

(A) Rainbow Ridge
(B) Borges Peninsula
(C) The Old Church Route
(D) Brilliant Boulevard

190. What does Mr. Fitzgerald suggest on his comment card?

(A) He didn't think the planning guide was very useful.
(B) He is a professional hiker.
(C) He purchased a one-month transportation card.
(D) He booked a hotel near the Visitor Center.

GO ON TO THE NEXT PAGE

Questions 191-195 refer to the following schedule, feedback form, and e-mail.

Solter Engineering Employee Orientation Schedule

9:00 - 9:30 A.M.	Meet with the induction group over breakfast. Overview of the day.
9:30 - 10:30 A.M.	Session 1: "Solter's history, mission, and value proposition" by Gemma Ball, Head of Marketing
10:30 - 11:30 A.M.	Session 2: "Solter's product lines, major markets, and main competitors" by Shaun Portillo, Lead Product Manager
11:30 - 1:00 P.M.	LUNCH BREAK
1:00 - 2:15 P.M.	Session 3: "Solter's acquisitions, partners, and alliances" by Karen Wallis, Head of Strategy
2:15 - 3:30 P.M.	Guest speaker: "What does the future of microprocessors look like? What are the implications" by Gary Koch, PhD
3:30 - 4:00 P.M.	Session 4: "Your new home: benefits, retirement, and promotions" by Tyler Guest, Human Resources Team
4:00 - 6:30 P.M.	Meet your team over dinner

Solter Engineering New Employee Orientation Feedback Form

Welcome to the Solter Engineering family! We would like to gather feedback on your recent orientation session. Your responses will have no bearing on your status at Solter Engineering and will strictly be used for bettering future sessions.

	Statement	Strongly Agree	Agree	Disagree	Strongly Disagree
1	I was well-informed on what the day will involve.			O	
2	I found the sessions useful in doing my job.			O	
3	I felt that the sessions were of appropriate length.		O		
4	I felt engaged and entertained by the speakers.				O
5	I was satisfied with the food and beverages.		O		

Additional comments:

I thought the only session that was useful was the one about what Solter Engineering actually sells. I think the other sessions could have been sent as an e-mail, in my honest opinion. I think there should have been more time dedicated to meeting our coworkers and bosses instead.

To	Karen Wallis
From	Laura North
Date	May 15
Subject	Your session

Dear Ms. Wallis,

Thank you once again for the excellent session you gave at the orientation. As I will be working in client management, I found the session extremely relevant to my work. However, if you have some time available, I would love to sit down and discuss Seraliss Technologies. I'm very eager to make a good impression here, so I would appreciate any help you can provide.

Thank you, and I look forward to hearing from you.

Sincerely,

Laura North

191. According to the schedule, who will discuss the company's philosophy?

(A) Mr. Guest
(B) Ms. Wallis
(C) Ms. Ball
(D) Mr. Portillo

192. According to the schedule, what will happen after 4:00 P.M.?

(A) A questionnaire about the company will be filled out.
(B) There will be a review of the content covered.
(C) The company president will hand out awards.
(D) Participants will meet some current employees.

193. What is indicated about the responses on the feedback form?

(A) They will be used to compensate the speakers.
(B) They will be used to improve future sessions.
(C) They will be sent to an independent company.
(D) They will be used to evaluate new employees.

194. What session did the new employee indicate enjoying most?

(A) Session 1
(B) Session 2
(C) Session 3
(D) Session 4

195. Why does Ms. North most likely ask Ms. Wallis about Seraliss Technologies?

(A) She also has a job interview there.
(B) She would like information on Solter Engineering's competitors.
(C) She has acquaintances who work at Seraliss Technologies.
(D) She will be working closely with Seraliss Technologies.

GO ON TO THE NEXT PAGE

Questions 196-200 refer to the following Web page and e-mails.

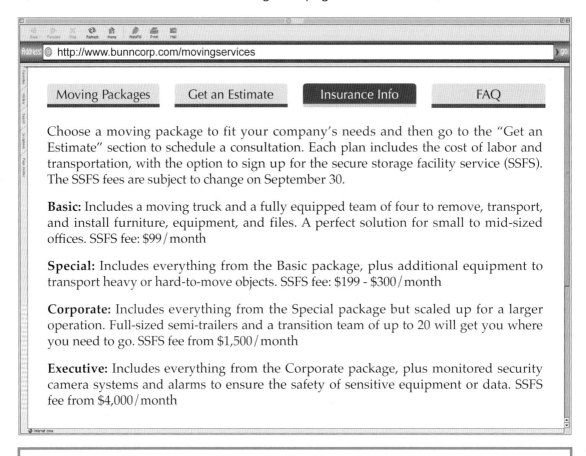

Address @ http://www.bunncorp.com/movingservices

| Moving Packages | Get an Estimate | Insurance Info | FAQ |

Choose a moving package to fit your company's needs and then go to the "Get an Estimate" section to schedule a consultation. Each plan includes the cost of labor and transportation, with the option to sign up for the secure storage facility service (SSFS). The SSFS fees are subject to change on September 30.

Basic: Includes a moving truck and a fully equipped team of four to remove, transport, and install furniture, equipment, and files. A perfect solution for small to mid-sized offices. SSFS fee: $99/month

Special: Includes everything from the Basic package, plus additional equipment to transport heavy or hard-to-move objects. SSFS fee: $199 - $300/month

Corporate: Includes everything from the Special package but scaled up for a larger operation. Full-sized semi-trailers and a transition team of up to 20 will get you where you need to go. SSFS fee from $1,500/month

Executive: Includes everything from the Corporate package, plus monitored security camera systems and alarms to ensure the safety of sensitive equipment or data. SSFS fee from $4,000/month

---

To: BMoore@kraussfinancial.com
From: BBunn@bunncorp.com
Date: July 2
Subject: First Phase of Relocation: Done

Dear Mr. Moore,

This is to confirm that our workers have successfully moved all of your company's equipment into our large storage warehouse on 2000 Huxley Drive. As agreed upon during our meeting last week and in accordance with your SSFS, the items will be stored there until July 31. And at approximately 10 A.M. on that day, we will transport them into your new office in the Crytech Building on 19724 Brookhurst Street.

Should you need to use the SSFS beyond July 31, you will have to give us prior notice at least five days before. Furthermore, you will be assessed a fee for every month that your items remain in our warehouse. The charge will be reflected in your bill on the first date of each month.

Sincerely,

Bradley Bunn
Bunn Corp

To:	BBunn@bunncorp.com
From:	BMoore@kraussfinancial.com
Date:	July 3
Subject:	RE: First Phase of Relocation: Done

Dear Mr. Bunn,

We appreciated how efficient and skilled your workers were during the move. We were especially happy to be able to observe and monitor our items when they were in transit through the alarm and camera system.

However, due to some urgent business, we had to revise the date of our move-in. Therefore, we now request that our equipment be transported to 19724 Brookhurst Street on Tuesday, August 29.

Also, does your storage warehouse have a temperature control system? I am a bit concerned that the heat and humidity from summer rains may cause some of our couches and tables to deteriorate.

Thanks again,

Barney Moore
Krauss Financial

---

196. According to Bunn Corp.'s Web page, what is true about the secure storage facility services?

(A) They are currently being discounted.
(B) Their prices vary by the moving package.
(C) They must be paid for in advance.
(D) Their fees are updated every six months.

197. What is the purpose of the first e-mail?

(A) To discuss a billing mistake
(B) To respond to a client's inquiry
(C) To ask for a deposit
(D) To provide an update on a project

198. What moving package did Mr. Moore probably select?

(A) Basic
(B) Special
(C) Corporate
(D) Executive

199. According to the second e-mail, what is Mr. Moore worried about?

(A) Revised contract conditions
(B) Damages to some furniture
(C) Increased fuel costs
(D) Access to a building

200. What is suggested about Bunn Corp.?

(A) Its head office will relocate to the Crytech Building.
(B) It will not be able to move additional equipment.
(C) It will charge Krauss Financial an extra fee on August 1.
(D) Its employees have received awards for their work.

Stop! This is the end of the test. If you finish before time is called, you may go back to Parts 5, 6, and 7 and check your work.

TEST 02

준비물: OMR 카드, 연필, 지우개, 시계
시험시간: RC 75분

나의 점수	
RC	
맞은 개수	
환산 점수	

TEST 01	TEST 02	TEST 03	TEST 04	TEST 05
_____점	_____점	_____점	_____점	_____점
TEST 06	**TEST 07**	**TEST 08**	**TEST 09**	**TEST 10**
_____점	_____점	_____점	_____점	_____점

점수 환산표

RC			
맞은 개수	환산 점수	맞은 개수	환산 점수
96-100	460-495	41-45	140-215
91-95	425-490	36-40	115-180
86-90	395-465	31-35	95-145
81-85	370-440	26-30	75-120
76-80	335-415	21-25	60-95
71-75	310-390	16-20	45-75
66-70	280-365	11-15	30-55
61-65	250-335	6-10	10-40
56-60	220-305	1-5	5-30
51-55	195-270	0	5-15
46-50	165-240		

READING TEST

In the Reading test, you will read a variety of texts and answer several different types of reading comprehension questions. The entire Reading test will last 75 minutes. There are three parts, and directions are given for each part. You are encouraged to answer as many questions as possible within the time allowed.

You must mark your answers on the separate answer sheet. Do not write your answers in your test book.

PART 5

Directions: A word or phrase is missing in each of the sentences below. Four answer choices are given below each sentence. Select the best answer to complete the sentence. Then mark the letter (A), (B), (C), or (D) on your answer sheet.

101. ------- no one has been hired for the client account manager position, we need to begin the search again.

(A) Despite
(B) Because
(C) Unless
(D) Also

102. All travelers on Atlantic Airways will receive reimbursement if ------- luggage is lost in transit.

(A) them
(B) their
(C) theirs
(D) they

103. Meilee Zhang was nominated for a promotion for her many ------- as a contract negotiator.

(A) competitors
(B) contributions
(C) computations
(D) considerations

104. The company executives are grateful ------- all the hard work and effort from all staff members.

(A) with
(B) much
(C) that
(D) for

105. ------- this morning's team meeting, Mr. Insel acknowledged the need for further research regarding international business practices.

(A) Upon
(B) Across
(C) With
(D) During

106. Each teapot is ------- constructed of porcelain or ceramic, depending on your needs.

(A) expertly
(B) expertise
(C) expert
(D) experts

107. Pearl Star Limited had diminishing returns in the first half of the year ------- still managed to gain profit for the calendar year.

(A) likewise
(B) but
(C) therefore
(D) both

108. All customer -------, no matter how minor, should always be answered promptly and politely.

(A) inquiries
(B) inquiring
(C) inquiry
(D) inquired

109. To gain a new perspective, Ellerton Security is conducting an ------- search for a new director of human resources.

(A) available
(B) external
(C) alternating
(D) approximate

110. The administrator of this office will remove any advertisements that ------- do not conform to the regulations of the university.

(A) clearing
(B) clearly
(C) clear
(D) cleared

111. Ali Gallery determines artwork for exhibition mainly by ------- of patron donations.

(A) petitions
(B) expenses
(C) means
(D) regards

112. Mr. Ramirez assured the directors that he would revise the document ------- by noon.

(A) ourselves
(B) themselves
(C) itself
(D) himself

113. The guest speaker insisted that addressing employee complaints ------- was one vital element for retaining staff.

(A) largely
(B) similarly
(C) consistently
(D) immensely

114. In order to make its servers instantly -------, the restaurant chain hired a well-known fashion designer to create stylish uniforms for its employees.

(A) identify
(B) identifying
(C) identifiable
(D) identification

115. Devon International is pleased to announce the expansion ------- its east training center.

(A) over
(B) as
(C) from
(D) of

116. The magazine article includes ------- on how to increase employee retention rate.

(A) tipping
(B) tipped
(C) tips
(D) tip

117. A few alterations in the garment's design ------- the manufacturer thousands of euros.

(A) saved
(B) examined
(C) intended
(D) prevented

118. Mr. Nguyen confirmed that he would respond to concerns regarding the new emissions tax -------

(A) prompt
(B) prompted
(C) promptly
(D) promptness

119. To receive a complimentary beverage at the theater café, guests must present a ------- admission ticket.

(A) moderate
(B) valid
(C) plausible
(D) determined

120. Whole Grains Grocery Store ------- résumés and cover letters for the cashier position until next Friday.

(A) accepted
(B) acceptable
(C) has been accepting
(D) will be accepting

GO ON TO THE NEXT PAGE

121. ------- in the Belknap Association is open to amateur as well as professional scientists.

(A) Allowance
(B) Endorsement
(C) Certification
(D) Membership

122. The manufacturing plant in Toronto reported that production figures reached their ------- rate ever in the last week of September.

(A) highness
(B) highest
(C) highly
(D) high

123. Because their line of work differs widely, the manufacturing team often works ------- of the sales team, much to the chagrin of the CEO.

(A) thoroughly
(B) independently
(C) equitably
(D) commendably

124. Mr. Chiu made two photocopies of the invoice, one to send out and the ------- to file.

(A) few
(B) each
(C) more
(D) other

125. Ms. Chun was instructed to pick ------- she concluded was the best security firm.

(A) if
(B) anything
(C) whichever
(D) that

126. The Titanium series of Duratek laptops can be dropped from 2 meters without losing -------.

(A) functioned
(B) functional
(C) functionally
(D) functionality

127. Ledgewood's latest line of kitchenware is finished ------- thin layers of gold paint for aesthetics.

(A) near
(B) under
(C) on
(D) with

128. Fortress Hill University was awarded a grant ------- provide financial aid to its less-privileged students.

(A) for
(B) hence
(C) so that
(D) in order to

129. All employees are required to ------- their social security numbers to qualify for medical insurance.

(A) perceive
(B) authenticate
(C) regulate
(D) convince

130. To ensure the safe delivery of the products, employees should remember to add an ample amount of packing peanuts ------- sealing the shipping boxes.

(A) and
(B) prior to
(C) since
(D) if not

PART 6

Directions: Read the texts that follow. A word, phrase, or sentence is missing in parts of each text. Four answer choices for each question are given below the text. Select the best answer to complete the text. Then mark the letter (A), (B), (C), or (D) on your answer sheet.

Questions 131-134 refer to the following notice.

Attention Wyandotte County Residents

Please note that Wyandotte County Public Works (WCPW) will be resurfacing major roads and highways in the county throughout the month of May in accordance with our annual maintenance schedule. Road resurfacing is planned for every Monday of this month between 3 A.M. and 5 A.M. -------. Also, in the days following the completion of
131.
resurfacing, the pavement will be soft, so slower driving speeds are recommended. This is ------- but cannot be avoided. County residents ------- longer commute times for
132. **133.**
about six weeks. WCPW will send out a similar announcement ------- the next yearly
134.
maintenance period, which normally occurs in late spring. Please contact WCPW at 555-1212 with any questions or concerns.

---

131. (A) During these times, motorists are prohibited from accessing these roads.
(B) The revised schedule will be posted as quickly as possible.
(C) As an alternative, county officials may choose to fund a bus route.
(D) Most businesses are closed between midnight and 6 A.M.

132. (A) ideal
(B) complete
(C) temporary
(D) cautious

133. (A) expecting
(B) have expected
(C) should expect
(D) expects

134. (A) since
(B) while
(C) against
(D) before

GO ON TO THE NEXT PAGE

Questions 135-138 refer to the following information.

Many of the ------- to *The Natural World* are veteran biologists who have collaborated
    135.
with our publication over an extended period. -------, we are always interested in
             136.
promoting the work of aspiring scientists. For every issue, we aim to feature at least
one to two submissions from a new researcher, but with our quarterly publishing
schedule, it is difficult to include every worthy article. Before you submit your work, it is
essential to familiarize yourself with our publication guidelines (available at naturalworld.
com/submissions), which detail our citation and formatting rules. -------.
             137.

Keep in mind that we make every effort to respond to all correspondence we receive,
but due to the high volume of submissions, we cannot always do so quickly. Because
of this, we have to ask you to be -------.
        138.

135. (A) contributing
(B) contributes
(C) contributors
(D) contribution

136. (A) In fact
(B) Even so
(C) In this case
(D) For example

137. (A) Most of our subscribers are
university professors and graduate
students.
(B) This month's issue will be delivered
within the next two weeks.
(C) We're impressed by your approach,
but we require more statistical
evidence.
(D) This will improve the chances that
your work is chosen.

138. (A) minor
(B) concise
(C) meticulous
(D) patient

Questions 139-142 refer to the following notice.

Brafton Entrepreneur Association

The Brafton Entrepreneur Association is accepting nominations for two special awards this year. Nominations -------- for both awards until August 18.
139.

The Disruptive Growth Award is to recognize a small business that has achieved exceptional growth in a short amount of time. Nominees may employ up to 50 people.
-------.
140.

The Community Outreach Award is to recognize businesses that have played a significant role ------- helping smaller businesses get off the ground. Businesses from
141.
all industries and sizes are eligible as long as the ------- were to smaller businesses
142.
located in the Brafton area.

To nominate businesses or to find out more about the awards, visit our website at www.beaawards.org.

---

139. (A) will be open
(B) were opened
(C) open
(D) are opening

140. (A) An applicant may be declined for any reason.
(B) The business should have been operating for less than three years.
(C) We would like to extend an invite for you to join our association.
(D) Overdue fees may be paid through our website.

141. (A) with
(B) about
(C) between
(D) in

142. (A) contributions
(B) examinations
(C) inspections
(D) revisions

GO ON TO THE NEXT PAGE

Questions 143-146 refer to the following article.

Yuccaville (August 9) — Row upon row of rooftop solar panels attest to the fact that Yuccaville has taken an interest in renewable energy. In fact, 5 percent of the power generated in the Yuccaville comes from solar energy these days, and that number is rising at a ------- rate. To a certain degree, this is because of the town's significant tax
143.
------- granted to solar panel owners. According to Brian Alvarez, CEO of Yuccaville
144.
Renewable Energy Solutions, more efficient batteries and easy-to-install panels have

------- made the technology more attractive. Mr. Alvarez anticipates that the number of
145.
solar panels in Yuccaville will increase dramatically in the future. --------.
146.

143. (A) temporary
(B) limited
(C) steady
(D) potential

144. (A) reduce
(B) reduced
(C) reducing
(D) reduction

145. (A) ever
(B) soon
(C) also
(D) much

146. (A) As a matter of fact, he believes that within a decade, almost all buildings will have solar panels.
(B) He believes this is one reason that fewer businesses have been opening in the Yuccaville.
(C) He worries about how the increased cost will affect sales.
(D) Furthermore, he has been very happy with the quality of the panels that he purchased last year.

PART 7

Directions: In this part you will read a selection of texts, such as magazine and newspaper articles, e-mails, and instant messages. Each text or set of texts is followed by several questions. Select the best answer for each question and mark the letter (A), (B), (C), or (D) on your answer sheet.

Questions 147-148 refer to the following invitation.

We are honored to invite you to this year's
David Conrad Memorial Marketing Seminar

Hosted by
James Nakamoto
Business Advisor at the Toronto Small Business Center (TSBC)
and owner of Alpine Grill

Subject: Digital Marketing
Time: June 28, 1:00 – 3:00 P.M.
Place: The Grand Hotel Conference Room

This seminar is available to all entrepreneurs in the Toronto area. All attendees must present a copy of their business registration certificate when signing up. Please call the TSBC for more information.

147. For whom is the invitation most likely intended?

(A) Marketing specialists
(B) Business owners
(C) Financial advisors
(D) Hotel managers

148. What are interested individuals asked to do?

(A) Provide a certificate
(B) Arrange a seminar room
(C) Call Mr. Nakamoto's restaurant
(D) Look over an event schedule

GO ON TO THE NEXT PAGE

Questions 149-150 refer to the following notice.

Remington Lawn Masters:
For Your Lawn Mowing and Gardening Needs

Thanks for purchasing the Lawn Master MM2500d. If you keep the following information in mind, your machine should work well for many years.

- Make sure to drain the tank of gasoline at the end of the mowing season. Old fuel can make the engine hard to start after a long winter.

- Clean the bottom of the mower regularly to prevent buildup. The blades can be filled with grass and dirt over time, causing malfunction.

- Replace the sparkplug every year. By changing this inexpensive, easy-to-replace component, you'll prevent the need for more expensive repairs.

- Get a periodic tune-up. A good way to ensure your machine lasts a long time is to take it into a repair shop regularly so that a professional can inspect it.

149. What is indicated about the blades of the Lawn Master MM2500d?

(A) They can become blocked.
(B) They are expensive to replace.
(C) They are only available from Remington.
(D) They can cut any type of grass.

150. What is NOT mentioned as a tip for lawnmower maintenance?

(A) Emptying the gas tank
(B) Using a specific cleaning product
(C) Buying a new part annually
(D) Visiting a specialist

Questions 151-153 refer to the following e-mail.

To	: Amos Reese <areese@gotomail.net>
From	: Doris Kim <dkim@eureek.com>
Date	: August 28
Subject	: RE: Reversing a charge

Dear Mr. Reese,

Thank you for contacting Eureek Finservices. —[1]—. We have looked into your request to reverse a charge, and we can confirm that we have flagged the charge for review. If successful, you will be credited for the original amount of $112.50 in your checking account ending in 7650. —[2]—. Therefore, please do not be alarmed if you do not hear from us immediately.

During the review process, we will be contacting the merchant for them to provide evidence that it has sent the goods to you. Unless satisfactory evidence is sent in, the review will be ruled in favor of you. —[3]—. At Eureek Finservices, our commitment is to you as our valued customer. Therefore, we will do our best to provide you with the best result in a timely manner. If you have not received an update within the next two weeks, please get in touch with us.

Thank you for your continued business with us, and we look forward to celebrating your tenth year of membership with us! —[4]—.

Sincerely,

Doris Kim, Customer Satisfaction Team

---

151. What is one purpose of the e-mail?

(A) To explain the steps involved in a process
(B) To encourage the usage of a new service
(C) To provide advice on an investment opportunity
(D) To request additional information on an inquiry

152. What is indicated about Mr. Reese?

(A) He is a former employee at Eureek Finservices.
(B) He runs a small online business from his home.
(C) He has been a member of Eureek Finservices for some time.
(D) He has previously been a victim of credit card fraud.

153. In which of the positions marked [1], [2], [3], and [4] does the following sentence best belong?

"The review can take up to two weeks."

(A) [1]
(B) [2]
(C) [3]
(D) [4]

GO ON TO THE NEXT PAGE

Questions 154-155 refer to the following postcard.

Annual Lantern Festival

From August 5 until August 11, the city of Oakman will be hosting our annual Lantern Festival. You will see elaborate, handmade lanterns on display, accompanied by live music. There will also be plenty of food stalls to choose from. Due to increased rainfall this year, the lanterns may be featured at Harbour Stadium instead.

The event is free to the public, so feel free to bring your entire family along. Please note that the tables in the food area can only seat four, so bear that in mind if you are at a large party. For more information, please visit www.oakman.govt.nz/events/lantern.

Place
Stamp
Here

154. What is indicated about the festival?

(A) Its location may change.
(B) Its attendance has increased.
(C) It has been featured on television.
(D) It also provides parking.

155. What is suggested about large groups?

(A) They must inform the organizers in advance.
(B) They can receive a discount on food orders.
(C) They may be charged a fee for attending.
(D) They may have to eat at different tables.

Questions 156-157 refer to the following text message chain.

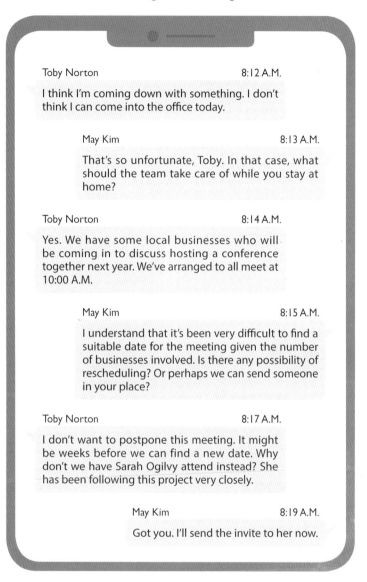

Toby Norton   8:12 A.M.

I think I'm coming down with something. I don't think I can come into the office today.

May Kim   8:13 A.M.

That's so unfortunate, Toby. In that case, what should the team take care of while you stay at home?

Toby Norton   8:14 A.M.

Yes. We have some local businesses who will be coming in to discuss hosting a conference together next year. We've arranged to all meet at 10:00 A.M.

May Kim   8:15 A.M.

I understand that it's been very difficult to find a suitable date for the meeting given the number of businesses involved. Is there any possibility of rescheduling? Or perhaps we can send someone in your place?

Toby Norton   8:17 A.M.

I don't want to postpone this meeting. It might be weeks before we can find a new date. Why don't we have Sarah Ogilvy attend instead? She has been following this project very closely.

May Kim   8:19 A.M.

Got you. I'll send the invite to her now.

156. What is suggested about Mr. Norton?

(A) He resides close to his office.
(B) He will go on vacation next week.
(C) He has recently been promoted.
(D) He is unable to attend a meeting.

157. At 8:19 A.M., what does Ms. Kim most likely mean when she writes, "Got you"?

(A) She will attend the meeting instead.
(B) She is unsure if Ms. Ogilvy should be involved.
(C) She agrees with Mr. Norton's suggestion.
(D) She thinks rescheduling is a better idea.

GO ON TO THE NEXT PAGE

Questions 158-160 refer to the following notice.

Douglas EasyBooks

Congratulations on purchasing the Douglas EasyBooks accounting program. Our application will save you time, allowing you to focus on being the best business you can be.

With your purchase, your business is eligible for a training seminar free of charge. This three-part online training series is a great way to educate your staff on how to use the software effectively.

These brief but helpful sessions are conducted by trainers who have utilized our product to simplify practices at their own firms. To reserve your training seminar, log on to Douglaseasybooks. com/training today.

---

158. What is one purpose of the notice?

(A) To recruit some trainers
(B) To advertise a new book
(C) To explain some fees
(D) To describe a service

159. According to the notice, what qualifications do the trainers possess?

(A) They have a graduate degree in economics.
(B) They have been employed at Douglas' EasyBooks for a long time.
(C) They helped develop the accounting program.
(D) They have experience using the accounting program.

160. The word "focus" in paragraph 1, line 2, is closest in meaning to

(A) concentrate
(B) direct
(C) adjust
(D) adopt

Questions 161-163 refer to the following press release.

PRESS RELEASE

Leonard Osgard
PR Director, Windermere Partners
losgard@windermerep.com

Marina (February 15) — Windermere Partners proudly announces the opening of its brand-new shopping area, Marina Square. —[1]—. Although many of the commercial units have been sold, ten retail spaces are still up for sale.

All retail spaces come, with an open floor plan for you to design to your liking with the option to add on extra features such as shelving, countertops, and partitions. —[2]—. In addition, all stores will be able to take advantage of the shopping center's free wireless Internet, security patrols to keep your business safe day and night, and on-site cleaning and maintenance assistance, along with many other conveniences.

Marina Square is more than just a shopping center; it's also a great entertainment destination. —[3]—. With multiple fine dining options and plenty of activities for the whole family to take part in, Marina Square is set to become the new hot spot in town.

Feel free to stop by Marina Square and have a look around. —[4]—. For an individual consultation, call 710-555-6214 to arrange an appointment.

---

161. What kind of business most likely is Windermere Partners?

(A) A public relations company
(B) A construction materials manufacturer
(C) A private security company
(D) A commercial property developer

162. What is indicated about the retail spaces?

(A) They include storage rooms.
(B) They have access to several services.
(C) They are designed to be environmentally friendly.
(D) They can be leased for a short period.

163. In which of the positions marked [1], [2], [3], and [4] does the following sentence best belong?

"We have showings every day beginning at 11 A.M. and ending at 5 P.M."

(A) [1]
(B) [2]
(C) [3]
(D) [4]

GO ON TO THE NEXT PAGE

Questions 164-167 refer to the following article.

NEW YORK (April 2) — Yesterday afternoon, Judge John Reinsdorf ruled that a merger between the nation's two leading accounting firms could go ahead despite objections from some experts. This means that Markkanen & Associates and Donovan ELX are now free to form what will be the country's largest accounting company, with over 300,000 employees.

"We're excited about what will happen when these two companies join forces," said Spencer Mitchell of Markkanen, who will most likely become CEO of the new firm to be known as Markkanen-Donovan. "We have a tremendous amount of know-how and two amazingly diverse client portfolios. This move will not only let us keep our New York and Los Angeles branches, but also make it possible to increase our reach worldwide. We're looking at setting up a new office outside of the U.S. in Singapore in the next year."

Mitchell has drawn the attention of press agencies around the country for his charity work, especially his efforts to promote small businesses in developing countries through microloans.

Mitchell said that Markkanen-Donovan plans to retain the entire staff of each company. "Every department has vital skills to bring to the table," he explained.

164. What is the main purpose of this article?

(A) To explain new tax regulations
(B) To report on the combining of two firms
(C) To discuss a legal case
(D) To advertise an accounting service

165. What does Markkanen-Donovan plan to do?

(A) Borrow some money
(B) Hold an executive board election
(C) Close one of its New York branches
(D) Expand to a new country

166. What is suggested about Mr. Mitchell?

(A) He is nationally recognized.
(B) He used to be a banker.
(C) He is based in Los Angeles.
(D) He owns a small business.

167. The word "reach" in paragraph 2, line 11, is closest in meaning to

(A) length
(B) arrival
(C) influence
(D) extension

Questions 168-171 refer to the following e-mail.

To:	Raiden Staff
From:	n.sullivan@raiden.com
Date:	Sunday, November 15
Subject:	Progress on Pipes
Attachment:	Workshop documents

Hello all,

The building will still be inaccessible on Tuesday because it's taking technicians longer than planned to replace the damaged water pipes. Please check your e-mail regularly for further updates. In addition, you are still required to maintain regular contact with your clients and take care of any other assignments while at home.

On the other hand, we will need to move Tuesday's workshop to sometime next week. During the workshop, we'll be discussing our quarterly sales and earnings. Attached to the e-mail, you'll find a detailed document regarding this, so please read it over carefully. Afterward, we will be having a company-wide dinner to celebrate the successful launch of our latest line of washers and dryers.

On a final note, I want to thank you all for your patience and dedication. I know that this repair has caused some unforeseen challenges, but I am confident that we will get through it.

Sincerely,

Nancy Sullivan
Raiden Corp.

168. What is mentioned about some water pipes?

(A) They are expensive to repair.
(B) They were initially inspected by Ms. Sullivan.
(C) They have been leaking for weeks.
(D) They will take more time to replace.

169. What are staff members expected to do on Tuesday?

(A) Work out of another location
(B) Visit some businesses
(C) Use a vacation day
(D) Come to the office later

170. What did Nancy Sullivan include with the e-mail?

(A) A dinner menu
(B) A client contact list
(C) An event calendar
(D) A financial report

171. What kind of business most likely is Raiden Corp.?

(A) A property management firm
(B) A home appliance producer
(C) A plumbing company
(D) An accounting business

GO ON TO THE NEXT PAGE

Questions 172-175 refer to the following online chat discussion.

Danny Sokolich	(8:13 A.M.)
Good morning, everyone. I'm not feeling well today, so I will be working from home today.	
Amy Burrows	(8:15 A.M.)
We were meant to meet regarding the product prototype today at 1 P.M. How will we accomplish that?	
Danny Sokolich	(8:17 A.M.)
Perhaps if somebody is able to set up videoconferencing, we can still meet virtually?	
Sean Evans	(8:19 A.M.)
I can get Ms. Berkahn to help with that. She has a lot of experience because she often videoconferences with our international suppliers.	
Amy Burrows	(8:21 A.M.)
I think Tessa Mulholland and Liam Jacobs should also be present. They know the most about the market we'll be entering, so we would really like their input.	
Danny Sokolich	(8:23 A.M.)
In that case, we should move the meeting to the conference room on the fifth floor. That should be able to accommodate everyone.	
Sean Evans	(8:24 A.M.)
You read my mind.	
Jaimee Berkahn	(8:24 A.M.)
I've set up videoconferencing in that room before, and it's quite easy. I can set it up for you before I have to head off to a meeting.	
Amy Burrows	(8:26 A.M.)
Please include Ms. Mulholland and Mr. Jacobs.	
Sean Evans	(8:27 A.M.)
I'll have to check their availability. In any case, I'll send invites out with the new location to the five of us.	
Danny Sokolich	(8:28 A.M.)
Excellent. They'll have some great insights into what we might have missed.	

SEND

172. What is suggested in the chat?

(A) Several products will be released simultaneously.
(B) The writers work from different countries.
(C) The meeting will not be postponed.
(D) A contract is due to be renewed.

173. Why most likely are the writers planning to meet?

(A) To organize a company event
(B) To provide an update on a project
(C) To discuss a product launch
(D) To meet with an international client

174. How many people will attend the meeting?

(A) Three
(B) Four
(C) Five
(D) Six

175. At 8:24 A.M., what does Mr. Evans most likely mean when he writes, "You read my mind"?

(A) He agrees with Mr. Sokolich about the meeting location.
(B) He thinks they do not need Ms. Berkahn's help.
(C) He would like to change the meeting time.
(D) He knows that Ms. Mulholland and Mr. Jacobs's input is valuable.

GO ON TO THE NEXT PAGE

Questions 176-180 refer to the following notice, form, and e-mail.

SUPPLY THE MASSES CONFERENCE

The third annual conference for consumer supplements, Supply the Masses, will take place on 4 November at the Hexagon Convention Hall. The conference will aim to cover some of the major trends identified in the consumer supplement market as well as highlight some new, exciting products in the pipeline.

The conference will feature a special guest, Dr. Aria Bradford. Unless you've been living under a rock, Dr. Bradford's work will be familiar to many of you. She is the founder of Thrillience and essentially wrote the book on how to market supplements effectively. She will be sharing some of her recent experiences in Europe, where she has been based.

There is a registration fee of $150 for members belonging to the Safer Supplements Alliance. Non-members are welcome to participate but will have to pay $200 for entrance instead. If you reserve your spot before 12 September, you will also receive an early bird discount of 10 percent.

SUPPLY THE MASSES CONFERENCE

Registration form

Last Name: Graves	**First Name:** Nate
Date: 19 September	**Member:** Yes:V No: ___
Company Name: RefresherFast	**Position:** Manager
Telephone: +51 555 1995	**Fax:** +51 555 1996
Company Billing Address: 459 Deerfield Drive New Bedford, MA 02740	**E-mail:** n.graves@refresherfast.com

To	Nate Graves
From	Ashraf Mackie
Date	21 September
Subject	Re: Supply the Masses Conference

Dear Mr. Graves,

We have looked into your request, and we can confirm that despite all tickets being sold out, you may transfer your ticket to your coworker Ms. Leigh Nash. Please note that this is due to exceptional circumstances. However, as Ms. Nash is not a member of the Safer Supplements Alliance, she must cover the difference in price between a member ticket and a non-member ticket. She is advised to complete that as soon as possible so that her ticket can be mailed out.

Thank you, and please let me know if you have further questions.

Regards,

Ashraf Mackie, Events Coordinator

176. In the notice, what is indicated about this year's Supply the Masses Conference?

(A) It will include catering services.
(B) It will feature an acclaimed speaker.
(C) It will provide product samples to guests.
(D) It will be conducted online.

177. How much did Mr. Graves likely pay to register himself for the conference?

(A) $250
(B) $200
(C) $150
(D) $100

178. Why did Mr. Mackie send an e-mail to Mr. Graves?

(A) To notify him of a decision that was made
(B) To suggest that a schedule be changed
(C) To invite him to give a presentation
(D) To request that an additional payment be made

179. According to the e-mail, what should Ms. Nash do?

(A) Join an alliance
(B) Respond to an e-mail
(C) Submit an application
(D) Make a payment

180. Where does Ms. Nash work?

(A) RefresherFast
(B) Hexagon Convention Hall
(C) Thrillience
(D) Safer Supplements Alliance

GO ON TO THE NEXT PAGE

Questions 181-185 refer to the following Web page and e-mail.

www.adventureexcursions.com/self-drivingtours

Adventure Excursions: South America
FAQ: Self-driving tours

Are visas required?
For EU citizens, you will be able to travel freely without a special visa as long as your passport is current. For citizens of other countries, please confirm the latest entry requirements with the relevant government authorities. Every traveler should be ready to present their passport on the first day of the tour for a photocopy. Subsequently, remember to keep it on hand to display whenever we pass through border security. An international driver's license and car insurance plan are also required.

Where do I pick up my vehicle, and where do I drop it off?
We will send our driver to the airport when you arrive. From there, you can drive yourself or rest in the support car. On your way out of the country, you can simply leave the vehicle with us at the airport. If you are not flying out immediately, you will need to organize your own means of transport to the airport.

What information do I need to be aware of?
Each excursion will be equipped with heavy-duty 4-wheel-drive vehicles capable of passing over rough terrain. Thirty days prior to your excursion, we will send an e-mail information on the exact make and model, along with a final itinerary with expected travel times, road conditions, and planned accommodations.

What should I pack?
It is important to bring versatile clothing. You will experience both humid jungles near sea level and snow-capped peaks at high altitudes. Pack accordingly.

TO:	jorge_montero@adventureexcursions.com
FROM:	moira_oriordan@iemail.com
DATE:	April 22
SUBJECT:	Self-driving tour

I booked a self-driving trip last week, which is due to run from August 7 to August 19. I've explored some pretty remote parts of Alaska, but I've never been to South America. As I'm taking a long flight over, I would like to see some additional sites after the excursion ends. If possible, I'd love to end my tour near Huascaran National Park and adjust the route around that. Also, could I ask you to help plan a backpacking trip there? I might need to rent some extra equipment for a few days. I understand the Cordillera Blanca mountains are quite beautiful. I'm open to suggestions, but I'd like to figure out the plan before I get there.

Best Regards,

Moira O'Riordan

181. What is implied about Adventure Excursions: South America's self-driving tours?

(A) They allow visitors to see more sites than a traditional tour.
(B) They are meant for people traveling in large groups.
(C) They go through predominately cool weather locations.
(D) They involve traveling to multiple countries.

182. According to the Web page, what should travelers do before the tour?

(A) Organize transportation to the tour office
(B) Fax a copy of their international driver's license
(C) Determine if a visa is necessary
(D) Get special travel vaccines

183. What will Ms. O'Riordan need to do if she changes her travel plans as described in her e-mail?

(A) Adjust a flight time
(B) Rent a different model
(C) Pay an additional service fee
(D) Arrange a trip to the airport

184. What is likely to happen in July?

(A) Ms. O'Riordan will receive detailed tour information.
(B) Mr. Montero will lead a tour of the Cordillera Blanca mountains.
(C) Mr. Montero will copy some travel documents.
(D) Ms. O'Riordan will rent a vehicle in Alaska.

185. In the e-mail, the phrase "figure out" in line 7 is closest in meaning to

(A) infer
(B) evaluate
(C) accept
(D) clarify

GO ON TO THE NEXT PAGE

Redtie Vehicle Repairs
A premium service at an affordable price

We provide a wide range of vehicle services, including repairs, assessments, painting, and cleaning. We can cater to all sorts of vehicles, including cars, trucks, vans, and more. Our policy is to always provide an honest quote before carrying out any work.

We are also proud to announce a merger with Total Autos. We will be moving forward under the Redtie brand together and — with our new logo — expanding our services to cover the greater Esmeralda area. All previous customers of Total Autos will see no changes to ongoing contracts and arrangements. If you have any questions about existing contracts or you wish to look at various contract options, please contact Joseph Castillo at jcastillo@redtie.com or 191-555-7915, Ext. 7.

Special promotion: to celebrate, we are providing a 15% discount on all contracts signed in July. For existing customers, 15% has already been deducted from your July bill.

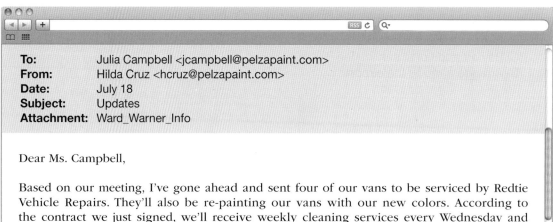

To:	Julia Campbell <jcampbell@pelzapaint.com>
From:	Hilda Cruz <hcruz@pelzapaint.com>
Date:	July 18
Subject:	Updates
Attachment:	Ward_Warner_Info

Dear Ms. Campbell,

Based on our meeting, I've gone ahead and sent four of our vans to be serviced by Redtie Vehicle Repairs. They'll also be re-painting our vans with our new colors. According to the contract we just signed, we'll receive weekly cleaning services every Wednesday and maintenance services every month. We signed a six-month contract, and we'll see how happy we are with their services before resigning.

Also, I am passing on the appropriate forms for our new hires, Terry Ward and Salvador Warner. It has their driver's licenses and bank information. They'll be coming in for training next week. They have prior experience, so the training portion shouldn't take long.

Sincerely,

Hilda Cruz
General Manager

★ ★ ★ ★ ★

Pelza Paint is new to the area, so I wasn't sure what to expect. However, I was renovating my store and decided to give them a call. Within minutes, they had organized an employee to come in and get started right away. The painter, Terry Ward, was nothing but professional and hardworking. She knew exactly what I had in mind and completed the job in just over a week. At a very reasonable price and with such terrific employees, I would recommend Pelza Paint in a heartbeat.

Bruce Schultz, 12 August

186. According to the advertisement, what is new at Redtie Vehicle Repairs?

(A) A business logo
(B) A contract term
(C) A website
(D) A type of service

187. Who most likely is Mr. Castillo?

(A) The head of sales
(B) The client account manager
(C) A marketing specialist
(D) A senior accountant

188. What does the e-mail indicate about Ms. Campbell and Ms. Cruz?

(A) They both drive Pelza Paint's vehicles.
(B) They have previously spoken about vehicle arrangements.
(C) They are planning on purchasing new vans.
(D) They will be advertising job openings next week.

189. What is most likely true about the contract Ms. Cruz mentions in her e-mail?

(A) It will be renewed in six months.
(B) It has not been signed yet.
(C) It received a discount on its price.
(D) It includes repairs free of charge.

190. What is suggested about the service that Mr. Schultz received?

(A) It was the cheapest option.
(B) It was delayed for some time.
(C) It involved a new employee.
(D) It was completed within three days.

GO ON TO THE NEXT PAGE

Johnson County to Renovate Water Pipe Network

(March 12) — Throughout the month of April, Johnson County Water District intends to upgrade several miles of copper pipes with new polyvinyl chloride (PVC) pipes in order to ensure that the county's water system continues to function in an optimal manner.

"The ability of PVC pipes to withstand greater water pressure will allow for better operation of laundry machines, dishwashers, and a variety of other consumer devices," said Mr. Sohel Khan, Johnson County Water District Supervisor. "The new pipes will also pose fewer potential environmental hazards than the old copper ones."

Several roads in the county will be completely inaccessible for 24-hour periods while the renovation is taking place. Water District officials are consulting with local store owners in hopes of agreeing upon a timetable that will avoid causing unnecessary problems for businesses. Constant revisions will be made to the schedule, which can be found on the County Clerk's Web site. Residents may also address comments and concerns to the County Clerk.

---

www.johnsoncountyclerk.gov

Water Pipe Renovation Schedule:

Saturday, April 4	Antioch Street
Sunday, April 5	Corinth Avenue
Saturday, April 11	Jameson Lane
Sunday, April 12	Cherokee Drive

After the renovation has been completed, a Johnson County Water District employee will visit your home or business to check the water pressure.

To	Ed Haber <eddie@eddiesbakery.com>
From	Anita Quackenbush <quackenbush@johnsoncountyclerk.gov>
Date	April 1
Subject	Inspection

Dear Mr. Haber,

As you may know, we will be renovating water lines on the street that runs along your store on Saturday, April 11. You should anticipate about 4 hours without running water that morning. We apologize for any inconvenience this may cause. A Water District technician is scheduled to visit your business the following day between 9 A.M. and 11 A.M. to confirm proper water pressure. If you need to arrange a different time, please notify us at 555-1212.

Best Regards,

Anita Quackenbush

191. According to the article, what is indicated about the new pipes?

(A) They are more affordable than copper pipes.
(B) They will make some equipment function better.
(C) They are going to be installed during the morning.
(D) They will be inspected on a frequent basis.

192. What does the article mention about the project schedule?

(A) It will be updated regularly.
(B) Mr. Khan created it.
(C) Some residents don't approve of it.
(D) It has some problems.

193. What will happen on April 4?

(A) A new county clerk director will be appointed.
(B) A road will be blocked.
(C) A business convention will be held.
(D) A city parade will take place.

194. What is implied about Mr. Haber's store?

(A) It has been closed for one week.
(B) It operates 24 hours a day.
(C) It is located on Jameson Lane.
(D) It has recently opened.

195. Who most likely is Ms. Quackenbush?

(A) A local business owner
(B) A construction worker
(C) A Water District technician
(D) A government employee

GO ON TO THE NEXT PAGE

Questions 196-200 refer to the following online form, e-mail, and Web page.

www.nguyensportswear.vn/service

Please fill out the information below, followed by your detailed feedback. Thank you for allowing us to serve you better.

Name: Hassina Boulmerka
E-mail: hassina.b@elwatan.vn
Phone number: 514-555-1212

Feedback:
I've been purchasing items from Nguyen Sportswear ever since you had your original offline shop in Ho Chi Minh City, and I have always been satisfied. For that reason, I was surprised and disappointed by my most recent order. Once the sweatshirt arrived, it was clear right away that it was made from a cheaper — and less comfortable — material than before. To make matters worse, after I had worn it just a couple of times, the fabric in the sleeve near the elbow wore down and tore open!

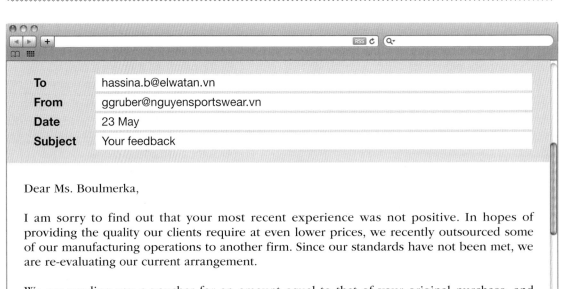

To	hassina.b@elwatan.vn
From	ggruber@nguyensportswear.vn
Date	23 May
Subject	Your feedback

Dear Ms. Boulmerka,

I am sorry to find out that your most recent experience was not positive. In hopes of providing the quality our clients require at even lower prices, we recently outsourced some of our manufacturing operations to another firm. Since our standards have not been met, we are re-evaluating our current arrangement.

We are sending you a voucher for an amount equal to that of your original purchase, and we would also like to offer you one of our popular 495-Z sweatshirts, free of charge, as an apology and a token of our appreciation. This item, created from our special durable fabric, is guaranteed to endure extreme conditions and last for a long time. Simply reply to this e-mail with your desired size and color.

We hope you will continue to do business with us in the future.

Best Regards,

Glenn Gruber
Client Service Associate

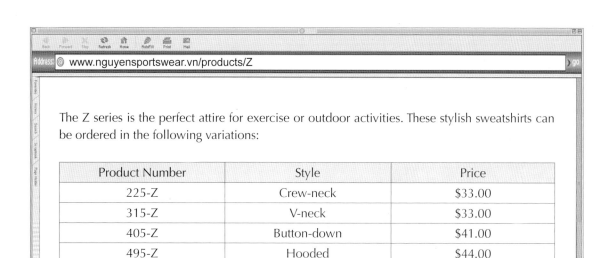

The Z series is the perfect attire for exercise or outdoor activities. These stylish sweatshirts can be ordered in the following variations:

Product Number	Style	Price
225-Z	Crew-neck	$33.00
315-Z	V-neck	$33.00
405-Z	Button-down	$41.00
495-Z	Hooded	$44.00

196. What is Ms. Boulmerka's main problem?

(A) Some prices have increased.
(B) The quality of an item has declined.
(C) An order was delivered late.
(D) A website did not work.

197. What is implied about some of Nguyen Sportswear's merchandise?

(A) They have been sold at a lower price than other product lines.
(B) They have been produced by another company.
(C) They are not designed for athletes.
(D) They are currently not in stock.

198. What is indicated about the Z series?

(A) It wears out more quickly than other items.
(B) It was manufactured in Ho Chi Minh City.
(C) It is made of a unique material.
(D) It recently added some new options.

199. What is Ms. Boulmerka asked to do?

(A) Provide her order preferences
(B) Drop by a store
(C) Use a different credit card
(D) Return some clothing items

200. What type of sweatshirt does Mr. Gruber offer to Ms. Boulmerka?

(A) Crew-neck
(B) V-neck
(C) Button-down
(D) Hooded

Stop! This is the end of the test. If you finish before time is called, you may go back to Parts 5, 6, and 7 and check your work.

TEST 03

준비물: OMR 카드, 연필, 지우개, 시계
시험시간: RC 75분

나의 점수	
RC	
맞은 개수	
환산 점수	

TEST 01	TEST 02	TEST 03	TEST 04	TEST 05
_____점	_____점	_____점	_____점	_____점
TEST 06	**TEST 07**	**TEST 08**	**TEST 09**	**TEST 10**
_____점	_____점	_____점	_____점	_____점

점수 환산표

RC			
맞은 개수	환산 점수	맞은 개수	환산 점수
96-100	460-495	41-45	140-215
91-95	425-490	36-40	115-180
86-90	395-465	31-35	95-145
81-85	370-440	26-30	75-120
76-80	335-415	21-25	60-95
71-75	310-390	16-20	45-75
66-70	280-365	11-15	30-55
61-65	250-335	6-10	10-40
56-60	220-305	1-5	5-30
51-55	195-270	0	5-15
46-50	165-240		

READING TEST

In the Reading test, you will read a variety of texts and answer several different types of reading comprehension questions. The entire Reading test will last 75 minutes. There are three parts, and directions are given for each part. You are encouraged to answer as many questions as possible within the time allowed.

You must mark your answers on the separate answer sheet. Do not write your answers in your test book.

PART 5

Directions: A word or phrase is missing in each of the sentences below. Four answer choices are given below each sentence. Select the best answer to complete the sentence. Then mark the letter (A), (B), (C), or (D) on your answer sheet.

101. ------- Ms. George or Mr. Baldwin will assume the position of director until a suitable replacement is found.

(A) Both
(B) Between
(C) Someone
(D) Either

102. Due to its ------- location in the province, Martenville has the largest train switch yard.

(A) center
(B) centering
(C) central
(D) centrally

103. Dr. Muniz is ------- to see the patient on Thursday at 5:15 P.M.

(A) comfortable
(B) probable
(C) available
(D) possible

104. With its new health facilities nearing -------, Fitness First is changing its focus to hiring qualified personal trainers.

(A) conception
(B) completion
(C) compilation
(D) competition

105. The schedule ------- in the chart is only an estimate, as the arrival time is subject to change depending on traffic conditions.

(A) show
(B) showing
(C) shown
(D) are shown

106. Donnelly Curtains' Web site was thoroughly tested by quality assurance specialists to make sure it works as -------.

(A) intentional
(B) intended
(C) intending
(D) to intend

107. Lisa Chen proofread the press release ------- prior to its publication.

(A) caution
(B) cautioned
(C) cautious
(D) cautiously

108. The laboratory manager is required to ensure proper ------- of all chemicals.

(A) store
(B) storable
(C) stores
(D) storage

109. ------- the rising cost of petroleum, the merchandising team is being advised to decrease the availability of free shipping.

(A) Of
(B) For
(C) Upon
(D) Given

110. The Canberra Photographers Association is a prominent group with very ------- members.

(A) lenient
(B) anonymous
(C) fundamental
(D) accomplished

111. This announcement is to inform passengers of ------- on carry-on luggage for international flights.

(A) limitations
(B) limit
(C) limiting
(D) limited

112. The customer survey results indicate that most people ------- Milkmade's strawberry drinking yogurt very satisfying.

(A) enjoy
(B) find
(C) sense
(D) correspond

113. The newly published novel by writer Dana Sandoval ------- as her best one ever.

(A) is regarded
(B) regarding
(C) regards
(D) to regard

114. This translated document must be officially notarized to verify that it ------- reflects the original source.

(A) correction
(B) corrected
(C) correctness
(D) correctly

115. Min-hee Park transformed her research on the ------- effects of physical exercise into a popular nonfiction film.

(A) favor
(B) favorable
(C) favorably
(D) favored

116. The company's sanitation standards for its production line extend ------- those of most other companies.

(A) far
(B) even
(C) more
(D) beyond

117. Nature Free's ------- launched skincare line received numerous awards for its formulation.

(A) newly
(B) supposedly
(C) subsequently
(D) repeatedly

118. Because the delivery was slightly damaged, the customers received a significant price ------- on their next shipment.

(A) reduction
(B) reducing
(C) reduced
(D) reduce

119. Top Post Stationery offers a range of ------- created greeting cards and gifts.

(A) tremendously
(B) neglectfully
(C) thoughtfully
(D) considerably

120. ------- her expertise in digital media trends, Ms. Kim became the lead manager of the marketing division.

(A) Although
(B) Then
(C) Despite
(D) Because of

GO ON TO THE NEXT PAGE

121. The association is ------- hesitant to approve the use of new pharmaceuticals before proper approval has been attained.

(A) understandably
(B) understandable
(C) understanding
(D) understand

122. New employees at Westmoreland Constructions must take a ------- training program on safe working practices.

(A) mandatory
(B) disconcerted
(C) charitable
(D) discrete

123. Mr. Briggs' program manual should prove ------- to customers who are unfamiliar with the new software.

(A) instructed
(B) instructions
(C) instructive
(D) instructively

124. The estimate for the hotel renovation will be sent this afternoon ------- we receive the contractor's measurements before noon.

(A) besides
(B) as long as
(C) predicting
(D) if not

125. Mindsweep, Inc., a rising ------- in AI technology, has already outperformed its main rival ICM in the market.

(A) competitor
(B) transfer
(C) detective
(D) order

126. The project manager position was posted on Youngstown Marketing's Web site since ------- of the project coordinators had sufficient experience.

(A) anybody
(B) other
(C) neither
(D) nobody

127. Many grocery stores offer prizes, such as home appliances, to loyal customers who ------- enough membership points.

(A) execute
(B) diffuse
(C) comprehend
(D) acquire

128. The packages of office supplies arrived just as the receptionist ------- for home.

(A) has been leaving
(B) has left
(C) was leaving
(D) leaves

129. The annual company trip to Fairfax will be held as planned ------- the rainy weather.

(A) in view of
(B) in spite of
(C) with respect to
(D) in light of

130. Entries must be submitted by the competition deadline to leave ------- time for judge deliberation.

(A) impaired
(B) adequate
(C) persistent
(D) compulsive

PART 6

Directions: Read the texts that follow. A word, phrase, or sentence is missing in parts of each text. Four answer choices for each question are given below the text. Select the best answer to complete the text. Then mark the letter (A), (B), (C), or (D) on your answer sheet.

Questions 131-134 refer to the following memo.

To: All Tectonia Staff
From: Brendan Chandler, Director of Human Resources
Date: October 15
Subject: Company newsletter

The first edition of our company newsletter ------- this week via e-mail. From this point
                                              131.
onwards, you can expect future issues on the first Monday of every month. The primary

------- of these newsletters is to bring employees closer together. Each issue will feature
132.
profiles and interviews of employees from various teams. The newsletters can serve as

starting points to get to know a little more about your colleagues. We hope you find the

newsletters ------- and make for a good start to the month. -------. Please send me an
            133.   **134.**
e-mail if you have any thoughts.

---

131. (A) to distribute
    (B) will be distributed
    (C) distribute
    (D) was distributing

132. (A) guideline
    (B) structure
    (C) origin
    (D) objective

133. (A) engaging
    (B) engaged
    (C) engage
    (D) engagement

134. (A) A copy can be saved on file for
       future use.
    (B) An invitation for the event has also
       been sent out.
    (C) We also invite any feedback on the
       first issue.
    (D) Vacancies can be viewed on the
       bulletin board.

GO ON TO THE NEXT PAGE

Questions 135-138 refer to the following e-mail.

To: Dominic Powell <dpowell@iu.edu>
From: Curtis Branson <branson@edental.com>
Date: October 27
Subject: Patient alerts

Dear Mr. Powell,

In hopes of ------- our patients as efficiently and conveniently as possible, we have
                135.
started offering the opportunity to receive notifications and reminders by using a mobile
application. Currently, we send you updates to your e-mail address. -------. If you would
                                                                  136.
like to try using the app or wish to discuss your ------- for notifications from us, please
                                                137.
give us a call at 858-555-1212.

------- aim is to provide patients with timely and helpful information about all aspects of
138.
dental care and to ensure an optimal patient experience at all times.

Curtis Branson
Office Manager
Elite Dental Clinic of Lenexa

135. (A) allowing
(B) serving
(C) improving
(D) thanking

136. (A) We believe that our clinic is the best
in the area.
(B) Remember to schedule at least one
yearly visit.
(C) E-mail alerts first became available
last year.
(D) No changes will be made if you are
satisfied with this arrangement.

137. (A) opted
(B) options
(C) optional
(D) optionally

138. (A) My
(B) Its
(C) Our
(D) Your

The Human Resources Team is requesting that all employees fill out a self-development

plan. The intent of the plan is ------- you with the flexibility to grow beyond your current
                                139.
role. The ------- will also help us understand what core capabilities the firm will have in
        140.
the future, which will help us plan our long-term future.

On the landing page of the plan, please start by indicating your role and tenure in the

company. -------. You will then be asked to rate each course on a scale of 1 to 5. -------,
        141.   **142.**
please refrain from leaving any of the fields blank. This may cause unexpected issues

when the system compiles your results.

---

139. (A) has provided
 (B) provided
 (C) to provide
 (D) provide

140. (A) initiatives
 (B) pitfalls
 (C) results
 (D) projects

141. (A) This information will be used to
  determine what options you are
  eligible for.
 (B) The cost of each course can be
  found at the bottom.
 (C) Concerns should be directed to Ms.
  Siemen.
 (D) The system is being trialed for the
  first time this year.

142. (A) Despite
 (B) Additionally
 (C) Therefore
 (D) Due to

GO ON TO THE NEXT PAGE

To: jake.fowler@crimpmail.com
From: order@esmondesoap.com
Date: July 12
Subject: Order 20773051

Dear Mr. Fowler,

Thank you ------- from the Esmonde Soap Company. We are confirming that we have
              143.
received your payment. Your order is now being prepared for -------. If you selected the
                                                              144.
regular courier option, you should expect to receive your goods in five to ten working

days. -------. Once your package ------- the warehouse, you will be sent a link that lets
       145.   **146.**
you track your package in real-time. If you have any questions about your order or if

you think something has gone wrong, please contact us at helpdesk@esmondesoap.

com.

Thank you for your business.

Sincerely,

Cassandra Nash
Esmonde Soap Company

---

143. (A) that ordered
(B) to order
(C) for ordering
(D) had been ordering

144. (A) extraction
(B) dispatch
(C) inspecting
(D) inquiry

145. (A) A cancellation fee will apply in this case.
(B) Inquiries should be directed to one of our sales representatives.
(C) Orders made during the holiday season may take longer.
(D) Our warehouses are located throughout the country.

146. (A) was left
(B) has been left
(C) left
(D) has left

PART 7

Directions: In this part you will read a selection of texts, such as magazine and newspaper articles, e-mails, and instant messages. Each text or set of texts is followed by several questions. Select the best answer for each question and mark the letter (A), (B), (C), or (D) on your answer sheet.

Questions 147-148 refer to the following information.

Due to popular demand, our loyalty program will no longer be restricted to one Baroque Hotels location. Instead, you will be able to redeem your points at any of our nationwide locations. Take advantage now to receive free room upgrades, discounted room services, and access to our private health facilities and swimming pools. We have plenty of additional services in the works, so check our Web site www.baroquehotels.com for the latest updates.

For more information on our list of offerings or if you would like clarification on anything, e-mail us with your questions. We also have our mobile app that can connect you to one of our employees.

Thank you for choosing Baroque Hotels.

147. For whom is the information most likely intended?

(A) Web development staff
(B) Front-desk staff
(C) Hotel guests
(D) Facility managers

148. According to the information, what has Baroque Hotels changed recently?

(A) Its program restrictions
(B) Its restaurant services
(C) Its guest facilities
(D) Its room prices

GO ON TO THE NEXT PAGE

Questions 149-150 refer to the following form.

RK Co.

Client: Top Ten Electronics
Address: 446 Cleveland Rd.
Attn: Angela Martin

Thank you again for your business. You'll find the bill for your October 30th service below. If you have any issues, don't hesitate to call Gerry Martin at (555) 212-9891.

Service/Product	Amount	Price Per Unit	Price
Fittings	x20 Faucets(Brass)	$20	$400
Pipe Installation	x10 Type L Piping(Copper)	$25	$250
Fixture Replacement	x4 Sinks(Porcelain)	$40	$160
Labor	35 hours	$25/hr	$875
Total $1,685			

149. What most likely is RK Co.?

(A) An electrical company
(B) A plumbing business
(C) A hardware store
(D) A metal manufacturer

150. What information was NOT included?

(A) The contact representative of RK Co.
(B) The number of workers involved
(C) The kind of pipes that were purchased
(D) The length of a project

Thank you for choosing Rison Electronics! To register your product, please complete the following steps:

1. Visit our Web site at www.risonelectronics.com/product_registration.
2. Login using the temporary ID and password included inside the product box.
3. Complete the form, including your name and e-mail address. You will also need to input the purchase date and the original country of purchase. Afterward, enter your product's serial number, which can be found on the back page of your instruction manual.
4. You will then be asked to make your own personal ID and password. Please use this information whenever you need to access your account.
5. Once everything is filled out, click on the "Submit" button. Your product is now registered under our warranty service.

RISON ELECTRONICS

151. For whom are the instructions most likely intended?

(A) Rison Electronics employees
(B) Product developers
(C) First-time customers
(D) Quality-control inspectors

152. What is the reader asked to do?

(A) Extend a warranty
(B) Update some log-in details
(C) Download some files
(D) Complete a survey

GO ON TO THE NEXT PAGE

Questions 153-154 refer to the following text message chain.

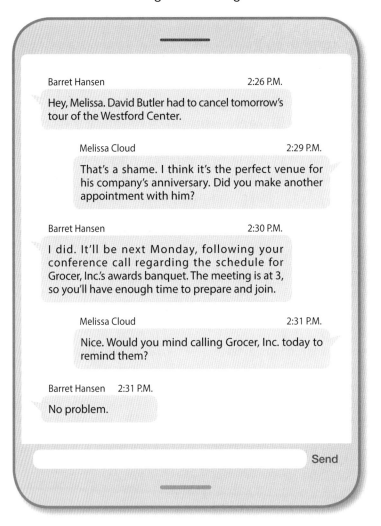

Barret Hansen   2:26 P.M.

Hey, Melissa. David Butler had to cancel tomorrow's tour of the Westford Center.

Melissa Cloud   2:29 P.M.

That's a shame. I think it's the perfect venue for his company's anniversary. Did you make another appointment with him?

Barret Hansen   2:30 P.M.

I did. It'll be next Monday, following your conference call regarding the schedule for Grocer, Inc.'s awards banquet. The meeting is at 3, so you'll have enough time to prepare and join.

Melissa Cloud   2:31 P.M.

Nice. Would you mind calling Grocer, Inc. today to remind them?

Barret Hansen   2:31 P.M.

No problem.

Send

---

153. What most likely is Ms. Cloud's profession?

(A) Maintenance worker
(B) Restaurant manager
(C) Event planner
(D) Personnel director

154. At 2:31 P.M., what does Ms. Cloud most likely mean when she writes, "Nice"?

(A) She is eager to visit a facility.
(B) She is excited to call Mr. Butler.
(C) She is pleased with the progress of a project.
(D) She is satisfied with Mr. Hansen's work.

Questions 155-157 refer to the following invoice.

DeLaurentis Security Systems

Billing Number: AHD84-1113
Appointment Date: March 25
Billed to: Antonia Brown (Due March 31)

On-Site Consultation (2 hours, $35/hour)	$70.00
Out-of-Area Service Request	$50.00
Subtotal	$120.00
Referral Code (25% off)	$24.00
Total Amount Due	$96.00

Let us know what you think about your appointment! Send us feedback on Sonya Young's service via our mobile app, DL Secure, today. If you have any concerns or need more information regarding our billing procedure, contact Thomas Nwamba at tnwamba@delaurentissecuritysys.com.

---

155. What is indicated on the bill?

(A) It was issued on March 31.
(B) A fee was charged for at-location service.
(C) A consultation price was recently raised.
(D) It was given to a private corporation.

156. Why most likely did Ms. Brown get a discount?

(A) She has purchased products from the company before.
(B) Her order was placed during a March promotion.
(C) Her consultation took less than three hours.
(D) A previous customer recommended the service to her.

157. Who most likely provided the consultation?

(A) Ms. Brown
(B) Mr. DeLaurentis
(C) Ms. Young
(D) Mr. Nwamba

GO ON TO THE NEXT PAGE

Questions 158-160 refer to the following advertisement.

Auckland Culinary Students' Test Kitchen Is Open for Dinner

Do you want that perfect gourmet experience without the usual price tag? —[1]—.

The Auckland Culinary School would like to make you dinner for just $10. For one full week at the beginning of every month, our students cook meals for the general public. The experience of running our Test Kitchen gives the students valuable experience in their field. —[2]—. To make sure your dining experience is up to our high standards, one of our top instructors will be in the kitchen to oversee the service.

Reservations for the Test Kitchen can be made in the last week of each month, but book quickly. Our location only has eight tables. —[3]—. You can use the Fork and Knife app to get a table before they run out.

Be aware that the student may require a little longer to get your dish exactly right. It should also be noted that the students are required to follow Test Kitchen recipes, so no substitutions or special requests will be taken. —[4]—.

---

158. What is indicated about instructors at the Auckland Culinary School?

(A) They work one week per month.
(B) They decide which students will cook.
(C) They supervise service at the Test Kitchen.
(D) They give students safety training.

159. What is NOT mentioned about the Test Kitchen?

(A) It can be reserved through an application.
(B) It has an outdoor dining area.
(C) It does not have much space for customers.
(D) It might take some time to serve dishes.

160. In which of the positions marked [1], [2], [3], and [4] does the following sentence best belong?

"Because of this, make sure to check the menu carefully if you have any dietary restrictions."

(A) [1]
(B) [2]
(C) [3]
(D) [4]

Questions 161-164 refer to the following brochure.

Rastlinn Center of Opportunities

About

The Rastlinn Center of Opportunities (RCO) assists local entrepreneurs by providing classes on the basics of running a business. Funded by the government, the classes are provided free of charge in order to promote entrepreneurial efforts in Rastlinn. Since our founding 20 years ago, we have already helped thousands of businesses get on their feet.

More than just classes

We offer much more than classes at RCO. You will be joining a community of like-minded individuals. We also have many prominent businesses such as MediCare Now, Market Insights, and Green Grocers sponsoring our events. By being part of our community, you can learn from the very best business leaders in the city while also nurturing important relationships.

Contact

For further information about what RCO can offer you, please contact Celia Flowers, Program Manager, at cflowers@rastlinnco.com or 303-555-6284. If you are interested in becoming one of our sponsors, please contact Israel Morrison, Head of Partnerships, at imorrison@rastlinnco.com or 303-555-6259.

Our Locations

North Shore: 48 Ferguson Close, Rastlinn, Montana
City Central: 166 Westfield Estate, Rastlinn, Montana
West Harbor: 501 Doncastle Road, Rastlinn, Montana

---

161. Whom does RCO want to help?

(A) Recruitment officers
(B) Business owners
(C) Job seekers
(D) Real estate agents

162. What is indicated about RCO?

(A) It aims to sustain a community.
(B) It was founded last year.
(C) It charges a membership fee.
(D) It has offices outside of Rastlinn.

163. What type of business is NOT mentioned in the brochure as being associated with RCO?

(A) A market research firm
(B) A supermarket
(C) A medical facility
(D) A logistics company

164. What should businesses do if they are interested in working with RCO?

(A) Attend a class
(B) Contact Mr. Morrison
(C) E-mail Ms. Flowers
(D) Visit one of the offices

GO ON TO THE NEXT PAGE

Questions 165-167 refer to the following letter.

Jean Rios · 15 Chandos Road · Coconino AZ 86046

13 July
Ronald Brown
Collective Images Ltd.
33 Shannon Gardens
Coconino AZ 86046

Dear Mr. Brown,

I am writing to apply for the position of photographer at Collective Images Ltd. For your convenience, I have attached my résumé and portfolio. My neighbor Morris Santos informed me of the position and suggested I apply for the role. Mr. Santos and I attended the same university and have had the same role since graduating. I believe he can vouch for my abilities.

To briefly describe myself, I am a passionate and hardworking person. From my portfolio, you will see a diverse range of works. I started off only doing portraits, but in my current position, I am now doing events such as fashion shows and grand openings. The reception to my shots has been terrific, and they have been featured in many publications.

I am looking to move on from my current role as I would like to take more of a managerial position. While my performance reviews from my boss have been stellar, something that draws the envy of my peers, the firm is small. It does not offer the kind of challenge I am now looking for. I believe Collective Images can highly benefit from my skillset, and I would enjoy the opportunity to discuss what I can provide.

Thank you, and I hope you consider my application.

Sincerely,
Jean Rios

165. What does Ms. Rios indicate about her current position?

(A) It requires Ms. Rios to work overtime often.
(B) It involves attending various events.
(C) It is sponsored by the local university.
(D) It is a relatively new position.

166. The word "featured" in paragraph 2, line 4, is closest in meaning to

(A) changed
(B) designated
(C) supported
(D) appeared

167. What is indicated about Ms. Rios?

(A) She is looking to relocate for a new job.
(B) She is applying to several different firms.
(C) She intends to attend additional classes.
(D) She receives high ratings from her boss.

GO ON TO THE NEXT PAGE

Questions 168-171 refer to the following text message chain.

Pablo Hammond   8:34 A.M.

I just received an update from the Baldwin family. I informed them that the weather might not hold up during the week. I explained that this would drastically increase the time it takes for the paint to dry. However, they would still like it done on Saturday. Andrea, do you have a rough estimate of how much paint we will need?

Andrea Lowe   8:36 A.M.

Right. I can help you with that.

Pablo Hammond   8:38 A.M.

Everett, can you draft up a quote for the work? You can reference some of our past works to help you.

Everett Stephens   8:42 A.M.

Great. I'll fill in everything except the cost of the paint. Will they be using our Peltier brand?

Pablo Hammond   8:51 A.M.

Actually, they live right by the beach. We've recommended a stronger, more durable brand.

Andrea Lowe   8:52 A.M.

I sent through the paint requirements based on their house size.

Everett Stephens   8:55 A.M.

I'll prepare the estimate.

Andrea Lowe   8:59 A.M.

The paint can get here by Thursday. Should I put in the order?

Pablo Hammond   9:04 A.M.

Yes, please. Make the delivery to the Baldwin residence. They said they would be home to receive the order.

Andrea Lowe   9:08 A.M.

OK. It should get there sometime around 5 P.M.

Pablo Hammond   9:11 A.M.

Thank you. I will let them know.

Send

168. For what type of business does Mr. Hammond work?

(A) A design firm
(B) A moving service
(C) A real estate agent
(D) A painting company

169. At 8:36 A.M., what does Ms. Lowe mean when she writes, "I can help you with that"?

(A) She will require some assistance.
(B) She will be busy throughout the day.
(C) She will prepare a document.
(D) She will suggest a new company.

170. According to the text message chain, what will happen on Thursday?

(A) Some products will be getting delivered.
(B) Some prices are expected to change.
(C) A contract will be signed.
(D) An inspector will be visiting the Baldwin family.

171. What will Ms. Lowe most likely do next?

(A) Consult with a colleague
(B) Replace a product
(C) Attend an interview
(D) Put in an order

GO ON TO THE NEXT PAGE

Questions 172-175 refer to the following article.

UNLIMITED VACATION?

Greg Waiters, Staff Writer

Workers often dream about going on vacations to get away from the stresses of their work. Unfortunately, a limited number of vacation days may not allow employees to get the rest and relaxation they need. —[1]—. Some companies, however, have begun offering their employees unlimited paid leave. Even though this policy may seem to put companies at a disadvantage, it has been shown to have a positive impact. Companies have noticed that their employees work harder, they are able to recruit and retain top talent, and they don't need to pay out unused vacation time since there is no fixed number of days to be taken.

Before implementing such measures, employers must ensure that the policy is well-understood and that expectations are realistic. —[2]—. This includes educating your company's employees on how the policy will benefit the company overall, as well as emphasizing that unlimited time off does not translate to any reduction in responsibility for getting their share of work done. Employees should also be clear on the proper procedure for taking days off of work. —[3]—. Employers should check on this regularly to make sure there are no issues. —[4]—.

172. For whom is the article mainly intended?

(A) Magazine writers
(B) Legal experts
(C) Travel agents
(D) Company executives

173. What is NOT stated as a benefit of unlimited vacation?

(A) It keeps a company from losing employees.
(B) It allows a company to save money.
(C) It increases productivity levels.
(D) It offers employees a telecommuting option.

174. According to the article, what should happen periodically?

(A) A review of a procedure
(B) A change in management
(C) A training seminar
(D) A discussion of job duties

175. In which of the positions marked [1], [2], [3], and [4] does the following sentence best belong?

"For instance, employees may need to request time off in advance if taking an extended holiday."

(A) [1]
(B) [2]
(C) [3]
(D) [4]

GO ON TO THE NEXT PAGE

TEST 03

Questions 176-180 refer to the following advertisement and e-mail.

MANDY'S MONITOR MARKET

Mandy's Monitor Market just celebrated its fifth birthday. To mark the occasion, we are offering discounts on all of our monitors for the next month.

Our current stock includes the following:

Model	Size	Price
21-FTE	21 inches	$150
24-MWF	24 inches	$225
27-AYM	27 inches	$270
29-KOZ	29 inches	$315

Order online by visiting mandysmonitor.com. Orders may also be placed by phone at 496-555-3736.

If you order more than one monitor, we will provide you with a complimentary keyboard, complete with wireless capabilities.

Upon ordering, you can expect to receive your item within seven working days. We also offer express shipping for an additional fee, which guarantees that your order will arrive within 48 hours.

To	Mandy's Monitor Market <help@mandysmonitor.com>
From	Leah Dixon <ldixon@coullsmail.com>
Date	17 June
Subject	A Big Compliment

I am writing this e-mail to express how satisfied I was following my order from Mandy's Monitor Market.

I recently moved here for my job, and I had to set up an office at home. Admittedly, I am not familiar with technology, which made me quite nervous. However, seeing your Web site made it so easy to find what I needed that I didn't even consider other businesses. I was expecting to pay much more than $270 for what I got, which was a pleasant surprise.

I realized after my order that I had set the delivery date to a day I would not be at home. Luckily, I managed to speak to a customer service representative, who was able to change the delivery date for me. He even threw in a free keyboard. Having received my monitor, my home office is now complete, and I could not be happier. I will absolutely be leaving a positive review on your Web site for future customers.

Leah Dixon

176. What is indicated about Mandy's Monitor Market?

(A) It had its most successful year last year.
(B) It has recently expanded into new regions.
(C) It is celebrating a special occasion.
(D) It advertises on the Internet.

177. How can customers obtain a free keyboard?

(A) By purchasing multiple items
(B) By filling out a form
(C) By referring a friend
(D) By entering a code

178. What size monitor did Ms. Dixon order?

(A) 21 inches
(B) 24 inches
(C) 27 inches
(D) 29 inches

179. In the e-mail, the word "consider" in paragraph 2, line 3, is closest in meaning to

(A) quantify
(B) figure out
(C) contemplate
(D) deal with

180. What does Ms. Dixon indicate?

(A) She will write about her experiences at Mandy's Monitor Market.
(B) She will change jobs in the near future.
(C) She has recently purchased a new home.
(D) She often travels internationally for work.

GO ON TO THE NEXT PAGE

QMC Construction Solutions, Inc.
Contreras Work Study Program

QMC Construction Solutions, Inc., based in Rancho Cucamonga, is looking for 15 promising students for the Contreras Work-Study Program (CWSP). Program participants will work in one of QMC's three facilities: San Bernardino, Riverside, or Rancho Cucamonga. For consideration, students should send a cover letter and CV to CWSP@qmcconstruction.com. Those selected for the program will be featured in a special article in *Inland Empire Business Journal* next month.

About the Program:
CWSP is the creation of Anthony Contreras, who wanted to commemorate the work of Guillermo M. Contreras, the original owner of QMC Construction Solutions. The program is designed to foster young architecture students to follow Guillermo Contreras' example, exploring and developing more effective solutions to design and construction problems. After completing his Master's degree in architecture, Guillermo Contreras opened QMC Construction Solutions, Inc. in partnership with his brother Edwin. As the years passed, he grew the small company into one of the most respected construction firms in Southern California. After leading the company for 35 years, he stepped down earlier this year to let his nephew, Anthony, take charge.

To: Jerry Skakal <JSkakal@desertcollege.edu>
From: Deanna Rogers <rogers@qmcbuilders.com>
Date: July 14
Subject: Details

Dear Mr. Skakal,

Congratulations on your acceptance to the Contreras Work Study Program. You will receive your official letter of acceptance and contract in the next few days. Concerning your question about accommodations, I certainly understand that you'd prefer not to make a 2-hour drive from your home in San Diego every day, but I'm afraid that we are unable to arrange the house for program participants. However, Rodrigo Carvalho, the program coordinator for the Riverside office, would be a good person to talk to about this. He was born and raised in Riverside, and he will probably have some suggestions for low-cost lodging there.

Once again, congratulations, and we look forward to working with you.

Best Regards,
Deanna Rogers
HR Specialist
QMC Construction Solutions, Inc.

181. Why was the notice posted?

    (A) To promote a corporate program
    (B) To seek a new company president
    (C) To report on a construction project
    (D) To advertise a magazine article

182. Who is Anthony Contreras?

    (A) A university administrator
    (B) The founder of a company
    (C) The leader of a business
    (D) A student intern

183. What is one purpose of Ms. Rogers' e-mail?

    (A) To discuss Mr. Skakal's contract
    (B) To recommend a real estate agency
    (C) To ask about an issue
    (D) To respond to an inquiry

184. What is true about Mr. Skakal?

    (A) He studies architecture.
    (B) He has met Mr. Carvalho before.
    (C) He will relocate to another office.
    (D) He wants to hire QMC Construction Solutions.

185. Where will Mr. Skakal work?

    (A) In San Bernardino
    (B) In Riverside
    (C) In Rancho Cucamonga
    (D) In San Diego

GO ON TO THE NEXT PAGE

Questions 186-190 refer to the following Web page, online form, and e-mail.

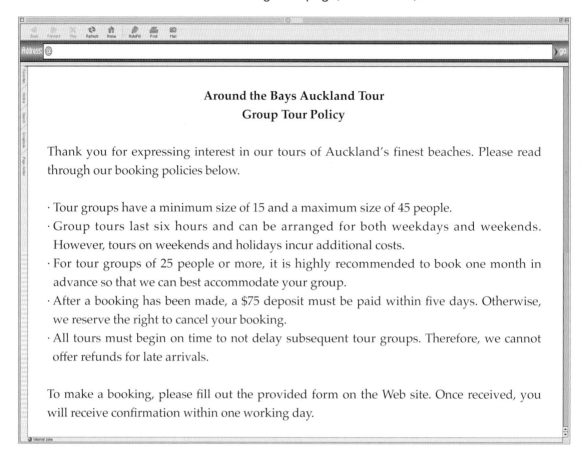

Around the Bays Auckland Tour
Group Tour Policy

Thank you for expressing interest in our tours of Auckland's finest beaches. Please read through our booking policies below.

· Tour groups have a minimum size of 15 and a maximum size of 45 people.
· Group tours last six hours and can be arranged for both weekdays and weekends. However, tours on weekends and holidays incur additional costs.
· For tour groups of 25 people or more, it is highly recommended to book one month in advance so that we can best accommodate your group.
· After a booking has been made, a $75 deposit must be paid within five days. Otherwise, we reserve the right to cancel your booking.
· All tours must begin on time to not delay subsequent tour groups. Therefore, we cannot offer refunds for late arrivals.

To make a booking, please fill out the provided form on the Web site. Once received, you will receive confirmation within one working day.

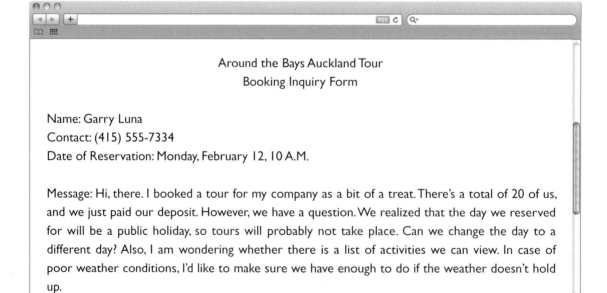

Around the Bays Auckland Tour
Booking Inquiry Form

Name: Garry Luna
Contact: (415) 555-7334
Date of Reservation: Monday, February 12, 10 A.M.

Message: Hi, there. I booked a tour for my company as a bit of a treat. There's a total of 20 of us, and we just paid our deposit. However, we have a question. We realized that the day we reserved for will be a public holiday, so tours will probably not take place. Can we change the day to a different day? Also, I am wondering whether there is a list of activities we can view. In case of poor weather conditions, I'd like to make sure we have enough to do if the weather doesn't hold up.

To: info@aroundthebays.co.nz
From: m.powell@aucklandtourgroup.co.nz
Date: Wednesday, January 28
Subject: Around the Bays

Dear team,

Management has decided that we have to start optimizing some of our costs. Based on a review of our services, we have found the average size of our tour groups to be an area of weakness. Therefore, we have decided that the following policy will be placed on the page:

· For groups smaller than 25, you may be placed in the same tour group along with other groups.

Can we ensure that this policy is posted by February 7? I'll be traveling to your office in the next week to explain how this will change the way we make bookings. If you have any questions before then, please let me know.

Thank you.

Milton Powell
Division Lead, Auckland Tour Group

186. What is suggested on the Web page about groups larger than 25?

(A) They may not be able to secure a tour date at the last minute.
(B) They will have access to exclusive tour packages.
(C) They must pay a larger deposit prior to the tour.
(D) They receive a group discount rate.

187. What policy did Mr. Luna most likely misunderstand?

(A) The amount of money required for the deposit
(B) The times and locations of the tour
(C) The reservation of particular dates in advance
(D) The days on which tours can be reserved

188. What does Mr. Luna ask Around the Bays to clarify?

(A) How many tour guides are available
(B) What activities are included in the tour
(C) What transportation options are possible
(D) When the payment for the tour is due

189. What is the purpose of Mr. Powell's e-mail?

(A) To arrange a partnership with a local company
(B) To request data on the usage of a service
(C) To clarify the cost breakdown of an operation
(D) To announce the inclusion of a new policy

190. What is suggested about Mr. Luna's group tour?

(A) It may include other groups.
(B) It may be eligible for a discount.
(C) It may be televised.
(D) It may follow a new route.

GO ON TO THE NEXT PAGE

Questions 191-195 refer to the following advertisement, e-mail, and information sheet.

MeiHua Bamboo

MeiHua Bamboo is proud to celebrate 25 years of offering top-quality bamboo products to China and the world!

Bamboo houses and furniture have been popular for thousands of years in Asia due to their beauty and durability. As a building material, it has many notable features:

1. Lightweight: Bamboo is much lighter than other building materials. This means it requires less labor to transport, store, and install most bamboo products.
2. Strength: Bamboo is far stronger than wood. In fact, it can withstand more pressure than concrete and almost as much tension as steel.
3. Easy Maintenance: Bamboo is quite durable and is more water-resistant than most woods. Therefore, it is not difficult to clean bamboo. For example, if you spill something on a bamboo floor, all you need to do is use a dry towel to clean it up.
4. Versatility: Despite its strength, bamboo is easy to cut and form into various shapes. That means we can work with you to custom-design just about anything you'd like to add to your home or business, from floors to cabinets, and even curtains!
5. Eco-Friendly: Bamboo is a completely renewable, non-polluting resource. Any leftover materials can be easily recycled or safely discarded.

To:	Giuseppine Nieddu
From:	Earl Doherty
Date:	June 27
Subject:	Bamboo Countertops

Dear Ms. Nieddu,

Thank you for meeting with me and showing me your design proposal for custom bamboo countertops. The countertops are different from anything I've ever seen, and I believe they will be a perfect addition to DDD's new chain of donuts and coffee shops in Canada.

My company's management team is of the same opinion, but they do have one question. We will be preparing and serving food and beverages on these countertops. Can you suggest a proper chemical solution to protect the surfaces? Naturally, we need to apply a solution that will keep the counters clean and attractive for a long time but, most importantly, provide the safest possible environment for food preparation and consumption.

Thanks in advance.

Earl Doherty
Doherty's Donut Domain (DDD), Inc.

Finishing Options for Bamboo Products

Finishing is the last step in the manufacture of bamboo items. Finishing simply involves covering the surface of the item with a chemical solution that only absorbs a small amount of water, dirt, and oil particles. When the solution dries, it protects the original surface from moisture and bacteria during use. Depending on how and where the product will be used, one of the following finishing products should be chosen.

Material	Durability	Food-Safe
Natural wax	Poor	Always
Water-based varnish	Excellent	Usually
Oil-based varnish	Very good	Never
Mineral oil	Very good	Always

191. What is mentioned about MeiHua?

(A) It is based in Canada.
(B) It can create customized merchandise.
(C) It will open this year.
(D) It makes furniture cleaning products.

192. Why did Mr. Doherty write the e-mail?

(A) To delay a delivery
(B) To schedule a meeting
(C) To request a recommendation
(D) To revise an order

193. Which feature of MeiHua's bamboo building materials did Ms. Nieddu and Mr. Doherty discuss?

(A) Feature 2
(B) Feature 3
(C) Feature 4
(D) Feature 5

194. According to the information sheet, what does finishing require?

(A) A smooth surface
(B) A cloth made of special material
(C) A cool environment
(D) A solution with low absorbency

195. Which finishing product will DDD, Inc. most likely choose?

(A) Natural wax
(B) Water-based varnish
(C) Oil-based varnish
(D) Mineral oil

GO ON TO THE NEXT PAGE

Questions 196-200 refer to the following invoice and e-mails.

Trilland Consulting

August 21
Customer No.: 4882

Due date: September 15

Milton Wood
374 Woodward Corner
Mylo, ND 58353

Service Date	Description	Reference Code	Amount
8/2	1-day process analysis	0095	$480
8/6	1-day software implementation	0075	$1,050
8/6	Team training session	0082	$250
TOTAL $1,780			

Thank you for choosing Trilland Consulting's North America division for your business needs. We hope you are satisfied with our service. If you have any inquiries about the invoice, please contact our billing department at invoice@trillandconsulting.com.

To	<invoice@trillandconsulting.com>
From	Milton Wood <mwood@centurytale.com>
Date	August 24
Subject	Inquiries

Dear Trilland Consulting,

I recently received some consulting from your group. It was headed by Paul Gibson, and we had a fantastic experience with him. He knew the ins and outs of all of the enterprise systems we were considering, and he helped us come to a decision. I would actually like to see if he will be available to help with another project we are considering. Would Mr. Gibon's schedule have time in September for some more work?

Also, I have a question regarding the invoice I was sent. When we first contacted Mr. Gibson regarding the extent of his services, we were informed that the 1-day software implementation service would also include a training session. However, on the invoice, it looks as though we were charged additionally for a training session. Is this a mistake, or was Mr. Gibson misinformed?

Thank you.
Milton Wood

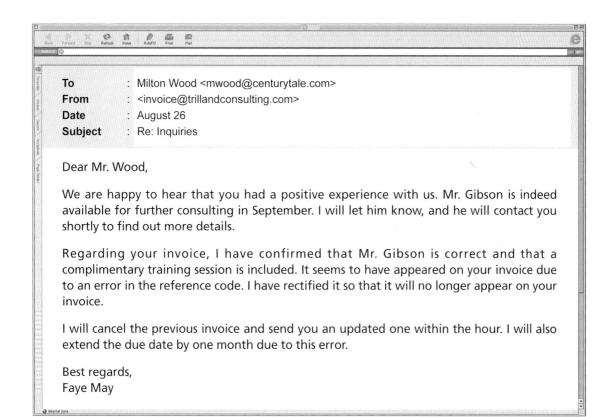

To : Milton Wood <mwood@centurytale.com>
From : <invoice@trillandconsulting.com>
Date : August 26
Subject : Re: Inquiries

Dear Mr. Wood,

We are happy to hear that you had a positive experience with us. Mr. Gibson is indeed available for further consulting in September. I will let him know, and he will contact you shortly to find out more details.

Regarding your invoice, I have confirmed that Mr. Gibson is correct and that a complimentary training session is included. It seems to have appeared on your invoice due to an error in the reference code. I have rectified it so that it will no longer appear on your invoice.

I will cancel the previous invoice and send you an updated one within the hour. I will also extend the due date by one month due to this error.

Best regards,
Faye May

196. What does the invoice imply about Trilland Consulting?

(A) It specializes in software-based solutions.
(B) It is currently hiring new consultants.
(C) It has operations in other countries.
(D) It has partnered with several software companies.

197. According to the first e-mail, what would Mr. Wood like to do?

(A) Receive further consultation
(B) Write a testimonial
(C) Issue a permit
(D) Visit a company

198. What code is Mr. Wood concerned about?

(A) 4882
(B) 0095
(C) 0075
(D) 0082

199. Who most likely is Ms. May?

(A) A consultant
(B) A recruitment agent
(C) A billing supervisor
(D) A software engineer

200. What is the due date on Mr. Wood's revised invoice?

(A) August 21
(B) August 26
(C) September 15
(D) October 15

Stop! This is the end of the test. If you finish before time is called, you may go back to Parts 5, 6, and 7 and check your work.

TEST 04

준비물: OMR 카드, 연필, 지우개, 시계
시험시간: RC 75분

나의 점수		
RC		
맞은 개수		
환산 점수		

TEST 01	TEST 02	TEST 03	TEST 04	TEST 05
_____점	_____점	_____점	_____점	_____점
TEST 06	**TEST 07**	**TEST 08**	**TEST 09**	**TEST 10**
_____점	_____점	_____점	_____점	_____점

점수 환산표

RC			
맞은 개수	환산 점수	맞은 개수	환산 점수
96-100	460-495	41-45	140-215
91-95	425-490	36-40	115-180
86-90	395-465	31-35	95-145
81-85	370-440	26-30	75-120
76-80	335-415	21-25	60-95
71-75	310-390	16-20	45-75
66-70	280-365	11-15	30-55
61-65	250-335	6-10	10-40
56-60	220-305	1-5	5-30
51-55	195-270	0	5-15
46-50	165-240		

READING TEST

In the Reading test, you will read a variety of texts and answer several different types of reading comprehension questions. The entire Reading test will last 75 minutes. There are three parts, and directions are given for each part. You are encouraged to answer as many questions as possible within the time allowed.

You must mark your answers on the separate answer sheet. Do not write your answers in your test book.

PART 5

Directions: A word or phrase is missing in each of the sentences below. Four answer choices are given below each sentence. Select the best answer to complete the sentence. Then mark the letter (A), (B), (C), or (D) on your answer sheet.

101. Before Ms. Lam submits the legal documents, she must ------- her manager.

(A) consult
(B) consults
(C) consulted
(D) consulting

102. The Builders Safety Group will examine the blueprints and provide ------- to the architects.

(A) opinion
(B) reaction
(C) feedback
(D) knowledge

103. Mindworks Ltd. has implemented several ------- reforms in its artificial intelligence ethics team.

(A) essence
(B) essentially
(C) essential
(D) essentialness

104. Having started only a week ago, Ms. LaPointe had a difficult time keeping ------- with the other physician's assistants.

(A) line
(B) track
(C) pace
(D) control

105. Denson Tech has launched a new vacuum cleaner that is more powerful and ------- than previous models.

(A) light
(B) lightly
(C) lighter
(D) lightest

106. Students ------- in attending the annual job fair should complete a registration form.

(A) interests
(B) interest
(C) interested
(D) interesting

107. The broadly advertised technology convention at the National Exhibition Center is ------- a large audience.

(A) calling
(B) suggesting
(C) happening
(D) attracting

108. Around 250 positions will be ------- when Peacock Publishers shuts down its operations in Arlington.

(A) eliminating
(B) eliminated
(C) eliminates
(D) eliminate

109. The Arcadia National Bank restorations are ------- to resume within the next three months.

(A) yet
(B) almost
(C) expected
(D) relevant

110. Ms. Salina's flight may not arrive on time ------- the wind shifts sooner than predicted.

(A) despite
(B) except
(C) since
(D) unless

111. The celebrity endorsements show ------- how stylish and fashionable our handbags are.

(A) like
(B) along
(C) around
(D) just

112. ------- business expenses will be reimbursed for all staff members working from home.

(A) Capable
(B) Reasoned
(C) Vacant
(D) Eligible

113. The appliances included in the sale were assembled at different factories, so they arrived -------.

(A) separately
(B) separates
(C) separating
(D) separate

114. Employees attending the convention in Houston were directed to make ------- for transportation, keep their receipts, and file reimbursement requests after they returned.

(A) pay
(B) to pay
(C) paying
(D) payments

115. Builders must wear hard hats at all times ------- on the construction site.

(A) while
(B) regrettably
(C) already
(D) before

116. ------- you need any assistance with your company e-mail, call Mr. Thapa in the IT team.

(A) Forward
(B) Whenever
(C) Therefore
(D) Likewise

117. ------- our Legal Department manager, Mr. Belfort, has just been appointed Director of Legal Affairs.

(A) Exclusively
(B) Candidly
(C) Formerly
(D) Exactly

118. This ------- lets you effectively launder all types of fabric without compromising on the cost.

(A) contentment
(B) efficiency
(C) administration
(D) detergent

119. Mr. Ahn, ------- his co-hosts, discusses current events around the world on their morning TV show.

(A) along with
(B) in case of
(C) as soon as
(D) in order to

120. Pyreen kitchen appliances will help your restaurant operate ------- no matter what cuisine you serve.

(A) smooth
(B) smoothed
(C) smoothing
(D) smoothly

GO ON TO THE NEXT PAGE

121. Although Merriman's dress shoes are made from synthetic leather, they are ------- softer and more durable than the genuine version.

(A) noticed
(B) noticing
(C) noticeable
(D) noticeably

122. Mr. Conde will decide if the firm's rate is too high for the ------- building design.

(A) organic
(B) careful
(C) exhausted
(D) proposed

123. Hahn Telecommunications, after its success in Kazakhstan, intends ------- its coverage across Central Asia.

(A) to broaden
(B) broad
(C) broadened
(D) have broadened

124. With numerous state-of-the-art features, the THR fitness tracker is most definitely ------- its price.

(A) right
(B) on
(C) worth
(D) within

125. The Flagstone Café ------- breakfast promotions on Sundays for the last decade.

(A) will be offering
(B) would have been offering
(C) has been offering
(D) is offering

126. Given the positive reviews from critics about her art exhibition, Ms. Griffin is expected to ------- gain international acclaim.

(A) after
(B) ahead
(C) soon
(D) very

127. Hill Sporting Goods customers who would like to ------- their purchases for another will be required to pay for the difference in price.

(A) fashion
(B) exchange
(C) corrode
(D) advertise

128. Virtually ------- number in Winston Sparks' original musical is noteworthy.

(A) recent
(B) whole
(C) best
(D) every

129. Duchene Investment Firm provides free consultations to help ------- business owners apply for loans.

(A) inexperienced
(B) indisputable
(C) unwilling
(D) unfamiliar

130. When members of the ------- arrive on Monday, Mr. Nichols will lead a city tour for them.

(A) rendition
(B) delegation
(C) objection
(D) designation

PART 6

Directions: Read the texts that follow. A word, phrase, or sentence is missing in parts of each text. Four answer choices for each question are given below the text. Select the best answer to complete the text. Then mark the letter (A), (B), (C), or (D) on your answer sheet.

Questions 131-134 refer to the following product review.

I was ------- to use new spreadsheet software because I didn't think any would have
131.
the same functionality as our current one. However, my company made the decision to

switch over to Zoro, so I gave it a go. I was ------- surprised.
132.

-------. Although it took a while, the manual explained it well enough. Then I tried doing
133.
some advanced functions such as forecasting our sales. The model the software

produced ended up being more accurate than before, which is why I would recommend

------- to other businesses despite the price.
134.

Although there are some features that are missing, the developers are constantly

working on updates. In my honest opinion, I think Zoro will be the new industry

standard at this rate.

131. (A) relucted
(B) reluctance
(C) reluctant
(D) reluctantly

132. (A) infrequently
(B) pleasantly
(C) arguably
(D) thoughtfully

133. (A) I expected to pay a higher price for that.
(B) Established businesses may already have their own software.
(C) Figuring out how to import my data was challenging at first.
(D) Zoro has been featured in some publications in the past.

134. (A) those
(B) many
(C) it
(D) them

GO ON TO THE NEXT PAGE

Questions 135-138 refer to the following article.

Safeguards and Precautions

The National Sculpture Gallery (NSG) makes every effort to protect the priceless works on display by carefully ------- the environment of the exhibits. Works made of wood are
135.
vulnerable to hot and dry conditions. -------, the gallery strictly controls the temperature
136.
of all areas. Nor does it display pieces outside during the summer months due to the

------- caused by the rainy season. -------. By making this effort to guard our priceless
137.   **138.**
collection, we hope to preserve the history and genius of our nation far into the future.

---

135. (A) conducting
(B) securing
(C) promoting
(D) monitoring

136. (A) Accordingly
(B) Previously
(C) Surprisingly
(D) Finally

137. (A) humidity
(B) humidify
(C) humid
(D) humidly

138. (A) Additionally, please refrain from touching any of the pieces on display.
(B) These will be exhibited again once they are returned to the gallery this fall.
(C) Sadly, some sculptures have been removed for emergency repairs.
(D) Some of the artworks are over 300 years old.

Questions 139-142 refer to the following product description.

DB Mallex's new "Anywhere" dress shirt is made of lightweight, odor-absorbing organic cotton perfect for traveling wherever you need to go. -------. The addition of flexible
139.
fabric on the ------- allows for greater mobility and comfort. The combination of stylish
140.
fit and breathability make it perfect whether you're in a meeting or on a hiking trail. This shirt comes with a reversible collar flap ------- provides an extra degree of versatility.
141.
Every purchase ------- from our headquarters in Wharton and is guaranteed to arrive
142.
anywhere in the country within 48 hours of ordering.

---

139. (A) This high-tech fabric stays wrinkle free and never needs ironing.
(B) Our company has been a leader in the fashion industry since 1982.
(C) The lightweight cotton pillowcase stays cool throughout the night.
(D) Its stylish design goes well with any style of shirt.

140. (A) buttons
(B) sleeves
(C) brim
(D) packaging

141. (A) still
(B) then
(C) such
(D) that

142. (A) have shipped
(B) had shipped
(C) were shipped
(D) will be shipped

GO ON TO THE NEXT PAGE

Questions 143-146 refer to the following notice.

Thank you for downloading the Trevea MyButler app. This app will help keep track of your incoming phone calls, text messages, and e-mails during your Trevea Air flight. To ------- whether your flight offers a complimentary WiFi, please check your booking
143.
confirmation form. You may also purchase WiFi access for $20 at any time. If the connection you have purchased does not meet your -------, you may request a refund.
144.

Please note that the WiFi connection is not suitable for Internet video streaming. Trevea Air recommends that you view our collection of in-flight movies and television shows available on your seat-back video screen. You are ------- more than welcome to use
145.
your personal device to watch your own movies or shows during the flight. We just ask that you set your devices to "Airplane Mode" before we take off. -------.
146.

143. (A) display
(B) confirm
(C) disclose
(D) select

144. (A) expecting
(B) expected
(C) expectations
(D) expects

145. (A) instead
(B) openly
(C) despite
(D) also

146. (A) Your dietary restrictions will be updated shortly.
(B) Weather conditions indicate that a delay may be possible.
(C) The app will utilize Bluetooth in the next update.
(D) We will remind you again before we depart.

PART 7

Directions: In this part you will read a selection of texts, such as magazine and newspaper articles, e-mails, and instant messages. Each text or set of texts is followed by several questions. Select the best answer for each question and mark the letter (A), (B), (C), or (D) on your answer sheet.

Questions 147-148 refer to the following advertisement.

> ## Deylano Allied Carpenters
> A local favorite for over 15 years
>
> If you've been thinking about some home renovations, save yourself the trouble by giving us a call. We have been in business for well over a decade, and there's a reason we're the only ones Deylano trusts. Whether you need your garden trimmed and maintained, you want to put in a new swimming pool, or you just need to fix a few things around the house, we can do it all.
>
> Go to www.deylanoallied.com/request and describe what you need. Based on your needs, we will give you a call with a quote. If you mention this advertisement, we will knock 15 percent off the total price. This offer is only valid until February 25, so what are you waiting for?

147. What is indicated about Deylano Allied Carpenters?

(A) They are currently fully booked until March.
(B) They have locations in other cities.
(C) Their workforce solely consists of Deylano citizens.
(D) Their services include conducting house repairs.

148. How can a discount be obtained from Deylano Allied Carpenters?

(A) By referring to an advertisement
(B) By becoming a member on the website
(C) By arranging multiple services
(D) By paying a deposit

GO ON TO THE NEXT PAGE ➡

Questions 149-150 refer to the following note.

A note from: Postal Plus

Your delivery is scheduled for 10 April. The size of the item being delivered means someone must be present. This is so that our employees can bring it into the house safely for you. Please ensure that you are at home between 9 A.M. to 11 A.M. to allow for delivery.

Sender: Longvale Buck
Package Identification Number: K932AE
Delivery to: Kendall Evans
        12 Delisle Avenue
        Mercer, Pennsylvania 16137

If you require a different delivery date, visit our website www.postalplus.com/mydelivery.

149. What is suggested about Ms. Evans's delivery?

(A) It was shipped from overseas.
(B) It is for a large item.
(C) It was delivered on 10 April.
(D) It contains fragile parts.

150. According to the note, what can Ms. Evans do on Postal Plus's website?

(A) Submit feedback on a service
(B) View the contents of a package
(C) Change a delivery date
(D) Track the progress of a delivery

Questions 151-153 refer to the following press release.

www.sparksvillearch.com/press_release

Looking for something fun to do with the entire family? The Museum of Archaeology now has extended hours on Saturday and Sunday nights until 9:00 P.M. Come and see some of our most popular exhibits including our numerous fossils and recently unearthed tools from the early settlers.

Additionally, from now until 28 April, we are waiving the price of admissions to our exhibit on Ancient Egypt. This is a limited-time offer, so take advantage while you can. We are also accepting bookings for our primitive art classes once again. Advance bookings are mandatory, and these can be made via our website.

The Museum of Archaeology provides ample outdoors parking as well as numerous cafés and restaurant options. Our gift shop has souvenirs for everyone, and proceeds from gift shop purchases go towards improving our range of exhibits.

151. What is suggested about The Museum of Archaeology?

(A) It has updated its website.
(B) It will be undergoing renovations soon.
(C) Its membership program has new requirements.
(D) Its hours of operation have been lengthened.

152. What most likely will happen after April 28?

(A) An exhibit will charge an admission fee.
(B) A holiday program will be announced.
(C) A gift shop will increase its prices.
(D) A parking lot will be closed off.

153. What is indicated about the art classes?

(A) They use tools shown in the exhibits.
(B) They must be booked ahead of time.
(C) They are only available in the evenings.
(D) They have an age restriction.

GO ON TO THE NEXT PAGE

Questions 154-155 refer to the following text message chain.

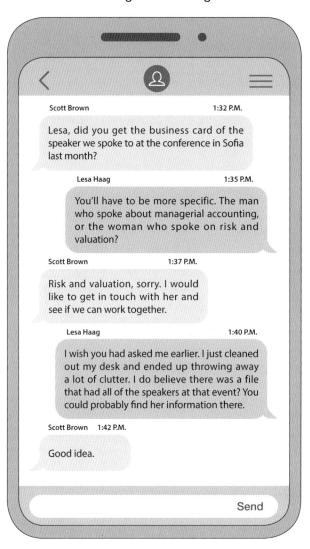

Scott Brown   1:32 P.M.

Lesa, did you get the business card of the speaker we spoke to at the conference in Sofia last month?

Lesa Haag   1:35 P.M.

You'll have to be more specific. The man who spoke about managerial accounting, or the woman who spoke on risk and valuation?

Scott Brown   1:37 P.M.

Risk and valuation, sorry. I would like to get in touch with her and see if we can work together.

Lesa Haag   1:40 P.M.

I wish you had asked me earlier. I just cleaned out my desk and ended up throwing away a lot of clutter. I do believe there was a file that had all of the speakers at that event? You could probably find her information there.

Scott Brown   1:42 P.M.

Good idea.

Send

154. What most likely was the subject of the conference in Sofia?

(A) Software design
(B) Architecture
(C) Finance
(D) Engineering

155. At 1:40 P.M., what does Ms. Haag most likely mean when she writes, "I wish you had asked me earlier"?

(A) She lost a copy of a requested contract.
(B) She is happy to fulfill Mr. Brown's request.
(C) She does not remember the details.
(D) She is unable to help Mr. Brown.

TRUENORTH DENTIST CLINIC
Patient Satisfaction Survey

How did you find out about us?
[ ] Newspaper   [ ] TV   [ ] Internet   [ ] Family/friends   [**V**] Other (specify below)

Directed to this clinic from my doctor

What was the purpose of your visit?

To get a wisdom tooth removed

How long did you have to wait for your procedure?

30 minutes, but I didn't book in advance

How well did the dentist explain the procedure?

Dentist helped me feel more comfortable

Would you use our services again? Please specify why.

Yes, the procedure went very smoothly, and the price was great

What would you like to see improved about our service? Please be specific.

Although I had the address to the clinic, it was difficult finding it. Perhaps some signs or arrows would help

To enter our draw for a free cleaning, please fill in your details:

Name: [Cara Luke]
E-mail: [cluke@pembton.com]

I consent to being sent details about special deals or discounts offered by TrueNorth Dentist Clinic.   [V]

Thank you for your feedback!

---

156. What difficulty does Ms. Luke mention?

(A) Finding the clinic
(B) Booking an appointment
(C) Parking her car
(D) Paying for the procedure

157. What does Ms. Luke allow TrueNorth Dentist Clinic to do?

(A) Suggest additional procedures
(B) Book her next appointment
(C) Send her promotional information
(D) Publish her testimony online

GO ON TO THE NEXT PAGE

Questions 158-161 refer to the following information.

Secondments Open at Stebry Consulting Group

—[1]—. In the thirty years Stebry Consulting Group has been in operation, we have partnered with over 50 clients located in 14 different countries. It is our mission to embrace different nationalities and cultures. As part of that mission, we are now offering secondments to work with one of our partners in various places around the world. —[2]—. This opportunity is available to employees with at least two years of work experience at Stebry.

All available positions can be viewed in the employee section of our company website. —[3]—. If you are interested in an opening, we ask that you carefully review the job requirements to ensure you meet them. If you feel that you do, your first step should be to speak to your manager. Upon obtaining your manager's approval, you should then contact Mr. Collins, who will then interview you for the position. —[4]—. As Mr. Collins heads our client relationship team, the decision to approve the secondment request ultimately rests with him.

158. What is the purpose of the information?

(A) To elicit a vote on a new policy
(B) To announce a recent decision
(C) To ask employees to check a report
(D) To describe an important result

159. How can employees find out about open positions at Stebry Consulting Group?

(A) By downloading a document
(B) By attending an interview
(C) By accessing a website
(D) By speaking to a manager

160. According to the information, what is a responsibility of Mr. Collins?

(A) Contacting international clients
(B) Forecasting quarterly sales
(C) Authorizing secondment requests
(D) Evaluating employee performances

161. In which of the positions marked [1], [2], [3], and [4] does the following sentence best belong?

"It is recommended that you prepare well for this."

(A) [1]
(B) [2]
(C) [3]
(D) [4]

Questions 162-165 refer to the following article.

Filling Up A Plate

At Cheesman Park

Eldorado, July 7 —— Hayward's took home the award for Best Tasting Food at the Backyard Cook-off at Cheesman Park last Friday. It won first place among 11 contestants.

The Backyard Cook-off is a popular event, drawing participating restaurants and spectators from all over the greater Eldorado area. After a short introduction from the event organizer, Malcolm Jones, cooks from all the establishments began smoking and grilling meats all around the park. Attendees were given the opportunity to sample different types of barbecue from each restaurant. They were then asked to rate the food they had sampled. Later that night, after all the ratings were reviewed, everyone gathered for the awards presentation.

Hayward's continued its string of successes at this year's event. Last year, their smoky pulled pork came in second, and the year before, their spicy chicken took third place. Be sure to try both when you visit their restaurant.

Hayward's recently celebrated its 10th anniversary in Eldorado. During its first year of business, Hayward's was just a barbecue smoker and a couple of picnic tables outside a local supermarket. Now, they operate in a space that fits up to 40 families.

Before Hayward's received their prize, the winners for second place and third place were announced. Rattlesnake Barbecue took home the latter honor, while Joe's Smokehouse won second for their brisket.

162. What kind of event is mentioned in the article?

(A) The opening of a new location in south Eldorado
(B) A food sale to collect donations for charity
(C) A celebration for a newly-elected government official
(D) A cooking competition featuring local businesses

163. According to the article, what probably happened on Friday night?

(A) Rattlesnake Barbecue moved to a new location.
(B) Joe's Smokehouse bought a new grill.
(C) Hayward's was given an award.
(D) Cheesman Park closed early for the day.

164. What is true about Hayward's?

(A) It raises its own chickens.
(B) It was recognized in two previous Backyard Cook-offs.
(C) It sells its products to supermarkets in the Eldorado area.
(D) It is owned by Malcolm Jones.

165. What is suggested about Rattlesnake Barbecue?

(A) It got lower ratings than Joe's Smokehouse.
(B) It was started by a chef who was previously employed at Hayward's.
(C) It is a family-run business.
(D) It is famous for its brisket dish.

GO ON TO THE NEXT PAGE

Questions 166-167 refer to the following Web page.

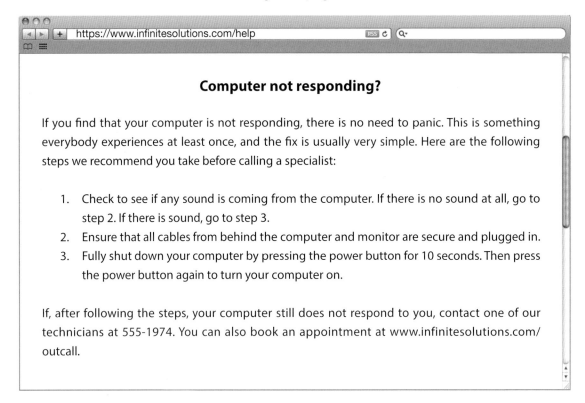

Computer not responding?

If you find that your computer is not responding, there is no need to panic. This is something everybody experiences at least once, and the fix is usually very simple. Here are the following steps we recommend you take before calling a specialist:

1. Check to see if any sound is coming from the computer. If there is no sound at all, go to step 2. If there is sound, go to step 3.
2. Ensure that all cables from behind the computer and monitor are secure and plugged in.
3. Fully shut down your computer by pressing the power button for 10 seconds. Then press the power button again to turn your computer on.

If, after following the steps, your computer still does not respond to you, contact one of our technicians at 555-1974. You can also book an appointment at www.infinitesolutions.com/outcall.

---

166. What does the Web page suggest about a computer freeze?

(A) It may lead to repair fees.
(B) It tends to happen with older models.
(C) It can only be fixed by specialists.
(D) It is a common occurrence.

167. What is NOT mentioned as a possible way to address a computer freeze?

(A) Installing an update
(B) Booking an appointment
(C) Restarting the computer
(D) Checking the cables

Avoiding Burnout

A recent study by Jarrett Partners has revealed that many office workers in Dover are feeling the effects of burnout. Many workers reported that over the past year, feelings of dissatisfaction, lack of motivation, and persistent tiredness are becoming more frequent. —[1]—. Dover has become a hotspot for many start-ups in the area, but this has also created an overly work-focused culture. Consequently, many companies are looking for ways to alleviate the effects of burnout.

One popular solution is to encourage more time off. A four-day work week has been trialed in many of the companies in the area, and the results have been positive. —[2]—. A three-day weekend has led to employees taking trips outside of Dover, which provides a way to take their busy minds off work. Employees reported coming back to work fresher and more motivated.

Another solution is to host fun events for employees. Events dispersed throughout the year break up the monotony of everyday work while also creating a sense of community within teams. Experts stress that events do not have to be expensive. Some ideas that don't break the bank include going on a company picnic or hosting a sporting event. —[3]—.

One more way is to allow employees to work from home on occasion. —[4]—. Sometimes, it is the commute to work that contributes to burnout. Allowing employees to work from home can eliminate the burden of commuting while still staying on top of their work.

All companies are at risk of losing valuable employees to burnout. However, by taking preemptive steps and providing support, burnout can be an issue of the past.

168. What is one purpose of the article?

(A) To contrast various working styles
(B) To disprove a misconception
(C) To discuss a common workplace issue
(D) To advertise a consulting service

169. What does the article suggest about many workers in Dover?

(A) They do not own their own vehicles.
(B) They report feeling tired often.
(C) They hold advanced university degrees.
(D) They frequently change jobs.

170. What is NOT mentioned in the article as a way to prevent burnout?

(A) Allowing employees to work from home
(B) Hosting occasional events
(C) Working fewer days
(D) Increasing salaries

171. In which of the positions marked [1], [2], [3], and [4] does the following sentence best belong?

"Not all burnout is attributable to what happens at work."

(A) [1]
(B) [2]
(C) [3]
(D) [4]

GO ON TO THE NEXT PAGE

TEST 04

Questions 172-175 refer to the following text message chain.

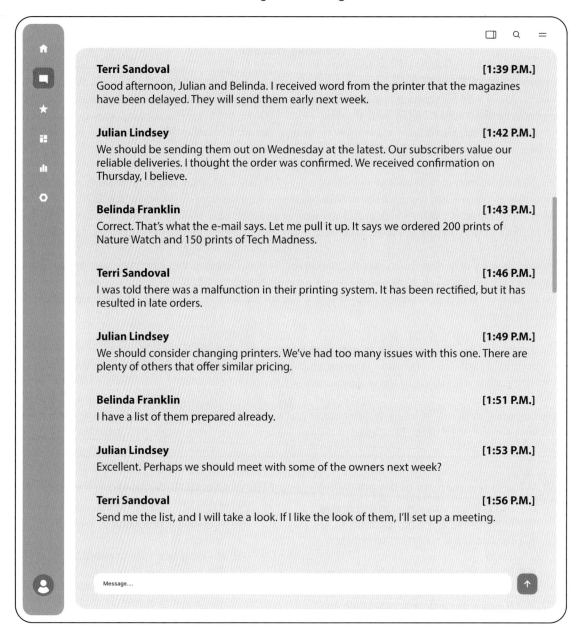

Terri Sandoval [1:39 P.M.]

Good afternoon, Julian and Belinda. I received word from the printer that the magazines have been delayed. They will send them early next week.

Julian Lindsey [1:42 P.M.]

We should be sending them out on Wednesday at the latest. Our subscribers value our reliable deliveries. I thought the order was confirmed. We received confirmation on Thursday, I believe.

Belinda Franklin [1:43 P.M.]

Correct. That's what the e-mail says. Let me pull it up. It says we ordered 200 prints of Nature Watch and 150 prints of Tech Madness.

Terri Sandoval [1:46 P.M.]

I was told there was a malfunction in their printing system. It has been rectified, but it has resulted in late orders.

Julian Lindsey [1:49 P.M.]

We should consider changing printers. We've had too many issues with this one. There are plenty of others that offer similar pricing.

Belinda Franklin [1:51 P.M.]

I have a list of them prepared already.

Julian Lindsey [1:53 P.M.]

Excellent. Perhaps we should meet with some of the owners next week?

Terri Sandoval [1:56 P.M.]

Send me the list, and I will take a look. If I like the look of them, I'll set up a meeting.

Message....

172. What type of work do the writers most likely do?

(A) Event photographers
(B) Magazine publishers
(C) Market researchers
(D) Printer manufacturers

173. When was an order confirmed?

(A) On Monday
(B) On Wednesday
(C) On Thursday
(D) On Saturday

174. At 1:43 P.M., what does Ms. Franklin most likely mean when she writes, "Let me pull it up"?

(A) She is updating a number on an invoice.
(B) She is sending out local deliveries.
(C) She is contacting a future subscriber.
(D) She is viewing an e-mail from a printer.

175. What will Ms. Sandoval most likely do next?

(A) Attend a meeting
(B) View a document
(C) Compile some results
(D) Cancel an order

TEST 04

GO ON TO THE NEXT PAGE

Questions 176-180 refer to the following flyer and letter.

Are you between the ages of 18 and 42, living in the Chicago area, and in need of some extra cash? Then, contact Mercer Research!

We at Mercer Research are looking for people to participate in paid focus group sessions, so we can obtain valuable input for our clients. If you are interested in any of the listings below, please visit www.mercerresearch.com/focusgroups to sign up. You will need to complete a questionnaire to confirm that you are a suitable candidate.

#G918 – Music lovers are wanted to give their opinions on a local band's new album. Participants will earn $75 for the 90-minute listening session.

#G929 – Electronics enthusiasts are wanted to test and review a brand-new tablet PC for two hours. After completing a short survey, attendees will earn $125 for their time.

#G951 – Parents of children under the age of five are invited to take part in a two-day focus group on toys. Meetings will last for three hours each day, and participants will earn $300 for their time.

#G996 – Sports fans are needed to give their opinions on the local professional baseball team. Both new and old fans are encouraged to sign up to attend a pair of one-hour discussions. In return, participants will receive $50 and two tickets to the next home game.

October 3

Jacob Tambor
1912 Farland Way
Chicago, IL 60606

Mr. Tambor,

You have been accepted to participate in session #G996. As our Web page states, you will be asked to attend two one-hour meetings set for August 18 at 12 P.M. and August 20 at 1 P.M. I will lead both of the sessions. Since time is limited, we ask that you watch a short video and fill out a survey before attending the session. This should allow for a more productive discussion.

Our building is currently undergoing a renovation project, so we will not be meeting at our main office. Instead, we have reserved a workspace in the city center (directions can be found on our website). Also, enclosed, you'll find a pass that will give you access to the building's parking garage.

In the event that you are unable to attend your session, it is important that you let us know as quickly as you can. This will allow us to notify an alternative candidate.

We appreciate your help and time.

Nathaniel Olsen

Nathaniel Olsen
Mercer Research

Enclosure

176. What is the purpose of the flyer?

    (A) To hire qualified research assistants

    (B) To promote a new marketing firm

    (C) To list upcoming athletic competitions

    (D) To advertise a discussion opportunity

177. How much will Mercer Research most likely pay Mr. Tambor?

    (A) $50

    (B) $75

    (C) $125

    (D) $300

178. What is implied about Mr. Olsen?

    (A) He needs to purchase a tablet PC.

    (B) He organizes focus groups.

    (C) He has a part-time job.

    (D) He works at a sports stadium.

179. What is included with the letter?

    (A) A building map

    (B) An application form

    (C) A parking pass

    (D) A meal coupon

180. What will Mercer Research do if Mr. Tambor cancels his appointment?

    (A) Contact another applicant

    (B) Send an information packet

    (C) Reschedule a meeting

    (D) Issue a full reimbursement

GO ON TO THE NEXT PAGE →

Questions 181-185 refer to the following questionnaire and e-mail.

QUESTIONNAIRE

Thank you for taking a moment to fill out our questionnaire. By doing so, you are helping us to better serve you here at Barkley's. In the form below, please check the box that indicates your level of satisfaction with each aspect.

(1=Poor, 2=Fair, 3=Average, 4=Good, 5=Excellent)

	1 2 3 4 5
How would you rate the store's atmosphere and cleanliness?	☐ ☐ ☐ ■ ☐
How would you rate the freshness of the ingredients used in your dish?	☐ ☐ ☐ ☐ ■
How would you rate your satisfaction compared to how much you paid for the food?	☐ ☐ ☐ ■ ☐
How would you rate the speed of the service you received?	☐ ☐ ☐ ☐ ■
How would you rate the staff's ability to answer your questions?	■ ☐ ☐ ☐ ☐
How would you rate your overall impression of Barkley's?	☐ ☐ ☐ ■ ☐

• How much did you spend today?: $75
• Age (optional):
14-21 ☐ / 22-29 ■ / 30-37 ☐ / 38-45 ☐ / 46-54 ☐ / 55+ ☐
• Name (optional): Miguel Nunez
• E-mail (optional): mnunez1@penmail.co.nz

TO: Miguel Nunez <mnunez1@penmail.co.nz>
FROM: Support Services <ss@barkleys.co.nz>
DATE: Tuesday, 4 August, 11:25 A.M.
SUBJECT: QUESTIONNAIRE
ATTACHMENT: coupon

Dear Mr. Nunez,

We would like to thank you for taking the time to fill out our questionnaire about Barkley's. We received feedback from a lot of people, and we value all of your opinions. This information provides us with an opportunity to learn and serve you better.

We are glad to see that your overall rating of Barkley's was satisfactory. We were, however, disappointed to see that the majority of the responses we received expressed negative impressions regarding the same aspect that you were unhappy with. I want to assure you that we are taking the necessary steps to correct this problem. A new employee education program will be starting in the near future.

To show our appreciation for your feedback, we would like you to have a coupon (attached to this e-mail) for 20 percent off your next purchase at any Barkley's location in the nation. As always, we thank you for your business.

Best,

Yasiel Sanders

181. What kind of business most likely is Barkley's?

    (A) An electronics store
    (B) A supermarket
    (C) A restaurant
    (D) A marketing agency

182. Which statement about Barkley's would Mr. Nunez most likely agree with?

    (A) It is reasonably priced.
    (B) It has a wide range of services.
    (C) It is in a convenient location.
    (D) It has experienced employees.

183. In the e-mail, the word "value" in paragraph 1, line 2, is closest in meaning to

    (A) calculate
    (B) appreciate
    (C) profit
    (D) emphasize

184. What most likely is Barkley's planning to do?

    (A) Clean the workplace more frequently
    (B) Lower prices on some of its merchandise
    (C) Offer a coupon to every customer who participates in a questionnaire
    (D) Train workers to be more knowledgeable about its products

185. What is implied about the questionnaire?

    (A) It must be filled out on the Internet.
    (B) Many customers have completed it.
    (C) It is updated every two years.
    (D) Mr. Sanders designed it.

GO ON TO THE NEXT PAGE

To: David Davis <daviddavis@orourkeschools.edu>
From: Maggie Jones <maggiejones@albanytours.ca>
Date: 6 March
Subject: April Tournament Estimate
Attachment: ORourke_April.pdf; EntertainmentOptions.pdf

Hi David,

We really enjoyed putting together the school trip this past December, and we appreciate the opportunity to make arrangements for the Edmonton Bears for this month's Provincial Hockey Playoffs. We were able to find a hotel near the venue to meet your request for an open-ended reservation, which I understand is required since the duration of the team's stay will be determined by the stage they reach in the competition.

You'll find an attachment that details the rates below. I've also included some pamphlets describing local tourist attractions and recommended activities.

I appreciate your continued business.

Best,

Maggie B. Jones

The Alpine Inn, Richview

Check-in Date: 21 April
Guests: Edmonton Bears (student-athletes, team managers, and coaches)
Contact Person: David Davis (818) 555-3143

Competition Round	Total Length of Stay	Total Room Rate Per Round
Round 1	5 nights	$10,000
Round 2	4 nights	$8,000
Round 3	3 nights	$6,000
Finals	2 nights	$4,000

Charges are due at the end of each stage. Your daily group rate is $2,000 per night.

To:	Maggie Jones <maggiejones@albanytours.ca>
From:	David Davis <daviddavis@orourkeschools.edu>
Date:	27 April
Subject:	April Event

Maggie,

Thanks for sending over the updated itemized bill for the team trip. My assistant visited your office earlier in the afternoon and dropped off a check for $6,000 as agreed. Regarding the trip, I want to thank you. Everything went very smoothly with lodging, food, and transportation, and we especially loved the horse-riding tour you suggested. The team had so much fun taking photos with the animals afterward.

I'll let you know about our next trip soon. It will likely be in October, but I'll fill you in when I get the details.

David Davis

186. Who most likely is Ms. Jones?

(A) A hockey coach
(B) A hotel employee
(C) A school official
(D) A travel agent

187. What is true about the room rates sent to Mr. Davis?

(A) They do not change by the length of stay.
(B) They include a free morning meal.
(C) They are only provided to sports teams.
(D) They have increased recently.

188. According to the second e-mail, what is indicated about Mr. Davis' payment?

(A) It was paid in person.
(B) It was made in installments.
(C) It was higher than expected.
(D) It was made for an October trip.

189. What did Mr. Davis most likely do with the pamphlets Ms. Jones sent?

(A) He updated the information.
(B) He distributed them to the Edmonton Bears.
(C) He requested that more copies be made of them.
(D) He emailed them to a colleague.

190. What was the last round of the competition that the Edmonton Bears participated in?

(A) Round 1
(B) Round 2
(C) Round 3
(D) Finals

GO ON TO THE NEXT PAGE

This chart summarizes the harvest seasons of some strawberry varieties commonly grown in New Zealand.

	Albion	Chandler	Galetta	Royal	San Andreas
October					✓
November	✓				✓
December	✓				✓
January	✓	✓			✓
February	✓	✓		✓	✓
March		✓		✓	✓
April		✓		✓	
May		✓	✓	✓	
June			✓		
July			✓		

Want to grow with Agility Farm Group?

· Strawberries can be harvested year-round in New Zealand, guaranteeing the tastiest and freshest fruit.

· With our new local variety, we are able to supply strawberries during the off-season which takes place after May. This eclipses even varieties with late harvests such as the Royal variety.

· Our farmers are scattered all throughout New Zealand. Purchasing from us means supporting New Zealand farmers.

· Many of our farmers grow strawberries inside sustainable greenhouses. This not only minimizes the impact weather has on our crops, but it also contributes to our mission of embedding sustainability into farming.

· The Agility Farm Group has made a name for itself in New Zealand as one that cares. We ensure that all batches with our brand on it meet the highest quality standards.

To	Agility Support <support@agilityfarms.co.nz>
From	Elmer Norton <enorton@thebasket.co.nz>
Date	2 April
Subject	Your strawberries

Dear Agility Farm Group:

We received our fifth shipment of Chandler strawberries from you last week. This is the first year we've sold this variety, and it's been a huge success. It seems that strawberries are trending these days because we are consistently selling out, often within a few days. Therefore, I'd like to see if we can increase the size of our orders. Could we receive some quotes?

Also, I have noticed that the Chandler variety can be found in other stores. I'd like to try something new that will bring even more people into the store. Would you have any other varieties that are in season at this time? If so, we'd like to get some orders in right away while strawberries are flying off the shelves!

Thank you.

Elmer Norton
Owner, The Basket

191. According to the chart, what strawberry variety has the longest harvest season?

(A) Albion
(B) Chandler
(C) Royal
(D) San Andreas

192. What does the Web page indicate about Agility Farm Group?

(A) Its farmers grow their strawberries indoors.
(B) Its full product range includes meat products.
(C) It was founded by a group of farmers.
(D) It only sells to specific stores in New Zealand.

193. What is most likely true about Galetta strawberries?

(A) They have a sweeter taste than other varieties.
(B) They are often difficult to ship in large quantities.
(C) They are a local variety grown in New Zealand.
(D) They are the most expensive variety.

194. Why did Mr. Norton send the e-mail?

(A) To suggest a meeting date
(B) To inquire about some prices
(C) To request some nutritional information
(D) To change a delivery date

195. What will Agility Support most likely suggest that Mr. Norton do?

(A) Order more Chandler strawberries
(B) Increase its prices
(C) Speak to a farmer
(D) Try Royal strawberries

GO ON TO THE NEXT PAGE

Questions 196-200 refer to the following advertisement, customer review, and e-mail.

Chaucomb Catering
Supplying only the best food for Nevada's busy workers
169-555-4977

Chaucomb Catering specializes in providing treats and beverages for businesses in the area. Every week, we send a basket of curated snacks and beverages to your workplace for your employees to enjoy.

We understand that health is an important priority. Therefore, we partner with only the best food and beverage vendors in the area who provide delicious but healthy products. We can also cater for allergies as well as those with vegetarian or vegan diets. In short, simply tell us what you would like, and we will be happy to accommodate your needs.

If you would like to test some of our products, call us today to arrange a sample basket to be delivered. Alternatively, visit our office at 712 Grove Crescent in Bristol. If you are interested in event-catering services, inquire about our MealCare Program. Find out why we have been in business for over 25 years by giving us a call.

Chaucomb Catering
★★★☆☆
August 18

I've heard a lot about Chaucomb Catering from other businesses in the area, so I finally decided to give it a go. I immediately saw why so many businesses were fiercely loyal to Chaucomb. Ms. Chaucomb took it upon herself to come into our office to meet our employees in order to understand what kind of products she should include. The price was admittedly higher than I had expected, but my employees managed to convince me. Given the proximity of their office, I was even more surprised that there was a delivery fee at all. However, the presentation of the basket was great, and it really boosted morale in the workplace.

I do have to mention a problem we did encounter. On some of the oatmeal cookies we were sent, we noticed that they were already stale. It caused a bit of embarrassment for us as we had offered a visiting client one of the cookies, and he mentioned it. I hope this is not a recurring problem for Chaucomb Catering.

Brian Garrett
bgarrett@franklinpartners.com

To	bgarrett@franklinpartners.com
From	chaucomb@chaucomb.com
Date	August 21
Subject	A message from Chaucomb Catering

Dear Mr. Garrett,

I would first like to thank you for giving Chaucomb Catering a chance. After reading your comment, I would like to extend my deepest apologies over your experience. The vendor we purchased the problematic items from has been on our radar for some time as we have heard similar problems from our other clients. We regretfully did not take action sooner, and for that, we would like to apologize. We have removed the vendor from our list until they rectify their quality issues.

To make up for that poor experience, we would like to offer you two free baskets as well as a 25 percent discount on our MealCare Program. We hope this shows how committed we are to keeping our customers happy.

Sincerely,

Barbara Chaucomb
Owner, Chaucomb Catering

196. According to the advertisement, who are Chaucomb Catering's clients?

(A) Multinational companies
(B) Local businesses
(C) Regional schools
(D) Government agencies

197. What aspect of Chaucomb Catering's service does Mr. Garrett praise in his review?

(A) The appearance
(B) The delivery time
(C) The cost
(D) The quality

198. What is suggested about Mr. Garrett?

(A) He has worked with Ms. Chaucomb in the past.
(B) He intends on hiring additional employees.
(C) His business is located in Bristol.
(D) His office recently underwent renovations.

199. What is indicated in the e-mail about Chaucomb Catering?

(A) It does not check the quality of its products.
(B) It received several complaints in the past.
(C) It intends on expanding its product line.
(D) It only works with local vendors.

200. What is one of the offers that Ms. Chaucomb extends to Mr. Garrett?

(A) An invite to an event
(B) A catalog of upcoming products
(C) A referral to a different vendor
(D) A discount on a catering service

Stop! This is the end of the test. If you finish before time is called, you may go back to Parts 5, 6, and 7 and check your work.

TEST 05

준비물: OMR 카드, 연필, 지우개, 시계
시험시간: RC 75분

나의 점수	
RC	
맞은 개수	
환산 점수	

TEST 01	TEST 02	TEST 03	TEST 04	TEST 05
_____점	_____점	_____점	_____점	_____점
TEST 06	TEST 07	TEST 08	TEST 09	TEST 10
_____점	_____점	_____점	_____점	_____점

점수 환산표

RC			
맞은 개수	환산 점수	맞은 개수	환산 점수
96-100	460-495	41-45	140-215
91-95	425-490	36-40	115-180
86-90	395-465	31-35	95-145
81-85	370-440	26-30	75-120
76-80	335-415	21-25	60-95
71-75	310-390	16-20	45-75
66-70	280-365	11-15	30-55
61-65	250-335	6-10	10-40
56-60	220-305	1-5	5-30
51-55	195-270	0	5-15
46-50	165-240		

READING TEST

In the Reading test, you will read a variety of texts and answer several different types of reading comprehension questions. The entire Reading test will last 75 minutes. There are three parts, and directions are given for each part. You are encouraged to answer as many questions as possible within the time allowed.

You must mark your answers on the separate answer sheet. Do not write your answers in your test book.

PART 5

Directions: A word or phrase is missing in each of the sentences below. Four answer choices are given below each sentence. Select the best answer to complete the sentence. Then mark the letter (A), (B), (C), or (D) on your answer sheet.

101. Takagawa Co. renovated the building by constructing a ------- outside dining area.

(A) beautifully
(B) beautiful
(C) beautify
(D) beauty

102. Push firmly ------- the bar with your hands to release the emergency door's locking mechanism.

(A) on
(B) at
(C) by
(D) up

103. Mr. Watson is responsible for accepting all produce or meat shipments when they ------- after regular business hours have ended.

(A) are delivered
(B) will deliver
(C) deliver
(D) are delivering

104. Seeing that your rent is now two weeks -------, you must pay an additional late fee as stated in the contract.

(A) valuable
(B) remaining
(C) overdue
(D) owed

105. The conversation with Mr. Davidson was ------- Biznet Magazine's best interview of the year.

(A) easy
(B) easiest
(C) easily
(D) easing

106. Eileen's Boutique ------- primarily to wholesale distributors but also accepts retail customers.

(A) has
(B) does
(C) alters
(D) sells

107. The training ------- have turned in their final evaluations of the recently hired interns for official approval.

(A) supervision
(B) supervisory
(C) supervisors
(D) supervisor

108. Ms. Sawyer's train arrived ------- late for her to participate in the luncheon.

(A) very
(B) quite
(C) so
(D) too

109. Cheetah Automobile's next electric car is expected to be ten times more efficient than its ------- one.

(A) anticipated
(B) prompt
(C) current
(D) hardest

110. The legal guarantee period for the BMV convertible is five years ------- 300 thousand kilometers, whichever takes place first.

(A) plus
(B) or
(C) but
(D) to

111. Moody Advertising praised Ms. Young and her team for exceeding the client's -------.

(A) expectations
(B) expectantly
(C) expecting
(D) expect

112. Hancock Financial Services never ------- client information to other parties without the account holder's authorization.

(A) locates
(B) manages
(C) collects
(D) discloses

113. Please contact the company that we ordered the coffee beans from to confirm we ------- recorded the quantity on the purchase form.

(A) solely
(B) directly
(C) originally
(D) correctly

114. The city of Morrison is inviting the public ------- in its plan to put up a new commemorative plaque celebrating the city's centennial.

(A) arrangement
(B) interest
(C) comment
(D) order

115. Harper Wallpaper is sold in a wide variety of patterns ------- any home.

(A) is suiting
(B) to suit
(C) suited
(D) suit

116. Considering the ------- call volume on Monday mornings, contacting our customer services may take longer than expected.

(A) multiple
(B) noisy
(C) heavy
(D) extended

117. For the majority of restaurants, retaining local customers is more ------- than attracting out-of-town visitors.

(A) profit
(B) profits
(C) profiting
(D) profitable

118. The Maynard Fine Art Museum requires that the ------- of recording devices be limited to the lobby and reception areas.

(A) category
(B) usage
(C) capacity
(D) period

119. Stowaway Storage Center apologized for the ------- difficulties that renters had with its electronic locking system.

(A) occasionally
(B) occasion
(C) occasioned
(D) occasional

120. Carmel Ltd. has hired a learning specialist to ------- its employee education and development programs.

(A) manage
(B) apprehend
(C) proclaim
(D) presume

GO ON TO THE NEXT PAGE

121. Mr. Griffon examined the applications for ------- who could handle the redesign project with a limited budget.

(A) him
(B) ours
(C) himself
(D) anyone

122. ------- complimentary guided tours, the art museum will offer new services for visitors.

(A) In addition to
(B) In comparison to
(C) Except
(D) Likewise

123. ------- three million people are projected to attend the World Football Tournament.

(A) Nearness
(B) Nearest
(C) Neared
(D) Nearly

124. The Southeast Asian Education Initiative believes that continued ------- between educators and families is critical.

(A) competence
(B) assistance
(C) compliance
(D) collaboration

125. With our network of freelancers, Transbridges can send an interpreter to help ------- there is a need.

(A) out
(B) wherever
(C) one another
(D) fast

126. ------- employees moderately improve their workplace productivity will BlueBox House be able to increase its revenues.

(A) Except
(B) Since
(C) Beginning
(D) Only if

127. Overton Research utilizes their findings from market surveys to base ------- promotional strategies on.

(A) itself
(B) its
(C) them
(D) theirs

128. Following the Web design workshop, participants stated that their site traffic was ------- higher.

(A) severely
(B) considerably
(C) necessarily
(D) willingly

129. ------- the expansion of the street is not complete, please use the rear entrance.

(A) In the event that
(B) Overall
(C) In response to
(D) Nevertheless

130. Tour guides in Boston receive formal training but should be generally ------- about the city's history.

(A) anticipated
(B) knowledgeable
(C) distinguished
(D) inventive

PART 6

Directions: Read the texts that follow. A word, phrase, or sentence is missing in parts of each text. Four answer choices for each question are given below the text. Select the best answer to complete the text. Then mark the letter (A), (B), (C), or (D) on your answer sheet.

Questions 131-134 refer to the following letter.

A message to our loyal customers:

Bullseye Appliances strives ------- high-quality products at affordable prices. In addition
131.
to our competitive costs, our tremendous customer service has made us the most

trusted chain of appliance retailers in the province. Bullseye's five locations have served

Ontarians ------- a collective total of 60 years.
132.

To enable us to provide you with the best possible service, we will close the Kitchener

location from May 8 to May 29 for remodeling. -------. Throughout this time, the store in
133.

neighboring Cambridge will remain open during the regular business -------. Let us
134.

know any questions or comments you might have. As always, we value your time and

your business.

Thank you,

Pablo Guaido

Owner and Founder, Bullseye Appliances

131. (A) to be offered
(B) to offer
(C) offered
(D) offering

132. (A) by
(B) within
(C) for
(D) between

133. (A) The store will remain open an hour later until May 31.
(B) All feedback will receive a response within 48 hours.
(C) This guarantee will be available for a limited time only.
(D) We would like to apologize in advance for any bother this causes.

134. (A) recruitment
(B) owners
(C) evaluations
(D) hours

GO ON TO THE NEXT PAGE

Questions 135-138 refer to the following advertisement.

Café Mazer's coffee has quickly become the city's ------- place to enjoy a cup of coffee.
                                                                    135.
Would you like the opportunity to find out how to ------- our special brand of coffee
                                                  136.
yourself? Owner Felicia Carter is inviting the public for a ------- of classes on the
                                                            137.
secrets to achieving the perfect cup of coffee. The classes draw from her experiences
in Ethiopia, long considered the birthplace of coffee. Classes will be held at Holbrook
College on Saturdays from 9:00 A.M. to 11:30 A.M. -------. Don't miss out! Sign up
                                                  138.
today by visiting our Web site at cafemazer.com/learnwithus.

135. (A) cleanest
(B) largest
(C) cheapest
(D) busiest

136. (A) brew
(B) brewing
(C) brewed
(D) brews

137. (A) layer
(B) section
(C) faculty
(D) series

138. (A) Franchising opportunities may be available in the future.
(B) Café Mazer will introduce a new menu soon.
(C) Spaces are limited, so reservations are mandatory.
(D) Ms. Carter has recently returned from an international conference.

Questions 139-142 refer to the following notice.

Notice to all Auto-Smart Customers:

When you have car windows replaced, you will notice an extra fee of $10 per window (or windshield) replaced. This fee is to cover the cost of auto glass disposal. ------- you **139.** indicate otherwise, we will go ahead and take care of the windows for you.

The combination of glass and plastic in car windows is tricky to work with, and improper disposal causes significant environmental damage. The good news is that these materials are perfect for carpet backing and insulation, as long as the windows are correctly -------. Just $10 covers this important process. **140.**

This payment is -------. You are free to take the old windows with you and handle **141.** everything yourself, in which case, we will not charge you. -------. **142.**

---

139. (A) Because
(B) While
(C) Unless
(D) Although

140. (A) recycles
(B) recycled
(C) recycling
(D) recyclable

141. (A) frequent
(B) expensive
(C) final
(D) voluntary

142. (A) We are confident that you will be very pleased with your new windows.
(B) Just remember to deal with the process in an eco-friendly way.
(C) If you notice cracks or other damages, you should contact customer service immediately.
(D) Yearly inspections are not required, but they are highly recommended.

GO ON TO THE NEXT PAGE

Questions 143-146 refer to the following notice.

Oliveira Antique Cinema requests that all electronic devices, including smartphones and smartwatches, be switched to silent mode and placed inside your pockets once the lights -------. Sounds may interfere with the viewer experience, and the use of devices
   143.
in a dark environment can be very distracting for nearby -------. The light from a screen,
                                                          144.
-------, can draw attention away from the film and onto your device.
145.

We understand that you may be expecting a call, or you do need to use your device.

-------. Afterward, you may quietly re-enter and return to your seat. Please make as little
146.
noise as possible to avoid disturbing the audience.

143. (A) have dimmed
(B) dims
(C) can dim
(D) dimmed

144. (A) patrons
(B) actors
(C) players
(D) witnesses

145. (A) however
(B) unless
(C) for instance
(D) consequently

146. (A) A refund may not be possible as a result.
(B) Any complaints about our policies should be directed to the front office.
(C) In such cases, please exit the theater and use the waiting room.
(D) Discounts are only offered to large groups that reserve in advance.

PART 7

Directions: In this part you will read a selection of texts, such as magazine and newspaper articles, e-mails, and instant messages. Each text or set of texts is followed by several questions. Select the best answer for each question and mark the letter (A), (B), (C), or (D) on your answer sheet.

Questions 147-148 refer to the following form.

Kurtz BBQ and Wings

Thanks for stopping by Kurtz BBQ and Wings. We'd appreciate it if you took a moment to fill out the survey below.

	Agree	Neutral	Disagree
The food looked and tasted great.		O	
The food was reasonably priced.	O		
I didn't have to wait too long.		O	
The service was friendly and helpful.	O		
The restaurant was exceptionally clean.		O	
The lighting and music were set to proper levels.			O

Name and contact info:
Gerald Brunswick
555 032-4592

Comments:
The restaurant was packed, but I was impressed with the service. Despite having a small staff, all our items arrived quickly and were prepared properly. It would have been better if the restaurant wasn't so dim. Some overhead fixtures would really help brighten up the place.

147. What did Mr. Brunswick indicate about his dining experience?

(A) The menu items were a good value for the price.
(B) His order was delayed for a few minutes.
(C) Some items arrived at the table cold.
(D) The portion sizes were large.

148. What improvement does Mr. Brunswick suggest?

(A) Additional staff should be hired.
(B) A loyalty card should be offered.
(C) Menu items should be better presented.
(D) More lighting should be installed.

GO ON TO THE NEXT PAGE

Questions 149-150 refer to the following online review.

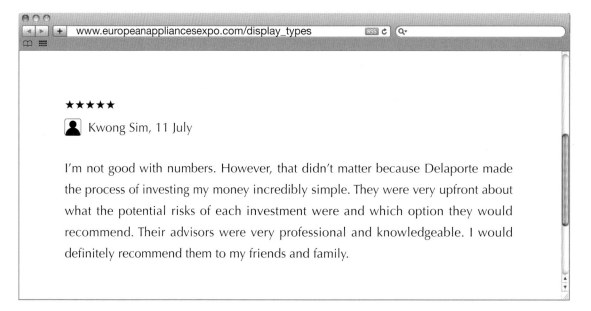

www.europeanappliancesexpo.com/display_types

★★★★★

Kwong Sim, 11 July

I'm not good with numbers. However, that didn't matter because Delaporte made the process of investing my money incredibly simple. They were very upfront about what the potential risks of each investment were and which option they would recommend. Their advisors were very professional and knowledgeable. I would definitely recommend them to my friends and family.

149. According to the online review, what service does the company provide?

(A) Product design
(B) Financial investing
(C) Market research
(D) Real estate

150. What does Mr. Sim express satisfaction with?

(A) The company's software
(B) The low fees
(C) The employees' conduct
(D) The payment process

Questions 151-153 refer to the following information.

Minim Coffee
Quality Coffee in a jiffy

With this container, you can enjoy twenty servings of Minim's very best coffee. Drink with confidence as every packet contains coffee beans sourced from sustainable farms in Papua New Guinea.

Brewing Instructions

1. Empty the contents of one packet into a mug
2. Pour hot water into the mug
3. Stir gently for three minutes

Your coffee is now ready to serve. In the instance you are unsatisfied with the product, you are eligible for a full refund at the place of purchase.

The product is good until 14 December.

151. Where is the information most likely printed?

(A) On an advertisement
(B) On a bowl
(C) On a box
(D) On a machine

152. What can customers do if they are not pleased with the product?

(A) Receive a refund
(B) Request an inspection
(C) Donate the contents
(D) Call the company

153. What does the information NOT mention about the product?

(A) Its health benefits
(B) Its date of expiration
(C) Its place of origin
(D) Its preparation

GO ON TO THE NEXT PAGE

Questions 154-155 refer to the following advertisement.

Erik Harrison Carpets is the most trusted carpet installer in Allegan. We offer a quick and convenient service that can work around your schedule. It's as simple as picking out the carpet you want, placing your order, and then letting us handle the rest. We have been operating for over twenty years, and we let our testimonials speak volumes about our work.

Stop by your closest Erik Harrison store to browse through our carpet options and discuss installation options. Alternatively, go to www.erikharrison.com/products and download our catalog. Once you have made your selection, request a consultation by sending us an e-mail. We will get back to you within two working days with a full quote and an estimated completion date for the work.

154. What is indicated about Erik Harrison Carpets?

(A) They also offer interior design services.
(B) They import their products from overseas.
(C) Their services can be requested without visiting a store.
(D) Their customers are eligible to become store members.

155. Why does the advertisement give details about the company's history?

(A) To provide justification for their high costs
(B) To emphasize their standing in the community
(C) To specify details included in their contracts
(D) To notify customers about recent trends

Questions 156-157 refer to the following online chat discussion.

Todd Campbell	(11:31 A.M.)
Vickie, did you see Ronnie's results from the focus group he ran? He sent an e-mail about it earlier this morning.	
Vickie Frank	(11:34 A.M.)
Yes. I was very surprised at some of the suggestions he made.	
Todd Campbell	(11:37 A.M.)
Right. The results will greatly affect how we should market this product. I think we need to have a meeting with the marketing team.	
Vickie Frank	(11:39 A.M.)
Exactly what I was thinking. We should invite Ronnie too. Should I email him?	
Todd Campbell	(11:42 A.M.)
I'm scheduled to have lunch with him today.	
Vickie Frank	(11:43 A.M.)
That works out nicely!	

156. What did Ronnie do?

(A) He had a meeting with the head of marketing.
(B) He gathered some feedback on a product.
(C) He finalized the plans for a new product.
(D) He requested an extension on a deadline.

157. At 11:42 A.M., what does Mr. Campbell most likely mean when he writes, "I'm scheduled to have lunch with him today"?

(A) He will be busy for the rest of the day.
(B) He is planning on taking a few days off.
(C) He will invite Ronnie to the meeting.
(D) He should prepare a meeting agenda.

GO ON TO THE NEXT PAGE

Questions 158-161 refer to the following advertisement.

LaVine Vision: Career Opportunity

The customer insight team at LaVine Vision has had a very exciting year, and we are eager to maintain this momentum. We are looking for enthusiastic candidates to join our growing team to gather important data from our valued customers. You will play a pivotal part in understanding what all of our customers want.

Responsibilities:
· Interact with customers to understand their needs
· Turn customer insights into actionable items
· Present findings to various teams and explain actions that should be made

Qualifications:
· Ability to engage with customers in a friendly manner
· Ability to identify patterns among large amounts of data
· Confidence and a bright demeanor
· Bachelor's degree, preferably in business, from an accredited university

If this is the opportunity you have been waiting for, send your résumé to careers@lavinevision.org.

Due to the volume of applications, we are unfortunately unable to respond to every applicant. Therefore, only shortlisted candidates will be contacted.

---

158. The word "part" in paragraph 1, line 4, is closest in meaning to

(A) power
(B) role
(C) act
(D) segment

159. What is the main responsibility of the advertised job?

(A) Creating advertisements
(B) Training employees
(C) Analyzing competitors
(D) Interviewing customers

160. What is one qualification listed in the job advertisement?

(A) Experience in data analysis
(B) A driver's license
(C) A degree from a university
(D) Knowledge of retail operations

161. What is suggested about LaVine Vision?

(A) Its job positions are competitive.
(B) Its CEO conducts the interviews.
(C) It has doubled in size since last year.
(D) It pays its employees a high salary.

Questions 162-164 refer to the following review.

---

https://agliooexpress.com/reviews

★★★★★

In my line of work, we use many different courier services. However, Aglioo Express was clearly a cut above the rest. — [1] —. We had commissioned a company to do an inspection on the house we were putting on the market. — [2] —. The company sent its results through Aglioo Express, and they said that Aglioo offered some of the lowest prices for its deliveries. — [3] —. Ever since hearing that, we started using Aglioo Express for all of our courier needs. I love that they require signing for every document. It really assures us that many confidential documents we send out remain that way. — [4] —. I would highly recommend everybody to use Aglioo Express for their courier needs.

Holly Barber, 13 March

---

162. For what type of business does Ms. Barber most likely work?

(A) A construction company
(B) A publishing house
(C) A consultancy firm
(D) A real estate agency

163. What does Ms. Barber like about Aglioo Express?

(A) Its attractive price plans
(B) Its secure deliveries
(C) Its hours of operation
(D) Its quick turnarounds

164. In which of the positions marked [1], [2], [3], and [4] does the following sentence best belong?

"We were in a rush because we had some interested buyers."

(A) [1]
(B) [2]
(C) [3]
(D) [4]

GO ON TO THE NEXT PAGE

Questions 165-167 refer to the following e-mail.

To: Cameron Howell <cameron.howell@electromail.com>

From: Dora Butler <dbutler@finplanners.com>

Date: February 17

Subject: Welcome

Dear Mr. Howell:

Thank you for subscribing to No-Stress Money's money management program. This is to confirm that we received your payment of $350, which allows access to our app for one year.

Using No-Stress Money, you now have all of the resources you will need to create and monitor your monthly budget at your fingertips. Our program comes with an array of videos, activities, and live one-on-one sessions to help you realize your goals. Whether you are saving for the holiday season, a vacation trip, or your first house, our program can be modified to fit your goal.

In the next week, one of our qualified advisors will organize a meeting time. This is an opportunity for you to discuss your aspirations. Our advisor will then help you get started with No-Stress Money and show you how to use the various tools we offer. Our advisor will also be checking in with you periodically to help you along the way.

I created No-Stress Money with the goal of helping everyone reach a healthier financial position. We offer a 90-day money-back guarantee. If you aren't happy with the program within 90 days, we will refund your money. On behalf of my entire team at No-Stress Money, thank you very much for your business.

Sincerely,

Dora Butler
No-Stress Money

165. What is indicated about No-Stress Money?

(A) Its team consists of six people.
(B) Its program is able to be customized.
(C) It won several awards last year.
(D) It is free to try for two months.

166. The word "realize" in paragraph 2, line 3, is closest in meaning to

(A) discover
(B) comprehend
(C) analyze
(D) achieve

167. Who most likely is Ms. Butler?

(A) A customer service agent
(B) A Web developer
(C) A company executive
(D) A financial advisor

Questions 168-171 refer to the following online chat discussion.

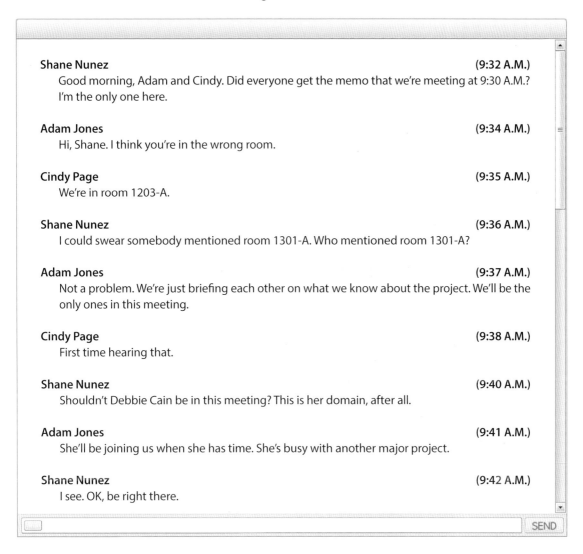

Shane Nunez	(9:32 A.M.)
Good morning, Adam and Cindy. Did everyone get the memo that we're meeting at 9:30 A.M.? I'm the only one here.	
Adam Jones	(9:34 A.M.)
Hi, Shane. I think you're in the wrong room.	
Cindy Page	(9:35 A.M.)
We're in room 1203-A.	
Shane Nunez	(9:36 A.M.)
I could swear somebody mentioned room 1301-A. Who mentioned room 1301-A?	
Adam Jones	(9:37 A.M.)
Not a problem. We're just briefing each other on what we know about the project. We'll be the only ones in this meeting.	
Cindy Page	(9:38 A.M.)
First time hearing that.	
Shane Nunez	(9:40 A.M.)
Shouldn't Debbie Cain be in this meeting? This is her domain, after all.	
Adam Jones	(9:41 A.M.)
She'll be joining us when she has time. She's busy with another major project.	
Shane Nunez	(9:42 A.M.)
I see. OK, be right there.	

SEND

168. What does Mr. Nunez need to do?

(A) Report to the correct room
(B) Reschedule the meeting
(C) Send out the meeting agenda
(D) Record a presentation

169. At 9:38 A.M., what does Ms. Page most likely mean when she writes, "First time hearing that"?

(A) She sent out a reminder e-mail.
(B) She has to leave the meeting early.
(C) She received a late invitation to the meeting.
(D) She is certain of the meeting location.

170. What is indicated about Ms. Cain?

(A) She is unaware of the meeting.
(B) She will lead multiple projects.
(C) She is fully occupied.
(D) She is currently on vacation.

171. How many people will be attending the meeting?

(A) Two
(B) Three
(C) Four
(D) Five

GO ON TO THE NEXT PAGE

SINDRI COMES TO MANITOBA

(March 19) — Sindri, the Canadian manufacturer known for making personal electronics, is moving its main production facility. Most of its production in Quebec will cease when the new state-of-the-art plant opens in Manitoba next July. —[1]—. The relocation coincides with Sindri's announcement of a new range of models, including a tablet PC.

"Our original model, the Sindri Book laptop, was tremendously popular when it came out seven years ago," said Claude McCleod, the company's founder and CEO. "Since we started selling our all-in-one desktop three years ago, we've received feedback from our customers that they were interested in something more portable," he continued. While sales of existing models remain strong, McCleod is confident that the new tablet will draw new demographics of customers to the company's products. —[2]—.

Sindri has distinguished itself by offering high-quality products without the usual steep price tags. —[3]—. Sindri has grown as demand for affordable consumer electronics has taken off and has been particularly strong in countries with developing economies. The company's internal polling suggests that the top reasons customers chose Sindri over their competitors were its products' warranty and reputation for reliability and their high price-performance ratio across all models. —[4]—. Find out more about the company's new line of products at their Web site sindri.com.

172. What does the article suggest about Sindri?

(A) It has manufacturing plants in multiple countries.
(B) It will operate two factories in Manitoba.
(C) It makes personal devices.
(D) It has been in business for over a decade.

173. What was the first product sold by Sindri?

(A) A smartwatch
(B) A desktop
(C) A tablet
(D) A laptop

174. What is indicated about Sindri customers?

(A) They are concerned about pricing.
(B) They are environmentally conscious.
(C) They prefer tablets to other products.
(D) They mostly live in developed countries.

175. In which of the positions marked [1], [2], [3], and [4] does the following sentence best belong?

"Younger people, and students, in particular, are likely customers."

(A) [1]
(B) [2]
(C) [3]
(D) [4]

GO ON TO THE NEXT PAGE

Questions 176-180 refer to the following advertisement and e-mail.

Chanthavong Thai Boxing Academy
12856 Salmon River Road
San Diego, CA 92129
858-555-1212

Thank you for your interest in Chanthavong Thai Boxing Academy. We are now accepting students for the coming year. Memberships will be effective from January 1 through December 31.

Class Levels:
- Just for Kicks (JFK): JFK students will get an introduction to kickboxing training Wednesday and Friday nights from 7:00 to 8:00 P.M. The class emphasizes conditioning and etiquette. Students will also learn three basic punches and two basic kicks.

- High Beginner Class (HBC): HBC students continue their study of Thai boxing on Monday and Wednesday nights from 7:30 to 8:30 P.M. Students will work mainly on the heavy bag ("sandbag"), and a variety of punching and kicking combinations will be introduced.

- Intermediate Boxing Training (IBT): IBT students will focus heavily on training with a partner. Sparring is encouraged but not mandatory. Class meets on Tuesday and Thursday nights from 6:00 P.M. to 7:00 P.M.

- Nak Muay Thai (NMT): NMT students are the Academy's competition team. Participation in the Academy's Winter Tournament and Summer Tournament is required, as is attendance at five weekly practices: Monday through Thursday from 8:00 P.M. to 9:00 P.M., and Saturdays from 4:00 P.M. to 6:00 P.M.

No classes are held on Sundays, but the Academy is open from 9:00 A.M. to 7:00 P.M. for independent practice.

All members get an academy T-shirt, free tickets to the semi-annual tournaments, and a 20 percent discount on gloves and other training supplies.

To: Diana Langley <dlangley@ujjp.com>
From: Sakda Khongsawatwaja <s.khongsawatwaja@ctba.com>
Date: December 12
Subject: Next year's memberships
Attachment: form.doc

Dear Ms. Langley,

We are very glad to have your son, Tony, and your daughter, Josephine, as students this coming year. We will start Tony out in the Just for Kicks (JFK) class — we're sure he'll love it and advance quickly!

Josephine, on the other hand, is qualified for our competition team. Since this involves hard training and full-contact sparring, we do require a special consent form from participants' parents. Please sign and return the attached form at the information session for parents on December 20.

Best Regards,

Sakda Khongsawatwaja
Head Instructor,
Chanthavong Thai Boxing Academy

176. What is NOT stated as a benefit for a Chanthavong Thai Boxing Academy membership?

(A) A free clothing item
(B) Complimentary admission to tournaments
(C) Reduced rates on personal instruction
(D) Discounted training equipment

177. What is mentioned about Chanthavong Thai Boxing Academy?

(A) It has morning classes.
(B) Its instructors are former professional athletes.
(C) It provides weekly practice opportunities.
(D) Its facility was recently expanded.

178. Why did Mr. Khongsawatwaja write to Ms. Langley?

(A) To announce her children's placements
(B) To ask that she pay her children's membership fee
(C) To advertise new merchandise at the academy
(D) To explain a new registration process

179. On what day will both of Ms. Langley's children most likely be at the academy?

(A) Monday
(B) Tuesday
(C) Wednesday
(D) Thursday

180. What will Josephine most likely do next year?

(A) Work part-time at a sports stadium
(B) Enter two competitions
(C) Participate in an information session
(D) Advance to the High Beginner Class

GO ON TO THE NEXT PAGE

Questions 181-185 refer to the following Web page and review.

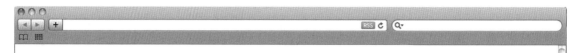

Two Incredible Events Brought to You by Radiance Entertainment

Hyannis vs. Dailey Cricket Match—13 August. In a rematch between the two finalists from last season, the Hyannis and Dailey cricket teams will be going head-to-head at North Harbor Stadium. Our $55 package for this game includes entry tickets, team jerseys of your choice, and a packed lunch consisting of a sandwich, a slice of cake, and a bottle of water. The game starts at 12:00 P.M. Transportation to and from the stadium is also included as part of the package. Reserve your place now!

A Night with Chopin—15 August. The Venice Troupe will be performing an original play titled "A Night with Chopin." Written by critically acclaimed writer Eva Lawson, the play has garnered some serious attention. For $75, we provide transportation, tickets, and a three-course meal at the Lula Roe Inn. Dinner will be served at approximately 6:30 P.M., and the play will begin at 7:30 P.M.

· Transportation to the events will depart from the Plata Building.
· Payments must be received prior to events; payment is available online.
· Cancellations are subject to our refund policy. Full refunds are given if cancellations are 24 hours prior to the event.

★★★★★
Peggy 19 June I decided to watch the Dailey basketball team play the Hancock basketball team as a family event. I personally found the sport hard to follow, but Edwin, our tour host, did a great job explaining what was happening. He made the experience terrific for my entire family, and I would absolutely go with Radiance Entertainment again.

★★★★★
Gustavo 17 August I recently watched "A Night with Chopin" by booking through Radiance Entertainment. That turned out to be a great decision. I enjoyed having a night out where somebody else took care of the logistics. Being taken to the restaurant and then to the play afterward was much better than trying to find a parking spot all night. Our tour guide, Natascha, was very organized and made sure we were on time.

★★★★★
Vanessa Cain 23 August It was incredibly difficult finding tickets for the Dailey-Hyannis cricket match. I could only find tickets through Radiance Entertainment. While the tickets were a bit pricier than I would have liked, it was well worth it. The experience was very smooth. In fact, our tour leader, Edwin, went out of his way to make sure we had everything we needed.

181. What is included with the tour package to North Harbor Stadium?

(A) A group photo
(B) A Dailey team photo
(C) A team jersey
(D) A Hyannis team cricket bat

182. What is indicated about Radiance Entertainment?

(A) It requires its customers to meet at the Plata Building prior to events.
(B) It plans on sponsoring more events in the future.
(C) It will raise the prices of its events next month.
(D) It offers partial refunds for canceled reservations.

183. What is suggested about the review writers?

(A) They received discounts for reserving as a group.
(B) They were previous clients of Radiance Entertainment.
(C) They were satisfied with Radiance Entertainment.
(D) They all booked the same event.

184. What is indicated about Gustavo?

(A) He indicated special dietary requirements.
(B) He paid $75 for his ticket.
(C) He drove his own car to the event.
(D) He attended his first professional play performance.

185. According to the reviews, what do Peggy and Vanessa Cain have in common?

(A) They frequently attend sporting events.
(B) They attended events with family members.
(C) They were given prizes for writing reviews.
(D) They had the same Radiance Entertainment host.

GO ON TO THE NEXT PAGE

Questions 186-190 refer to the following Web page, text message, and review.

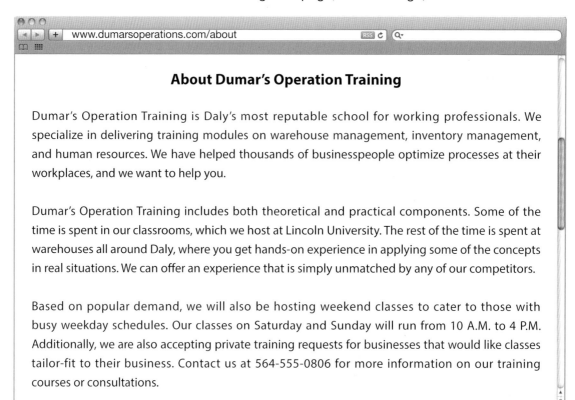

About Dumar's Operation Training

Dumar's Operation Training is Daly's most reputable school for working professionals. We specialize in delivering training modules on warehouse management, inventory management, and human resources. We have helped thousands of businesspeople optimize processes at their workplaces, and we want to help you.

Dumar's Operation Training includes both theoretical and practical components. Some of the time is spent in our classrooms, which we host at Lincoln University. The rest of the time is spent at warehouses all around Daly, where you get hands-on experience in applying some of the concepts in real situations. We can offer an experience that is simply unmatched by any of our competitors.

Based on popular demand, we will also be hosting weekend classes to cater to those with busy weekday schedules. Our classes on Saturday and Sunday will run from 10 A.M. to 4 P.M. Additionally, we are also accepting private training requests for businesses that would like classes tailor-fit to their business. Contact us at 564-555-0806 for more information on our training courses or consultations.

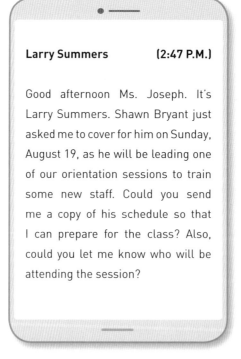

Larry Summers   **(2:47 P.M.)**

Good afternoon Ms. Joseph. It's Larry Summers. Shawn Bryant just asked me to cover for him on Sunday, August 19, as he will be leading one of our orientation sessions to train some new staff. Could you send me a copy of his schedule so that I can prepare for the class? Also, could you let me know who will be attending the session?

www.dumarsoperations.com/testimonials

Dumar's Operation Training Customer Testimonials

I've been thinking about taking classes at Dumar's Operation Training for some time, but I wasn't sure how beneficial it would be for my business. I saw that you started offering tailored classes, so I immediately signed my team up. Our team wasn't sure what to think at first, but Larry did a great job showing how some of the concepts would directly benefit our business. In the end, everyone was glad to have attended the class despite it being held on a Sunday. I would highly recommend Dumar's Operation Training to any business wanting to improve how they work.

Willie Carroll

186. What does the Web page indicate about Dumar's Operation Training?

(A) It was founded over ten years ago.
(B) It delivers its training courses in an online setting.
(C) It will open its own classrooms next year.
(D) It caters to people who are currently working.

187. According to the text message, what will Mr. Bryant do on August 19?

(A) Attend a special event
(B) Train some employees
(C) Travel out of town
(D) Meet with Ms. Joseph

188. What is suggested about Mr. Bryant?

(A) He is Dumar's Operation Training's most experienced employee.
(B) He recently started working on Sundays.
(C) He prefers teaching smaller classes.
(D) He has a second job as a warehouse manager.

189. According to the review, what was Mr. Carroll concerned about?

(A) High tuition fees
(B) Ineffective teaching methods
(C) An inconvenient location
(D) Relevance of the content

190. What is most likely true about Mr. Carroll?

(A) He will sign up for additional classes.
(B) He received a discount on the tuition fees.
(C) He had to reschedule his session.
(D) He was taught by a substitute instructor.

GO ON TO THE NEXT PAGE

Sherbrooke Gazette

March 9 — A new skating rink is being created in downtown Sherbrooke between Rue Papineau and Rue Eymard. Construction of Leopold Arena started six months ago. Steven Fontaine, who works in the Quebec branch of the French company, Ayoub, is the mastermind behind the Arena's unique design.

Ayoub has built sports complexes in both North America and Western Europe. Because of concerns that construction of the rink would run into delays, Ayoub CEO Jean-Baptiste Charpentier has offered a cash incentive to all Canadian staff if Leopold Arena is finished in time to host the Bantam Sherbrooke International Hockey Tournament. The tournament is scheduled for the end of next January.

People who back the creation of the new arena believe that it will give the area's economy a much-needed boost. Ayoub is employing more than 100 Sherbrooke residents to help build the facility. And City Councilor Yvette Sevigny points out that ice hockey will be a long-term revenue source. In addition to ticket sales, local businesses are sure to benefit as fans purchase food, lodging, and souvenirs in Sherbrooke.

To	Steven Fontaine <fontaine@ayoub.ca>
From	David Harrachi <harrachi@ayoub.fr>
Date	January 12
Subject	Update

Hi Steven,

Just a quick note to congratulate you on having Leopold Arena ready for the big tournament. I'm sure all the Canadian staff are delighted, as is Mr. Charpentier, who is looking forward to meeting with you again during your next visit to corporate headquarters.

Sincerely,
David Harrachi
Executive Assistant

Hotel Caméléon
Feb 19 by Armand Boucher

My favorite hockey team made it to the finals at the Bantam Sherbrooke International Tournament, so of course, I had to come here and cheer them on. Such an exciting time!

Hotel Caméléon was very welcoming to all the hockey fans in town for the event and a great place to celebrate afterward. I was especially impressed with the special "victory dinner" that the hotel's restaurant prepared on the last night of the tournament. We came to attend the hockey games, but honestly, it would be worth a trip back to Sherbrooke just to have that food again. The place is a little noisy since it's located right next to a busy shopping and entertainment district. But overall, Hotel Caméléon has been a great place to stay, and I would highly recommend it.

191. Why was the article written?

(A) To compare construction companies
(B) To discuss a decline in tourists
(C) To introduce a building project
(D) To advertise a rental property

192. In the article, the word "back" in paragraph 3, line 1, is closest in meaning to

(A) reverse
(B) support
(C) assist
(D) turn

193. What is suggested in the e-mail?

(A) Employees in Canada will receive a bonus.
(B) Mr. Charpentier will visit the Quebec region.
(C) Ayoub will sponsor some hockey players.
(D) Mr. Fontaine will be offered a promotion.

194. What is probably true about Armand Boucher?

(A) He knows Mr. Charpentier.
(B) He works near Sherbrooke.
(C) He has visited Leopold Arena.
(D) He used to be a professional athlete.

195. What did Mr. Boucher especially like about Hotel Caméléon?

(A) The fitness facilities
(B) The spacious rooms
(C) The souvenir store
(D) The evening meal

GO ON TO THE NEXT PAGE

➡

Questions 196-200 refer to the following e-mails and coupon proof sheet.

To: Kelly Hansen
From: Calvin Hunt
Date: May 13
Subject: Promotional coupons
Attachment: Coupon_proof_sheet

Kelly,

I am sending over the drafts for the coupons we will send out next month. Our hope is that for every week of June, there will be a new coupon for customers to use. This should drive a lot of new business towards our store. Here is what we have planned for June:

Week 1: 15% off all diagnoses and repairs
Week 2: Free phone case and charger with a purchase of a phone
Week 3: 10 gigabytes of data free with any purchase
Week 4: 2-month subscription to our movie streaming service when you sign up for at least six months

Please take a look and see if anything needs to be changed. Thank you.

Calvin Hunt
Marketing Team, GoGizmo

Need A Repair?
15% OFF all diagnoses and repairs
Promo code: FIXIT

Disclaimer: Coupons only good for this week. Terms and conditions apply. See the back of the coupon for more details. When in doubt, call GoGizmo at 555-1333.

Need Data?
Get 10 Gigabytes of data free with any purchase
Promo code: INET

Disclaimer: Coupons only good for this week. Terms and conditions apply. See the back of the coupon for more details. When in doubt, call GoGizmo at 555-1333.

Accessorize
Free phone case and charger with any phone purchase
Promo code: GEAR

Disclaimer: Coupons only good for this week. Terms and conditions apply. See the back of the coupon for more details. When in doubt, call GoGizmo at 555-1333.

All You See
2-month subscription if you sign up for 6 months
Promo code: ALLUC

Disclaimer: Coupons only good for this week. Terms and conditions apply. See the back of the coupon for more details. When in doubt, call GoGizmo at 555-1333.

To:	Calvin Hunt
From:	Kelly Hansen
Date:	May 15
Subject:	RE: Promotional coupons

Hello, Calvin,

I love the concept of coupons. Do you have a copy of our terms and conditions? I'll have to see them first before I officially sign off on these. Also, I think it makes more sense to promote the purchase of phones from the very beginning of the month. That way, those new customers can take advantage of our other coupons. Other than that, everything looks great. Please also send me the updated sales numbers, and I'll see if we are on track for our targets.

Thank you.

Kelly Hansen

196. What is the purpose of the first e-mail?

(A) To confirm a meeting
(B) To clarify a product
(C) To request a review
(D) To modify a schedule

197. In Mr. Hunt's proposed schedule, what code would be used during Week 3?

(A) FIXIT
(B) INET
(C) GEAR
(D) ALLUC

198. What does the disclaimer indicate about the coupons?

(A) They do not have an expiry date.
(B) They are available in limited numbers.
(C) They cannot be used with online sales.
(D) They may be subject to other provisions.

199. According to the second e-mail, what most likely is Ms. Hansen's job?

(A) Marketing lead
(B) Web developer
(C) Legal advisor
(D) Product designer

200. What week does Ms. Hansen want to offer free phone cases and chargers?

(A) Week 1
(B) Week 2
(C) Week 3
(D) Week 4

Stop! This is the end of the test. If you finish before time is called, you may go back to Parts 5, 6, and 7 and check your work.

준비물: OMR 카드, 연필, 지우개, 시계
시험시간: RC 75분

나의 점수	
RC	
맞은 개수	
환산 점수	

TEST 01	TEST 02	TEST 03	TEST 04	TEST 05
_____점	_____점	_____점	_____점	_____점
TEST 06	TEST 07	TEST 08	TEST 09	TEST 10
_____점	_____점	_____점	_____점	_____점

점수 환산표

RC			
맞은 개수	환산 점수	맞은 개수	환산 점수
96-100	460-495	41-45	140-215
91-95	425-490	36-40	115-180
86-90	395-465	31-35	95-145
81-85	370-440	26-30	75-120
76-80	335-415	21-25	60-95
71-75	310-390	16-20	45-75
66-70	280-365	11-15	30-55
61-65	250-335	6-10	10-40
56-60	220-305	1-5	5-30
51-55	195-270	0	5-15
46-50	165-240		

READING TEST

In the Reading test, you will read a variety of texts and answer several different types of reading comprehension questions. The entire Reading test will last 75 minutes. There are three parts, and directions are given for each part. You are encouraged to answer as many questions as possible within the time allowed.

You must mark your answers on the separate answer sheet. Do not write your answers in your test book.

PART 5

Directions: A word or phrase is missing in each of the sentences below. Four answer choices are given below each sentence. Select the best answer to complete the sentence. Then mark the letter (A), (B), (C), or (D) on your answer sheet.

101. As a result of Marie Speer's able leadership, the Smartphone Department has achieved rapid -------.

(A) growth
(B) grower
(C) growing
(D) grow

102. Your clothing items should be delivered ------- 48 hours, but it may take up to four business days.

(A) next
(B) into
(C) within
(D) plus

103. The Marchand Choir stands out because the singers know ------- to blend their individual singing styles.

(A) this
(B) many
(C) how
(D) after

104. The director of strategy would like one of the ------- to revise the company profile.

(A) schemes
(B) types
(C) editors
(D) amendments

105. Henderson Inc. ------- questions about the appointment of Nora Hale as the new CEO this Wednesday.

(A) to answer
(B) answering
(C) will answer
(D) is answered

106. To cater to high customer demand on weekends, Paul's Café will be open ------- 11 P.M.

(A) on
(B) under
(C) into
(D) until

107. A coworker of ------- wants to attend Ken Strickland's keynote address in Berlin this summer.

(A) mine
(B) myself
(C) my
(D) me

108. Toucon Manufacturing is one of the premier car manufacturers with offices in more than fifty -------.

(A) positions
(B) associations
(C) locations
(D) circumstances

109. ------- its membership rewards program, Tesseract Communcations' service rates are regarded as exorbitant by many.

(A) Thanks to
(B) Far from
(C) Despite
(D) During

110. Eighty percent of doctors ------- that General Department's antibacterial hand wash is better than the competitors'.

(A) favor
(B) assure
(C) confess
(D) agree

111. An archive of ------- for forensic analysts was recently retrieved from the organization's servers.

(A) resources
(B) resourceful
(C) resourcefully
(D) resourced

112. When requesting reimbursement, employees must fill out this form and provide receipts for the ------- purchases.

(A) exposed
(B) forwarded
(C) gained
(D) listed

113. Unless you are using a virtual private network, ------- changing your password is advised.

(A) regularized
(B) regulation
(C) regularly
(D) regular

114. Ms. O'Driscoll has a speaking ------- on Friday, October 13.

(A) recruitment
(B) term
(C) topic
(D) engagement

115. Our department has enough budget, but we cannot order ------- office supplies until next month.

(A) addition
(B) additions
(C) additionally
(D) additional

116. Although she ------- the complete sales report, Ms. Orrin was still satisfied with the results of the recent online promotion.

(A) has not seen
(B) had not seen
(C) was not seen
(D) is not seeing

117. Aherran Chocolatier's trendy new iced chocolate is the ------- of a recent consulting session with a market research firm.

(A) productive
(B) productivity
(C) produce
(D) product

118. Jun Lin loved to travel around the world but ------- imagined he would found his own international resort chain.

(A) after
(B) whereas
(C) never
(D) therefore

119. ------- she started at NPM Production, Ms. Ramirez was an assistant creative director at Cooper Media.

(A) Even if
(B) Since
(C) In case
(D) Before

120. The department enjoyed being shown ------- the manufacturing plant by Mr. Suzuki.

(A) up
(B) over
(C) in
(D) around

GO ON TO THE NEXT PAGE

121. Similar experiments conducted at Yorktown University laboratories yielded ------- results.

(A) to conflict
(B) conflicting
(C) conflicts
(D) conflict

122. Trevino Architecture's design of the city hall building features ------- parking and a theater on the 5th floor.

(A) pertinent
(B) underground
(C) abundant
(D) diligent

123. Before the update was available, users had been sending inquiries about bugs ------- the Michaelson Bank's smartphone application.

(A) affected
(B) affecting
(C) are affecting
(D) were affected

124. The Gensian range and oven combo is Albi Kitchenwares' most ------- priced configuration.

(A) reasonably
(B) definitely
(C) sparsely
(D) approximately

125. Profits ------- sales of plastic sheets rose by five percent this quarter.

(A) from
(B) out
(C) within
(D) up

126. The panel will discuss their documentary film and answer questions from the audience -------.

(A) afterward
(B) alike
(C) behind
(D) of late

127. Ms. Sheridan will arrive late since she ------- thought that the press conference was scheduled for tomorrow.

(A) mistaken
(B) mistook
(C) mistaking
(D) mistakenly

128. For the consumer study, customers were ------- into groups according to their age and employment status.

(A) classified
(B) finished
(C) enhanced
(D) assessed

129. If all of your paperwork is -------, the temporary working visa should take less than a week to issue.

(A) on call
(B) in order
(C) on duty
(D) in advance

130. Our team will look over the software functions this week and update ------- that needs revision.

(A) any
(B) one
(C) if
(D) someone

PART 6

Directions: Read the texts that follow. A word, phrase, or sentence is missing in parts of each text. Four answer choices for each question are given below the text. Select the best answer to complete the text. Then mark the letter (A), (B), (C), or (D) on your answer sheet.

Questions 131-134 refer to the following e-mail.

To: Adam Campbell <adamc@netmail.com>
From: Russell Bridges <rbridges@ascendworks.com>
Date: June 8
Subject: Exterior painting

Dear Mr. Campbell,

Thank you for choosing Ascend Works for your -------. Based on our assessment of the
131.
work to be done, the work will take two weeks, and we can provide a quote of $7,500.

-------. This job will be handled by our team of highly experienced painters. They will
132.
take care of -------, from purchasing the right paint to cleaning up after the job is
133.
completed. If you have any questions, please give me a call, and I will be happy to

discuss anything ------- you. Thank you for your interest, and we look forward to
134.
working with you soon.

Best regards,

Russell Bridges
Sales Manager

131. (A) accommodation
(B) renovation
(C) instruction
(D) supervision

132. (A) An on-site inspection should be
conducted prior to starting.
(B) Our work portfolio should be sent
over to you shortly.
(C) Customer reviews help us
continuously improve our service.
(D) This includes two coats of paint on
the interior and exterior walls.

133. (A) everything
(B) those
(C) else
(D) much

134. (A) with
(B) like
(C) about
(D) from

GO ON TO THE NEXT PAGE

Questions 135-138 refer to the following warranty card.

Metta Handbags

72 Woodlands Spinney · San Saba, Texas 76832 · United States of America Metta

Handbags is proud of its reputation as a high-end manufacturer of luxury handbags. We take the utmost care to personally craft each one with the best available materials. If you receive a product from us that you think is ------, contact us to file a report.
135.

This policy only applies to items purchased from one of our physical stores ------ or
136.
from our online retail store. Any purchases made should come with a purchase ID.

------. Please note that the warranty policy does not cover damages arising from
137.
misuse of the product by the user or if the bag has been ------ to harsh chemicals.
138.

---

135. (A) subpar
(B) creative
(C) tolerable
(D) astounding

136. (A) direction
(B) direct
(C) directed
(D) directly

137. (A) Our stores offer a variety of payment plan options.
(B) Delivery times for online purchases can take up to five working days.
(C) All product reports must be filed using the given ID.
(D) Metta Handbags has won several awards for our innovative designs.

138. (A) varied
(B) subject
(C) handled
(D) suited

Questions 139-142 refer to the following article.

Hogan Named CEO of Frontier Fabric

Frontier Fabric, the state's largest supplier of textiles, has recently announced that Linda Hogan will be assuming the CEO position. "Ms. Hogan has demonstrated -------
139.
time and time again throughout her tenure, and we have no doubt we are making the right decision," said Gregory Schmidt, the company's spokesperson.

Ms. Hogan brings over 20 years of experience in the textile industry. She most recently oversaw Fronter Fabric's overseas expansion efforts. -------. "I ------- elated when the
140.   **141.**
role was offered to me. I'm very excited for this opportunity," said Ms. Hogan.

Based in Sardinia, Frontier Fabric partners with independent textile manufacturers to supply clothing companies ------- the county with the finest materials.
142.

---

139. (A) excellent
(B) excelled
(C) excellence
(D) excel

140. (A) It secured a sizable market share under her leadership.
(B) Prices for textiles have gone up due to shortages.
(C) More experienced members may be available.
(D) The management team recently held a vote.

141. (A) am
(B) could have been
(C) was
(D) have been

142. (A) across
(B) into
(C) against
(D) along

GO ON TO THE NEXT PAGE

Questions 143-146 refer to the following letter.

January 5

Dana Wilkinson
12654 Salmon River Road
San Diego, CA 92129

Dear Ms. Wilkinson,

This letter is to remind you that your membership at the Golf and Tennis Club (GTC) expired last month. If you do not plan to continue your membership, please let ------- know so that we may update our records. However, if you would like to extend, I should **143.** mention that we are currently offering a 30 percent discount on membership renewals. This means that for just $2,000, you would have one more year of full membership including ------- of GTC's swimming pool. -------. To renew your membership, ------- **144.** **145.** **146.** submit the application form enclosed here.

We look forward to keeping you as a valued member here at GTC.

Sincerely,

Kelso Montburg
Director of Membership Services
ENCLOSURE

---

143. (A) her
(B) him
(C) them
(D) us

144. (A) use
(B) uses
(C) used
(D) using

145. (A) Please reply by January 10 to take advantage of this deal.
(B) You can ignore this letter if you have already paid your bill.
(C) We offer personal instruction sessions twice a week.
(D) A confirmation e-mail regarding your membership cancellation will be sent to you shortly.

146. (A) extremely
(B) simply
(C) clearly
(D) apparently

PART 7

Directions: In this part you will read a selection of texts, such as magazine and newspaper articles, e-mails, and instant messages. Each text or set of texts is followed by several questions. Select the best answer for each question and mark the letter (A), (B), (C), or (D) on your answer sheet.

Questions 147-148 refer to the following voucher.

Luigi Angelo's

We at Luigi Angelo's are pleased to announce that the remodeling of our Chester Park location is now complete. Please join us at 196 Yosemite Way as we reopen our doors to the public. Bring this voucher any time between March 3 and March 9 to receive a complimentary garden salad when ordering a fountain drink and one of our homemade pasta dishes. Limit one coupon per table.

---

147. What is true about Luigi Angelo's?
(A) It has a vegetable garden.
(B) It will open a new location in March.
(C) It makes its own pasta.
(D) It recently expanded its menu offerings.

148. What is implied about the voucher?
(A) It can be applied to delivery orders.
(B) All Luigi Angelo's locations will accept it.
(C) Diners will receive a free drink with it.
(D) It is only valid for one week.

GO ON TO THE NEXT PAGE →

Questions 149-150 refer to the following article.

Turner Institute Wants You

The Turner Institute is looking for research assistants who have a deep knowledge of agricultural sciences and a background in farm management. Go to www.turnercropinitiative.org to find out more about the requirements for the project and to apply online. Or, if you want to apply in person, visit the institute, located at 2425 Lyndale Road, and ask for Nicole Sessions.

The institute, founded by Dr. Jackson Sparrow, aims to feed the whole world by creating, testing, and promoting open-source seeds that will grow wholesome, pest-resistant crops.

149. What is the purpose of this article?

(A) To explain a farming method
(B) To request volunteers for market testing
(C) To celebrate a scientist's retirement
(D) To announce some job openings

150. Who most likely is Ms. Sessions?

(A) A graduate student
(B) An institute employee
(C) An agriculture professor
(D) A local journalist

Questions 151-152 refer to the following notice.

Haynes Apparel Grand Reopening

Construction on our beautiful, modern facility at 2117 East Highway is complete. So after two months of absence, we're pleased to announce that Haynes Apparel will be relocating to the Tri-state Area on April 1.

The East Highway location will be in the heart of downtown. This will mean that the store will be more accessible to customers throughout the metro region.

To celebrate Haynes Apparel's reopening, we will be holding a special event on April 1. The first 50 customers to arrive when the store opens at 10:00 A.M. will be entered in a raffle. We will draw the names of two lucky winners who will be rewarded with $500 gift cards. Come on down! This is an event you won't want to miss!

And don't forget to check out our online store at www.haynesapparel.com.

---

151. According to the notice, why is Haynes Apparel relocating?

(A) To be situated in a more convenient area
(B) To attract a different group of customers
(C) To offer a wider range of clothing items
(D) To provide a faster delivery service

152. How will Haynes Apparel celebrate its reopening on April 1?

(A) By giving online discounts
(B) By opening earlier than usual
(C) By revealing a new product
(D) By distributing some prizes

GO ON TO THE NEXT PAGE

Questions 153-154 refer to the following text message chain.

Andre Lawrence   1:55 P.M.

Hey, have you left the restaurant yet?

Olga Furtak   1:57 P.M.

I had trouble finding parking. I just walked in.

Andre Lawrence   1:58 P.M.

Actually, that's good to hear. I just found out that five employees from the Griggs branch will be joining us for lunch, not two.

Olga Furtak   1:59 P.M.

No problem. I'll pick up enough sandwiches for everyone attending. Should I get anything else?

Andre Lawrence   2:00 P.M.

That should be it. We have enough plates and utensils at the office.

153. At 1:58 P.M., what does Mr. Lawrence most likely mean when he writes, "Actually, that's good to hear"?

(A) He is satisfied with some menu options.
(B) He thinks a restaurant is a good meeting place.
(C) He contacted Ms. Furtak in time to provide some information.
(D) He is happy that Ms. Furtak is transferring to the Griggs branch.

154. What will Ms. Furtak probably do next?

(A) Buy plates and utensils
(B) Visit a different business
(C) Order additional food
(D) Contact a supervisor

Questions 155-157 refer to the following e-mail.

To	JiwooP@flash.net
From	JohnRothko@updikehomestore.com
Date	March 15
Subject	Issue with Delivery

Ms. Park,

Your copy of Updike Home Store's fall catalog was sent out last week. However, the package was given back to us with a note saying "Return to Sender."

We want you to have the catalog so that you don't miss out on this fall's exclusive offers. Given the purchases you've made in the past, you may want to know about our new range of patio chairs and tables. Please provide us with your current home address so that we can mail you the catalog again as well as a discount voucher worth $50.

In addition, we have improved our customer support services. Now, instead of calling, you have the option of using our new online chat feature to talk with our representatives. Of course, you can still call our support center at 555-3093 with any issues you have about your order.

We are looking forward to hearing from you.

John Rothko
General Manager, Updike Home Store

155. Why was the e-mail sent?

(A) To request new contact information
(B) To follow up on a job application
(C) To apologize for a damaged item
(D) To describe a revised refund policy

156. What is indicated about Ms. Park?

(A) She has moved to another city recently.
(B) She has bought furniture from Updike Home Store before.
(C) She requested a discount voucher.
(D) She used an old catalog to purchase a product.

157. What is a change Updike Home Store recently made?

(A) The support center is now available 24 hours a day.
(B) Home installation fees have been lowered.
(C) Some unpopular product lines have been discontinued.
(D) Customer inquiries can be addressed through a chat service.

GO ON TO THE NEXT PAGE

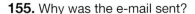

Questions 158-160 refer to the following Web page.

Our Delivery Policy

Big Turtle Clothiers' express service guarantees overnight delivery for all orders made in Maine placed before 6 P.M. Overnight delivery orders must be made online on our website to be eligible. However, please bear in mind before you order that you may be charged different delivery fees depending on how far you are from our distribution center. Our regular delivery service is also available, but orders may take up to 7 working days to arrive.

Destination	Express/ Delivery Time	Standard/Delivery Time
Newport (Harmony, Dexter, Corinth, Bradford)	$6.50/ Overnight	No charge/3 business days
Dixmont (Thorndike, Jackson, Monroe)	$8.30/ Overnight	No charge/5 business days
Dedham (Orrington, Holden, Bucksport)	Not available	$3.50/5 business days
Out of State	Not available	$7.50 and up/ 7 business days

---

158. What is NOT indicated about Big Turtle Clothiers?

(A) It offers an express delivery service.
(B) It has a distribution center in Maine.
(C) It is selling its products overseas.
(D) It delivers to some areas free of charge.

159. The word "placed" in paragraph 1, line 2, is closest in meaning to

(A) submitted
(B) devised
(C) presented
(D) handled

160. What is the minimum cost to send an order to another state?

(A) $3.50
(B) $6.50
(C) $7.50
(D) $8.30

Questions 161-163 refer to the following invitation.

Sunday, April 10 from Noon to 4 P.M.

**Come Commemorate 200 years of Chesterton
at the Civic Heritage Museum!**

This year is our town's bicentennial anniversary. To honor 200 years of history, the museum is presenting a commemorative event that celebrates the unique culture and heritage of our community over the years. All donors who have supported the Civic Heritage Museum are invited to come for an afternoon of film, fine dining, and a first look at our newest exhibit. Enjoy presentations and panel discussions featuring noted scholars, with a keynote speech by Professor Chloe Emmerich of Chesterton University. And you won't want to miss the screening of acclaimed director Geoffrey Maxwell's documentary film *From Frontier to Front Yard*. Lunch and beverages will be provided by Twin Rivers Pub. All profits from ticket and food sales will go to the town's Future Filmmakers project.

To reserve a ticket, visit www.chestertonCHM.com/bookings. Keep in mind that they must be purchased at least 48 hours in advance, and only a limited number are available.

---

161. For whom is the invitation most likely intended?

(A) History professors
(B) Chesterton town officials
(C) Past contributors
(D) Film students

162. The word "over" in paragraph 1, line 3, is closest in meaning to

(A) above
(B) more
(C) beyond
(D) through

163. What is true about the event?

(A) It will only sell a certain number of tickets.
(B) It features a free lunch.
(C) It will include a speech on film history.
(D) It is held on an annual basis.

GO ON TO THE NEXT PAGE

Questions 164-167 refer to the following online chat discussion.

David Villa [1:02 P.M.]

Hey, guys. I need to ask for a favor. I'm supposed to work the night shift tonight, but I'm not feeling too well. Would it be possible to swap shifts with anyone?

Allison Costello [1:04 P.M.]

I wouldn't mind taking the hours, but I won't be able to make it to the hotel until 9. I have a dinner appointment at 7 in downtown Haverford. If Ms. Wahlberg is fine with me starting the shift a bit later, I can cover for you.

Lamar Jackson [1:06 P.M.]

I'd help you out, David, but I already purchased tickets to the evening showing of that new film, Halfway There. Hopefully, someone else can help.

David Villa [1:08 P.M.]

Allison, that's not a bad idea, but I'm worried Ms. Wahlberg would reject it. She's really serious about having enough people at the front desk at all times of the day.

Allison Costello [1:09 P.M.]

True. David, why don't you contact Ms. Wahlberg and check if someone who is already there can work a little longer?

Jessica Choi [1:12 P.M.]

Hi, all, I would've replied earlier, but we got really busy. I'll be happy to stay later and wait until Allison gets here.

Allison Costello [1:14 P.M.]

That sounds like a good plan. Do you think it will be OK with Ms. Wahlberg?

David Villa [1:18 P.M.]

I just got off the phone with her. Ms. Walhberg doesn't mind at all. Thanks for your support, everyone.

Allison Costello [1:19 P.M.]

Sure thing. See you later, Jessica.

Message....

164. Where do the writers work?

    (A) At a theater
    (B) At a hospital
    (C) At a restaurant
    (D) At a hotel

165. What is probably true about all the writers?

    (A) They work for the same supervisor.
    (B) They will have dinner together.
    (C) They regularly watch movies.
    (D) They all live in Haverford.

166. At 1:18 P.M., what does Mr. Villa mean when he writes, "Ms. Walhberg doesn't mind at all"?

    (A) She does not like a plan.
    (B) She can pick him up.
    (C) She will cover his shift for one week.
    (D) She is fine with a scheduling change.

167. Who will end work later than originally intended this evening?

    (A) David Villa
    (B) Lamar Jackson
    (C) Allison Costello
    (D) Jessica Choi

GO ON TO THE NEXT PAGE

Questions 168-171 refer to the following e-mail.

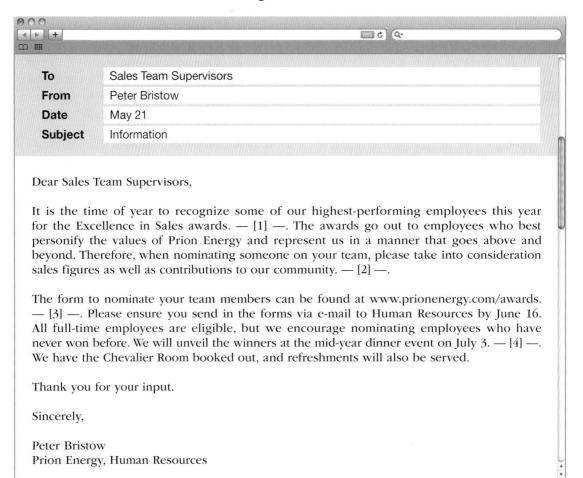

To   Sales Team Supervisors
From   Peter Bristow
Date   May 21
Subject   Information

Dear Sales Team Supervisors,

It is the time of year to recognize some of our highest-performing employees this year for the Excellence in Sales awards. — [1] —. The awards go out to employees who best personify the values of Prion Energy and represent us in a manner that goes above and beyond. Therefore, when nominating someone on your team, please take into consideration sales figures as well as contributions to our community. — [2] —.

The form to nominate your team members can be found at www.prionenergy.com/awards. — [3] —. Please ensure you send in the forms via e-mail to Human Resources by June 16. All full-time employees are eligible, but we encourage nominating employees who have never won before. We will unveil the winners at the mid-year dinner event on July 3. — [4] —. We have the Chevalier Room booked out, and refreshments will also be served.

Thank you for your input.

Sincerely,

Peter Bristow
Prion Energy, Human Resources

168. What is the purpose of the e-mail?

(A) To announce a change to a plan
(B) To ask for nominations of employees
(C) To call for a vote on a venue
(D) To reiterate a new policy

169. What will happen on July 3?

(A) Some tickets will be ordered.
(B) Some requirements will be explained.
(C) Some nominations will be collected.
(D) Some award recipients will be announced.

170. What is indicated about the ceremony?

(A) It will include some guest speakers.
(B) Food and beverages will be provided.
(C) Dates have not been confirmed.
(D) It will be held outdoors.

171. In which of the positions marked [1], [2], [3], and [4] does the following sentence best belong?

"We have also provided a copy of the document."

(A) [1]
(B) [2]
(C) [3]
(D) [4]

GO ON TO THE NEXT PAGE

Questions 172-175 refer to the following article.

Restoration Project Back on Track

Garo (October 21) — It has been a tumultuous time for Garo residents as the project to restore the iconic Sigil Building has been anything but smooth. Fortunately, Cashera Builders—the firm undertaking the project—has announced that the project is back on schedule.

When Cashera Builders first released its proposal to restore the building, it received mixed reviews. Residents considered the timeframe to be unrealistic and also believed that the cost would be substantially higher than stated. — [1] —. Armanda Way, CEO of Cashera Builders, said, "At Cashera, we believe in making the most out of our available resources. People saw impossible promises, but we were confident we could deliver." Ms. Way noted that her firm has always been recognized as one of the leaders in the building industry. — [2] —.

Cashera Builders' proposed timeline and cost were met with the required scrutiny from a panel of experts back in January. Although experts spent much time debating, the proposal was ultimately passed. An important factor that swung the vote in Cashera's favor was its portfolio. — [3] —.

The project initially faced considerable delays due to factors beyond Cashera's control. Poor weather conditions for an extended period meant work had to be delayed. Thankfully, the project is now back on track thanks to the relentless efforts of the building team. — [4] —.

The current project status is available for public viewing. Any member of the public may also request further information or make any comments. Please visit www.garocouncil.gov.au/sigil for all relevant links.

172. According to the article, what was an initial concern about restoring the Sigil Building?

(A) The short time required
(B) The increase in road congestion
(C) The potential for damages
(D) The need for council approval

173. What is suggested about the proposal submitted by Cashera Builders?

(A) It had to be modified several times.
(B) It was submitted past the deadline.
(C) It was approved unanimously.
(D) It was reviewed by many experts.

174. What has been made available online?

(A) Cashera's portfolio
(B) Budget approval requests
(C) The original proposal
(D) The progress of the project

175. In which of the positions marked [1], [2], [3], and [4] does the following sentence best belong?

"Its past restoration projects constituted significant parts of it."

(A) [1]
(B) [2]
(C) [3]
(D) [4]

GO ON TO THE NEXT PAGE

Questions 176-180 refer to the following flyer and e-mail.

Idalou Urban Market
Invites all Craftspeople

The Idalou Urban Market is returning to Skyline Park from June 12 to 15. Craftspeople will have the chance to show off their talents and products. Every year we have seen the number of visitors increase, and we expect the same this year. In previous years, only Texas-based artisans were eligible to participate, but we have modified the rules to include everyone regardless of the state they live in.

To apply, please do the following:

1. Go to www.idaloumarket.com/register and fill out the form. For those planning to share a stand, one form can be used for both parties. However, the $35 registration fee still applies to both sellers.

2. Upload no more than 10 photos of the items you plan to display at the market. Please name the files as such: item description_seller name.

The final day to submit the necessary documents is April 20. If you have been approved, an e-mail will be sent to you by May 2. These people will need to pay the remaining stand management fee of $525 by May 16. This fee includes four five-foot-long tables to be used as you wish. The images that you provide will be displayed on our website under the "Exhibitors" tab along with a link to your homepage.

TO: e.orville@idaloumarket.com
FROM: rin.takai@takaisupply.com
CC: henry.reiss@reissphotos.net
DATE: May 9
SUBJECT: Urban Market

Hello,

I, along with my stall partner, Henry Reiss, received the approval e-mails, and we are thrilled to be a part of this year's festivities. We have sent the payment for our shared stand via bank transfer using the account number on your website. We can't wait to hear more about this year's event.

I had the chance to partake in the event last year, and I really enjoyed the tutorials that some artisans provided. Will there be something similar to that this year? Please let us know if there is because I would love to show the audience how we produce some of our crafts.

Sincerely,

Rin Takai

176. When will approval e-mails be sent?

(A) April 20
(B) May 2
(C) May 16
(D) June 12

177. What does the flyer indicate about the Idalou Urban Market?

(A) It offers complimentary parking for all attendees.
(B) Its online page promotes the participating craftspeople.
(C) It is being held for the first time.
(D) It does not charge for admission.

178. What is suggested about Ms. Takai and Mr. Reiss?

(A) They filled out different forms.
(B) They will need extra tables.
(C) They both paid a $35 fee.
(D) They offer video tutorials.

179. What is probably true about Ms. Takai?

(A) Her crafts were popular last year.
(B) Her work was featured in a magazine.
(C) She does not have an online page.
(D) She resides in Texas.

180. In the e-mail, what does Ms. Takai ask about?

(A) The possibility of demonstrating some skills
(B) The dimensions of her stall
(C) Contact information of other artists
(D) Acceptable forms of payment

GO ON TO THE NEXT PAGE

Questions 181-185 refer to the following e-mails.

To	ASG Conference Attendees
From	Conrad Waters
Date	April 23
Subject	ASG Conference Update

Dear ASG Conference Attendees:

This is to let you know that the ASG Conference has been greenlit for May 20 to May 23 at the Cloverfield Hotel. The hotel is located in the heart of Ashburton with plenty of transportation options.

If you booked a room together with your ticket, you will have received a confirmation e-mail from the Cloverfield Hotel. There are still some rooms left. If you have changed your mind and you would like a room, please let me know as soon as possible. Additionally, we understand that some of our attendees need assistance with transportation. Respond to this e-mail with your time of arrival, and we can accommodate your requests.

The conference will kick off at 12 P.M. on May 20 with a speech from this year's organizer. Afterward, you are free to explore the city with your colleagues for the day. The talks and presentations will commence bright and early on May 21 at 9 A.M. When the schedule is finalized, we will post it on the website.

Thank you.

Conrad Waters
Event Coordinator
S&P Food Group

To	Conrad Waters
From	Ethel Elliott
Date	April 24
Subject	RE: ASG Conference Update

Dear Mr. Waters:

Thank you for the confirmation e-mail. I am very much looking forward to seeing you in person after speaking to you so many times over the phone. I will arrive in Ashburton on Friday at 11 A.M.

Is it too late to reserve a room? My plans to stay with a former colleague fell through, so I'm suddenly in need. Additionally, I'll be bringing some samples of our work during my talk, so it would make things a lot more convenient. If not, it's not a problem. I'm sure I can figure something out.

Thank you for your help.

Best regards,

Ethel Elliott
Senior Product Designer
Magnum Opus Inc.

181. What is the purpose of the first e-mail?

(A) To change a schedule
(B) To request payment from travelers
(C) To send out a list of venues
(D) To confirm event details

182. What does Mr. Waters indicate about May 20?

(A) The events will start in the morning.
(B) A tour of the city will be provided.
(C) There is only one event planned.
(D) It will require the use of a vehicle.

183. In the first e-mail, the word "accommodate" in paragraph 2, line 5, is closest in meaning to

(A) handle
(B) gratify
(C) contain
(D) determine

184. What will Mr. Waters most likely do for Ms. Elliott?

(A) Refer her to a colleague
(B) Attempt to secure a lodging option
(C) Prepare a detailed schedule
(D) Hire a private car service

185. What does the second e-mail suggest about Ms. Elliott?

(A) She helped organize the event.
(B) She was one of the first to be invited.
(C) She recently received a promotion.
(D) She will be one of the speakers.

GO ON TO THE NEXT PAGE

Questions 186-190 refer to the following notice, article, and e-mail.

Attention Bradbury Art Museum Patrons:

From time to time, during Pioneer City's upcoming renovations on 41st Street, the museum's entrance will be blocked. Unfortunately, this means that the museum will sometimes have to close. Please visit the museum's website for the most up-to-date information regarding this schedule.

Please remember that there are other museums downtown, such as the Museum of Modern History or the Stamp Museum. The renovations are expected to be completed by July 31. We're sorry for the disruptions this will cause.

Pioneer City Observer

(September 2) — After nearly two months of renovations that carried over until late August, work on 41st Street has finally finished. Bradbury Art Museum can finally breathe easy, as it saw its visitor numbers significantly drop during this period. In addition to resuming its normal schedule, the museum will soon unveil a new addition. Thanks to funding from the City Council, the museum was finally able to finish its own construction project of a scenic courtyard that has a stage reserved for live concerts and shows.

To celebrate, Bradbury Art Museum will host a free music festival in the new courtyard on October 20. Acts that are scheduled to attend include Charles Liou's Jazz Messengers and saxophonist Ann Sandman. All attendees will be entered into a raffle for gifts.

In the event of inclement weather, the event may be rescheduled for October 22. Check www.bradburymuseum.org/events for more details.

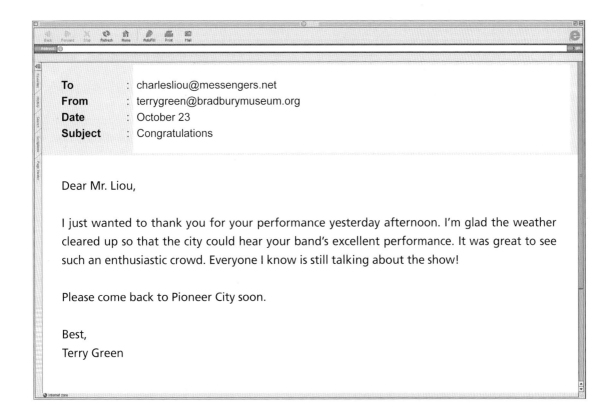

To : charlesliou@messengers.net
From : terrygreen@bradburymuseum.org
Date : October 23
Subject : Congratulations

Dear Mr. Liou,

I just wanted to thank you for your performance yesterday afternoon. I'm glad the weather cleared up so that the city could hear your band's excellent performance. It was great to see such an enthusiastic crowd. Everyone I know is still talking about the show!

Please come back to Pioneer City soon.

Best,

Terry Green

186. What is the notice mainly about?

(A) An upcoming building closure
(B) Increased membership fees
(C) A museum job opening
(D) Customer service policies

187. What is implied about the street renovation project?

(A) It began in August.
(B) It required more funds.
(C) It was overseen by Mr. Green.
(D) It took longer than anticipated.

188. According to the article, what was constructed at the museum?

(A) A parking lot
(B) An entertainment area
(C) A gift shop
(D) An indoor theater

189. What does the article state as one feature of the festival?

(A) A food sampling event
(B) A new art exhibition
(C) A prize drawing
(D) An auction

190. What is suggested about the festival?

(A) It had to be postponed.
(B) It was only open to local residents.
(C) It will be held every year.
(D) It did not attract many attendees.

GO ON TO THE NEXT PAGE

Satoru Suite
Book Viewings Now!

A recently renovated building in the heart of Eden Park, Satoru Suite is the ideal spot for young businesses wanting to create an office presence in Hamilton. We've made a number of additions to ensure that your business has everything it needs to thrive. All of our units include access to communal meeting rooms, conference halls, as well as a shared cafeteria. On the top floors are our premium offerings, which include the same facilities but with the addition of a private gym.

Our central location ensures easy access by subway or bus. Satoru Suite is also located near several restaurants and cafés for additional eating options. Our most recent addition to the building includes a supermarket where you can conveniently do your shopping before or after work.

Our website includes photos as well as the ability to book a viewing. Our units are going quickly, so book your space today!

To:	Tracy Cowell <tcowell@satorusuite.com>
From:	Mindy Howard <mhoward@dratmostpartners.com>
Date:	September 17
Subject:	Maintenance fees

Hello Ms. Cowell,

I have been in touch with you regarding securing some space at Satoru Suite. My interior design business is really in need of new clients, and I think the big problem is that our current office is simply too remote. I really like where Satoru Suite is, and the extra feature offered to the top-floor tenants is a huge plus for me. Does the $3,000 monthly rent include maintenance fees for cleaning and supplies?

Sincerely,

Mindy Howard

To:	Mindy Howard <mhoward@dratmostpartners.com>
From:	Tracy Cowell <tcowell@satorusuite.com>
Date:	September 17
Subject:	RE: Maintenance fees

Dear Ms. Howard,

Thank you for your interest in Satoru Suite. Our prices do include all maintenance fees as well as utilities. While this would normally add around $300 to most rent prices, our price already includes everything.

I would also like to mention that this is a great time to consider moving in. To celebrate the reopening of our facilities, we are waiving the first month's rent for all tenants who sign up in the next two months. Please note that we do have to run a background check on you before we approve your application, and this will cost $100.

Sincerely,

Tracy Cowell
Leasing Agent, Satoru Suite

191. Who most likely will use the advertised spaces?

(A) Warehouse staff
(B) Government employees
(C) Factory laborers
(D) Office workers

192. According to the advertisement, what is available within Satoru Suite?

(A) A grocery store
(B) A library
(C) A post office
(D) A café

193. What additional special feature does Ms. Howard suggest she is interested in?

(A) A corner office
(B) An exercise facility
(C) A shared kitchen
(D) A conference hall

194. Why most likely does Ms. Howard want to move her business out of its current location?

(A) The business has added more employees.
(B) The rent has recently been raised.
(C) The office is under construction.
(D) The place is too far from other businesses.

195. How much of a discount is offered to Ms. Howard?

(A) $300
(B) $400
(C) $2,700
(D) $3,000

GO ON TO THE NEXT PAGE

FOR IMMEDIATE RELEASE
7 February

Contact: Wesley Mcguire
wmcguire@wyndhaminn.com

(Du Bois) — The Wyndham Inn on Thames Terrace will officially be reopening its doors to visitors once again following a lengthy renovation period. While the renovations were slated to finish in November, poor weather meant the project to expand the inn's ballroom area was delayed. Starting 16 February, its new ballroom will be available for large groups of 30 or more guests to book out. Food and catering services from neighboring restaurant, Canopy Plaza, can also be reserved for events or conferences.

The Wyndham Inn Manager Olga Hampton said, "We're very excited to show the public the changes we've made here. We've redone many parts of the inn and integrated some state-of-the-art technology into our rooms." The Wyndham Inn offers 60 guest rooms, meeting rooms, an executive lounge, and complimentary Wi-Fi.

To:	Olga Hampton
From:	Gordon Wallace
Date:	12 February
Subject:	Reservation request

Hi, Olga.

Thank you for forwarding the request from the Du Bois Engineers Association (DEA) about hosting their annual awards event in The Wyndham Inn's ballroom. I heard they were considering hosting it in the first week of March, but I'm not sure that will be possible. I'd like to push it back if possible. For one, the catering arm of our restaurant is relatively new, and I'm not confident we can handle such a large event this early. Second, we are in the process of finding a new head chef. Ideally, I'd like to push the event back a month. In any case, please let me know when a date has been finalized. Based on the date, I will let you know if I anticipate any issues.

Thank you,

Gordon

The Du Bois Engineers Association (DEA) is proud to recognize Ms. Caldwell as this year's winner of the Engineering Achievement Award. Please join us as we celebrate this achievement as well as share some of our learnings over the past year.

Friday, 15 April, 6:00 P.M.
Saddleback House, Lionel Road Conference Center
174 Cairn Square, Du Bois

Last year's award winner, Martin Ross, will deliver the opening speech while DEA President Beverly Graves will present the award.

Please let us know if you will be attending by emailing event coordinator Derek Kim at dkim@deadubois.com.

196. What does the press release announce?

(A) The reopening of an inn
(B) The acceptance of an award
(C) The launching of a new service
(D) The hiring of a new manager

197. According to the press release, what does The Wyndham Inn offer?

(A) A garden tour
(B) An exercise facility
(C) An Internet connection
(D) A swimming pool

198. What is suggested about the reservation request Mr. Wallace received?

(A) It is for an event with at least 30 guests.
(B) It has already been confirmed.
(C) It will not require catering services.
(D) It will require some special equipment.

199. According to the invitation, who will receive a prize?

(A) Mr. Kim
(B) Mr. Ross
(C) Ms. Caldwell
(D) Ms. Graves

200. What is suggested about the DEA event?

(A) It will finish at 6:00 P.M.
(B) It has been moved to a different date.
(C) It has invited additional speakers.
(D) It will be televised.

Stop! This is the end of the test. If you finish before time is called, you may go back to Parts 5, 6, and 7 and check your work.

TEST 07

준비물: OMR 카드, 연필, 지우개, 시계
시험시간: RC 75분

<table>
<tr><td colspan="5" align="center">나의 점수</td></tr>
<tr><td colspan="5" align="center">RC</td></tr>
<tr><td colspan="2">맞은 개수</td><td colspan="3"></td></tr>
<tr><td colspan="2">환산 점수</td><td colspan="3"></td></tr>
<tr><td>TEST 01</td><td>TEST 02</td><td>TEST 03</td><td>TEST 04</td><td>TEST 05</td></tr>
<tr><td>_____점</td><td>_____점</td><td>_____점</td><td>_____점</td><td>_____점</td></tr>
<tr><td>TEST 06</td><td>TEST 07</td><td>TEST 08</td><td>TEST 09</td><td>TEST 10</td></tr>
<tr><td>_____점</td><td>_____점</td><td>_____점</td><td>_____점</td><td>_____점</td></tr>
</table>

점수 환산표

RC			
맞은 개수	환산 점수	맞은 개수	환산 점수
96-100	460-495	41-45	140-215
91-95	425-490	36-40	115-180
86-90	395-465	31-35	95-145
81-85	370-440	26-30	75-120
76-80	335-415	21-25	60-95
71-75	310-390	16-20	45-75
66-70	280-365	11-15	30-55
61-65	250-335	6-10	10-40
56-60	220-305	1-5	5-30
51-55	195-270	0	5-15
46-50	165-240		

READING TEST

In the Reading test, you will read a variety of texts and answer several different types of reading comprehension questions. The entire Reading test will last 75 minutes. There are three parts, and directions are given for each part. You are encouraged to answer as many questions as possible within the time allowed.

You must mark your answers on the separate answer sheet. Do not write your answers in your test book.

PART 5

Directions: A word or phrase is missing in each of the sentences below. Four answer choices are given below each sentence. Select the best answer to complete the sentence. Then mark the letter (A), (B), (C), or (D) on your answer sheet.

101. Professional fashion designers often ------- their color choices to heighten the aesthetic quality.

(A) vary
(B) varying
(C) can be varied
(D) were varied

102. Mr. Maxwell messaged ------- director for more information on the company's relocation.

(A) he
(B) his
(C) him
(D) himself

103. The concert organizers ------- planned to hold the event at Dartmoor College, but it was deemed too remote.

(A) evenly
(B) originally
(C) relatively
(D) excellently

104. The recommended ------- of nutrient intake depends on the person's age and gender.

(A) allows
(B) allowed
(C) allowing
(D) allowance

105. The Sultan Financial Group's website will be inaccessible ------- the hours of 2 A.M. and 4 A.M.

(A) in
(B) since
(C) among
(D) between

106. Prospective students are required to submit letters of recommendation on top of the other required -------.

(A) matters
(B) documents
(C) policies
(D) directions

107. For guidelines on preparing the project proposal, please refer to the ------- instructions attached to this request.

(A) helpfully
(B) helpful
(C) helping
(D) helped

108. Thanks to her 10-year experience at SKG Accounting, Mrs. Ho has a ------- understanding of business tax consulting.

(A) potential
(B) preliminary
(C) thorough
(D) misleading

109. Ms. Clark confirmed with marketing that the consumer report is ------- finished.

(A) almost
(B) too
(C) little
(D) closely

110. Even though progress on the new space engine has been advancing -------, it will still be ready to launch next year.

(A) slowly
(B) nearly
(C) typically
(D) graciously

111. Mr. Ponchartrain, ------- is away on business, left Ms. Hyun in charge of the Carter account.

(A) which
(B) whose
(C) that
(D) who

112. Ms. Guelph ------- the seminar with the results of the latest marketing survey.

(A) concluding
(B) will conclude
(C) was concluded
(D) conclude

113. Randit Corporation's history of 30 years of ------- service is unique in the industry.

(A) reliable
(B) relied
(C) relying
(D) rely

114. ------- the final contract had been signed, Ms. Cheng thanked the negotiators for their time and effort.

(A) Soon
(B) After
(C) If
(D) While

115. Utility companies have ------- been offering online bill-paying services to make the process more convenient.

(A) increased
(B) increasingly
(C) increases
(D) increasing

116. ------- the building supplies were delivered late, the construction staff worked quickly and kept the project on schedule.

(A) Not all
(B) Also
(C) Contrary to
(D) Although

117. While the auditor has valued the artwork at $50,000, the owner may be willing to ------- if you can pay by wire transfer.

(A) diminish
(B) negotiate
(C) include
(D) contradict

118. After a sample group described Route 1 Shoes' current commercial as -------, the company decided to film a new version.

(A) forgot
(B) forgetful
(C) forgettable
(D) forgetting

119. Patrons of the Zahir Gallery have the ------- to receive a five percent discount on their next purchase by registering for our newsletter.

(A) opportunity
(B) value
(C) consideration
(D) skill

120. At the press conference, the city officials often ------- to questions from reporters with a sense of humor.

(A) apply
(B) publicize
(C) respond
(D) report

GO ON TO THE NEXT PAGE

121. Papillion, Inc. will enter ------- a business contract with Lunae Corporations, once they renegotiate some of the finer points of the document.

(A) that
(B) quite
(C) into
(D) through

122. Aiming ------- its market share, Hazel's Boutique hopes to open 34 new branches by the end of the year.

(A) expanding
(B) expansion
(C) expanded
(D) to expand

123. Ms. Fontaine had a conflict with the conference since she was ------- required to be present at a meeting on that date.

(A) yet
(B) already
(C) rather
(D) not

124. All employees must consult with Ms. Lee before requesting any ------- to the contract.

(A) shreds
(B) preferences
(C) allotments
(D) revisions

125. Employee feedback on the new company headquarters ------- by the board of directors.

(A) seeking
(B) used to seek
(C) sought
(D) was sought

126. Sales figures for our new laptop have increased ------- over the past six months.

(A) significantly
(B) significance
(C) significant
(D) to signify

127. We will be constructing an additional exhibition space ------- the generous donations of our patrons.

(A) as well as
(B) by the way
(C) thanks to
(D) so long as

128. The job application process at the Meadowlark Hotel and Resort Group is -------, so we encourage starting as soon as you can.

(A) complicated
(B) complication
(C) complicating
(D) complicates

129. Many people find the wait before seeing the dentist for their routine checkup almost -------.

(A) unbearable
(B) irresistible
(C) inexplicable
(D) unbeatable

130. Many manufacturers are producing more energy-efficient air conditioners ------- stricter government regulations.

(A) prior to
(B) inasmuch as
(C) as a result of
(D) further from

PART 6

Directions: Read the texts that follow. A word, phrase, or sentence is missing in parts of each text. Four answer choices for each question are given below the text. Select the best answer to complete the text. Then mark the letter (A), (B), (C), or (D) on your answer sheet.

Questions 131-134 refer to the following memo.

To: drivers@canberratransport.gov.au
From: Harold Strahan
Date: May 7
Subject: Vehicle assessment

To All Drivers,

As I mentioned last week, representatives from the mayor's office ------- an assessment
131.
of our bus fleet. They plan to determine ------- motor coaches and transport vans
132.
should be replaced in the coming year.

It would be helpful if you assist us with this -------. When you have time, inform us of
133.
any problems that have persistently occurred when operating your vehicle. Please send
this information to the management team via e-mail at mgmt@canberratransport.gov.
au. -------. We only need the vehicle's registration number, model year, and a short
134.
summary of the issue.

We always appreciate your dedication.

131. (A) was administering
(B) administer
(C) will have administered
(D) will be administering

132. (A) some
(B) each
(C) whom
(D) which

133. (A) tour
(B) model
(C) matter
(D) space

134. (A) We were surprised by the extent of the damage reported.
(B) An exact technical explanation is not necessary.
(C) The repairs will be performed as swiftly as possible.
(D) You will receive a $100 bonus if the person you referred is hired.

GO ON TO THE NEXT PAGE

Questions 135-138 refer to the following e-mail.

To: team@algermuseum.com
From: qat@algermuseum.com
Date: March 17
Subject: Exhibit Texts

Dear Curators,

As we have mentioned in previous e-mails, Alger Museum is making a large effort to increase visitors. We have spoken to some popular museums, and I suggest we follow an interesting -------. Many of these museums indicated that visitors do not pay close
135.
attention to exhibits that have a lot of text. -------.
136.

The implication for us is that many of our exhibits feature descriptions that are too long and difficult to read. I looked at a few of them, and they were all ------- 200 words.
137.
Additionally, we frequently use very technical words. Other museums revamped their descriptions to only contain about 50 words. Based on the success they have had, I think we should keep our texts short and -------. That way, each exhibit won't feel as
138.
burdensome.

---

135. (A) suggest
(B) suggesting
(C) suggested
(D) suggestion

136. (A) Visitors tend to come in groups.
(B) In fact, it is a deterrent.
(C) The museum is busiest on the weekends.
(D) I did not approve of that change.

137. (A) only
(B) until
(C) between
(D) at least

138. (A) comfortable
(B) simple
(C) excessive
(D) crucial

Lab Equipment: Glass Beaker Protocols

Due to its superior reusability, most of our lab equipment is made out of glass rather than plastic. -------, dissimilar to plastic, glass is quite fragile. As a result, special
139.
precautions need to be taken when performing experiments using tools composed of glass. In particular, when loading and unloading glass containers from the centrifuge, perform a brief check to ensure they are not chipped, scratched, or otherwise compromised. -------. While we are in the process of removing all equipment that does
140.
not meet the highest tolerance standards, including flasks ------- of soda-lime glass,
141.
some do remain in circulation. Should you come across one, do not attempt to use it. It is unlikely to be properly calibrated. Just remember to carefully wrap it in paper and place it in the green recycling box instead of the receptacle for normal -------.
142.

---

139. (A) In short
(B) On the other hand
(C) In this case
(D) Presumably

140. (A) This is one notable advantage that plastic containers have over the glass.
(B) Glass beakers must be allowed to fully dry before use.
(C) They will need to be stored separately in the future.
(D) Before doing so, read all of the safety guidelines first.

141. (A) made
(B) make
(C) making
(D) makes

142. (A) process
(B) amount
(C) waste
(D) arrangement

TEST 07

GO ON TO THE NEXT PAGE

Questions 143-146 refer to the following advertisement.

If your business is ready to expand beyond your local market, posting an advertisement in the classified ads section on The Pacific Times is the best way to ------- with buyers
143.
across the Asia-Pacific region. The ------- has held the highest readership in the region
144.
for over ten years. If you are interested, go to pacifictimes.com/advertise and choose from the various options available. -------. You can then submit your request, and one of
145.
our helpful team members will provide you with a full quote. -------, we are partnered
146.
with several local papers in various countries, who will also print your advertisement in their international section. This will provide the best value for your money.

---

143. (A) connective
(B) connecting
(C) connect
(D) connected

144. (A) emulation
(B) revelation
(C) foundation
(D) publication

145. (A) You can decide on the size, color, and position of your advertisement.
(B) An online version can also be accessed.
(C) Our editors sometimes contribute their own opinions.
(D) The cost of advertisements have risen steadily.

146. (A) Consequently
(B) However
(C) Additionally
(D) Hitherto

PART 7

Directions: In this part you will read a selection of texts, such as magazine and newspaper articles, e-mails, and instant messages. Each text or set of texts is followed by several questions. Select the best answer for each question and mark the letter (A), (B), (C), or (D) on your answer sheet.

Questions 147-148 refer to the following online article.

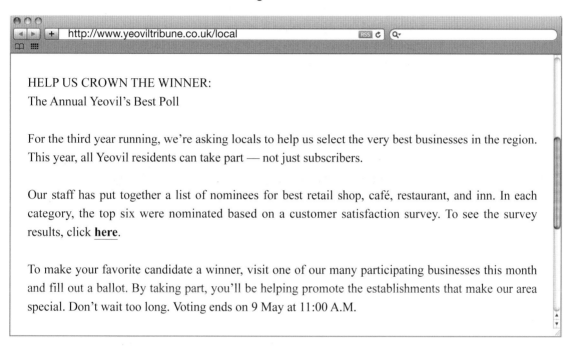

HELP US CROWN THE WINNER:
The Annual Yeovil's Best Poll

For the third year running, we're asking locals to help us select the very best businesses in the region. This year, all Yeovil residents can take part — not just subscribers.

Our staff has put together a list of nominees for best retail shop, café, restaurant, and inn. In each category, the top six were nominated based on a customer satisfaction survey. To see the survey results, click **here**.

To make your favorite candidate a winner, visit one of our many participating businesses this month and fill out a ballot. By taking part, you'll be helping promote the establishments that make our area special. Don't wait too long. Voting ends on 9 May at 11:00 A.M.

147. What was the main purpose of this article?

(A) To ask businesses to donate money
(B) To encourage readers to make a choice
(C) To promote a new magazine subscription
(D) To name the winners of a contest

148. What is indicated about Yeovil's Best Poll?

(A) It can be taken online.
(B) It offers a cash incentive to participants.
(C) It has six categories.
(D) It is conducted at several locations.

GO ON TO THE NEXT PAGE

Questions 149-150 refer to the following advertisement.

Thinking about your next project?
Check out Mike's Supply Shed to save yourself some money!

We receive pieces of wood, various metals, and old furniture from all over the town. Once here, everything goes through our thorough cleaning and repairing process. Not only do we slash the prices on everything, but all proceeds will also go towards cleaning up the city. Save money while also supporting a good cause!

149. What is mentioned about Mike's Supply Shed?

(A) It receives its materials through donations.
(B) It limits the amount each customer can buy.
(C) It is funded by the local council.
(D) It was founded last year.

150. What is true about the items at Mike's Supply Shed?

(A) They can be purchased online.
(B) They can be delivered for an additional fee.
(C) Their quality is thoroughly checked.
(D) Their prices are reduced.

The Supreme Multi-Tool – Everything You Need, Right In Your Pocket

$50.00

TOOLS

Needle-nose Pliers – Great for reaching into compact spaces and holding small objects

Wire Stripper – Safely strip the plastic coating around all types of wires

Knife – Made with high-carbon stainless steel that can cut through tough materials

Spring-action Scissors – Springs assist the cutting action and reduce hand strain

Can and Bottle Opener – Easily open canned goods or bottled drinks

Medium Screwdriver – Loosen or tighten any flathead screw

Includes a leather case for easy carrying in your pocket

151. What is mentioned about the needle-nose pliers?

(A) They can be used in tight areas.
(B) They cut through different types of materials.
(C) They tighten loose screws.
(D) They open metal containers.

152. What is indicated about The Supreme Multi-Tool?

(A) It comes in many colors.
(B) It comes with an accessory.
(C) It has a lifetime warranty.
(D) It has an easy-to-read manual.

GO ON TO THE NEXT PAGE

Questions 153-155 refer to the following blog post.

To sell your products, you must first understand your customers

As a business, your primary goal is to increase sales. This is typically done by creating products that fulfill some kind of need. Therefore, in order to be a successful business, you must first understand who your customers are and what they want. — [1] —. Here is how you can do just that.

Step 1: Identify your customers
The first step to understanding your own business is to find out who are the people buying your products. This can be as simple as observing your store and seeing who comes through the doors. You should be able to notice what the gender ratio of your customers is as well as what demographic they belong to. — [2] —. Knowing who your customers are helps you refine and focus your company's strategy.

Step 2: Ask why
Why do your customers buy your products? Is it because you offer the cheapest products, or is there another reason? Knowing what your customers like about your products will help you improve or create future products. Surveys can help immensely in gathering the necessary data. By asking customers to fill out surveys — perhaps you can reward them with a small discount — you can have access to a wealth of information. — [3] —.

Step 3: Refine your products
Using the information you have collected about your customers, you are now ready to improve your business. If you have learned that your customers care about price, see how you can cut costs on your products. Also, using what you know about who your customers are, design some advertising campaigns catering to those specific groups. — [4] —.

---

153. For whom is the blog post intended?

(A) Customers looking to find new businesses
(B) Firms who want to expand into new areas
(C) Manufacturers who need to reduce overhead
(D) Businesses that want to increase revenues

154. According to the blog post, why are surveys recommended?

(A) They provide an outlet for customers to make demands.
(B) They show that the company cares about what its customers think.
(C) They give insight into what customers value about the brand.
(D) They are relatively easy to do compared to other data-gathering techniques.

155. In which of the positions marked [1], [2], [3], and [4] does the following sentence best belong?

"Research has found that customers like brands that understand them."

(A) [1]
(B) [2]
(C) [3]
(D) [4]

Questions 156-157 refer to the following text message chain.

Pam Graham   9:05 A.M.

Hi, Lewis. I have a bit of an emergency. My car just broke down.

    Lewis Holt   9:06 A.M.

    Would you like me to take the lead on the meeting instead?

Pam Graham   9:08 A.M.

Yes, please. The clients will be meeting us downstairs.

Pam Graham   9:09 A.M.

Meet them in the lobby and then take them to the meeting room.

    Lewis Holt   9:11 A.M.

    Are the contracts ready to be signed?

Pam Graham   9:14 A.M.

Right. I forgot to tell you. They will be bringing the contracts to us instead. Can you make sure to get them?

    Lewis Holt   9:15 A.M.

    Got it. Anything else?

Pam Graham   9:17 A.M.

That will be all. Thank you. I'll take care of the rest.

    Lewis Holt 9:18 A.M.

    Great.

156. Why does Ms. Graham contact Mr. Holt?

(A) To request him to send a document
(B) To send a proposed schedule
(C) To confirm a meeting venue
(D) To inform him of a dilemma

157. At 9:15 A.M., what does Mr. Holt most likely mean when he writes, "Got it"?

(A) He has understood the instructions Ms. Graham has given.
(B) He invited a manager to attend the meeting.
(C) He will read the latest e-mails exchanged with the clients.
(D) He received the documents prior to the meeting.

GO ON TO THE NEXT PAGE

Questions 158-160 refer to the following memo.

To: All Camcom Staff
From: Katie Comstock, Vice President
Date: September 1
Subject: Rhonda Hanna

I am happy to tell everyone that Rhonda Hanna will be taking on the role of Director of Sales. Ms. Hanna is a graduate of Pennsylvania State and joined us after working for Boston's Ernst and Sawyer for six years.

Last summer, Ms. Hanna joined the Outside Sales Department. She immediately made an impact, nearly doubling sales numbers, which had previously been flat. Her leadership helped us win the GloboTech contract and made her team one of the highest-earning departments in the company.

Ms. Hanna's new position will be officially announced on Monday. And to celebrate her promotion, I've booked the private banquet room at Dorsia this Thursday. I've heard from many of you about their famous lobster stew, so I can't wait to try it. Seating is limited, so make sure to email Terry Wright by this afternoon if you plan on coming.

158. Why was the memo posted?

(A) To announce the signing of a contract
(B) To advertise a job opening
(C) To introduce a new coworker
(D) To publicize a staff member's promotion

159. What is mentioned about the Outside Sales Department?

(A) It has given its members a pay raise.
(B) Its employees will regularly attend training sessions.
(C) Its revenue has increased significantly.
(D) It will relocate to the Boston branch.

160. What is implied about Dorsia?

(A) It is popular with Camcom personnel.
(B) It has very limited hours.
(C) It does not have private seating.
(D) It serves only seafood.

Questions 161-164 refer to the following e-mail.

To	Alexa Ramirez <ramrez@gibbs.com>
CC	Beth Park <part@gibbs.com>
From	Jesse Auerbach <auerbach@gibbs.com>
Date	July 8
Subject	Assistance Required

Ms. Ramirez,

I could use your assistance with an important project. —[1]—. My team is responsible for developing the new system. Colbert Medical will be used to track patient records. Due to a lack of experienced staff on hand, we are behind schedule. —[2]—. To keep things running smoothly, I need you to take charge of our migration software for now.

I already spoke with your department head, Beth Park, who told me I could use you for a few weeks. —[3]—.

As you'll encounter a lot of sensitive information while doing this task, I'll need to go over some non-disclosure forms with you. Why don't you come by my office on the 40th floor this afternoon? —[4]—. I'd also like to have you join our meeting next Monday to introduce you to the team.

Best,

Jesse Auerbach

161. What most likely is Ms. Ramirez's profession?

(A) Construction manager
(B) Medical doctor
(C) Job recruiter
(D) Computer programmer

162. What has Mr. Auerbach asked for?

(A) Additional funds for a project
(B) A collection of patient records
(C) The temporary help of an employee
(D) The floor plan of a vacant office

163. Why does Mr. Auerbach want to meet with Ms. Ramirez?

(A) To provide some training
(B) To discuss some forms
(C) To introduce a new product
(D) To hold an evaluation

164. In which of the positions marked [1], [2], [3], and [4] does the following sentence best belong?

"She said her department would be fine without you this month."

(A) [1]
(B) [2]
(C) [3]
(D) [4]

GO ON TO THE NEXT PAGE

Questions 165-167 refer to the following letter.

Sirius International

Dear Stafford Residents,

At Sirius International, we have a mission to provide everyone access to food products from all around the world at an affordable price. To that end, we have plans to open up a store right here in Stafford. Before we can do that, we need your help in convincing the city government to grant us permission to open up shop.

We chose Stafford because of the many requests we received from residents in this area. Having to travel to other provinces to buy international food products can be very burdensome. Additionally, opening up shop here will create many jobs for the community while at the same time increasing traffic to the area. Our goal is to become a big part of the Stafford community.

You can help us achieve our mission by logging on to www.siriusintl.com/projects. You can view our full proposal for a new store in Stafford. If you would like to support us, simply sign the proposal with your name.

With much thanks,

Ellen Robbins, Sirius International

165. According to the letter, how will Stafford residents benefit from the new Sirius International location?

(A) They will receive a discount on all store goods.
(B) They will be able to shop online on the website.
(C) They will receive weekly payments from the city government.
(D) They will not have to travel to purchase international goods.

166. What is suggested about Stafford?

(A) It does not have a store that sells foreign goods.
(B) It does not host any festivals or events to attract tourists.
(C) It is conveniently located next to a seaport.
(D) It is experiencing a shortage of jobs for its residents.

167. According to the letter, why should readers visit a website?

(A) To apply for a job at a store
(B) To show support for a proposal
(C) To get in touch with Ms. Robbins
(D) To view a full list of goods

Questions 168-171 refer to the following e-mail.

To:	b.obafemi@lwmail.com
From:	sandra.lukacs@renosmith.com
Date:	May 29
Subject:	Re: Blueprints

Ms. Obafemi,

I appreciate your quick response regarding the blueprints. I think we made a lot of progress when we met last Friday. Your home improvement store will soon become a reality.

According to the proposed dimensions of the shop and the specifications we've discussed, it's getting clearer what moves we now need to make going forward. I've noted the funding issues you mentioned. Still, I think we have enough for the granite exterior and tiling with the right cost-effective components. I'll send over the full itemized estimate by next Tuesday. Let me know after you've had a chance to assess it line by line. We can then schedule a meeting to make any necessary revisions, and you can sign off on everything.

We're also scheduled to rent the heavy excavation equipment from July 1 to 7. Contact me right away if there is any reason that these dates don't work for you because I have to obtain the work permits beforehand. Due to city regulations, I will need to get special authorization to operate such noisy machinery in an otherwise residential area.

It's a pleasure working together, and thanks once again for choosing Reno-Smith as your partner on this important project.

Sincerely,

Sandra Lukacs

168. What is the purpose of the e-mail?

(A) To request the approval of some documents
(B) To detail the next stage of a project
(C) To explain some additions to a plan
(D) To outline the total cost of a project

169. What is suggested about Ms. Obafemi?

(A) She owns a successful store.
(B) She has a restricted budget.
(C) She needs to apply for a permit.
(D) She wants to relocate her business.

170. According to the e-mail, what should Ms. Obafemi do to prepare for the next meeting?

(A) Create a blueprint
(B) Review some figures
(C) Purchase some materials
(D) Sign a contract

171. Why does Ms. Lukacs mention heavy equipment?

(A) To confirm that it will be available on requested dates
(B) To make sure that she has a large enough construction crew
(C) To make sure that regulations are being followed
(D) To confirm that it will fit in the building's dimensions

GO ON TO THE NEXT PAGE

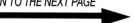

Questions 172-175 refer to the following online chat discussion.

Charlie Stokes   (11:07 A.M.)

The schedule for the charity lunches should be viewable on the website. It has a password on it because it's for internal use only. Here's the password: clunch07

Jamie Wade   (11:18 A.M.)

I took a quick look. The Fortune Group normally purchases tickets for all of its employees. It's always our biggest contributor.

Sheldon Padilla   (11:22 A.M.)

They hired more people this year too. I don't think the Earnest Room will be big enough. We should move them to the Reverence Room.

Charlie Stokes   (11:25 A.M.)

Understood. I'll change that right now. Sheldon, I remember asking you to compile a list of confirmed attendees. Can you send that to me now?

Jamie Wade   (11:27 A.M.)

Once the rooms have been confirmed, I'll mail out the tickets as well as the schedules. Just let me know.

Charlie Stokes   (11:31 A.M.)

For the big raffle, how will we announce the winners? Will we have to bring everybody to the lobby and announce the winners using a microphone?

Sheldon Padilla   (11:35 A.M.)

I can have our tech team set up televisions in each room. That way, our guests can eat while we do the raffle.

Jamie Wade   (11:39 A.M.)

Why didn't I think of that?

SEND

172. What does Mr. Stokes mention about a schedule?

    (A) It needs to be confirmed by Mr. Wade.
    (B) It has already been sent out.
    (C) It should not be shared with the public.
    (D) It contains several images.

173. Why does Mr. Padilla suggest moving The Fortune Group to a different room?

    (A) It is expected to have many attendees.
    (B) It will arrive earlier than other guests.
    (C) It has paid an additional fee.
    (D) It requires special equipment.

174. What does Mr. Stokes ask Mr. Padilla to do?

    (A) Confirm a menu
    (B) Nominate an event manager
    (C) Make a reservation
    (D) Send a list of guests

175. At 11:39 A.M., what does Ms. Wade most likely mean when she writes, "Why didn't I think of that"?

    (A) She prefers Mr. Padilla's suggestion.
    (B) She thinks the event should be pushed back.
    (C) She is concerned about the high cost.
    (D) She would like to change the raffle.

GO ON TO THE NEXT PAGE

Questions 176-180 refer to the following book review and e-mail.

The Enigmatic Floor by Willis Nguyen
reviewed by Kristina Bryan

The Enigmatic Floor is Willis Nguyen's latest book following a three-year break. Inspired by an event that took place in his grandfather's village, the book tells the story of Andre Vasquez, a local painter whose talents are hidden from the world. One day, Andre mysteriously disappears from the village without a trace. When an inspector arrives to investigate where Andre went, he soon finds out that Andre left clues as to where he was going in his paintings. The entire village unites to decode Andre's messages and find out where he is. Although the pacing felt slow at times, the ending is well worth it. Nguyen masterfully ties in elements of suspense and drama to tell an engaging and moving story.

To	Willis Nguyen <wnguyen@comostudios.com>
From	Leigh Oliver <l.oliver@fletcher.edu>
Date	July 8
Subject	Re: Invitation

Dear Mr. Nguyen,

Thank you once again for agreeing to visit Fletcher University and give a guest lecture to the students in my contemporary writing class on Tuesday, August 2. Many of them have aspirations to become writers themselves, so they are ecstatic you've agreed to come. They'll have a lot of questions about the ideating process and how you come up with such engaging plots. Everybody also wants to know how much of the painter's disappearance was real!

You mentioned you would be taking bus number nine to the campus. It will drop you off directly outside the main gates. I will be waiting outside at one o'clock, and we can walk over to Elberta Hall together.

Yours,

Leigh Oliver

176. What is indicated about Mr. Nguyen's novel?

(A) It is based on a true story.
(B) It was Mr. Nguyen's first book.
(C) It won a prestigious award.
(D) It has been published in two languages.

177. In the book review, the word "ties" in paragraph 1, line 8, is closest in meaning to

(A) matches
(B) fixes
(C) blends
(D) attaches

178. What is suggested about the students in a contemporary writing class?

(A) They will graduate at the end of the year.
(B) They have read The Enigmatic Floor.
(C) They live near Elberta Hall.
(D) They attend evening classes.

179. Who most likely is Ms. Oliver?

(A) A university professor
(B) A lawyer
(C) A bus driver
(D) An editor

180. What does the e-mail imply about Mr. Nguyen?

(A) He has met Ms. Oliver previously.
(B) He attended Fletcher University.
(C) He will have to cancel a prior arrangement.
(D) He will ride public transportation on August 2.

GO ON TO THE NEXT PAGE

Questions 181-185 refer to the following article and e-mail.

HYDESVILLE (13 October) — After months of ongoing delays, Echo Rock Isles (ERI) is officially opening its doors on the first of November. The shopping plaza will feature twenty stores, numerous restaurants and cafés, and plenty of entertainment options. The stores all have one thing in common, which is that they are all international companies making their foray into New Zealand.

Big Turtle Clothiers, based in Malaysia, was among the first stores to secure a location at

ERI. "We made a big splash in Asia, and we are hoping to expand our presence in the greater Asia-Pacific region. ERI sounded like the perfect opportunity for us to do that," said Alyssa Cohen, founder of Big Turtle Clothiers.

ERI is open from 9:00 A.M. to 6:00 P.M. Monday through Friday, and 10:00 A.M. to 8:00 P.M. on the weekends. Parking is available at levels B1 and B2.

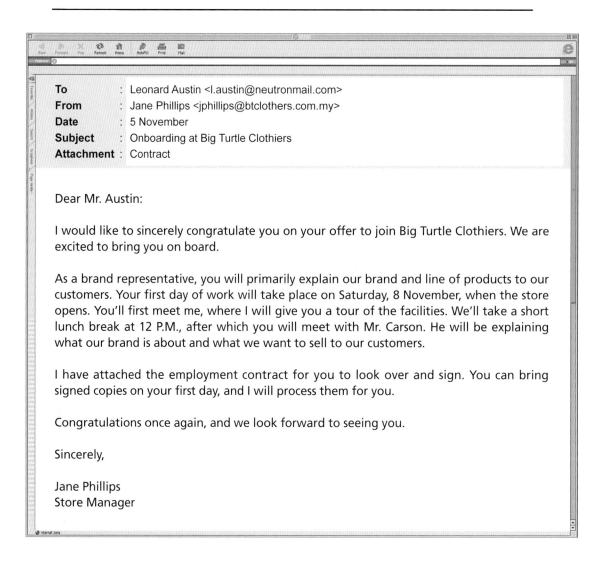

To : Leonard Austin <l.austin@neutronmail.com>
From : Jane Phillips <jphillips@btclothers.com.my>
Date : 5 November
Subject : Onboarding at Big Turtle Clothiers
Attachment : Contract

Dear Mr. Austin:

I would like to sincerely congratulate you on your offer to join Big Turtle Clothiers. We are excited to bring you on board.

As a brand representative, you will primarily explain our brand and line of products to our customers. Your first day of work will take place on Saturday, 8 November, when the store opens. You'll first meet me, where I will give you a tour of the facilities. We'll take a short lunch break at 12 P.M., after which you will meet with Mr. Carson. He will be explaining what our brand is about and what we want to sell to our customers.

I have attached the employment contract for you to look over and sign. You can bring signed copies on your first day, and I will process them for you.

Congratulations once again, and we look forward to seeing you.

Sincerely,

Jane Phillips
Store Manager

181. What is one purpose of the article?

(A) To highlight the disruptions caused by the construction
(B) To announce the opening of a new complex
(C) To advertise a product at Big Turtle Clothiers
(D) To detail the history of a new building

182. What is suggested about Big Turtle Clothiers?

(A) It opened for business last year.
(B) It donates proceeds to several charities.
(C) It is hiring a new store manager.
(D) It is new to the New Zealand market.

183. What did Ms. Phillips send to Mr. Austin?

(A) Meeting agendas
(B) Work documents
(C) A product catalog
(D) A map of the facilities

184. When does Mr. Austin need to arrive at the store?

(A) At 9:00 A.M.
(B) At 10:00 A.M.
(C) At 12:00 P.M.
(D) At 6:00 P.M.

185. What will Mr. Austin do on Saturday afternoon?

(A) Meet with Mr. Carson
(B) Tour Echo Rock Isles
(C) Sign a contract
(D) Meet with customers

GO ON TO THE NEXT PAGE

Questions 186-190 refer to the following e-mail, form, and article.

To:	All
From:	HR Team
Date:	13 February
Subject:	Emerging Leaders Initiative
Attachment:	Application Form

Any staff member who has been with JTB Motors for less than two years is invited to sign up for a new leadership initiative, which will pair a select group of 20 junior workers with some of the most experienced staff members at the company. The program aims to provide junior staff with an opportunity to refine their skill sets and build networks, preparing them for the next step in their careers. Participants will be matched with mentors solely based on their areas of expertise and professional responsibilities. From April, each pair will meet up regularly for at least an hour every week.

To be selected for this program, fill out the attachment and email it to the Emerging Leaders Initiative Coordinator, Daria Donnelly, by 25 February. Selected applicants will receive an acceptance e-mail from Ms. Donnelly on 3 March.

**Emerging Leaders
Application Form**

Name: Ned Griffin
Department: Product Development
Staff ID: N_Griffin

Career Goals and Professional Focus
I want to learn more about the process of designing products localized for international markets and how to better present those ideas to my managers in an appealing way. Any career advice would be welcome.

Availability
Afternoons from Wednesday through Friday

JTB Motors Quarterly

Emerging Leaders Initiative Bears Fruit

Veteran creative director Phillip Jackson was curious to see what would happen when the human resources team reached out last spring to see if he would mentor one of the company's younger employees. He was hopeful, but he did not expect it to be so rewarding. "After working with Mr. Griffin, I feel happier coming into work every day knowing that I am helping an up-and-coming employee. My only regret is that I did not have someone giving me advice when I started here all those years ago," said Jackson.

For his part, Mr. Griffin says, "I was looking for someone to show me how to pitch my design ideas." Since joining the program, he says several of his designs have been put to use, including an integral part of an electric engine. He is more confident and now knows what it takes to rise in the ranks of JTB Motors. "I have never had clearer goals, nor have I been more fulfilled in the office, and it is all thanks to Mr. Jackson."

The program will be expanding. If you would like to participate, reach out to Daria Donnelly in Human Resources.

---

186. What does the e-mail suggest about the initiative?

(A) There will be a limited number of participants.
(B) It is intended for Product Development staff.
(C) It was requested by the company's newer employees.
(D) Participants will be required to attend a networking event.

187. How will junior staff members most likely be chosen?

(A) They will be recommended by their supervisors.
(B) They will be interviewed by potential mentors.
(C) They will be selected based on their education background.
(D) They will be assessed by Ms. Donnelly.

188. What is suggested about Mr. Griffin?

(A) He has been transferred to Mr. Jackson's department.
(B) He has submitted his design proposal to overseas clients.
(C) He has worked at JTB Motors for less than two years.
(D) He has recently earned a new promotion.

189. What is most likely true about Mr. Jackson?

(A) He has been a mentor for several employees.
(B) He works in the Human Resources Department.
(C) He is one of the company's longest-serving employees.
(D) He has international Product Development experience.

190. How have both Mr. Griffin and Mr. Jackson benefited from the initiative?

(A) More defined goals
(B) Pay increases
(C) Improved job fulfillment
(D) Better job security

GO ON TO THE NEXT PAGE

Questions 191-195 refer to the following e-mails and event information.

To:	Joseph Lucchese
From:	XiaoHui Huang
Date:	July 12
Subject:	August 12 Poster
Attachment:	Poster Content

Hi Joseph,

Per our conversation, here is the content to be displayed on the poster. We'll need at least 100 copies to post around various locations at each of our branches. After reviewing the template you provided, I think we should go with "hot pink" for the background and "baby blue" for the majority of the lettering. But also, let's use a fancy font for the lecturers' names so that they catch people's attention.

To make sure that management is on the same page, let's make sure to show them a sample far in advance of the celebration. Do you think you can have one ready by next week?

Thanks,

XiaoHui Huang,
Program Organizer

ErgoBuff Laboratories
35th Year of Recognizing Excellence

Overlook Hotel, August 12, 7 - 10 P.M.

7:00 P.M. - 7:15 P.M.	Opening remarks by CEO Tony Bibbo
7:15 P.M. - 8:15 P.M.	Dinner and Musical Performance by Juan Talavera
8:15 P.M. - 8:45 P.M.	Special Lecture 1: The Gym as a Way of Life by Roger Severen, Vice President of Marketing, Silver's Gym.
8:45 P.M. - 9:15 P.M.	Special Lecture 2: The Future of the Nutritional Supplement Industry by Professor Ernest Jung of Tamaulipas University.
9:15 P.M. - 9:45 P.M.	Presentations
9:45 P.M. - 10:00 P.M.	Closing remarks

Recipients:

Philip Bain	Outstanding Business Development
Shruti Chandrashekar	Top Sales
Rebecca Wilson	Silver Anniversary
Eileen Vogel	Best New Idea

To	XiaoHui Huang
From	Eric Eilenberger
Date	July 19
Subject	Content for August 12 Poster

Hi XiaoHui,

I reviewed the proposed design for the poster, and it looks good overall. With the bright background and font colors, it certainly has a more cheerful feel to it than the posters we've put up in past years! From their job titles, the guest lecturers certainly look impressive as well.

Just one note: The recipient for the Silver Anniversary is given to someone who has been with the company for more than 25 years. Most likely, this individual is in a senior management position. Aside from that, the current order is fine. Before you finalize anything, though, be sure to get Mr. Bibbo's approval. In addition, confirm that every name on the poster is written correctly. It is a special event, after all.

The print shop we use is usually very busy during this time of year. Therefore, it is crucial that you maintain frequent contact with the shop. Two years back, the program organizer took too long to place the order that the posters came on the day of the event.

Eric Eilenberger
HR Manager

191. Whose name will most likely be shown in a special style in the poster?

(A) Tony Bibbo's
(B) Ernest Jung's
(C) Juan Talavera's
(D) Eileen Vogel's

192. In the first e-mail, the word "far" in paragraph 2, line 1, is closest in meaning to

(A) distant
(B) long
(C) deep
(D) stretched

193. What event will be held on August 12?

(A) An awards ceremony
(B) A managers' conference
(C) A branch opening
(D) A product launch

194. What is suggested about Ms. Wilson?

(A) She will provide entertainment at the August 12 event.
(B) She has been employed at ErgoBuff for over 25 years.
(C) She used to work as an event organizer.
(D) She supervises the Human Resources Department.

195. What does Mr. Eilenberger ask Ms. Huang to do?

(A) Choose a different vendor
(B) Order more supplies
(C) Check that some information is correct
(D) Modify the color of a background

GO ON TO THE NEXT PAGE

Questions 196-200 refer to the following notice and e-mails.

An art exhibition will be held from June 15 until June 19 in Bee Spring Plaza, Colorado. This annual event has proven to be extremely popular among locals and tourists alike, attracting some 25,000 people every year.

We are inviting artists from across the country to exhibit their art to the world. The exhibition will feature the 80 best artists selected by our jury. Last year, over 1,000 artists competed for a spot at the exhibition, so get your application in today. Go to www.beespringplaza.org and download the application form. As part of your application, you must attach images of five original pieces of art as well as a $50 application fee. Completed applications should be then uploaded to the website or submitted by e-mail. We require all applications to be received by March 10 to receive consideration. If you are selected for our exhibition, you will be notified by April 5 at the latest.

Booth sizes and fees are as follows:
· 8-foot-by-8-foot booth for $300
· 8-foot-by-12-foot booth for $450
· 12-foot-by-12-foot booth for $525
· 16-foot-by-16-foot booth for $700

NOTE: All artists must organize their own transportation of artworks to the venue. We will not take responsibility for damaged artwork.

To:	Ray Dawson <rdawson@dawsonworks.com>
From:	Veronica Murphy <vmurphy@beespringplaza.org>
Date:	April 1
Subject:	Bee Spring Plaza Art Exhibition
Attachment:	Contract

Dear Mr. Dawson,

Congratulations! We would be delighted to invite you to feature your artwork at this year's Bee Spring Plaza Art Exhibition. Your paintings capturing Colorado's diverse landscapes stunned the judges, and we think they will resonate with many of the locals. We have attached a contract along with this e-mail. In order to accept the invitation, please sign and return the contract to us by April 30. Along with the contract, please also include the booth fee as well as a short biography of yourself. The biography should be around 200 words or less.

We will also be holding meet-and-greet sessions, where you can meet the guests and answer any questions. We will be holding the sessions by the picnic area at 4:00 P.M. from Wednesday, June 15, through Saturday, June 18. If you would be interested in participating, please also specify which date works best for you. We are looking forward to seeing you at the exhibition.

Sincerely,

Veronica Murphy, Director
Bee Spring Plaza

To: Veronica Murphy <vmurphy@beespringplaza.org>
From: Ray Dawson <rdawson@dawsonworks.com>
Date: April 3
Subject: RE: Bee Spring Plaza Art Exhibition
Attachment: Contract; Dawson_Bio

Dear Ms. Murphy,

Thank you for the opportunity to showcase my work at Bee Spring Plaza. I am very happy to accept the invitation. I am sending over the signed contract as well as a short biography of myself. I have also sent over the required $450 for the booth.

I am also very interested in attending the meet-and-greet sessions. Ideally, I would like to attend the Friday session as I may not be available on Saturday.

Sincerely,

Ray Dawson

196. In the notice, what is indicated about the Bee Spring Plaza Art Exhibition?

(A) It is an indoor event.
(B) It invites artists from around the world.
(C) It charges an admission fee.
(D) It is held once a year.

197. What does the notice suggest about the event?

(A) Artworks can be sold during the event.
(B) The dates are subject to change.
(C) Applicants receive a discount on booth fees.
(D) The screening process is competitive.

198. What does the first e-mail indicate about Mr. Dawson?

(A) He paints landscapes.
(B) He helped organize the exhibition.
(C) He grew up in Colorado.
(D) He is a photographer.

199. What size booth will Mr. Dawson most likely use?

(A) A 8-foot-by-8-foot booth
(B) A 8-foot-by-12-foot booth
(C) A 12-foot-by-12-foot booth
(D) A 16-foot-by-16-foot booth

200. On what day will Mr. Dawson most likely participate in a meet-and-greet session?

(A) June 15
(B) June 16
(C) June 17
(D) June 18

Stop! This is the end of the test. If you finish before time is called, you may go back to Parts 5, 6, and 7 and check your work.

준비물: OMR 카드, 연필, 지우개, 시계
시험시간: RC 75분

나의 점수		
RC		
맞은 개수		
환산 점수		

TEST 01	TEST 02	TEST 03	TEST 04	TEST 05
_____점	_____점	_____점	_____점	_____점
TEST 06	**TEST 07**	**TEST 08**	**TEST 09**	**TEST 10**
_____점	_____점	_____점	_____점	_____점

점수 환산표

RC			
맞은 개수	환산 점수	맞은 개수	환산 점수
96-100	460-495	41-45	140-215
91-95	425-490	36-40	115-180
86-90	395-465	31-35	95-145
81-85	370-440	26-30	75-120
76-80	335-415	21-25	60-95
71-75	310-390	16-20	45-75
66-70	280-365	11-15	30-55
61-65	250-335	6-10	10-40
56-60	220-305	1-5	5-30
51-55	195-270	0	5-15
46-50	165-240		

READING TEST

In the Reading test, you will read a variety of texts and answer several different types of reading comprehension questions. The entire Reading test will last 75 minutes. There are three parts, and directions are given for each part. You are encouraged to answer as many questions as possible within the time allowed.

You must mark your answers on the separate answer sheet. Do not write your answers in your test book.

PART 5

Directions: A word or phrase is missing in each of the sentences below. Four answer choices are given below each sentence. Select the best answer to complete the sentence. Then mark the letter (A), (B), (C), or (D) on your answer sheet.

101. For decades, Margate College has been ------- in supporting local youth organizations through annual fundraising events.

(A) activities
(B) activists
(C) actively
(D) active

102. The demonstration of Feder Corporation's new consumer electronics line ------- a lot of attention at the technology expo.

(A) generate
(B) generating
(C) is generated
(D) has generated

103. HR team members may use the Marketing Department's photocopier while ------- is being repaired.

(A) them
(B) their
(C) they
(D) theirs

104. Mr. Coulson will organize the ceremony and press conference for the ------- of the new headquarters.

(A) openness
(B) opening
(C) opener
(D) open

105. ------- 5,000 people visited Kowloon Finance's website yesterday.

(A) Over
(B) Well
(C) Any
(D) Other

106. Management is ------- focused on the plan to improve employee morale in the workplace.

(A) exclude
(B) exclusion
(C) exclusively
(D) exclusive

107. Calumet Construction's proposal to remodel the Rotherton Museum received ------- by the management this morning.

(A) obedience
(B) decision
(C) approval
(D) reaction

108. Every item ------- at nearly $100 comes with a discount voucher.

(A) pricing
(B) prices
(C) priced
(D) pricey

109. Any amount charged after the 20th of every month will be reflected on the ------- month's statement.

(A) developing
(B) incoming
(C) following
(D) accompanying

110. To ensure the best quality, Mason Electronics conducts ------- durability and temperature tests of its smartphones.

(A) more rigorously
(B) rigorously
(C) rigorous
(D) rigor

111. Guests are invited ------- the newly opened ancient Greek-Roman wing of the Montcrew Museum.

(A) tours
(B) having toured
(C) to tour
(D) touring

112. Dr. Rangit will be in his office for short ------- from 1 P.M. to 6 P.M. on Thursday.

(A) consults
(B) consultants
(C) consultant
(D) consultations

113. Sales soared after the promotional event, ------- the store manager will consider offering more special deals.

(A) only if
(B) as though
(C) however
(D) so

114. With the Deerfield University's digital library, students can ------- thousands of e-books and databases virtually.

(A) accessed
(B) accessing
(C) accesses
(D) access

115. An early novel draft by Scottish author Giles Fitzpatrick was purchased by a private collector today ------- an unknown amount.

(A) to
(B) for
(C) over
(D) out

116. The garden located in the ------- significant Van Tassel Building is open to visitors every weekend.

(A) history
(B) historian
(C) historical
(D) historically

117. Intercity buses from Guangzhou to Shenzhen depart the terminals at 30-minute -------.

(A) arrangements
(B) interchanges
(C) sectors
(D) intervals

118. The Costa Sol Produce Company announced a record-high crop yield of avocados ------- an unusually wet spring and summer.

(A) apart from
(B) caused by
(C) depending on
(D) exempt from

119. Users can enjoy a free 7-day trial of our smartphone application ------- deciding to sign up for a long-term plan.

(A) besides
(B) later
(C) before
(D) though

120. Please submit a photograph and a ------- of the damaged product if you would like us to process your refund.

(A) description
(B) determination
(C) definition
(D) detriment

GO ON TO THE NEXT PAGE

121. The warehouse manager told the shipping department that ------- more employees relocated, they would have to work additional hours.

(A) whenever
(B) upon
(C) until
(D) even

122. The delivery date and time forecasted by the shipping company were on target and -------.

(A) precision
(B) preciseness
(C) precise
(D) precisely

123. ------- and unit price were factored equally in selecting ABM Computers for our new notebooks.

(A) Accommodation
(B) Estimation
(C) Reliability
(D) Dependency

124. ------- interest in the seminar series on ancient Egyptian art failed to meet expectations, it was quickly canceled.

(A) Unless
(B) Obviously
(C) Since
(D) Due to

125. There is ------- more essential to preserving good nutrition than drinking 2 liters of water daily.

(A) nothing
(B) whenever
(C) other
(D) either

126. The visual effects team cannot provide proper graphics ------- the most recent update for the video editing software.

(A) without
(B) against
(C) past
(D) above

127. All customer calls ------- to ensure the quality of the service provided.

(A) recording
(B) recorded
(C) have been recording
(D) are recorded

128. ------- happens next in Mr. Briggs' career, he gained a lot of experience as a surveyor at DK Engineering.

(A) Whatever
(B) Everything
(C) Which
(D) Regardless

129. Wonder Grow tulip bulbs should be planted ------- eight weeks after the peak summer season.

(A) in case of
(B) as well
(C) at least
(D) even if

130. Staff members who leave the company forgo unclaimed health benefits ------- receive reimbursement for unused paid sick leaves.

(A) as a result
(B) in fact
(C) therefore
(D) but

PART 6

Directions: Read the texts that follow. A word, phrase, or sentence is missing in parts of each text. Four answer choices for each question are given below the text. Select the best answer to complete the text. Then mark the letter (A), (B), (C), or (D) on your answer sheet.

Questions 131-134 refer to the following advertisement.

Are you looking for the latest fashions?

Do you care about the environmental impact of your choices?

If so, you need to visit Eka's Boutique. -------. This includes recycled cotton, wool, and
                                               131.
three types of silk. We guarantee you'll like what you see!

We at Eka's Boutique always care ------- our products' sources. This is ------- we only
                                  132.   **133.**
offer clothing made in verified manufacturing facilities. To learn more and view our

------- catalogue, please go to our website, www.ekasboutique.co.uk.
134.

131. (A) Our boutique recently signed a contract with the local textile factory.
(B) We have dresses, jackets, and other fashionable items made from sustainable fabrics.
(C) Our boutique is conveniently located in Fashion Valley.
(D) We are open from 10:00 A.M. to 8:00 P.M., seven days a week.

132. (A) to
(B) on
(C) along
(D) about

133. (A) why
(B) where
(C) how
(D) when

134. (A) completed
(B) complete
(C) completely
(D) completeness

GO ON TO THE NEXT PAGE

Questions 135-138 refer to the following memo.

From: Fred Dixon, Human Resources
To: All Employees
Date: July 12
Subject: Office Closing

In preparation for the mid-year employee ------- on Saturday, July 29, we will be closing
                                        135.
the office off at 3:00 P.M. on Friday, July 28. Therefore, we ask that you plan on working

from home that day ------- you have a meeting. If you do, please send us an e-mail so
                   136.
that we can accommodate your request. Regarding the event, we have sent out the

invitations to everyone. If you have not received one yet, please let us know -------.
                                                                              137.
Finally, we are still taking recommendations for catering services in the area. -------.
                                                                               138.

---

135. (A) function
(B) broadcast
(C) instructions
(D) evaluations

136. (A) after
(B) so
(C) although
(D) unless

137. (A) immediately
(B) immediacy
(C) immediate
(D) immediateness

138. (A) The items belong in the storage
closet.
(B) A list of suggestions was acquired.
(C) July is often a busy time for
businesses.
(D) If you know a place, please let us
know.

To: board@regrowthfoundation.org
From: ian@regrowthfoundation.org
Date: December 8
Subject: Financial Report
Attachment: financialreport_12_8.pdf

Dear Members of the Board,

I have finished preparing our annual financial report, and I am sharing it with everyone. Please take a look and if you have any questions, you can bring them up at the end-of-year board meeting next week. -------.
139.

The main takeaway is that our financial position -------. While we did bring in a lot more
140.
money through our various events, pay close attention to our expenses. They have risen every year for the past five years. We, therefore, need to plan some cost-cutting -------. Finally, we will have to estimate how much money we expect to receive in
141.
corporate donations this year. This is necessary in order for us to establish our budgets for next year. We exceeded our donation goals last year, but I'd like us to err on the side of caution. Setting ------- goals is usually good, but it may also create unrealistic
142.
expectations.

---

139. (A) If you cannot attend, please email me your questions.
(B) I have addressed that concern in a previous e-mail.
(C) The change will need to go through an official procedure.
(D) Attendance has been fairly low every year.

140. (A) should not be declining
(B) is declining
(C) may have been declining
(D) could have declined

141. (A) measures
(B) areas
(C) concerns
(D) events

142. (A) unlikely
(B) dangerous
(C) competing
(D) ambitious

GO ON TO THE NEXT PAGE

Questions 143-146 refer to the following article.

PIERCE (17 June)—Primord Fitness will be launching a new watch in partnership with
------- giant Lifegate. Known for its expertise in creating ------- fitness programs,
143.   **144.**
Primord now wants to help customers reach their fitness goals faster. So after
collaborating with the programming team at Lifegate, Primord ------- new software for
145.
its watch that records data during a user's exercise. -------.
146.

Some lucky customers got to trial the watch earlier this month. "The trial went well, and
we learned a lot ourselves," said company spokesperson Mr. Jeff Jensen. "Now that we
have ironed out the finer details, we feel confident that the watches are ready to enter
the market," he added.

143. (A) technology
(B) accounting
(C) education
(D) advertising

144. (A) personalize
(B) personalized
(C) personally
(D) personalization

145. (A) endorsed
(B) requested
(C) contracted
(D) included

146. (A) Key information, such as workout
time and calories burned, is stored.
(B) Further testing will be required to
confirm the results.
(C) Availability is usually weak during
the colder months.
(D) A manual is available on the
company's website.

PART 7

Directions: In this part you will read a selection of texts, such as magazine and newspaper articles, e-mails, and instant messages. Each text or set of texts is followed by several questions. Select the best answer for each question and mark the letter (A), (B), (C), or (D) on your answer sheet.

Questions 147-148 refer to the following information.

To All Electric Avenue Listeners!

Now, our listeners can access the show on all major online streaming platforms.

- Stream our content any time
- Play our entire catalog free of charge

Search "Electric Avenue" on your music subscription service. Or tune in to WCCRB to hear us live from 8 P.M. to midnight.

147. What is the main purpose of the information?

(A) To announce a new streaming platform
(B) To publicize a special live event
(C) To advertise a new option for fans
(D) To attract new listeners to a radio station

148. What is indicated about the streaming service?

(A) Listeners can access the show 24 hours a day.
(B) It requires listeners to pay a monthly fee.
(C) It is only available to certain listeners.
(D) Listeners need to activate an account via e-mail.

GO ON TO THE NEXT PAGE

Questions 149-150 refer to the following text message chain.

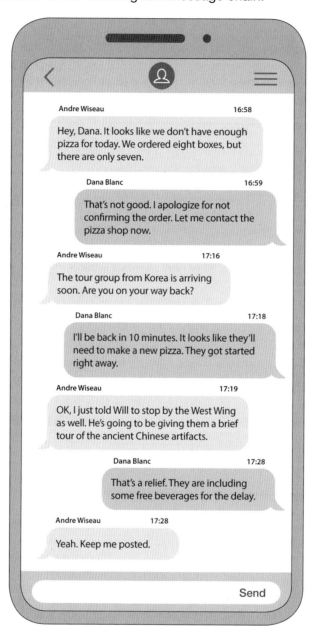

Andre Wiseau 16:58

Hey, Dana. It looks like we don't have enough pizza for today. We ordered eight boxes, but there are only seven.

Dana Blanc 16:59

That's not good. I apologize for not confirming the order. Let me contact the pizza shop now.

Andre Wiseau 17:16

The tour group from Korea is arriving soon. Are you on your way back?

Dana Blanc 17:18

I'll be back in 10 minutes. It looks like they'll need to make a new pizza. They got started right away.

Andre Wiseau 17:19

OK, I just told Will to stop by the West Wing as well. He's going to be giving them a brief tour of the ancient Chinese artifacts.

Dana Blanc 17:28

That's a relief. They are including some free beverages for the delay.

Andre Wiseau 17:28

Yeah. Keep me posted.

Send

149. What is probably true about Mr. Wiseau?

(A) He is overseeing a tour group.
(B) He is skilled at making pizzas.
(C) He is employed at a history museum.
(D) He is going to purchase some beverages.

150. At 17:18, what does Ms. Blanc mean when she writes, "They got started right away"?

(A) Some drinks are being refilled.
(B) A new tour group just arrived.
(C) Some guests have begun eating a meal.
(D) An order is being handled quickly.

Learn to operate heavy equipment with us!

We at Sunbelt Training specialize in the training of heavy equipment operations such as forklifts and cranes, and we have been growing at an incredible rate. Demand is now higher than ever for heavy equipment operators. With us, you'll be guaranteed employment, or we'll refund your tuition.

Our six-month course will have you on your feet and ready to work as a heavy equipment operator. Here's the incredible package we are offering:

◆ A three-day schedule where you can choose from:
  - Morning Classes: Monday/Wednesday/Friday, 8:00 A.M. to 12 P.M.
  - Evening Classes: Tuesday/Thursday/Saturday, 6:00 P.M. to 10 P.M.
◆ Free transportation to and from the training center
◆ Reduced tuition rates if you have been unemployed for longer than six months
◆ Our award-winning coaching system, where we will match you up with an experienced operator. Your coach will guide you through everything you will learn and help you prepare for the exams.
◆ Ongoing professional help, where we will find employment for you upon completion of the course as well as give advice on how to move up in the industry

Ready to start a new chapter of your life with us?

Come on down to our information nights where you can find out more!

| Session one | Tuesday, September 8 |
| Session two | Saturday, September 12 |

For more information, visit us at www.sunbelttraining.com or simply call 425-555-4685.

---

151. According to the brochure, what is a benefit of working as a heavy equipment operator?

(A) No weekend shifts
(B) High international demand
(C) Ease of employment
(D) Low cost of entry

152. Who is eligible for a reduced class cost?

(A) Those who have been unemployed
(B) Natives of the area
(C) People under the age of 35
(D) Holders of university degrees

153. According to the brochure, what is emphasized about the classes?

(A) They have the lowest tuition rates in the industry.
(B) They contain a self-learning component.
(C) They are taught by an award-winning instructor.
(D) They include a mentorship program.

154. What is offered by Sunbelt Training?

(A) Job interview practice
(B) Career advancement advice
(C) A tuition loan scheme
(D) Résumé templates

GO ON TO THE NEXT PAGE

Questions 155-157 refer to the following announcement.

SAVE THE REEF

The Australian Department of the Environment and Energy (ADEE) is holding a global fundraiser to save the Great Barrier Reef. —[1]—. A goal of $10 million (AUD) by the end of the month has been set, and friends from all over the world are encouraged to contribute to help preserve one of the great natural wonders of the world. —[2]—. Money raised will be applied towards research on how to better protect the Reef from threats such as rising sea temperatures and the increased frequency of severe weather events. —[3]—.

To learn more about what you can do to save the Reef, visit www.environment.gov.au/savethereef/info. —[4]—.

Show your support today!

155. Why was the announcement written?

(A) To explain a new energy plan
(B) To advertise a monthly deal
(C) To request a donation
(D) To report on a new research finding

156. What is implied about the Great Barrier Reef?

(A) It is home to various sea creatures.
(B) It is being affected by climate change.
(C) It is Australia's biggest tourist attraction.
(D) It is closed to the public.

157. In which of the positions marked [1], [2], [3], and [4] does the following sentence best belong?

"In addition, some of it will be used to help improve the water quality in the surrounding area."

(A) [1]
(B) [2]
(C) [3]
(D) [4]

Questions 158-160 refer to the following job advertisement.

Museum Curator Job Opening

POSITION
Montreal National Art Museum is in need of an experienced individual for its Ancient Art Department. Responsibilities of the curator include acquiring artifacts, care and display of collections, as well as educating and informing visitors of the exhibits.

QUALIFICATIONS
Candidates need at least two years of work experience in a museum or gallery setting. In addition, successful candidates will have the ability to speak French fluently. Candidates must also hold a university degree or equivalent in a subject such as fine arts or art history. Although a graduate degree is not necessary, it is an added bonus.

HOW TO APPLY
Visit our website at www.montrealart.com/jobs/ancientart to fill out an application.

CONTACT
If you have any questions or would like to learn more about the position, please email our HR manager at janlopez@montrealart.com.

---

158. What is a necessary qualification for the job?

(A) A graduate degree
(B) Strong communication skills
(C) Proficiency in a specific language
(D) Experience in teaching fine arts

159. The word "bonus" in paragraph 2, line 4, is closest in meaning to

(A) prize
(B) advantage
(C) commission
(D) compensation

160. How can more information about the job be acquired?

(A) By attending a career fair
(B) By contacting an employee
(C) By going to a museum
(D) By visiting a home page

GO ON TO THE NEXT PAGE

Questions 161-164 refer to the following online chat discussion.

Manuel Aguilar [9:32 A.M.]
Hello, Thelma. I was taking a look at the front page before we send it to the printers. The picture looks great, but our cover story doesn't feature enough opinions from citizens in the area. The story would really benefit from more personal accounts.

Thelma Lambert [9:34 A.M.]
Hi, Manuel. I was concerned that the article was getting too long. I did conduct some interviews, so we do have the option of including them. Perhaps I can use a smaller image to fit in more text.

Manuel Aguilar [9:36 A.M.]
I see. What are you thinking?

Thelma Lambert [9:39 A.M.]
I'll go ahead and add some interviews to the article. Then, I'll play around with the size of the image. Also, I think we should consider changing the sort of paper we use. Improved newsprint paper would make our photographs really stand out.

Manuel Aguilar [9:42 A.M.]
We have considered that in the past. How would that affect our costs?

Thelma Lambert [9:45 A.M.]
I was thinking we would only use it on the outside pages of our paper. It shouldn't affect how much we have to charge for our papers.

Manuel Aguilar [9:47 A.M.]
Sounds great. I'll get some quotes from our printer and get back to you about that.

SEND

---

161. What most likely is Ms. Lambert's job?

(A) Project manager
(B) Commercial lawyer
(C) Real estate agent
(D) News reporter

162. At 9:36 A.M., what does Mr. Aguilar most likely want to know when he writes, "What are you thinking"?

(A) How many interviews took place
(B) When the deadline for a project is
(C) Whether additional details can be included
(D) If a client should be contacted

163. Why does Ms. Lambert want to use improved newsprint paper?

(A) It improves the images.
(B) It is environmentally friendly.
(C) It provides more protection.
(D) It is more cost-efficient.

164. What does Ms. Lambert suggest about the cost?

(A) It should be revised in the future.
(B) It may need customer input.
(C) It is already too high.
(D) It will not be a significant amount.

Rules for Using Elkton Community Workspaces

Elkton start-up companies who would like to utilize our workspaces at 102 George Park must agree to the following rules:

· Workspaces are taken on a first-come, first-served basis. While there is no charge, you are not permitted to reserve a spot ahead of time.

· Participating businesses using our workspaces must sign in using the sheet provided. You may not use the workspaces for other purposes such as studying. The workspaces should be a place for start-up businesses to mingle and co-operate with one another. Therefore, we are designating these areas solely for business.

· Workspaces should be cleaned up after use. We ask that businesses who use this service clean up after themselves so that another business may use the area. Users caught not cleaning up may receive a warning, which may result in a fine.

165. What are participants expected to do?

(A) Assist other businesses
(B) Reserve a spot
(C) Fill in a sheet
(D) Register a business

166. According to the notice, why would a participant receive a warning?

(A) For studying at a workspace
(B) For not cleaning an area
(C) For creating excess noise
(D) For receiving outside funding

GO ON TO THE NEXT PAGE

Questions 167-168 refer to the following article.

Affinity Views, an up-and-comer in the advertising space, has drawn some scrutiny in recent months due to its controversial advertising strategies. The Commerce Commission has made it clear that if the company continues to breach the Fair Trading Act, actions will be taken against them. It is with this in mind that Affinity Views has hired Mr. Gordon to help keep the company in line. Affinity Views' latest campaign involved dropping fake money from a helicopter as a viral advertising campaign. The campaign was met with criticism, with the public commenting that such a stunt was shortsighted and dangerous. Mr. Gordon intends on leveraging his vast experience to ensure that the company only generates good publicity. He has hinted that next year will present a new image for the company. Despite the controversies, Affinity Views has posted its highest numbers yet. Its revenues for last year totaled $15 million, of which $5 million was earned overseas. The company expects its overseas accounts to grow considerably next year.

167. Why did Affinity Views hire Mr. Gordon?

(A) To manage the company's overseas expansion
(B) To keep the company in compliance
(C) To organize the company's finances
(D) To increase the company's publicity

168. How much money did Affinity Views earn last year?

(A) $5 million
(B) $10 million
(C) $12.5 million
(D) $15 million

Sparkle Again

First, make sure to absorb and wipe away excess residue from the spill with a paper towel. Then, apply a small amount of the solution to the fabric. Gently rub the Sparkle Again solution in a circular motion. The stain will begin to lighten and disappear. Reapply if the stain is still visible.

Sparkle Again uses all-natural ingredients to keep your clothes from discoloring. For best results, apply it immediately after a spill. It is highly recommended that you only apply Sparkle Again to non-delicate fabrics, as it may ruin clothes made from other materials.

To get more information and for videos on how to use Sparkle Again, visit our website at www. sparkleagain.com/howto. If you'd like to talk to one of our friendly customer support agents directly, please call +(41) 555-8274 or email us at cs@sparkleagain.com.

---

169. What is the purpose of Sparkle Again?

(A) To polish surfaces
(B) To lighten colors
(C) To eliminate stains
(D) To prevent odors

170. According to the instructions, what is important to do when using the product?

(A) Avoid using it on delicate fabrics
(B) Avoid applying it multiple times
(C) Allow it to dry once on the clothing
(D) Allow it to absorb all of the liquid

171. What is indicated about Sparkle Again?

(A) The product contains synthetic ingredients.
(B) The company provides tutorials on its website.
(C) The product can be purchased online or in stores.
(D) The company will reimburse customers for damaged clothing.

TEST 08

Questions 172-175 refer to the following Web page.

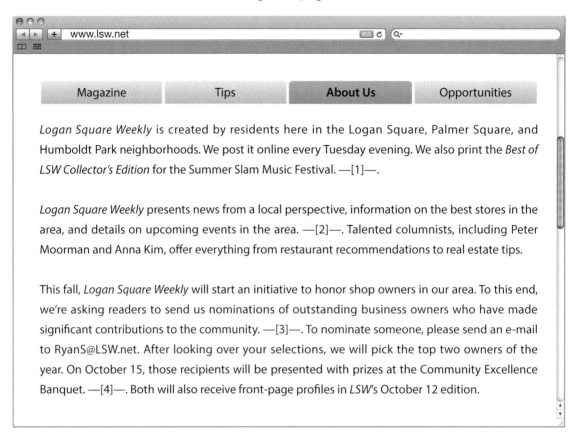

| Magazine | Tips | **About Us** | Opportunities |

Logan Square Weekly is created by residents here in the Logan Square, Palmer Square, and Humboldt Park neighborhoods. We post it online every Tuesday evening. We also print the *Best of LSW Collector's Edition* for the Summer Slam Music Festival. —[1]—.

Logan Square Weekly presents news from a local perspective, information on the best stores in the area, and details on upcoming events in the area. —[2]—. Talented columnists, including Peter Moorman and Anna Kim, offer everything from restaurant recommendations to real estate tips.

This fall, *Logan Square Weekly* will start an initiative to honor shop owners in our area. To this end, we're asking readers to send us nominations of outstanding business owners who have made significant contributions to the community. —[3]—. To nominate someone, please send an e-mail to RyanS@LSW.net. After looking over your selections, we will pick the top two owners of the year. On October 15, those recipients will be presented with prizes at the Community Excellence Banquet. —[4]—. Both will also receive front-page profiles in *LSW*'s October 12 edition.

172. What is the purpose of the Web page?

(A) To advertise a community publication
(B) To describe a restaurant opening
(C) To explain a local election
(D) To announce a concert schedule

173. What new feature is being announced?

(A) A new column for financial advice
(B) A Web chat service
(C) A plan to recognize store owners
(D) A property listing page

174. What will happen on October 15?

(A) An article will be published.
(B) City officials will be appointed.
(C) A new shop will open.
(D) Prizes will be distributed.

175. In which of the positions marked [1], [2], [3], and [4] does the following sentence best belong?

"As always, it will be available for purchase for $1 throughout the event."

(A) [1]
(B) [2]
(C) [3]
(D) [4]

GO ON TO THE NEXT PAGE

Questions 176-180 refer to the following e-mail and invoice.

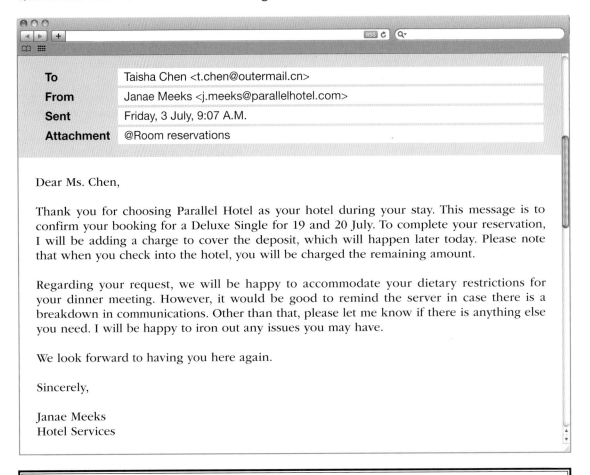

To	Taisha Chen <t.chen@outermail.cn>
From	Janae Meeks <j.meeks@parallelhotel.com>
Sent	Friday, 3 July, 9:07 A.M.
Attachment	@Room reservations

Dear Ms. Chen,

Thank you for choosing Parallel Hotel as your hotel during your stay. This message is to confirm your booking for a Deluxe Single for 19 and 20 July. To complete your reservation, I will be adding a charge to cover the deposit, which will happen later today. Please note that when you check into the hotel, you will be charged the remaining amount.

Regarding your request, we will be happy to accommodate your dietary restrictions for your dinner meeting. However, it would be good to remind the server in case there is a breakdown in communications. Other than that, please let me know if there is anything else you need. I will be happy to iron out any issues you may have.

We look forward to having you here again.

Sincerely,

Janae Meeks
Hotel Services

Parallel Hotel · 15 Ryecroft Field · Pennsylvania 15057

Guest: Taisha Chen
Address: 293 Bradford Manor, Elma, New York

Room No.	516	Room Rate	$375/night
Arrival	17 July	Departure	20 July

Date	Description	Charge
17-20 July	Room Charge	$1,125
17 July	Room Service	$30
18 July	Restaurant Dinner	$250
18 July	Room Service	$25
19 July	Restaurant Lunch	$50
20 July	Airport Dropoff	$30
	TOTAL	$1,510

176. What did Ms. Meeks most likely do on 3 July?

(A) She canceled an appointment.
(B) She called Ms. Chen's office.
(C) She charged Ms. Chen's credit card.
(D) She purchased advertising space.

177. In the e-mail, the phrase "iron out" in paragraph 2, line 4, is closest in meaning to

(A) execute
(B) handle
(C) develop
(D) ideate

178. What is suggested about Ms. Chen's stay at the Parallel Hotel?

(A) It was her first time visiting Parallel Hotel.
(B) It was more expensive than she anticipated.
(C) It was cut short due to an emergency.
(D) It was earlier than originally planned.

179. When did Ms. Chen most likely attend a meeting?

(A) July 17
(B) July 18
(C) July 19
(D) July 20

180. What is indicated about the Parallel Hotel?

(A) It offers an airport chauffeur service.
(B) It is the oldest hotel in Pennsylvania.
(C) It is owned and operated by Ms. Meeks.
(D) It has recently increased its prices.

GO ON TO THE NEXT PAGE

Questions 181-185 refer to the following Web page and e-mail.

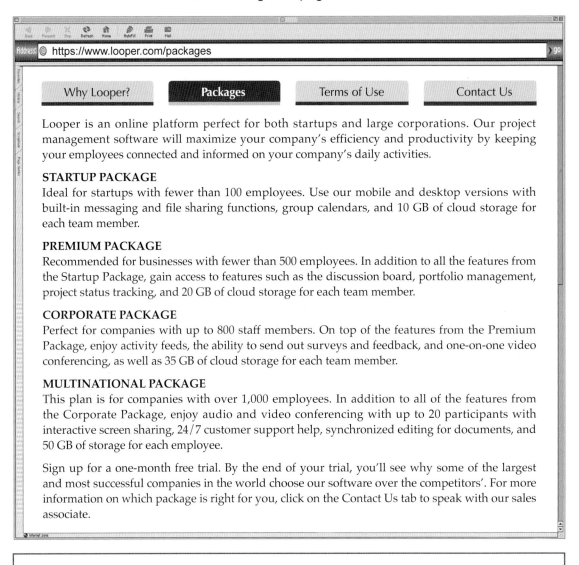

https://www.looper.com/packages

| Why Looper? | **Packages** | Terms of Use | Contact Us |

Looper is an online platform perfect for both startups and large corporations. Our project management software will maximize your company's efficiency and productivity by keeping your employees connected and informed on your company's daily activities.

STARTUP PACKAGE
Ideal for startups with fewer than 100 employees. Use our mobile and desktop versions with built-in messaging and file sharing functions, group calendars, and 10 GB of cloud storage for each team member.

PREMIUM PACKAGE
Recommended for businesses with fewer than 500 employees. In addition to all the features from the Startup Package, gain access to features such as the discussion board, portfolio management, project status tracking, and 20 GB of cloud storage for each team member.

CORPORATE PACKAGE
Perfect for companies with up to 800 staff members. On top of the features from the Premium Package, enjoy activity feeds, the ability to send out surveys and feedback, and one-on-one video conferencing, as well as 35 GB of cloud storage for each team member.

MULTINATIONAL PACKAGE
This plan is for companies with over 1,000 employees. In addition to all of the features from the Corporate Package, enjoy audio and video conferencing with up to 20 participants with interactive screen sharing, 24/7 customer support help, synchronized editing for documents, and 50 GB of storage for each employee.

Sign up for a one-month free trial. By the end of your trial, you'll see why some of the largest and most successful companies in the world choose our software over the competitors'. For more information on which package is right for you, click on the Contact Us tab to speak with our sales associate.

TO: a.crosby@looper.com
FROM: p.malkin@capsun.ca
DATE: May 19
SUBJECT: Looper Packages

Dear Ms. Crosby,

My name is Paul Malkin, and I'm the Chief Strategy Officer at Capsun Industries. We have been using Looper for the past five years, and I can't stress enough how important your software has been to our growth. We've recently finalized plans to expand, and we will soon have over 1,300 staff members across Canada. We've made good use of the cloud storage that your company offers, but we're going to be needing more than 35 GB per employee now, as well as a better way to track work progress. Do you have anything that is tailored to this?

I look forward to your response.

Paul Malkin
Chief Strategy Officer
Capsun Industries

181. How would Looper software most likely be used?

(A) For hiring new employees
(B) For advertising goods online
(C) For providing assistance to clients
(D) For improving staff productivity

182. What is true about Looper?

(A) Its products are used by major companies.
(B) It has merged with Capsun Industries.
(C) Its first line of software was released five years ago.
(D) It has over 200 employees.

183. What is the purpose of the e-mail?

(A) To confirm the purchase of an item
(B) To get advice on selecting a product
(C) To complain about some program issues
(D) To request an updated user manual

184. Which product will Ms. Crosby most likely recommend?

(A) The Startup Package
(B) The Premium Package
(C) The Corporate Package
(D) The Multinational Package

185. In the e-mail, the word "stress" in paragraph 1, line 2, is closest in meaning to

(A) anticipate
(B) worry
(C) emphasize
(D) pressure

GO ON TO THE NEXT PAGE

Questions 186-190 refer to the following e-mail, advertisement, and note.

To	Ashraf Bhagat (Flotech Pakistan)
From	Lew Burns (Flotech UK)
Date	5 December
Subject	Awad Engineering

Hi Ashraf,

I've just heard that you are preparing for a visit from Awad Engineering. The UK branch of Flotech Consulting has been working with Awad Engineering for many years here in London, and they are looking forward very much to a good relationship with the Flotech Pakistan team as well. I think you will find them very easy to work with.

Concerning the meal you are planning for them on 12 January, I should mention that several of the engineers have rather strict dietary restrictions. You'll want to keep this in mind when making arrangements.

Give me a call if you have any questions.

Thanks,
-Lew

Darbar Catering
Karachi

When you want to plan the perfect event, Darbar Catering is at your service. Our company has delighted clients in Karachi since 1955, providing the finest food and beverages for both corporate and family gatherings.

Why Darbar? Well, this is what makes us stand out:
*Customized decorations, including your company's logo
*A global menu featuring Western, South Asian, and Chinese favorites
*Special menus that can be created to suit a variety of food preferences
*Dance floor setup and music entertainment services available on request

Our services are available daily, noon to 10 P.M.

For more details, please give us a call at (92) 0213-555-1212.

Bilal Resort
An Avaricor Group Hotel

January 12

Dear Mr. Opfel,

Welcome to Pakistan: I hope you had a pleasant flight from London! My team and I would be honored if you would join us at 12:30 P.M. for a special luncheon in Rainbow Hall on the second floor of this resort. We're looking forward to getting to know you a bit over some good food before heading out to the construction site.

In the meantime, please give me a call at (92) 0304-551-2522 if I may be of assistance.

Yours faithfully,
Ashraf Bhagat

186. Why was the e-mail sent?

(A) To discuss the terms of a new contract
(B) To cooperate with another branch about a client
(C) To recommend a candidate for an engineering position
(D) To reschedule a client lunch meeting

187. What feature of Darbar Catering makes it the most suitable vendor for the event?

(A) Its affordable services
(B) Its large venues
(C) Its customized menus
(D) Its entertainment choices

188. According to the advertisement, what type of event would Darbar Catering be least likely to assist with?

(A) An awards dinner
(B) A corporate breakfast
(C) A holiday celebration
(D) A graduation party

189. Where does Mr. Opfel most likely work?

(A) At Awad Engineering
(B) At Darbar Catering
(C) At Flotech Consulting
(D) At Avaricor Group

190. Where was Mr. Opfel most likely given the note?

(A) At the front desk of a resort
(B) At a social gathering hosted by Flotech
(C) At the departure gate of the London airport
(D) At the head office of Awad Engineering

GO ON TO THE NEXT PAGE

Questions 191-195 refer to the following Web page and e-mails.

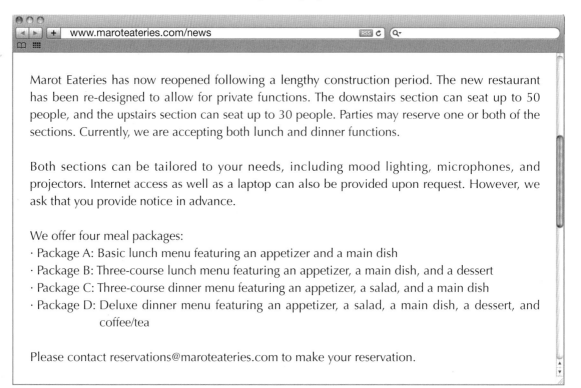

Marot Eateries has now reopened following a lengthy construction period. The new restaurant has been re-designed to allow for private functions. The downstairs section can seat up to 50 people, and the upstairs section can seat up to 30 people. Parties may reserve one or both of the sections. Currently, we are accepting both lunch and dinner functions.

Both sections can be tailored to your needs, including mood lighting, microphones, and projectors. Internet access as well as a laptop can also be provided upon request. However, we ask that you provide notice in advance.

We offer four meal packages:
· Package A: Basic lunch menu featuring an appetizer and a main dish
· Package B: Three-course lunch menu featuring an appetizer, a main dish, and a dessert
· Package C: Three-course dinner menu featuring an appetizer, a salad, and a main dish
· Package D: Deluxe dinner menu featuring an appetizer, a salad, a main dish, a dessert, and coffee/tea

Please contact reservations@maroteateries.com to make your reservation.

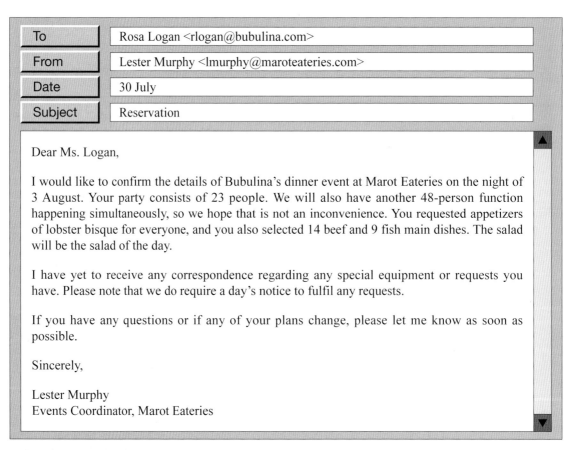

To	Rosa Logan <rlogan@bubulina.com>
From	Lester Murphy <lmurphy@maroteateries.com>
Date	30 July
Subject	Reservation

Dear Ms. Logan,

I would like to confirm the details of Bubulina's dinner event at Marot Eateries on the night of 3 August. Your party consists of 23 people. We will also have another 48-person function happening simultaneously, so we hope that is not an inconvenience. You requested appetizers of lobster bisque for everyone, and you also selected 14 beef and 9 fish main dishes. The salad will be the salad of the day.

I have yet to receive any correspondence regarding any special equipment or requests you have. Please note that we do require a day's notice to fulfil any requests.

If you have any questions or if any of your plans change, please let me know as soon as possible.

Sincerely,

Lester Murphy
Events Coordinator, Marot Eateries

To: Lester Murphy <lmurphy@maroteateries.com>
From: Rosa Logan <rlogan@bubulina.com>
Date: 31 July
Subject: RE: Reservation

Dear Mr. Murphy:

Thank you for the confirmation. First of all, we understand there will be another event going on. I hope the noise won't be much of an issue. Additionally, I do have some changes to request. We have been fortunate to have been granted a bonus for having a fantastic quarter. Therefore, we would like to celebrate by having a great meal. Can I add on the chocolate mousse and coffee and tea for everyone? Also, I do intend on handing out awards to my employees. I don't need a projector or anything as a microphone will be sufficient.

Thank you for your help.

Rosa Logan
Marketing Lead
Bubulina

191. What does the Web page indicate about Marot Eateries?

(A) It offers vegan options.
(B) It has been renovated.
(C) It is under new management.
(D) It is new to the area.

192. What is one purpose of the first e-mail?

(A) To confirm details of an upcoming event
(B) To revise the contents of a new menu
(C) To request advance payment of a service
(D) To schedule an appointment with management

193. What is suggested about the Bubulina event?

(A) It may have more attendees than expected.
(B) It is held annually at the same restaurant.
(C) It will be held in the upstairs section.
(D) It will feature a speech by Mr. Murphy.

194. What meal option will most likely be served at the award dinner?

(A) Package A
(B) Package B
(C) Package C
(D) Package D

195. What equipment does Ms. Logan request?

(A) Special lights
(B) A projector
(C) A microphone
(D) A laptop

GO ON TO THE NEXT PAGE

Questions 196-200 refer to the following online forum posts and e-mail.

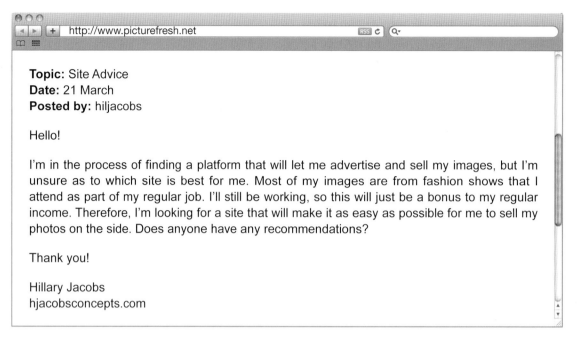

Topic: Site Advice
Date: 21 March
Posted by: hiljacobs

Hello!

I'm in the process of finding a platform that will let me advertise and sell my images, but I'm unsure as to which site is best for me. Most of my images are from fashion shows that I attend as part of my regular job. I'll still be working, so this will just be a bonus to my regular income. Therefore, I'm looking for a site that will make it as easy as possible for me to sell my photos on the side. Does anyone have any recommendations?

Thank you!

Hillary Jacobs
hjacobsconcepts.com

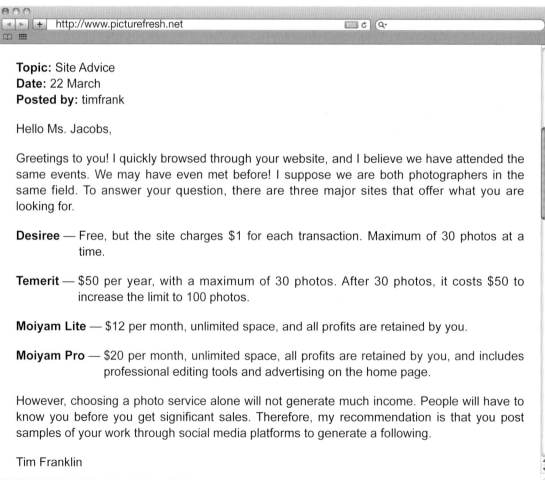

Topic: Site Advice
Date: 22 March
Posted by: timfrank

Hello Ms. Jacobs,

Greetings to you! I quickly browsed through your website, and I believe we have attended the same events. We may have even met before! I suppose we are both photographers in the same field. To answer your question, there are three major sites that offer what you are looking for.

Desiree — Free, but the site charges $1 for each transaction. Maximum of 30 photos at a time.

Temerit — $50 per year, with a maximum of 30 photos. After 30 photos, it costs $50 to increase the limit to 100 photos.

Moiyam Lite — $12 per month, unlimited space, and all profits are retained by you.

Moiyam Pro — $20 per month, unlimited space, all profits are retained by you, and includes professional editing tools and advertising on the home page.

However, choosing a photo service alone will not generate much income. People will have to know you before you get significant sales. Therefore, my recommendation is that you post samples of your work through social media platforms to generate a following.

Tim Franklin

To	hjacobs@hjacobsconcepts.com
From	helpdesk@moiyam.com
Date	25 March
Subject	A Warm Welcome

Dear Ms. Jacobs,

Thank you for signing up for Moiyam Pro! Your page has been created and is available for you to start uploading now. The URL is www.moiyam.com/hillary_jacobs. Your username is "hillary_jacobs," and your password is "pl2&f9Vm$a." Once you log in, you will be prompted to change your password. Ensure that you use a strong password that uses a combination of numbers, letters, and symbols.

Before customers can view your page, you will need to set up your profile first. This will require you to upload a picture of yourself and provide a short biography. To set up your profile, log into your account and click on the link at the top that says "Profile." If you experience difficulties with the site, please let us know.

Kind regards,
The Moiyam Team

196. Why did Ms. Jacobs write the first forum post?

(A) She is looking for guides on photo editing.
(B) She plans on teaching a photography class.
(C) She wants to expand her professional network.
(D) She would like to supplement her income.

197. On what type of photography does Mr. Franklin focus?

(A) Fashion
(B) Nature
(C) Architecture
(D) Animals

198. What does Mr. Franklin suggest Ms. Jacobs to do?

(A) Pay for advertising
(B) Share her work online
(C) Attend large events
(D) Partner with local businesses

199. How much will Ms. Jacobs pay annually?

(A) $0
(B) $50
(C) $144
(D) $240

200. According to the e-mail, what must Ms. Jacobs do to make her portfolio page public?

(A) Change her password
(B) Fill in some information
(C) Verify her account
(D) Speak to a customer service representative

Stop! This is the end of the test. If you finish before time is called, you may go back to Parts 5, 6, and 7 and check your work.

TEST 09

준비물: OMR 카드, 연필, 지우개, 시계
시험시간: RC 75분

나의 점수	
RC	
맞은 개수	
환산 점수	

TEST 01	TEST 02	TEST 03	TEST 04	TEST 05
_____점	_____점	_____점	_____점	_____점
TEST 06	TEST 07	TEST 08	TEST 09	TEST 10
_____점	_____점	_____점	_____점	_____점

점수 환산표

RC			
맞은 개수	환산 점수	맞은 개수	환산 점수
96-100	460-495	41-45	140-215
91-95	425-490	36-40	115-180
86-90	395-465	31-35	95-145
81-85	370-440	26-30	75-120
76-80	335-415	21-25	60-95
71-75	310-390	16-20	45-75
66-70	280-365	11-15	30-55
61-65	250-335	6-10	10-40
56-60	220-305	1-5	5-30
51-55	195-270	0	5-15
46-50	165-240		

READING TEST

In the Reading test, you will read a variety of texts and answer several different types of reading comprehension questions. The entire Reading test will last 75 minutes. There are three parts, and directions are given for each part. You are encouraged to answer as many questions as possible within the time allowed.

You must mark your answers on the separate answer sheet. Do not write your answers in your test book.

PART 5

Directions: A word or phrase is missing in each of the sentences below. Four answer choices are given below each sentence. Select the best answer to complete the sentence. Then mark the letter (A), (B), (C), or (D) on your answer sheet.

101. The airport shuttle will take the passengers ------- to the hotel.

(A) directors
(B) directing
(C) direction
(D) directly

102. Duoyi's most popular fitness tracker ------- a state-of-the-art GPS system.

(A) exercises
(B) challenges
(C) features
(D) contends

103. To find out more about how you can save money on home insurance, call -------.

(A) now
(B) greatly
(C) lately
(D) then

104. Ms. Pangchorn will answer her e-mails when she ------- from her trip on Wednesday.

(A) return
(B) returning
(C) returns
(D) had returned

105. We sent out a feedback request to all of our clients, but ------- refused to respond.

(A) more
(B) many
(C) yet
(D) often

106. The graphic designer made ------- to the company's logo for the ad campaign.

(A) duplications
(B) revisions
(C) installations
(D) complications

107. Before sending the final copy to the publisher, make sure it has the approval ------- the editors.

(A) with
(B) of
(C) over
(D) around

108. Ball's Kitchen Goods repurposed its recycled plastic and glass into chandeliers in an ------- to draw attention to global warming.

(A) attempt
(B) attempting
(C) attempts
(D) attempted

109. Until the board of directors can ------- a replacement, Pete Watkins will serve as the acting vice president.

(A) associate
(B) entitle
(C) select
(D) accomplish

110. The Shamrock Marathon has been canceled due to ------- high temperatures this week.

(A) exceed
(B) exceeding
(C) excess
(D) excessively

111. Cornwall Barriers is ------- a week-long shutdown of its production facilities so that they may be inspected for safety.

(A) generating
(B) implementing
(C) inducing
(D) arbitrating

112. Due to a lack of time, the company's programmers have not updated the mobile application -------.

(A) continually
(B) shortly
(C) firmly
(D) recently

113. Before emailing the contract to the vendor, the supplier noticed it required some ------- modifications.

(A) finally
(B) finalize
(C) finalist
(D) final

114. From next Monday, the coffee shop will close ------- as the owner, Mr. Walsh, goes on a holiday.

(A) adequately
(B) temporarily
(C) formerly
(D) comparatively

115. The personnel interviews revealed that most of the staff members have ------- in the management.

(A) confidence
(B) incentive
(C) courage
(D) sincerity

116. The top five candidates for the marketing officer position will be contacted ------- they are chosen.

(A) as soon as
(B) along with
(C) rather than
(D) on behalf of

117. ------- inquiries must be addressed to the Operations Department.

(A) Internal
(B) Organized
(C) Favored
(D) Recovered

118. Most West Oak Furniture staff members left early due to inclement weather conditions ------- a few who helped board up the store.

(A) justly
(B) in case of
(C) except for
(D) already

119. Mr. Valdez will ------- how to operate the new laser cutting machine once it is installed.

(A) attempt
(B) assist
(C) demonstrate
(D) reassure

120. Project managers monitor all steps ------- the workflow to ensure all processes are on track.

(A) throughout
(B) between
(C) beneath
(D) inward

GO ON TO THE NEXT PAGE

121. In spite of recent uncertainty in the rubber industry, demand for vehicle tires has remained fairly -------.

(A) unpredictable
(B) complacent
(C) stable
(D) strict

122. The man who is coming to pick up a birthday cake should be informed that ------- is in the refrigerator.

(A) he
(B) him
(C) his
(D) himself

123. ------- each session with a possible vendor, the interviewers should set aside some time to discuss their thoughts.

(A) Afterwards
(B) Beyond
(C) Following
(D) Outside

124. Ms. Chu will implement the new filing system with the ------- of the administration staff.

(A) assistance
(B) assistant
(C) assisted
(D) assist

125. ------- a rigorous study schedule is best, Lahp's tutoring services provide wisdom you may be lacking.

(A) While
(B) Both
(C) Either
(D) That

126. A ------- deadline for the final project has been set for the first week of May, but it will depend on the schedule for senior week.

(A) certain
(B) slack
(C) tentative
(D) prompt

127. Hiroko Mifune, ------- financial support has made the new city park possible, will give a speech at the dedication ceremony.

(A) whose
(B) whoever
(C) who
(D) whom

128. Budget changes impacting employee incentives ------- to the CEO right away.

(A) should be submitted
(B) will be submitting
(C) may have submitted
(D) has been submitted

129. Clothing from Monique's High Fashions sometimes costs ------- more than the manufacturer's suggested retail price.

(A) so
(B) this
(C) very
(D) much

130. The greater emphasis on reaching a younger ------- stems from extensive market research.

(A) implementation
(B) clientele
(C) radius
(D) phase

PART 6

Directions: Read the texts that follow. A word, phrase, or sentence is missing in parts of each text. Four answer choices for each question are given below the text. Select the best answer to complete the text. Then mark the letter (A), (B), (C), or (D) on your answer sheet.

Questions 131-134 refer to the following article.

TRA, Inc. Appoints New Director

Tokyo (10 March) — In a press conference this morning, a TRA representative announced that Hiro Musashi will take over as Director of Client Relations. Mr. Musashi will manage a department ------- business relationships with domestic and international
                                                    131.
companies.

TRA President Aiko Ogawa stated, "We look forward to working with Mr. Musashi, and we know he will ------- us to expand into different regions and create new
                        132.
partnerships." -------. When he was the business relations manager at Wango
                133.
Solutions, he helped increase annual sales by an average of 5 percent every year.

TRA offers ------- for commercial computer networks in major cities across Japan. It
            134.
also services other areas in Asia and Europe.

131. (A) develops
    (B) that develops
    (C) its development
    (D) is developing

132. (A) enable
    (B) discern
    (C) inform
    (D) profit

133. (A) Mr. Musashi will be transferring to the headquarters in Tokyo.
    (B) Mr. Musashi was previously the president of Wango Solutions.
    (C) Mr. Musashi will be welcomed at a corporate party.
    (D) Mr. Musashi joins TRA with nearly 20 years of industry experience.

134. (A) content
    (B) support
    (C) gifts
    (D) courses

GO ON TO THE NEXT PAGE

Questions 135-138 refer to the following memo.

To: All employees
From: Administration
Date: 8 April
Subject: New recycling bins

We promised that we will be making a bigger step towards sustainability in the office this year. You ------- some colored bins around the office. We will be recycling
135.
everything used in this office and sending it to a processing plant. The blue one is for glass, the yellow one is for cans, and the red one is for plastic. If you forget the -------
136.
associated with each color, there are helpful symbols on the sides of the bins. Please note that not all items can be recycled. -------. When in doubt, it is better to place these
137.
in the rubbish bin. Thank you for your ------- in helping us stay green.
138.

135. (A) would see
(B) would have seen
(C) may have seen
(D) did see

136. (A) categories
(B) indicators
(C) images
(D) solutions

137. (A) Additional bins will be installed later in the year.
(B) Staff should pay attention to the time of day.
(C) The initiative will bring up our sustainability scores.
(D) This includes items that still contain traces of food.

138. (A) production
(B) motive
(C) part
(D) faith

TBD Financial's new Endeavor card rewards you for investing in yourself.

TBD Financial is excited to offer a rewards credit card for business owners that lets you accrue points from day-to-day business expenses, ranging from ordering inventory to buying new office furniture. Now, you can start saving up for that next vacation while you work. Why ------- for a card that only rewards you for dining out at restaurants or
139.
going to the movies? ------- the Endeavor card turns 1.5 percent of every purchase into
140.
points, it provides double that for key business expenses, such as office supplies, gas, and mobile services. It's the best choice for ------- individuals whose main priority is
141.
their own business. Sign up with TBD Financial today to take advantage of our special $500 signing bonus. -------.
142.

---

139. (A) settling
(B) settled
(C) settle
(D) settlement

140. (A) Moreover
(B) Despite
(C) While
(D) Then

141. (A) they
(B) those
(C) this
(D) that

142. (A) This amazing offer expires on March 1, so don't wait.
(B) The Endeavor card does not offer bonus points for restaurant expenses.
(C) Expenses related to transportation do not generate points.
(D) Each person you refer will also receive the introductory gift.

GO ON TO THE NEXT PAGE

Questions 143-146 refer to the following advertisement.

Get the perfect rest every night on one of our ShapeShift luxury mattresses. Our patented memory foam will constantly adjust to your position for maximum comfort. Its ability to disperse ------- ensures you stay cool and comfortable. No matter what
143.
mattress size you are looking for, we have the perfect size for you. -------. ShapeShift
144.
luxury mattresses are manufactured in Pocopson and come with a 10-year warranty. We are confident you ------- our mattress the minute you lie down. We are so confident
145.
that we are offering a 30-day money-back guarantee, no questions asked. Simply tell us you are unhappy with your purchase, and we will send ------- to pick up the
146.
mattress.

143. (A) heat
(B) light
(C) energy
(D) sound

144. (A) Shipping fees may also vary depending on your location.
(B) This promotion will last until the end of the year.
(C) We can also cater for custom sizes.
(D) Sales of our mattresses have been strong.

145. (A) love
(B) will love
(C) have loved
(D) are loving

146. (A) one
(B) them
(C) someone
(D) yourself

PART 7

Directions: In this part you will read a selection of texts, such as magazine and newspaper articles, e-mails, and instant messages. Each text or set of texts is followed by several questions. Select the best answer for each question and mark the letter (A), (B), (C), or (D) on your answer sheet.

Questions 147-148 refer to the following information.

A complete list of our lunch and dinner options has been provided. Use the form provided in your room to check off the items you would like to order. When you are done, simply place the form outside your door and let reception know. Please note that our services start at 7:00 A.M. and finish at 8:00 P.M. We will be unable to process any orders placed outside of these hours. Payments will be settled at the end of your stay. Your final bill will include an itemized list of services you ordered during your stay.

147. For whom is the information most likely intended?

(A) Hotel receptionists
(B) Kitchen staff
(C) Travel agents
(D) Hotel guests

148. What is mentioned about the service?

(A) It must be paid for using cash.
(B) It is only available during certain hours.
(C) It can be used at a discounted rate.
(D) It includes additional charges for delivery.

GO ON TO THE NEXT PAGE

Questions 149-150 refer to the following Web page.

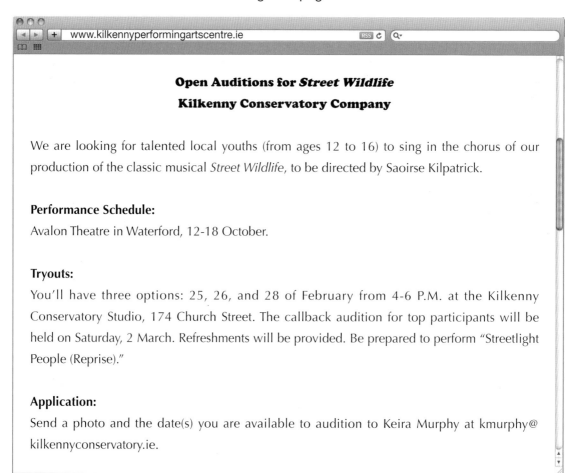

www.kilkennyperformingartscentre.ie

Open Auditions for *Street Wildlife*
Kilkenny Conservatory Company

We are looking for talented local youths (from ages 12 to 16) to sing in the chorus of our production of the classic musical *Street Wildlife*, to be directed by Saoirse Kilpatrick.

Performance Schedule:

Avalon Theatre in Waterford, 12-18 October.

Tryouts:

You'll have three options: 25, 26, and 28 of February from 4-6 P.M. at the Kilkenny Conservatory Studio, 174 Church Street. The callback audition for top participants will be held on Saturday, 2 March. Refreshments will be provided. Be prepared to perform "Streetlight People (Reprise)."

Application:

Send a photo and the date(s) you are available to audition to Keira Murphy at kmurphy@ kilkennyconservatory.ie.

149. According to the Web page, who should get in touch with Ms. Murphy?

(A) Singers
(B) Models
(C) Directors
(D) Artists

150. What is suggested about *Street Wildlife*?

(A) It was written by Ms. Kilpatrick.
(B) It was originally performed in Waterford.
(C) It will be performed in October.
(D) It will be performed three times.

TO	ugrant@baltor.com
FROM	jingram@hae.com
DATE	September 5
SUBJECT	Milton Hotel Accommodations

Dear Trade Show Vendor,

First and foremost, the team here at the Household Appliances Exposition (HAE) would like to thank you for your participation this year. I'm excited to inform you that we have negotiated with the nearby Milton Hotel to give all vendors a discounted rate on accommodations. All HAE vendors will be given a 20 percent discount during their stays at the Milton. In your official HAE vendor confirmation letter, you will see a unique ID number for your company. To apply the discount, enter this number in the promo code box when reserving your room through the hotel's website. We encourage you to take advantage of this deal quickly as the hotel is sure to run out of rooms.

Janette Ingram

151. Who most likely is Janette Ingram?

(A) A hotel manager
(B) A travel agent
(C) An event coordinator
(D) A business owner

152. How can an ID number be used?

(A) To enter a facility
(B) To receive a price reduction
(C) To purchase an appliance
(D) To access a membership account

GO ON TO THE NEXT PAGE

Questions 153-154 refer to the following text message chain.

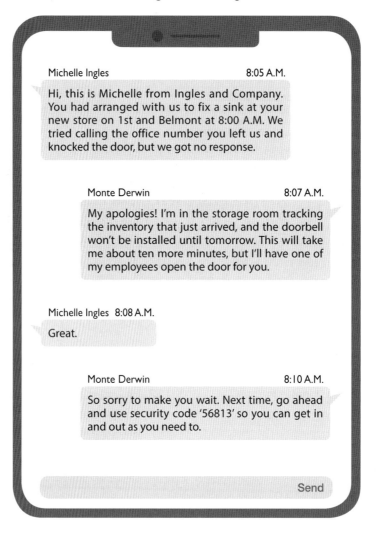

Michelle Ingles   8:05 A.M.

Hi, this is Michelle from Ingles and Company. You had arranged with us to fix a sink at your new store on 1st and Belmont at 8:00 A.M. We tried calling the office number you left us and knocked the door, but we got no response.

Monte Derwin   8:07 A.M.

My apologies! I'm in the storage room tracking the inventory that just arrived, and the doorbell won't be installed until tomorrow. This will take me about ten more minutes, but I'll have one of my employees open the door for you.

Michelle Ingles 8:08 A.M.

Great.

Monte Derwin   8:10 A.M.

So sorry to make you wait. Next time, go ahead and use security code '56813' so you can get in and out as you need to.

Send

153. What was scheduled at 8:00 A.M.?

(A) An inventory meeting
(B) A doorbell installation
(C) A plumbing repair
(D) A product delivery

154. At 8:07 A.M., why most likely does Mr. Derwin write, "My apologies!"?

(A) He forgot a store could not be accessed.
(B) He is unsure when he can help Ms. Ingles.
(C) He thought Ms. Ingles would come the next day.
(D) He expected an employee to share a security code.

Questions 155-157 refer to the following e-mail.

To: Jane Shepheard <jshepheard@bibbomail.com>
From: Tad Maynor <tad83@destinationstore.com>
Subject: Greetings
Date: 2 January
Attachment: j_shepheard

Dear Ms. Shepheard,

It's good to have you on the team. As we discussed in person, you will be assuming the role of assistant manager at our Oaklands Park location, 1774 Barksdale Road. As far as training goes, you are scheduled to begin on 22 January. Please go to the 21st floor of our headquarters that morning at 8:00 A.M. There, you'll be undergoing the mandatory Destination Store training with several new colleagues for one week. The course will familiarize you with the company's product range and our core philosophy. During this time, your work schedule will be from 9 A.M. to 6 P.M. After the orientation concludes, you'll be assigned your regular shift at the store and will be able to sign up for company benefits, including the retirement plan.

For now, we need you to fill in the attached document. By completing and signing it, you acknowledge that you understand and accept your new role and responsibilities. Email me right away if you have any questions.

Best of Luck,

Tad Maynor
Personnel Director

155. Why did Mr. Maynor write the e-mail?

(A) To discuss plans for a store promotion
(B) To explain a retirement policy
(C) To give details about a position
(D) To reschedule a meeting

156. According to Mr. Maynor, what will probably happen after one week?

(A) Ms. Shepheard will attend a celebration.
(B) Ms. Shepheard's wages will be increased.
(C) Ms. Shepheard will relocate to a different city.
(D) Ms. Shepheard's work hours will be adjusted.

157. What did Mr. Maynor include in the e-mail?

(A) An agreement form
(B) An insurance brochure
(C) An orientation agenda
(D) A product catalog

GO ON TO THE NEXT PAGE

TEST 09

Questions 158-160 refer to the following e-mail.

To:	emacpherson@naismith.org
From:	Carl@customizedcookwarehouse.com
Subject:	Order #234-19887
Date:	April 2

Mr. Macpherson,

This e-mail is in reference to your recent order. —[1]—. Unfortunately, the item listed below has already sold out:

"Customized Kitchen" Professional Ceramic Non-Stick Fry Pan Set, $150

We would like to apologize for the confusion this may cause. —[2]—. We strive to provide a seamless user experience; however, we do occasionally run into issues. —[3]—. Our last remaining set was purchased by another customer a few hours ago. Due to a delay in processing their payment, our inventory system was not properly updated to reflect that the item was out of stock. This is a rare but unfortunate error, which we are working to address.

We have refunded the points used to make the purchase to your Cookwarehouse.com account. Please verify that these appear on our website, but do allow two to six hours for the reimbursement to process. —[4]—.

Best Regards,

Carl Weizen
Customized Cookwarehouse Customer Relations

---

158. What is the main purpose of this e-mail?

(A) To mention an item cannot be purchased
(B) To report that an order will be delayed
(C) To promote a sale on a certain product
(D) To confirm that a shipment has been delivered

159. What is Mr. Macpherson asked to do?

(A) Provide a new form of payment
(B) Check an online account
(C) Email the customer relations team
(D) Use a special discount code

160. In which of the positions marked [1], [2], [3], and [4] does the following sentence best belong?

"This has occurred in your case."

(A) [1]
(B) [2]
(C) [3]
(D) [4]

Questions 161-163 refer to the following memo.

MEMO

To: All BrightSide Marketing employees
From: Candice Harris, General Manager
Date: August 19
Subject: Re: Sponsorships

This year, BrightSide Marketing is making a huge charitable contribution to the city of Severn. Through a partnership with Woodlawn High School, our employees will have the opportunity to serve as mentors for some of the students.

The gist of the program is that students will be matched with one of our employees, who will spend the day at work together. It will be an opportunity for the students to see what it's like working in an office while also gaining valuable work experience. Afterward, you can stay in touch with your mentee and provide them with support. The event will run throughout September, so if you are too busy then, please send Ms. Henry an e-mail. That way, she can mark you as ineligible. The program will be announced at Woodlawn High School soon, and I will pass on the newspaper article about it in a future e-mail.

---

161. What is the purpose of the memo?

(A) To inform employees about a charitable program
(B) To announce a potential merger with a rival
(C) To encourage more productive meetings at work
(D) To advise employees to take regular breaks

162. What group of employees should contact Ms. Henry?

(A) Those who would like to change teams
(B) Those who are new to the company
(C) Those who attended Woodlawn High School
(D) Those who will be unable to participate

163. According to the memo, what follow-up information will be sent?

(A) A detailed schedule
(B) A sign-up sheet
(C) A formal announcement
(D) A list of students

GO ON TO THE NEXT PAGE

Questions 164-167 refer to the following online chat discussion.

Edith Crawley [12:38 P.M.]

Hey, Joan and Dave. Have either of you seen the latest data on the FPX-2220 air conditioner we're about to release?

Joan Mitchell [12:39 P.M.]

Just did. I was surprised that it could cool faster while also being more energy-efficient.

Dave Edison [12:40 P.M.]

I know! It's a shame I won't be able to show it at my meeting with Baez Systems.

Joan Mitchell [12:40 P.M.]

I emailed a copy to everyone in the department.

Edith Crawley [12:42 P.M.]

That's scheduled for 3:30, though. You should have enough time to pick out the most pertinent graphs and put them into a slideshow.

Dave Edison [12:44 P.M.]

The problem is I'm giving a training seminar at 1:00, and I'll have to drive out to Baez's new main office immediately after. It's almost 30 miles away now.

Edith Crawley [12:45 P.M.]

I'd take care of it for you, but I'm already on my way to the airport.

Joan Mitchell [12:46 P.M.]

I'm on it. I'll make a file with the best charts and put it on a flash drive. Just make sure to pick it up from my desk before you go.

Edith Crawley [12:48 P.M.]

I hope the meeting is a success. If Baez agrees to a major purchase, it will definitely be worth celebrating.

Dave Edison [12:51 P.M.]

I appreciate your support!

SEND

---

164. What most likely is Mr. Edison's profession?

(A) Computer programmer
(B) Project manager
(C) Sales agent
(D) Repair technician

165. What will happen at 3:30 P.M.?

(A) A flight will take off.
(B) An application will be submitted.
(C) A meeting will be held.
(D) An award will be given.

166. What is implied about Baez Systems?

(A) It will soon release a new product.
(B) Ms. Crawley has many clients there.
(C) Mr. Edison was once employed there.
(D) Its headquarters was recently relocated.

167. At 12:46 P.M., what does Ms. Mitchell most likely mean when she writes, "I'm on it"?

(A) She will conduct a training session.
(B) She will send an e-mail.
(C) She will gather some data.
(D) She will create some visual aids.

The Rise of Suzanne Shore

Five years ago, Suzanne Shore was a receptionist at a small company. Today Ms. Shore is the founder and owner of a New York-based business, Shore's Delights. — [1] —. The company sold 5,000,000 meal kits last year and is on track to sell even more this year.

— [2] —. When her company had to let Ms. Shore go, she rented out a small apartment in Steuben. With her passion for cooking, she started preparing meal kits for her busy friends who did not have time to fix their own meals. — [3] —.

By chance, a new neighbor moved in next to her. The neighbor happened to be Justin Rice, the managing director of Wharton Financials. "I told him about these meal kits I had been preparing, and his eyes just lit up," said Ms. Shore. — [4] —. Mr. Rice, who is well-known for his entrepreneur scene, saw a big opportunity in Ms. Shore. After renting a commercial kitchen, hiring some employees, and setting up a website, orders started flooding in.

"We're just getting started. We are putting together plans to distribute our products all across America," said Ms. Shore.

---

168. What is suggested about Ms. Shore?

(A) She lives with her family.
(B) She did not intend on starting a business.
(C) She recently moved to New York.
(D) She has worked in the hospitality industry before.

169. What is NOT mentioned as a reason for Ms. Shore's success?

(A) A university degree
(B) A fortunate encounter
(C) A hobby
(D) The Internet

170. What is implied about Mr. Rice?

(A) He does not cook meals at home.
(B) He previously worked in real estate.
(C) He often travels out of state for business.
(D) He helped launch Ms. Shore's business.

171. In which of the positions marked [1], [2], [3], and [4] does the following sentence best belong?

"For a modest monthly fee, the company sends meal kits all across New York."

(A) [1]
(B) [2]
(C) [3]
(D) [4]

GO ON TO THE NEXT PAGE

Worldwide Eats

By Jack Bowman

SYDNEY (30 March) — Last month, we asked our readers to weigh in on the places to eat around town to form the Sydney Bucket List, a list of the best places to eat. As the results came in, one thing was clear: Sydney citizens are embracing the many varieties of international dishes that have propped up in the area. The most popular and interesting restaurants were compiled, and awards were presented to the city's top eateries.

The winner of the grand prize for most popular restaurant went to Chada Thai, which received the most number of first-place votes. A new player to the restaurant business, Chada Thai made a name for itself with owner Mr. Sukkasem's authentic recipes. "My parents ran a restaurant in Thailand. They taught me everything I know so that I can introduce native dishes to Sydney," said Mr. Sukkasem, in his interview.

Min-Hee Lee received an honourable mention for her restaurant, Nolbune. Hailing from South Korea, Ms. Lee stated that receiving a mention in the newspaper felt like an incredible achievement. Ms. Lee moved to Australia when she was 20, and her restaurant has been a staple part of Sydney dining experience for over 15 years now. Nolbune serves authentic Korean dishes ranging from fried chicken to various soups.

One of the more unusual names to make the list went to The Melting Pot, which received votes thanks to its unique concept. Rather than having a static menu, restaurant owner Oliver Carroll rotates guest chefs from all over Sydney every month. "Before I received my Australian citizenship, I spent a lot of time in immigrant communities. It helped me create connections with chefs from all over the world." Mr. Carroll is planning on opening a second location in Melbourne, which is expected to open in August.

The full list including interviews from all of the winners is available on *The Sydney Times* website at www.sydneytimes.com.au.

172. What is one purpose of the article?

(A) To investigate the cost of eating at restaurants
(B) To compare popular restaurants in Sydney
(C) To interview chefs on the value of good nutrition
(D) To highlight winners of a community restaurant vote

173. What is indicated about Chada Thai?

(A) It is known for its catering service.
(B) It is a relatively new restaurant.
(C) It requires patrons to book in advance.
(D) It offers discounts for children.

174. What do Ms. Lee and Mr. Carroll have in common?

(A) They were trained as professional chefs.
(B) They are both from overseas.
(C) They own multiple businesses in the city.
(D) They opened restaurants in the same area.

175. What is suggested about *The Sydney Times*?

(A) It publishes its list of winners online.
(B) It holds a community vote every month.
(C) It is the oldest newspaper in Sydney.
(D) It has experienced a decrease in subscribers.

GO ON TO THE NEXT PAGE

Questions 176-180 refer to the following Web page and review.

http://www.starshotcameras.com/products

Whether photography is your hobby, passion, or career, Starshot Cameras has got what you need. We offer a wide variety of cameras. However, all of our cameras are customizable based on your exact needs.

H2C — This is our default camera, which is particularly suited for beginners to photography. It is extremely intuitive to use and is compatible with many devices. Armed with a 16-megapixel camera, you'll be able to take images that come out beautifully. The H2C is the perfect stepping stone into the world of photography.

42C — A step above the H2C, the 42C comes with everything the H2C does except with more storage capabilities as well as the ability to manually focus the camera. This small detail helps you capture the exact shot you want rather than relying on the camera's autofocus feature.

K2P — The K2P is the first level of our commercial-use cameras. It features an impressive 30-megapixel camera, three interchangeable lenses for different zoom settings, and a long battery life. The K2P is perfect for budding photographers wanting to take their photography to the next level. Some installation of hardware and software is required.

P4X — The P4X is our high-end camera for commercial use. It features our highest megapixel camera at 45, and this camera is built to last. It is watertight and durable to the wear and tear of everyday use. It also comes with an array of lenses and cases all packed in a container for convenient carrying.

Visit your closest Starshot Cameras store today. Our sales representatives will gladly help you purchase the perfect camera for you.

I've only recently started taking my photography seriously, and I was nervous about having to buy some expensive equipment. I received a recommendation from my neighbor, who is a professional photographer. She said that Starshot's default camera would make an excellent starting point. Thanks to help from Velma Potter, I had a very smooth in-store experience. I ended up going for a camera that lets me have a bit more control over my shots as I often get frustrated at most autofocus features. Besides, the price difference between it and the basic camera was not as big as I thought. I'm very happy with my purchase!

Jim Frank

176. What does the Web page indicate about Starshot Cameras?

(A) It only sell cameras designed for commercial use.
(B) They can be tailored to exact specifications.
(C) They can only be bought at Starshot Cameras stores.
(D) They are renowned for their quality.

177. What feature does the 42C have that the H2C lacks?

(A) Adjustable lenses
(B) Manual focus
(C) Removable battery
(D) Resistance to water

178. In the Web page, the word "Armed" in paragraph 2, line 2, is closest in meaning to

(A) Carried
(B) Specialized
(C) Equipped
(D) Designed

179. What product did Mr. Frank most likely buy?

(A) H2C
(B) 42C
(C) K2P
(D) P4X

180. Who most likely is Ms. Potter?

(A) A Starshot Cameras sales representative
(B) The owner of Starshot Cameras
(C) Mr. Frank's neighbor
(D) A wildlife photographer

GO ON TO THE NEXT PAGE

Questions 181-185 refer to the following e-mail and flyer.

To: Quality Assurance Team <qc@techquest.com>
From: Barry Walker <b.walker@techquest.com>
Date: Tuesday, November 2
Subject: Upcoming workshops
Attachment: Flyer

Dear Team,

I am sending a flyer explaining the one-day workshops taking place next week. These one-day workshops will be an ongoing event as part of the CEO's new initiative. Unfortunately, the second session clashes with our weekly team meeting. However, you should still be able to attend one of the other times. The person running the workshops has written several books on the topic and is one of the most respected minds in the field. While the workshops are not mandatory, I think everyone would highly benefit from attending.

Thank you.

Barry Walker
Head of Quality Assurance

November Professional Development Workshop

This month's workshop will help employees understand the concepts behind forecasting and how we can use our past sales data to create our own forecasts. Our coordinator will be going over how to use spreadsheet software to prepare these in her workshop.

Coordinator: Emma Drake is a data scientist at ITO Corporation. She regularly speaks at international conferences and is a consultant at many big firms.

Upcoming Sessions (from 10:30 A.M. to 3:30 P.M.):
Monday, November 8
Wednesday, November 10
Thursday, November 11

There is a cap on the number of people who can sign up for each session. To sign up, please contact Alfred Ballard (ext. 792) in Human Resources. Once registered, workshop materials will be sent to your work inboxes one hour prior to the start time.

181. What is the purpose of the e-mail?

    (A) To encourage attendance at a workshop
    (B) To request details about a meeting
    (C) To address a recent decision
    (D) To notify a team about a change

182. When will Mr. Walker's team have its next team meeting?

    (A) On November 2
    (B) On November 8
    (C) On November 10
    (D) On November 11

183. What does Mr. Walker indicate about Ms. Drake?

    (A) She is highly knowledgeable in her field.
    (B) She attended the same university.
    (C) She consulted for the quality assurance team.
    (D) She recently started a new role.

184. What is the goal of the November workshop?

    (A) To teach employees about a new technique
    (B) To revise work safety and health standards
    (C) To improve communication among employees
    (D) To inform employees about some important trends

185. When will workshop participants receive their materials?

    (A) At 9:30 A.M.
    (B) At 10:30 A.M.
    (C) At 2:30 P.M.
    (D) At 3:30 P.M.

GO ON TO THE NEXT PAGE →

Questions 186-190 refer to the following e-mail, business card, and online review.

To	Ruth Bryant <rbryant@palumork.com>
From	Webb Physiotherapy <help@webbphys.com>
Date	February 12
Subject	Appointment

Dear Ms. Bryant,

This message is to confirm that we have received your deposit. Your appointment is now confirmed for 10 A.M. on February 15 at Webb Physiotherapy.

As you were referred from a hospital, please bring any scans taken as well as your reference letter from the hospital. This will help with diagnosing your injured ankle. Until a proper diagnosis is made, we recommend having somebody assist you to and from the practice. Dr. Erica Moore will be conducting some tests to examine the extent of the damage.

We hope to see you soon.

Sincerely,
Melinda Russell
Receptionist, Webb Physiotherapy

Webb Physiotherapy

12 Eider Drive, Lost River
Custer, Idaho, 83255
info@webbphys.com

Practice hours:
11 A.M. to 6 P.M., Monday to Friday
12 P.M. to 3 P.M., on Saturday
9 A.M. to 1 P.M., on Sunday

Who are we? Read about our history at www.webbphys.com.

To book appointments or consultations, fill out an online form at www.webbphys.com/form.

We accept major credit cards, and we also offer payment plans.

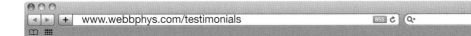

I must have visited two other physiotherapists, who told me my ankle was fine. I decided to visit Webb Physiotherapy, and Dr. Henry Wallace was finally able to diagnose my problem. I've been away from work since I injured my ankle on a school trip to Montana. Coincidentally, Dr. Wallace is a Montana native like me, and we actually grew up in the same town! However, he went overseas to study physiotherapy and gained a lot of work experience in Spain. Having only returned last year, he has brought a lot of new diagnoses and practices into Webb Physiotherapy. He was able to alleviate some of the discomfort I had been feeling in my ankle. I'm now ready to return to school for my work again.

The experience I had at Webb Physiotherapy was excellent, and I would absolutely recommend it to everyone.

Ruth Bryant, February 18

186. In the e-mail, what is Ms. Bryant asked to do?

(A) Sign a document
(B) Bring some assistance
(C) Make a payment
(D) Refer a friend

187. When is Ms. Bryant's appointment?

(A) On Monday
(B) On Wednesday
(C) On Saturday
(D) On Sunday

188. According to the business card, how should patients schedule an appointment with Webb Physiotherapy?

(A) By writing an e-mail
(B) By calling the office
(C) By downloading an app
(D) By filling out a form

189. What is suggested about Dr. Wallace?

(A) He was not originally scheduled for Ms. Bryant's appointment.
(B) He is also attending university while he works.
(C) He is not originally from the Montana area.
(D) He has worked at Webb Physiotherapy for over two years.

190. What does the online review indicate about Ms. Bryant?

(A) She knew Dr. Wallace growing up.
(B) She works at a school.
(C) She got injured playing sports.
(D) She recently returned from overseas.

TEST 09

GO ON TO THE NEXT PAGE

Questions 191-195 refer to the following article, Web page, and online order form.

BROOKLYN (September 25) — A recently launched app is changing the way people eat in the Williamsburg neighborhood. Thrive Fresh is a food delivery app started by a local Jason Vernon. The app gives users access to detailed nutritional and sourcing information on hundreds of menu items from a diverse range of local kitchens. For a monthly fee, it can also track users' orders and make dietary recommendations based on their needs and preferences.

Mr. Vernon got the idea when he noticed how greasy the food from traditional delivery services tended to be. "Whenever my former coworkers and I stayed late at work—which was quite often—we would order food, but it hardly ever had any fresh ingredients. Most of us tried to watch what we ate, but when it came to delivery, we were in the dark."

In response, Mr. Vernon developed a system that promoted transparency and wellness. Thrive Fresh works with local food providers that exclusively sell organic dishes. Its wide variety of healthy options and affordable prices have helped the service build a large and loyal customer base. The app still only delivers to users in the Williamsburg area but will expand to the rest of New York City in December.

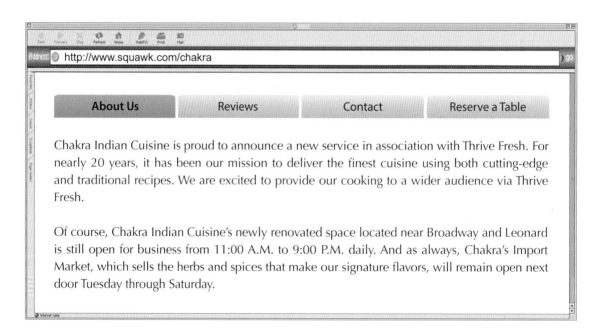

http://www.squawk.com/chakra

| **About Us** | Reviews | Contact | Reserve a Table |

Chakra Indian Cuisine is proud to announce a new service in association with Thrive Fresh. For nearly 20 years, it has been our mission to deliver the finest cuisine using both cutting-edge and traditional recipes. We are excited to provide our cooking to a wider audience via Thrive Fresh.

Of course, Chakra Indian Cuisine's newly renovated space located near Broadway and Leonard is still open for business from 11:00 A.M. to 9:00 P.M. daily. And as always, Chakra's Import Market, which sells the herbs and spices that make our signature flavors, will remain open next door Tuesday through Saturday.

Thrive Fresh Order Confirmation

Order:
Manpasand Quinoa Salad $7.00
Spinach Kofta Curry $12.00
Dal Makhani $13.00

Food $32.00
Membership Discount -$3.20
Tax $1.06
Total $29.86
(Payment at the door via credit card)

Name: Jill Klein
Address: 169 Lynch St., Apartment 3B
Phone: 718-555-9922
Delivery Time: Between 14:35-14:50, September 29

191. What is the article mainly about?

(A) What diet plan will help readers lead a healthy lifestyle
(B) Where inexpensive groceries can be bought
(C) How a meal service app was founded
(D) Why a restaurant became successful

192. According to the article, what is one reason Thrive Fresh is popular?

(A) Its quick delivery times
(B) Its high-quality user interface
(C) Its 24-hour availability
(D) Its reasonable prices

193. What is announced on Chakra Indian Cuisine's Web page?

(A) A new location
(B) A business partnership
(C) Some job openings
(D) Some upcoming renovations

194. What is most likely true about Chakra Indian Cuisine?

(A) It only sells organic dishes.
(B) It is only available through Thrive Fresh.
(C) It has been open for 20 years.
(D) It has multiple locations.

195. What is implied about Ms. Klein?

(A) She follows a strict nutritional plan.
(B) She is one of Mr. Vernon's colleagues.
(C) She lives in Williamsburg.
(D) She is hosting an event on September 29.

GO ON TO THE NEXT PAGE

Questions 196-200 refer to the following brochure and e-mails.

Nevardo's

Just outside Palm Springs in the desert community of Cathedral City, Nevardo's provides a perfect location for any seminar, party, or ceremony. Situated at the edge of the gorgeous Indian Canyon Nature Preserve, it features breathtaking views from its spacious patio lounge.

Inside, the Coachella Room hosts groups of up to 150 people, and the Agua Caliente Hall can comfortably fit 250 attendees. For conferences, the Joshua Tree Room works well for groups of up to 75 participants, or larger turnouts can be accommodated in the newly restored Lucille Ball Auditorium, which can seat 100. The latter two are fully equipped with top-quality audio-visual equipment to ensure a successful presentation.

Our award-winning buffet, the Nopalitos Grill, serves up a fantastic array of Mexican and Southwestern dishes. Make sure to check out our special Cinco de Mayo menu on May 5!

For more information, check out our website www.nevardos.com.

We offer a special Local Partner discount of 30 percent to Coachella Valley businesses on certain days. For details, call 760-555-1212.

To: Dan Chan <dchan@charpentierfinancial.com>
From: Fadila Boumaza <fboumaza@charpentierfinancial.com>
Date: January 4
Subject: Merger Celebration Plan

Dear Mr. Chan,

I checked out that place, Nevardo's, you mentioned in Monday's meeting, and I think it would be perfect for our corporate merger party. The location's really scenic, and since we've got a lot of guests, now over 200, attending from out of town, it's a fine opportunity to show visitors the beauty of the desert. They have an appropriate space available on May 11, May 25, and May 27. The first date is when they offer a substantial discount for local companies like ours.

Please confirm with Accounting and let me know when they say it's okay to make the reservation. However, we shouldn't wait too long. The place is already booked up through April, and these openings in May will probably be filled up quickly, too.

Thanks,

Fadila

To:	Fadila Boumaza <fboumaza@charpentierfinancial.com>
From:	Dan Chan <dchan@charpentierfinancial.com>
Date:	January 4
Subject:	Re: Merger Celebration Plan

Fadila,

Thank you for the details regarding Nevardo's. After talking with the accounting manager, we decided to go with the date when we can receive a reduced rate. This will be good for our budget. Please call Nevardo's and book the venue.

Dan Chan

HR Director, Charpentier Financial

---

196. According to the brochure, what is true about Nevardo's?

(A) It plans to remodel an auditorium.
(B) It has recently updated its restaurant menu.
(C) It is in downtown Palm Springs.
(D) It is suitable for various kinds of events.

197. What does Ms. Boumaza indicate about the corporate merger party?

(A) It will be held on multiple dates.
(B) It requires approval from others.
(C) It will include a video presentation.
(D) It may be postponed.

198. Where will the corporate merger party most likely be held?

(A) In the Coachella Room
(B) In the Agua Caliente Hall
(C) In the Joshua Tree Room
(D) In the Lucille Ball Auditorium

199. Why is Ms. Boumaza worried?

(A) The price of a venue may increase.
(B) A location may be too inconvenient.
(C) Many guests have not confirmed their attendance.
(D) The most ideal room may become unavailable.

200. When will Charpentier Financial's party most likely take place?

(A) On May 5
(B) On May 11
(C) On May 25
(D) On May 27

Stop! This is the end of the test. If you finish before time is called, you may go back to Parts 5, 6, and 7 and check your work.

준비물: OMR 카드, 연필, 지우개, 시계
시험시간: RC 75분

나의 점수	
RC	
맞은 개수	
환산 점수	

TEST 01	TEST 02	TEST 03	TEST 04	TEST 05
_____점	_____점	_____점	_____점	_____점
TEST 06	TEST 07	TEST 08	TEST 09	TEST 10
_____점	_____점	_____점	_____점	_____점

점수 환산표

RC			
맞은 개수	환산 점수	맞은 개수	환산 점수
96-100	460-495	41-45	140-215
91-95	425-490	36-40	115-180
86-90	395-465	31-35	95-145
81-85	370-440	26-30	75-120
76-80	335-415	21-25	60-95
71-75	310-390	16-20	45-75
66-70	280-365	11-15	30-55
61-65	250-335	6-10	10-40
56-60	220-305	1-5	5-30
51-55	195-270	0	5-15
46-50	165-240		

READING TEST

In the Reading test, you will read a variety of texts and answer several different types of reading comprehension questions. The entire Reading test will last 75 minutes. There are three parts, and directions are given for each part. You are encouraged to answer as many questions as possible within the time allowed.

You must mark your answers on the separate answer sheet. Do not write your answers in your test book.

PART 5

Directions: A word or phrase is missing in each of the sentences below. Four answer choices are given below each sentence. Select the best answer to complete the sentence. Then mark the letter (A), (B), (C), or (D) on your answer sheet.

101. Mr. McKinney was chosen to give a keynote speech at the conference, but ------- had to turn down the offer.

(A) he
(B) his
(C) him
(D) himself

102. Mr. Klein is ------- of job applications that contain even the slightest grammatical errors.

(A) criticize
(B) critical
(C) critics
(D) critic

103. At Kraven Law School, six months of legal internship ------- for certification as a graduate student.

(A) require
(B) will require
(C) are required
(D) has required

104. Diners can try ------- dishes all year round at the newly opened Merchant Bistro.

(A) dominant
(B) abundant
(C) exceptional
(D) excessive

105. Ms. Silva thinks that the review in *Viewer Digest* will bring positive ------- to her production company's latest project.

(A) publicize
(B) publicist
(C) publicity
(D) publicized

106. ------- the annual inspection has been completed, the warehouse crew can begin installing the additional shelving units.

(A) With that
(B) In order that
(C) In that
(D) Now that

107. Ms. Clarke was elected mayor for ------- running a popular campaign.

(A) successfully
(B) successful
(C) succeed
(D) succeeded

108. Ms. Kim ------- the new advertisement campaign in the latest issue of *Design Monthly*.

(A) focused
(B) cared
(C) answered
(D) included

109. ------- October 3, all gold-level passengers can cancel their flights free of charge.

(A) Effectiveness
(B) Effectively
(C) Effective
(D) Effecting

110. Mr. Zhukov replaced his car remote since it had not been working -------.

(A) deliberately
(B) actively
(C) properly
(D) moderately

111. Ms. Romanov became a valued resource at Robertson Ltd. ------- increasing its distribution network.

(A) therefore
(B) from
(C) by
(D) along

112. After Ms. Park's film, viewers are encouraged to stay for a short -------.

(A) participation
(B) discussion
(C) attendance
(D) concurrence

113. The office space will be cleaned ------- the workers remove the furniture.

(A) all
(B) or
(C) only
(D) once

114. Owing to the ------- pipe burst, businesses within a 200-meter radius were forced to close when raw sewage flowed into the streets.

(A) appropriate
(B) sudden
(C) impending
(D) immediate

115. The research and development department at Helvetica Corp. rewards employee -------.

(A) innovatively
(B) innovation
(C) innovative
(D) innovator

116. The SAC artists-in-residence program brings together artists of ------- disciplines, thus giving them the opportunity to exchange ideas.

(A) vary
(B) various
(C) variously
(D) variation

117. You can open a savings account ------- our latest smartphone banking app.

(A) through
(B) during
(C) under
(D) about

118. All community swimming pools must ------- by certified lifeguards to operate.

(A) monitor
(B) monitors
(C) are monitoring
(D) be monitored

119. The senior research analyst is ------- concerned with the small growth rate of the semiconductor industry in recent years.

(A) justifiably
(B) justifying
(C) justified
(D) justifiable

120. For safety reasons, visitors to the Militech plant must be ------- while on site.

(A) consulted
(B) escorted
(C) presented
(D) supported

GO ON TO THE NEXT PAGE

121. The caterers will evaluate all of the produce suppliers' bids and select ------- that suits their menu.

(A) few
(B) each
(C) one
(D) several

122. Thanks to its ------- design, the new Strom smartphone can comfortably fit in the user's pocket.

(A) compact
(B) vague
(C) rigid
(D) significant

123. Ms. Denali will be attending the media conference ------- she can gain valuable insight into the industry.

(A) so that
(B) in pursuit of
(C) with respect to
(D) or

124. Visitor numbers at the Natural History Museum increased ------- following the opening of the new dinosaur exhibit.

(A) strictly
(B) exactly
(C) rapidly
(D) closely

125. Guests are offered a complimentary gift basket with seven different types of fruit or cheese, ------- they prefer.

(A) rather
(B) everyone
(C) whichever
(D) both

126. Barrow Road, Inc. ------- that its heaters are the most energy-efficient in the industry.

(A) compares
(B) claims
(C) features
(D) inquires

127. Kayleigh Traylor's bespoke furniture is crafted ------- durable mahogany, then coated with varnish for a natural sheen.

(A) over
(B) ahead of
(C) in case of
(D) from

128. Monetary compensation will be provided for vendors working on public holidays ------- all relevant parties have agreed otherwise.

(A) additionally
(B) unless
(C) moreover
(D) whereas

129. At Wasson Inc., we are honored to be ------- officially as a trusted member of the Huvier Province Business Network.

(A) enlarged
(B) recognized
(C) progressed
(D) accomplished

130. In the televised interview with Channel 8's "News at Nine," the ------- of this year's most popular smartphone application will discuss how he came up with the idea of *Cent Saver*.

(A) developer
(B) user
(C) negotiator
(D) administrator

PART 6

Directions: Read the texts that follow. A word, phrase, or sentence is missing in parts of each text. Four answer choices for each question are given below the text. Select the best answer to complete the text. Then mark the letter (A), (B), (C), or (D) on your answer sheet.

Questions 131-134 refer to the following notice.

If you wish ------- a subscriber to our online movie streaming service, we will require
    131.
you to update your personal details. To do so, start by going onto our website, logging
in using your credentials, and accessing your ------- page. At the top of the page, select
                                               132.
the "My Details" tab. Click the "Update My Details" ------- and fill in the form. -------.
                                                     133.   **134.**

131. (A) remains
    (B) in remaining
    (C) to remain
    (D) remained

132. (A) account
    (B) accounting
    (C) accounted
    (D) accountings

133. (A) point
    (B) link
    (C) rank
    (D) scene

134. (A) A stable Internet connection is recommended for a pleasant viewing experience.
    (B) New releases will be displayed on the home page.
    (C) The holiday period will affect the hours our customer service team is available.
    (D) You will have to verify your details using an acceptable form of identification.

GO ON TO THE NEXT PAGE

Questions 135-138 refer to the following e-mail.

To: Eric Bollman <ebollman@leihouma.com>
From: Nancy Jensen <njensen@leihouma.com>
Subject: Water Issue
Date: Monday, September 10

Welcome to Leihouma's San Francisco branch. I am in charge of ensuring that you adjust well to this new location.

-------. I am sorry that your bathroom sink is not working. I have arranged for a
   135.
technician to come by your place tomorrow at 7 A.M., but this can be canceled if the issue is resolved before -------; please advise if this is the case. Also, be sure to present
                136.
your company ------- when the technician visits your home.
         137.

I ------- you again to follow up and make sure that everything is working properly
 138.
tomorrow morning.

Best Regards,

Nancy Jensen
HR Representative

---

135. (A) Ichiro Plumbing Co.'s representative can meet with you next Friday at 3 P.M.
   (B) The water delivery service will be complimentary for the first month only.
   (C) The quality of our drinking water has greatly improved.
   (D) I got your message that you need to call for a plumber.

136. (A) early
   (B) fast
   (C) then
   (D) there

137. (A) status
   (B) identification
   (C) video
   (D) permit

138. (A) email
   (B) had emailed
   (C) will email
   (D) would have emailed

Questions 139-142 refer to the following article.

DRG Awards Top Performers

Dawson Restaurant Group (DRG) has recognized its highest-performing locations for the month of April. For the fourth ------- month, the top award went to the Appling
<u>139.</u>
location, which achieved the highest sales while simultaneously topping the scores on the customer satisfaction surveys. "It's just an incredible achievement by ------- there,"
<u>140.</u>
DRG's president Colleen Payne commented.

Two other locations were also highlighted. The Stewardson location recorded the largest increase in sales this month, while the Damascus location organized a community fundraiser. -------. "We always encourage our locations to help the
<u>141.</u>
community," said Ms. Payne. "------- being new to the community, the Damascus
<u>142.</u>
location is committed to improving the city of Rockbridge."

---

139. (A) succeed
(B) success
(C) successively
(D) successive

140. (A) any
(B) her
(C) everyone
(D) other

141. (A) New locations will be opening up next year.
(B) The funds went to build a town hall.
(C) Employee retention should be our new focus.
(D) Customers are most drawn to the appealing designs.

142. (A) Alongside
(B) Supposedly
(C) Despite
(D) Unlike

GO ON TO THE NEXT PAGE

Questions 143-146 refer to the following e-mail.

To: staff@hbcentertainment.com
From: Amanda Nguyen
Subject: Jakob Bernal's new position
Date: November 21

Good morning,

I'm both deeply proud and a little sad to inform you all that Jakob Bernal will be moving on from HBC Entertainment to join Etten Media as Vice President of Operations. His ------- day here will be Thursday, January 31.
143.

Throughout Jakob's time at our company, he has been a big part of the production team. Especially over the course of the last two years, he has guided some of our biggest and most successful projects. In that time, he ------- strong and lasting
144.
friendships with so many of us at HBC Entertainment. His passion and leadership have been something we could count on. -------.
145.

If you can make the time over the next few days, please reach out to Jakob. I think we should all wish him good luck and ------- success in his new position.
146.

Best,

Amanda Nguyen
CEO

---

143. (A) next
    (B) nearest
    (D) latest
    (D) last

144. (A) formed
    (B) should form
    (C) forms
    (D) will form

145. (A) He developed a program in collaboration with Khepri Faried.
    (B) HR conducted an extensive search for a qualified candidate.
    (C) He previously worked in the media and design team at DeBrunye, Inc.
    (D) I'm sure we'll all miss his quick wit, good humor, and dedication.

146. (A) continued
    (B) continue
    (C) continuation
    (D) continues

PART 7

Directions: In this part you will read a selection of texts, such as magazine and newspaper articles, e-mails, and instant messages. Each text or set of texts is followed by several questions. Select the best answer for each question and mark the letter (A), (B), (C), or (D) on your answer sheet.

Questions 147-148 refer to the following notice.

Lend-a-Device Organization

If you have old computers or laptops lying around your house, now is your chance to make a difference. We are a charitable organization that sends unused electronic devices to the needy to help them get ahead in life. Your dusty computer could literally change lives by giving a child the opportunity to learn valuable computer skills. Call us at 555-1977, and we will arrange to pick up any devices you no longer need. Once a time and date is decided, simply leave the equipment in a labeled box outside your home, and our drivers will come and collect. Remove some clutter around your house while also making a difference!

---

147. What is the purpose of the notice?
(A) To request a discount on a provided service
(B) To encourage people to donate electronics
(C) To suggest that a new policy be added
(D) To advertise a new form of learning

148. What are people asked to do with their devices?
(A) Check that they still work
(B) Hand them into a participating store
(C) Write down the specifications
(D) Place them in a box

GO ON TO THE NEXT PAGE

Questions 149-150 refer to the following advertisement.

Belinda's Banishing Balm

The official release of Belinda's Banishing Balm was a huge shock to us. Although we expected strong demand due to the holiday season, we did not anticipate selling out so quickly. The good news is that we will receive the next batch of our balm next month, and we are offering a special discount to everyone who pre-orders.

The balm is derived from only natural ingredients such as aloe. It is guaranteed to moisturize and protect your skin like no other product. Order yours today and experience it for yourself!

149. What kind of product is being promoted?

(A) A diet supplement
(B) A hair product
(C) A stain remover
(D) A skin moisturizer

150. What is stated about the price of the product?

(A) It has been reduced for early buyers.
(B) It will not change until the next holiday season.
(C) It has increased due to high demand.
(D) It will change depending on the batch.

Make traveling for business trips simple and stylish with the Converge TravelFree.

The slim design of the Converge TravelFree has plenty of room to fit your laptop and meeting notes. — [1] —. While roomy inside, it measures in at 17 X 22 X 42 centimeters, allowing it to easily fit underneath your plane seat. Its outer layer provides cushioning to protect your possessions. — [2] —. Additionally, it is made out of material that repels water. This means that even in heavy rain, your backpack and possessions will stay dry. There is also a hidden compartment inside. — [3] —.

All Converge products come with a two-year warranty. — [4] —. If you find any defects or your bag is damaged, simply go to your closest Converge store with proof of purchase, and we will provide you with a replacement.

151. What type of company is Converge?

(A) A security products firm
(B) A backpack manufacturer
(C) A furniture company
(D) A fitness equipment maker

152. What is stated about the Converge TravelFree?

(A) It is suitable for use in rainy weather.
(B) It comes in a variety of colors.
(C) It often goes on sale every year.
(D) It can be ordered online.

153. In which of the positions marked [1], [2], [3], and [4] does the following sentence best belong?

"It's the perfect place to store your credit cards and passports."

(A) [1]
(B) [2]
(C) [3]
(D) [4]

GO ON TO THE NEXT PAGE

Questions 154-156 refer to the following Web page.

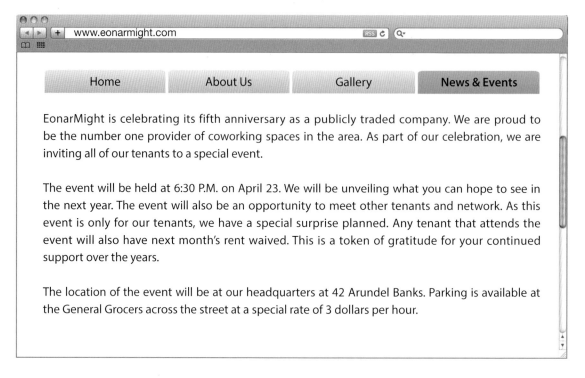

EonarMight is celebrating its fifth anniversary as a publicly traded company. We are proud to be the number one provider of coworking spaces in the area. As part of our celebration, we are inviting all of our tenants to a special event.

The event will be held at 6:30 P.M. on April 23. We will be unveiling what you can hope to see in the next year. The event will also be an opportunity to meet other tenants and network. As this event is only for our tenants, we have a special surprise planned. Any tenant that attends the event will also have next month's rent waived. This is a token of gratitude for your continued support over the years.

The location of the event will be at our headquarters at 42 Arundel Banks. Parking is available at the General Grocers across the street at a special rate of 3 dollars per hour.

154. What is indicated about EonarMight?

(A) It is located near a supermarket.
(B) It charges higher prices than its competitors.
(C) It holds celebrations every year.
(D) It has recently had a change in leadership.

155. What is NOT true about the event being advertised?

(A) It is an invite-only event.
(B) It will provide benefits to attendees.
(C) It requires the payment of an entry fee.
(D) It is celebrating a momentous day.

156. The word "hope" in paragraph 2, line 1, is closest in meaning to

(A) covet
(B) prefer
(C) desire
(D) expect

Questions 157-158 refer to the following text message chain.

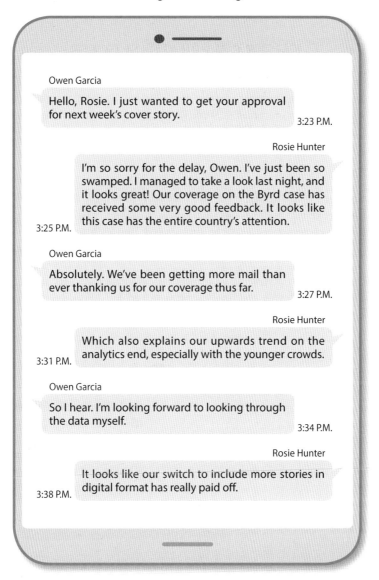

Owen Garcia

Hello, Rosie. I just wanted to get your approval for next week's cover story.

3:23 P.M.

Rosie Hunter

I'm so sorry for the delay, Owen. I've just been so swamped. I managed to take a look last night, and it looks great! Our coverage on the Byrd case has received some very good feedback. It looks like this case has the entire country's attention.

3:25 P.M.

Owen Garcia

Absolutely. We've been getting more mail than ever thanking us for our coverage thus far.

3:27 P.M.

Rosie Hunter

Which also explains our upwards trend on the analytics end, especially with the younger crowds.

3:31 P.M.

Owen Garcia

So I hear. I'm looking forward to looking through the data myself.

3:34 P.M.

Rosie Hunter

It looks like our switch to include more stories in digital format has really paid off.

3:38 P.M.

157. For what type of business do the writers most likely work?

(A) An accounting firm
(B) An online store
(C) A restaurant
(D) A newspaper

158. At 3:34 P.M., what does Mr. Garcia most likely mean when he writes, "So I hear"?

(A) He is also aware of the recent popularity.
(B) He would like confirmation of the information he has just heard.
(C) He thinks the upwards trend may have a different cause.
(D) He believes that managers have misinterpreted something.

GO ON TO THE NEXT PAGE

Questions 159-160 refer to the following article.

KAISER CELEBRATES SUCCESS

TOLEDO (September 3)—Kaiser Partners, a homegrown legal services firm, is celebrating an important milestone in the firm's history. Kaiser Partners has made this year's list of Top 100 Companies to Work For. Kaiser Partners was originally founded over 50 years ago by Bill Chandler, who ran the firm as a one-person operation here in Toledo. For 20 years, Mr. Chandler made a name for himself as an expert in corporate takeovers.

It was only when his daughter, Charlotte Chandler, joined the firm in 1980 where it began to grow exponentially. Today, the firm is still wholly owned by the Chandler household. However, just last year, the firm named Tonya Bowen, its first non-family member, as its CEO, with Ms. Chandler taking a step back to tend to her health.

Kaiser Partners is still the nation's go-to firm for corporate takeovers and acquisitions, but according to Ms. Bowen, the firm has plans to become a household name in every facet of legal services.

159. What is the main purpose of the article?

(A) To provide the history of a company
(B) To speculate on the prospects of a company
(C) To discuss the impact of a legal service
(D) To critique a company's ownership structure

160. What is currently true about Kaiser Partners?

(A) It is a family-owned business.
(B) It has only practiced legal services in Toledo.
(C) It has its headquarters overseas.
(D) It is the only firm practicing corporate takeovers.

Questions 161-163 refer to the following e-mail.

To:	mailinglist@topmall.com
From:	Top Mall
Date:	12 October
Subject:	Announcement

Top Mall is a leader in online retailing, providing a wide range of products to countries around the world. Because of the high traffic volume our site receives, we must continuously upgrade our servers to ensure a pleasant shopping experience.

Therefore, on 15 October, from 3 A.M. to 11 A.M. GMT, our website will be down to perform these upgrades. During this time, users will not be able to browse our inventory, access their shopping carts, or make changes to their orders. Our customer service agents, however, will be available to answer your questions and concerns in English, Chinese, and Spanish. Unfortunately, some account information may not be available during this process. We appreciate your understanding.

After 15 October, we will be even better able to assist you with all of your shopping needs. Top Mall will also start offering our customers a weekly newsletter with information on special offers and promotions. Sign up online to have it sent directly to your e-mail, and we will also send you a discount voucher good for 15 percent off your next purchase.

161. Why was the e-mail sent?

(A) To confirm an order
(B) To introduce a new product
(C) To announce a system upgrade
(D) To provide a shipping update

162. What is indicated about the Top Mall?

(A) Its website is easy to use.
(B) Its staff can speak several languages.
(C) It has offices in several countries.
(D) It was highly rated by customers.

163. How can readers receive a coupon?

(A) By upgrading an online service
(B) By subscribing to a newsletter
(C) By spending over a certain amount
(D) By calling a customer service agent

GO ON TO THE NEXT PAGE

Questions 164-167 refer to the following online chat discussion.

Rosemary Patton   9:12 A.M.
As you know, last week was an anomaly for many reasons. To get Perry caught up to speed, we had a mysterious illness going around the office, which caused some employees to miss work. What this has meant is that we missed some of our milestones. Particularly, the software side of things is coming along quite slowly.

Santiago Morrison   9:14 A.M.
We fell behind because the client is taking quite a long time to get back to us. We need confirmation on some of the specifications before we can begin work. I've been waiting for a response for over a week.

Rosemary Patton   9:16 A.M.
OK. I will need a copy of your correspondences as soon as possible. That way, I can let the client know that the project may be compromised unless they respond faster.

Perry Frazier   9:18 A.M.
Check your inbox in a minute, Rosemary. Also, I am going to voice my concern over the manpower available for this project. I think we are understaffed.

Faith Morris   9:20 A.M.
I'm in agreeance. I've contacted human resources to try find us some more developers.

Santiago Morrison   9:22 A.M.
I have some interviews lined up. The candidates look very promising, so I'm feeling optimistic.

Rosemary Patton   9:23 A.M.
Great. I will follow up with human resources on how the search is going. Santiago, can you let me know when the interviews are?

Message....

164. What most likely is Ms. Patton's job?

    (A) A customer representative
    (B) A project manager
    (C) A magazine writer
    (D) A product designer

165. What is suggested about Mr. Frazier?

    (A) He recently changed jobs.
    (B) He contracted an illness.
    (C) He has been away from work.
    (D) He will go on vacation next week.

166. At 9:18 A.M., what does Mr. Frazier most likely mean when he writes, "Check your inbox in a minute"?

    (A) He has scheduled a meeting with Ms. Patton.
    (B) He is unable to gain access to his e-mails.
    (C) He expects to be late to his meeting today.
    (D) He has forwarded Ms. Patton the requested information.

167. What will Ms. Patton most likely do before the workday ends?

    (A) Organize an interview with a colleague
    (B) Revise some workplace policies
    (C) Inform a client about a possible delay
    (D) Update an existing schedule

GO ON TO THE NEXT PAGE

Questions 168-171 refer to the following e-mail.

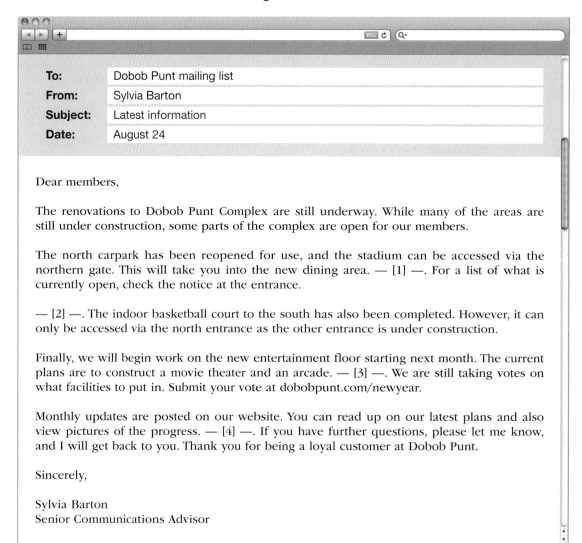

To: Dobob Punt mailing list

From: Sylvia Barton

Subject: Latest information

Date: August 24

Dear members,

The renovations to Dobob Punt Complex are still underway. While many of the areas are still under construction, some parts of the complex are open for our members.

The north carpark has been reopened for use, and the stadium can be accessed via the northern gate. This will take you into the new dining area. — [1] —. For a list of what is currently open, check the notice at the entrance.

— [2] —. The indoor basketball court to the south has also been completed. However, it can only be accessed via the north entrance as the other entrance is under construction.

Finally, we will begin work on the new entertainment floor starting next month. The current plans are to construct a movie theater and an arcade. — [3] —. We are still taking votes on what facilities to put in. Submit your vote at dobobpunt.com/newyear.

Monthly updates are posted on our website. You can read up on our latest plans and also view pictures of the progress. — [4] —. If you have further questions, please let me know, and I will get back to you. Thank you for being a loyal customer at Dobob Punt.

Sincerely,

Sylvia Barton
Senior Communications Advisor

168. What is the purpose of the e-mail?

(A) To hire employees to work on a building
(B) To provide an update on a project
(C) To announce the approval of new facilities
(D) To survey opinions on a budget request

169. What is indicated about Dobob Punt Complex?

(A) It has two entrances.
(B) It is the largest building in the area.
(C) It charges an entry fee for non-members.
(D) It plans to open a second complex.

170. Which of the following does the e-mail NOT ask members to do?

(A) Ask some questions
(B) Check a notice
(C) Vote on a decision
(D) Submit a photo

171. In which of the positions marked [1], [2], [3], and [4] does the following sentence best belong?

"Despite some unexpected delays, the gymnasium has been completed."

(A) [1]
(B) [2]
(C) [3]
(D) [4]

GO ON TO THE NEXT PAGE

Questions 172-175 refer to the following Web page.

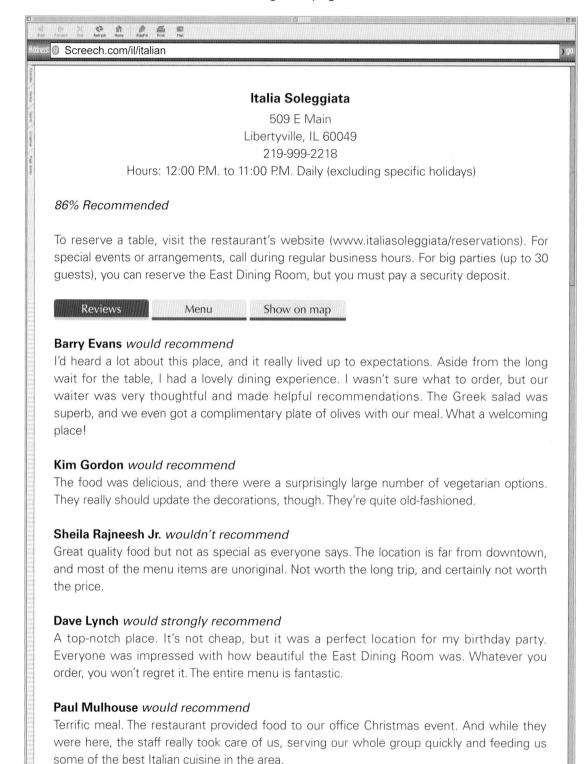

Italia Soleggiata

509 E Main
Libertyville, IL 60049
219-999-2218
Hours: 12:00 P.M. to 11:00 P.M. Daily (excluding specific holidays)

86% Recommended

To reserve a table, visit the restaurant's website (www.italiasoleggiata/reservations). For special events or arrangements, call during regular business hours. For big parties (up to 30 guests), you can reserve the East Dining Room, but you must pay a security deposit.

Reviews	Menu	Show on map

Barry Evans *would recommend*
I'd heard a lot about this place, and it really lived up to expectations. Aside from the long wait for the table, I had a lovely dining experience. I wasn't sure what to order, but our waiter was very thoughtful and made helpful recommendations. The Greek salad was superb, and we even got a complimentary plate of olives with our meal. What a welcoming place!

Kim Gordon *would recommend*
The food was delicious, and there were a surprisingly large number of vegetarian options. They really should update the decorations, though. They're quite old-fashioned.

Sheila Rajneesh Jr. *wouldn't recommend*
Great quality food but not as special as everyone says. The location is far from downtown, and most of the menu items are unoriginal. Not worth the long trip, and certainly not worth the price.

Dave Lynch *would strongly recommend*
A top-notch place. It's not cheap, but it was a perfect location for my birthday party. Everyone was impressed with how beautiful the East Dining Room was. Whatever you order, you won't regret it. The entire menu is fantastic.

Paul Mulhouse *would recommend*
Terrific meal. The restaurant provided food to our office Christmas event. And while they were here, the staff really took care of us, serving our whole group quickly and feeding us some of the best Italian cuisine in the area.

172. What did Barry Evans like the most about Italia Soleggiata?

(A) The restaurant's interior
(B) The variety of vegetarian options
(C) The good customer service
(D) The discount coupons

173. What is most likely true about the reservation made by Dave Lynch?

(A) It required a security deposit.
(B) It was made on a website.
(C) It was made after 11 P.M.
(D) It qualified for a discount.

174. What is indicated about Italia Soleggiata?

(A) It offers a catering service.
(B) It will open a downtown location.
(C) It operates every day of the year.
(D) It serves Italian food exclusively.

175. On what aspect of the restaurant do all the reviewers agree?

(A) The taste of the dishes
(B) The quality of the decorations
(C) The spacious parking lot
(D) The affordable menu items

GO ON TO THE NEXT PAGE

TO: employees@bellingercorp.com
FROM: Petra Stojakovic <petras@bellingercorp.com>
SUBJECT: Reallocation of parking spaces
DATE: 22 April

Attention Staff:

This e-mail is to remind you that construction of the new Bellinger Corp. R&D Facility will commence on 29 April.

Starting 27 April, parking lots J and K will be inaccessible until 9 July, the estimated date of completion. Employees allocated to lots J and K will receive a temporary "visitor" parking permit allowing them to park their vehicles in the visitor garage. The Facilities Management Department will deliver these permits to your desk by noon tomorrow. Please place the permits on the passenger side of your front windshield.

The street leading up to parking lots J and K will be closed off due to the creation of a construction access road. In addition, the main entrance to the security office and flower garden will be closed. An alternate entry point will be available for both locations.

In order to reduce the number of incoming cars, we urge everyone to avoid these areas unless you have urgent business. Remember, when using the temporary entrance, please use the painted walkway only.

Thank you for your cooperation.

Best regards,

Petra Stojakovic
Facilities Management

WELCOME TO BELLINGER CORP.
BUILDING INFORMATION DESK

IMPORTANT NOTICE:
PARKING LOTS J & K WILL BE CLOSED UNTIL 1 AUGUST

Employees who are assigned to these lots but have not been given a temporary permit must visit the security office as soon as possible. An employee ID badge and a vehicle registration form are necessary.

Vehicles parked near designated work zones, such as the construction site or loading areas, are subject to be towed. Cars that are parked in lots without the proper permit will be issued a $30 penalty per day.

Staff members are on hand to help you.

176. Why are some parking lots being closed?

(A) They will only be available for visitors.
(B) They are being cleaned and repainted.
(C) Some construction work is starting soon.
(D) A company is using them for an event.

177. According to the e-mail, who will receive a temporary parking permit?

(A) People who normally park in lots J and K
(B) People who are touring the R&D Facility
(C) People who are interviewing for a job at Bellinger Corp.
(D) People who register for one with the Facilities Department

178. Why should employees try to avoid visiting the security office?

(A) So that guests can access an information desk
(B) So that security personnel can perform an inspection
(C) So that they can enjoy the garden
(D) So that there will be less traffic

179. What changed after the e-mail was sent on April 22?

(A) Which parking lots are inaccessible
(B) How long some parking lots will be inaccessible
(C) When employees will receive their parking permits
(D) Where parking permits should be placed

180. According to the notice, why might a staff member's vehicle be towed?

(A) If it is parked in the garage after July 9
(B) If it is parked next to a loading area
(C) If it does not have a parking permit
(D) If it is parked in the guest lot

GO ON TO THE NEXT PAGE

Questions 181-185 refer to the following press release and e-mail.

Press Release
Contact: media@ropavieja.com

Phoenix, March 15 – Ropavieja Retailers announced that next week, they will launch a spring recruitment drive in hopes of placing 700 new employees in its 80 branches by June 1. Ropavieja is looking to add salespeople and cashiers in all of its locations. The retail chain is known for its excellent compensation, as well as benefits such as tuition assistance and daycare.

Ropavieja branches in select cities will also hold information sessions, led by regional managers, every Wednesday evening in April. Those who attend will have a chance to ask questions about the company and discuss career opportunities in individual interviews. To reserve a spot for a session, send an e-mail to recruit@ropavieja.com by March 22. Visit www.ropavieja.com for a complete list of job openings.

Ropavieja started out as a small shop in downtown Tucson 20 years ago. These days, it has branches all over North America, and is set to open one more in El Centro, California, in the coming weeks.

To	Steve Henry <shenry@bkmail.com>
From	Brad Narukawa <narukawa@ropavieja.com>
Subject	Details
Date	April 10

Dear Mr. Henry,

It was nice meeting you last Wednesday night. Based on our meeting, I would like to meet again to discuss a possible opportunity to work as a sales manager for us in Southern California. Letty Cantu, our Director of Sales, will also be at the interview.

Are you free on April 12 in the afternoon? Please give me a call at (505) 555-1212 to confirm.

Best Regards,

Brad Narukawa

181. According to the press release, what will Ropavieja Retailers begin soon?

(A) A new product promotion
(B) A major hiring campaign
(C) A company merger
(D) An executive board election

182. What is implied about Ropavieja Retailers?

(A) Its president will be resigning.
(B) Its budget will be decreased.
(C) Its first store is in California.
(D) Its business is growing.

183. What should people interested in a Wednesday evening event do?

(A) Make a reservation
(B) Download some forms
(C) Visit a company's head office
(D) Research information about tuition

184. What is the purpose of the e-mail?

(A) To promote a new service
(B) To discuss a project timeline
(C) To announce an upcoming sale
(D) To arrange an appointment

185. What is suggested about Brad Narukawa?

(A) He was born in El Centro.
(B) He was recently hired at Ropavieja Retailers.
(C) He is a regional manager.
(D) He is relocating to a new branch.

GO ON TO THE NEXT PAGE

Questions 186-190 refer to the following e-mail, Web page, and article.

To:	Mildred Roberson
From:	Perry Barrett
Date:	21 March
Subject:	Changing offices

You raised some very interesting points in your e-mail, Mildred. I have been concerned about the constantly rising price of rent in this area. It doesn't make much sense for us to keep paying such high rates, especially since we are shifting more towards working from home. We don't need an office in a premium location. I'd rather pay the lowest rent possible while still staying within Renburton city. We should use the money saved to pay higher salaries in order to attract more talent.

I do have a concern about moving. If we move out of our current location, I do wonder if that will affect the prestige of our firm. Having an office in the tallest tower in Renburton has done wonders for us in the past. I will have to consider whether saving money on rent is worth the possible loss in reputation. Let's meet later on today to discuss this in more detail.

Perry

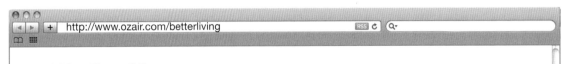

http://www.ozair.com/betterliving

Available Office Buildings

385 Argosy Close
Enjoy being a part of history by being in the oldest building in Penrose. Easily accessible from nearby highways and public transportation options.

16 Wessex Courtyard
One floor available. Fit for a large business. Tenancy comes with dedicated parking spaces for executives.

97 Stonefield Road
A brand new building with plenty of spaces to fill. Plans to open a cafeteria on the ground floor. Excellent chance to network with many new businesses.

45 Crescent Street
Located in the heart of Renburton. A great fifth-floor view of the city. Located across the street from a mall. Walking distance to the subway station.

879 Grigg Lane
Located just off the edge of the city. Close proximity to many suburbs for great commuting options. Plenty of access to nearby carparks as well as bus stops.

Renburton Stays Hot

RENBURTON (25 September) — Despite ever-increasing rent prices due to a surge in business in the area, the city has continued to attract and retain businesses. Clearly, the benefits of staying in the area are outweighing the hefty costs.

We spoke to the owner of Fizdale Designs, a business that has been in the Renburton area for the past five years. Owner Perry Barrett spoke about his decision to stay in the area.

"We debated moving our office elsewhere because the rent prices have been out of control," said Barrett. "In the end, we decided that it's a small price to pay to stay in Renburton in the midst of fantastic economic growth. Besides, many of our employees grew up here, and they wouldn't dream of leaving."

Fizdale Designs did recently make the decision to move offices within Renburton. According to Barrett, this was a strategic decision.

"We realized that we need to bring in new clients. There are so many new businesses popping up, and we want to connect with them," said Barrett. "We've had the same clients since the beginning. These guys are big, established companies. They're great, but we also want to work with a diverse range of clients."

---

186. What is the purpose of the e-mail?

(A) To convey urgency in a pending change
(B) To discuss the possibility of a relocation
(C) To request feedback on a new project
(D) To inquire about a new management system

187. What feature of 45 Crescent Street would meet one of Mr. Barrett's requirements?

(A) Its access to highways
(B) Its facilities
(C) Its cost
(D) Its location

188. What does the article indicate about Renburton?

(A) Its economy has been flourishing in recent years.
(B) It offers generous tax cuts to new businesses.
(C) Its buildings are overdue for renovations.
(D) It has been featured in business magazines.

189. Which location was most likely chosen by Fizdale Designs?

(A) 385 Argosy Close
(B) 16 Wessex Courtyard
(C) 97 Stonefield Road
(D) 45 Crescent Street

190. What does the article suggest about the clients of Fizdale Designs?

(A) They tend to pay higher prices than other companies.
(B) They do not often visit the office of Fizdale Designs.
(C) They have been with Fizdale Designs for a long time.
(D) They are located in the Renburton area.

GO ON TO THE NEXT PAGE

Questions 191-195 refer to the following Web page, e-mail, and memo.

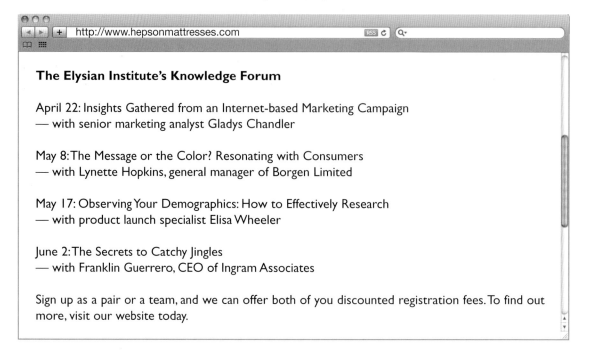

The Elysian Institute's Knowledge Forum

April 22: Insights Gathered from an Internet-based Marketing Campaign
— with senior marketing analyst Gladys Chandler

May 8: The Message or the Color? Resonating with Consumers
— with Lynette Hopkins, general manager of Borgen Limited

May 17: Observing Your Demographics: How to Effectively Research
— with product launch specialist Elisa Wheeler

June 2: The Secrets to Catchy Jingles
— with Franklin Guerrero, CEO of Ingram Associates

Sign up as a pair or a team, and we can offer both of you discounted registration fees. To find out more, visit our website today.

To: ewheeler@launchpad.com
From: Calm Waves Air
Date: May 28
Subject: Flight confirmation and itinerary

Dear Ms. Wheeler,

Thank you for choosing Calm Waves Air. Your flights are now confirmed, and the details are shown below.

Departure: June 21

Flight number	Departing	Arriving
185	Baltimore, 8:50 A.M.	Denver, 12:43 P.M.
760	Denver, 2:10 P.M.	Seattle, 4:46 P.M.

Departure: June 24

Flight number	Departing	Arriving
241	Seattle, 7:25 A.M.	Oklahoma City, 11:13 A.M.
697	Oklahoma City, 1:08 P.M.	Baltimore, 6:02 P.M.

MEMO

To: All Kavelock Staff
From: Marjorie Ellis, Head of Strategy
Date: June 19
Subject: RE: Reports

This week, we will be visited by Elisa Wheeler, who just gave an excellent presentation at the Elysian Knowledge Forum. She will be building off her original talk and explaining how the concepts can be applied to Kavelock. In light of this, I want us to suspend any planning we've done for Cataria until after Ms. Wheeler's visit. Instead, I want everybody here to watch her talk, which is available online. That way, we can already plan what questions we may have for her ahead of time.

191. What general topic do all of the webinars address?

(A) Data collection
(B) Product design
(C) Efficient practices
(D) Advertising strategies

192. According to the Web page, what can participants do to receive a discount?

(A) Sign up as a group
(B) Nominate a speaker
(C) Register for the event early
(D) Purchase multiple webinars

193. What is one purpose of the memo?

(A) To request voluntary speakers
(B) To schedule a celebration event
(C) To re-prioritize some work
(D) To collect feedback on a product

194. What most likely is the subject of the upcoming event at Kavelock?

(A) Conducting research
(B) Optimizing cost structures
(C) Securing real estate
(D) Internet advertising

195. Where is Kavelock most likely located?

(A) In Baltimore
(B) In Denver
(C) In Seattle
(D) In Oklahoma City

GO ON TO THE NEXT PAGE

Questions 196-200 refer to the following e-mail, flyer, and schedule.

To	Christine Walters <christine@maddux.com>
From	Julian Kojima <julian@maddux.com>
Date	April 30
Subject	Team-building Event

Dear Christine,

I trust that you're doing well. I know it can be rather challenging to keep track of everything at first, but I'm certain you will get the hang of it soon. Every year, around this time, our administrative coordinator organizes a company-wide event. I believe we discussed it when you interviewed in February. In past years, we have gone to soccer games and taken hikes in the national park, among other things. It's a great chance to get to know one another outside of work.

This year, I think it would be nice to go to a concert. Many employees are big music fans and have been talking about the outdoor concert series in Leeper Pavilion. It would need to be a concert on a weekday, and it should be a jazz show. We have $400 budgeted for this year. And, after a quick look at the pricing, it looks like that will be sufficient to get every employee a ticket.

If you need any help, Scott can help you with this. He has helped organize the event in the past.

Regards,

Julian Kojima
President, Maddux Industries

Join us for an evening to remember
at Leeper Pavilion

Concert tickets are available at reduced rates for large groups. Savings start when you buy 12 or more, and the more, the merrier! As a bonus, your group will be admitted to the venue early, receive complimentary refreshments, and will be entered into a contest to win VIP access to the backstage area to meet the artists.

Group Rates
- 12 tickets for $240
- 25 tickets for $375
- 50 tickets for $650
- 100 tickets for $1,200

Call or text 219-555-5040 if you have any questions.

Springtime in Leeper Pavilion
May Concert Schedule

Performer	Date	Day	Genre	Time
Merrion-Clark Ensemble	May 11	Saturday	Jazz	4:30 P.M.
Hill Street Seven	May 16	Thursday	Jazz	7:00 P.M.
Marcia Barton Quintet	May 26	Sunday	Classical	2:00 P.M.
Elkhart Philharmonic	May 29	Wednesday	Classical	8:00 P.M.

Tickets are now on sale at **www.leeperpavilion.gov/concertseries**.

196. What was the main reason Mr. Kojima emailed Ms. Walters?

(A) To invite her on a team-building hike
(B) To introduce a new filing protocol
(C) To instruct her to arrange an outing
(D) To inform her of his upcoming vacation

197. What does the e-mail suggest about Ms. Walters?

(A) She was recently hired at Maddux.
(B) She will be relocating to work on a new project.
(C) She has attended a performance at Leeper Pavilion.
(D) She is a fan of jazz music.

198. According to the flyer, what is an advantage of buying tickets in bulk?

(A) Lower ticket prices
(B) VIP seating
(C) Discounted concessions
(D) Gift bags

199. How many employees does Maddux Industries most likely have?

(A) 12
(B) 25
(C) 50
(D) 100

200. On what date will Maddux Industries hold their event?

(A) May 11
(B) May 16
(C) May 26
(D) May 29

Stop! This is the end of the test. If you finish before time is called, you may go back to Parts 5, 6, and 7 and check your work.

ANSWER SHEET

TEST 02

READING (Part V -VII)

NO.	ANSWER A B C D	NO.	ANSWER A B C D	NO.	ANSWER A B C D	NO.	ANSWER A B C D	NO.	ANSWER A B C D
101	Ⓐ Ⓑ Ⓒ Ⓓ	121	Ⓐ Ⓑ Ⓒ Ⓓ	141	Ⓐ Ⓑ Ⓒ Ⓓ	161	Ⓐ Ⓑ Ⓒ Ⓓ	181	Ⓐ Ⓑ Ⓒ Ⓓ
102	Ⓐ Ⓑ Ⓒ Ⓓ	122	Ⓐ Ⓑ Ⓒ Ⓓ	142	Ⓐ Ⓑ Ⓒ Ⓓ	162	Ⓐ Ⓑ Ⓒ Ⓓ	182	Ⓐ Ⓑ Ⓒ Ⓓ
103	Ⓐ Ⓑ Ⓒ Ⓓ	123	Ⓐ Ⓑ Ⓒ Ⓓ	143	Ⓐ Ⓑ Ⓒ Ⓓ	163	Ⓐ Ⓑ Ⓒ Ⓓ	183	Ⓐ Ⓑ Ⓒ Ⓓ
104	Ⓐ Ⓑ Ⓒ Ⓓ	124	Ⓐ Ⓑ Ⓒ Ⓓ	144	Ⓐ Ⓑ Ⓒ Ⓓ	164	Ⓐ Ⓑ Ⓒ Ⓓ	184	Ⓐ Ⓑ Ⓒ Ⓓ
105	Ⓐ Ⓑ Ⓒ Ⓓ	125	Ⓐ Ⓑ Ⓒ Ⓓ	145	Ⓐ Ⓑ Ⓒ Ⓓ	165	Ⓐ Ⓑ Ⓒ Ⓓ	185	Ⓐ Ⓑ Ⓒ Ⓓ
106	Ⓐ Ⓑ Ⓒ Ⓓ	126	Ⓐ Ⓑ Ⓒ Ⓓ	146	Ⓐ Ⓑ Ⓒ Ⓓ	166	Ⓐ Ⓑ Ⓒ Ⓓ	186	Ⓐ Ⓑ Ⓒ Ⓓ
107	Ⓐ Ⓑ Ⓒ Ⓓ	127	Ⓐ Ⓑ Ⓒ Ⓓ	147	Ⓐ Ⓑ Ⓒ Ⓓ	167	Ⓐ Ⓑ Ⓒ Ⓓ	187	Ⓐ Ⓑ Ⓒ Ⓓ
108	Ⓐ Ⓑ Ⓒ Ⓓ	128	Ⓐ Ⓑ Ⓒ Ⓓ	148	Ⓐ Ⓑ Ⓒ Ⓓ	168	Ⓐ Ⓑ Ⓒ Ⓓ	188	Ⓐ Ⓑ Ⓒ Ⓓ
109	Ⓐ Ⓑ Ⓒ Ⓓ	129	Ⓐ Ⓑ Ⓒ Ⓓ	149	Ⓐ Ⓑ Ⓒ Ⓓ	169	Ⓐ Ⓑ Ⓒ Ⓓ	189	Ⓐ Ⓑ Ⓒ Ⓓ
110	Ⓐ Ⓑ Ⓒ Ⓓ	130	Ⓐ Ⓑ Ⓒ Ⓓ	150	Ⓐ Ⓑ Ⓒ Ⓓ	170	Ⓐ Ⓑ Ⓒ Ⓓ	190	Ⓐ Ⓑ Ⓒ Ⓓ
111	Ⓐ Ⓑ Ⓒ Ⓓ	131	Ⓐ Ⓑ Ⓒ Ⓓ	151	Ⓐ Ⓑ Ⓒ Ⓓ	171	Ⓐ Ⓑ Ⓒ Ⓓ	191	Ⓐ Ⓑ Ⓒ Ⓓ
112	Ⓐ Ⓑ Ⓒ Ⓓ	132	Ⓐ Ⓑ Ⓒ Ⓓ	152	Ⓐ Ⓑ Ⓒ Ⓓ	172	Ⓐ Ⓑ Ⓒ Ⓓ	192	Ⓐ Ⓑ Ⓒ Ⓓ
113	Ⓐ Ⓑ Ⓒ Ⓓ	133	Ⓐ Ⓑ Ⓒ Ⓓ	153	Ⓐ Ⓑ Ⓒ Ⓓ	173	Ⓐ Ⓑ Ⓒ Ⓓ	193	Ⓐ Ⓑ Ⓒ Ⓓ
114	Ⓐ Ⓑ Ⓒ Ⓓ	134	Ⓐ Ⓑ Ⓒ Ⓓ	154	Ⓐ Ⓑ Ⓒ Ⓓ	174	Ⓐ Ⓑ Ⓒ Ⓓ	194	Ⓐ Ⓑ Ⓒ Ⓓ
115	Ⓐ Ⓑ Ⓒ Ⓓ	135	Ⓐ Ⓑ Ⓒ Ⓓ	155	Ⓐ Ⓑ Ⓒ Ⓓ	175	Ⓐ Ⓑ Ⓒ Ⓓ	195	Ⓐ Ⓑ Ⓒ Ⓓ
116	Ⓐ Ⓑ Ⓒ Ⓓ	136	Ⓐ Ⓑ Ⓒ Ⓓ	156	Ⓐ Ⓑ Ⓒ Ⓓ	176	Ⓐ Ⓑ Ⓒ Ⓓ	196	Ⓐ Ⓑ Ⓒ Ⓓ
117	Ⓐ Ⓑ Ⓒ Ⓓ	137	Ⓐ Ⓑ Ⓒ Ⓓ	157	Ⓐ Ⓑ Ⓒ Ⓓ	177	Ⓐ Ⓑ Ⓒ Ⓓ	197	Ⓐ Ⓑ Ⓒ Ⓓ
118	Ⓐ Ⓑ Ⓒ Ⓓ	138	Ⓐ Ⓑ Ⓒ Ⓓ	158	Ⓐ Ⓑ Ⓒ Ⓓ	178	Ⓐ Ⓑ Ⓒ Ⓓ	198	Ⓐ Ⓑ Ⓒ Ⓓ
119	Ⓐ Ⓑ Ⓒ Ⓓ	139	Ⓐ Ⓑ Ⓒ Ⓓ	159	Ⓐ Ⓑ Ⓒ Ⓓ	179	Ⓐ Ⓑ Ⓒ Ⓓ	199	Ⓐ Ⓑ Ⓒ Ⓓ
120	Ⓐ Ⓑ Ⓒ Ⓓ	140	Ⓐ Ⓑ Ⓒ Ⓓ	160	Ⓐ Ⓑ Ⓒ Ⓓ	180	Ⓐ Ⓑ Ⓒ Ⓓ	200	Ⓐ Ⓑ Ⓒ Ⓓ

ANSWER SHEET

TEST 01

READING (Part V -VII)

NO.	ANSWER A B C D	NO.	ANSWER A B C D	NO.	ANSWER A B C D	NO.	ANSWER A B C D	NO.	ANSWER A B C D
101	Ⓐ Ⓑ Ⓒ Ⓓ	121	Ⓐ Ⓑ Ⓒ Ⓓ	141	Ⓐ Ⓑ Ⓒ Ⓓ	161	Ⓐ Ⓑ Ⓒ Ⓓ	181	Ⓐ Ⓑ Ⓒ Ⓓ
102	Ⓐ Ⓑ Ⓒ Ⓓ	122	Ⓐ Ⓑ Ⓒ Ⓓ	142	Ⓐ Ⓑ Ⓒ Ⓓ	162	Ⓐ Ⓑ Ⓒ Ⓓ	182	Ⓐ Ⓑ Ⓒ Ⓓ
103	Ⓐ Ⓑ Ⓒ Ⓓ	123	Ⓐ Ⓑ Ⓒ Ⓓ	143	Ⓐ Ⓑ Ⓒ Ⓓ	163	Ⓐ Ⓑ Ⓒ Ⓓ	183	Ⓐ Ⓑ Ⓒ Ⓓ
104	Ⓐ Ⓑ Ⓒ Ⓓ	124	Ⓐ Ⓑ Ⓒ Ⓓ	144	Ⓐ Ⓑ Ⓒ Ⓓ	164	Ⓐ Ⓑ Ⓒ Ⓓ	184	Ⓐ Ⓑ Ⓒ Ⓓ
105	Ⓐ Ⓑ Ⓒ Ⓓ	125	Ⓐ Ⓑ Ⓒ Ⓓ	145	Ⓐ Ⓑ Ⓒ Ⓓ	165	Ⓐ Ⓑ Ⓒ Ⓓ	185	Ⓐ Ⓑ Ⓒ Ⓓ
106	Ⓐ Ⓑ Ⓒ Ⓓ	126	Ⓐ Ⓑ Ⓒ Ⓓ	146	Ⓐ Ⓑ Ⓒ Ⓓ	166	Ⓐ Ⓑ Ⓒ Ⓓ	186	Ⓐ Ⓑ Ⓒ Ⓓ
107	Ⓐ Ⓑ Ⓒ Ⓓ	127	Ⓐ Ⓑ Ⓒ Ⓓ	147	Ⓐ Ⓑ Ⓒ Ⓓ	167	Ⓐ Ⓑ Ⓒ Ⓓ	187	Ⓐ Ⓑ Ⓒ Ⓓ
108	Ⓐ Ⓑ Ⓒ Ⓓ	128	Ⓐ Ⓑ Ⓒ Ⓓ	148	Ⓐ Ⓑ Ⓒ Ⓓ	168	Ⓐ Ⓑ Ⓒ Ⓓ	188	Ⓐ Ⓑ Ⓒ Ⓓ
109	Ⓐ Ⓑ Ⓒ Ⓓ	129	Ⓐ Ⓑ Ⓒ Ⓓ	149	Ⓐ Ⓑ Ⓒ Ⓓ	169	Ⓐ Ⓑ Ⓒ Ⓓ	189	Ⓐ Ⓑ Ⓒ Ⓓ
110	Ⓐ Ⓑ Ⓒ Ⓓ	130	Ⓐ Ⓑ Ⓒ Ⓓ	150	Ⓐ Ⓑ Ⓒ Ⓓ	170	Ⓐ Ⓑ Ⓒ Ⓓ	190	Ⓐ Ⓑ Ⓒ Ⓓ
111	Ⓐ Ⓑ Ⓒ Ⓓ	131	Ⓐ Ⓑ Ⓒ Ⓓ	151	Ⓐ Ⓑ Ⓒ Ⓓ	171	Ⓐ Ⓑ Ⓒ Ⓓ	191	Ⓐ Ⓑ Ⓒ Ⓓ
112	Ⓐ Ⓑ Ⓒ Ⓓ	132	Ⓐ Ⓑ Ⓒ Ⓓ	152	Ⓐ Ⓑ Ⓒ Ⓓ	172	Ⓐ Ⓑ Ⓒ Ⓓ	192	Ⓐ Ⓑ Ⓒ Ⓓ
113	Ⓐ Ⓑ Ⓒ Ⓓ	133	Ⓐ Ⓑ Ⓒ Ⓓ	153	Ⓐ Ⓑ Ⓒ Ⓓ	173	Ⓐ Ⓑ Ⓒ Ⓓ	193	Ⓐ Ⓑ Ⓒ Ⓓ
114	Ⓐ Ⓑ Ⓒ Ⓓ	134	Ⓐ Ⓑ Ⓒ Ⓓ	154	Ⓐ Ⓑ Ⓒ Ⓓ	174	Ⓐ Ⓑ Ⓒ Ⓓ	194	Ⓐ Ⓑ Ⓒ Ⓓ
115	Ⓐ Ⓑ Ⓒ Ⓓ	135	Ⓐ Ⓑ Ⓒ Ⓓ	155	Ⓐ Ⓑ Ⓒ Ⓓ	175	Ⓐ Ⓑ Ⓒ Ⓓ	195	Ⓐ Ⓑ Ⓒ Ⓓ
116	Ⓐ Ⓑ Ⓒ Ⓓ	136	Ⓐ Ⓑ Ⓒ Ⓓ	156	Ⓐ Ⓑ Ⓒ Ⓓ	176	Ⓐ Ⓑ Ⓒ Ⓓ	196	Ⓐ Ⓑ Ⓒ Ⓓ
117	Ⓐ Ⓑ Ⓒ Ⓓ	137	Ⓐ Ⓑ Ⓒ Ⓓ	157	Ⓐ Ⓑ Ⓒ Ⓓ	177	Ⓐ Ⓑ Ⓒ Ⓓ	197	Ⓐ Ⓑ Ⓒ Ⓓ
118	Ⓐ Ⓑ Ⓒ Ⓓ	138	Ⓐ Ⓑ Ⓒ Ⓓ	158	Ⓐ Ⓑ Ⓒ Ⓓ	178	Ⓐ Ⓑ Ⓒ Ⓓ	198	Ⓐ Ⓑ Ⓒ Ⓓ
119	Ⓐ Ⓑ Ⓒ Ⓓ	139	Ⓐ Ⓑ Ⓒ Ⓓ	159	Ⓐ Ⓑ Ⓒ Ⓓ	179	Ⓐ Ⓑ Ⓒ Ⓓ	199	Ⓐ Ⓑ Ⓒ Ⓓ
120	Ⓐ Ⓑ Ⓒ Ⓓ	140	Ⓐ Ⓑ Ⓒ Ⓓ	160	Ⓐ Ⓑ Ⓒ Ⓓ	180	Ⓐ Ⓑ Ⓒ Ⓓ	200	Ⓐ Ⓑ Ⓒ Ⓓ

READING (Part V-VII)

NO.	ANSWER	NO.	ANSWER	NO.	ANSWER	NO.	ANSWER	NO.	ANSWER
	A B C D		A B C D		A B C D		A B C D		A B C D
101	Ⓐ Ⓑ Ⓒ Ⓓ	121	Ⓐ Ⓑ Ⓒ Ⓓ	141	Ⓐ Ⓑ Ⓒ Ⓓ	161	Ⓐ Ⓑ Ⓒ Ⓓ	181	Ⓐ Ⓑ Ⓒ Ⓓ
102	Ⓐ Ⓑ Ⓒ Ⓓ	122	Ⓐ Ⓑ Ⓒ Ⓓ	142	Ⓐ Ⓑ Ⓒ Ⓓ	162	Ⓐ Ⓑ Ⓒ Ⓓ	182	Ⓐ Ⓑ Ⓒ Ⓓ
103	Ⓐ Ⓑ Ⓒ Ⓓ	123	Ⓐ Ⓑ Ⓒ Ⓓ	143	Ⓐ Ⓑ Ⓒ Ⓓ	163	Ⓐ Ⓑ Ⓒ Ⓓ	183	Ⓐ Ⓑ Ⓒ Ⓓ
104	Ⓐ Ⓑ Ⓒ Ⓓ	124	Ⓐ Ⓑ Ⓒ Ⓓ	144	Ⓐ Ⓑ Ⓒ Ⓓ	164	Ⓐ Ⓑ Ⓒ Ⓓ	184	Ⓐ Ⓑ Ⓒ Ⓓ
105	Ⓐ Ⓑ Ⓒ Ⓓ	125	Ⓐ Ⓑ Ⓒ Ⓓ	145	Ⓐ Ⓑ Ⓒ Ⓓ	165	Ⓐ Ⓑ Ⓒ Ⓓ	185	Ⓐ Ⓑ Ⓒ Ⓓ
106	Ⓐ Ⓑ Ⓒ Ⓓ	126	Ⓐ Ⓑ Ⓒ Ⓓ	146	Ⓐ Ⓑ Ⓒ Ⓓ	166	Ⓐ Ⓑ Ⓒ Ⓓ	186	Ⓐ Ⓑ Ⓒ Ⓓ
107	Ⓐ Ⓑ Ⓒ Ⓓ	127	Ⓐ Ⓑ Ⓒ Ⓓ	147	Ⓐ Ⓑ Ⓒ Ⓓ	167	Ⓐ Ⓑ Ⓒ Ⓓ	187	Ⓐ Ⓑ Ⓒ Ⓓ
108	Ⓐ Ⓑ Ⓒ Ⓓ	128	Ⓐ Ⓑ Ⓒ Ⓓ	148	Ⓐ Ⓑ Ⓒ Ⓓ	168	Ⓐ Ⓑ Ⓒ Ⓓ	188	Ⓐ Ⓑ Ⓒ Ⓓ
109	Ⓐ Ⓑ Ⓒ Ⓓ	129	Ⓐ Ⓑ Ⓒ Ⓓ	149	Ⓐ Ⓑ Ⓒ Ⓓ	169	Ⓐ Ⓑ Ⓒ Ⓓ	189	Ⓐ Ⓑ Ⓒ Ⓓ
110	Ⓐ Ⓑ Ⓒ Ⓓ	130	Ⓐ Ⓑ Ⓒ Ⓓ	150	Ⓐ Ⓑ Ⓒ Ⓓ	170	Ⓐ Ⓑ Ⓒ Ⓓ	190	Ⓐ Ⓑ Ⓒ Ⓓ
111	Ⓐ Ⓑ Ⓒ Ⓓ	131	Ⓐ Ⓑ Ⓒ Ⓓ	151	Ⓐ Ⓑ Ⓒ Ⓓ	171	Ⓐ Ⓑ Ⓒ Ⓓ	191	Ⓐ Ⓑ Ⓒ Ⓓ
112	Ⓐ Ⓑ Ⓒ Ⓓ	132	Ⓐ Ⓑ Ⓒ Ⓓ	152	Ⓐ Ⓑ Ⓒ Ⓓ	172	Ⓐ Ⓑ Ⓒ Ⓓ	192	Ⓐ Ⓑ Ⓒ Ⓓ
113	Ⓐ Ⓑ Ⓒ Ⓓ	133	Ⓐ Ⓑ Ⓒ Ⓓ	153	Ⓐ Ⓑ Ⓒ Ⓓ	173	Ⓐ Ⓑ Ⓒ Ⓓ	193	Ⓐ Ⓑ Ⓒ Ⓓ
114	Ⓐ Ⓑ Ⓒ Ⓓ	134	Ⓐ Ⓑ Ⓒ Ⓓ	154	Ⓐ Ⓑ Ⓒ Ⓓ	174	Ⓐ Ⓑ Ⓒ Ⓓ	194	Ⓐ Ⓑ Ⓒ Ⓓ
115	Ⓐ Ⓑ Ⓒ Ⓓ	135	Ⓐ Ⓑ Ⓒ Ⓓ	155	Ⓐ Ⓑ Ⓒ Ⓓ	175	Ⓐ Ⓑ Ⓒ Ⓓ	195	Ⓐ Ⓑ Ⓒ Ⓓ
116	Ⓐ Ⓑ Ⓒ Ⓓ	136	Ⓐ Ⓑ Ⓒ Ⓓ	156	Ⓐ Ⓑ Ⓒ Ⓓ	176	Ⓐ Ⓑ Ⓒ Ⓓ	196	Ⓐ Ⓑ Ⓒ Ⓓ
117	Ⓐ Ⓑ Ⓒ Ⓓ	137	Ⓐ Ⓑ Ⓒ Ⓓ	157	Ⓐ Ⓑ Ⓒ Ⓓ	177	Ⓐ Ⓑ Ⓒ Ⓓ	197	Ⓐ Ⓑ Ⓒ Ⓓ
118	Ⓐ Ⓑ Ⓒ Ⓓ	138	Ⓐ Ⓑ Ⓒ Ⓓ	158	Ⓐ Ⓑ Ⓒ Ⓓ	178	Ⓐ Ⓑ Ⓒ Ⓓ	198	Ⓐ Ⓑ Ⓒ Ⓓ
119	Ⓐ Ⓑ Ⓒ Ⓓ	139	Ⓐ Ⓑ Ⓒ Ⓓ	159	Ⓐ Ⓑ Ⓒ Ⓓ	179	Ⓐ Ⓑ Ⓒ Ⓓ	199	Ⓐ Ⓑ Ⓒ Ⓓ
120	Ⓐ Ⓑ Ⓒ Ⓓ	140	Ⓐ Ⓑ Ⓒ Ⓓ	160	Ⓐ Ⓑ Ⓒ Ⓓ	180	Ⓐ Ⓑ Ⓒ Ⓓ	200	Ⓐ Ⓑ Ⓒ Ⓓ

READING (Part V-VII)

NO.	ANSWER	NO.	ANSWER	NO.	ANSWER	NO.	ANSWER	NO.	ANSWER
	A B C D		A B C D		A B C D		A B C D		A B C D
101	Ⓐ Ⓑ Ⓒ Ⓓ	121	Ⓐ Ⓑ Ⓒ Ⓓ	141	Ⓐ Ⓑ Ⓒ Ⓓ	161	Ⓐ Ⓑ Ⓒ Ⓓ	181	Ⓐ Ⓑ Ⓒ Ⓓ
102	Ⓐ Ⓑ Ⓒ Ⓓ	122	Ⓐ Ⓑ Ⓒ Ⓓ	142	Ⓐ Ⓑ Ⓒ Ⓓ	162	Ⓐ Ⓑ Ⓒ Ⓓ	182	Ⓐ Ⓑ Ⓒ Ⓓ
103	Ⓐ Ⓑ Ⓒ Ⓓ	123	Ⓐ Ⓑ Ⓒ Ⓓ	143	Ⓐ Ⓑ Ⓒ Ⓓ	163	Ⓐ Ⓑ Ⓒ Ⓓ	183	Ⓐ Ⓑ Ⓒ Ⓓ
104	Ⓐ Ⓑ Ⓒ Ⓓ	124	Ⓐ Ⓑ Ⓒ Ⓓ	144	Ⓐ Ⓑ Ⓒ Ⓓ	164	Ⓐ Ⓑ Ⓒ Ⓓ	184	Ⓐ Ⓑ Ⓒ Ⓓ
105	Ⓐ Ⓑ Ⓒ Ⓓ	125	Ⓐ Ⓑ Ⓒ Ⓓ	145	Ⓐ Ⓑ Ⓒ Ⓓ	165	Ⓐ Ⓑ Ⓒ Ⓓ	185	Ⓐ Ⓑ Ⓒ Ⓓ
106	Ⓐ Ⓑ Ⓒ Ⓓ	126	Ⓐ Ⓑ Ⓒ Ⓓ	146	Ⓐ Ⓑ Ⓒ Ⓓ	166	Ⓐ Ⓑ Ⓒ Ⓓ	186	Ⓐ Ⓑ Ⓒ Ⓓ
107	Ⓐ Ⓑ Ⓒ Ⓓ	127	Ⓐ Ⓑ Ⓒ Ⓓ	147	Ⓐ Ⓑ Ⓒ Ⓓ	167	Ⓐ Ⓑ Ⓒ Ⓓ	187	Ⓐ Ⓑ Ⓒ Ⓓ
108	Ⓐ Ⓑ Ⓒ Ⓓ	128	Ⓐ Ⓑ Ⓒ Ⓓ	148	Ⓐ Ⓑ Ⓒ Ⓓ	168	Ⓐ Ⓑ Ⓒ Ⓓ	188	Ⓐ Ⓑ Ⓒ Ⓓ
109	Ⓐ Ⓑ Ⓒ Ⓓ	129	Ⓐ Ⓑ Ⓒ Ⓓ	149	Ⓐ Ⓑ Ⓒ Ⓓ	169	Ⓐ Ⓑ Ⓒ Ⓓ	189	Ⓐ Ⓑ Ⓒ Ⓓ
110	Ⓐ Ⓑ Ⓒ Ⓓ	130	Ⓐ Ⓑ Ⓒ Ⓓ	150	Ⓐ Ⓑ Ⓒ Ⓓ	170	Ⓐ Ⓑ Ⓒ Ⓓ	190	Ⓐ Ⓑ Ⓒ Ⓓ
111	Ⓐ Ⓑ Ⓒ Ⓓ	131	Ⓐ Ⓑ Ⓒ Ⓓ	151	Ⓐ Ⓑ Ⓒ Ⓓ	171	Ⓐ Ⓑ Ⓒ Ⓓ	191	Ⓐ Ⓑ Ⓒ Ⓓ
112	Ⓐ Ⓑ Ⓒ Ⓓ	132	Ⓐ Ⓑ Ⓒ Ⓓ	152	Ⓐ Ⓑ Ⓒ Ⓓ	172	Ⓐ Ⓑ Ⓒ Ⓓ	192	Ⓐ Ⓑ Ⓒ Ⓓ
113	Ⓐ Ⓑ Ⓒ Ⓓ	133	Ⓐ Ⓑ Ⓒ Ⓓ	153	Ⓐ Ⓑ Ⓒ Ⓓ	173	Ⓐ Ⓑ Ⓒ Ⓓ	193	Ⓐ Ⓑ Ⓒ Ⓓ
114	Ⓐ Ⓑ Ⓒ Ⓓ	134	Ⓐ Ⓑ Ⓒ Ⓓ	154	Ⓐ Ⓑ Ⓒ Ⓓ	174	Ⓐ Ⓑ Ⓒ Ⓓ	194	Ⓐ Ⓑ Ⓒ Ⓓ
115	Ⓐ Ⓑ Ⓒ Ⓓ	135	Ⓐ Ⓑ Ⓒ Ⓓ	155	Ⓐ Ⓑ Ⓒ Ⓓ	175	Ⓐ Ⓑ Ⓒ Ⓓ	195	Ⓐ Ⓑ Ⓒ Ⓓ
116	Ⓐ Ⓑ Ⓒ Ⓓ	136	Ⓐ Ⓑ Ⓒ Ⓓ	156	Ⓐ Ⓑ Ⓒ Ⓓ	176	Ⓐ Ⓑ Ⓒ Ⓓ	196	Ⓐ Ⓑ Ⓒ Ⓓ
117	Ⓐ Ⓑ Ⓒ Ⓓ	137	Ⓐ Ⓑ Ⓒ Ⓓ	157	Ⓐ Ⓑ Ⓒ Ⓓ	177	Ⓐ Ⓑ Ⓒ Ⓓ	197	Ⓐ Ⓑ Ⓒ Ⓓ
118	Ⓐ Ⓑ Ⓒ Ⓓ	138	Ⓐ Ⓑ Ⓒ Ⓓ	158	Ⓐ Ⓑ Ⓒ Ⓓ	178	Ⓐ Ⓑ Ⓒ Ⓓ	198	Ⓐ Ⓑ Ⓒ Ⓓ
119	Ⓐ Ⓑ Ⓒ Ⓓ	139	Ⓐ Ⓑ Ⓒ Ⓓ	159	Ⓐ Ⓑ Ⓒ Ⓓ	179	Ⓐ Ⓑ Ⓒ Ⓓ	199	Ⓐ Ⓑ Ⓒ Ⓓ
120	Ⓐ Ⓑ Ⓒ Ⓓ	140	Ⓐ Ⓑ Ⓒ Ⓓ	160	Ⓐ Ⓑ Ⓒ Ⓓ	180	Ⓐ Ⓑ Ⓒ Ⓓ	200	Ⓐ Ⓑ Ⓒ Ⓓ

ANSWER SHEET

TEST 08

READING (Part V-VII)

NO.	ANSWER	NO.	ANSWER	NO.	ANSWER	NO.	ANSWER
	A B C D		A B C D		A B C D		A B C D
101	Ⓐ Ⓑ Ⓒ Ⓓ	121	Ⓐ Ⓑ Ⓒ Ⓓ	141	Ⓐ Ⓑ Ⓒ Ⓓ	181	Ⓐ Ⓑ Ⓒ Ⓓ
102	Ⓐ Ⓑ Ⓒ Ⓓ	122	Ⓐ Ⓑ Ⓒ Ⓓ	142	Ⓐ Ⓑ Ⓒ Ⓓ	182	Ⓐ Ⓑ Ⓒ Ⓓ
103	Ⓐ Ⓑ Ⓒ Ⓓ	123	Ⓐ Ⓑ Ⓒ Ⓓ	143	Ⓐ Ⓑ Ⓒ Ⓓ	183	Ⓐ Ⓑ Ⓒ Ⓓ
104	Ⓐ Ⓑ Ⓒ Ⓓ	124	Ⓐ Ⓑ Ⓒ Ⓓ	144	Ⓐ Ⓑ Ⓒ Ⓓ	184	Ⓐ Ⓑ Ⓒ Ⓓ
105	Ⓐ Ⓑ Ⓒ Ⓓ	125	Ⓐ Ⓑ Ⓒ Ⓓ	145	Ⓐ Ⓑ Ⓒ Ⓓ	185	Ⓐ Ⓑ Ⓒ Ⓓ
106	Ⓐ Ⓑ Ⓒ Ⓓ	126	Ⓐ Ⓑ Ⓒ Ⓓ	146	Ⓐ Ⓑ Ⓒ Ⓓ	186	Ⓐ Ⓑ Ⓒ Ⓓ
107	Ⓐ Ⓑ Ⓒ Ⓓ	127	Ⓐ Ⓑ Ⓒ Ⓓ	147	Ⓐ Ⓑ Ⓒ Ⓓ	187	Ⓐ Ⓑ Ⓒ Ⓓ
108	Ⓐ Ⓑ Ⓒ Ⓓ	128	Ⓐ Ⓑ Ⓒ Ⓓ	148	Ⓐ Ⓑ Ⓒ Ⓓ	188	Ⓐ Ⓑ Ⓒ Ⓓ
109	Ⓐ Ⓑ Ⓒ Ⓓ	129	Ⓐ Ⓑ Ⓒ Ⓓ	149	Ⓐ Ⓑ Ⓒ Ⓓ	189	Ⓐ Ⓑ Ⓒ Ⓓ
110	Ⓐ Ⓑ Ⓒ Ⓓ	130	Ⓐ Ⓑ Ⓒ Ⓓ	150	Ⓐ Ⓑ Ⓒ Ⓓ	190	Ⓐ Ⓑ Ⓒ Ⓓ
111	Ⓐ Ⓑ Ⓒ Ⓓ	131	Ⓐ Ⓑ Ⓒ Ⓓ	151	Ⓐ Ⓑ Ⓒ Ⓓ	191	Ⓐ Ⓑ Ⓒ Ⓓ
112	Ⓐ Ⓑ Ⓒ Ⓓ	132	Ⓐ Ⓑ Ⓒ Ⓓ	152	Ⓐ Ⓑ Ⓒ Ⓓ	192	Ⓐ Ⓑ Ⓒ Ⓓ
113	Ⓐ Ⓑ Ⓒ Ⓓ	133	Ⓐ Ⓑ Ⓒ Ⓓ	153	Ⓐ Ⓑ Ⓒ Ⓓ	193	Ⓐ Ⓑ Ⓒ Ⓓ
114	Ⓐ Ⓑ Ⓒ Ⓓ	134	Ⓐ Ⓑ Ⓒ Ⓓ	154	Ⓐ Ⓑ Ⓒ Ⓓ	194	Ⓐ Ⓑ Ⓒ Ⓓ
115	Ⓐ Ⓑ Ⓒ Ⓓ	135	Ⓐ Ⓑ Ⓒ Ⓓ	155	Ⓐ Ⓑ Ⓒ Ⓓ	195	Ⓐ Ⓑ Ⓒ Ⓓ
116	Ⓐ Ⓑ Ⓒ Ⓓ	136	Ⓐ Ⓑ Ⓒ Ⓓ	156	Ⓐ Ⓑ Ⓒ Ⓓ	196	Ⓐ Ⓑ Ⓒ Ⓓ
117	Ⓐ Ⓑ Ⓒ Ⓓ	137	Ⓐ Ⓑ Ⓒ Ⓓ	157	Ⓐ Ⓑ Ⓒ Ⓓ	197	Ⓐ Ⓑ Ⓒ Ⓓ
118	Ⓐ Ⓑ Ⓒ Ⓓ	138	Ⓐ Ⓑ Ⓒ Ⓓ	158	Ⓐ Ⓑ Ⓒ Ⓓ	198	Ⓐ Ⓑ Ⓒ Ⓓ
119	Ⓐ Ⓑ Ⓒ Ⓓ	139	Ⓐ Ⓑ Ⓒ Ⓓ	159	Ⓐ Ⓑ Ⓒ Ⓓ	199	Ⓐ Ⓑ Ⓒ Ⓓ
120	Ⓐ Ⓑ Ⓒ Ⓓ	140	Ⓐ Ⓑ Ⓒ Ⓓ	160	Ⓐ Ⓑ Ⓒ Ⓓ	200	Ⓐ Ⓑ Ⓒ Ⓓ

ANSWER SHEET

TEST 07

READING (Part V-VII)

NO.	ANSWER	NO.	ANSWER	NO.	ANSWER	NO.	ANSWER
	A B C D		A B C D		A B C D		A B C D
101	Ⓐ Ⓑ Ⓒ Ⓓ	121	Ⓐ Ⓑ Ⓒ Ⓓ	141	Ⓐ Ⓑ Ⓒ Ⓓ	181	Ⓐ Ⓑ Ⓒ Ⓓ
102	Ⓐ Ⓑ Ⓒ Ⓓ	122	Ⓐ Ⓑ Ⓒ Ⓓ	142	Ⓐ Ⓑ Ⓒ Ⓓ	182	Ⓐ Ⓑ Ⓒ Ⓓ
103	Ⓐ Ⓑ Ⓒ Ⓓ	123	Ⓐ Ⓑ Ⓒ Ⓓ	143	Ⓐ Ⓑ Ⓒ Ⓓ	183	Ⓐ Ⓑ Ⓒ Ⓓ
104	Ⓐ Ⓑ Ⓒ Ⓓ	124	Ⓐ Ⓑ Ⓒ Ⓓ	144	Ⓐ Ⓑ Ⓒ Ⓓ	184	Ⓐ Ⓑ Ⓒ Ⓓ
105	Ⓐ Ⓑ Ⓒ Ⓓ	125	Ⓐ Ⓑ Ⓒ Ⓓ	145	Ⓐ Ⓑ Ⓒ Ⓓ	185	Ⓐ Ⓑ Ⓒ Ⓓ
106	Ⓐ Ⓑ Ⓒ Ⓓ	126	Ⓐ Ⓑ Ⓒ Ⓓ	146	Ⓐ Ⓑ Ⓒ Ⓓ	186	Ⓐ Ⓑ Ⓒ Ⓓ
107	Ⓐ Ⓑ Ⓒ Ⓓ	127	Ⓐ Ⓑ Ⓒ Ⓓ	147	Ⓐ Ⓑ Ⓒ Ⓓ	187	Ⓐ Ⓑ Ⓒ Ⓓ
108	Ⓐ Ⓑ Ⓒ Ⓓ	128	Ⓐ Ⓑ Ⓒ Ⓓ	148	Ⓐ Ⓑ Ⓒ Ⓓ	188	Ⓐ Ⓑ Ⓒ Ⓓ
109	Ⓐ Ⓑ Ⓒ Ⓓ	129	Ⓐ Ⓑ Ⓒ Ⓓ	149	Ⓐ Ⓑ Ⓒ Ⓓ	189	Ⓐ Ⓑ Ⓒ Ⓓ
110	Ⓐ Ⓑ Ⓒ Ⓓ	130	Ⓐ Ⓑ Ⓒ Ⓓ	150	Ⓐ Ⓑ Ⓒ Ⓓ	190	Ⓐ Ⓑ Ⓒ Ⓓ
111	Ⓐ Ⓑ Ⓒ Ⓓ	131	Ⓐ Ⓑ Ⓒ Ⓓ	151	Ⓐ Ⓑ Ⓒ Ⓓ	191	Ⓐ Ⓑ Ⓒ Ⓓ
112	Ⓐ Ⓑ Ⓒ Ⓓ	132	Ⓐ Ⓑ Ⓒ Ⓓ	152	Ⓐ Ⓑ Ⓒ Ⓓ	192	Ⓐ Ⓑ Ⓒ Ⓓ
113	Ⓐ Ⓑ Ⓒ Ⓓ	133	Ⓐ Ⓑ Ⓒ Ⓓ	153	Ⓐ Ⓑ Ⓒ Ⓓ	193	Ⓐ Ⓑ Ⓒ Ⓓ
114	Ⓐ Ⓑ Ⓒ Ⓓ	134	Ⓐ Ⓑ Ⓒ Ⓓ	154	Ⓐ Ⓑ Ⓒ Ⓓ	194	Ⓐ Ⓑ Ⓒ Ⓓ
115	Ⓐ Ⓑ Ⓒ Ⓓ	135	Ⓐ Ⓑ Ⓒ Ⓓ	155	Ⓐ Ⓑ Ⓒ Ⓓ	195	Ⓐ Ⓑ Ⓒ Ⓓ
116	Ⓐ Ⓑ Ⓒ Ⓓ	136	Ⓐ Ⓑ Ⓒ Ⓓ	156	Ⓐ Ⓑ Ⓒ Ⓓ	196	Ⓐ Ⓑ Ⓒ Ⓓ
117	Ⓐ Ⓑ Ⓒ Ⓓ	137	Ⓐ Ⓑ Ⓒ Ⓓ	157	Ⓐ Ⓑ Ⓒ Ⓓ	197	Ⓐ Ⓑ Ⓒ Ⓓ
118	Ⓐ Ⓑ Ⓒ Ⓓ	138	Ⓐ Ⓑ Ⓒ Ⓓ	158	Ⓐ Ⓑ Ⓒ Ⓓ	198	Ⓐ Ⓑ Ⓒ Ⓓ
119	Ⓐ Ⓑ Ⓒ Ⓓ	139	Ⓐ Ⓑ Ⓒ Ⓓ	159	Ⓐ Ⓑ Ⓒ Ⓓ	199	Ⓐ Ⓑ Ⓒ Ⓓ
120	Ⓐ Ⓑ Ⓒ Ⓓ	140	Ⓐ Ⓑ Ⓒ Ⓓ	160	Ⓐ Ⓑ Ⓒ Ⓓ	200	Ⓐ Ⓑ Ⓒ Ⓓ

ANSWER SHEET

TEST 10

READING (Part V-VII)

NO.	ANSWER	NO.	ANSWER	NO.	ANSWER	NO.	ANSWER	NO.	ANSWER
	A B C D		A B C D		A B C D		A B C D		A B C D
101	Ⓐ Ⓑ Ⓒ Ⓓ	121	Ⓐ Ⓑ Ⓒ Ⓓ	141	Ⓐ Ⓑ Ⓒ Ⓓ	161	Ⓐ Ⓑ Ⓒ Ⓓ	181	Ⓐ Ⓑ Ⓒ Ⓓ
102	Ⓐ Ⓑ Ⓒ Ⓓ	122	Ⓐ Ⓑ Ⓒ Ⓓ	142	Ⓐ Ⓑ Ⓒ Ⓓ	162	Ⓐ Ⓑ Ⓒ Ⓓ	182	Ⓐ Ⓑ Ⓒ Ⓓ
103	Ⓐ Ⓑ Ⓒ Ⓓ	123	Ⓐ Ⓑ Ⓒ Ⓓ	143	Ⓐ Ⓑ Ⓒ Ⓓ	163	Ⓐ Ⓑ Ⓒ Ⓓ	183	Ⓐ Ⓑ Ⓒ Ⓓ
104	Ⓐ Ⓑ Ⓒ Ⓓ	124	Ⓐ Ⓑ Ⓒ Ⓓ	144	Ⓐ Ⓑ Ⓒ Ⓓ	164	Ⓐ Ⓑ Ⓒ Ⓓ	184	Ⓐ Ⓑ Ⓒ Ⓓ
105	Ⓐ Ⓑ Ⓒ Ⓓ	125	Ⓐ Ⓑ Ⓒ Ⓓ	145	Ⓐ Ⓑ Ⓒ Ⓓ	165	Ⓐ Ⓑ Ⓒ Ⓓ	185	Ⓐ Ⓑ Ⓒ Ⓓ
106	Ⓐ Ⓑ Ⓒ Ⓓ	126	Ⓐ Ⓑ Ⓒ Ⓓ	146	Ⓐ Ⓑ Ⓒ Ⓓ	166	Ⓐ Ⓑ Ⓒ Ⓓ	186	Ⓐ Ⓑ Ⓒ Ⓓ
107	Ⓐ Ⓑ Ⓒ Ⓓ	127	Ⓐ Ⓑ Ⓒ Ⓓ	147	Ⓐ Ⓑ Ⓒ Ⓓ	167	Ⓐ Ⓑ Ⓒ Ⓓ	187	Ⓐ Ⓑ Ⓒ Ⓓ
108	Ⓐ Ⓑ Ⓒ Ⓓ	128	Ⓐ Ⓑ Ⓒ Ⓓ	148	Ⓐ Ⓑ Ⓒ Ⓓ	168	Ⓐ Ⓑ Ⓒ Ⓓ	188	Ⓐ Ⓑ Ⓒ Ⓓ
109	Ⓐ Ⓑ Ⓒ Ⓓ	129	Ⓐ Ⓑ Ⓒ Ⓓ	149	Ⓐ Ⓑ Ⓒ Ⓓ	169	Ⓐ Ⓑ Ⓒ Ⓓ	189	Ⓐ Ⓑ Ⓒ Ⓓ
110	Ⓐ Ⓑ Ⓒ Ⓓ	130	Ⓐ Ⓑ Ⓒ Ⓓ	150	Ⓐ Ⓑ Ⓒ Ⓓ	170	Ⓐ Ⓑ Ⓒ Ⓓ	190	Ⓐ Ⓑ Ⓒ Ⓓ
111	Ⓐ Ⓑ Ⓒ Ⓓ	131	Ⓐ Ⓑ Ⓒ Ⓓ	151	Ⓐ Ⓑ Ⓒ Ⓓ	171	Ⓐ Ⓑ Ⓒ Ⓓ	191	Ⓐ Ⓑ Ⓒ Ⓓ
112	Ⓐ Ⓑ Ⓒ Ⓓ	132	Ⓐ Ⓑ Ⓒ Ⓓ	152	Ⓐ Ⓑ Ⓒ Ⓓ	172	Ⓐ Ⓑ Ⓒ Ⓓ	192	Ⓐ Ⓑ Ⓒ Ⓓ
113	Ⓐ Ⓑ Ⓒ Ⓓ	133	Ⓐ Ⓑ Ⓒ Ⓓ	153	Ⓐ Ⓑ Ⓒ Ⓓ	173	Ⓐ Ⓑ Ⓒ Ⓓ	193	Ⓐ Ⓑ Ⓒ Ⓓ
114	Ⓐ Ⓑ Ⓒ Ⓓ	134	Ⓐ Ⓑ Ⓒ Ⓓ	154	Ⓐ Ⓑ Ⓒ Ⓓ	174	Ⓐ Ⓑ Ⓒ Ⓓ	194	Ⓐ Ⓑ Ⓒ Ⓓ
115	Ⓐ Ⓑ Ⓒ Ⓓ	135	Ⓐ Ⓑ Ⓒ Ⓓ	155	Ⓐ Ⓑ Ⓒ Ⓓ	175	Ⓐ Ⓑ Ⓒ Ⓓ	195	Ⓐ Ⓑ Ⓒ Ⓓ
116	Ⓐ Ⓑ Ⓒ Ⓓ	136	Ⓐ Ⓑ Ⓒ Ⓓ	156	Ⓐ Ⓑ Ⓒ Ⓓ	176	Ⓐ Ⓑ Ⓒ Ⓓ	196	Ⓐ Ⓑ Ⓒ Ⓓ
117	Ⓐ Ⓑ Ⓒ Ⓓ	137	Ⓐ Ⓑ Ⓒ Ⓓ	157	Ⓐ Ⓑ Ⓒ Ⓓ	177	Ⓐ Ⓑ Ⓒ Ⓓ	197	Ⓐ Ⓑ Ⓒ Ⓓ
118	Ⓐ Ⓑ Ⓒ Ⓓ	138	Ⓐ Ⓑ Ⓒ Ⓓ	158	Ⓐ Ⓑ Ⓒ Ⓓ	178	Ⓐ Ⓑ Ⓒ Ⓓ	198	Ⓐ Ⓑ Ⓒ Ⓓ
119	Ⓐ Ⓑ Ⓒ Ⓓ	139	Ⓐ Ⓑ Ⓒ Ⓓ	159	Ⓐ Ⓑ Ⓒ Ⓓ	179	Ⓐ Ⓑ Ⓒ Ⓓ	199	Ⓐ Ⓑ Ⓒ Ⓓ
120	Ⓐ Ⓑ Ⓒ Ⓓ	140	Ⓐ Ⓑ Ⓒ Ⓓ	160	Ⓐ Ⓑ Ⓒ Ⓓ	180	Ⓐ Ⓑ Ⓒ Ⓓ	200	Ⓐ Ⓑ Ⓒ Ⓓ

ANSWER SHEET

TEST 09

READING (Part V-VII)

NO.	ANSWER	NO.	ANSWER	NO.	ANSWER	NO.	ANSWER	NO.	ANSWER
	A B C D		A B C D		A B C D		A B C D		A B C D
101	Ⓐ Ⓑ Ⓒ Ⓓ	121	Ⓐ Ⓑ Ⓒ Ⓓ	141	Ⓐ Ⓑ Ⓒ Ⓓ	161	Ⓐ Ⓑ Ⓒ Ⓓ	181	Ⓐ Ⓑ Ⓒ Ⓓ
102	Ⓐ Ⓑ Ⓒ Ⓓ	122	Ⓐ Ⓑ Ⓒ Ⓓ	142	Ⓐ Ⓑ Ⓒ Ⓓ	162	Ⓐ Ⓑ Ⓒ Ⓓ	182	Ⓐ Ⓑ Ⓒ Ⓓ
103	Ⓐ Ⓑ Ⓒ Ⓓ	123	Ⓐ Ⓑ Ⓒ Ⓓ	143	Ⓐ Ⓑ Ⓒ Ⓓ	163	Ⓐ Ⓑ Ⓒ Ⓓ	183	Ⓐ Ⓑ Ⓒ Ⓓ
104	Ⓐ Ⓑ Ⓒ Ⓓ	124	Ⓐ Ⓑ Ⓒ Ⓓ	144	Ⓐ Ⓑ Ⓒ Ⓓ	164	Ⓐ Ⓑ Ⓒ Ⓓ	184	Ⓐ Ⓑ Ⓒ Ⓓ
105	Ⓐ Ⓑ Ⓒ Ⓓ	125	Ⓐ Ⓑ Ⓒ Ⓓ	145	Ⓐ Ⓑ Ⓒ Ⓓ	165	Ⓐ Ⓑ Ⓒ Ⓓ	185	Ⓐ Ⓑ Ⓒ Ⓓ
106	Ⓐ Ⓑ Ⓒ Ⓓ	126	Ⓐ Ⓑ Ⓒ Ⓓ	146	Ⓐ Ⓑ Ⓒ Ⓓ	166	Ⓐ Ⓑ Ⓒ Ⓓ	186	Ⓐ Ⓑ Ⓒ Ⓓ
107	Ⓐ Ⓑ Ⓒ Ⓓ	127	Ⓐ Ⓑ Ⓒ Ⓓ	147	Ⓐ Ⓑ Ⓒ Ⓓ	167	Ⓐ Ⓑ Ⓒ Ⓓ	187	Ⓐ Ⓑ Ⓒ Ⓓ
108	Ⓐ Ⓑ Ⓒ Ⓓ	128	Ⓐ Ⓑ Ⓒ Ⓓ	148	Ⓐ Ⓑ Ⓒ Ⓓ	168	Ⓐ Ⓑ Ⓒ Ⓓ	188	Ⓐ Ⓑ Ⓒ Ⓓ
109	Ⓐ Ⓑ Ⓒ Ⓓ	129	Ⓐ Ⓑ Ⓒ Ⓓ	149	Ⓐ Ⓑ Ⓒ Ⓓ	169	Ⓐ Ⓑ Ⓒ Ⓓ	189	Ⓐ Ⓑ Ⓒ Ⓓ
110	Ⓐ Ⓑ Ⓒ Ⓓ	130	Ⓐ Ⓑ Ⓒ Ⓓ	150	Ⓐ Ⓑ Ⓒ Ⓓ	170	Ⓐ Ⓑ Ⓒ Ⓓ	190	Ⓐ Ⓑ Ⓒ Ⓓ
111	Ⓐ Ⓑ Ⓒ Ⓓ	131	Ⓐ Ⓑ Ⓒ Ⓓ	151	Ⓐ Ⓑ Ⓒ Ⓓ	171	Ⓐ Ⓑ Ⓒ Ⓓ	191	Ⓐ Ⓑ Ⓒ Ⓓ
112	Ⓐ Ⓑ Ⓒ Ⓓ	132	Ⓐ Ⓑ Ⓒ Ⓓ	152	Ⓐ Ⓑ Ⓒ Ⓓ	172	Ⓐ Ⓑ Ⓒ Ⓓ	192	Ⓐ Ⓑ Ⓒ Ⓓ
113	Ⓐ Ⓑ Ⓒ Ⓓ	133	Ⓐ Ⓑ Ⓒ Ⓓ	153	Ⓐ Ⓑ Ⓒ Ⓓ	173	Ⓐ Ⓑ Ⓒ Ⓓ	193	Ⓐ Ⓑ Ⓒ Ⓓ
114	Ⓐ Ⓑ Ⓒ Ⓓ	134	Ⓐ Ⓑ Ⓒ Ⓓ	154	Ⓐ Ⓑ Ⓒ Ⓓ	174	Ⓐ Ⓑ Ⓒ Ⓓ	194	Ⓐ Ⓑ Ⓒ Ⓓ
115	Ⓐ Ⓑ Ⓒ Ⓓ	135	Ⓐ Ⓑ Ⓒ Ⓓ	155	Ⓐ Ⓑ Ⓒ Ⓓ	175	Ⓐ Ⓑ Ⓒ Ⓓ	195	Ⓐ Ⓑ Ⓒ Ⓓ
116	Ⓐ Ⓑ Ⓒ Ⓓ	136	Ⓐ Ⓑ Ⓒ Ⓓ	156	Ⓐ Ⓑ Ⓒ Ⓓ	176	Ⓐ Ⓑ Ⓒ Ⓓ	196	Ⓐ Ⓑ Ⓒ Ⓓ
117	Ⓐ Ⓑ Ⓒ Ⓓ	137	Ⓐ Ⓑ Ⓒ Ⓓ	157	Ⓐ Ⓑ Ⓒ Ⓓ	177	Ⓐ Ⓑ Ⓒ Ⓓ	197	Ⓐ Ⓑ Ⓒ Ⓓ
118	Ⓐ Ⓑ Ⓒ Ⓓ	138	Ⓐ Ⓑ Ⓒ Ⓓ	158	Ⓐ Ⓑ Ⓒ Ⓓ	178	Ⓐ Ⓑ Ⓒ Ⓓ	198	Ⓐ Ⓑ Ⓒ Ⓓ
119	Ⓐ Ⓑ Ⓒ Ⓓ	139	Ⓐ Ⓑ Ⓒ Ⓓ	159	Ⓐ Ⓑ Ⓒ Ⓓ	179	Ⓐ Ⓑ Ⓒ Ⓓ	199	Ⓐ Ⓑ Ⓒ Ⓓ
120	Ⓐ Ⓑ Ⓒ Ⓓ	140	Ⓐ Ⓑ Ⓒ Ⓓ	160	Ⓐ Ⓑ Ⓒ Ⓓ	180	Ⓐ Ⓑ Ⓒ Ⓓ	200	Ⓐ Ⓑ Ⓒ Ⓓ

파고다 토익 RC

실전 1000제 | 정답·해석

PAGODA Books

파고다 토익 RC

실전 1000제 정답·해석

TEST 01

PART 5   P. 16

101 Kaiser 미디어와 Gaulish 신문사는 회계연도 초에 합병한다는 합의에 도달했다.

102 GHM 사의 규정에 따라, 모든 직원들은 출장 2개월 이내에 정식으로 환급을 신청해야 한다.

103 Raymond Howles에 의해 연출된 밴드의 최신 뮤직비디오가 어제 첫선을 보였다.

104 Ms. Kitigoe는 조립 라인을 점검한 후, 그녀는 그것을 더 효율적으로 운영할 방법을 제안할 것이다.

105 엘리베이터는 비상시인 경우를 제외하면 항시 사용될 수 있다.

106 초반의 비난에도 불구하고, Covington 시 축제는 인기 있는 행사였다.

107 수요일에 있을 세미나는 지역 관리자들이 직원들을 효율적으로 채용하고, 관리하고, 독려하는 능력을 평가하는 데 도움이 될 것이다.

108 Silvercove 리조트는 쉽게 갈 수 있으며 자체 셔틀버스 서비스가 있다.

109 Mountaindell 민박집의 주인은 방문객들이 인터넷에 올리는 모든 후기에 직접 답한다.

110 Van Tassel Media는 다른 제작사들에 비해 상당히 작지만, 다큐멘터리 영화로는 거의 틀림없이 국내 최고에 속한다.

111 올 봄 저희 West 음악 축제로 초대합니다. 거기에서 저희 신곡이 처음으로 연주될 것입니다.

112 Somoza 사의 마케팅 부서는 온라인에서 미치는 영향력을 높이기 위해서 새로운 디지털 전략을 시행할 예정이다.

113 Rocket Bikes의 사장은 공장 직원들에게 빠른 생산 가동에 대해 그들을 칭찬하는 이메일을 발송했다.

114 누락된 허가증 때문에, Ms. Cheung은 그 부지에 새로운 건물을 지으려는 신청을 기각했다.

115 각 직원의 휴가를 동일한 일정표에 적어놓고 관리하면 유용하다.

116 Shackleton 사의 어느 누구도 회사 주차장 공사 문제에 대해 Garrett Nguyen보다 더 열심히 로비를 하지 않았다.

117 사무실 인터넷 연결이 충분히 빠르지 않았어서, 직원들은 CEO 연설의 생중계 영상 피드를 시청할 수 없었다.

118 매출 수요가 무엇일지 예측할 때는, 오차범위를 포함하는 것을 기억하세요.

119 우리 지역 공급업체는 우리가 현지에서 필요로 한 원료를 가지고 있지 않았기 때문에, 우리는 대신 더 규모가 큰 공급업체에서 그것들을 주문했다.

120 회사 경영진은 향후 몇 달간 경영전략부서에서 예상한 이윤을 보기를 희망한다.

121 학생들은 월 단위로 자신의 지도 교사와 연락해야 한다.

122 예술가의 복제품을 원본과 함께 꼼꼼히 살펴본 후, 비평가는 두 작품의 구별되는 특성들을 구분할 수 있었다.

123 프로모션 안내판이 이번 주부터 전시될 수 있지만, 세일 마지막 날에는 반드시 치워져야 한다.

124 제안이 프로젝트로 선정될 지의 여부와 상관없이, 모든 제출물은 2년간 데이터베이스에 보관된다.

125 고객에 관한 민감한 개인 정보가 들어 있으니 이 파일을 안전하게 저장해 놓으시기 바랍니다.

126 Epperson 사진 도서관은 이미 1만 장이 넘는 사진을 소장하고 있으며, 새로운 사진이 업로드되면서 계속해서 늘어날 것이다.

127 Tyson 기업 연구센터에 따르면, 직원들에게 유연한 일정을 선택하도록 허용하는 것은 업무 성과를 향상시킨다.

128 Barnum F&B의 사명은 최고급 식품을 생산하되 가격을 저렴하게 유지하는 것이다.

129 지역 뉴스 채널의 토요일 방송에는 스포츠 스타 Steffanie Grove와의 독점 인터뷰가 포함될 것이다.

130 금리가 내려가면서 부동산을 구입하려는 사람 수가 갑작스럽게 급증했다.

PART 6   P. 19

131-134번은 다음 공지에 관한 문제입니다.

> 소중한 고객님께,
>
> 아쉽게도 이번 주 일요일인 7월 12일이 Fresh 'n Fragrant's Gardner 지점에서 커피를 **131. 즐길 수 있는** 마지막 기회가 될 것임을 알려드립니다. 수년간 이용해 주신 것에 깊은 감사의 말씀 드립니다. Gardner 주민들이 바쁜 일과 중에 재충전하는 장소였던 것을 **132. 그리워할** 것입니다. 하지

만 저희는 Lake Shore와 Mahwah 지점에서 영업을 계속합니다. **133. 남은 지점에서 계속해서 모든 분을 모실 수 있게 되길 바랍니다.**

이곳에 있는 동안 보내주신 지속적인 **134. 성원**에 다시 한번 감사드립니다. 진정으로 대단한 여정이었고, 여러분이 없었더라면 해내지 못했을 것입니다.

Fresh 'n Fragrant 운영진 일동

133 (A) 지원서는 홈페이지에서 다운받을 수 있습니다.
(B) 개조 공사가 완료되면 신메뉴가 공개될 예정입니다.
(C) 남은 지점에서 계속해서 모든 분을 모실 수 있게 되길 바랍니다.
(D) 주문이 잘못된 경우 즉시 저희 팀에 알려주십시오.

135-138번은 다음 이메일에 관한 문제입니다.

수신: vasquez@watertown.gov
발신: shenderson@bryantconsulting.com
날짜: 12월 3일
제목: 웹사이트 피드백
첨부: 분석 자료

Ms. Vasquez께,

아래 공간에 귀 도시의 시립 웹사이트에 대한 제 동료들의 의견을 요약해 드립니다.

전반적으로, 그들은 웹사이트가 예상만큼 **135. 효과적이지 않다고** 생각했습니다. 사용 편의를 위해 디자인을 간소화하여, 외관을 단순화하는 것이 도움이 될 것입니다. 또한 그들은 사이트 **136. 전체에** 버그가 지속적으로 나타나, 페이지가 아주 느리게 로딩되는 것을 발견했습니다.

그들은 또한 첫 페이지에 사용된 사진을 보완할 것을 권장했습니다. **137. 이미지만으로 사용자의 주의를 끄는 것은 어렵습니다.** 이에, 사용자에게 웹사이트 사용법을 안내하는 간략하면서도, 전문가 수준의 동영상을 올리는 것이 자원의 좋은 활용이 될 것입니다. **138. 또한,** 사용자들이 실시간으로 도움을 요청할 수 있는 라이브 채팅 기능을 추가할 것을 권장했습니다.

문의사항이 있으시면, 저에게 알려주세요.

Spencer Henderson 드림

137 (A) 이 사진들은 더 높은 해상도로 게시되어야 합니다.
(B) 제대로 된 파일 명명 프로토콜이 없으면 이미지 파일들은 엉망이 됩니다.
(C) 사진은 전문 사진작가가 찍은 것처럼 보이지 않습니다.
(D) 이미지만으로 사용자의 주의를 끄는 것은 어렵습니다.

139-142번은 다음 편지에 관한 문제입니다.

7월 16일

Derek Hunter
인사부
Milltek Systems, Inc.

Mr. Hunter께,

최근 귀하의 웹사이트에 올라온 엔지니어 매니저 공석에 관해 문의 드리고 싶습니다. 저는 Milltek Systems의 엔지니어링 **139. 팀** 관리자로 귀중한 인재가 될 것이라 자신합니다.

140. 저는 관련 분야에서 수 년의 경험을 가지고 있습니다. 현재는 Tappco Machinery에서 프로젝트 매니저로 근무하고 있는데, 거의 10년 간 농업 및 산업 분류 기계류를 설계해왔습니다. 이 **141. 전**에는 AgroTec Engineering에서 근무했었는데, 그곳에서 제분 및 제빵 애플

리케이션을 위한 전산화 과정을 개발했습니다.

제 이력서를 첨부해 드리며, 이력서에는 제 경력과 자격증들에 대한 더 많은 정보가 **142. 담겨 있습니다.** 이 내용이 귀사와 잘 맞는다고 생각하신다면, 만나뵙고 더 심도있게 이야기를 나누고 싶습니다.

Edwin Dearing 드림
동봉물재중

140 **(A) 저는 관련 분야에서 수 년의 경험을 가지고 있습니다.**
(B) 귀하는 이 직무에 공학 학위가 필수라고 하셨습니다.
(C) 저의 예전 직장동료들로부터 이메일 몇 통을 받으셨을 겁니다.
(D) 좀 더 적합한 자리가 생기면 저에게 알려주세요.

143-146번은 다음 기사에 관한 문제입니다.

Celtzer Goods, 낙관적인 목표를 넘어서다

CHASTANG (3월 19일) — Celtzer Goods에서 3월 26일에 50번째 지점을 개장할 장소를 확보했다. 신규 **143. 매장**은 Southgate Grove에 있는 New Lynn 몰의 맞은편에 있다. 역사적인 이정표 통과를 기념하여 라이브 음악과 기타 엔터테인먼트를 포함한 행사가 예정되어 있다. Chastang의 주민이 아니어도 아쉬워할 것은 없다. 전국 **144. 에 걸친** 모든 Celtzer 지점에서 자체 축하 행사를 개최할 예정이다. 모든 지점에 기프트 카드와 선물 주머니를 비롯해 다양한 경품도 마련될 것이다.

Celtzer Goods는 50년 전에 Simon Celtzer가 호주에서 자신의 상점을 차리겠다는 단순한 사명을 가지고 설립되었다. **145. 그** 목표는 이제 영국은 물론 뉴질랜드까지 확장되었다. **146. Celtzer Goods는 조만간 새로운 시장으로의 진출을 내다보고 있다.**

146 (A) 지원서는 직원에게 문의한다.
(B) Celtzer Goods는 조만간 새로운 시장으로의 진출을 내다보고 있다.
(C) 사전 통지가 있으면 조기 입장이 가능할 수 있다.
(D) 수출 비용은 수년에 걸쳐 상승했다.

PART 7

P. 23

147-148번은 다음 온라인 채팅 대화문에 관한 문제입니다.

Fannie Robertson [오후 4시 12분]
안녕하세요. 기술 지원부의 Ms. Robertson입니다. 오늘 무엇을 도와드릴까요?

Carl Walker [오후 4시 13분]
안녕하세요. 제 노트북에 충전기를 하나 더 사고 싶어요. 집에서 직장으로 가지고 다녀야 하는 게 싫어요. **(147)** 도와주실 수 있나요?

Fannie Robertson [오후 4시 14분]
그럼요. 노트북 모델 번호를 알고 계신가요? 시리얼 번호도 괜찮습니다.

Carl Walker [오후 4시 16분]
방금 찾아봤어요. Florian X3예요.

Fannie Robertson [오후 4시 17분]
좋습니다. 제가 시스템으로 검색해 볼게요. 잠깐이면 됩니다.

Carl Walker [오후 4시 18분]
괜찮아요.

Fannie Robertson [오후 4시 23분]
기다려 주셔서 감사합니다. 부품 번호 36MU45를 주문하셔야 합니다. 편리하시도록 제가 장바구니에 넣어 드렸습니다. 그러면, 준비되실 때 '지금 주문'만 클릭하시면 됩니다.

Carl Walker [오후 4시 24분]
아주 좋아요. 도와주셔서 감사합니다.

Fannie Robertson [오후 4시 24분]
아닙니다, Mr. Walker. 오늘 다른 도움이 필요한 건 있으세요?[148]

Carl Walker [오후 4시 25분]
없습니다. 그럼 가 볼게요.[148]

147 Mr. Walker는 왜 노트북 충전기를 주문하고 싶어하는가?
(A) 자신의 충전기를 잃어버렸다.
(B) 곧 있을 출장에 하나 필요할 것이다.
(C) 동료에게 선물을 할 생각이다.
(D) 사무실에 하나 놓고 싶다.

148 오후 4시 25분에, Mr. Walker가 "그럼 가 볼게요"라고 할 때 무엇을 의미하는가?
(A) Ms. Robertson의 사무실로 갈 것이다.
(B) 더 낮은 가격에 동일한 제품을 찾았다.
(C) 더 이상 도움이 필요하지 않다.
(D) 충전기를 주문할 수 없다.

149-150번은 다음 명함에 관한 문제입니다.

프리랜서 사진작가 Max Ortiz

· Ashford 잡지에서 수상 경력을 보유한 사진작가
· **인생에서 가장 특별한 개인적인 또는 업무적인 순간을 영원히 남기는 작업을 전문으로 함**[149]
· 가장 흔히 사용되는 사진 편집 소프트웨어 전문가

궁금한 사항이나 문의 사항은 715-555-4896번으로 전화주시거나 me@ortizservices.com으로 이메일을 보내주세요.
수상 내역을 비롯한 전체 이력은 www.ortizservices.com/biography 에서 확인하시기 바랍니다.[150]

---

149 Mr. Ortiz는 무엇을 촬영하겠는가?
(A) 식당 음식
(B) 역사 명소
(C) 기업 행사
(D) 야생 동물

150 명함에 따르면, Mr. Ortiz의 웹사이트에서 볼 수 있는 것은 무엇인가?
(A) 인터뷰
(B) 소프트웨어 설명서
(C) 세부 일정
(D) 그의 이력

151-153번은 다음 이메일에 관한 문제입니다.

수신: Emerton 취업 박람회 입장권 소지자
발신: Darrell Fletcher
날짜: 6월 14일
제목: 중요 공지

참석자 수가 급증하여 Emerton 취업 박람회 장소가 변경되었음을 알려드립니다.[151] 이제 새로운 장소는 기차역 옆에 위치한 컨벤션 홀이 될 것입니다. 불편을 끼쳐드려 죄송합니다.

7월 5일에 개최되는 Emerton 취업 박람회는 학생과 성인 모두에게 채용 담당자와 사업주를 만날 수 있는 아주 좋은 기회가 됩니다. 주요 기업에서 모두 참석할 예정입니다. 기업 내 새롭게 떠오르는 역할에 대해 알게 되면서 직업적인 인맥을 쌓을 수 있는 훌륭한 기회입니다.

일부 인근 교외지역에서 참석하는 분들을 행사장으로 수송하는 버스

가 마련될 예정입니다. 귀하의 교외 지역이 포함되는지 알아보시려면, www.emertoncity.gov/careerfair에서 버스 노선도를 다운받으시길 바랍니다. 입장권은 저희 웹사이트에서 25달러에 판매 중입니다. **현금으로 지불하시려면, Emerton 시청으로 오셔야 합니다.**[152] **구입한 입장권에 대한 환불은 조건에 따라 다릅니다.**[153]

Darrell Fletcher 드림
행사 진행자

151 이메일의 목적은 무엇인가?
(A) 위치 변경을 알리려고
(B) 비공식 설문조사를 실시하려고
(C) 사람들에게 규정 변경을 알리려고
(D) 신규 사업체를 광고하려고

152 이메일에 따르면, 누가 Emerton 시청으로 가야 하는가?
(A) 자신의 사업체를 운영하는 사람들
(B) 행사 기획에 경험이 있는 사람들
(C) 현금으로 입장권을 구입하고 싶은 사람들
(D) 지인을 데려가고 싶은 사람들

153 세 번째 단락, 네 번째 줄의 단어, "subject to"와 의미상 가장 가까운 것은?
(A) ~로 간주되는
(B) ~에서 독점적인
(C) 특유의
(D) ~에 달려 있는

154-155번은 다음 광고에 관한 문제입니다.

Bee Knee 음악 학교
2/30 Jellicoe Lane, Causeway Street
Rutherford, NC 28018

새로운 악기를 배우는 데 늦은 때란 없습니다. Bee Knee 음악 학교에서는 모든 연령의 학습자에게 피아노, 바이올린, 기타 레슨을 제공합니다. **악기를 가지고 있지 않아도 됩니다. 스튜디오에 오시면 저희 악기를 대여해 드립니다.**[154] 현재 워크숍, 레슨, 그리고 기술을 연마할 수 있도록 연습실에서의 연습 시간까지 패키지로 제공합니다.

12세 이하 어린이:
· 초급 수준의 피아노 또는 바이올린 그룹 레슨. 각 레슨은 30분 동안 진행되며, 그룹 규모는 어린이 최대 6명입니다.

십대 및 성인:
· **초급자를 위한 피아노, 바이올린, 또는 기타 일대일 레슨. 각 레슨은 45분 동안 진행됩니다.**[155]
· 고급 수준 학생의 경우, 저희에게 연락해 주시면 적합한 개인 교사를 찾아드립니다.

오늘 www.beekneeschool.com을 방문하셔서 당신의 음악 여정을 시작해 보세요.

---

154 Bee Knee 음악 학교에 관하여 언급된 것은 무엇인가?
(A) 새로운 교수법을 사용한다.
(B) 학생들에게 악기를 제공한다.
(C) 온라인 플랫폼을 통해서도 레슨을 제공한다.
(D) 학생을 대회에 준비시키는 것을 전문으로 한다.

155 초급 수준의 성인 학습자에게는 무엇이 제공되는가?
(A) 가정 방문 레슨
(B) 성인 학습자용 교재 시리즈
(C) 자격을 갖춘 멘토
(D) 45분간 일대일 레슨

156-158번은 다음 공지에 관한 문제입니다.

공지: 봄맞이 콘서트 최신 정보

저희가 올해 콘서트를 위해 벌인 추가 프로모션으로, 거의 1,200명의 사람들이 올 것으로 예상하고 있습니다. 현재 장소는 1,000명만 수용할 수 있기에, 이를 바탕으로 저희 지휘자가 장소를 변경하기로 결정했습니다. **(156)/(157)** 확정되는 대로 새로운 장소에 대한 세부 정보를 제공해드릴 예정입니다. 또한, 공연에 합류하는 새로운 얼굴이 있습니다. 저희는 Chatham 시 오케스트라와 협력하고 있어, 단원 몇 명이 공연에 참여하고 싶어 합니다. 모두 경험이 아주 풍부하기에, 어떤 모습을 보여줄 것인지 기대됩니다. 또한, 저희가 곧 공식 프로그램을 보내드릴 예정입니다. 이번 주까지 수령하지 못한 경우, kbazemore@popilorc.com으로 이메일을 보내주세요. 마지막으로, 저희는 다가오는 금요일에 직원 회의를 갖습니다. 모두 연습하고 싶은 선호 날짜 목록을 가지고 회의에 참석해 주시기 바랍니다. **(158)** 그렇게 하면, 회의에서 시간을 많이 절감할 수 있습니다.

---

156 공지는 누구를 위해 작성되었는가?
(A) 오케스트라 단원
(B) 공무원
(C) 공연 참석자
(D) 행사 진행자

157 공지에서 언급된 것은 무엇인가?
(A) 행사 가격이 올해 낮아졌다.
(B) 예상 관중을 수용하기에 원래 장소가 너무 작다.
(C) 제안된 프로그램은 전에 공연된 적이 있다.
(D) 공연이 자선 행사의 일환이다.

158 금요일 회의에서 어떤 주제가 논의되겠는가?
(A) 무대를 설치할 자원봉사자
(B) 잠재적인 연습 일자
(C) 장소 추천
(D) 행사용 출장 연회 준비

159-160번은 다음 웹 페이지에 관한 문제입니다.

---

http://www.boodletrainingsolutions.com/about

BTS			
홈	작업	서비스	소개

Boodle Training Solutions 소개

오늘날 같이 변화무쌍한 세상에서는 직원들이 일어나고 있는 커다란 변화를 알고 있도록 하는 것이 아주 중요합니다. Boodle Training Solutions에서는 바로 그것을 제공해 드립니다. **(159)** 당신의 직원들을 교육하도록 고안된 맞춤 프로그램입니다. 필요하신 것만 저희에게 알려주시면, 동영상과 애니메이션으로 가득한 완전 맞춤형 프로그램을 설계해 드립니다.

운영 방식은 다음과 같습니다. 저희와 예약을 확정하시면, 저희는 Boodle Team을 파견해 귀사의 관리자를 만나게 됩니다. **(160C)** 회의는 온라인으로도 진행될 수 있습니다. **(160D)** 귀사의 요구사항을 파악하면, 저희는 동영상 제작자, 학습 설계자, 진행자로 구성된 팀을 이용해 어디서도 볼 수 없는 몰입형 교육 자료를 제작합니다. 저희 프로그램은 전세계에서 찬사를 받았습니다. **(160A)** 지금 예약하셔서 귀사의 직원에게 필요한 정보를 알려주세요!

---

159 웹 페이지에 따르면, 회사는 왜 BTS 프로그램을 사용해야 하는가?
(A) 직장 내 직원 사기를 진작하기 위해
(B) 가격을 인상해 수익을 높이기 위해
(C) 직원들에게 변경사항을 알려주기 위해
(D) 의사 결정 과정을 파악하기 위해

160 BTS에 관하여 알 수 없는 것은?
(A) 과거에 해외 고객이 있었다.
(B) 비교적 신생 기업이다.
(C) 요구사항을 파악하기 위해 고객에게 팀을 파견한다.
(D) 디지털 방식으로 서비스를 제공한다.

161-163번은 다음 이메일에 관한 문제입니다.

수신: 마케팅팀 전원
발신: Alan Chang
날짜: 1월 12일
제목: 최신정보

모두 안녕하세요.

몇 가지 매우 좋은 소식이 있습니다. Dunkirk 항공의 취항지들을 홍보하는 우리 캠페인이 큰 성공을 거뒀습니다. —[1]—. Dunkirk 사의 웹사이트는 최근 Christchurch와 Napier 시로 가는 여행을 예약하려는 수많은 방문객으로 인해 높은 접속량을 경험하고 있습니다. **(161)** —[2]—.

하지만 이제, 우리는 Morton & Alonzo 프로젝트에 집중해야 합니다. 우리의 과제는 그들의 새 스포츠음료가 젊은 운동선수들에게 안성맞춤인 음료라는 걸 보여주는 것입니다. —[3]—. 그러나, 우리가 회사 외부 사람들을 만나기 전에, **(163)** TV 광고 아이디어 회의를 했으면 합니다. 오늘 퇴근 전에, 목요일 오전과 오후 중 언제 모이는 게 좋을지 단체 채팅방으로 메시지를 보내주세요. **(162)** —[4]—. 전원 참석하여 아이디어를 제시해주시기 바랍니다. 지난번처럼 잘 협력한다면, 이번 캠페인이 Dunkirk 프로젝트보다 훨씬 더 큰 성공을 거둘 수 있을 거라 믿습니다.

Alan Chang 드림
마케팅담당 이사

---

161 Dunkirk 항공 캠페인이 성공적이었다는 증거로 무엇이 언급되는가?
(A) 회원 가입의 증가
(B) 긍정적인 고객 후기의 수
(C) 휴가 예약의 양
(D) 항공요금 인하

162 Mr. Chang은 마케팅 직원들에게 무엇을 하라고 요청하는가?
(A) 설문조사를 만들라고
(B) 참석 가능 시간을 확인해 달라고
(C) 여행사에 연락하라고
(D) 소비자 보고서를 읽으라고

163 [1], [2], [3], [4]로 표시된 곳 중 다음 문장이 들어가기에 가장 적절한 곳은 어디인가?

"이를 위해, 운동선수들과 영양 상담가들을 모두 인터뷰할 계획입니다."

(A) [1]
(B) [2]
(C) [3]
(D) [4]

164-167번은 다음 온라인 채팅 대화문에 관한 문제입니다.

Tony Gandolfini [오후 7시 45분]
모두 안녕하세요. 제가 이 동네에 새로 이사 왔는데요, 여기가 질문을 하기에 좋은 곳이라고 들었습니다. **(164)** 창문을 직접 설치해보신 분 계신가요?

Sam Rockwell [오후 7시 47분]
Glenview 동네 채팅방에 오신 걸 환영해요, Tony. **(164)** 작업을 직접 하실 계획인가요? 제가 작년에 다락에 창문을 새로 달았어요. 하지만 그런 일을 다시 할지는 잘 모르겠어요. **(165)**

Tony Gandolfini [오후 7시 48분]
제가 알아본 바로는, 직접 하면 돈을 많이 절감할 수 있는 것 같아서요. 하지만 솔직히 제가 이런 일을 해본 적이 없어요.

Deidre Stapleton [오후 7시 52분]
이런 종류의 작업을 잘 하신다면, 다른 사람이 하는 걸 몇 번 본 후에 창문을 설치하는 게 가능해요. 하지만 매우 정확하게 해야 해요. 실수하면 창문 일부를 망가뜨리기 쉽거든요.

Sam Rockwell [오후 7시 53분]
저는 할 때 먼저 www.yourhouseproj.com에서 온라인 자료들을 많이 읽어보고 안내 동영상도 먼저 봤어요. 하지만 전 다음 번에는 전문가를 고용할 것 같아요.⁽¹⁶⁵⁾

Sam Rockwell [오후 7시 54분]
Deidre, 이런 프로젝트를 많이 맡아봤나요? Tony가 혼자 작업을 할 수 있게 조언 좀 해주시겠어요?

Tony Gandolfini [오후 7시 54분]
그건 매우 도움이 됩니다. 조언 감사 드려요.

Deidre Stapleton [오후 7시 55분]
제가 창문과 외장재 사업을 하거든요.⁽¹⁶⁶⁾ 그 작업을 권할지 여부는 몇 가지에 달려 있어요. Tony, 새 창문을 설치하시나요, 아니면 쓰던 걸 제거하셔야 하나요? 그리고 알맞은 연장을 확실히 모두 가지고 계신가요?

Tony Gandolfini [오후 7시 55분]
창문 하나만 교체하려고 했는데, 새내기 집주인이 하기에는 고생스러운 일 같네요. Deidre, 당신 회사 전화번호를 알려주시겠어요?⁽¹⁶⁷⁾

Deidre Stapleton [오후 7시 57분]
저희가 기꺼이 도와드릴게요. 제 사무실 번호는 555-4220이에요. 저와 얘기 했다고만 말씀하시면 돼요.

164 채팅방은 누구를 대상으로 하는가?
(A) 함께 휴가 가는 사람들
(B) 같은 사무실에서 근무하는 사람들
(C) 같은 수업을 듣는 사람들
(D) 같은 지역에 사는 사람들

165 오후 7시 47분에, Mr. Rockwell이 "하지만 그런 일을 다시 할지는 잘 모르겠어요"라고 할 때 무엇을 의미하겠는가?
(A) 전문가를 고용하지 않은 것을 후회한다.
(B) 프로젝트에 너무 많은 비용이 들었다고 생각했다.
(C) 신뢰할 수 없는 자재를 구매했다.
(D) 집을 다시 꾸며야 한다.

166 Ms. Stapleton에 관하여 무엇이 사실이겠는가?
(A) Mr. Gandolfini와 함께 근무한다.
(B) 창문 설치 경험이 있다.
(C) 정기적으로 www.yourhouseproj.com에 동영상을 업로드한다.
(D) 새로 집을 장만했다.

167 Mr. Gandolfini는 이후에 무엇을 하겠는가?
(A) 파손된 창문을 교체할 것이다.
(B) 교육용 동영상을 시청할 것이다.
(C) 사업체에 전화할 것이다.
(D) 가격 견적을 검토할 것이다.

168-171번은 다음 기사에 관한 문제입니다.

Herbert McGraw는 다른 음악 강사들과 비교하면 정말 독특하다. 그는 **경력의 대부분을 Roth & Stein Associates에서 성공한 변호사로 보낸 후,**⁽¹⁶⁸⁾ 갑자기 음악으로 관심을 돌렸다. —[1]—. McGraw는 초등학교 때 학교 공부를 따라가느라 애를 먹었다. 그러나 중학교 시절부터 학교 음

악 프로그램이 그의 흥미를 끌었다. 음악에 대한 그의 열정은 학업에 대한 집중력을 향상하는 데 도움을 주기도 했다. **그래서 자신의 고향 학군에서 모든 음악 프로그램 예산을 삭감했다는 것을 알았을 때, 자신이 무언가를 해야 한다고 생각했다.**⁽¹⁶⁹⁾ —[2]—. 그 '무언가'는 음악 스튜디오 To the Beat가 되었다.

음악 스튜디오는 도시 중심부에 위치하여, 지역 학생들이 쉽게 이용할 수 있다. 무엇보다 좋은 것은 McGraw가 학생들에게 모든 것을 무료로 제공한다는 점이다.

—[3]—. McGraw의 스튜디오에는 상상할 수 있는 거의 모든 종류의 악기가 갖춰져 있으며, 학생들이 가져다 연주하도록 권장된다. To the Beat는 매일 학생들에게 자신의 재능을 발견하고 음악을 통해 자신을 표현할 기회를 제공한다. "고향의 학교들이 음악 프로그램들을 없앤다는 말을 듣고 화가 났어요,"라고 McGraw는 말했다.⁽¹⁶⁹⁾ "저는 음악이 학업과 인생에서 중요한 기능을 한다는 것을 경험으로 알고 있어요. 단지 이 일에 장기적으로 자금을 댈 방법을 찾을 수 있길 바랄 뿐인데, 그 부분이 쉽지 않을 듯 해요."⁽¹⁷¹⁾ —[4]—.

수상 경력이 있는 밴드 The Jamming Camels는 이 아이들을 도우려는 McGraw의 노력에 대한 이야기를 들었다. 그들은 지지를 표하기 위해 McGraw와 To the Beat 음악 스튜디오에 금액을 비공개로 기부했다.⁽¹⁷⁰⁾

168 Herbert McGraw는 어디에서 직장생활을 시작하는가?
(A) 광고회사
(B) 법률 분야
(C) 음악산업
(D) 교육 분야

169 Herbert McGraw의 고향에서 무엇이 변화했는가?
(A) 관광객의 수
(B) 학교 프로그램의 수
(C) 일부 부동산의 가격
(D) 지역의 인구 규모

170 To the Beat에 관하여 사실인 것은 무엇인가?
(A) 최근 Roth & Stein Associates를 고용했다.
(B) The Jamming Camels로부터 일부 자금지원을 받았다.
(C) 지역 학군에 물품을 기부할 것이다.
(D) 수상경력이 있는 밴드와 함께 앨범을 녹음할 것이다.

171 [1], [2], [3], [4]로 표시된 곳 중 다음 문장이 들어가기에 가장 적절한 곳은 어디인가?

"그러나 지금 예상치 못했던 곳으로부터 도움이 왔다."

(A) [1]
(B) [2]
(C) [3]
(D) [4]

172-175번은 다음 구인 광고에 관한 문제입니다.

Bekai Boutique에서 직원을 채용합니다

Bekai Boutique에서는 직업 그 이상을 제공합니다. 국내에서 최고로 신뢰 받는 고급 의류 공급업체로서 저희와 함께 일하면 성취감을 느끼며 일할 수 있습니다. 저희가 최고의 직원 복지 기준을 유지하며 계속해서 상을 받는 이유를 직접 알아보세요.⁽¹⁷²⁾ 저희는 다음 직책을 채용합니다.

매장 관리자: 업무에는 전반적인 매장 운영, **프로모션 및 행사 계획 및 실시,**^(173C) 고객 불만 경청 및 처리,^(173A) 본사와의 협업,^(173D) 직원 교육이 포함됩니다. 정규직이며, 화요일부터 토요일까지 근무.

재고 관리 전문가: 업무에는 재고 수준 기록, 필요 시 물품 주문, 필요 시 주문품 개봉 작업, 전반적인 창고 청소 업무가 포함됩니다. 시간제 근무이며, 주말 근무 필수.

인테리어 디자이너: 업무에는 월별 주제에 맞춰 매장 꾸미기 및 매주 진열 변경이 포함됩니다. 의류점에서의 이전 경력은 필수입니다. **자가용과 운전 면허증이 있어야 합니다.**(174) 시즌 프로모션 시기에는 야근을 할 수도 있습니다.

판매 직원: 업무에는 고객과 교류하기, 고객이 제품을 찾고 구매하도록 지원하기, 계산대 직원과 협업하기가 포함됩니다. 시간제 근무이며, 월요일부터 금요일 근무.

모든 직책에 경쟁력 있는 급여와 유연한 근무 일정을 제공합니다.(175) 관심 있으시면, Jim Richardson에게 jrichardson@bekai.com으로 이력서와 자기소개서를 보내주시기 바랍니다.

172 광고에서 Bekai Boutique에 관해 언급한 것은 무엇인가?
(A) 좋은 회사라고 인정받아왔다.
(B) 제품 라인을 확대할 계획이다.
(C) 최근 경영진을 교체했다.
(D) 다른 나라에서 영업한다.

173 매장 관리자의 업무로 언급되지 않은 것은?
(A) 고객 문제 해결하기
(B) 신규 재고품 주문하기
(C) 특별 행사 운영하기
(D) 다른 직원과 소통하기

174 Bekai Boutique의 인테리어 디자이너에 관하여 알 수 있는 것은?
(A) 고객에게 의견을 받는다.
(B) 특수 소프트웨어 사용법을 배워야 한다.
(C) 자주 출장을 가야 할 수도 있다.
(D) 다른 직책보다 근무 시간이 더 적다.

175 광고된 모든 직책에 관하여 언급된 것은 무엇인가?
(A) 서로 다른 일정에 맞출 수 있다.
(B) 휴가 상여를 받게 된다.
(C) 정규직이다.
(D) 유급 휴가를 받는다.

176-180번은 다음 웹 페이지와 이메일에 관한 문제입니다.

www.alphalumenstar.co.uk/review/LU-X/ad52d

Huntsdale 식물원 안내서

방문해주셔서 감사 드립니다! **Grand 중앙역과 도시 내 가장 유명한 호텔 및 레스토랑에서 짧은 도보 거리에 위치한**(176) Huntsdale 식물원은 방문객들에게 도시를 떠나지 않고도 휴식을 취하고 자연의 아름다움을 경험할 수 있는 훌륭한 방법을 선사합니다. 식물원 방문을 최대한 활용하고 싶은 분들은 투어 또한 이용하실 수 있습니다. 자동차 및 자전거 주차공간이 충분히 마련되어 있습니다. 저희 식물원 뷔페 샐러드 바에서의 점심식사는 어떠신가요?

요금표:

입장단계	금액	입장 권한
General	5달러	주 식물원과 온실
Deluxe	10달러	General 입장 구역 + 일본 정원 투어
Executive	15달러	Deluxe 입장 구역 + 유기농 농장 투어
VIP	25달러	Executive 입장 구역 + 야생동물 쇼(179)

야생동물 쇼:(180)
치타를 만나요: 대도시의 큰 고양이과 동물들 (1월 - 3월)
아름다운 코요테: 코요테, 여우 및 늑대 (4월 - 6월)

대탈출: 고릴라, 침팬지와 Orlando 오랑우탄 (7월 - 9월)
어둠이 내린 공원: 야행성 사막 동물들 (10월 - 12월)(180)

수신: HPers@huntsdalegarden.org
발신: Damian@indioschools.edu
날짜: 11월 6일
제목: 예정된 방문

Mr. Pers께,

저는 Indio 중학교 자연 클럽(IMSNC)의 설립자인 Leticia Damian입니다. 이름에서 짐작하시겠지만, 저희 클럽은 자연계 및 그것이 직면한 생태 문제들에 대한 어린 학생들의 인식 증대를 추구합니다.(178)

저희는 11월 22일 식물원을 방문할 계획입니다. 현재, 최소 20명의 회원이 참석할 예정이고, 참석자들은 일본정원과 현지 유기농 농장 견학에 관심을 보였습니다.(179)

저는 저희가 계획한 투어의 일부로 이 장소들에 입장할 수 있는지를 확인받고 싶었습니다.(177) 또한 쇼가 예정되어 있다면, 저희는 현재 진행 중인 야생동물 쇼를 관람하고 싶습니다.(179)/(180) 이 조건들을 충족하려면 저희가 어떤 종류의 티켓을 구입해야 할지 알려주세요.(177)

Leticia Damian 드림
멘토 교직원, IMSNC

176 Huntsdale 식물원에 관하여 알 수 있는 것은 무엇인가?
(A) 최근 식당을 오픈했다.
(B) 대규모 단체에 할인을 제공한다.
(C) 편리한 장소에 위치한다.
(D) 자전거 투어를 허용한다.

177 이메일의 목적은 무엇인가?
(A) 투어 선택사항에 대해 문의하려고
(B) 클럽 창단을 발표하려고
(C) 방문 일정을 변경하려고
(D) 멘토 교직원으로서 Ms. Damian의 역할을 설명하려고

178 Ms. Damian에 따르면, IMSNC는 무엇인가?
(A) 오락 프로그램
(B) 정부 부처
(C) 교환학생 기관
(D) 환경 교육 단체

179 IMSNC는 어떤 종류의 입장권을 선택하겠는가?
(A) General
(B) Deluxe
(C) Executive
(D) VIP

180 IMSNC 회원들은 어떤 공연을 보겠는가?
(A) 치타를 만나요
(B) 아름다운 코요테
(C) 대탈출
(D) 어둠이 내린 공원

181-185번은 다음 온라인 안내와 이메일에 관한 문제입니다.

Ratdom Limited

구매 절차

Ratdom Limited를 대표하여 주문할 때는 다음 단계를 순서대로 따라야 합니다.

1단계: 주문의 내역, 수량(181D), 빈도(181A)와 필수 배송일(181B)을 포함한 필요사항을 자세히 살펴봅니다.(181)

2단계: 재무팀에 연락해 가용 예산을 설정합니다.

3단계: 승인된 공급사 명단을 참조하여 최적 업체를 선택합니다.

4단계: 선택된 공급사와 조건을 협의합니다.

5단계: 확정된 주문 세부내역을 구매 담당자에게 보내고 승인된 구매 주문서를 받습니다.(184)

6단계: 공급사에 승인된 주문서를 제출합니다.(184)

7단계: 공급사로부터 영수증을 받는 즉시, 지불을 처리합니다.

수신: oliver_shelton@ratdom.com
발신: alison_holloway@ratdom.com
날짜: 8월 19일
제목: 최신 소식

Mr. Shelton께,

몹시 필요한 서버 업그레이드를 알아봐 주셔서 감사합니다. 저희가 몇 년 째 하드웨어 업그레이드를 하지 않아서, 저희에게 상대적으로 약한 부분이라고 생각했습니다.(182) 저희 최고 전략 책임자이신 Ms. Cruz께서 고품질 장비로 유명한 업체가 좋으시다고 의견을 주셨습니다.(183) 그런 점에서 저희가 Fieldtron을 선택한 데 만족해 하실 것 같습니다.(183)

제가 그 회사에 아주 익숙하고, 구매 주문서에 서명하는 게 편합니다. Fieldtron의 제품이 저희 예산 범위에 들어오는 게 도움이 되네요. 이 이메일에 제 서명이 들어간 주문서를 첨부해 드립니다.(184)

저희는 또한 기계도 일부 업그레이드를 고려할 것임을 알려드립니다. 이에, 저희가 과거에 이용해 본 제조사 명단을 보내드립니다.(185) 그쪽에 연락하셔서 저희 요건을 기준으로 제공할 수 있는 것을 알아봐 주세요.

감사합니다.

Alison Holloway

---

181 설명서 1단계에서 수행하지 않아도 되는 일은 무엇인가?
(A) 주문 빈도 선택하기
(B) 주문 배송일 결정하기
(C) 소요 금액 산출하기
(D) 필요 제품 개수 기록하기

182 Fieldtron에서는 무엇을 생산하겠는가?
(A) 보호 장비
(B) 서버 하드웨어
(C) 차량 부품
(D) 공장 부품

183 Ms. Cruz에 관하여 암시되는 것은 무엇인가?
(A) Fieldtron 장비가 품질이 좋다고 생각한다.
(B) 출장을 갈 예정이다.
(C) 최근 현 직책으로 승진했다.
(D) 모든 주문에 승인해줘야 한다.

184 Fieldtron과의 작업에서 Mr. Shelton의 다음 단계는 무엇이 되겠는가?
(A) 4단계
(B) 5단계
(C) 6단계
(D) 7단계

185 Ms. Holloway는 Mr. Shelton에게 무엇을 제공할 것인가?
(A) 아는 제조사 이름
(B) 조직도
(C) 업데이트된 가격표
(D) 설문조사 결과

186-190번은 다음 계획 안내서, 정보문, 의견카드에 관한 문제입니다.

San Lorenzo: 방문기간 최대한 즐기기

몇 시간 들르시거나 잠시 머물러보세요. 어느 쪽이든 San Lorenzo 시에 마음을 뺏기실 겁니다. 아래와 같은 방문일정을 추천해 드립니다.

반일 투어
Main가 113번지에 있는 San Lorenzo 관광 안내소에 가셔서 도시의 역사에 관한 짧은 강연을 들어보세요.(186)/(188) 그리고 나서 시내 명소들에 방문객들을 태우고 내려주는 투어버스에 타세요.

종일 투어
반일 투어의 모든 활동 외에, 관광 안내소 바로 건너편에 있는 Phoenix 궁전에 가보세요.(186) 매일 정오부터 일몰 시까지 궁전과 궁전 식물원에서 가이드와 함께 하는 투어를 이용하실 수 있습니다. 아름다운 기념품을 위해 기념품점도 꼭 방문해주세요.

수일 투어(하루 이상)
위에 열거한 모든 활동을 하신 후,(188) 시내 및 주변지역에서 도보 관광을 하시면서 San Lorenzo에 관해 더 알아보세요.

San Lorenzo의 산책로

Rainbow 산마루(10.3km)
대부분 오르막인 이 10.3km의 하이킹은 항만에서 출발하여 시내를 지나 Rainbow 산마루 공원의 경치 좋은 절벽까지 이어집니다. 시내 최고 전경을 보기에 안성맞춤이지만, 초보 등산객들에게는 부담스럽습니다.(189)

Borges 반도(6.1km)
이 6.1km 산책로는 Borges 야생보호구역 근처의 완만한 언덕들을 통과하여 지나갑니다. 두꺼운 나뭇잎은 산책로에 빛이 많이 들지 않는다는 것을 의미하므로, 일몰 전에 돌아오세요.(187)

옛 교회 경로(1.7km)
성 Catherine 교회에서 성 Jessica 교회까지의 자갈이 깔린 길을 따라 경치를 감상하면서 걸어보세요. 1.7km의 수월한 평지길입니다.

Brilliant 대로(2.1km)
박물관 구역에서 Crimson 타워에 이르는 인기 경로입니다. 거리를 따라 쇼핑과 식사를 즐겨 보세요. 이 2.1km 경로는 밤에 약간 붐빌 수 있습니다.

San Lorenzo 관광 안내소
의견 카드

이름: Scottie Fitzgerald(188)
방문일: 8월 1일-2일(188)/(190)

메시지:
우리 가족은 San Lorenzo 여행이 정말 좋았습니다. 그 도시를 방문해본 적이 없어서, 관광 안내소에서 받은 계획 안내서에 나온 추천사항들을 그대로 따랐는데, 정말 도움이 되었습니다. 토요일과 일요일 모두 시내에서 보내면서 구경을 많이 했습니다.(188) 투어버스는 돈이 아깝지 않더군요. 저희가 가보지 않은 유일한 산책로는 가장 길고 가장 어려운 코스였습니다. 저희 아이들이 아직 그런 것을 하기에는 너무 어리거든요. 하지만 조만간 가보고 싶습니다.(189) 물론 제가 첫날 구매한 San Lorenzo 교통카드가 8월 말일에 만료되기 전에 갈 수 있다면 좋겠네요.(190)

---

186 계획 안내서에서는 Phoenix 궁전에 관하여 무엇을 언급하는가?
(A) 주민에게 할인을 제공한다.
(B) 입장료를 받지 않는다.
(C) Main가에 위치한다.
(D) San Lorenzo에서 가장 오래된 장소이다.

187 산책로 정보에 따르면, Borges 반도 산책로에 관하여 사실인 것은?
(A) 도시 전경을 볼 수 있다.
(B) 그늘진 구역이다.
(C) 밤에 매우 아름답다.
(D) 초보자가 이용하면 안 된다.

188 Mr. Fitzgerald는 도시를 방문했을 때 무엇을 처음으로 했겠는가?
(A) 투어버스를 탔을 것이다.
(B) 궁전을 방문했을 것이다.
(C) 강연을 들었을 것이다.
(D) 하이킹을 갔을 것이다.

189 Mr. Fitzgerald는 나중에 어느 산책로에서 하이킹을 할 계획인가?
(A) Rainbow 산마루
(B) Borges 반도
(C) 옛 교회 경로
(D) Brilliant 대로

190 Mr. Fitzgerald는 의견 카드에서 무엇을 암시하는가?
(A) 계획 안내서가 매우 유용했다고 생각하지 않는다.
(B) 전문 등산가이다.
(C) 한 달짜리 교통카드를 구입했다.
(D) 관광 안내소 근처의 호텔을 예약했다.

191-195번은 다음 일정표, 피드백 양식, 이메일에 관한 문제입니다.

Solter Engineering 직원 오리엔테이션 일정표	
오전 9시 - 9시 30분	소개 그룹과 조찬 하루 일정 개요
오전 9시 30분 - 10시 30분	세션 1: 'Solter의 연혁, 사명, 가치 제안'을 주제로 한 마케팅 부장 Gemma Ball의 강연(191)
오전 10시30분 - 11시 30분	세션 2: "Solter의 제품군, 주요 시장, 주 경쟁사'에 관한 리드 제품 매니저 Shaun Portillo의 강연(194)
오전 11시 30분 - 오후 1시	점심 시간
오후 1시 - 2시 15분	세션 3: "Solter의 인수, 협력사, 제휴사'에 관한 전략 부장 Karen Wallis의 강연(195)
오후 2시 15분 - 3시 30분	초청 연사: '마이크로프로세서의 미래 모습은? 그 영향에 대하여'를 주제로 한 Gary Koch 박사의 강연
오후 3시 30분 - 4시	세션 4: '새로운 안식처: 복리후생, 퇴직, 승진'에 관한 인사팀 Tyler Guest의 강연
오후 4시 - 6시 30분	팀원들과 만찬(192)

Solter Engineering 신입 직원 오리엔테이션 피드백 양식

Solter Engineering의 가족이 되신 것을 환영합니다! 최근 받으신 오리엔테이션 세션에 대한 귀하의 피드백을 받아보고자 합니다. **귀하의 답변은 Solter Engineering에서의 귀하의 지위와는 무관하며 향후 더 나은 세션을 만들기 위한 용도로만 엄격히 사용될 것입니다.**(193)

	내용	매우 동의함	동의함	동의하지 않음	매우 동의하지 않음
1	하루 일정의 진행 사항을 잘 알고 있었다.			O	
2	내 업무를 수행하는 데 세션이 유용하다고 느꼈다.			O	
3	세션의 길이가 적당하다고 느꼈다.		O		
4	연사들이 관심과 흥미를 갖게 했다.				O
5	음식 및 음료가 만족스러웠다.		O		

추가 의견:

제가 생각하기에 유일하게 유용했던 세션은 Solter Engineering에서 실제로 판매하는 제품을 다룬 세션이었습니다.(194) 솔직한 의견으로, 다른 세션은 이메일로 보내 줬어도 됐다고 봅니다. 대신에 동료 및 상사와 만나는 데 더 많은 시간을 할애 했었어야 한다고 봅니다.

수신: Karen Wallis
발신: Laura North
날짜: 5월 15일
제목: 귀하의 세션

Ms. Wallis께,

오리엔테이션 때 훌륭한 강연을 해주셔서 다시 한번 감사드립니다. 저는 고객 관리 부서에서 일할 예정이라, 세션이 제 업무와 아주 관련이 높다고 느꼈습니다. 하지만 시간을 잠시 내주실 수 있다면, 만나 뵙고 Seraliss Technologies에 대해 이야기 나누는 시간을 갖고 싶습니다.(195) 저는 이곳에 좋은 인상을 남기고 싶다는 마음이 너무 간절해서, 어떤 도움이라도 주실 수 있다면 감사하겠습니다.

감사드리며, 답장 기다리겠습니다.

Laura North 드림

191 일정표에 따르면, 누가 회사의 철학에 대해 이야기할 것인가?
(A) Mr. Guest
(B) Ms. Wallis
(C) Ms. Ball
(D) Mr. Portillo

192 일정표에 따르면, 오후 4시 이후에는 무슨 일이 있을 것인가?
(A) 회사에 관한 설문지를 작성할 것이다.
(B) 앞서 다룬 내용을 다시 살펴볼 것이다.
(C) 회사 사장이 상을 나눠줄 것이다.
(D) 참가자들은 현 직원들을 일부 만날 것이다.

193 피드백 양식에 있는 답변에 관하여 언급된 것은?
(A) 연사들에게 보상하는데 사용될 것이다.
(B) 향후 세션을 개선하는데 사용될 것이다.
(C) 독립 회사로 발송될 것이다.
(D) 신입 직원을 평가하는 데 사용될 것이다.

194 신입 직원은 어떤 세션을 가장 즐거워했다고 언급하는가?
(A) 세션 1
(B) 세션 2
(C) 세션 3
(D) 세션 4

195 Ms. North는 Ms. Wallis에게 Seraliss Technologies에 관하여 왜 물어보겠는가?
(A) 거기서도 면접을 본다.
(B) Solter Engineering의 경쟁사에 관한 정보를 알고 싶다.
(C) Seraliss Technologies에서 근무하는 지인이 있다.
(D) Seraliss Technologies와 긴밀히 협력하게 될 것이다.

196-200번은 다음 웹 페이지와 이메일들에 관한 문제입니다.

http://www.bunncorp.com/movingservices

| 이사 패키지 | 견적 요청 | 보험 정보 | 자주 묻는 질문 |

귀사의 필요에 맞는 이사 패키지를 선택하신 후, '견적 요청' 페이지로 가서서 상담을 예약하세요. 각 요금제에는 인건비와 운송비가 포함되며, 안전 보관시설 서비스(SSFS) 신청은 선택사항입니다. SSFS 요금은 9월 30일에 변경될 수 있습니다.

기본형: 운송 트럭과 가구 및 장비, 파일을 해체 및 운송, 설치하는 4인으로 구성된 장비를 갖춘 팀을 포함. 중소 규모 사무실에 안성맞춤. **SSFS 요금: 99달러/월**(196)

특별형: 기본형 패키지의 모든 내용을 포함하면서, 무겁거나 옮기기 힘든 물건 운송을 위한 추가 장비 포함. **SSFS 요금: 199 - 300달러/월**(196)

기업형: 특별형 패키지의 모든 내용을 포함하면서, 더 규모가 큰 작업에 맞춰 확장. 대형 세미트레일러와 최대 20명으로 구성된 운송팀이 필요하신 곳으로 모셔다 드립니다. **SSFS 요금: 월 1,500달러부터**(196)

고급형: 기업형 패키지의 모든 내용을 포함하면서, **민감한 장비나 데이터의 안전보장을 위한 보안 카메라 감시 시스템과 경보기 포함.**(198) SSFS **요금: 월 4,000달러부터**(196)

수신: BMoore@kraussfinancial.com
발신: BBunn@bunncorp.com
날짜: 7월 2일
제목: 이전 첫 단계: 완료

Mr. Moore께,

저희 직원들이 귀사의 모든 장비를 Huxley Drive 2000번지에 있는 저희 대형 보관창고로 성공적으로 옮겼음을 알려드립니다. 지난 주 회의에서의 합의 사항과 귀사의 SSFS에 따라, 물품은 7월 31일까지 그곳에 보관됩니다. 그날 오전 10시경에 Brookhurst Street 19724번지, Crytech 빌딩에 있는 귀사의 새 사무실로 물품을 옮겨드리겠습니다.(197)

7월 31일 이후에도 SSFS를 이용하셔야 한다면, 저희에게 최소 5일 전 사전통지를 해주셔야 합니다. 또한, 물건이 창고에 있는 동안 매월 요금이 부과될 것입니다. 요금은 매월 1일에 청구서에 반영됩니다.(200)

Bradley Bunn 드림
Bunn 사

수신: BBunn@bunncorp.com
발신: BMoore@kraussfinancial.com
날짜: 7월 3일
제목: 회신: 이전 첫 단계 완료

Mr. Bunn께,

이사를 하는 동안 귀사 직원들이 보여준 효율성과 노련함에 감사 드립니다. **특히 운송 중 경보기와 카메라 시스템을 통해 저희 물품을 관찰 및 감시할 수 있다는 점이 만족스러웠습니다.**(198)

그러나 긴급한 업무로 인해, 저희는 이사 들어가는 날짜를 변경해야 했습니다. 그래서, 이제 저희 장비를 8월 29일 화요일에 Brookhurst Street 19724번지로 옮겨주실 것을 요청드립니다.(200)

그리고 보관창고에 온도 조절장치가 있나요? 여름 장마철 열기와 습기로 저희 소파나 테이블이 손상될까 봐 약간 염려됩니다.(199)

다시 한번 고맙습니다.

Barney Moore 드림
Krauss 금융

---

196 Bunn 사 웹 페이지에 따르면, 안전 보관시설 서비스에 관하여 사실인 것은?
(A) 현재 할인 중이다.
(B) 이사 패키지에 따라 가격이 다르다.
(C) 사전에 비용을 지불해야 한다.
(D) 요금이 6개월마다 업데이트된다.

197 첫 번째 이메일의 목적은 무엇인가?
(A) 청구서상의 실수를 이야기하기 위해
(B) 고객의 문의사항에 응답하기 위해
(C) 보증금을 요청하기 위해
(D) 프로젝트에 대한 최신정보를 제공하기 위해

198 Mr. Moore는 어떤 이사 패키지를 선택했겠는가?
(A) 기본형
(B) 특별형
(C) 기업형
(D) 고급형

199 두 번째 이메일에 따르면, Mr. Moore는 무엇에 관하여 걱정하는가?
(A) 개정된 계약 조건
(B) 일부 가구의 손상
(C) 증가된 연료비
(D) 건물에의 출입

200 Bunn 사에 관하여 알 수 있는 것은?
(A) 본사가 Crytech 빌딩으로 이전할 것이다.
(B) 추가 장비를 옮기지 못할 것이다.
(C) 8월 1일에 Krauss 금융에 추가 비용을 청구할 것이다.
(D) 직원들이 업무에 대해 상을 받았다.

TEST 02

PART 5
P. 48

101 (B)	102 (B)	103 (B)	104 (D)	105 (D)	106 (A)
107 (B)	108 (A)	109 (B)	110 (B)	111 (C)	112 (D)
113 (C)	114 (C)	115 (B)	116 (C)	117 (A)	118 (C)
119 (B)	120 (D)	121 (D)	122 (B)	123 (B)	124 (D)
125 (C)	126 (D)	127 (D)	128 (D)	129 (B)	130 (B)

PART 6
P. 51

131 (A)	132 (C)	133 (C)	134 (D)	135 (C)	136 (B)
137 (D)	138 (C)	139 (A)	140 (B)	141 (D)	142 (A)
143 (C)	144 (D)	145 (C)	146 (A)		

PART 7
P. 55

147 (B)	148 (A)	149 (A)	150 (B)	151 (A)	152 (C)
153 (B)	154 (A)	155 (C)	156 (C)	157 (C)	158 (D)
159 (D)	160 (A)	161 (D)	162 (B)	163 (D)	164 (B)
165 (D)	166 (C)	167 (C)	168 (D)	169 (D)	170 (D)
171 (B)	172 (C)	173 (C)	174 (C)	175 (D)	176 (B)
177 (C)	178 (A)	179 (D)	180 (D)	181 (D)	182 (C)
183 (D)	184 (A)	185 (D)	186 (A)	187 (B)	188 (B)
189 (C)	190 (C)	191 (B)	192 (A)	193 (B)	194 (C)
195 (D)	196 (B)	197 (B)	198 (C)	199 (A)	200 (D)

PART 5
P. 48

101 고객 계정 관리자 직책에 채용된 사람이 없기 때문에, 우리는 다시 물색을 시작해야 한다.

102 Atlantic 항공의 모든 이용객은 이동 중에 자신의 수하물이 분실되면 배상을 받게 된다.

103 Meilee Zhang은 계약 협상가로서 행한 수많은 기여로 승진 후보자로 지명되었다.

104 회사 임원들은 전 직원의 모든 수고와 노력에 감사해 한다.

105 오늘 오전 부서 회의 동안 Mr. Insel은 해외 사업 관행에 관한 추가 조사의 필요성을 인정했다.

106 각각의 차 주전자는 필요에 따라 자기나 도자기로 전문적으로 만들어진다.

107 Pearl Star 사는 상반기에 수익 절감을 겪었지만, 그래도 올해 가까스로 수익을 얻었다.

108 모든 고객 문의들은, 아무리 사소할지라도, 항상 신속하고 정중하게 답변되어야 한다.

109 새로운 시각을 얻기 위해, Ellerton Security에서는 신임 인사부 이사를 외부에서 찾고 있다.

110 이 사무실 관리인은 대학교 규정에 명백히 맞지 않는 광고를 모두 삭제할 것이다.

111 Ali 갤러리는 주로 후원자들의 기부로 전시 작품을 결정한다.

112 Mr. Ramirez는 임원들에게 정오까지 그가 직접 문서를 수정하겠다고 장담했다.

113 초청 연사는 직원 고충을 지속적으로 다루어주는 것이 직원을 유지하는 한 가지 필수요소였다고 역설했다.

114 서빙 직원들을 즉시 알아볼 수 있도록, 그 레스토랑 체인은 멋진 직원 유니폼 제작을 위해 유명 패션 디자이너를 고용했다.

115 Devon International은 동부 훈련 센터의 확장을 발표하게 되어 기쁘다.

116 잡지 기사는 직원 유지율을 늘리는 방법에 관한 조언을 담고 있다.

117 의류 디자인에의 몇 가지 변경으로 제조사는 수천 유로를 절감할 수 있었다.

118 Mr. Nguyen은 새로운 배출세에 관한 우려에 즉시 대응할 것임을 확인해줬다.

119 극장 카페에서 무료 음료를 받으려면, 방문객은 유효한 입장권을 제시해야 한다.

120 Whole Grains 식료품점은 다음주 금요일까지 계산원 직책을 위한 이력서 및 자기소개서를 받을 것이다.

121 Belknap 협회의 회원 자격은 전문 과학자들뿐만 아니라 아마추어 과학자들에게도 열려 있다.

122 Toronto에 있는 제조공장은 9월 마지막 주에 생산량이 사상 최고치에 도달했다고 발표했다.

123 업무 분야가 완전히 다르기 때문에, CEO에게는 유감스럽게도 제조팀은 보통 영업팀과 독립적으로 일한다.

124 Mr. Chiu는 송장을 2부 복사했는데, 하나는 발송용이고 나머지는 보관용이다.

125 Ms. Chun은 그녀가 가장 좋은 보안회사라고 판단한 어느 회사든지 고르라고 지시받았다.

126 Duratek 노트북 Titanium 시리즈는 2미터 높이에서 떨어뜨려도 기능을 잃지 않는다.

127 Ledgewood의 최신 주방 제품은 미적 외관을 위해 얇은 금색 칠로 마무리된다.

128 Fortress Hill 대학교는 소외계층의 학생들에게 학자금 지원을 제공하기 위해 보조금을 받았다.

129 의료보험 자격을 얻으려면 모든 직원은 자신의 사회보장번호를 인증해야 한다.

130 제품의 안전 배송을 보장하기 위해, 직원들은 운송용 상자를 밀봉하기 전에 충분한 양의 포장용 충전재를 추가하는 것을 기억해야 한다.

PART 6
P. 51

131-134번은 다음 공지에 관한 문제입니다.

Wyandotte 카운티 주민 여러분께 알려드립니다.

Wyandotte 카운티 공공사업부(WCPW)가 연간 보수작업 일정에 따라 5월 한 달 내내 카운티 내 주요 도로와 고속도로의 재포장 작업을 진행한다는 점에 유의하시기 바랍니다. 도로재포장은 이달 매주 월요일 오전 3시부터 오전 5시 사이로 계획되어 있습니다. **131. 운전자 여러분은 이 시간대에 도로 사용이 금지됩니다.** 또한 재포장 작업 완료 후 며칠 동안은 노

면이 무른 상태이기 때문에, 속도를 더 줄여서 운전하실 것을 권장합니다. 이것은 **132. 일시적이지만** 피할 수는 없는 일입니다. 카운티 주민 여러분은 약 6주 동안은 통근 시간을 더 길게 **133. 잡으셔야 합니다.** WCPW는 다음 연례 보수작업 기간 **134. 전에** 이와 유사한 공지문을 발송할 것인데, 이는 보통 늦봄경입니다. 문의사항이나 기타 의견이 있으시면, WCPW에 555-1212로 연락 주시기 바랍니다.

131 (A) 운전자 여러분은 이 시간대에 도로 사용이 금지됩니다.
　　(B) 되도록 신속히 수정된 일정표를 게재하겠습니다.
　　(C) 대안으로, 카운티 공무원들은 버스 노선에 자금 지원하는 것을 선택할 수 있습니다.
　　(D) 자정에서 오전 6시 사이에는 대부분의 사업체들이 문을 닫습니다.

135-138번은 다음 정보에 관한 문제입니다.

<The Natural World>의 많은 **135. 기고가들은** 오랜 기간 동안 저희 출판물과 함께 작업해온 베테랑 생물학자들입니다. **136. 그렇지만,** 저희는 항상 미래 과학자들의 작품을 알리는 데 관심이 있습니다. 저희는 모든 호에 새로운 연구자의 제출작을 적어도 1~2개 싣는 것을 목표로 하고 있지만, 저희의 분기별 출판 일정으로는 모든 훌륭한 글을 싣는 것이 어렵습니다. 작업물을 제출하시기 전에, 저희 출판물 지침을 숙지하시는 것이 매우 중요한데(naturalworld.com/submissions에서 보실 수 있습니다), 여기에 인용 및 서식 규칙이 자세히 나와 있습니다. **137. 이는 귀하의 작업물이 선택될 가능성을 높여줄 것입니다.**

저희는 수령하는 모든 서신에 답하기 위해 최선의 노력을 다하고 있다는 것을 기억해 주십시오. 하지만 많은 양의 제출물로 인해, 저희는 항상 빠르게 답을 드릴 수는 없습니다. 이로 인해, 저희는 여러분께 **138. 인내심을 가지고 기다려 주시기를** 요청 드립니다.

137 (A) 저희 구독자 대부분은 대학교수 및 대학원생들입니다.
　　(B) 이번 달 출간호는 앞으로 2주 내 발송될 것입니다.
　　(C) 귀하의 접근법에 깊은 인상을 받았습니다만, 더 많은 통계적인 증거를 필요로 합니다.
　　(D) 이는 귀하의 작업물이 선택될 가능성을 높여줄 것입니다.

139-142번은 다음 공지에 관한 문제입니다.

Brafton 기업가 협회

올해 Brafton 기업가 협회는 두 개의 특별상에 후보 추천을 받고 있습니다. 두 가지 상에 대한 추천은 8월 18일까지 **139. 열려 있을 예정입니다.**

혁신적 성장 상은 짧은 시간 안에 놀라운 성장을 거둔 중소기업을 표창하는 상입니다. 후보 기업은 최대 50명까지 고용할 수 있습니다. **140. 기업은 영업을 시작한 지 3년 미만이어야 합니다.**

지역사회 봉사 상은 중소기업이 궤도에 오르도록 돕는 데 큰 **141. 역할을** 한 기업을 표창하는 상입니다. **142. 기여가** Brafton 지역에 위치한 중소기업에 이뤄진 것이라면, 모든 업종 및 규모의 기업이 후보에 오를 수 있습니다.

기업을 추천하거나 상에 관해 보다 자세한 내용을 알아보시려면, 저희 웹사이트 www.beaawards.org를 방문해 주세요.

140 (A) 지원자는 어떤 사유로든 거부될 수 있습니다.
　　(B) 기업은 영업을 시작한 지 3년 미만이어야 합니다.
　　(C) 귀하를 우리 협회에 초대하고자 합니다.
　　(D) 연체 수수료는 당사 웹사이트를 통해 지불할 수 있습니다.

143-146번은 다음 기사에 관한 문제입니다.

Yuccaville (8월 9일) — 옥상에 나란히 줄지어있는 태양 전지판들은 Yuccaville이 재생 가능 에너지에 관심을 가지고 있다는 사실을 증명한다. 사실, 오늘날 Yuccaville에서 생산되는 전력의 5%는 태양열에서 비롯되고, 그 수치는 **143. 꾸준한** 속도로 증가하고 있다. 이는 어느 정도 태양열 전지판 소유주들에게 주어지는, 마을의 상당한 세금 **144. 감면** 때문이다. Yuccaville Renewable Energy Solutions의 CEO인 Brian Alvarez에 따르면, 보다 효율적인 배터리와 설치가 용이한 판 **145. 또한** 이 기술을 더 매력적으로 만들어주었다. Mr. Alvarez는 Yuccaville에 있는 태양 전지판의 수는 미래에 엄청나게 증가할 것으로 예상한다. **146. 사실, 그는 10년 내 거의 모든 건물들이 태양 전지판을 보유하게 될 것이라고 믿는다.**

146 (A) 사실, 그는 10년 내 거의 모든 건물들이 태양 전지판을 보유하게 될 것이라고 믿는다.
　　(B) 그는 이것이 Yuccaville에서 비즈니스를 시작하려는 업체들이 점점 더 줄어드는 이유 중 하나라고 생각한다.
　　(C) 그는 증가된 비용이 판매에 어떤 영향을 미칠지에 관해 염려한다.
　　(D) 게다가, 그는 작년에 구입한 전지판의 품질에 매우 만족해왔다.

PART 7
P. 55

147-148번은 다음 초대장에 관한 문제입니다.

올해의 **David Conrad 기념 마케팅 세미나**에
귀하를 초대하게 되어 영광입니다.

Toronto 중소기업센터(TSBC)의 기업고문이자 Alpine Grill의 사장인
James Nakamoto가 진행합니다.

주제: 디지털 마케팅
일시: 6월 28일 오후 1~3시
장소: 그랜드 호텔 콘퍼런스룸

이 세미나는 Toronto 지역의 모든 사업가들에게 열려있습니다. (147) 참석하시는 모든 분들은 등록하실 때 사업자등록증 사본을 제출해야 합니다. (148) 더 자세한 정보를 알아보시려면 TSBC로 전화 주십시오.

147 초대장은 누구를 대상으로 하겠는가?
　　(A) 마케팅 전문가
　　(B) 사업주
　　(C) 재정 고문
　　(D) 호텔 매니저

148 관심 있는 사람들은 무엇을 하라고 요청 받는가?
　　(A) 증명서를 제공하라고
　　(B) 세미나실을 준비하라고
　　(C) Mr. Nakamoto의 레스토랑으로 전화하라고
　　(D) 행사 일정을 살펴보라고

149-150번은 다음 안내문에 관한 문제입니다.

Remington Lawn Masters:
잔디 깎기 및 정원관리 필수품

Lawn Master MM2500d를 구매해주셔서 감사 드립니다. 다음 정보를 유념하시면, 기계는 오랫동안 잘 작동할 것입니다.

- 잔디 깎기 기간이 끝나면 반드시 휘발유 탱크를 비워주세요. (150A) 오래된 연료는 긴 겨울이 지난 후 엔진 시동을 어렵게 할 수 있습니다.

- 이물질이 쌓이는 것을 방지하기 위해 정기적으로 기계 바닥을 청소해주세요. 시간이 지나면서 칼날에 풀이나 먼지가 쌓여, 오작동을 유발할 수 있습니다.(149)

- 매년 점화 플러그를 교체해주세요.(150C) 저렴하고 교체가 용이한 이 부품을 바꾸는 것으로, 더 큰 비용이 드는 수리를 예방할 수 있습니다.

- 주기적으로 점검을 받으세요. 기계의 수명을 보장하는 좋은 방법은 정기적으로 수리점에 가져가서 전문가의 점검을 받는 것입니다.(150D)

149 Lawn Master MM2500d의 칼날에 관하여 언급된 것은?
(A) 막힐 수 있다.
(B) 교체비용이 많이 든다.
(C) Remington에서만 구할 수 있다.
(D) 어떤 종류의 잔디라도 깎을 수 있다.

150 잔디 깎는 기계 관리의 팁으로 언급되지 않은 것은?
(A) 연료탱크를 비우는 것
(B) 특정 청소제품을 사용하는 것
(C) 매년 새 부품을 구매하는 것
(D) 전문가를 찾아가는 것

151-153번은 다음 이메일에 관한 문제입니다.

수신: Amos Reese <areese@gotomail.net>
발신: Doris Kim <dkim@eureek.com>
날짜: 8월 28일
제목: 회신: 요금 반환

Mr. Reese께,

Eureek Finservices에 연락해 주셔서 감사 드립니다. —[1]—. 귀하의 요금 반환 요청을 확인했으며, 해당 요금에 검토 요청 표시를 해놓았습니다. 잘 처리된다면, 7650으로 끝나는 귀하의 당좌 예금 계좌로 원금 112.50 달러가 입금됩니다. —[2]—. 이에, 저희에게 바로 소식이 없더라도, 걱정하지 마시기 바랍니다.(153)

검토가 이뤄지는 동안, 저희는 업체에 연락해 귀하께 상품을 발송한 증거 자료 제출을 요청할 것입니다.(151) 만족스러운 증거가 제출되지 않으면, 검토작업에 대한 판결은 귀하께 유리하게 날 것입니다. —[3]—. Eureek Finservices의 책무는 귀하를 귀중한 고객으로 모시는 것입니다. 따라서 저희는 적시에 최상의 결과를 제공해드리기 위해 최선을 다할 것입니다. 향후 2주 내 새로운 소식을 받지 못하시는 경우, 저희에게 연락해 주시기 바랍니다.

지속적인 이용에 감사 드리며, 귀하의 회원 가입 10주년을 축하 드리게 되길 고대합니다!(152) —[4]—.

Doris Kim 드림, 고객 만족팀

151 이메일의 한 가지 목적에 해당하는 것은?
(A) 과정에 포함되는 단계를 설명하려고
(B) 신규 서비스 이용을 독려하려고
(C) 투자 기회에 관한 조언을 제공하려고
(D) 문의 관련 추가 정보를 요청하려고

152 Mr. Reese에 관하여 언급된 것은?
(A) Eureek Finservices의 전 직원이다.
(B) 집에서 소규모 온라인 사업체를 운영한다.
(C) 상당한 기간 동안 Eureek Finservices의 회원이었다.
(D) 이전에 신용카드 사기를 당한 적이 있다.

153 [1], [2], [3], [4]로 표시된 곳 중 다음 문장이 들어가기에 가장 적절한 곳은 어디인가?

"검토에는 최대 2주까지 소요될 수 있습니다."

(A) [1]
(B) [2]
(C) [3]
(D) [4]

154-155번은 다음 엽서에 관한 문제입니다.

연례 연등 축제

8월 5일부터 8월 11일까지, Oakman시에서 연례 연등 축제를 개최합니다. 전시되어 있는 정교한 수제 연등을 보실 수 있으며, 라이브 음악도 들으실 수 있습니다. 선택하실 수 있는 수많은 음식 가판대도 있을 것입니다. 올해 늘어난 강우량으로 인해, 연등은 Harbour Stadium에 대신 마련될 수도 있습니다.(154)

행사는 무료로 공개되므로, 온 가족 모두 오셔도 됩니다. 식사 구역에 있는 테이블은 4인석뿐이니, 일행이 많다면 이점 유념해 주시기 바랍니다.(155) 더 자세한 정보는 www.oakman.govt.nz/events/lantern을 방문해 주시기 바랍니다.

이곳에 우표를 붙이세요

_____
_____
_____
_____

154 축제에 대하여 언급된 것은 무엇인가?
(A) 장소가 바뀔 수 있다.
(B) 참석자 수가 늘어났다.
(C) 텔레비전에 소개됐다.
(D) 주차도 제공한다.

155 대규모 일행에 관하여 알 수 있는 것은 무엇인가?
(A) 주최측에 사전에 알려야 한다.
(B) 음식 주문 시 할인을 받을 수 있다.
(C) 참가비가 부과될 수 있다.
(D) 서로 다른 테이블에서 먹어야 할 수도 있다.

156-157번은 다음 문자메시지 대화에 관한 문제입니다.

Toby Norton [오전 8시 12분]
제가 몸이 안 좋아서요. 오늘 사무실에 못 나갈 것 같아요.(156)

May Kim [오전 8시 13분]
안 됐네요, Toby. 그러면, 못 나오시는 동안 팀에서 뭘 처리해야 하죠?

Toby Norton [오전 8시 14분]
네. 내년에 함께 개최하는 콘퍼런스 건을 논의하러 현지 사업체에서 방문할 예정이에요. 오전 10시에 모두 만나기로 되어 있어요.(156)

May Kim [오전 8시 15분]
참여 업체 수 때문에 적절한 회의 날짜를 찾느라 아주 힘들었던 걸로 알아요. 일정을 변경할 가능성이 있나요? 아니면 당신 자리에 누군가를 보낼까요?

Toby Norton [오전 8시 17분]
이 회의는 연기하고 싶지 않아요. 새로운 날짜를 찾는데 몇 주는 걸릴 수 있어요. Sarah Ogilvy를 대신 참석하게 하는 건 어때요? 이 프로젝트를 아주 가까이서 지켜봐 왔어요.(157)

May Kim [오전 8시 19분]
알았어요. 지금 그녀를 초대할게요.(157)

156 Mr. Norton에 관하여 알 수 있는 것은?

(A) 사무실 근처에 거주한다.

(B) 다음 주에 휴가 갈 예정이다.

(C) 최근에 승진했다.

(D) 회의에 참석할 수 없다.

157 오전 8시 19분에, Ms. Kim이 "알았어요"라고 할 때 무엇을 의미하겠는가?

(A) 대신 회의에 참석할 것이다.

(B) Ms. Ogilvy가 참여해야 할지 확신이 서지 않는다.

(C) Mr. Norton의 제안에 동의한다.

(D) 일정을 다시 잡는 게 더 낫다고 생각한다.

158-160번은 다음 안내문에 관한 문제입니다.

Douglas EasyBooks

Douglas EasyBooks 회계 프로그램 구매를 축하 드립니다.(159) 저희 응용 프로그램은 귀하의 시간을 절감해주어, 귀하의 사업체가 최고가 되는 데 집중할 수 있게 해줄 것입니다.(160)

이번 구매로, 귀하의 사업체는 무료로 교육 세미나를 받으실 수 있습니다.(158) 3회로 구성된 이 온라인 교육 시리즈는 소프트웨어를 효과적으로 사용하는 방법에 관해 직원들을 교육할 수 있는 아주 좋은 방법입니다.

짧지만 유익한 이 세미나는 자사에서 업무를 간소화하는데 저희 제품을 활용한 강사들에 의해 실시됩니다.(159) 교육 세미나를 예약하시려면, 오늘 Douglaseasybooks.com/training에 로그인해 주세요.

---

158 안내문의 목적은 무엇인가?

(A) 강사들을 모집하기 위해

(B) 신간도서를 광고하기 위해

(C) 요금에 대하여 설명하기 위해

(D) 서비스에 대하여 설명하기 위해

159 안내문에 따르면, 강사들은 어떤 자격을 갖추고 있는가?

(A) 경제학 석사학위가 있다.

(B) Douglas' EasyBooks에서 장기간 근무해왔다.

(C) 회계 프로그램 개발을 도왔다.

(D) 회계 프로그램을 사용해본 경험이 있다.

160 첫 번째 단락, 두 번째 줄의 단어 "focus"와 의미상 가장 가까운 것은?

(A) 집중하다

(B) 지시하다

(C) 조정하다

(D) 채택하다

161-163번은 다음 보도자료에 관한 문제입니다.

보도 자료

Leonard Osgard

홍보이사, Windermere Partners

losgard@windermerep.com

Marina (2월 15일) — Windermere Partners는 자사 신규 쇼핑구역, Marina Square의 개관을 자랑스럽게 발표합니다. —[1]—. 대부분의 점포가 판매되었지만, 10곳의 소매 점포가 아직 판매 중입니다.(161)

모든 소매 공간은 선반, 작업대, 그리고 파티션과 같은 별도의 요소들을 추가할 옵션이 있어 여러분이 취향에 맞게 설계할 수 있도록 개방형 평면도로 제공됩니다. —[2]—. 또한, 모든 상점은 쇼핑센터에서 제공하는 무료 무선 인터넷과, 사업장을 밤낮으로 안전하게 지켜줄 보안순찰대, 그리고 현장 청소 및 유지보수 지원 혜택을 비롯해 기타 다른 편의 사항들을 누리실 수 있을 것입니다.(162)

Marina Square는 단순한 쇼핑센터 그 이상입니다. 훌륭한 복합 오락 공간이기도 합니다. —[3]—. 다수의 파인다이닝 공간과 온 가족이 참여할 수 있는 다양한 액티비티를 갖춘 Marina Square는 도시 내 새로운 명소가 될 것입니다.

Marina Square에 오셔서 부담 없이 한 번 둘러보세요. —[4]—. 개별 상담을 원하시면, 710-555-6214로 전화하셔서 상담예약을 하시기 바랍니다.(163)

---

161 Windermere Partners는 어떤 종류의 사업체이겠는가?

(A) 홍보 회사

(B) 건축 자재 제조사

(C) 사설 보안회사

(D) 상업 부동산 개발회사

162 소매 공간에 관하여 언급된 것은 무엇인가?

(A) 창고 공간을 포함한다.

(B) 몇몇 서비스를 이용할 수 있다.

(C) 환경친화적으로 설계된다.

(D) 단기로 임대될 수 있다.

163 [1], [2], [3], [4]로 표시된 곳 중 다음 문장이 들어가기에 가장 적절한 곳은 어디인가?

"저희는 공개를 매일 오전 11시에 시작하여 오후 5시까지 합니다."

(A) [1]

(B) [2]

(C) [3]

(D) [4]

164-167번은 다음 기사에 관한 문제입니다.

NEW YORK (4월 2일) — 어제 오후, 판사 John Reinsdorf는 일부 전문가들의 반대에도 불구하고 국내 시장을 선도하는 두 회계법인의 합병이 진행되어도 좋다고 판결했다. 이는 Markkanen & Associates와 Donovan ELX가 이제 자유롭게 30만명 이상의 직원을 보유한 국내 최대 회계법인을 구성할 수 있다는 것을 의미한다.(164)

Markkanen의 Spencer Mitchell은 "이 두 회사가 힘을 합칠 때 일어날 일이 기대됩니다."라고 말했는데, 그는 Markkanen-Donovan으로 알려질 새로운 회사의 CEO가 될 가능성이 높다. "우리는 엄청난 양의 노하우와 놀라울 정도로 다양한 고객 포트폴리오를 2개나 가지고 있습니다. 이 변화는 New York과 Los Angeles 지점을 유지시켜줄 뿐만 아니라, 우리의 영향력을 전 세계로 넓혀 나갈 수 있도록 해줄 것입니다.(167) 우리는 내년에 미국을 벗어나 싱가포르에 새 지사를 설립하는 것을 검토 중입니다."(165)

Mitchell은 자선사업, 특히 소액 대출을 통해 개발도상국의 영세기업을 지원해주는 활동으로 전국 언론사의 관심을 끌었다.(166)

Mitchell은 Markkanen-Donovan이 각 회사의 전 직원을 유지할 계획이라고 밝혔다. 그는 "모든 부서가 회사에 기여할 필수 기술을 가지고 있습니다."라고 설명했다.

---

164 이 기사의 주요 목적은 무엇인가?

(A) 새로운 조세규정을 설명하기 위해

(B) 두 회사의 합병에 관해 보도하기 위해

(C) 법률 소송에 대해 논의하기 위해

(D) 회계 서비스를 광고하기 위해

165 Markkanen-Donovan은 무엇을 할 계획인가?

(A) 자금 대출

(B) 이사회 선거 주최

(C) New York 지점 중 한 곳의 폐쇄

(D) 다른 나라로의 확장

166 Mr. Mitchell에 관하여 알 수 있는 것은?
(A) 전국적으로 알려져 있다.
(B) 은행원이었다.
(C) Los Angeles에서 근무한다.
(D) 작은 사업체를 소유하고 있다.

167 두 번째 단락, 열한 번째 줄의 단어 "reach"와 의미상 가장 가까운 것은?
(A) 길이
(B) 도착
(C) 영향력
(D) 연장

168-171번은 다음 이메일에 관한 문제입니다.

발신: n.sullivan@raiden.com
수신: Raiden 직원
제목: 파이프 건 진행상황
날짜: 11월 15일, 일요일
첨부: 워크숍 문서

모두 안녕하세요.

기술자가 손상된 수도관을 교체하는 작업이 계획보다 오래 걸려 화요일에도 건물을 이용할 수 없을 예정입니다. (168)/(169) 새로운 소식이 있는지 이메일을 정기적으로 확인해주십시오. 또한 여러분은 고객들과 정기적인 연락을 유지하고, 그 밖의 다른 업무들을 자택에서 처리하셔야 합니다. (169)

반면, 저희는 화요일 워크숍을 다음주로 옮겨야 할 것입니다. 워크숍에서는 분기별 매출 및 수익에 대해 논의할 것입니다. 이와 관련된 자세한 내용은 이메일에 첨부된 문서에 있으니, 자세히 읽어주시기 바랍니다. (170) 논의 후에는, 세탁기 및 건조기 신규 라인의 성공적인 출시를 축하하는 전사차원의 저녁식사 자리가 있을 예정입니다. (171)

마지막으로, 저는 여러분 모두의 인내와 헌신에 감사 드립니다. 이번 수리가 예측하지 못한 어려움을 야기시켰다는 것을 잘 알고 있습니다만, 저는 우리가 그것을 잘 헤쳐나갈 것이라고 믿습니다.

Nancy Sullivan 드림
Raiden 사

---

168 수도관에 관하여 언급된 것은 무엇인가?
(A) 수리하는 데 비용이 많이 든다.
(B) 초반에 Ms. Sullivan이 점검했다.
(C) 몇 주간 누수가 있었다.
(D) 교체하는데 시간이 더 걸릴 것이다.

169 직원들은 화요일에 무엇을 할 예정인가?
(A) 다른 장소에서 근무할 것이다.
(B) 몇몇 사업체를 방문할 것이다.
(C) 휴가를 쓸 것이다.
(D) 사무실에 늦게 올 것이다.

170 Nancy Sullivan은 이메일에 무엇을 첨부했는가?
(A) 저녁식사 메뉴
(B) 고객 연락 명단
(C) 행사일정 달력
(D) 재무 보고서

171 Raiden 사는 어떤 종류의 업체겠는가?
(A) 자산관리 회사
(B) 가전제품 제조사
(C) 수도배관회사
(D) 회계사무소

172-175번은 다음 온라인 채팅 대화문에 관한 문제입니다.

Danny Sokolich (오전 8시 13분)
모두, 좋은 아침이에요. 제가 오늘 몸이 안 좋아서 재택 근무를 할 거예요. (172)

Amy Burrows (오전 8시 15분)
오늘 오후 1시에 시제품 건으로 회의가 있었어요. (173) 그건 어떻게 하죠? (172)

Danny Sokolich (오전 8시 17분)
화상 회의 자리를 마련해 주실 수 있으면, 화상으로 만날까요? (172)

Sean Evans (오전 8시 19분)
Ms. Berkahn께 도움 받을 수 있어요. 해외 공급사와 화상 회의를 많이 하셔서 경험이 많으세요.

Amy Burrows (오전 8시 21분)
Tessa Mulholland, Liam Jacobs도 참석해야 할 거 같아요. 저희가 진출하려는 시장에 대해 가장 잘 알고 계셔서, 그분들 의견을 들으면 정말 좋을 거예요. (173)

Danny Sokolich (오전 8시 23분)
그렇다면, 5층 회의실로 자리를 옮겨야 해요. 그래야 모두 수용할 수 있을 거예요. (175)

Jaimee Berkahn (오전 8시 24분)
제가 그 방에서 화상회의를 세팅해봤는데, 꽤 간단해요. 제가 회의 가기 전에 세팅할 수 있어요.

Sean Evans (오전 8시 24분)
제 마음을 읽으셨네요. (175)

Amy Burrows (오전 8시 26분)
Ms. Mulholland랑 Mr. Jacobs도 포함해 주세요.

Sean Evans (오전 8시 27분)
그분들이 시간이 되는지 확인해야 해요. 어찌됐든, 저희 5명한테는 새로운 장소로 초대를 보낼게요. (172)/(174)

Danny Sokolich (오전 8시 28분)
좋아요. 저희가 놓쳤을 지도 모르는 걸 그분들이 짚어 주실 거예요.

---

172 대화에서 알 수 있는 것은 무엇인가?
(A) 몇 가지 제품이 동시에 출시될 것이다.
(B) 작성자들은 서로 다른 국가에서 근무한다.
(C) 회의는 연기되지 않을 것이다.
(D) 계약서가 갱신될 예정이다.

173 작성자들은 왜 만날 계획을 세우겠는가?
(A) 회사 행사를 준비하려고
(B) 프로젝트에 대한 업데이트를 제공하려고
(C) 제품 출시에 대해 논의하려고
(D) 해외 고객과 만나려고

174 몇 명이 회의에 참석할 것인가?
(A) 3명
(B) 4명
(C) 5명
(D) 6명

175 오전 8시 24분에, Sean Evans가 "제 마음을 읽으셨네요"라고 할 때 무엇을 의미하겠는가?
(A) 회의 장소에 관해 Mr. Sokolich와 같은 생각이다.
(B) Ms. Berkahn의 도움이 필요하지 않다고 생각한다.
(C) 회의 시간을 변경하고 싶어한다.
(D) Ms. Mulholland와 Mr. Jacobs의 의견이 소중하다는 것을 알고 있다.

176-180번은 다음 공지, 양식, 이메일에 관한 문제입니다.

SUPPLY THE MASSES 콘퍼런스

제 3회 Supply the Masses 소비자 보충제 연례 콘퍼런스가 11월 4일 Hexagon 컨벤션 홀에서 개최됩니다. 이 콘퍼런스의 목표는 소비자 보충제 시장에 나온 주요 트렌드를 일부 다루면서, 호기심을 불러일으키는 개발 단계의 신제품을 몇 가지 소개하는 것입니다.

콘퍼런스에는 **Dr. Aria Bradford**가 특별 게스트로 참석합니다. 세상과 담쌓고 살고 계시지 않는다면, 많은 분들이 Dr. Bradford의 연구에 익숙하실 겁니다. **(176)** Thrillience의 설립자시고, 보충제의 효과적인 마케팅 방법을 주제로 책을 쓰셨습니다. 그녀는 자신이 거주해온 유럽에서 최근 겪었던 일들을 일부 공유해줄 겁니다.

Safer Supplements Alliance 소속 회원에게는 150달러의 등록비가 있습니다. **(177)** 비회원도 참여하실 수 있지만 대신에 200달러의 입장료를 지불하셔야 합니다. 9월 12일 이전에 자리를 예약하실 경우, 조기 예매 10퍼센트 할인을 받으실 수 있습니다.

SUPPLY THE MASSES 콘퍼런스

등록 양식

성: Graves **(177)**		이름: Nate	
날짜: 9월 19일		회원: 예: V**(177)** 아니요:	
회사명: RefresherFast**(180)**		직책: 관리자	
전화번호: +51 555 1995		팩스: +51 555 1996	
회사 청구서 발송주소: 459 Deerfield Drive New Bedford, MA 02740		이메일: n.graves@refresherfast.com	

수신: Nate Graves
발신: Ashraf Mackie
날짜: 9월 21일
제목: 회신: Supply the Masses 콘퍼런스

Mr. Graves께,

귀하의 요청사항을 검토해 보았으며, 전체 티켓이 매진되었지만, 귀하께서 티켓을 동료인 Ms. Leigh Nash께 이양하실 수 있음을 확인 드립니다. **(178)/(180)** 이는 예외 상황으로 인한 것임을 유념해 주시기 바랍니다. 하지만, Ms. Nash께서 Safer Supplements Alliance의 회원이 아니시기에, 회원용 티켓과 비회원용 티켓 가격 간 차액을 감당해 주셔야 합니다. 티켓을 발송해드릴 수 있도록 그녀가 가능한 한 빨리 마무리해 주시길 권장 드립니다. **(179)**

감사드리고, 추가 문의사항이 있으시면 저에게 말씀해 주세요.

Ashraf Mackie 드림, 행사 진행자

176 공지에서, 올해의 Supply the Masses 콘퍼런스에 관하여 언급된 것은 무엇인가?
(A) 음식 공급 서비스를 포함할 것이다.
(B) 호평 받은 연사가 참석할 것이다.
(C) 손님들에게 제품 샘플을 제공할 것이다.
(D) 온라인으로 실시될 것이다.

177 Mr. Graves는 자신의 콘퍼런스 등록비로 얼마를 지불했겠는가?
(A) 250달러
(B) 200달러
(C) 150달러
(D) 100달러

178 Mr. Mackie는 Mr. Graves에게 왜 이메일을 보냈는가?
(A) 정해진 결정에 대해 알려주려고
(B) 일정을 바꾸는 걸 제안하려고
(C) 프레젠테이션을 해달라고 요청하려고
(D) 추가 결제를 해야 한다고 요구하려고

179 이메일에 따르면, Ms. Nash는 무엇을 해야 하는가?
(A) 협회에 가입해야 한다.
(B) 이메일에 답장해야 한다.
(C) 신청서를 제출해야 한다.
(D) 지불해야 한다.

180 Ms. Nash는 어디서 일하는가?
(A) RefresherFast
(B) Hexagon 콘벤션 홀
(C) Thrillience
(D) Safer Supplements Alliance

181-185번은 다음 웹 페이지와 이메일에 관한 문제입니다.

---

www.adventureexcursions.com/self-drivingtours

어드벤처 여행: 남미
자주 묻는 질문: 자가운전 투어

비자가 필요한가요?(182)
유럽연합 시민의 경우, 여권이 유효한 한 특별 비자 없이 자유롭게 여행할 수 있습니다. 기타 국가 시민의 경우, 관련 정부당국에 최신 입국 요건을 확인하십시오. **(182)** 모든 여행자는 투어 첫 날 복사를 위해 여권을 제시할 준비가 되어 있어야 합니다. 이후, 국경 보안을 통과할 때마다 보여주도록 소지해야 함을 기억하시기 바랍니다. **(181)** 국제 운전면허증과 자동차 보험증서 또한 필요합니다.

차량을 어디서 픽업하고, 어디에 반납하나요?
도착하실 때 저희가 운전기사를 공항으로 보내드립니다. 거기서부터 직접 운전하시거나 지원차량에서 휴식을 취할 수 있습니다. **출국하실 때는**, 공항에서 저희에게 차량을 주시기만 하면 됩니다. 바로 비행기를 타는 게 아니라면, 공항으로 가는 교통수단을 직접 마련하셔야 합니다. **(183)**

어떤 정보를 알고 있어야 하나요?
각 여행에는 험난한 지형을 통과할 수 있는 튼튼한 사륜구동 차량이 제공됩니다. **여행 30일 전, 저희는 예상 이동시간 및 도로 상태, 예정 숙소가 포함된 최종 여행일정과 함께 정확한 제조사 및 모델에 관한 정보를 이메일로 보내드립니다. (184)**

무엇을 싸야 하나요?
다용도로 활용할 수 있는 옷을 가져오는 게 중요합니다. 해수면 근처의 습한 정글과 높은 고도의 눈 덮인 산꼭대기를 모두 경험하시게 됩니다. 그에 맞게 짐을 싸주세요.

수신: jorge_montero@adventureexcursions.com
발신: moira_oriordan@iemail.com
날짜: 4월 22일
제목: 자가운전 투어

저는 지난주 자가운전 여행을 예약했는데, 8월 7일부터 8월 19일까지 진행될 예정입니다. **(184)** 저는 알래스카의 꽤 외진 지역들은 탐험했었지만, 남미에는 가본 적이 없습니다. 장거리 비행을 하기 때문에, 여행이 끝난 후에 몇몇 장소들을 더 보고 싶습니다. 가능하다면, **Huascaran 국립공원** 근처에서 제 투어를 마무리하고, 그 근방으로 루트를 조정하고 싶습니다. **(183)** 그리고, 거기서 배낭여행 계획하는 걸 도와주실 수 있으신가요? 저는 며칠 간 추가 장비를 대여해야 할지도 몰라요. 저는 Cordillera

Blanca 산이 꽤 아름다운 걸로 알고 있습니다. 저는 제안을 환영하지만, **제가 그곳에 가기 전에 계획을 세우고 싶습니다.**(185)

Moira O'Riordan 드림

181 <어드벤처 여행: 남미의 자가운전 투어>에 관하여 알 수 있는 것은?
(A) 방문객들이 전통적인 관광보다 더 많은 장소들을 볼 수 있게 해준다.
(B) 대규모로 여행하는 사람들을 위한 것이다.
(C) 주로 날씨가 서늘한 장소들을 통과한다.
(D) 여러 국가로의 여행을 포함한다.

182 웹 페이지에 따르면, 여행자들은 투어 전에 무엇을 해야 하는가?
(A) 투어사무실로 가는 교통편을 준비해야 한다.
(B) 국제운전면허증 사본을 팩스로 보내야 한다.
(C) 비자가 필요한지 알아내야 한다.
(D) 특정 여행 백신을 맞아야 한다.

183 이메일에 설명된 대로 여행 계획을 변경한다면 Ms. O'Riordan은 무엇을 해야 하는가?
(A) 비행시간을 조정해야 한다.
(B) 다른 모델을 대여해야 한다.
(C) 추가 서비스 요금을 지불해야 한다.
(D) 공항으로 가는 방법을 마련해야 한다.

184 7월에 무슨 일이 있겠는가?
(A) Ms. O'Riordan이 상세한 투어정보를 받을 것이다.
(B) Mr. Montero가 Cordillera Blanca 산 투어를 이끌 것이다.
(C) Mr. Montero가 몇 가지 여행 서류를 복사할 것이다.
(D) Ms. O'Riordan이 알래스카에서 차를 빌릴 것이다.

185 이메일에서 일곱 번째 줄의 구 "figure out"과 의미상 가장 가까운 것은?
(A) 추론하다
(B) 평가하다
(C) 받아들이다
(D) 명확하게 하다

186-190번은 다음 광고, 이메일, 고객 후기에 관한 문제입니다.

Redtie 자동차 수리
저렴한 가격으로 최고의 서비스를

저희는 수리, 점검, 도장, 청소를 비롯하여 광범위한 자동차 서비스를 제공합니다. 승용차, 트럭, 밴 등을 포함해 온갖 종류의 차량에 맞춰 드립니다. 작업을 수행하기 전에 언제나 정직한 견적을 제공하는 것이 저희의 방침입니다.

또한 저희는 Total Autos와의 합병을 알려드리게 되어 영광입니다. **저희는 Redtie 브랜드 하에서 함께 나아갈 것이며, 새로운 로고 하에 Esmeralda 근교 지역까지 서비스를 확장할 예정입니다.**(186) Total Autos의 기존 고객은 모두 현재 진행 중인 계약 및 약정에 변화가 없을 것입니다. **현재 계약에 관해 궁금한 점이 있거나 다양한 계약 옵션을 살펴보고 싶으시면, Joseph Castillo에게 jcastillo@redtie.com이나 191-555-7915, 내선번호 7로 연락해 주시기 바랍니다.**(187)

특별 프로모션: 축하의 의미로, **7월에 체결되는 모든 계약에 15퍼센트 할인을 제공합니다.**(189) 기존 고객의 경우, 7월 청구서에서 15퍼센트가 이미 공제 처리되었습니다.

수신: Julia Campbell <jcampbell@pelzapaint.com>
발신: Hilda Cruz <hcruz@pelzapaint.com>
제목: 업데이트
날짜: **7월 18일**(189)
첨부: Ward_Warner_Info

Ms. Campbell께,

저희 회의에 기반하여, 제가 밴 네 대를 Redtie 자동차 수리점에서 정비받도록 보냈습니다.(188) 그쪽에서 새로운 색상으로 도장 작업도 진행할 예정입니다. 저희가 얼마 전 서명한 계약서에 따라, 수요일마다 주간 세차 서비스와 한 달에 한 번씩 점검 서비스를 받게 됩니다. **6개월로 계약했으니, 재계약하기 전까지 서비스 만족도를 지켜봅시다.**(189)

그리고, 신입 사원 Terry Ward와 Salvador Warner의 관련 양식을 전달해 드립니다.(190) 이들의 운전면허증과 은행 정보가 들어 있어요. 이들은 다음주에 교육을 받으러 올 예정이에요. 사전 경력이 있으니 교육이 오래 걸리지는 않을 겁니다.

Hilda Cruz 드림
총괄 관리자

Pelza Paint는 지역에서 신규 업체라, 크게 기대하진 않았어요. 하지만 저희 매장을 개조하면서 그곳에 연락해보기로 했죠. 몇 분만에 직원을 보내서 바로 작업에 착수하더군요. **도장공 Terry Ward는 전문성 있고 근면했습니다.**(190) 제 속마음을 꿰뚫어보고 일주일 정도 만에 작업을 마쳤습니다. 아주 합리적인 가격에 그토록 뛰어난 직원을 갖춘 Pelza Paint를 무조건 추천합니다.

Bruce Schultz, 8월 12일

---

186 광고에 따르면, Redtie 자동차 수리점에서 새로워진 사항은?
(A) 사업체 로고
(B) 계약 조건
(C) 웹 사이트
(D) 서비스 유형

187 Mr. Castillo는 누구겠는가?
(A) 영업 부장
(B) 고객 관리자
(C) 마케팅 전문가
(D) 수석 회계사

188 이메일에서는 Ms. Campbell과 Ms. Cruz에 관해 무엇을 언급하는가?
(A) 둘 다 Pelza Paint의 차량을 운전한다.
(B) 자동차 약정에 관해 이전에 이야기를 나눴다.
(C) 신규 밴을 구입하려고 계획하고 있다.
(D) 다음 주에 구인 공고를 올릴 예정이다.

189 Ms. Cruz가 이메일에서 언급한 계약 내용 중 무엇이 사실이겠는가?
(A) 6개월 후 갱신할 것이다.
(B) 아직 서명하지 않았다.
(C) 가격을 할인 받았다.
(D) 무료 수리를 포함한다.

190 Mr. Schultz가 받은 서비스에 관하여 알 수 있는 것은?
(A) 가장 저렴한 종류였다.
(B) 한동안 지연되었다.
(C) 신입 직원과 관련됐다.
(D) 3일도 안 돼 완료되었다.

Johnson 카운티, 수도관 보수작업 실시

(3월 12일) — 4월 한달 동안, Johnson 카운티 수자원 공사는 자치주의 수도시스템이 최적의 방식으로 계속 작동할 수 있도록 수 마일의 구리관을 새로운 폴리염화비닐(PVC)관으로 업그레이드할 계획입니다.

"더 강한 수압에도 견딜 수 있는 PVC 수도관은 세탁기, 식기세척기 및 다른 다양한 종류의 소비자 가전제품들이 더 잘 작동할 수 있게 해줍니다."(191)라고 Johnson 카운티 수자원 공사 감독관인 Mr. Sohel Khan 은 말합니다. "또한 새로운 수도관은 예전의 구리 수도관보다 더 적은 잠재적 환경 오염원을 내포합니다."

카운티에 있는 몇몇 도로들은 보수작업이 진행되는 24시간 동안 전면 봉쇄될 것입니다.(193) 수자원 공사 관리들은 업체들에 불필요한 문제 야기를 방지할 일정표에 동의를 얻으려는 희망으로 지역 상인들과 협의 중에 있습니다.(195) 일정은 계속 변경될 것이며, 이는 County Clerk 웹 사이트에서 확인하실 수 있습니다.(192) 주민들은 또한 County Clerk에 의견 및 우려사항들을 올릴 수 있습니다.

---

www.johnsoncountyclerk.gov

수도관 보수 일정:

4월 4일, 토요일	Antioch Street(193)
4월 5일, 일요일	Corinth Avenue
4월 11일, 토요일	Jameson Lane(194)
4월 12일, 일요일	Cherokee Drive

보수작업이 마무리된 후, Johnson 카운티 수자원 공사 직원이 수압 확인을 위해 귀하의 자택 또는 사업장을 방문할 것입니다.

수신: Ed Haber <eddie@eddiesbakery.com>
발신: Anita Quackenbush <quackenbush@johnsoncountyclerk.gov>(195)
날짜: 4월 1일
제목: 점검

Mr. Haber께,

아시다시피, 저희는 4월 11일 토요일 귀하의 점포를 지나는 도로 수도관에 보수공사를 진행합니다.(194) 그날 오전 약 4시간 동안 수돗물이 공급되지 않음을 예상하셔야 합니다. 이 작업으로 불편을 드려 죄송합니다. 수자원 공사 기술자는 수압이 적절한지를 확인하기 위해 다음날 오전 9시에서 11시 사이 귀하의 사업장을 방문할 예정입니다. 다른 시간으로 일정을 잡으셔야 한다면, 저희에게 555-1212번으로 알려주시기 바랍니다.(195)

Anita Quackenbush 드림

---

191 기사에 따르면, 새로운 수도관에 관하여 언급된 것은?
(A) 구리관보다 더 저렴하다.
(B) 일부 기기가 더 잘 작동하게 해 줄 것이다.
(C) 오전에 설치될 것이다.
(D) 자주 점검될 것이다.

192 기사에서 프로젝트 일정에 관하여 언급한 것은?
(A) 정기적으로 업데이트될 것이다.
(B) Mr. Khan이 만들었다.
(C) 일부 주민들이 찬성하지 않는다.
(D) 몇 가지 문제가 있다.

193 4월 4일에 무슨 일이 일어날 것인가?
(A) 새로운 카운티 서기 관리자가 임명될 것이다.
(B) 도로가 봉쇄될 것이다.
(C) 비즈니스 컨벤션이 열릴 것이다.
(D) 도시 퍼레이드가 있을 것이다.

194 Mr. Haber의 매장에 관하여 알 수 있는 것은?
(A) 일주일 동안 영업을 하지 않았다.
(B) 하루 24시간 영업한다.
(C) Jameson Lane에 위치한다.
(D) 최근 문을 열었다.

195 Ms. Quackenbush는 누구겠는가?
(A) 지역 사업주
(B) 건설 노동자
(C) 수자원 공사 기술자
(D) 공무원

---

www.nguyensportswear.vn/service

다음 정보를 작성해주신 후에, 자세한 의견을 적어주세요. 저희가 더 나은 서비스를 제공해 드릴 수 있게 해주셔서 감사 드립니다.

이름: Hassina Boulmerka
이메일: hassina.b@elwatan.vn
전화번호: 514-555-1212

의견:
저는 Ho Chi Minh City에 첫 오프라인 매장이 생겼을 때부터 Nguyen Sportswear에서 물건을 구매해왔고, 항상 만족했습니다. 이런 이유로, 가장 최근에 주문한 물건에 놀라고 실망했습니다. 스웨트셔츠가 도착했을 때, 딱 봐도 전보다 더 저렴하고 덜 편안한 재질로 만들어졌다는 게 분명했습니다. 설상가상으로, 겨우 몇 번 입고 나니 팔꿈치 쪽 소매 천이 닳아서 터져버렸습니다!(196)

수신: hassina.b@elwatan.vn
발신: ggruber@nguyensportswear.vn
날짜: 5월 23일
제목: 고객님의 의견

Ms. Boulmerka께,

귀하의 가장 최근의 경험이 긍정적이지 못했다는 것을 알게 되어 유감입니다. 훨씬 더 낮은 가격에 고객들이 요구하는 품질을 제공하려는 바람으로, 저희는 최근 일부 제조 공정을 다른 회사에 위탁했습니다.(197) 저희의 기준이 충족되지 않아, 저희는 현재의 방식을 재평가하는 중입니다.

초기 구매하신 물품가격에 해당하는 상품권을 보내드리며, 사과와 감사의 표시로 저희 인기상품 중 하나인 495-Z 스웨트셔츠도 무료로 드리고자 합니다.(200) 내구성이 강한 특별 직물로 만들어진 이 제품은(198) 극한의 환경을 견딜 수 있고 오래 사용하실 수 있음을 보장합니다. 이 이메일에 답장으로 원하시는 사이즈와 색상을 알려주세요.(199)

앞으로도 계속 저희와 거래해주시기 바랍니다.

Glenn Gruber 드림
고객서비스 직원

---

www.nguyensportswear.vn/products/Z

Z 시리즈는 운동 또는 야외활동에 완벽한 의복입니다. 이 멋진 스웨트셔츠는 다음 종류 중에 주문하실 수 있습니다.

제품 번호	스타일	가격
225-Z	크루넥	33.00달러
315-Z	브이넥	33.00달러
405-Z	버튼다운	41.00달러
495-Z	**후드(200)**	44.00달러

196 Ms. Boulmerka의 주요 문제는 무엇인가?

(A) 가격이 인상되었다.

(B) 제품의 품질이 저하되었다.

(C) 주문품이 늦게 배송되었다.

(D) 웹사이트가 작동하지 않았다.

197 Nguyen Sportswear의 일부 상품에 관하여 알 수 있는 것은?

(A) 다른 제품군보다 더 낮은 가격에 판매되었다.

(B) 다른 회사에서 생산했다.

(C) 선수용으로 디자인되지 않았다.

(D) 현재 재고가 없다.

198 Z 시리즈에 관하여 언급된 것은?

(A) 다른 제품들보다 더 빨리 닳는다.

(B) Ho Chi Minh City에서 제조되었다.

(C) 독특한 재료로 만들어진다.

(D) 최근에 새로운 옵션을 추가했다.

199 Ms. Boulmerka는 무엇을 하라고 요청 받는가?

(A) 주문 선호 사항을 알려달라고

(B) 매장에 들르라고

(C) 다른 신용카드를 사용하라고

(D) 의류제품을 반품하라고

200 Mr. Gruber는 Ms. Boulmerka에게 어떤 종류의 스웨트셔츠를 제공하는가?

(A) 크루넥

(B) 브이넥

(C) 버튼다운

(D) 후드

TEST 03

PART 5   P. 78

101 적합한 후임자를 찾을 때까지 Ms. George나 Mr. Baldwin 중 한 명이 이 사직을 맡을 것이다.

102 지역 내 중심 위치로 인해, Martenville에는 최대 규모의 열차 조차장이 있다.

103 Dr. Muniz는 목요일 오후 5시 15분에 환자를 진찰할 수 있다.

104 새로운 보건시설의 완공이 가까워지면서, Fitness First는 자격을 갖춘 개인 트레이너 채용으로 초점을 옮기고 있다.

105 도착시간은 교통상황에 따라 달라질 수 있기에, 표에 나온 일정은 예상치일 뿐이다.

106 Donnelly Curtains의 웹 사이트는 의도한 대로 확실히 작동할 수 있도록 품질 보증 전문가에게 철저하게 검사받았다.

107 Lisa Chen은 보도자료를 발표하기 전에 신중히 교정을 보았다.

108 실험실 관리자는 모든 화학약품의 올바른 보관을 확실히 해야 한다.

109 증가하는 석유 비용을 고려하여, 상품 판매 부서는 무료 배송의 이용 가능성을 줄이라고 권고받고 있다.

110 Canberra 사진작가 협회는 매우 뛰어난 구성원들로 이루어진 저명한 단체이다.

111 이 공지는 승객들에게 국제 항공편의 휴대용 수화물에 대한 규제사항들을 알리기 위함입니다.

112 고객 설문조사 결과는 대부분의 사람들이 Milkmade 딸기 요거트가 매우 만족스럽다고 여긴다는 것을 보여준다.

113 새로 출간된 Dana Sandoval 작가의 소설은 그녀의 작품 중 역대 최고로 평가받는다.

114 이 번역 문서는 원래 출처를 정확하게 반영하고 있는지 확인하기 위해 공식적으로 공증받아야 한다.

115 Min-hee Park는 신체 운동의 긍정적인 효과에 대한 자신의 연구를 인기 논픽션 영화로 만들었다.

116 그 회사의 생산라인에 대한 위생 관리 기준은 대부분의 다른 회사들의 기준을 뛰어넘는다.

117 Nature Free에서 새롭게 출시한 스킨케어 제품은 제형으로 수많은 상을 받았다.

118 배송품이 살짝 훼손되었기 때문에, 고객들은 다음 배송에 대한 상당한 가격 할인을 받았다.

119 Top Post 문구는 사려 깊게 만들어진 다양한 축하카드 및 선물들을 제공한다.

120 디지털 미디어 트렌드에 관한 전문성으로 인해, Ms. Kim은 마케팅 부서의 책임자가 되었다.

121 협회에서는 제대로 된 승인을 얻기 전 신약 사용을 승인하는 것을 당연히 주저한다.

122 Westmoreland Constructions의 신입사원은 안전 근무 규정에 관한 필수 교육을 받아야 한다.

123 Mr. Briggs의 프로그램 설명서는 새로운 소프트웨어에 익숙하지 않은 고객들에게 유익하다고 판명될 것이다.

124 저희가 도급업자의 측정치를 정오 전에 받는 한, 호텔 개조 견적서는 오늘 오후 발송될 것입니다.

125 인공지능 기술의 신흥 경쟁상대인 Mindsweep 사는 이미 주요 경쟁사인 ICM을 시장에서 넘어섰다.

126 프로젝트 담당자들 중 충분한 경력을 가진 사람이 아무도 없었기에, 프로젝트 관리자 직책이 Youngstown Marketing의 웹 사이트에 공고로 올라왔다.

127 많은 식료품점에서는 충분한 멤버십 포인트를 획득한 단골 고객에게 전자제품 같은 경품을 제공한다.

128 접수 담당자가 막 퇴근하려고 할 때 사무용품 배송품이 도착했다.

129 비 오는 날씨에도 불구하고 Fairfax로의 연례 회사 야유회는 계획대로 진행될 것이다.

130 심사위원이 심의할 충분한 시간을 남겨놓을 수 있도록 출품작은 대회 마감일까지 제출되어야 한다.

PART 6   P. 81

131-134번은 다음 회람에 관한 문제입니다.

수신: Tectonia 전 직원
발신: Brendan Chandler, 인사부 이사
날짜: 10월 15일
제목: 사보

사보 창간호가 이번 주에 이메일로 **131. 배포될 겁니다.** 앞으로 매달 첫 번째 월요일에 다음 호를 예상하실 수 있습니다. 사보의 주된 **132. 목적은** 직원들을 더 가깝게 만드는 것입니다. 매 호에는 다양한 부서 직원들의 프로필과 인터뷰가 수록될 예정입니다. 사보는 여러분의 동료들에 대해 조금 더 알아가는 출발점이 되어줄 겁니다. 사보가 여러분에게 **133. 흥미로우며,** 한 달을 기분 좋게 시작하는 데 도움이 되길 바랍니다. **134. 더불어, 창간호에 대한 여러분의 의견을 요청드립니다.** 의견이 있으면 저에게 이메일을 보내주시길 바랍니다.

134 (A) 사본은 추후 사용할 수 있도록 파일에 저장할 수 있습니다.
(B) 이벤트 초대장도 발송되었습니다.
(C) 더불어, 창간호에 대한 여러분의 의견을 요청드립니다.
(D) 공석은 게시판에서 열람할 수 있습니다.

135-138번은 다음 이메일에 관한 문제입니다.

수신: Dominic Powell <dpowell@iu.edu>
발신: Curtis Branson <branson@edental.com>
날짜: 10월 27일
제목: 환자 알림 서비스

Mr. Powell께,

최대한 효율적이고도 편리하게 환자분들을 **135. 모시려는** 바람으로, 저희는 휴대폰 앱을 이용하여 알림과 공지를 받아보실 수 있는 혜택을 제공하기 시작했습니다. 현재 저희는 이메일 주소로 귀하께 최신정보를 보내드리고 있습니다. **136. 이 방식에 만족하신다면, 그 어떤 변경도 없을 것입니다.** 귀하께서 앱을 사용해보고 싶거나, 저희가 드리는 알림 서비스의 **137. 선택사항들에** 대해 상의하고 싶으시면, 858-555-1212번으로 전화해 주시기 바랍니다.

138. 저희의 목표는 환자분들께 치과 치료와 관련된 모든 것에 관한 시기적절하고 유용한 정보를 제공하고 항상 최상의 치료 경험을 보장해드리는 것입니다.

Curtis Branson
사무장
Lenexa Elite 치과

136 (A) 저희는 저희 병원이 이 지역에서 최고라고 믿습니다.
(B) 적어도 일년에 한 번 방문 일정을 잡는 것을 기억하십시오.
(C) 이메일 알림 서비스는 작년에 처음 시작됐습니다.
(D) 이 방식에 만족하신다면, 그 어떤 변경도 없을 것입니다.

139-142번은 다음 공지에 관한 문제입니다.

인사팀에서는 전 직원 여러분께서 자기 계발 계획서를 작성해 주시기를 요청 드립니다. 계획서의 목적은 여러분께 현재의 역할을 뛰어넘어 성장할 유연성을 **139. 제공해 드리는 것입니다.** **140. 결과는** 회사가 앞으로 어떤 핵심 역량을 갖게 될지를 저희가 파악하는 데도 도움을 주어, 장기적인 미래의 계획을 세우는 데 도움이 될 것입니다.

계획서의 첫 화면에서 회사 내 여러분의 역할 및 근속 기간을 입력하며 시작해 주세요. **141. 이 정보는 여러분이 어떤 옵션에 해당되는지 결정하는 데 이용됩니다.** 그런 다음 각 과정에 1부터 5점 사이로 평가하라는 안내를 받게 됩니다. **142. 또한,** 모든 항목을 공란으로 비워 두지 마세요. 이는 시스템에서 결과를 합산할 때 예기치 못한 문제를 야기할 수 있습니다.

141 **(A) 이 정보는 여러분이 어떤 옵션에 해당되는지 결정하는 데 이용됩니다.**
(B) 각 과정의 비용은 하단에서 확인할 수 있습니다.
(C) 문제는 Ms. Siemen에게 전달되어야 합니다.
(D) 이 시스템은 올해 처음으로 시험되고 있습니다.

143-146번은 다음 이메일에 관한 문제입니다.

수신: jake.fowler@crimpmail.com
발신: order@esmondesoap.com
날짜: 7월 12일
제목: 주문 20773051

Mr. Fowler께,

Esmonde Soap Company에서 **143. 주문해 주셔서** 감사드립니다. 귀하의 지불을 수령했음을 확인해 드립니다. 귀하의 주문은 이제 **144. 발송**을 위해 준비되고 있습니다. 일반 택배 옵션을 선택하셨다면, 상품을 영업일 기준 5-10일 이내에 받아보실 겁니다. **145. 연휴철에 이루어진 주문은 시간이 더 걸릴 수 있습니다.** 귀하의 물품이 창고에서 **146. 출발하면,** 물품을 실시간으로 추적할 수 있는 링크가 전송됩니다. 주문 관련 문의사항이 있거나 무언가 잘못된 부분이 있다는 생각이 드시면, helpdesk@esmondesoap.com으로 연락해 주시기 바랍니다.

이용해 주셔서 감사합니다.

Cassandra Nash 드림
Esmonde Soap Company

145 (A) 이 경우 취소 수수료가 부과됩니다.
(B) 문의 사항은 당사 영업 담당자에게 전달해야 합니다.
(C) 연휴철에 이루어진 주문은 시간이 더 걸릴 수 있습니다.
(D) 우리 창고는 전국에 걸쳐 있습니다.

PART 7

P. 85

147-148번은 다음 정보에 관한 문제입니다.

대중의 요구로 인해, 이제 저희 로열티 프로그램이 더 이상 Baroque 호텔 한 지점에만 한정되지 않게 됩니다. 대신에, 전국 어느 지점에서나 포인트를 이용할 수 있습니다. **(147)/(148)** 지금 무료 객실 업그레이드, 룸 서비스 할인, 전용 운동시설 및 수영장을 이용해 보세요. **(147)** 준비 중에 있는 추가 서비스도 많으니, 저희 웹 사이트 www.baroquehotels.com에서 최신 업데이트를 확인하세요.

제공 서비스 목록에 대한 더 자세한 정보나 설명이 필요한 부분이 있으시면, 문의사항을 이메일로 보내주세요. 또한 저희 직원과 연결해드리는 모바일 앱도 이용할 수 있습니다.

Baroque 호텔을 선택해 주셔서 감사합니다.

147 정보는 누구를 대상으로 하겠는가?
(A) 웹 개발 직원
(B) 프론트데스크 직원
(C) 호텔 손님
(D) 시설 관리자

148 정보에 따르면, Baroque 호텔은 최근 무엇을 변경했는가?
(A) 프로그램 제한 규정
(B) 레스토랑 서비스
(C) 투숙객 이용시설
(D) 객실 가격

149-150번은 다음 양식에 관한 문제입니다.

RK Co.

고객: Top Ten 전자
주소: Cleveland Rd. 446번지
수신: Angela Martin

거래해 주셔서 다시 한번 감사 드립니다. 아래는 10월 30일에 이용하신 서비스에 대한 청구서입니다. 문제가 있으시면, 언제든지 Gerry Martin에게 (555) 212-9891로 전화하시기 바랍니다. **(150A)**

서비스/제품**(149)**	수량**(149)**	개당 가격	가격
부속품	수도꼭지(황동) x20	20달러	400달러
파이프 설치	L자관(구리) x10**(150C)**	25달러	250달러
설비 교체	개수대(도자기) x4	40달러	160달러
공임	35시간**(150D)**	25달러/시간	875달러
	총 1,685달러		

149 RK Co.는 무엇이겠는가?
(A) 전기회사
(B) 배관업체
(C) 철물점
(D) 금속 제조업체

150 어떤 정보가 포함되지 않았는가?
(A) RK Co. 담당직원
(B) 관여 직원의 수
(C) 구매된 파이프의 종류
(D) 프로젝트 기간

151-152번은 다음 설명서에 관한 문제입니다.

Rison 전자를 선택해주셔서 감사합니다! 귀하의 상품을 등록하려면, **(151)** 다음의 단계를 따라주시기 바랍니다.

1. 저희 웹 사이트 www.risonelectronics.com/product_registration 을 방문하십시오.
2. **제품 상자에 포함된 임시 ID와 비밀번호로 로그인 하십시오. (152)**
3. 귀하의 이름과 이메일 주소를 포함하여 양식을 작성하십시오. 구입일자와 최초 구입한 국가 역시 입력하셔야 합니다. 그 다음, 귀하가 구입한 제품의 시리얼넘버를 입력하세요. 시리얼넘버는 설명서 마지막 페이지에 있습니다.
4. 그리고 나면, 개인 ID와 비밀번호를 만들라는 안내를 받게 되실 겁니다. **(152)** 귀하의 계정에 접속할 때마다 이 정보를 이용하십시오.
5. 작성이 모두 완료되면, "제출" 버튼을 클릭하십시오. 귀하의 상품은 이제 저희 보증서비스에 등록되었습니다.

RISON 전자

151 설명서는 누구를 대상으로 하겠는가?
(A) Rison 전자 직원
(B) 제품 개발자
(C) 신규 고객
(D) 품질 검사관

152 독자는 무엇을 하라고 요청받는가?
(A) 보증기간을 연장하라고
(B) 로그인 정보를 갱신하라고
(C) 몇몇 파일을 다운로드 하라고
(D) 설문조사를 작성하라고

153-154번은 다음 문자 메시지 대화에 관한 문제입니다.

Barret Hansen (오후 2시 26분)
저기, Melissa. David Butler가 내일 하려고 했던 Westford 센터 투어를 취소했어요.

Melissa Cloud (오후 2시 29분)
아쉽네요. 그분 회사 기념 행사 장소로 완벽한 것 같은데 말이죠. **(153)** 새로 약속을 잡았나요?**(154)**

Barret Hansen (오후 2시 30분)
네. 다음 주 월요일이에요, Grocer 사 시상식 연회 일정에 관한 전화회의 이후로요.**(153)/(154)** 회의가 3시니까, 준비하고 합류하시는 데 시간이 충분할 거예요.

Melissa Cloud (오후 2시 31분)
좋아요.**(154)** 오늘 Grocer 사에 전화해서 다시 안내 좀 해주시겠어요?

Barret Hansen (오후 2시 31분)
알았어요.

153 Ms. Cloud의 직업은 무엇이겠는가?
(A) 시설 관리 근로자
(B) 식당 지배인
(C) 행사 기획자
(D) 인사 담당자

154 오후 2시 31분에, Ms. Cloud가 "좋아요"라고 할 때 무엇을 의미하겠는가?
(A) 시설을 방문하고 싶다.
(B) Mr. Butler와 통화하는 것이 기대된다.
(C) 프로젝트의 진행이 만족스럽다.
(D) Mr. Hansen의 일처리에 만족한다.

155-157번은 다음 청구서에 관한 문제입니다.

DeLaurentis 보안 시스템

청구 번호: AHD84-1113
예약일: 3월 25일
청구 대상: Antonia Brown (3월 31일까지 지불)

현장 상담 (2시간, 35달러/시간당)	70.00달러
지역 외 서비스 요청	50.00달러**(155)**
소계	120.00달러
추천 코드(25퍼센트 할인)	24.00달러**(156)**
총 주문액	96.00달러

예약에 관한 귀하의 의견을 저희에게 알려주세요! 오늘 저희 모바일 앱 DL Secure로 Sonya Young의 서비스에 대한 피드백을 저희에게 보내주세요.**(157)** 청구 절차와 관련하여 우려사항이 있으시거나 더 많은 정보가 필요하시면, Thomas Nwamba에게 tnwamba@delaurentissecuritysys.com으로 연락해 주십시오.

155 청구서에서 언급된 것은?
(A) 3월 31일에 발행되었다.
(B) 현장 서비스 요금이 부과되었다.
(C) 상담료가 최근 인상되었다.
(D) 민간기업에게 제공되었다.

156 Ms. Brown은 왜 할인을 받았겠는가?
(A) 전에 회사에서 제품을 구입한 적이 있다.
(B) 주문이 3월 프로모션 기간에 이루어졌다.
(C) 상담이 3시간을 넘지 않았다.
(D) 이전 고객이 그녀에게 서비스를 추천했다.

157 누가 상담을 제공했겠는가?
(A) Ms. Brown
(B) Mr. DeLaurentis
(C) Ms. Young
(D) Mr. Nwamba

158-160번은 다음 광고에 관한 문제입니다.

Auckland 요리학교 학생들의 실습용 식당에서
저녁식사 이용 가능

금액 부담 없이 미식을 경험해보고 싶으신가요? —[1]—.

Auckland 요리학교에서 단 10달러에 저녁식사를 만들어드립니다. 매월 첫째 주 내내 저희 학생들이 일반인들에게 음식을 요리해드립니다. 실습용 식당의 운영 경험은 저희 학생들에게 해당 분야에서의 소중한 경험을 제공해 줍니다. —[2]—. 식사 경험이 저희의 높은 기준에 부합할 수 있도록, 저희 최고 강사진 중 한 명이 식당에서 서비스를 감독할 것입니다.(158)

실습용 식당은 매월 마지막 주에 예약이 가능하나, 일찍 하시기 바랍니다. 저희 매장에는 테이블이 8개밖에 없습니다.(159C) —[3]—. Fork and Knife 앱을 이용해 마감되기 전에 예약하실 수 있습니다.(159A)

학생이 요리를 제대로 준비하는 데 시간이 조금 더 걸릴 수 있다는 점을 유의해 주시기 바랍니다.(159D) 또한 학생들은 실습용 식당의 조리법을 준수해야 하기에, 대체식단이나 특별 요청은 받을 수 없다는 점도 양해해주시기 바랍니다.(160) —[4]—.

---

158 Auckland 요리학교 강사들에 관하여 언급된 것은?
(A) 한 달에 일주일 근무한다.
(B) 어느 학생이 요리할지 결정한다.
(C) 실습용 식당에서 서비스를 감독한다.
(D) 학생들에게 안전교육을 해준다.

159 실습용 식당에 관하여 언급되지 않은 것은?
(A) 앱으로 예약할 수 있다.
(B) 야외 식사공간이 있다.
(C) 고객들이 앉을 공간이 많지 않다.
(D) 요리가 나오는 데 시간이 걸릴 수 있다.

160 [1], [2], [3], [4]로 표시된 곳 중 다음 문장이 들어가기에 가장 적절한 곳은 어디인가?

"이러한 이유로, 식단 제한사항이 있으시면 반드시 메뉴를 주의 깊게 확인하시기 바랍니다."

(A) [1]
(B) [2]
(C) [3]
(D) [4]

161-164번은 다음 안내 책자에 관한 문제입니다.

Rastlinn 기회 센터

소개
Rastlinn 기회 센터(RCO)에서는 사업체 운영에 필요한 기본적인 것들에 관한 수업을 제공해 지역 사업가에게 도움을 드립니다.(161) Rastlinn 내 기업 활동 촉진을 위해, 수업은 정부의 재정 지원을 받아 무료로 제공됩니다. 저희는 20년 전 설립 이래로 수천 곳의 사업체가 자립하도록 도왔습니다.

수업 그 이상을 드립니다
RCO에서는 수업 그 이상을 제공합니다. 같은 뜻을 가진 분들이 모여 만든 공동체에 가입하게 됩니다.(162) 또한 MediCare Now,(163C) Market Insights,(163A) Green Grocers(163B)처럼 저희 행사를 후원하는 유명 기업도 많습니다.(163) 저희 공동체의 일원이 되시면, 도시 내 최고의 기업가에게 배우면서, 중요한 관계도 맺을 수 있습니다.(162)

연락
RCO에서 제공하는 것에 관한 더 자세한 정보는 프로그램 매니저 Celia Flowers에게 cflowers@rastlinnco.com이나 303-555-6284로 연락해 주세요. 후원사가 되고 싶으시면, 후원 담당인 Israel Morrison에게 imorrison@rastlinnco.com이나 303-555-6259로 연락 주시기 바랍니다.(164)

지점
North Shore: 48 Ferguson Close, Rastlinn, Montana
City Central: 166 Westfield Estate, Rastlinn, Montana
West Harbor: 501 Doncastle Road, Rastlinn, Montana

---

161 RCO에서는 누구를 돕고 싶어 하는가?
(A) 채용 담당자
(B) 사업주
(C) 구직자
(D) 부동산 중개인

162 RCO에 관하여 언급된 것은?
(A) 공동체 유지를 목표로 한다.
(B) 작년에 설립됐다.
(C) 회비를 부과한다.
(D) Rastlinn 외부에 사무실이 있다.

163 안내 책자에서 RCO와 관련된 종류의 업체로 언급하지 않은 것은?
(A) 시장 조사 기관
(B) 슈퍼마켓
(C) 의료 시설
(D) 물류 회사

164 RCO와 협업하고 싶은 기업은 무엇을 해야 하는가?
(A) 수업에 참석해야 한다.
(B) Mr. Morrison에게 연락해야 한다.
(C) Ms. Flowers에게 이메일을 보내야 한다.
(D) 사무실을 방문해야 한다.

165-167번은 다음 편지에 관한 문제입니다.

Jean Rios · 15 Chandos Road · Coconino AZ 86046

7월 13일
Ronald Brown
Collective Images Ltd.
33 Shannon Gardens
Coconino AZ 86046

Mr. Brown께,

Collective Images Ltd.의 사진 작가 직책에 지원하고자 서신을 드립니다. 귀하의 편의를 위해 제 이력서와 포트폴리오를 첨부해 드립니다. 제 이웃 Morris Santos가 직책에 대해 알려주며 저에게 역할에 지원하라고 제안했습니다. Mr. Santos와 저는 같은 대학을 다녔고, 졸업 후 같은 일을 해 왔습니다. 그가 제 능력을 보증해 줄 수 있습니다.

간략하게 제 설명을 드리자면, 저는 열정 넘치고, 근면 성실한 사람입니다. 제 포트폴리오에서 광범위한 종류의 작품을 보실 수 있습니다. **처음 시작할 때는 인물 사진 작업만 했지만, 이제 현재 직책에서는 패션쇼와 개장식 같은 행사를 하고 있습니다.(165)** 제 사진에 대한 반응은 아주 좋았고, 수많은 출간물에 실렸습니다.(166)

저는 관리직을 더 맡고 싶기에 현재 직무에서 이동하고자 합니다. **제 상사에게 받은 업무 평가는 동료들의 선망을 받을 정도로 좋지만,(167)** 회사의 규모가 작습니다. 그곳에서는 현재 제가 찾고 있는 종류의 도전을 제공하지 않습니다. Collective Images에서 제가 가진 다양한 능력으로 커다란 이익을 얻게 될 것이라 믿으며, 제가 제공할 수 있는 것에 대해 논의할 기회를 얻을 수 있다면 좋겠습니다.

감사드리며, 제 지원서를 고려해 주시길 바랍니다.

Jean Rios 드림

---

165 Ms. Rios는 자신의 현 직책에 대해 무엇을 언급하는가?
(A) Ms. Rios가 자주 초과근무를 하도록 요구한다.
(B) 다양한 행사 참석을 포함한다.
(C) 지역 대학교의 후원을 받는다.
(D) 비교적 새로운 직책이다.

166 두 번째 단락, 네 번째 줄의 단어, "featured"와 의미상 가장 가까운 것은?
(A) 바뀐
(B) 지명된
(C) 지원받은
(D) (신문 등에) 나온

167 Ms. Rios에 관하여 언급된 것은?
(A) 새 직장을 위해 이동하려고 한다.
(B) 여러 다른 회사에 지원하고 있다.
(C) 추가 수업을 들을 계획이다.
(D) 자신의 상사에게 높은 평가를 받는다.

168-171번은 다음 문자메시지 대화에 관한 문제입니다.

Pablo Hammond (오전 8시 34분)
방금 Baldwin 가족에게 소식을 받았어요. 제가 주중에 날씨가 수그러들지 않을 지도 모른다고 그쪽에 알려줬어요. 이럴 경우 페인트가 마르는데 걸리는 시간이 대폭 늘어날 거라고 설명해줬어요. 그런데도 그들이 여전히 토요일에 하길 원하세요. [168] Andrea, 페인트가 얼마나 필요할지 대략 계산해 줄래요? [169]

Andrea Lowe (오전 8시 36분)
네. 제가 도와드릴 수 있어요. [169]

Pablo Hammond (오전 8시 38분)
Everett, 견적서 초안을 작성해 줄래요? 저희가 예전에 했던 작업으로 참조하면 돼요.

Everett Stephens (오전 8시 42분)
그럼요. 페인트 비용만 빼고 모두 채워 놓을게요. Peltier 브랜드로 사용하는 건가요?

Pablo Hammond (오전 8시 51분)
실은, 그분들이 해변가 바로 옆에 사세요. 더 강하고, 내구성 좋은 브랜드로 추천해드렸어요.

Andrea Lowe (오전 8시 52분)
집 크기를 바탕으로 필요한 페인트를 보내 드렸어요.

Everett Stephens (오전 8시 55분)
제가 견적서를 준비할게요.

Andrea Lowe (오전 8시 59분)
페인트는 목요일까지 여기로 받아볼 수 있어요. 제가 주문 넣을까요? [170]/[171]

Pablo Hammond (오전 9시 04분)
네, 그렇게 해주세요. Baldwin 주택으로 배송해주세요. 주문품을 받으러 집에 계신다고 하셨어요. [170]

Andrea Lowe (오전 9시 08분)
알았어요. 오후 5시쯤 도착할 거에요. [170]

Pablo Hammond (오전 9시 11분)
고마워요. 제가 그분들께 알릴게요.

---

168 Mr. Hammond는 어떤 종류의 사업체에서 일하는가?
(A) 디자인 회사
(B) 이사서비스 업체
(C) 부동산 중개소
(D) 도장업체

169 오전 8시 36분에, Ms. Lowe가 "제가 도와드릴 수 있어요"라고 할 때 무엇을 의미하는가?
(A) 지원이 필요할 것이다.
(B) 하루 종일 바쁠 것이다.
(C) 문서를 준비할 것이다.
(D) 새로운 회사를 제안할 것이다.

170 문자메시지 대화에 따르면, 목요일에 무슨 일이 있을 것인가?
(A) 일부 상품이 배송될 예정이다.
(B) 일부 가격이 변경될 예정이다.
(C) 계약이 체결될 것이다.
(D) 검사관이 Baldwin 가족을 방문할 것이다.

171 Ms. Lowe는 다음으로 무엇을 하겠는가?
(A) 동료와 상의할 것이다.
(B) 제품을 교체할 것이다.
(C) 면접에 참석할 것이다.
(D) 주문을 넣을 것이다.

172-175번은 다음 기사에 관한 문제입니다.

무제한 휴가?

Greg Waiters, 전속작가

근로자들은 종종 업무 스트레스로부터 벗어나 휴가를 떠나는 것을 꿈꾼다. 아쉽게도, 한정된 휴가 일수는 직원들에게 필요한 만큼의 휴식과 여가를 허용하지 않을지도 모른다. ―[1]―. 하지만 일부 회사에서 직원들에게 무제한 유급 휴가를 제공하기 시작했다. 이 제도가 회사에 불리하게 작용할 것처럼 보일 수 있지만, 긍정적인 영향을 주는 것으로 드러났다. 회사는 직원들이 더 열심히 근무한다는 것과, [173C] 핵심 인재를 채용 및 유지할 수 있다는 점, [173A] 그리고 사용해야 하는, 정해진 휴가 일수가 없으므로, 미사용 휴가에 대해 비용을 지급할 필요가 없다는 점에 주목했다. [173B]

이러한 정책을 실행하기 전, 고용주들은 반드시 이 제도가 모두의 이해를 기반으로 하고 있으며, 기대치가 현실적인지를 확실히 해야 한다. [172] ―[2]―. 이는 무제한 휴가가 각자의 업무 할당량에 대한 책임 축소를 의미하지 않음을 강조하는 것과 더불어, 자사 직원들에게 이 제도가 전반적으로 회사에 어떠한 이득을 가져다 줄 것인지에 대해 교육하는 것을 포함한다. 직원들은 휴가를 사용하는 올바른 절차에 대해서도 명확히 인지해야 한다. [175] ―[3]―. 고용주들은 이 부분에 대해 문제가 없도록 정기적으로 확인해야 한다. [174] ―[4]―.

---

172 기사는 주로 누구를 대상으로 하는가?
(A) 잡지 작가
(B) 법률 전문가
(C) 여행사 직원
(D) 회사 임원진

173 무제한 휴가의 이점으로 언급되지 않은 것은?
(A) 회사로 하여금 직원을 잃지 않게 해준다.
(B) 회사가 비용을 절감할 수 있도록 한다.
(C) 생산성을 증가시킨다.
(D) 직원들에게 재택근무 옵션을 제공한다.

174 기사에 따르면, 주기적으로 무엇이 이루어져야 하는가?
(A) 절차에 대한 검토
(B) 관리방식의 변경
(C) 교육 세미나
(D) 업무에 대한 논의

175 [1], [2], [3], [4]로 표시된 곳 중 다음 문장이 들어가기에 가장 적절한 곳은 어디인가?

"예를 들면, 직원들은 장기휴가 사용 시, 미리 휴가를 신청해야 할지도 모른다."

(A) [1]
(B) [2]
(C) [3]
(D) [4]

176-180번은 다음 광고와 이메일에 관한 문제입니다.

MANDY'S 모니터 마켓

Mandy's 모니터 마켓이 딱 5주년을 맞이했습니다.[176] 이를 기념하기 위해, 다음 한 달간 전 모니터 제품에 대해 할인을 제공합니다.

현재 저희가 보유한 제품은 다음과 같습니다.

모델	크기	가격
21-FTE	21인치	150달러
24-MWF	24인치	225달러
27-AYM	**27인치**	**270달러**[178]
29-KOZ	29인치	315달러

mandysmonitor.com을 방문하셔서 온라인으로 주문하세요. 496-555-3736으로 전화 주문도 가능합니다.

모니터를 두 대 이상 주문하시면, 무선 기능이 들어간 무료 키보드를 제공해 드립니다.[177]

주문 후 영업일 기준 7일 이내에 제품을 받아보실 수 있습니다. 추가 요금을 내시면 빠른 배송도 제공해 드리며, 48시간 내 주문품 도착을 보장합니다.

수신: Mandy's Monitor Market <help@mandysmonitor.com>
발신: Leah Dixon <ldixon@coullsmail.com>
날짜: 6월 17일
제목: 찬사

Mandy's Monitor Market에서 주문한 후 얼마나 만족스러운지 전하고 싶어 이 이메일을 드립니다.

저는 직장 때문에 최근 이곳으로 이사 왔고, 홈 오피스를 차려야 했습니다. 솔직히 제가 기계를 잘 다룰 줄 몰라서 걱정이 많이 됐습니다. **하지만 귀사의 웹사이트를 보니 저에게 필요한 것을 쉽게 찾을 수 있어서 다른 업체는 고려조차 하지 않았습니다.[179]** 제가 주문한 것에 270달러보다 훨씬 더 많이 지불할 줄 알았는데, 기분 좋은 깜짝 선물이었습니다.[178]

주문을 하고 나서 제가 집을 비우는 날짜로 배송일을 지정한 것을 깨달았습니다. 다행히, 고객 서비스 직원과 통화 연결이 돼서 배송일을 변경할 수 있었어요. 심지어 무료 키보드까지 보내 주셨죠. 모니터를 받고 나니, 이제야 제 홈 오피스가 완성됐고, 이렇게 행복할 수가 없네요. **미래 고객들을 위해 귀사 웹 사이트에 긍정적인 후기를 꼭 남길 겁니다.[180]**

Leah Dixon

---

176 Mandy's Monitor Market에 관하여 언급된 것은?
(A) 작년에 가장 성공적인 한 해를 보냈다.
(B) 최근 새로운 지역으로 진출했다.
(C) 특별한 날을 축하하고 있다.
(D) 인터넷에서 광고한다.

177 고객은 어떻게 무료 키보드를 받을 수 있는가?
(A) 제품을 여러 개 구매해서
(B) 양식을 작성해서
(C) 친구를 추천해서
(D) 코드를 입력해서

178 Ms. Dixon은 어떤 크기의 모니터를 주문했는가?
(A) 21인치
(B) 24인치
(C) 27인치
(D) 29인치

179 이메일에서 두 번째 단락, 세 번째 줄의 단어, "consider"와 의미상 가장 가까운 것은?
(A) 수량화하다
(B) 알아내다
(C) 고려하다
(D) 처리하다

180 Ms. Dixon은 무엇을 언급하는가?
(A) Mandy's 모니터 마켓에서 자신이 겪은 일을 글로 쓸 것이다.
(B) 가까운 미래에 직장을 옮길 것이다.
(C) 최근 새로운 집을 구입했다.
(D) 업무상 자주 해외로 출장 간다.

181-185번은 다음 공고와 이메일에 관한 문제입니다.

QMC 건설 솔루션 주식회사
Contreras 체험학습 프로그램

Rancho Cucamonga에 본사를 둔 QMC 건설 솔루션 주식회사는 Contreras 체험학습 프로그램(CWSP)에 참여할 15명의 전도유망한 학생들을 모집하고 있습니다.[181] 프로그램 참가자들은 San Bernardino, Riverside, 또는 Rancho Cucamonga에 있는 3곳의 QMC 시설들 중 한 곳에서 근무하게 될 것입니다.[185] 검토를 원할 경우, 학생들은 CWSP@qmcconstruction.com으로 자기소개서와 이력서를 보내야 합니다. 프로그램에 선발된 사람들은 다음 달 발행되는 <Inland Empire 비즈니스 저널>의 특집 기사에 실립니다.

프로그램 소개:
CWSP는 Anthony Contreras가 창설한 것으로, 그는 QMC 건설 솔루션의 원 소유자인 Guillermo M. Contreras의 업적을 기리고자 하였습니다.[182] 이 프로그램은 Guillermo Contreras의 정신을 받들어 젊은 건축학도를 양성하기 위해 만들어져,[184] 디자인과 건축 문제에 보다 효과적인 해결책을 모색하고 개발합니다. 건축학 석사학위 취득 후, Guillermo Contreras는 자신의 형제인 Edwin과 공동으로 QMC 건설 솔루션 주식회사를 설립했습니다. 해를 거듭하며 그는 소규모 회사를 남부 캘리포니아에서 가장 훌륭한 건설회사들 중 하나로 성장시켰습니다. **그는 35년간 경영 일선에 있다 올해 초 자리에서 물러났고, 자신의 조카 Anthony에게 자리를 물려줬습니다.[182]**

수신: Jerry Skakal <JSkakal@desertcollege.edu>
발신: Deanna Rogers <rogers@qmcbuilders.com>
날짜: 7월 14일
제목: 세부사항

Mr. Skakal께,

Contreras 체험학습 프로그램에 합격하신 것에 축하드립니다.[184] 귀하는 앞으로 수일 내 합격통지서 및 계약서를 받게 됩니다. 숙소에 대해 문의 주신 것과 관련하여, 저는 귀하가 매일 San Diego의 자택에서 두 시간씩 운전하여 통근하는 것을 원치 않으실 것에 전적으로 동감합니다만, 아쉽게도 저희는 프로그램 참가자들께 숙소를 제공해드릴 수가 없습니다.[183]

하지만, Riverside 사무실에 있는 프로그램 담당자 Rodrigo Carvalho와 이 문제에 대해 상의해 보세요. 그는 Riverside에서 태어나고 자라서, 아마 그곳의 저렴한 숙소에 대한 정보를 알고 있을 거예요. (185)

다시 한번 축하드리며, 저희는 귀하와 함께 일하기를 기대하고 있겠습니다.

Deanna Rogers 드림
HR 전문가
QMC 건설 솔루션 주식회사

181 공지는 왜 게시되었는가?
(A) 회사 프로그램을 홍보하기 위해
(B) 새로운 사장을 구하기 위해
(C) 건축 프로젝트에 대해 보고하기 위해
(D) 잡지 기사를 광고하기 위해

182 Anthony Contreras는 누구인가?
(A) 대학교 행정직원
(B) 회사 설립자
(C) 기업 대표
(D) 학생 인턴

183 Ms. Rogers가 보낸 이메일의 한 가지 목적에 해당하는 것은?
(A) Mr. Skakal의 계약서에 대해 논의하려고
(B) 부동산 중개업소를 추천하려고
(C) 문제에 대해 물어보려고
(D) 문의에 답하려고

184 Mr. Skakal에 관하여 사실인 것은?
(A) 건축학을 공부한다.
(B) 전에 Mr. Carvalho를 만난 적이 있다.
(C) 다른 사무실로 이동할 것이다.
(D) QMC 건설 솔루션을 고용하고 싶어한다.

185 Mr. Skakal은 어디서 일할 것인가?
(A) San Bernardino에서
(B) Riverside에서
(C) Rancho Cucamonga에서
(D) San Diego에서

186-190번은 다음 웹 페이지, 온라인 양식, 이메일에 관한 문제입니다.

Around the Bays Auckland 여행사
그룹 투어 정책

Auckland의 아름다운 해변 투어에 관심을 보여주셔서 감사합니다. 아래 예약 정책을 읽어 주시기 바랍니다.

· 투어 인원은 최소 15명에서 최대 45명입니다.
· **그룹 투어는 6시간 동안 진행되며 평일과 주말 모두 진행 가능합니다. 하지만 주말 및 휴일 투어에는 추가 비용이 발생합니다.** (187)
· **25명 이상의 투어 그룹인 경우, 귀하의 단체를 최선으로 수용할 수 있도록 한 달 전에 미리 예약해 주시기를 적극 권해 드립니다.** (186)
· 예약을 완료한 후, 5일 이내에 보증금 75달러를 지불해야 합니다. 그렇지 않으면, 저희가 예약을 취소할 권리가 있습니다.
· 다음 투어 그룹에 지연이 발생하지 않도록 모든 투어는 정시에 시작해야 합니다. 따라서 늦게 도착하는 경우에 대해서는 환불해 드릴 수 없습니다.

예약하시려면, 웹 사이트에 제공된 양식을 작성해 주십시오. 접수되면, 근무일 기준 하루 이내에 확인 연락을 받게 됩니다.

Around the Bays Auckland 투어
예약 문의 양식

이름: Garry Luna
연락처: (415) 555-7334
예약일: 2월 12일, 월요일, 오전 10시 (190)

내용: 안녕하세요. 제가 일종의 선물로 회사 앞으로 투어를 예약했습니다. 총 20명이고, 보증금만 지불한 상태입니다. (190) 그런데, 궁금한 게 있어요. 저희가 예약한 날이 공휴일이라서 투어를 진행하지 못한다는 걸 알게 됐습니다. 다른 날로 변경할 수 있을까요? (187) 또, 저희가 살펴볼 만한 활동 목록이 있는지 궁금합니다. 악천후인 경우, 날씨가 받쳐주지 않는다면 할 거리가 충분했으면 합니다. (188)

수신: info@aroundthebays.co.nz
발신: m.powell@aucklandtourgroup.co.nz
날짜: 1월 28일 수요일
제목: Around the Bays

팀원 여러분께,

경영진 측에서 일부 비용의 최적화를 시작해야 한다고 결정을 내렸습니다. 서비스 후기를 바탕으로, 우리 투어 그룹의 평균 규모가 약점이라는 것을 파악했습니다. 따라서, 다음과 같은 정책을 페이지에 싣기로 했습니다. (189)

· 25명 미만 단체인 경우, 다른 단체와 같은 투어 그룹에 배치할 수 있습니다. (190)

2월 7일까지 이 정책이 게시되도록 할 수 있나요? (190) 제가 다음주에 사무실에 가서 예약 방식이 어떻게 바뀔지 설명하겠습니다. 그 전에 궁금한 점이 있으면, 저에게 알려주세요.

감사합니다.

Milton Powell
지부장, Auckland Tour Group

---

186 25명 이상인 단체에 관하여 웹 페이지에서 알 수 있는 것은?
(A) 임박해서 투어 날짜를 잡지 못할 수도 있다.
(B) 전용 투어 패키지를 이용할 수 있을 것이다.
(C) 투어 전에 보증금을 더 많이 지불해야 한다.
(D) 단체 할인을 적용 받는다.

187 Mr. Luna는 어떤 정책을 잘못 알았겠는가?
(A) 보증금으로 내야 하는 금액
(B) 투어 시간 및 장소
(C) 특정 날짜 사전 예약
(D) 투어 예약이 가능한 날짜

188 Mr. Luna는 Around the Bays에 무엇을 알려달라고 요청하는가?
(A) 가용한 투어 가이드 수
(B) 투어에 포함되는 활동
(C) 이용 가능한 교통 수단
(D) 투어 요금 지불 시점

189 Mr. Powell이 보낸 이메일의 목적은 무엇인가?
(A) 현지 업체와 제휴를 맺으려고
(B) 서비스 사용에 관한 자료를 요청하려고
(C) 운영비 세부내역을 명확히 설명하려고
(D) 새로운 정책의 포함을 알리려고

190 Mr. Luna의 그룹 투어에 관하여 알 수 있는 것은?
(A) 다른 그룹을 포함할 수 있다.
(B) 할인받을 수 있다.
(C) 텔레비전에 방송될 수 있다.
(D) 새로운 경로를 따를 수 있다.

191-195번은 다음 광고, 이메일, 그리고 정보문에 관한 문제입니다.

MeiHua Bamboo

MeiHua Bamboo는 25년 간 최고 품질의 대나무 제품들을 중국과 전 세계에 공급해 온 것을 축하하게 되어 영광입니다!

대나무로 제작한 집과 가구는 그 아름다움과 내구성으로 인해 수천 년간 아시아에서 사랑받아 왔습니다. 건축 자재로서 대나무는 많은 주목할만한 특성을 갖고 있습니다.

1. **가벼움:** 대나무는 그 어떤 건축 자재보다 훨씬 가볍습니다. 이는 대부분의 대나무 제품들을 옮기고, 보관하고, 설치하는 데 힘이 덜 든다는 것을 의미합니다.
2. **견고함:** 대나무는 목재보다 훨씬 더 강합니다. 사실, 콘크리트보다 더 강한 압력을 견딜 수 있으며, 거의 강철만큼의 장력을 갖고 있습니다.
3. **쉬운 관리:** 대나무는 상당히 내구성이 좋고, 대부분의 목재보다 수분에 더 강합니다. 따라서 대나무를 청소하는 것은 어렵지 않습니다. 예를 들어, 대나무 바닥에 무언가를 흘리면, 마른 걸레로 닦아주기만 하면 됩니다.
4. **활용성:** 대나무는 그 견고함에도 불구하고 쉽게 절단할 수 있고, 다양한 형태로 변형될 수 있습니다. 이는 바닥재부터 캐비닛, 심지어 커튼에 이르기까지 집이나 사업장에 추가하고 싶은 제품은 무엇이든지 저희가 주문 제작해드릴 수 있음을 의미합니다! [191]/[193]
5. **친환경:** 대나무는 완벽히 재사용이 가능하며, 무공해 자원입니다. 남은 자재들은 쉽게 재활용되거나 안전하게 폐기될 수 있습니다.

수신: Giuseppine Nieddu
발신: Earl Doherty
제목: 대나무 조리대
날짜: 6월 27일

Ms. Nieddu께,

저와의 만남에 시간을 내주시고, 주문제작 대나무 조리대의 설계 제안서를 보여주셔서 감사드립니다. [193] 조리대는 이제까지 제가 본 것들과 다르고, 저는 그 조리대가 캐나다 내 신규 DDD 도넛 및 커피 체인점에 아주 잘 어울릴 거라고 생각합니다.

저희 회사 경영진도 같은 의견입니다만, 한가지 문의사항이 있습니다. 저희는 이 조리대 위에서 음식 및 음료를 준비하고 제공할 거예요. **표면을 보호할만한 적당한 화학 용액을 제안해주실 수 있으신가요?** [192] 당연히, 저희는 오랜 시간 동안 조리대를 깨끗하고 보기 좋게 유지해주되, 무엇보다 중요한 것은 음식 준비 및 섭취에 가장 안전한 환경을 제공할 용액을 써야 합니다. [195]

미리 감사의 말씀 드립니다.

Earl Doherty
Doherty's Donut Domain (DDD) 사

대나무 제품용 마감 옵션

마감은 대나무 용품 제작의 마지막 단계입니다. **마감은 아주 소량의 물, 먼지, 오일 입자만을 흡수하는 화학 용액으로 제품의 표면을 덧바르는 것입니다.** [194] 용액이 건조되면서, 사용 중에 생긴 습기나 박테리아로부터 원래의 표면을 보호해줍니다. 제품이 어떻게, 어디서 사용될지에 따라, 다음의 마감 제품들 중 하나를 선택하시면 됩니다.

재료	내구성	식품 안전
천연 왁스	약함	항상
수성 광택제	우수	보통
유성 광택제	매우 좋음	해당 없음
미네랄 오일	**매우 좋음**	**항상** [195]

191 MeiHua에 관하여 언급된 것은?
(A) 캐나다에 본사를 두고 있다.
(B) 주문제작 상품을 만들 수 있다.
(C) 올해 오픈할 것이다.
(D) 가구 세척 제품을 만든다.

192 Mr. Doherty는 왜 이메일을 썼는가?
(A) 배송을 미루기 위해
(B) 회의 일정을 잡기 위해
(C) 추천을 요청하기 위해
(D) 주문을 수정하기 위해

193 Ms. Nieddu와 Mr. Doherty는 MeiHua 대나무 건축자재의 어떤 특성에 대해 논의했는가?
(A) 특성 2
(B) 특성 3
(C) 특성 4
(D) 특성 5

194 정보문에 따르면, 마감에 필요한 것은?
(A) 매끈한 표면
(B) 특수 직물로 만들어진 천
(C) 시원한 환경
(D) 흡수율이 낮은 용액

195 DDD 사는 어떤 마감제품을 선택하겠는가?
(A) 천연왁스
(B) 수성 광택제
(C) 유성 광택제
(D) 미네랄 오일

196-200번은 다음 송장과 이메일들에 관한 문제입니다.

Trilland 컨설팅

8월 21일
고객 번호: 4882

지불 기한: 9월 15일 [200]

Milton Wood
374 Woodward Corner
Mylo, ND 58353

서비스 일자	내용	참조 코드	액수
8/2	1일 공정 분석	0095	480달러
8/6	1일 소프트웨어 구현	0075	1,050달러
8/6	**부서 교육**	0082 [198]	250달러
	총액 1,780달러		

귀하의 사업 요구에 Trilland 컨설팅의 북미 지사를 선택해 주셔서 감사합니다. [196] 저희 서비스에 만족하시길 바랍니다. 송장에 대해 문의사항이 있으시면, 청구 부서인 invoice@trillandconsulting.com으로 연락해 주시기 바랍니다.

수신: <invoice@trillandconsulting.com>
발신: Milton Wood <mwood@centurytale.com>
날짜: 8월 24일
제목: 문의

Trilland 컨설팅 담당자님께,

저는 최근 귀하의 그룹에서 컨설팅을 받았습니다. Paul Gibson이 주도했는데, 그분과 함께한 경험은 아주 놀라웠습니다. 저희가 고려했던 모든 사업 시스템을 구석구석 알고 계셨고, 저희가 결정을 내리도록 도와주셨습니다. **실은, 저희가 고려 중에 있는 다른 프로젝트에도 그분이 도움을 주실 수 있는지 알고 싶습니다.** (197) 9월 중 Mr. Gibon의 일정에서 추가 작업을 할 시간이 있을까요?

그리고, 제가 받은 송장과 관련해서 궁금한 점이 있습니다. **서비스 범위와 관련해 Mr. Gibson께 처음 연락했을 때, 저희는 1일 소프트웨어 구현 서비스가 교육에도 포함되는 걸로 안내 받았습니다. 하지만, 송장에는 저희에게 교육 비용이 추가 청구된 것처럼 보입니다.** (198) 이건 실수인가요, 아니면 Mr. Gibson께서 잘못 알고 계신 건가요?

감사합니다.
Milton Wood

수신: Milton Wood <mwood@centurytale.com>
발신: <invoice@trillandconsulting.com>
날짜: 8월 26일
제목: 회신: 문의

Mr. Wood께,

저희와의 경험이 긍정적이셨다니 기쁩니다. 실제로 9월 추가 컨설팅을 Mr. Gibson께 받으실 수 있습니다. 제가 그분께 알려드리면, 그분께서 세부 내용 파악차 조만간 귀하께 연락드릴 것입니다.

송장에 관해서는 Mr. Gibson이 맞고, 무료 교육이 포함되어 있는 것을 확인했습니다. 참조 코드상 오류로 인해 귀하의 송장에 표시된 것 같습니다. 송장에 더 이상 나타나지 않도록 제가 정정했습니다.

제가 이전 송장을 취소하고 한 시간 안에 최신본으로 보내드리겠습니다. (199) **또한 이 오류로 인해 지불 기한을 한 달 연장해 드릴 것입니다.** (200)

Faye May 드림

---

196 Trilland 컨설팅에 관하여 송장에서 알 수 있는 것은?
(A) 소프트웨어 기반 솔루션을 전문으로 한다.
(B) 현재 신규 컨설턴트를 채용 중이다.
(C) 여러 국가에서 운영한다.
(D) 소프트웨어 회사 몇 곳과 제휴를 맺었다.

197 첫 번째 이메일에 따르면, Mr. Wood는 무엇을 하고 싶어하는가?
(A) 추가 상담을 받고 싶어한다.
(B) 후기를 쓰고 싶어한다.
(C) 허가증을 발급하고 싶어한다.
(D) 회사를 방문하고 싶어한다.

198 Mr. Wood는 어떤 코드에 대해 염려하는가?
(A) 4882
(B) 0095
(C) 0075
(D) 0082

199 Ms. May는 누구겠는가?
(A) 컨설턴트
(B) 채용 대리인
(C) 청구서 발송 관리자
(D) 소프트웨어 엔지니어

200 Mr. Wood의 수정된 송장의 지불 기한은 며칠인가?
(A) 8월 21일
(B) 8월 26일
(C) 9월 15일
(D) 10월 15일

TEST 04

PART 5
P. 110

101 (A)	102 (C)	103 (C)	104 (C)	105 (C)	106 (C)
107 (D)	108 (B)	109 (C)	110 (D)	111 (D)	112 (D)
113 (A)	114 (D)	115 (A)	116 (B)	117 (C)	118 (D)
119 (A)	120 (D)	121 (C)	122 (C)	123 (A)	124 (C)
125 (C)	126 (C)	127 (B)	128 (D)	129 (A)	130 (B)

PART 6
P. 113

131 (C)	132 (B)	133 (C)	134 (C)	135 (D)	136 (A)
137 (A)	138 (A)	139 (A)	140 (B)	141 (D)	142 (D)
143 (B)	144 (C)	145 (A)	146 (D)		

PART 7
P. 117

147 (D)	148 (A)	149 (B)	150 (D)	151 (D)	152 (A)
153 (B)	154 (C)	155 (D)	156 (A)	157 (C)	158 (B)
159 (C)	160 (C)	161 (D)	162 (D)	163 (C)	164 (B)
165 (A)	166 (C)	167 (D)	168 (D)	169 (B)	170 (D)
171 (B)	172 (C)	173 (C)	174 (B)	175 (B)	176 (D)
177 (D)	178 (B)	179 (C)	180 (D)	181 (B)	182 (A)
183 (B)	184 (B)	185 (B)	186 (D)	187 (A)	188 (A)
189 (B)	190 (C)	191 (B)	192 (A)	193 (C)	194 (B)
195 (D)	196 (B)	197 (A)	198 (C)	199 (B)	200 (D)

PART 5
P. 110

101 Ms. Lam은 법률 문서를 제출하기 전에 관리자와 상의해야 한다.

102 Builders Safety Group은 설계도를 검토하여 건축가들에게 피드백을 제공할 것이다.

103 Mindworks 사에서는 인공지능 윤리 팀에 몇 가지 필수 개혁을 시행했다.

104 겨우 일주일 전에 일을 시작한 Ms. LaPointe는 다른 보조의사들을 따라가는 데 어려움을 겪었다.

105 Denson Tech는 이전 모델보다 더 강력하고 더 가벼운 새로운 진공 청소기를 출시했다.

106 연례 취업박람회 참석에 관심 있는 학생들은 등록 양식을 작성해야 한다.

107 국립 전시 센터에서 열리는 널리 광고된 기술 컨벤션은 많은 관중을 끌어 모으고 있다.

108 Peacock Publishers가 Arlington 지역에서 운영을 중단하면 약 250개 정도의 일자리가 없어질 것이다.

109 Arcadia 국립은행의 복원작업은 앞으로 3개월 안에 재개될 것으로 예상된다.

110 바람이 예상보다 빨리 바뀌지 않으면, Ms. Salina의 항공편은 제시간에 도착하지 않을지도 모른다.

111 유명 인사의 추천은 저희 핸드백이 얼마나 멋지고 유행하는 스타일인지 정확하게 보여줍니다.

112 재택근무하는 모든 직원에게 자격 조건에 부합하는 업무 경비에 대한 상환이 이루어질 것이다.

113 판매에 포함된 가전제품들은 여러 공장들에서 조립되었기 때문에 따로따로 도착했다.

114 Houston에서 열리는 컨벤션에 참석하는 직원들은 교통비를 결제하고, 영수증을 보관하고, 복귀 후 환불 신청서를 제출하라고 안내받았다.

115 건축업자들은 건설현장에 있는 동안 항상 안전모를 착용해야 한다.

116 회사 이메일에 도움이 필요하면 언제든지 IT팀의 Mr. Thapa에게 전화 주세요.

117 예전에 우리 법무 부장이었던 Mr. Belfort가 방금 법무 이사로 임명되었다.

118 이 세제는 비용에 타협하지 않고 모든 종류의 직물을 효과적으로 세탁하게 해 준다.

119 Mr. Ahn은 아침 TV쇼에서 자신의 공동 진행자들과 함께 전 세계 현안에 관해 이야기를 나눈다.

120 Pyreen 주방용품점은 어떤 요리를 제공하든 귀하의 식당이 순조롭게 운영되게 도와줄 것입니다.

121 Merriman의 정장 구두는 인조 가죽으로 만들어지지만, 천연 가죽보다 현저히 더 부드럽고 튼튼하다.

122 Mr. Conde는 제안된 건물 설계에 대한 회사의 요금이 너무 높은 것인지 결정할 것이다.

123 Hahn Telecommunications는 Kazakhstan에서 성공한 이후 서비스 구역을 중앙 아시아 전역으로 넓힐 계획이다.

124 수많은 최신 기능을 갖춘 THR의 피트니스 트래커는 확실히 가격만큼의 가치가 있다.

125 Flagstone 카페는 지난 10년간 일요일에 조식 판촉행사를 제공해오고 있다.

126 그녀의 미술 전시회에 관한 비평가들의 호평을 고려하면, Ms. Griffin은 조만간 국제적인 찬사를 얻을 것으로 예상된다.

127 구입한 제품을 다른 것으로 교환하고자 하는 Hill Sporting Goods의 고객들은 가격상 차액을 지불해야 할 것이다.

128 Winston Sparks의 오리지널 뮤지컬 속 거의 모든 곡이 주목할만하다.

129 Duchene 투자회사는 경험이 부족한 사업주들이 대출 신청하는 것을 돕기 위해 무료 상담을 제공한다.

130 월요일에 대표단 위원들이 도착하면, Mr. Nichols가 그들에게 시내 관광을 시켜줄 것이다.

PART 6
P. 113

131-134번은 다음 제품 후기에 관한 문제입니다.

저는 새로운 스프레드시트 소프트웨어를 사용하는 걸 **131. 망설였는데**, 저희가 현재 사용하는 것 같은 기능을 가진 건 없을 거라고 생각했거든요. 그런데, 저희 회사에서 Zoro로 바꾸기로 결정하면서 써보게 됐죠. **132. 기분 좋게 놀랐습니다.**

133. 제 데이터를 불러오는 방법을 파악하는 게 처음에는 어려웠습니다. 시간은 좀 걸렸지만, 매뉴얼에 비교적 잘 설명되어 있더군요. 그 다음에는 매출 예상치 도출 같은 고급 기능을 일부 사용해 봤습니다. 소프트웨어

에서 도출한 모델이 전에 사용하던 것보다 더 정확한 결과를 냈는데, 바로 그 이유로 저는 그 가격에도 불구하고 다른 업체들보다 **134. 그것을 추천**합니다.

빠진 기능들이 몇 개 있긴 하지만, 개발자들이 계속해서 업데이트 작업을 하고 있습니다. 솔직한 의견으로는 이런 식이라면 Zoro가 새로운 산업 표준이 될 것 같습니다.

133 (A) 저는 그것에 대해 더 높은 가격을 지불할 것으로 예상했습니다.
(B) 기존 기업은 이미 자체 소프트웨어를 보유하고 있을 수 있습니다.
(C) 제 데이터를 불러오는 방법을 파악하는 게 처음에는 어려웠습니다.
(D) Zoro는 과거에 일부 간행물에 실렸습니다.

135-138번은 다음 기사에 관한 문제입니다.

<안전 장치 및 예방 조치>

국립 조각 갤러리(NSG)는 전시 환경을 세심히 **135. 모니터링**하여 전시 중인 귀중한 작품을 보호하기 위해 최선을 다하고 있습니다. 나무로 만들어진 작품들은 덥고 건조한 환경에 취약합니다. **136. 따라서,** 갤러리에서는 모든 구역의 온도를 엄격히 통제합니다. 또한, 우기로 인한 **137. 습도**로 인해 여름에는 외부에 작품을 전시하지 않습니다. **138. 또한, 전시 중인 작품을 만지지 마십시오.** 저희는 귀중한 소장품을 지키려 이러한 노력을 함으로써, 역사와 국가의 유산을 먼 미래까지 보존되길 바랍니다.

---

138 **(A) 또한, 전시 중인 작품을 만지지 마십시오.**
(B) 이것들은 올 가을에 갤러리로 돌아오면 다시 전시될 것입니다.
(C) 아쉽게도, 일부 조각품은 긴급 수리를 위해 치워졌습니다.
(D) 일부 미술품은 300년이 넘었습니다.

139-142번은 다음 상품 설명에 관한 문제입니다.

DB Mallex의 새로 나온 "Anywhere" 와이셔츠는 가볍고 냄새를 흡수하는 유기농 면으로 만들어져 어느 곳을 가든 적합합니다. **139. 이 첨단 직물은 구김이 가지 않아 다림질이 필요 없습니다.** **140. 소매** 부분에 유연한 원단을 추가하여 활동성과 편안함을 향상시켰습니다. 세련된 핏과 통기성이 결합되어 회의에서도, 등산에서도 안성맞춤입니다. 이 셔츠에는 광범위한 활용도를 제공하 **141. 는,** 양면으로 사용 가능한 칼라 플랩이 있습니다. 모든 구매는 Wharton의 본사에서 **142. 발송되며** 국내 어디든 주문 후 48시간 내 배송을 보장합니다.

---

139 (A) 이 첨단 직물은 구김이 가지 않아 다림질이 필요 없습니다.
(B) 우리 회사는 1982년부터 패션 산업의 선두주자였습니다.
(C) 가벼운 면 베개커버는 밤새 시원하게 유지됩니다.
(D) 세련된 디자인은 어떤 스타일의 셔츠와도 잘 어울립니다.

143-146번은 다음 공지에 관한 문제입니다.

Trevea MyButler 앱을 다운로드 해주셔서 감사합니다. 이 앱은 Trevea Air로 비행하는 동안 수신되는 전화, 문자 메시지, 이메일 추적을 도와줍니다. 항공편 무료 와이파이를 제공하는지 **143. 확인하시려면,** 예약 확정서를 확인해 주세요. 언제든지 20달러에 와이파이 이용권을 구입하실 수도 있습니다. 구입한 접속이 **144. 기대**에 미치지 못할 경우 환불을 요구하실 수 있습니다.

와이파이 접속은 인터넷 동영상 스트리밍에는 적합하지 않다는 점에 유의해 주시기 바랍니다. Trevea Air에서는 좌석 등받이 화면으로 이용할 수 있는 기내 영화 및 TV 프로그램 시청을 권장드립니다. 비행 중 개인 기기로 혼자만의 영화나 프로그램을 보는 것 **145. 도** 얼마든지 환영합니다. 이륙 전에 기기를 '비행기 모드'로만 설정해 주시기 바랍니다. **146. 출발 전에 한번 더 안내해 드리겠습니다.**

---

146 (A) 귀하의 식이 제한이 곧 업데이트됩니다.
(B) 기상 조건에 따라 지연이 발생할 수 있습니다.
(C) 앱은 다음 업데이트에서 블루투스를 이용할 것입니다.
(D) 출발 전에 한번 더 안내해 드리겠습니다.

PART 7

P. 117

147-148번은 다음 광고에 관한 문제입니다.

Deylano Allied Carpenters
15년 넘게 현지인의 사랑을 받아온 곳

주택 개조를 생각해 오셨다면, 저희에게 전화 주셔서 수고를 덜어보세요. 저희는 10년 훨씬 넘게 운영해오고 있으며, Deylano에서 저희를 유일하게 신뢰하는 데는 이유가 있습니다. **정원 손질 및 관리가 필요하거나, 새 수영장을 설치하고 싶거나, 주택에 소소하게 수리가 필요한 경우에도 저희가 모두 해결해 드릴 수 있습니다.**(147)

www.deylanoallied.com/request를 방문하셔서 무엇이 필요한지 알려 주세요. 저희가 귀하의 요구사항에 맞춰 견적서를 작성해 연락드립니다. **이 광고를 언급하시면, 총 금액에서 15퍼센트를 할인해 드립니다.**(148) 이 제안은 2월 25일까지만 유효하니, 망설이지 마세요!

---

147 Deylano Allied Carpenters에 관하여 언급된 것은?
(A) 현재 3월까지 예약이 마감되었다.
(B) 다른 도시에 지점이 있다.
(C) 직원이 Deylano 시민으로만 이루어져 있다.
(D) 서비스에 주택 수리가 포함된다.

148 어떻게 Deylano Allied Carpenters에서 할인을 받을 수 있는가?
(A) 광고를 언급해서
(B) 웹사이트에 회원 가입해서
(C) 여러 서비스를 의뢰해서
(D) 보증금을 지불해서

149-150번은 다음 메모에 관한 문제입니다.

메모: Postal Plus

귀하의 물품은 4월 10일에 배송될 예정입니다. **배송되는 물품의 크기로 인해 반드시 사람이 상주해야 합니다.**(149) 이는 저희 직원이 집 안으로 안전하게 가져다 드리기 위함입니다. 배송 받으실 수 있도록 오전 9시에서 11시 사이에는 집에 계시기 바랍니다.

발송인: Longvale Buck
소포 식별 번호: K932AE
수취인: Kendall Evans
　　　　12 Delisle Avenue
　　　　Mercer, Pennsylvania 16137

다른 배송일이 필요한 경우, 저희 웹사이트 www.postalplus.com/mydelivery를 방문해 주세요.(150)

---

149 Ms. Evans의 배송에 관하여 알 수 있는 것은?
(A) 해외에서 배송됐다.
(B) 대형 물품이다.
(C) 4월 10일에 배송되었다.
(D) 깨지기 쉬운 부품이 들어 있다.

150 메모에 따르면, Ms. Evans는 Postal Plus 웹 사이트에서 무엇을 할 수 있는가?
(A) 서비스 후기를 제출할 수 있다.
(B) 소포 내용물을 볼 수 있다.
(C) 배송일을 변경할 수 있다.
(D) 배송 진행상황을 추적할 수 있다.

151-153번은 다음 언론 보도에 관한 문제입니다.

www.sparksvillearch.com/press_release

온 가족이 함께 할 즐길 거리를 찾고 있나요? **고고학 박물관에서 이제 토요일과 일요일에는 밤 9시까지 운영 시간을 연장했습니다.**[(151)] 오셔서 수많은 화석과 최근 발굴된 초기 정착민의 도구를 포함해 저희의 최고 인기 전시품을 관람하세요.

뿐만 아니라, 지금부터 4월 28일까지 고대 이집트 전시 입장료를 면제해 드립니다.[(152)] 한정된 기간 동안 주어지는 기회이므로, 가능하실 때 이용하세요. 또한 원시 미술 수업 예약도 다시 한번 받고 있습니다. 사전 예약은 필수이며, 웹사이트를 통해 할 수 있습니다.[(153)]

고고학 박물관에서는 수많은 카페 및 레스토랑뿐만 아니라 충분한 야외 주차장을 제공합니다. 저희 기프트숍에는 모든 분들을 위한 기념품이 구비되어 있으며, 기프트숍의 구매로 발생되는 수익금은 전시품의 다양성을 개선하는 데 사용됩니다.

151 고고학 박물관에 관하여 알 수 있는 것은?
(A) 웹사이트를 업데이트했다.
(B) 곧 수리에 들어갈 예정이다.
(C) 회원제 프로그램에 새로운 요건이 생겼다.
(D) 운영 시간이 연장됐다.

152 4월 28일 이후에 무슨 일이 일어나겠는가?
(A) 전시에서 입장료를 부과한다.
(B) 휴일 프로그램이 발표된다.
(C) 기프트숍에서 가격을 인상한다.
(D) 주차장이 폐쇄된다.

153 미술 수업에 관하여 언급된 것은?
(A) 전시에서 보여준 도구를 사용한다.
(B) 사전에 예약해야 한다.
(C) 저녁에만 들을 수 있다.
(D) 나이 제한이 있다.

154-155번은 다음 문자 메시지 대화에 관한 문제입니다.

Scott Brown (오후 1시 32분)
Lesa, 지난달 Sofia에서 열린 콘퍼런스에서 우리가 대화했던 연사 명함 받았어요?[(154)/(155)]

Lesa Haag (오후 1시 35분)
더 구체적으로 알려주세요. 관리 회계에 관해 발표한 남자분인가요, 아니면 리스크 및 가치 평가에 관해 발표한 여자분말인가요?[(154)]

Scott Brown (오후 1시 37분)
리스크 및 가치 평가요, 죄송해요. 그분한테 연락해서 함께 일할 수 있는지 알아보고 싶어요.

Lesa Haag (오후 1시 40분)
더 일찍 물어 보셨으면 좋았을 텐데. 제가 방금 책상을 치우면서 잡동사니는 잔뜩 버렸거든요.[(155)] 제가 알기론 그 행사 때 전체 연사를 정리한 파일이 있을걸요? 거기서 그 분 정보를 찾으실 수 있을 거예요.

Scott Brown (오후 1시 42분)
좋은 생각이에요.

154 Sofia에서 열린 콘퍼런스의 주제는 무엇이었겠는가?
(A) 소프트웨어 설계
(B) 건축
(C) 재무
(D) 공학

155 오후 1시 40분에, Ms. Haag가 "더 일찍 물어 보셨으면 좋았을 텐데"라고 할 때 무엇을 의미하겠는가?
(A) 요청 받은 계약서 사본을 분실했다.
(B) Mr. Brown의 요청을 들어줘서 기쁘다.
(C) 세부내용을 기억하지 못한다.
(D) Mr. Brown을 도와줄 수 없다.

156-157번은 다음 설문조사에 관한 문제입니다.

TRUENORTH 치과
환자 만족도 조사

저희에 대해 어떻게 알게 되셨나요?
[ ] 신문 [ ] TV [ ] 인터넷 [ ] 가족/친구 [V] 기타 (아래에 구체적으로 작성해 주세요)
주치의를 통해 이 치과로 바로 안내 받았습니다.

방문 목적은 무엇이었습니까?
사랑니 발치

치료 받는데 얼마나 오래 기다리셨습니까?
30분이었지만, 미리 예약하지 않았습니다.

치과의사는 치료에 대해 얼마나 잘 설명해주었습니까?
의사 선생님은 제가 더 편안할 수 있게 도와 주셨습니다.

저희 서비스를 다시 이용하시겠습니까? 이유를 구체적으로 작성해 주세요.
예, 치료가 아주 순조롭게 진행됐고, 비용도 좋았습니다.

저희 서비스에 대해 어떤 점이 개선되길 바라십니까? 구체적으로 작성해 주세요.
병원 주소를 알고 있었지만, 찾기가 힘들었습니다. 아마 표지판이나 화살표가 있다면 유용할 것 같습니다.[(156)]

무료 스케일링 추첨에 응모하시려면, 귀하의 정보를 작성해 주십시오.
이름: [Cara Luke]
이메일: [cluke@pembton.com]

저는 TrueNorth 치과에서 제공하는 특가나 할인 정보 수신에 동의합니다. [V][(157)]

귀하의 의견에 감사드립니다!

156 Ms. Luke는 어떤 어려움을 언급하는가?
(A) 병원을 찾는 일
(B) 진료를 예약하는 일
(C) 주차하는 일
(D) 치료비를 지불하는 일

157 Ms. Luke는 TrueNorth 치과에서 무엇을 하도록 허용하는가?
(A) 추가 치료를 제안하도록
(B) 다음 진료를 예약하도록
(C) 판촉 정보를 보내도록
(D) 온라인에 자신의 후기를 올리도록

158-161번은 다음 정보에 관한 문제입니다.

Stebry 컨설팅 그룹에서 파견근무 기회를 드립니다

—[1]—. Stebry 컨설팅 그룹은 지난 30년간 운영되어왔으며, 14개국 50개 이상의 고객사와 제휴를 맺고 있습니다. 저희의 사명은 서로 다른 국적과 문화를 포용하는 것입니다. **그러한 사명의 일환으로, 저희는 현재 전세계 다양한 곳에 있는 저희 협력사에서 파견 근무를 할 기회를 제공하고 있습니다.**(158) —[2]—. 이러한 기회는 Stebry에서 최소 2년 이상 근무 경력이 있는 직원이 지원 가능합니다.

지원 가능한 모든 직책은 당사 웹사이트의 직원란에서 볼 수 있습니다.(159) —[3]—. 모집 직책에 관심 있으시면, 반드시 자격요건을 충족하는지 주의 깊게 살펴봐주시기 바랍니다. 충족한다고 판단되신다면, 첫 번째 단계로 하실 일은 관리자에게 이야기하는 것입니다. 관리자의 승인을 받고 나서 바로 Mr. Collins께 연락하시면, Mr. Collins가 해당 직책에 대해 귀하를 면접하게 됩니다.(161) —[4]—. Mr. Collins께서 당사 고객 관리팀을 책임지고 있기에, 파견 근무 요청에 대한 승인 권한은 최종적으로 그분에게 달려 있습니다.(160)/(161)

158 안내문의 목적은 무엇인가?
(A) 신규 정책에 대한 투표를 유도하는 것
(B) 최근의 결정사항을 공지하는 것
(C) 직원들에게 보고서 확인을 요청하는 것
(D) 중요한 결과를 설명하는 것

159 Stebry 컨설팅 그룹 내 공석에 대해 직원들이 어떻게 알아낼 수 있는가?
(A) 문서를 다운받아서
(B) 면접에 참석해서
(C) 웹사이트를 방문해서
(D) 관리자에게 이야기해서

160 안내문에 따르면, Mr. Collins의 업무는 무엇인가?
(A) 해외 고객에게 연락하는 것
(B) 분기별 매출을 전망하는 것
(C) 임시파견 요청을 승인하는 것
(D) 직원 실적을 평가하는 것

161 [1], [2], [3], [4]로 표시된 곳 중 다음 문장이 들어가기에 가장 적절한 곳은 어디인가?

"이에 대해 제대로 준비하실 것을 권장 드립니다."

(A) [1]
(B) [2]
(C) [3]
(D) [4]

162-165번은 다음 기사에 관한 문제입니다.

Cheesman 공원에서 접시 채우기

Eldorado, 7월 7일 — Hayward's가 지난 주 금요일 Cheesman 공원에서 열린 뒤뜰 요리대회에서 최고 요리상을 차지했다.(162)/(163) 11개의 참가업체들 중 1위를 차지했다.

뒤뜰 요리대회는 인기 있는 행사로, Eldorado 지역 전역에서 참가식당과 관람객을 끌어 모으고 있다.(162) 행사 진행자 Malcolm Jones의 간단한 소개말에 이어, 모든 식당에서 온 요리사들이 공원 이곳 저곳에서 고기를 훈제하고 굽기 시작했다. 참석자들은 각 식당이 내놓은 다양한 종류의 바비큐를 맛볼 기회를 얻었다. 그리고 나서 맛본 음식을 평가해달라고 요청받았다. 그날 밤, 평가가 전부 검토된 후, 시상식을 위해 모두 한자리에 모였다.(163)

Hayward's는 올해 행사에서도 성공을 이어갔다. **작년에는 훈제 폴드 포크로 2위를 차지했고, 그 전 해에는 매운 치킨으로 3위에 올랐다.**(164) 이 식당을 방문한다면 반드시 두 요리를 모두 먹어봐야 한다.

Hayward's는 최근 Eldorado에서 10주년 기념행사를 가졌다. 영업 첫 해에 Hayward's는 동네 슈퍼마켓 바깥에 놓은 바비큐 훈제통 하나와 피크닉 테이블 몇 개가 전부였다. 이제는 최대 40가정을 수용할 수 있는 공간에서 영업한다.

Hayward's가 수상하기 전에, 2위와 3위 입상자들이 발표되었다. Rattlesnake Barbecue가 3위의 영예를 가져갔으며, Joe's Smokehouse가 양지머리요리로 2위를 차지했다.(165)

162 기사에 어떤 종류의 행사가 언급되는가?
(A) Eldorado 남부의 새 지점 개점
(B) 자선기금 모금을 위한 식품 판매
(C) 새로 선출된 정부 관료를 위한 축하행사
(D) 지역 업체들이 참가하는 요리대회

163 기사에 따르면, 금요일 밤에는 무슨 일이 있었겠는가?
(A) Rattlesnake Barbecue가 새로운 장소로 이전했다.
(B) Joe's Smokehouse에서 새 그림을 구입했다.
(C) Hayward's가 상을 받았다.
(D) Cheesman 공원이 일찍 폐장했다.

164 Hayward's에 관하여 사실인 것은?
(A) 직접 닭을 사육한다.
(B) 이전 두 번의 뒤뜰 요리대회에서 상을 받았다.
(C) Eldorado 지역의 슈퍼마켓들에게 상품을 판매한다.
(D) Malcolm Jones가 소유하고 있다.

165 Rattlesnake Barbecue에 관하여 알 수 있는 것은?
(A) Joe's Smokehouse보다 낮은 평점을 받았다.
(B) 이전에 Hayward's에서 근무했던 요리사에 의해 시작되었다.
(C) 가족이 운영하는 사업체이다.
(D) 양지머리요리로 유명하다.

166-167번은 다음 웹 페이지에 관한 문제입니다.

https://www.infinitesolutions.com/help

컴퓨터에 반응이 없나요?

컴퓨터에 반응이 없다면, 당황할 필요가 없습니다. **누구나 한번쯤은 겪는 일이며,**(166) 해결책은 보통 아주 간단합니다. 전문가를 부르기 전에 다음과 같은 조치를 취해보시기를 권장합니다:

1. 컴퓨터에서 소리가 나는지 확인합니다. 아무 소리도 나지 않는다면, 2단계로 이동하세요. 소리가 난다면, 3단계로 이동하세요.
2. 컴퓨터와 모니터 뒤편의 모든 케이블이 제대로 전원에 연결되어 있는지 확인합니다.(167D)
3. 전원버튼을 10초간 눌러서 컴퓨터를 완전히 종료합니다. 그런 다음 전원 버튼을 다시 눌러 컴퓨터를 켭니다.(167C)

조치를 취해본 후에도 컴퓨터에 계속 응답이 없으면, 저희 기술자에게 555-1974로 연락하십시오. www.infinitesolutions.com/outcall에서도 예약할 수 있습니다.(167B)

166 컴퓨터가 멈추는 것에 대해 웹페이지에서 암시하는 것은?
(A) 수리비로 이어질 수 있다.
(B) 구형 모델에서 발생하는 편이다.
(C) 전문가만 고칠 수 있다.
(D) 흔히 일어나는 일이다.

167 컴퓨터가 멈추는 현상을 해결할 수 있는 방법으로 언급되지 않은 것은?
(A) 업데이트 설치하기
(B) 예약하기
(C) 컴퓨터 다시 시작하기
(D) 케이블 확인하기

168-171번은 다음 직장 기사에 관한 문제입니다.

번아웃 방지하기

Jarrett Partners에서 실시한 최근 연구에 따르면, Dover 내 많은 사무 직원들이 번아웃의 영향을 받고 있다고 한다.[(168)/(169)] 수많은 근로자가 지난 1년간 불만, 동기 부족, 지속적인 피로감을 느끼는 일이 더 잦아지고 있다고 했다.[(169)] —[1]—. Dover는 지역 내 많은 스타트업 회사들에 핫 스폿이 되었지만, 이는 지나치게 일 중심적인 문화를 양산하기도 했다. 그 결과, 많은 회사에서 번아웃의 영향을 완화할 방법을 물색하고 있다.

인기 있는 해결책 한 가지는 휴가를 더 쓰도록 장려하는 것이다. 주 4일 근무제가 지역 내 많은 회사에서 시험 삼아 실시되었으며,[(170C)] 결과는 긍정적이었다. —[2]—. 3일의 주말이 생기며 직원들은 Dover 외곽으로 여행을 떠나게 됐는데, 이는 분주한 마음을 업무에서 쉬게 하는 방법을 제공해준다. 직원들은 보다 생기와 의욕을 갖고 업무에 복귀하게 된다고 알렸다.

또다른 해결책은 직원을 위한 즐거운 행사를 주최하는 것이다.[(170B)] 일년 내내 분산된 행사는 일상적인 업무의 단조로움을 해소하면서 부서 내 공동체 의식을 만들어준다. 전문가는 행사에 돈이 많이 들 필요는 없다고 강조한다. 큰 돈이 들지 않는 아이디어로는 회사 야유회를 가거나 체육 행사를 개최하는 것이 있다. —[3]—.

직원들에게 이따금 재택근무를 허용하는 것도 한 방법이다.[(170A)] —[4]—. 때로는 직장으로의 통근이 번아웃에 일조하기도 한다.[(171)] 직원들에게 재택근무를 하도록 허용하면, 통근의 부담은 덜면서 자신의 업무를 꿰고 있게 할 수 있다.

모든 회사는 번아웃으로 귀중한 직원을 잃을 위험에 처해 있다. 하지만 선제적인 조치를 취하고 지원을 제공하면, 번아웃은 과거의 일이 될 수 있다.

---

168 기사의 목적에 해당하는 것은 무엇인가?
(A) 다양한 업무 방식을 대조하기 위해
(B) 잘못된 인식을 반증하기 위해
(C) 공통적인 직장 문제에 대해 논의하기 위해
(D) 컨설팅 서비스를 광고하기 위해

169 Dover 내 많은 근로자에 관하여 기사에서 알 수 있는 것은 무엇인가?
(A) 자신의 차량을 가지고 있지 않다.
(B) 자주 피로를 느낀다고 전한다.
(C) 고급 대학 학위를 가지고 있다.
(D) 직장을 자주 바꾼다.

170 번아웃을 예방하는 방법으로 기사에 언급되지 않은 것은?
(A) 직원들에게 재택 근무를 허용하는 것
(B) 이따금 행사를 주최하는 것
(C) 더 적은 일수를 근무하는 것
(D) 급여를 인상하는 것

171 [1], [2], [3], [4]로 표시된 곳 중 다음 문장이 들어가기에 가장 적절한 곳은 어디인가?

"모든 번아웃이 직장에서 일어나는 일 때문은 아니다."

(A) [1]
(B) [2]
(C) [3]
(D) [4]

172-175번은 다음 문자메시지 대화문에 관한 문제입니다.

Terri Sandoval [오후 1시 39분]
안녕하세요, Julian, Belinda. 잡지가 지연됐다는 소식을 인쇄업자에게 들었어요. 그쪽에서 다음주 초에 발송할 거예요.[(172)]

Julian Lindsey [오후 1시 42분]
늦어도 수요일에는 발송해야 해요.[(172)] 구독자는 저희의 신뢰 배송을 중요하게 생각해요. 저는 주문이 확인된 줄 알았어요. 제가 알기로는 저희가 목요일에 확인 받았거든요.[(173)/(174)]

Belinda Franklin [오후 1시 43분]
맞아요.[(173)/(174)] 이메일에 그렇게 적혀 있어요. 제가 열어 볼게요. 저희가 Nature Watch 200부랑 Tech Madness 150부를 주문했다고 되어 있어요.[(174)]

Terri Sandoval [오후 1시 46분]
그쪽 인쇄 시스템에 문제가 있다고 들었어요. 바로잡긴 했지만, 주문이 늦어졌어요.

Julian Lindsey [오후 1시 49분]
인쇄소 교체를 고려해야 해요. 이곳에서 문제가 너무 많았어요. 비슷한 금액을 제시하는 다른 곳이 많아요.

Belinda Franklin [오후 1시 51분]
제가 이미 명단을 마련해 놨어요.

Julian Lindsey [오후 1시 53분]
잘됐네요. 다음 주에 사장 몇 명을 만나봐야겠죠?

Terri Sandoval [오후 1시 56분]
명단을 보내주시면, 제가 살펴볼게요.[(175)] 겉보기에 마음에 들면, 회의를 잡을게요.

---

172 작성자들은 어떤 종류의 일을 하겠는가?
(A) 행사 사진작가
(B) 잡지 발행인
(C) 시장 조사원
(D) 프린터 제조업자

173 주문은 언제 확인되었는가?
(A) 월요일에
(B) 수요일에
(C) 목요일에
(D) 토요일에

174 오후 1시 43분에, Ms. Franklin이 "제가 열어 볼게요"라고 할 때 무엇을 의미하겠는가?
(A) 송장에 있는 숫자를 갱신하고 있다.
(B) 지역 배송분을 발송하고 있다.
(C) 장래 구독자에게 연락하고 있다.
(D) 인쇄소에서 보낸 이메일을 살펴보고 있다.

175 Ms. Sandoval은 다음으로 무엇을 하겠는가?
(A) 회의에 참석할 것이다.
(B) 서류를 살펴볼 것이다.
(C) 일부 결과를 취합할 것이다.
(D) 주문을 취소할 것이다.

176-180번은 다음 전단지와 편지에 관한 문제입니다.

18세에서 42세 사이이며 Chicago 지역에 거주하고, 약간의 여유 돈이 필요하신가요? 그렇다면 Mercer 리서치에 연락하세요!

Mercer 리서치에서는 고객사를 위한 소중한 의견을 얻기 위해 유급 포커스그룹 세션에 참여하실 분들을 찾고 있습니다. [176]/[178] 아래 목록에서 관심 있는 것이 있으시면, www.mercerresearch.com/focusgroups에서 신청해 주세요. 귀하께서 적합한 지원자인지 확인하기 위한 설문지를 작성하셔야 합니다.

#G918 – 지역 밴드의 신규 앨범에 대해 의견을 주실 음악 애호가를 찾습니다. 참가자들은 90분 동안 청취하시고 75달러를 받게 됩니다.

#G929 – 2시간 동안 태블릿 PC 신제품을 테스트 및 리뷰해주실 전자제품 애호가를 찾습니다. 참석자들은 간단한 설문을 작성한 후, 내주신 시간에 대한 보상으로 125달러를 받게 됩니다.

#G951 – 5세 이하의 자녀를 둔 부모님들을 이틀간 진행되는 장난감 주제의 포커스 그룹에 초대합니다. 모임은 하루 3시간 동안 진행되며, 참가자들은 내주신 시간에 대한 보상으로 300달러를 받게 됩니다.

#G996 – 지역 프로야구팀에 의견을 주실 스포츠 팬을 모십니다. 새로운 팬과 오랜 팬 모두 2회로 진행되는 1시간 분량의 토론회에 참석을 신청하실 수 있습니다. 참가자들은 보상으로 50달러와 다음 홈경기 입장권 2매를 받게 됩니다. [177]

10월 3일

Jacob Tambor
1912 Farland Way
Chicago, IL 60606

Mr. Tambor께,

귀하는 #G996 모임의 참가자로 선정되셨습니다. 웹 페이지에 나와 있는 대로, 8월 18일 오후 12시와 8월 20일 오후 1시로 예정된 1시간 동안의 모임에 2회 참석하셔야 합니다. [177] **모임은 모두 제가 주재합니다.** [178] 시간이 한정되어 있으므로, 모임에 참석하시기 전에 짧은 동영상을 보시고 설문지 작성을 요청드립니다. 이는 더 생산적인 토론을 가능하게 해줄 것입니다.

저희 건물에 현재 보수작업이 진행 중이라서, 본사에서 모이지 않을 것입니다. 대신, 시 중심부에 있는 작업공간을 하나 예약했습니다(약도는 웹 사이트에서 확인하실 수 있습니다). **또한, 그 건물 주차장에 출입하실 수 있는 주차권을 동봉해드렸습니다.** [179]

신청하신 모임에 참석하실 수 없는 경우, 되도록 빨리 저희에게 알려주시는 것이 중요합니다. 그래야 저희도 대체 지원자에게 통보할 수 있습니다. [180]

시간 내어 도와주셔서 감사드립니다.

Nathaniel Olsen [178]

Nathaniel Olsen

Mercer 연구소

동봉물 재중

---

176 전단지의 목적은 무엇인가?
(A) 자격을 갖춘 보조 연구원을 채용하는 것
(B) 새 마케팅 회사를 홍보하는 것
(C) 곧 있을 운동경기들을 나열하는 것
(D) 토론 기회를 광고하는 것

177 Mercer 리서치는 Mr. Tambor에게 얼마를 지불하겠는가?
(A) 50달러
(B) 75달러
(C) 125달러
(D) 300달러

178 Mr. Olsen에 관하여 알 수 있는 것은?
(A) 태블릿 PC를 구입해야 한다.
(B) 포커스그룹을 조직한다.
(C) 파트타임으로 일한다.
(D) 스포츠 경기장에서 근무한다.

179 편지에 무엇이 포함되어 있는가?
(A) 건물 안내도
(B) 신청서
(C) 주차권
(D) 식권

180 Mr. Tambor가 약속을 취소하면 Mercer 리서치는 무엇을 할 것인가?
(A) 다른 지원자에게 연락할 것이다.
(B) 자료집을 발송할 것이다.
(C) 회의 일정을 다시 잡을 것이다.
(D) 전액 환불해줄 것이다.

181-185번은 다음 설문지와 이메일에 관한 문제입니다.

설문지

시간을 내어 설문지를 작성해주셔서 감사 드립니다. 설문에 응해주시면, 이곳 Barkley's에서 귀하에게 더 나은 서비스를 제공해 드리는 데 도움을 주시게 됩니다. 아래 양식에서 항목별 만족도를 나타내는 칸에 표시해주시기 바랍니다.

(1=매우 나쁨, 2=나쁨, 3=보통, 4=좋음, 5=매우 좋음)

	1	2	3	4	5
매장 분위기와 청결을 어떻게 평가하시겠습니까?	☐	☐	☐	■	☐
요리에 사용된 재료의 신선도를 어떻게 평가하시겠습니까? [181]	☐	☐	☐	☐	■
음식 값으로 지불한 금액 대비 귀하의 만족도를 어떻게 평가하시겠습니까? [181]/[182]	☐	☐	☐	■	☐
받으신 서비스의 속도를 어떻게 평가하시겠습니까?	☐	☐	☐	☐	■
문의사항에 응답하는 직원들의 능력을 어떻게 평가하시겠습니까? [184]	■	☐	☐	☐	☐
Barkley's에 대한 전체적인 인상을 어떻게 평가하시겠습니까?	☐	☐	☐	■	☐

- 오늘 얼마를 지불하셨습니까? : 75달러
- 나이(선택사항)
  14-21 ☐ /22-29 ■ /30-37 ☐ /38-45 ☐ /46-54 ☐ /55+ ☐
- 이름(선택사항): Miguel Nunez
- 이메일(선택사항): mnunez1@penmail.co.nz

수신: Miguel Nunez <mnunez1@penmail.co.nz>
발신: Support Services <ss@barkleys.co.nz>
제목: 설문지
날짜: 8월 4일 화요일, 오전 11시 25분
첨부파일: 쿠폰

Mr. Nunez께,

시간을 내어 Barkley's에 관한 설문지를 작성해주셔서 감사 드립니다. 저희는 많은 분께 피드백을 받았고, 여러분 모두의 의견을 소중하게 생각합니다. [183]/[185] 이 정보는 저희에게 배움과 더 나은 서비스를 제공할 기회를 줍니다.

Barkley's에 대한 귀하의 전체적인 평가가 만족이었다는 사실에 기쁩니다. 하지만, 저희가 받은 응답 중 대다수에서 귀하가 만족하지 못했던 것과 동일한 항목에 관해 부정적인 인상을 표현했다는 점에서 실망스러웠습니다. 저희는 이 문제를 바로잡는 데 필요한 조치를 취하고 있음을 귀하께 확실히 말씀 드리고 싶습니다. 조만간 새로운 직원교육 프로그램이 시작됩니다.[184]

응답에 대한 감사의 표시로, 다음 번 구매 시 Barkley's 전국 어느 지점에서든 할인 받을 수 있는 20 퍼센트 할인 쿠폰(이메일에 첨부)을 드리고자 합니다. 항상 이용해주셔서 감사 드립니다.

Yasiel Sanders 드림

181 Barkley's는 어떤 종류의 사업체이겠는가?
(A) 전자제품 매장
(B) 슈퍼마켓
(C) 식당
(D) 마케팅 대행사

182 Mr. Nunez는 Barkley's에 관한 어떤 진술에 동의하겠는가?
(A) 가격이 합리적이다.
(B) 서비스가 다양하다.
(C) 위치가 편리하다.
(D) 직원들이 노련하다.

183 이메일에서 첫 번째 단락, 두 번째 줄의 단어 "value"와 의미상 가장 가까운 것은?
(A) 계산하다
(B) 진가를 알아보다
(C) 이익을 얻다
(D) 강조하다

184 Barkley's는 무엇을 하려고 계획하고 있겠는가?
(A) 사업장을 더 자주 청소할 것이다.
(B) 일부 상품의 가격을 낮출 것이다.
(C) 설문조사에 참여하는 모든 고객에게 쿠폰을 제공할 것이다.
(D) 직원들이 제품에 대해 더 잘 알도록 교육할 것이다.

185 설문지에 관하여 알 수 있는 것은?
(A) 인터넷으로 작성되어야 한다.
(B) 많은 고객들이 작성했다.
(C) 2년마다 업데이트된다.
(D) Mr. Sanders가 설계했다.

186-190번은 다음 이메일들과 요금표에 관한 문제입니다.

수신: David Davis <daviddavis@orourkeschools.edu>
발신: **Maggie Jones <maggiejones@albanytours.ca>**[186]
날짜: 3월 6일
제목: 4월 대회 견적
첨부: ORourke_4월.pdf; 오락옵션.pdf

안녕하세요, David.

지난 12월 수학여행 준비도 정말 즐겁게 해드렸는데, 이번 달 Edmonton Bears의 주 하키 플레이오프를 준비해드릴 기회도 주셔서 고맙습니다.[186]/[190] 제가 이해하기로 팀의 투숙 기간이 대회 진출 단계에 따라 결정될 것이라 무기한 예약이 필요한데, 저희가 대회 장소 인근에서 이러한 요청을 수용해줄 수 있는 호텔을 찾았습니다.[190]

아래에 요금을 상세히 설명해놓은 첨부문서가 있습니다. 그리고 지역 관광명소와 추천 액티비티를 설명하는 팸플릿도 몇 개 넣어드렸습니다.[189]

계속 거래해주셔서 감사 드립니다.

Maggie B. Jones 드림

Richview시 Alpine 호텔

체크인 날짜: 4월 21일[190]
투숙객: Edmonton Bears (학생 선수들, 팀 매니저들 및 코치들)
담당자: David Davis (818) 555-3143

대회 라운드	총 투숙기간	라운드별 총 객실요금
1라운드	5박	10,000달러
2라운드	4박	8,000달러
3라운드	3박	6,000달러[190]
파이널	2박	4,000달러

요금은 매 경기가 끝날 때 지급하시기 바랍니다. **일일 단체요금은 1박에 2,000달러입니다.**[187]

수신: Maggie Jones<maggiejones@albanytours.ca>
발신: David Davis<daviddavis@orourkeschools.edu>
날짜: 4월 27일
제목: 4월 행사

Maggie께,

팀 여행의 최신 항목별 청구서를 보내주셔서 감사합니다. **제 비서가 오늘 오후에 당신의 사무실을 방문해서 합의한대로 6,000달러 수표를 전해드렸습니다.**[188]/[190] 여행과 관련해서 감사의 말씀을 드리고 싶습니다. 숙박과 식사, 교통의 모든 면이 매우 원활하게 진행되었고, 특히 제안해주신 승마 투어가 정말 좋았습니다. 끝나고 팀원들이 동물과 사진을 찍으면서 아주 즐거운 시간을 보냈습니다.[189]

다음 여행에 관해 곧 알려드리겠습니다. 10월이 될 것 같지만, 자세한 내용이 들어오면 알려드리겠습니다.

David Davis

186 Ms. Jones는 누구겠는가?
(A) 하키 코치
(B) 호텔 직원
(C) 교직원
(D) 여행사 직원

187 Mr. Davis에게 발송된 객실 요금에 관하여 사실인 것은?
(A) 투숙기간에 따라 변경되지 않는다.
(B) 무료 아침식사를 포함한다.
(C) 스포츠팀에게만 제공된다.
(D) 최근에 인상되었다.

188 두 번째 이메일에 따르면, Mr. Davis의 지불에 관하여 언급된 것은?
(A) 만나서 지불되었다.
(B) 할부로 이루어졌다.
(C) 예상보다 높았다.
(D) 10월 여행 대금이었다.

189 Mr. Davis는 Ms. Jones가 보낸 팸플릿으로 무엇을 했겠는가?
(A) 정보를 갱신했다.
(B) Edmonton Bears에 배포했다.
(C) 더 제작해줄 것을 요청했다.
(D) 동료에게 이메일로 보냈다.

190 Edmonton Bears가 참가한 대회의 마지막 라운드는 무엇인가?
(A) 1라운드
(B) 2라운드
(C) 3라운드
(D) 파이널

191-195번은 다음 표, 웹 페이지, 이메일에 관한 문제입니다.

이 도표는 뉴질랜드에서 흔히 재배되는 딸기 품종의 수확철을 요약해서 보여줍니다.

	Albion	Chandler	Galetta[193]	Royal[195]	San Andreas[191]
10월					✓
11월	✓				✓
12월	✓				✓
1월	✓	✓			✓
2월	✓	✓		✓	✓
3월		✓		✓	✓
4월		✓		✓	
5월		✓	✓	✓	
6월			✓		
7월			✓		

Agility 농장 그룹에서 재배하고 싶으세요?

· 뉴질랜드에서는 딸기를 일년 내내 수확할 수 있어, 가장 맛있고 신선한 과일을 보장합니다.

· 저희의 새로운 지역 품종으로 5월 이후 시작되는 비수기에 딸기를 공급해 드립니다.[193] 이는 Royal 같은 수확이 늦은 품종조차도 능가합니다.

· 저희 농부들은 뉴질랜드 전역에 흩어져 있습니다. 저희 제품을 구입하시면 뉴질랜드 농가를 지원하게 됩니다.

· 상당수 농부는 친환경 온실에서 딸기를 재배합니다.[192] 이는 농작물에 날씨가 미치는 영향을 최소화할 뿐만 아니라 농업에 지속 가능성을 주입한다는 저희의 사명에도 기여합니다.

· Agility 농장 그룹은 뉴질랜드에서 관심을 갖는 기업으로 유명해졌습니다. 저희는 저희 브랜드를 사용하는 모든 제품이 최고의 품질 기준을 충족할 것을 보장합니다.

수신: Agility 고객 지원팀 <support@agilityfarms.co.nz>
발신: Elmer Norton <enorton@thebasket.co.nz>
날짜: 4월 2일[195]
제목: 귀사의 딸기

Agility 농장 그룹 귀하,

저희는 지난 주 귀사에서 보낸 Chandler 딸기의 5회차 배송분을 수령했습니다. 이 품종은 올해 처음으로 판매했는데, 대성공을 거뒀습니다. 특히 요 며칠 들어 계속해서 완판되는 걸 보니, 요즘 딸기가 유행인 것 같습니다. 그래서 저희가 주문량을 늘릴 수 있는지 알고 싶습니다. 견적을 받아 볼 수 있을까요?[194]

그리고, Chandler 품종이 다른 상점에도 있다는 걸 알게 됐습니다. 저는 매장에 더 많은 사람들을 오게 할만한 새로운 것을 시도해 보고 싶습니다. 지금 시기에 제철인 다른 품종도 가지고 계시나요?[195] 그러시다면, 딸기가 날개 돋치게 팔리고 있는 지금 당장 주문을 넣고 싶습니다!

감사합니다.

Elmer Norton
The Basket 사장

191 표에 따르면, 어떤 딸기 품종의 수확기가 가장 긴가?
(A) Albion
(B) Chandler
(C) Royal
(D) San Andreas

192 웹 페이지에서 Agility 농장 그룹에 관해 언급하는 것은?
(A) 농부들이 실내에서 딸기를 재배한다.
(B) 전체 제품군에 육류를 포함한다.
(C) 몇 명의 농부들이 설립했다.
(D) 뉴질랜드 내 특정 상점에만 판매한다.

193 Galetta 딸기에 관해서 무엇이 사실이겠는가?
(A) 다른 품종보다 더 달다.
(B) 대량 수송이 힘들 때가 종종 있다.
(C) 뉴질랜드에서 재배되는 지역 품종이다.
(D) 가장 비싼 품종이다.

194 Mr. Norton은 왜 이메일을 보냈는가?
(A) 회의 날짜를 제안하려고
(B) 가격을 문의하려고
(C) 영양 정보를 요청하려고
(D) 배송일을 변경하려고

195 Agility 고객지원 팀은 Mr. Norton에게 무엇을 하라고 제안하겠는가?
(A) Chandler 딸기를 더 주문하라고
(B) 가격을 인상하라고
(C) 농부와 논의해 보라고
(D) Royal 딸기를 시도해 보라고

196-200번은 다음 광고, 고객 후기, 이메일에 관한 문제입니다.

Chaucomb Catering
Nevada의 바쁜 근로자를 위해 오직 최고의 음식만을 제공합니다
169-555-4977

Chaucomb Catering은 지역 내 기업체에 간식 및 음료를 제공하는 것을 전문으로 합니다.[196] 직원들이 즐길 수 있도록 매주 정성스럽게 구성한 스낵과 음료가 담긴 바구니를 일터로 보내드립니다.

저희는 건강이 중요한 우선순위라는 것을 잘 알고 있습니다. 따라서, 저희는 지역 내 맛있으면서도 건강한 제품을 제공하는 최고의 식품 및 음료 판매 업체와만 제휴를 맺습니다. 또한 가볍든, 엄격하든, 채식을 하는 분도, 알레르기가 있는 경우에도 맞춰드릴 수 있습니다. 요컨대, 저희에게 원하는 것만 알려주시면, 얼마든지 요구사항에 맞춰드리겠습니다.

저희 제품을 경험해보고 싶으신 경우, 오늘 저희에게 전화해 주시면 샘플 바구니 배송 일정을 잡아 드립니다. 아니면, Bristol의 Grove Crescent 712번지에 있는 저희 사무실에 방문해 주세요.[198] 행사 케이터링 서비스에 관심이 있으시면, 저희의 MealCare Program에 대해 문의해 주세요.[200] 저희에게 전화하셔서 저희가 25년 넘게 영업하고 있는 이유를 직접 경험해 보시기 바랍니다.

Chaucomb Catering
★★★☆☆
8월 18일

지역 내 다른 사업체로부터 Chaucomb Catering에 대한 이야기를 많이 들어왔기에, 드디어 한번 경험해보기로 결심했습니다. 왜 그렇게나 많은 기업에서 Chaucomb을 열렬히 애용하는지 바로 알겠더군요. 어떤 종류의 제품을 포함해야 할지 파악하기 위해 Ms. Chaucomb께서 직접 저희 사무실로 오셔서 직원들을 만났습니다. 확실히 가격은 제가 예상했던 것보다 높았지만, 저는 직원들한테 설득 당했습니다. 그쪽 사무실과 아주 가깝다는 점을 고려하면, 배송비가 있다는 사실에 더 놀라긴 했습니다.[198] 하지만, 바구니의 외형은 아주 훌륭했고 직장 내 사기를 높여주었습니다.[197]

다만 우리가 겪은 문제를 하나 언급해야겠습니다. 우리가 받은 오트밀 쿠키 중 일부에서 쾌쾌한 냄새가 났습니다. 방문한 고객에게 쿠키를 대접했는데 고객이 그 문제를 언급했다는 점에서 저희로서는 다소 당혹스러웠습니다. Chaucomb Catering에서 이런 문제가 다시는 생기지 않길 바랍니다.

Brian Garrett
bgarrett@franklinpartners.com

수신: bgarrett@franklinpartners.com
발신: chaucomb@chaucomb.com
날짜: 8월 21일
제목: Chaucomb Catering에서 메시지 드립니다

Mr. Garrett께,

무엇보다도 Chaucomb Catering에 기회를 주신 데 대해 감사의 말씀을 드립니다. 귀하의 의견을 읽은 후, 겪으신 일에 대해 깊은 사과의 말씀을 드리고 싶습니다. **저희는 다른 고객에서 비슷한 문제를 들었던 지라, 저희가 문제의 제품을 구입한 판매업체를 한동안 주시하고 있던 상황이었습니다.** (199) 유감스럽게도 저희가 더 일찍 조치를 취하지 못했습니다. 그 점에 대해 죄송하다는 말씀을 드리고 싶습니다. 품질 문제를 시정할 때까지 해당 업체를 목록에서 삭제했습니다.

형편없는 경험을 만회해 드리고자, 저희 MealCare Program의 25퍼센트 할인권과 더불어, 바구니 2개를 무료로 제공해 드리고 싶습니다. (200) 이를 통해 고객 만족을 향한 저희의 헌신을 알아주셨으면 하는 바람입니다.

Barbara Chaucomb 드림
Chaucomb Catering 사장

196 광고에 따르면, Chaucomb Catering의 고객은 누구인가?
(A) 다국적 기업
(B) 현지 기업체
(C) 지역 학교
(D) 정부 기관

197 Mr. Garrett은 후기에서 Chaucomb Catering 서비스의 어떤 측면에 대해 칭찬하는가?
(A) 외관
(B) 배송 시간
(C) 요금
(D) 품질

198 Mr. Garrett에 관하여 알 수 있는 것은?
(A) 과거에 Ms. Chaucomb과 일한 적이 있다.
(B) 직원을 추가로 채용하려고 한다.
(C) 사업체가 Bristol에 위치한다.
(D) 최근 사무실을 개조했다.

199 이메일에서 Chaucomb Catering에 관하여 언급하는 것은?
(A) 제품의 품질을 점검하지 않는다.
(B) 과거에 불만을 여러 번 받았다.
(C) 제품 라인을 확대할 계획이다.
(D) 현지 판매업체하고만 거래한다.

200 Ms. Chaucomb이 Mr. Garrett에게 베푼 제안에 해당하는 것은?
(A) 행사 초대
(B) 출시 예정 제품 카탈로그
(C) 다른 판매업체 추천
(D) 케이터링 서비스 할인

TEST 05

PART 5   P. 140

101 Takagawa 사는 아름다운 야외 식사 공간을 만들어서 건물을 개조했다.

102 비상문의 잠금 장치를 풀려면 손으로 빗장 위를 세게 미세요.

103 Mr. Watson은 정규 영업 시간이 끝난 후 배송되는 모든 농산물 또는 육류 수송품의 접수를 담당한다.

104 현재 귀하의 임차료 지불 기한이 2주 지났다는 점에서, 계약서에 명시된 바와 같이 추가 연체료를 지불하셔야 합니다.

105 Mr. Davidson과의 대화는 단연 Biznet 잡지의 올해 인터뷰 중 최고였다.

106 Eileen 부티크는 주로 도매 유통업자에게 판매하지만, 소매 고객도 받는다.

107 교육 감독관들은 공식 승인을 위해 최근 채용된 인턴들에 대한 최종 평가를 제출했다.

108 Ms. Sawyer가 탄 기차는 너무 늦게 도착해서 그녀는 오찬에 참석할 수 없었다.

109 Cheetah Automobile의 다음 전기차는 현재 모델보다 10배 더 효율적일 것으로 예상된다.

110 BMV 컨버터블 자동차의 법적 보증기간은 5년 또는 30만 킬로미터인데, 어느 쪽이든 먼저 발생하는 것으로 한다.

111 Moody 광고회사는 고객이 기대수준을 뛰어넘은 것에 대해 Ms. Young과 그녀의 팀을 칭찬했다.

112 Hancock 금융 서비스는 계정 소유자의 허가 없이 절대 고객 정보를 다른 당사자들에게 공개하지 않는다.

113 우리가 구매 양식에 수량을 정확하게 기록했는지 확인하려면 원두를 주문한 업체에 연락하시기 바랍니다.

114 Morrison 시는 시 창립 100주년을 기념하는 새로운 기념 명판을 세우려는 계획에 대해 대중의 의견을 묻고 있다.

115 Harper 벽지는 어떤 가정에든 어울리도록 매우 다양한 패턴으로 판매된다.

116 월요일 오전의 많은 통화량을 고려해 볼 때, 고객 서비스팀과의 통화연결이 예상보다 더 오래 걸릴 수 있다.

117 레스토랑 대부분에게는 현지 고객을 유지하는 것이 외부 방문객을 유치하는 것보다 더 수익이 좋다.

118 Maynard 미술관은 기록장치의 사용이 로비와 접수구역으로 한정되어야 한다고 요구한다.

119 Stowaway 보관센터는 임차인들이 전자 잠금장치로 인해 가끔 겪는 어려움에 대해 사과했다.

120 Carmel 사는 직원 교육개발 프로그램을 관리할 학습 전문가를 고용했다.

121 Mr. Griffon은 한정된 예산으로 재설계 프로젝트를 맡을 누군가를 찾기 위해 지원서들을 검토했다.

122 무료 가이드 투어뿐만 아니라, 미술관에서는 방문객을 위한 신규 서비스를 제공할 것이다.

123 거의 3백만명의 사람들이 세계 축구 토너먼트에 참석할 것으로 예상된다.

124 동남 아시아 교육 계획은 교육자들과 가족들 간 지속적인 공동 작업이 매우 중요하다고 믿는다.

125 프리랜서 네트워크를 갖추고 있어, Transbridges에서는 수요가 있는 곳은 어디든지 도움을 줄 통역사를 보낼 수 있다.

126 직원들이 직장 생산성을 적당히 높여야만 BlueBox House에서 매출을 늘릴 수 있을 것이다.

127 Overton Research에서는 자사 홍보전략의 기반을 잡는 데 시장 조사 결과를 활용한다.

128 웹 디자인 워크숍 이후, 참가자들은 자신들의 사이트 접속량이 상당히 많아졌다고 말했다.

129 도로 확장이 완료되지 않은 경우에는, 뒷문을 이용해 주시기 바랍니다.

130 Boston의 관광 가이드들은 정식 교육을 받지만 도시의 역사에 관해 대체로 많이 알아야 한다.

PART 6   P. 143

131-134번은 다음 편지에 관한 문제입니다.

> 오랜 고객님께 드리는 메시지:
>
> Bullseye 가정용품점은 저렴한 가격에 고품질의 상품을 **131. 제공해 드리기 위해** 노력합니다. 경쟁력 있는 가격과 더불어, 엄청난 고객서비스로 저희는 지역 내 가장 신뢰받는 가정용품 체인점이 되었습니다. Bullseye 내 5곳의 지점은 도합 60년 **132. 동안** 온타리오 주민들에게 서비스를 제공해 왔습니다.

최상의 서비스를 제공해 드리기 위해, 저희는 5월 8일부터 5월 29일까지 리모델링으로 Kitchener 지점의 문을 닫습니다. **133. 이로 인해 생겨나는 모든 불편에 미리 사과 드립니다.** 이 기간 동안, 인근의 Cambridge 매장이 정규 영업 **134. 시간** 동안 계속 영업할 것입니다. 문의사항이나 의견이 있으시면 저희에게 알려주세요. 저희는 항상 귀하의 시간과 거래를 소중히 여깁니다.

감사합니다.

Pablo Guaido
소유주 겸 창립자, Bullseye 가정용품점

133 (A) 매장은 5월 31일까지 한 시간 더 영업을 할 것입니다.
(B) 모든 의견에는 48시간 내 답변을 드립니다.
(C) 이 보증은 제한된 기간 동안만 이용할 수 있습니다.
(D) 이로 인해 생겨나는 모든 불편에 미리 사과 드립니다.

135-138번은 다음 광고에 관한 문제입니다.

Café Mazer의 커피는 순식간에 도시에서 커피 한 잔을 즐기기에 가장 **135. 붐비는** 장소가 됐습니다. 저희의 특별한 커피를 직접 **136. 만드는** 방법을 알고 싶으신가요? 주인인 Felicia Carter가 완벽한 한잔의 커피를 얻는 비결을 다루는 **137. 일련의** 강의에 일반인을 초대합니다. 수업은 오래도록 커피의 본고장으로 여겨지는 에티오피아에서 얻은 그녀의 경험을 바탕으로 합니다. 수업은 토요일 오전 9시부터 오전 11시 30분까지 Holbrook College에서 열립니다. **138. 자리가 한정적이어서, 예약은 필수입니다.** 놓치지 마세요! 오늘 저희 웹 사이트 cafemazer.com/learnwithus를 방문하셔서 등록하세요.

138 (A) 미래에 프랜차이즈 기회가 생길 수 있습니다.
(B) Café Mazer는 곧 신메뉴를 선보일 예정입니다.
(C) 자리가 한정적이어서, 예약은 필수입니다.
(D) Ms. Carter는 최근에 국제 회의에서 돌아왔습니다.

139-142번은 다음 공지에 관한 문제입니다.

Auto-Smart 고객 여러분께 알려드립니다.

자동차 창문을 교체하실 때, 교체되는 창문(혹은 전면유리) 한 장당 10달러의 추가 요금이 발생합니다. 이 요금은 자동차 유리 처리 비용을 부담하기 위한 것입니다. 달리 명시 **139. 하지 않으면,** 이대로 창문 작업을 진행해 처리하겠습니다.

자동차 창문에서의 유리와 플라스틱의 조합은 다루기가 까다로우며, 부적절한 처리는 심각한 환경 피해를 유발합니다. 희소식은 창문이 제대로 **140. 재활용되기만** 한다면, 이 자재가 카펫 뒷판과 단열 처리용으로 안성맞춤이라는 것입니다. 단 10달러로 이렇게 중요한 과정을 처리할 수 있습니다.

이 비용의 지불은 **141. 자율**입니다. 폐창문을 가져가셔서 모든 것을 직접 처리하셔도 되며, 이 경우 저희는 비용을 청구하지 않습니다. **142. 환경친화적인 방식으로 처리하는 것만 기억해주십시오.**

142 (A) 새 창문이 매우 마음에 드실 거라고 확신합니다.
(B) 환경친화적인 방식으로 처리하는 것만 기억해주십시오.
(C) 균열이나 기타 손상을 발견하시는 경우, 즉시 고객 서비스 부서로 연락하셔야 합니다.
(D) 연례 점검이 필수는 아니지만, 매우 권장됩니다.

143-146번은 다음 공지에 관한 문제입니다.

Oliveira Antique Cinema에서는 조명이 **143. 어두워지면** 스마트폰 및 스마트 워치를 비롯한 전자 기기 일체를 무음 모드로 전환하고 주머니 안에 넣어 주실 것을 요청 드립니다. 소리는 관객의 경험을 방해할 수 있으며, 어두운 환경에서 기기를 사용하면 가까이 있는 **144. 고객**의 집중을 흐트러뜨릴 수 있습니다. **145. 예를 들어,** 화면의 불빛은 영화에서 여러분의 기기로 주의를 분산시킬 수 있습니다.

기다리는 전화가 있거나 기기를 사용해야 하는 경우가 있다는 점을 잘 알고 있습니다. **146. 그런 경우에는 극장 밖으로 나가서 대기실을 이용해 주시기 바랍니다.** 그 뒤에 재입장해서 자리로 돌아가실 수 있습니다. 관객에게 방해가 되지 않도록 최대한 소리를 내지 말아 주세요.

146 (A) 결과적으로 환불이 불가능할 수 있습니다.
(B) 저희 정책에 대한 모든 불만 사항은 접수처로 전달되어야 합니다.
(C) 그런 경우에는 극장 밖으로 나가서 대기실을 이용해 주시기 바랍니다.
(D) 할인은 사전 예약하는 대규모 단체에게만 제공됩니다.

PART 7

P. 147

147-148번은 다음 양식에 관한 문제입니다.

Kurtz BBQ and Wings

Kurtz BBQ and Wings에 들러주셔서 감사합니다. 잠시 시간을 내어 아래 설문지를 작성해 주시면 감사하겠습니다.

	그렇다	보통	그렇지 않다
음식이 근사해 보였고 맛있었다.		O	
음식 가격은 적당했다.	O⁽¹⁴⁷⁾		
오래 기다릴 필요가 없었다.		O	
서비스는 친절했고 도움이 되었다.	O		
식당은 아주 깔끔했다.		O	
조명과 음악이 적당한 수준이었다.			O

이름 및 연락처:
Gerald Brunswick
555 032-4592

의견:
식당엔 사람이 꽉 차 있었지만, 저는 서비스에 감명받았습니다. 직원 수가 적었음에도, 저희 음식이 모두 빨리 나왔고, 제대로 준비되었습니다. **식당이 너무 어둡지 않았더라면 더 좋았을 것 같아요. 천장 조명이 몇 개 있다면 장소를 밝게 하는데 매우 도움이 될 거예요.**⁽¹⁴⁸⁾

147 Mr. Brunswick은 자신의 식사 경험에 관하여 무엇을 언급하는가?
(A) 메뉴 항목들은 값어치가 있었다.
(B) 주문이 몇 분 지연되었다.
(C) 일부 음식이 식어서 나왔다.
(D) 음식 양이 많았다.

148 Mr. Brunswick은 어떤 개선을 제안하는가?
(A) 추가 직원이 고용되어야 한다.
(B) 상용 고객 카드가 제공되어야 한다.
(C) 메뉴 항목들이 더 잘 보여져야 한다.
(D) 더 많은 조명이 설치되어야 한다.

149-150번은 다음 온라인 후기에 관한 문제입니다.

---

www.europeanappliancesexpo.com/display_types

Kwong Sim, 7월 11일

저는 숫자에 약합니다. 그런데 Delaporte에서 제 돈을 투자하는 과정을 엄청나게 간단하게 만들어줘서 문제되지 않았습니다. 투자별로 어떤 잠재 위험이 있고 어떤 옵션을 추천하는지에 대해 아주 솔직하게 알려줬습니다.[149] 그곳에서 조언해주시는 분들은 아주 전문적이고 지식이 풍부했습니다.[150] 가족과 친구에게 강력 추천합니다.

---

149 온라인 후기에 따르면, 회사에서 어떤 서비스를 제공하는가?
(A) 상품 디자인
(B) 재무 투자
(C) 시장 조사
(D) 부동산

150 Mr. Sim은 무엇에 만족을 표하는가?
(A) 회사 소프트웨어
(B) 낮은 요금
(C) 직원의 행동
(D) 결제 과정

151-153번은 다음 안내문에 관한 문제입니다.

Minim 커피
질 좋은 커피를 순식간에

이 용기로, 최고의 Minim 커피를 20잔 드실 수 있습니다.[151] 모든 봉지에는 파푸아뉴기니의 지속 가능한 농장에서 공급받은 커피 빈이 들어 있으니 믿고 드시면 됩니다.[153C]

커피 제조 방법[153D]

1. 한 봉지에 든 내용물을 머그잔에 넣으세요.
2. 머그잔에 뜨거운 물을 부으세요.
3. 3분간 살살 저어주세요.

이제 커피를 드시면 됩니다. 제품에 불만족하신 경우에는 구입하신 장소에서 전액 환불 받으실 수 있습니다.[152]

제품은 12월 14일까지 유효합니다.[153B]

---

151 안내문은 어디에 인쇄되어 있겠는가?
(A) 광고에
(B) 그릇에
(C) 상자에
(D) 기계에

152 고객은 제품에 만족하지 않으면 무엇을 할 수 있는가?
(A) 환불할 수 있다.
(B) 점검을 요청할 수 있다.
(C) 내용물을 기부할 수 있다.
(D) 회사에 전화할 수 있다.

153 안내문에서 제품에 관해 언급하지 않은 것은?
(A) 건강상 이점
(B) 유효기간
(C) 원산지
(D) 준비과정

154-155번은 다음 광고에 관한 문제입니다.

Erik Harrison Carpets는 Allegan에서 가장 신뢰받는 카펫 설치 업체입니다. 고객의 일정에 맞춰 빠르고 편리한 서비스를 제공합니다. 원하는 카펫을 고르고, 주문을 넣은 후, 나머지는 저희에게 맡기시면 됩니다. 저희는 20년 넘게 운영해왔으며, 저희 작업에 관한 추천 글이 많은 것을 알려줍니다.[155]

가까운 Erik Harrison 매장에 들르셔서 카펫을 구경하시고 설치 옵션을 상의하세요. 아니면, www.erikharrison.com/products에서 카탈로그를 다운받으셔도 됩니다. 선택을 마치면, 이메일로 상담을 요청하세요. 영업일 기준 2일 이내에 전체 견적서와 예상 작업 완료일을 알려드립니다.[154]

---

154 Erik Harrison Carpets에 관해서 언급된 것은?
(A) 인테리어 디자인 서비스도 제공한다.
(B) 해외에서 제품을 수입한다.
(C) 매장 방문 없이 서비스를 요청할 수 있다.
(D) 고객은 매장 회원이 될 수 있다.

155 왜 광고에서 회사의 역사에 관해 자세히 알려주는가?
(A) 높은 비용에 대한 정당성을 부여하려고
(B) 지역 사회 내 입지를 강조하려고
(C) 계약서에 포함된 세부 사항을 명시하려고
(D) 고객에게 최근 트렌드를 알려주려고

156-157번은 다음 온라인 채팅 대화문에 관한 문제입니다.

Todd Campbell (오전 11시 31분)
Vickie, Ronnie가 진행한 포커스 그룹의 결과 봤어요? 아까 아침에 이메일을 보냈더라고요.[156]

Vickie Frank (오전 11시 34분)
네. 제안한 몇 가지 의견을 보고 깜짝 놀랐어요.

Todd Campbell (오전 11시 37분)
맞아요. 결과는 이 제품의 광고 방식에 큰 영향을 줄 거예요. 마케팅 팀하고 회의를 해야 할 것 같아요.

Vickie Frank (오전 11시 39분)
저도 그 생각을 하고 있었어요. Ronnie도 불러야 해요. 제가 이메일을 보내야 할까요?[157]

Todd Campbell (오전 11시 42분)
제가 오늘 같이 점심을 먹을 예정이에요.[157]

Vickie Frank (오전 11시 43분)
잘 됐네요!

---

156 상Ronnie는 무엇을 했는가?
(A) 마케팅 팀장과 회의를 했다.
(B) 제품 피드백을 취합했다.
(C) 신상품 계획을 확정했다.
(D) 마감 기한 연장을 요청했다.

157 오전 11시 42분에, Mr. Campbell이 "제가 오늘 같이 점심을 먹을 예정이에요"라고 할 때 무엇을 의미하겠는가?
(A) 하루 종일 바쁠 것이다.
(B) 며칠 휴가를 쓸 계획이다.
(C) Ronnie를 회의에 초대할 것이다.
(D) 회의 안건을 준비해야 한다.

158-161번은 다음 광고에 관한 문제입니다.

LaVine Vision: 취업 기회

LaVine Vision의 고객 파악팀은 아주 흥미진진한 한 해를 보냈으며, 이러한 기세를 유지하고자 합니다. 저희는 성장하는 저희 팀에 합류해 저희의 소중한 고객 관련 중요한 정보를 수집해주실 열정 넘치는 지원자를 모집합니다. 모든 고객이 원하는 것을 이해하는 데 중추적인 역할을 맡게 됩니다.⁽¹⁵⁸⁾

담당 업무:
· 고객과의 소통을 통한 요구사항 파악⁽¹⁵⁹⁾
· 고객에 관해 파악한 정보를 실행 가능 항목으로 전환
· 다양한 팀에 결과를 전달하고 필요 조치 안내

자격 요건:
· 고객에게 친절하게 대하는 능력
· 방대한 자료에서 양식을 찾는 능력
· 자신감 있고 밝은 태도
· 공인 대학교 학사학위, 경영학 전공 선호⁽¹⁶⁰⁾

이 기회를 기다리고 계셨다면, careers@lavinevision.org로 이력서를 보내주세요.

지원서 규모로 인해, 안타깝게도 모든 지원자에게 회신해 드릴 수 없습니다.⁽¹⁶¹⁾ 이에, 최종 후보에 오른 분들에게만 연락드릴 예정입니다.

---

158 첫 번째 단락, 네 번째 줄의 단어, "part"와 의미상 가장 가까운 것은?
(A) 힘
(B) 역할
(C) 행동
(D) 부분

159 광고된 일자리의 주요 업무는 무엇인가?
(A) 광고 제작
(B) 직원 교육
(C) 경쟁사 분석
(D) 고객 면담

160 구인 광고에 열거된 자격 사항에 해당하는 것은?
(A) 데이터 분석 경험
(B) 운전면허증
(C) 대학 학위
(D) 소매업 관련 지식

161 LaVine Vision에 관하여 알 수 있는 것은?
(A) 해당 직책에 경쟁이 치열하다.
(B) CEO가 면접을 본다.
(C) 작년부터 규모가 두 배가 됐다.
(D) 직원에게 높은 급여를 준다.

162-164번은 다음 후기에 관한 문제입니다.

---

https://agliooexpress.com/reviews

★★★★★

업무상 저희는 다양한 택배 서비스를 많이 이용합니다. 하지만 Aglioo Express는 확실히 단연 최고였습니다. — [1] —. **저희가 시장에 내놓은 주택 점검을 어떤 회사에 의뢰한 적이 있었습니다.^{(162)/(164)}** — [2] —. 그 회사에서 Aglioo Express로 결과를 보내면서, Aglioo에서 최저 배송비를 제시했다고 말해줬어요. — [3] —. 그 말을 들은 후로, 저희는 모든 택배 건에 Aglioo Express를 이용하기 시작했어요. **저는 그곳에서 모든 문서에 서명을 요구하는 게 아주 마음에 듭니다. 저희가 발송하는 수많은 기밀 문서가 그 상태로 유지된다고 안심시켜 주거든요.⁽¹⁶³⁾** — [4] —. 모든 사람에게 Aglioo Express를 택배사로 이용하라고 강력 추천하고 싶습니다.

Holly Barber, 3월 13일

---

162 Ms. Barber는 어떤 업종에 종사하겠는가?
(A) 건설사
(B) 출판사
(C) 컨설팅 회사
(D) 부동산 중개

163 Ms. Barber는 Aglioo Express의 어떤 점을 좋아하는가?
(A) 좋은 가격
(B) 안전 배송
(C) 영업 시간
(D) 빠른 처리

164 [1], [2], [3], [4]로 표시된 곳 중 다음 문장이 들어가기에 가장 적절한 곳은 어디인가?

"관심 있는 구매자들이 있어서 급한 상황이었어요."

(A) [1]
(B) [2]
(C) [3]
(D) [4]

165-167번은 다음 이메일에 관한 문제입니다.

수신: Cameron Howell <cameron.howell@electromail.com>
발신: Dora Butler⁽¹⁶⁷⁾ <dbutler@finplanners.com>
날짜: 2월 17일
제목: 환영합니다

Mr. Howell께,

No-Stress Money의 자금 운영 프로그램을 구독해 주셔서 감사합니다. 귀하의 납입금 350달러를 수령했음을 알려드리며, 일년간 저희 앱을 이용하실 수 있습니다.

이제 No-Stress Money를 이용하시면, 월별 예산을 만들고 모니터링하는데 필요한 모든 자원을 편하게 이용하실 수 있습니다. **저희 프로그램에는 다수의 동영상, 액티비티, 실시간 일대일 수업이 제공되어 귀하가 목표를 달성하도록 도와드립니다.⁽¹⁶⁶⁾ 저축의 목적이 연휴든, 휴가 여행이든, 생애 첫 주택이든 상관없이, 저희 프로그램은 귀하의 목표에 맞춰 조정 가능합니다.⁽¹⁶⁵⁾**

다음 주에 저희 공인 자문이 회의 시간을 잡을 것입니다. 이는 귀하의 목표에 대해 논의할 수 있는 기회입니다. 그 다음으로, 저희 자문은 귀하가 No-Stress Money로 시작하도록 도와드리며, 저희가 제공하는 다양한 도구 사용법을 보여드릴 겁니다. 자문은 또한 귀하께서 제대로 진행하실 수 있게 정기적으로 점검해 드릴 것입니다.

저는 모든 사람이 보다 탄탄한 재정 상황에 도달할 수 있도록 도우려는 목표로 No-Stress Money를 만들었습니다.⁽¹⁶⁷⁾ 저희는 90일 환불 보증을 제공합니다. 90일 이내 프로그램에 만족하지 않으시면, 환불해 드립니다. **No-Stress Money의 저희 팀 전체를 대표하여, 이용해 주셔서 대단히 감사드립니다.⁽¹⁶⁷⁾**

Dora Butler 드림
No-Stress Money

---

165 No-Stress Money에 관하여 언급된 것은?
(A) 팀은 6명으로 이루어져 있다.
(B) 고객 맞춤형 프로그램이다.
(C) 작년에 다수의 상을 받았다.
(D) 두 달 간 무료로 이용해 볼 수 있다.

166 두 번째 단락, 세 번째 줄의 단어, 'realize'와 의미상 가장 가까운 것은?
(A) 발견하다
(B) 이해하다
(C) 분석하다
(D) 달성하다

167 Ms. Butler는 누구겠는가?
(A) 고객 서비스 직원
(B) 웹 개발자
(C) 기업 중역
(D) 재정 고문

168-171번은 다음 온라인 채팅 대화문에 관한 문제입니다.

Shane Nunez (오전 9시 32분)
Adam, Cindy, 안녕하세요. 오전 9시 30분에 회의한다는 회람 모두 받았나요? 저만 여기 와 있네요.[171]

Adam Jones (오전 9시 34분)
안녕하세요, Shane. 다른 방에 계신 것 같아요.[168]

Cindy Page (오전 9시 35분)
저희는 1203-A에 있어요.

Shane Nunez (오전 9시 36분)
맹세컨대 누군가 1301-A라고 했어요. 누가 1301-A호라고 했어요?[169]

Adam Jones (오전 9시 37분)
괜찮아요. 프로젝트에 관해 각자 아는 내용에 대해 말하고 있어요. 이 회의는 저희끼리만 할 거예요.[171]

Cindy Page (오전 9시 38분)
처음 듣네요.[169]

Shane Nunez (오전 9시 40분)
Debbie Cain이 이 회의에 있어야 하지 않아요?[170] 어쨌거나 그 분 관할이잖아요.

Adam Jones (오전 9시 41분)
시간 되면 합류하실 거예요. 다른 주요 프로젝트를 하느라 바쁘세요.[170]

Shane Nunez (오전 9시 42분)
그렇군요. 알았어요. 금방 갈게요.[168]

---

168 Mr. Nunez는 무엇을 해야 하는가?
(A) 맞는 방으로 가야 한다.
(B) 회의 일정을 다시 잡아야 한다.
(C) 회의 안건을 발송해야 한다.
(D) 프레젠테이션을 녹화해야 한다.

169 오전 9시 38분에, Ms. Page가 "처음 듣네요"라고 할 때 무엇을 의미하겠는가?
(A) 자신이 알림 이메일을 발송했다.
(B) 회의에서 일찍 자리를 떠야 한다.
(C) 회의에 늦게 초대받았다.
(D) 회의 장소에 대해 확신한다.

170 Ms. Cain에 관하여 언급된 것은?
(A) 회의에 대해 모르고 있다.
(B) 여러 프로젝트를 이끌 것이다.
(C) 짬 낼 틈 없이 바쁘다.
(D) 현재 휴가 중이다.

171 회의에 몇 명이 참석할 예정인가?
(A) 2명
(B) 3명
(C) 4명
(D) 5명

172-175번은 다음 기사에 관한 문제입니다.

Sindri, Manitoba에 오다

(3월 19일) — 개인 가전제품을 만드는 것으로 유명한 캐나다 생산업체 Sindri가 주요 생산 시설을 옮길 예정이다.[172] 내년 7월 신규 첨단공장이 Manitoba에 오픈하면 Quebec에서 이루어지는 생산 대부분이 중단될 것이다. —[1]—. 이전은 태블릿 PC를 포함해 Sindri의 다양한 새로운 모델들의 발표와 맞물려 있다.

"저희 최초 모델인 Sindri Book 노트북 컴퓨터는 7년 전 출시됐을 때 인기가 엄청났습니다.[173]"라고 회사 창립자이자 CEO인 Claude McCleod가 말했다. "저희가 3년 전 일체형 데스크톱 판매를 시작하면서 좀 더 휴대하기 좋은 것에 관심이 있다는 고객들의 피드백을 받았습니다."라고 덧붙였다. 기존 모델들 판매가 여전히 강세를 보이고 있지만, McCleod는 새로운 태블릿이 새로운 고객층을 회사 제품으로 끌어들일 것이라고 확신한다.[175] —[2]—.

Sindri는 일반적인 비싼 가격표가 붙지 않은 고품질 상품을 내놓으며 두각을 나타냈다. —[3]—. Sindri는 적당한 가격대의 소비자 가전제품에 대한 수요가 증가하면서 성장했으며, 특히 개발도상국들에서 강세를 보였다. 회사의 사내 여론조사에서는 고객들이 경쟁사 대비 Sindri를 선택한 가장 큰 이유는 품질보증과 신뢰성에 대한 평판, 그리고 전 모델의 높은 가성비임을 보여준다.[174] —[4]—. 회사의 신규 상품라인에 대한 자세한 내용은 웹 사이트 sindri.com에서 확인할 수 있다.

---

172 기사는 Sindri에 관해 무엇을 암시하는가?
(A) 여러 국가에 제조공장이 있다.
(B) Manitoba에 2개의 공장을 운영할 것이다.
(C) 개인용 기기를 만든다.
(D) 영업한지 10년이 넘었다.

173 Sindri에서 판매한 최초의 상품은 무엇이었는가?
(A) 스마트 워치
(B) 데스크톱 컴퓨터
(C) 태블릿
(D) 노트북 컴퓨터

174 Sindri 고객들에 관하여 언급된 것은?
(A) 가격에 관심이 있다.
(B) 환경을 의식한다.
(C) 다른 제품들보다 태블릿을 선호한다.
(D) 대부분 선진국에 산다.

175 [1], [2], [3], [4]로 표시된 곳 중 다음 문장이 들어가기에 가장 적절한 곳은 어디인가?

"젊은 사람들, 특히 학생들이 고객일 가능성이 높다."

(A) [1]
(B) [2]
(C) [3]
(D) [4]

176-180번은 다음 광고와 이메일에 관한 문제입니다.

Chanthavong 무에타이 아카데미
12856 Salmon River Road
San Diego, CA 92129
858-555-1212

Chanthavong 무에타이 아카데미에 관심을 가져주셔서 감사드립니다. 저희는 현재 내년도 학생을 모집 중입니다. 회원권은 1월 1일부터 12월 31일까지 유효합니다.

수업 단계:

- **기초 수업(JFK):** JFK 학생들은 수요일과 금요일 저녁 7시부터 8시까지 킥복싱 훈련에 입문하게 됩니다.[(179)] 이 수업은 적응훈련과 예절을 강조합니다. 학생들은 3가지 기본 주먹기술과 2가지 기본 발차기도 배웁니다.

- **초급 수업(HBC):** HBC 학생들은 월요일과 수요일 저녁 7시 30분부터 8시 30분까지 무에타이 공부를 계속합니다. 주로 펀치백(샌드백)으로 연습하며, 다양한 주먹기술과 발차기의 조합을 배우기 시작합니다.

- **중급 복싱 트레이닝(IBT):** IBT 학생들은 파트너와 함께 하는 훈련에 주로 집중합니다. 스파링이 권장되지만 의무는 아닙니다. 수업은 화요일과 목요일 저녁 6시부터 7시까지입니다.

- **낙무에타이(NMT):** NMT 학생들은 아카데미의 대회 준비반입니다. 아카데미의 동계 및 하계 대회 참가가 필수이며,[(180)] 주 5회의 연습에도 출석해야 합니다. 월요일부터 목요일까지는 오후 8시부터 9시까지, 토요일은 오후 4시부터 6시까지입니다.[(179)]

일요일에는 수업이 없지만, 개별 연습을 위해 오전 9시부터 오후 7시까지 아카데미를 개방합니다.[(177)]

모든 회원들은 아카데미 티셔츠와[(176A)] 연 2회 있는 대회의 무료 티켓,[(176B)] 글러브 및 기타 훈련용품에 대한 20퍼센트 할인을 받게 됩니다.[(176D)]

수신: Diana Langley <dlangley@ujjp.com>
발신: Sakda Khongsawatwaja <s.khongsawatwaja@ctba.com>
날짜: 12월 12일
제목: 내년도 회원권
첨부파일: 양식.doc

Ms. Langley께,

다가오는 해에 아드님 Tony와 따님 Josephine을 학생으로 맞이하게 되어 매우 기쁩니다. Tony는 기초 수업(JFK)으로 시작시키겠습니다. 분명 좋아하고 금방 발전할 것입니다![(178)/(179)]

반면, Josephine은 대회 준비반에 들어갈 자격이 됩니다.[(178)/(179)/(180)] 이 수업은 힘든 훈련과 실전 스파링을 수반하기 때문에, 참가자 부모님의 특별 동의서가 필요합니다. 첨부해드린 양식에 서명하셔서 12월 20일에 있는 학부모 설명회 때 제출해 주시기 바랍니다.

Sakda Khongsawatwaja 드림
수석 사범
Chanthavong 무에타이 아카데미

176 Chanthavong 무에타이 아카데미 회원의 혜택으로 언급되지 않은 것은?
(A) 무료 의상
(B) 무료 대회 입장
(C) 개인 교습비 할인
(D) 훈련장비 할인

177 Chanthavong 무에타이 아카데미에 관하여 언급된 것은?
(A) 오전 수업이 있다.
(B) 강사들이 전 프로선수 출신이다.
(C) 매주 연습기회를 제공한다.
(D) 시설이 최근 확장되었다.

178 Mr. Khongsawatwaja는 왜 Ms. Langley에게 편지를 썼는가?
(A) 자녀들의 반배치를 알려주려고
(B) 자녀들의 회비 납입을 요청하려고
(C) 아카데미의 신규 상품을 광고하려고
(D) 새로운 등록절차를 설명하려고

179 어느 요일에 Ms. Langley의 자녀들이 모두 아카데미에 있겠는가?
(A) 월요일
(B) 화요일
(C) 수요일
(D) 목요일

180 Josephine은 내년에 무엇을 하겠는가?
(A) 스포츠 경기장에서 시간제로 근무할 것이다.
(B) 두 개의 대회에 참가할 것이다.
(C) 설명회에 참석할 것이다.
(D) 초급 수업으로 올라갈 것이다.

181-185번은 다음 웹 페이지와 후기에 관한 문제입니다.

Radiance Entertainment에서 놀라운 두 가지 행사를 선보입니다.

Hyannis와 Dailey의 크리켓 경기—8월 13일. 지난 시즌 결승 진출 두 팀인 Hyannis와 Dailey 크리켓 팀이 재대결로 North Harbor 경기장에서 정면 대결을 펼칩니다. 55달러짜리 경기 패키지에는 입장권과 선택할 수 있는 팀 셔츠 그리고 샌드위치, 케이크 한 조각, 생수 한 병으로 구성된 점심 도시락이 포함됩니다.[(181)] 경기는 오후 12시에 시작합니다. 경기장을 오가는 교통편 역시 패키지에 포함되어 있습니다. 지금 바로 자리를 예약하세요!

쇼팽과 함께 하는 밤—8월 15일. Venice 극단이 '쇼팽과 함께 하는 밤'이라는 제목의 독창적인 희곡을 공연합니다. 비평가들의 극찬을 받는 작가인 Eva Lawson이 집필한 희곡은 엄청난 관심을 모았습니다. 75달러에, 교통편, 티켓, Lula Roe Inn에서의 세 가지 코스로 된 식사를 제공합니다.[(184)] 저녁 식사는 오후 6시 30분경에 제공되며, 공연은 오후 7시 30분에 시작합니다.

· 행사장까지의 교통편은 Plata Building에서 출발합니다.[(182)]
· 결제는 행사 전에 이루어져야 하며, 온라인으로 가능합니다.
· 취소는 환불 규정의 적용을 받습니다. 행사 24시간 전 취소 시 전액 환불됩니다.

Peggy 6월 19일 저는 가족 행사로 Dailey 농구팀과 Hancock 농구팀의 경기를 관람하기로 했습니다. 제 개인적으로는 그 스포츠를 잘 이해하지 못하는데, 저희 투어 주최자인 Edwin이 일어나는 상황을 아주 잘 설명해 주셨습니다.[(183)/(185)] 그분은 저희 가족 모두의 경험을 최고로 만들어 주셨기에, 저는 다음에도 무조건 Radiance Entertainment를 선택할 겁니다.

Gustavo 8월 17일 저는 최근 Radiance Entertainment를 통해 예약해서 '쇼팽과 함께 하는 밤'을 관람했습니다. 그건 탁월한 결정이었습니다. 저는 다른 사람이 계획을 짜 준 밤 외출을 즐겼습니다.[(183)] 레스토랑으로 이동됐다가 그 후엔 연극을 보러 간 것은 저녁 내내 주차 자리를 찾으러 다닌 것보다 훨씬 더 좋았습니다.[(184)] 저희 투어 가이드인 Natascha는 아주 체계적이었고, 저희가 늦지 않게 해주셨습니다.

Vanessa Cain 8월 23일 Dailey-Hyannis의 크리켓 경기 티켓을 구하는 건 엄청나게 어려웠습니다. Radiance Entertainment를 통해서만 티켓을 구할 수 있었습니다. 제가 만족할만한 수준보다 티켓 가격이 좀 더 비쌌지만, 그만한 가치가 있었습니다.[(183)] 아주 원활한 경험이었습니다. 사실, 저희 투어 지도자인 Edwin은 두 팔 걷고 나서서 저희에게 필요한 것을 모두 챙겨주셨습니다.[(185)]

181 North Harbor 경기장의 투어 패키지에는 무엇이 포함되어 있는가?
(A) 단체 사진
(B) Dailey 팀 사진
(C) 팀 셔츠
(D) Hyannis 팀 크리켓용 방망이

182 Radiance Entertainment에 관하여 언급된 것은?
(A) 고객들은 행사 전 Plata Building에서 만나야 한다.
(B) 앞으로 더 많은 행사를 후원할 계획이다.
(C) 다음 달에 행사 가격을 인상할 것이다.
(D) 예약 취소에 대해 부분 환불을 제공한다.

183 후기 작성자에 관하여 알 수 있는 것은?
(A) 단체 예약으로 할인을 받았다.
(B) 이전에 Radiance Entertainment의 고객이었다.
(C) Radiance Entertainment에 만족해했다.
(D) 모두 같은 행사를 예약했다.

184 Gustavo에 관하여 언급된 것은?
(A) 특별식 요청을 명시했다.
(B) 자신의 티켓 가격으로 75달러를 지불했다.
(C) 행사장에 자신의 차를 운전해서 갔다.
(D) 첫 번째 전문 연극 공연에 참석했다.

185 후기에 따르면 Peggy와 Vanessa Cain의 공통점은 무엇인가?
(A) 스포츠 경기를 자주 보러 간다.
(B) 가족과 함께 행사에 참석했다.
(C) 후기 작성으로 경품을 받았다.
(D) 동일한 Radiance Entertainment의 진행자를 만났다.

186-190번은 다음 웹페이지, 문자 메시지, 후기에 관한 문제입니다.

www.dumarsoperations.com/about

Dumar's Operation Training 소개

Dumar's Operation Training은 Daly에서 가장 평판 좋은 직업 전문가 학교입니다. (186) 저희는 창고 관리, 재고 관리, 인사에 관한 교육 모듈을 제공하는 것을 전문으로 합니다. 저희는 수천 명의 사업가가 자신의 일터에서 과정을 최대한 활용할 수 있도록 도와드렸고, 여러분에게도 도움을 드리고 싶습니다.

Dumar's Operation Training은 이론과 실습 요소를 모두 포함합니다. 일부 시간은 교실에서 보내게 되는데, Lincoln 대학교에서 진행합니다. 나머지 시간은 Daly 곳곳의 창고에서 보내며, 이곳에서는 실제 상황에서 개념을 적용하는 직접적인 경험을 하게 됩니다. 그야말로 어떤 경쟁 기관과도 비교할 수 없는 경험을 제공해 드립니다.

대중의 요구에 따라, 평일 일정이 바쁘신 분들에 맞춰 주말 수업도 진행할 예정입니다. 토요일과 일요일 수업은 오전 10시부터 오후 4시까지 진행됩니다. (188) 게다가, 자사 비즈니스용 맞춤 수업을 원하는 기업을 위해 개별 교육 신청도 받고 있습니다. 교육 과정에 대한 보다 자세한 정보나 상담을 원하시면 564-555-0806으로 연락해 주십시오.

Larry Summers (190) (오후 2시 47분)

Ms. Joseph, 안녕하세요. 저는 Larry Summers라고 합니다. **Shawn Bryant**가 신입 사원을 교육하는 오리엔테이션 세션 중 하나를 진행하게 되어, 저에게 8월 19일 일요일에 대신 해달라고 부탁했습니다. (187)/(188)/ (190) 제가 수업을 준비할 수 있게 그의 일정표를 보내 주시겠어요? 그리고, 누가 수업에 참석하는지도 알려주실 수 있으신가요?

www.dumarsoperations.com/testimonials

Dumar's Operation Training 고객 추천의 글

저는 Dumar's Operation Training에서 수강해볼까 생각했었는데, 제 사업체에 얼마나 도움이 될지 확신이 들지 않았습니다. 맞춤 수업 제공을

시작한다는 글을 보고, 바로 우리 팀을 등록했습니다. (189) 우리 팀은 처음에 어떻게 생각해야 할지 몰랐는데, Larry는 개념이 어떻게 우리 사업에 즉각 이익을 가져다 주는지 아주 잘 보여줬습니다. (190) 결국, 일요일에 진행되었음에도 전원이 수업에 참석한 것을 아주 만족해 했습니다. 작업 방식을 개선하고 싶은 모든 기업에 Dumar's Operation Training을 적극 추천합니다.

Willie Carroll

186 웹페이지에서 Dumar's Operation Training에 대해 언급한 것은?
(A) 설립된 지 10년이 넘었다.
(B) 온라인으로 교육 수업을 제공한다.
(C) 내년에 자체 강의실을 열 것이다.
(D) 현재 일하는 사람들에게 적합하다.

187 문자 메시지에 따르면, Mr. Bryant는 8월 19일에 무엇을 할 것인가?
(A) 특별 행사에 참석할 것이다.
(B) 직원들을 교육할 것이다.
(C) 다른 도시로 출장 갈 것이다.
(D) Ms. Joseph과 만날 것이다.

188 Mr. Bryant에 관하여 알 수 있는 것은?
(A) Dumar's Operation Training에서 가장 경력이 많은 직원이다.
(B) 최근 일요일에 근무하기 시작했다.
(C) 소규모 수업을 하는 것을 선호한다.
(D) 부업으로 창고 관리자 일을 한다.

189 후기에 따르면, Mr. Carroll은 무엇에 대해 우려했는가?
(A) 비싼 수업료
(B) 비효율적인 교수법
(C) 불편한 위치
(D) 내용의 적절성

190 Mr. Carroll에 관하여 무엇이 사실이겠는가?
(A) 추가 수업을 등록할 것이다.
(B) 수업료를 할인받았다.
(C) 그녀의 수업 일정을 변경해야만 했다.
(D) 대체 강사의 수업을 들었다.

191-195번은 다음 기사, 이메일, 온라인 후기에 관한 문제입니다.

Sherbrooke 신문

3월 9일 — Rue Papineau와 Rue Eymard 사이 Sherbrooke 시내에 새로운 아이스링크장이 건립 중이다. (191) Leopold 경기장 건설은 6개월 전에 시작되었다. 프랑스 회사 Ayoub의 Quebec 지사에서 근무하는 Steven Fontaine이 경기장의 독특한 설계의 지휘자이다.

Ayoub는 북미와 서유럽에서 스포츠 복합단지를 만들어왔다. Ayoub의 CEO인 Jean-Baptiste Charpentier는 링크장 공사가 지연될 수 있다는 우려 때문에, Leopold 경기장이 Bantam Sherbrooke 국제 하키 대회를 주최할 수 있게 제때에 완공되면, (194) 모든 캐나다 직원들에게 현금 인센티브를 준다고 제안했다. (193) 대회는 내년 1월 말로 예정되어 있다.

새로운 경기장의 건립을 지지하는 사람들은 그것이 지역 경제에 매우 필요한 부양책이 될 것이라고 믿는다. (192) Ayoub는 시설 건립을 돕기 위해 100명이 넘는 Sherbrooke 주민을 고용하고 있다. 또한 시의원 Yvette Sevigny는 아이스하키가 장기적인 수입원이 될 것이라고 언급한다. 티켓 판매뿐만 아니라, 팬들이 Sherbrooke에서 음식과 숙박, 기념품 등을 구매할 때 지역 사업체들도 분명 이득을 볼 것이다.

수신: Steven Fontaine <fontaine@ayoub.ca>
발신: David Harrachi <harrachi@ayoub.fr>
날짜: 1월 12일
제목: 새로운 소식

안녕하세요, Steven

큰 대회에 맞춰 Leopold 경기장을 준비하신 것에 축하의 말씀 짧게 드립니다. 모든 캐나다 직원들도 Mr. Charpentier만큼 기뻐할 것이라 확신합니다. **(193)/(194)** 그는 당신이 다음 번 회사 본사를 방문할 때 다시 만나기를 기대하고 있습니다.

David Harrachi 드림
비서실장

---

www.quebecstays.ca/reviews_hotels_sherbrooke

후기 → Sherbrooke의 호텔들

Caméléon 호텔
2월 19일, **Armand Boucher 작성(194)**

제가 가장 좋아하는 하키팀이 Bantam Sherbrooke 국제 대회에서 결승에 진출해서, 저는 당연히 이곳에 와서 응원해야 했습니다. **(194)** 정말 흥미진진한 시간이었습니다!

Caméléon 호텔은 경기를 보러 지역에 온 모든 하키팬들을 따뜻이 맞이해 주었으며, 이후의 축하자리도 훌륭했습니다. 특히 호텔 식당에서 대회 마지막 날 저녁에 마련해준 특별 '승리 만찬'에 감명받았습니다. **(195)** 저희는 하키 시합을 보러 온 것이었지만, 솔직히 그 음식만 다시 먹기 위해서라도 Sherbrooke은 다시 올 만한 가치가 있습니다. 붐비는 쇼핑 및 유흥가 바로 옆에 위치해서, 약간 시끄럽기는 합니다. 그러나 전체적으로 Caméléon 호텔은 투숙하기 매우 좋은 곳이었기에, 저는 적극 추천합니다.

191 기사는 왜 작성되었는가?
(A) 건설 회사들을 비교하기 위해
(B) 관광객 수의 감소를 논의하기 위해
(C) 건축 프로젝트를 소개하기 위해
(D) 임대용 부동산을 광고하기 위해

192 기사에서 세 번째 단락, 첫 번째 줄의 단어 "back"과 의미상 가장 가까운 것은?
(A) 뒤집다
(B) 지지하다
(C) 돕다
(D) 돌리다

193 이메일에서 알 수 있는 것은?
(A) 캐나다에 있는 직원들이 보너스를 받을 것이다.
(B) Mr. Charpentier가 Quebec 지역을 방문할 것이다.
(C) Ayoub가 몇몇 하키 선수들을 후원할 것이다.
(D) Mr. Fontaine이 승진을 제안받을 것이다.

194 Armand Boucher에 관하여 무엇이 사실이겠는가?
(A) Mr. Charpentier를 안다.
(B) Sherbrooke 인근에서 근무한다.
(C) Leopold 경기장을 방문했다.
(D) 프로 운동선수였다.

195 Mr. Boucher는 Caméléon 호텔의 무엇을 특히 마음에 들어 했는가?
(A) 운동 시설
(B) 널찍한 객실
(C) 기념품 가게
(D) 저녁 식사

196-200번은 다음 이메일들과 쿠폰 교정지에 관한 문제입니다.

수신: Kelly Hansen
발신: Calvin Hunt
날짜: 5월 13일
제목: 프로모션 쿠폰
첨부: 쿠폰 교정지

Kelly께,

저희가 다음 달에 발송할 쿠폰 초안을 보내드릴게요. 저희가 바라는 건 6월 동안 매주 고객이 사용할 새로운 쿠폰이 생기는 거예요. 이렇게 하면 수많은 신규 사업체를 저희 가게로 끌어들이게 될 거예요. 저희 6월 계획은 다음과 같습니다.

1주차: 모든 진단 및 수리 15퍼센트 할인
2주차: 전화기 구매 시 무료 휴대폰 케이스 및 충전기 제공**(200)**
3주차: 모든 구매에 데이터 10 기가바이트 무료 제공**(197)**
4주차: 6개월 이상 가입 시 영화 스트리밍 서비스 2개월 구독권 제공

수정이 필요한 부분이 있는지 살펴봐 주세요. (196) 감사합니다.

Calvin Hunt
마케팅팀, GoGizmo

수리가 필요하세요?	데이터가 필요하세요?
모든 진단 및 수리에 15퍼센트 할인	모든 구매 시 데이터 10기가바이트 무료 이용
쿠폰 번호: FIXIT	쿠폰 번호: INET**(197)**
면책 조항: 이번 주만 유효한 쿠폰입니다. **이용약관이 적용됩니다.(198)** 자세한 내용은 쿠폰 뒷면을 확인해 주세요. 불확실한 경우, 555-1333으로 GoGizmo에게 전화해 주세요.	면책 조항: 이번 주만 유효한 쿠폰입니다. **이용약관이 적용됩니다.(198)** 자세한 내용은 쿠폰 뒷면을 확인해 주세요. 불확실한 경우, 555-1333으로 GoGizmo에게 전화해 주세요.
액세서리로 꾸며 보세요	무엇이든 보세요
모든 휴대폰 구매 시 무료 휴대폰 케이스 및 충전기 제공**(197)**	6개월 등록 시 2개월 구독권
쿠폰 번호: GEAR	쿠폰 번호: ALLUC
면책 조항: 이번 주만 유효한 쿠폰입니다. **이용약관이 적용됩니다.(198)** 자세한 내용은 쿠폰 뒷면을 확인해 주세요. 불확실한 경우, 555-1333으로 GoGizmo에게 전화해 주세요.	면책 조항: 이번 주만 유효한 쿠폰입니다. **이용약관이 적용됩니다.(198)** 자세한 내용은 쿠폰 뒷면을 확인해 주세요. 불확실한 경우, 555-1333으로 GoGizmo에게 전화해 주세요.

수신: Calvin Hunt
발신: Kelly Hansen
날짜: 5월 15일
제목: 회신: 프로모션 쿠폰

Calvin, 안녕하세요.

쿠폰 컨셉이 아주 마음에 드네요. 계약 조건 사본을 가지고 계신가요? **제가 정식 승인하기 전에 먼저 살펴봐야 합니다. (199)** 그리고, 제 생각엔 월초부터 휴대폰 구입을 독려하는 게 더 말이 될 것 같습니다. **(200)** 그렇게 하면, 신규 고객들이 다른 쿠폰으로 혜택을 볼 수 있어요. 그 외에는 전부 훌륭해 보여요. **최신 판매 수치도 저에게 보내주시면, 목표량을 향해 잘 진행되고 있는지 살펴볼게요.(199)**

감사합니다.

Kelly Hansen

196 첫 번째 이메일의 목적은 무엇인가?
(A) 회의를 확정하려고
(B) 제품을 명확히 설명하려고
(C) 검토를 요청하려고
(D) 일정을 수정하려고

197 Mr. Hunt가 제안한 일정에서 3주차에는 어떤 코드가 사용되겠는가?
(A) FIXIT
(B) INET
(C) GEAR
(D) ALLUC

198 면책 조항에서는 쿠폰에 관해 무엇을 언급하는가?
(A) 만료일이 없다.
(B) 이용 가능한 횟수가 한정되어 있다.
(C) 온라인 판매에서 사용할 수 없다.
(D) 다른 조항의 적용을 받을 수 있다.

199 두 번째 이메일에 따르면, Ms. Hansen의 직업은 무엇이겠는가?
(A) 마케팅 팀장
(B) 웹 개발자
(C) 법률 고문
(D) 제품 개발자

200 Ms. Hansen은 몇 주차에 휴대폰 케이스와 충전기를 제공하기를 원하는가?
(A) 1주차
(B) 2주차
(C) 3주차
(D) 4주차

TEST 06

PART 5
P. 170

101 (A) **102** (C) **103** (C) **104** (C) **105** (C) **106** (D)
107 (A) **108** (C) **109** (C) **110** (D) **111** (A) **112** (D)
113 (C) **114** (D) **115** (B) **116** (B) **117** (D) **118** (C)
119 (D) **120** (D) **121** (B) **122** (B) **123** (B) **124** (A)
125 (A) **126** (A) **127** (D) **128** (A) **129** (D) **130** (A)

PART 6
P. 173

131 (B) **132** (D) **133** (A) **134** (A) **135** (A) **136** (D)
137 (C) **138** (B) **139** (C) **140** (A) **141** (C) **142** (A)
143 (D) **144** (A) **145** (A) **146** (B)

PART 7
P. 177

147 (C) **148** (D) **149** (D) **150** (B) **151** (A) **152** (D)
153 (C) **154** (C) **155** (A) **156** (B) **157** (D) **158** (C)
159 (A) **160** (C) **161** (C) **162** (D) **163** (A) **164** (D)
165 (A) **166** (D) **167** (C) **168** (B) **169** (D) **170** (B)
171 (C) **172** (A) **173** (B) **174** (A) **175** (C) **176** (B)
177 (B) **178** (C) **179** (D) **180** (A) **181** (D) **182** (C)
183 (A) **184** (B) **185** (D) **186** (A) **187** (D) **188** (B)
189 (C) **190** (A) **191** (D) **192** (A) **193** (B) **194** (D)
195 (D) **196** (A) **197** (C) **198** (A) **199** (C) **200** (B)

PART 5
P. 170

101 Marie Speer의 훌륭한 리더십의 결과, 스마트폰 부서는 빠른 성장을 이루었다.

102 의류 상품은 48시간 이내에 배송되어야 하지만, 최대 4 영업일까지 걸릴 수도 있다.

103 Marchand 합창단이 돋보이는데, 이는 단원들이 각자의 창법을 조합하는 법을 알고 있기 때문이다.

104 전략 책임자는 편집자 중 한 명이 회사 프로필을 수정하기를 원한다.

105 Henderson Inc.에서 이번주 수요일에 Nora Hale을 신임 대표이사로 임명하는 것에 관한 질문에 답변할 것이다.

106 주말에 높은 고객 수요에 부응하기 위해 Paul's Café에서는 밤 11시까지 영업할 것이다.

107 내 동료 한 명은 올 여름 베를린에서 하는 Ken Strickland의 기조 연설에 참석하고 싶어한다.

108 Toucon Manufacturing은 50개가 넘는 장소에 사무실을 보유한 최고 자동차 제조사 중 하나이다.

109 회원 리워드 프로그램에도 불구하고, Tesseract Communcations의 이용요금은 많은 사람들에게 과하다고 여겨진다.

110 의사들의 80%는 General Department의 항균 손세정 비누가 경쟁업체들의 것보다 더 좋다는 점에 동의한다.

111 법의학 분석가를 위한 자료 보관소가 최근 기관 서버에서 검색되었다.

112 상환 신청을 할 때, 직원들은 이 양식을 작성하고 열거된 구매내역에 대한 영수증을 제공해야 한다.

113 가상 사설 통신망을 사용하지 않으신다면, 비밀번호를 정기적으로 변경하는 것이 권장됩니다.

114 Ms. O'Driscoll은 10월 13일 금요일에 연설 일정이 있다.

115 우리 부서는 예산이 충분하지만, 다음 달까지는 추가 사무용품을 주문할 수 없다.

116 Ms. Orrin은 완전한 매출보고서를 보지 못했지만, 그래도 최근 온라인 홍보 결과에 만족해 했다.

117 Aherran Chocolatier의 유행하는 신상 아이스 초코는 최근 시장조사 기관과 컨설팅을 거쳐 나온 상품이다.

118 Jun Lin은 전세계를 여행하는 것을 좋아했지만 본인 소유의 해외 리조트 체인을 설립하리라고는 상상도 못했다.

119 Ms. Ramirez가 NPM Production에서 일을 시작하기 전에, 그녀는 Cooper Media에서 광고 제작 부감독이었다.

120 부서는 Mr. Suzuki의 안내에 따라 제조 공장을 둘러보는 것을 즐겼다.

121 Yorktown 대학교 연구소에서 실시한 유사한 실험이 모순된 결과를 도출했다.

122 Trevino Architecture의 시청사 설계도는 지하 주차장과 5층에 있는 극장을 특징으로 한다.

123 업데이트를 이용할 수 있기 전에, 이용자들은 Michaelson 은행 스마트폰앱에 영향을 미친 오류에 관한 문의를 보냈었다.

124 Gensian 복합 오븐렌지는 Albi 주방용품에서 가장 합리적인 가격의 상품이다.

125 이번 분기에 플라스틱 시트의 매출에서 비롯된 수익이 5퍼센트 상승했다.

126 패널은 다큐멘터리 영화에 관해 토론하고 그 뒤 관객의 질문에 답할 것이다.

127 Ms. Sheridan은 기자 회견이 내일로 예정되어 있다고 잘못 생각했기에 늦게 도착할 것이다.

128 소비자 연구를 위해 고객들은 연령 및 고용 상태에 따라 여러 그룹으로 분류되었다.

129 모든 서류가 유효하다면, 임시 취업 비자를 발급하는 데 일주일도 걸리지 않을 것이다.

130 우리 팀에서 이번 주에 소프트웨어 기능을 검토하고 수정이 필요한 부분을 업데이트할 것이다.

PART 6
P. 173

131-134번은 다음 이메일에 관한 문제입니다.

수신: Adam Campbell <adamc@netmail.com>
발신: Russell Bridges <rbridges@ascendworks.com>
날짜: 6월 8일
제목: 외부 도장

TEST 06

Mr. Campbell께,

귀하의 **131. 보수**에 Ascend Works를 선택해 주셔서 감사합니다. 저희가 산정한 필요 작업에 근거해 작업은 2주가 소요되며, 7,500달러로 견적을 제공해 드릴 수 있습니다. **132. 여기에는 실내 및 실외 벽에 페인트 이중 칠이 포함됩니다.** 이 작업은 경력이 풍부한 도장공으로 구성된 저희 팀에서 작업합니다. 적절한 페인트를 구매하는 것부터 작업이 마무리된 후 정리하는 일까지 **133. 모든 것**을 처리해 드립니다. 궁금한 점이 있으시면, 저에게 전화 주시면 기꺼이 무엇이든 귀하 **134. 와** 의논해 드리겠습니다. 관심을 가져주셔서 감사드리며, 조만간 함께 하게 되길 바랍니다.

Russell Bridges 드림
매장 관리자

---

132 (A) 현장점검은 착공 전에 실시되어야 합니다.
　　 (B) 저희 작업 포트폴리오가 곧 귀하에게 전달될 것입니다.
　　 (C) 고객 리뷰는 서비스를 지속적으로 개선하는 데 도움이 됩니다.
　　 (D) 여기에는 실내 및 실외 벽에 페인트 이중 칠이 포함됩니다.

135-138번은 다음 보증서에 관한 문제입니다.

> **Metta 핸드백**
>
> 72 Woodlands Spinney · San Saba, Texas 76832 · 미국
>
> Metta 핸드백은 고급 명품 핸드백 제조업체라는 명성을 자랑스럽게 여깁니다. 저희는 시중에서 구할 수 있는 최고의 소재로 최상의 주의를 기울여 하나하나 손수 공들여 만듭니다. 저희 제품을 받아보시고 **135. 수준이 떨어진다**는 생각이 드신다면, 저희에게 연락해 신고해 주세요.
>
> 이 정책은 저희 오프라인 매장에서 **136. 직접** 구입했거나 온라인 소매점에서 구입한 제품에 한해 적용됩니다. 모든 구입에는 구매 식별번호가 제공됩니다. **137. 전 제품은 지정 식별번호로 신고가 이루어져야 합니다.** 사용자의 제품 오용으로 발생한 훼손이나 가방이 강력한 화학물질에 노출 **138. 당한** 경우에는 품질 보증 정책으로 보장되지 않는 점에 유의해 주시기 바랍니다.

137 (A) 저희 매장은 다양한 지불 계획 옵션을 제공합니다.
　　 (B) 온라인 구매품의 배송 시간은 영업일 기준 최대 5일이 소요될 수 있습니다.
　　 (C) 전 제품은 지정 식별번호로 신고가 이루어져야 합니다.
　　 (D) Metta 핸드백은 혁신적인 디자인으로 다수의 상을 수상했습니다.

139-142번은 다음 기사에 관한 문제입니다.

> **Hogan, Frontier Fabric의 CEO에 임명되다**
>
> 국내 최대 직물 공급사인 Frontier Fabric에서 최근 Linda Hogan이 CEO직을 맡게 된다고 발표했다. "Ms. Hogan은 재임 기간 내내 거듭해서 **139. 탁월함**을 입증했기에, 저희가 옳은 결정을 내린다는 데 한 치의 의심도 없습니다."라고 회사의 대변인인 Gregory Schmidt가 말했다.
>
> Ms. Hogan은 섬유 산업에서 20년이 넘는 경력을 가지고 있다. 가장 최근에는 Fronter Fabric의 해외 진출 활동을 감독했다. **140. 회사는 그녀의 진두지휘 하에 상당한 시장 점유율을 확보했다.** "역할을 제안 받았을 때 아주 기뻤 **141. 습니다.** 이러한 기회에 기대가 많이 됩니다."라고 Ms. Hogan은 말했다.
>
> Sardinia에 본사를 둔 Frontier Fabric은 개별 섬유 제조공장과 제휴를 맺고 카운티 **142. 전역**의 의류 업체에 최고급 소재를 공급한다.

140 (A) 회사는 그녀의 진두지휘 하에 상당한 시장 점유율을 확보했다.
　　 (B) 부족 사태로 인해 직물 가격이 상승했다.
　　 (C) 경험이 더 많은 구성원을 이용할 수 있다.
　　 (D) 경영진은 최근에 투표를 실시했다.

143-146번은 다음 편지에 관한 문제입니다.

> 1월 5일
>
> Dana Wilkinson
> 12654 Salmon River Road
> San Diego, CA 92129
>
> Ms. Wilkinson께,
>
> 귀하의 Golf and Tennis 클럽(GTC) 회원권이 지난달에 만료되었음을 다시 알려드립니다. 회원권을 지속하지 않을 계획이시라면, **143. 저희에게** 알려주셔서 저희쪽 기록을 갱신할 수 있게 해주시기 바랍니다. 그러나, 연장을 원하신다면, 현재 회원권 갱신에 대해 30% 할인을 제공하고 있다는 사실을 알려드리고자 합니다. 이는 단 2,000달러로 GTC 수영장 **144. 이용**을 포함하는 정회원 자격을 1년 더 유지하게 됨을 의미합니다. **145. 이 혜택을 받으시려면 1월 10일까지 답장해주시기 바랍니다.** 회원권을 갱신하시려면, **146. 단지** 여기 동봉해드린 신청서를 제출해 주시면 됩니다.
>
> 저희 GTC의 소중한 고객으로 계속 남아주시기를 기대합니다.
>
> 진심을 담아,
>
> Kelso Montburg
> 회원서비스 책임자
> 동봉물재중

145 (A) 이 혜택을 받으시려면 1월 10일까지 답장해주시기 바랍니다.
　　 (B) 이미 청구대금을 지불하셨다면 이 편지는 무시하셔도 좋습니다.
　　 (C) 주 2회 개인 교육을 제공합니다.
　　 (D) 회원권 취소에 관한 확인 이메일이 곧 발송될 것입니다.

PART 7
P. 177

147-148번은 다음 쿠폰에 관한 문제입니다.

> **Luigi Angelo's**
>
> Luigi Angelo's는 Chester 공원 지점의 리모델링이 이제 완료되었음을 알려드리게 되어 기쁩니다. 다시 문을 열어 여러분을 맞이하오니 Yosemite Way 196번지로 방문해 주세요. **3월 3일에서 3월 9일 사이에 아무 때나 이 쿠폰을 가져오시면**(148) 일반 음료와 수제 파스타 요리 중 하나(147) 주문 시 가든 샐러드를 무료로 드실 수 있습니다. 테이블당 한 장의 쿠폰만 사용하실 수 있습니다.

147 Luigi Angelo's에 관하여 사실인 것은 무엇인가?
　　 (A) 채소밭이 있다.
　　 (B) 3월에 새 지점을 열 것이다.
　　 (C) 직접 파스타를 만든다.
　　 (D) 최근에 제공 메뉴를 확대했다.

148 쿠폰에 관하여 알 수 있는 것은 무엇인가?
　　 (A) 배달 주문에 적용할 수 있다.
　　 (B) Luigi Angelo's 전 지점에서 사용할 수 있다.
　　 (C) 손님들이 그것으로 무료 음료를 받을 수 있다.
　　 (D) 일주일 동안만 유효하다.

149-150번은 다음 기사에 관한 문제입니다.

> ### Turner 연구소에서 귀하를 원합니다. (149)
>
> Turner 연구소에서는 농업과학에 조예가 깊고 농장 운영 경험이 있는 보조 연구원을 찾고 있습니다. (149) 프로젝트 자격요건에 대해 더 자세히 알아보고 온라인으로 지원하시려면 www.turnercropinitiative.org를 방문해 주세요. 또는 방문 지원을 원하시면, Lyndale로 2425번지에 있는 연구소로 오셔서, Nicole Sessions를 찾으시기 바랍니다. (150)
>
> Dr. Jackson Sparrow에 의해 설립된 연구소는 건강에 좋고 해충에 강한 작물을 재배하는 오픈 소스 종자를 개발 및 시험, 홍보함으로써 전세계에 식량을 공급하는 것을 목표로 합니다.

149 기사의 목적은 무엇인가?
(A) 재배 방식을 설명하기 위해
(B) 시장성 테스트를 위해 자원봉사자들을 요청하기 위해
(C) 과학자의 은퇴를 축하하기 위해
(D) 일자리를 공지하기 위해

150 Ms. Sessions는 누구겠는가?
(A) 대학원생
(B) 연구소 직원
(C) 농업대학 교수
(D) 지역 언론인

151-152번은 다음 공지에 관한 문제입니다.

> ### Haynes 의류 재개장
>
> 동부 고속도로 2117번지에 있는 저희의 아름다운 현대적인 시설 공사가 완료되었습니다. 따라서 2개월 동안 여러분의 곁을 떠나 있던 저희 Haynes 의류는 4월 1일에 Tri-state 지역으로 이전하게 됨을 기쁘게 알려드립니다.
>
> 동부 고속도로 지점은 시내 중심부에 위치하게 됩니다. 이는 도시 전역에 있는 고객이 매장을 이용하기 더 쉬워진다는 것을 의미합니다. (151)
>
> Haynes 의류 재개장을 기념하기 위해, 저희는 4월 1일에 특별행사를 개최합니다. 오전 10시 개장 시간에 입장하는 고객 선착순 50명은 경품 추첨행사에 응모됩니다. 500달러 상품권을 받게 될 행운의 주인공 2명을 추첨합니다. (152) 오세요! 이 행사를 놓치지 마세요!
>
> 그리고 저희 온라인 상점 www.haynesapparel.com을 둘러보시는 것도 잊지 마세요.

151 공지에 따르면, Haynes 의류는 왜 이전하는가?
(A) 더 편리한 장소에 위치하기 위해
(B) 다른 고객층을 유치하기 위해
(C) 더욱 다양한 의류를 제공하기 위해
(D) 더 빠른 배송서비스를 제공하기 위해

152 Haynes 의류는 4월 1일에 어떻게 재개장을 기념할 것인가?
(A) 온라인 할인을 제공해서
(B) 평소보다 일찍 문을 열어서
(C) 신상품을 공개해서
(D) 경품을 나눠줘서

153-154번은 다음 문자 메시지 대화에 관한 문제입니다.

> **Andre Lawrence [오후 1시 55분]**
> 저기, 식당에서 벌써 나오셨나요?
>
> **Olga Furtak [오후 1시 57분]**
> 주차장을 찾느라 애먹었어요. 지금 막 들어왔어요. (153)
>
> **Andre Lawrence [오후 1시 58분]**
> 그럼 잘됐네요. Griggs 지점 직원 2명이 아니라 5명이 저희와 함께 점심 식사를 할 거라는 걸 방금 알았어요. (153)/(154)
>
> **Olga Furtak [오후 1시 59분]**
> 문제없어요. 참석자들이 모두 먹을 수 있게 샌드위치를 충분히 가져갈게요. (154) 더 사야 할 게 있나요?
>
> **Andre Lawrence [오후 2시 00분]**
> 그거면 될 거예요. 접시와 식기류는 사무실에 충분히 있으니까요.

153 오후 1시 58분에, Mr. Lawrence가 "그럼 잘됐네요"라고 할 때 무엇을 의미하겠는가?
(A) 메뉴 종류에 만족한다.
(B) 식당이 좋은 만남의 장소라고 생각한다.
(C) Ms. Furtak에게 정보를 제공하기에 적당한 때에 연락했다.
(D) Ms. Furtak가 Griggs 지점으로 전근간다는 것에 만족한다.

154 Ms. Furtak는 다음에 무엇을 하겠는가?
(A) 접시와 식기류를 살 것이다
(B) 다른 사업체를 방문할 것이다
(C) 음식을 추가로 주문할 것이다
(D) 상사에게 연락할 것이다

155-157번은 다음 이메일에 관한 문제입니다.

> 수신: JiwooP@flash.net
> 발신: JohnRothko@updikehomestore.com
> 날짜: 3월 15일
> 제목: 배송 문제
>
> Ms. Park께,
>
> 고객님의 Updike 홈스토어 가을 카탈로그가 지난주에 발송되었습니다. 그러나 '발신인에게 반송'이라는 메모와 함께 저희에게 돌아왔습니다.
>
> 올 가을 독점 제공 혜택들을 놓치지 않도록 카탈로그를 받아보시기 바랍니다. 고객님의 과거 구매이력으로 볼 때, 신규 테라스 의자 및 테이블 제품군에 관심 있으실 것 같습니다. (156) 저희가 50달러 상당의 할인쿠폰과 함께 카탈로그를 다시 보내드릴 수 있도록 현 주소지를 알려주시기 바랍니다. (155)
>
> 아울러, 저희 고객지원 서비스가 개선되었습니다. 이제 전화통화 대신, 신규 온라인 채팅 기능을 통해서도 저희 직원과 상담하실 수 있습니다. (157) 물론, 주문관련 문제에 대해 저희 지원센터에 555-3093번으로 전화주셔도 됩니다.
>
> 연락 기다리겠습니다.
>
> John Rothko
> 총지배인, Updike 홈스토어

155 이메일은 왜 발송되었는가?
(A) 새 연락처를 요청하기 위해
(B) 입사지원에 대한 후속논의를 하기 위해
(C) 파손품에 대해 사과하기 위해
(D) 개정된 환불정책에 관해 설명하기 위해

156 Ms. Park에 관하여 언급된 것은 무엇인가?

(A) 최근에 다른 도시로 이사했다.

(B) 이전에 Updike 홈스토어에서 가구를 구입한 적이 있다.

(C) 할인쿠폰을 요청했다.

(D) 예전 카탈로그를 보고 제품을 구매했다.

157 최근 Updike 홈스토어에서 무엇을 변경했는가?

(A) 이제 고객지원센터를 24시간 내내 이용할 수 있다.

(B) 가정 설치비가 인하되었다.

(C) 일부 비인기 제품군이 단종되었다.

(D) 고객 문의사항이 채팅서비스를 통해 처리될 수 있다.

158-160번은 다음 웹 페이지에 관한 문제입니다.

배송 정책

Big Turtle Clothiers의 속달 서비스는 Maine 지역에서 오후 6시 전에 이루어진 모든 주문 건에 대해 익일 배송을 보장합니다.(158A)/(158B)/(159) 익일 배송을 받으려면 저희 웹사이트를 통해 온라인으로 주문이 들어와야 합니다. 하지만 주문하기 전 저희 물류 센터에서의 거리에 따라 배송비가 차등 부과될 수 있다는 점을 유념해 주시기 바랍니다.(158B) 일반 배송 서비스도 이용 가능하지만, 주문품이 도착하기까지 최대 7 영업일이 소요될 수 있습니다.

목적지	속달/배송 시간	일반/배송 시간
Newport (Harmony, Dexter, Corinth, Bradford)	6.50달러/익일 배송	무료(158D)/3 영업일
Dixmont (Thorndike, Jackson, Monroe)	8.30달러/익일 배송	무료(158D)/5 영업일
Dedham (Orrington, Holden, Bucksport)	이용 불가	3.50달러/5 영업일
타 주(160)	이용 불가	7.50달러부터(160)/7 영업일

---

158 Big Turtle Clothiers에 관하여 언급되지 않은 것은 무엇인가?

(A) 속달 배송 서비스를 제공한다.

(B) Maine에 물류 센터가 있다.

(C) 해외로 제품을 판매한다.

(D) 일부 지역에 무료로 배송한다.

159 첫 번째 단락, 두 번째 줄의 단어, "placed"와 의미상 가장 가까운 것은?

(A) 제출됐다

(B) 고안됐다

(C) 제시됐다

(D) 다뤄졌다

160 다른 주로 주문을 발송하는 최소 비용은 얼마인가?

(A) 3.50달러

(B) 6.50달러

(C) 7.50달러

(D) 8.30달러

161-163번은 다음 초대장에 관한 문제입니다.

4월 10일 일요일, 정오부터 오후 4시까지

시립 문화유산 박물관에 오셔서 Chesterton의 200주년을 기념해 주세요!

올해는 우리 도시가 200주년이 되는 해입니다. 200년의 역사를 기리기 위해, 박물관에서 수년간 보존해온 우리 지역 사회의 독특한 문화 및 유산을 기념하는 행사를 개최합니다.(162) 시립 문화유산 박물관을 후원해 주신 모든 기부자 여러분을 영화 및 고급 식사, 그리고 저희 최신 전시의 최초 관람을 즐길 수 있는 오후로 초대합니다.(161) Chesterton 대학교 Chloe Emmerich 교수의 기조연설과 함께, 저명한 학자들이 참여하는 프레젠테이션과 패널 토론을 즐기십시오. 그리고 Geoffrey Maxwell 감독의 다큐멘터리 영화 <From Frontier to Front Yard>의 상영을 놓치지 마세요. 점심과 음료는 Twin Rivers Pub에서 공급합니다. 모든 티켓 및 음식 판매 수익은 시의 <미래 영화제작자> 프로젝트에 사용됩니다.티켓을 예약하시려면, www.chestertonCHM.com/bookings를 방문해 주세요. 최소 48시간 전에 미리 구입하셔야 하고 수량이 한정되어 있다는 것을 명심하시기 바랍니다.(163)

---

161 초대장은 누구를 대상으로 하겠는가?

(A) 역사 교수들

(B) Chesterton 시 공무원들

(C) 과거 기부자들

(D) 영화를 공부하는 학생들

162 첫 번째 단락, 세 번째 줄의 단어, "over"와 의미상 가장 가까운 것은?

(A) ~보다 위에

(B) 더 많은

(C) ~를 너머

(D) ~내내

163 행사에 관하여 사실인 것은 무엇인가?

(A) 일정한 수의 티켓만을 판매할 것이다.

(B) 무료 점심을 제공한다.

(C) 영화사에 관한 연설이 있을 것이다.

(D) 매년 개최된다.

164-167번은 다음 온라인 채팅 대화문에 관한 문제입니다.

David Villa [오후 1시 02분]

여러분. 부탁할 게 있어요. 제가 원래 오늘 야간근무인데, 몸 상태가 별로 좋지 않네요. 누구 저와 근무시간을 좀 바꿔주실 수 있을까요?

Allison Costello [오후 1시 04분]

제가 바꿔드리고 싶은데, 호텔에 9시는 되어야 도착할 거예요.(164) Haverford 시내에서 7시에 저녁 약속이 있거든요. 제가 약간 늦게 근무를 시작하는 걸 Ms. Wahlberg가 괜찮다고 하신다면,(165) 제가 대신 할게요.

Lamar Jackson [오후 1시 06분]

David, 제가 도와드리고 싶은데, 새 영화 <Halfway There>의 저녁 상영 티켓을 이미 사놔서요. 누군가 다른 분이 도와드릴 수 있으면 좋겠네요.

David Villa [오후 1시 08분]

Allison, 그거 나쁘지 않은 생각인데요, Ms. Wahlberg가 거절하실까 봐 걱정되네요.(165) 안내 데스크에 항상 충분한 수의 직원이 있는 걸 정말 중요하게 생각하시거든요.

Allison Costello [오후 1시 09분]

맞아요. David, Ms. Wahlberg에게 연락해서 지금 근무 중인 사람 중에 잠깐 더 일할 수 있는 사람이 있는지 알아보는 게 어때요?(166)

Jessica Choi [오후 1시 12분]
모두 안녕하세요. 더 일찍 답변을 드렸어야 했는데, 너무 바빴어요. 제가 좀 더 있으면서 Allison이 올 때까지 기다릴게요. **(166)/(167)**

Allison Costello [오후 1시 14분]
좋은 계획인 것 같아요. Ms. Wahlberg도 괜찮다고 하실 것 같나요? **(166)**

David Villa [오후 1시 18분]
방금 그 분과 통화했어요. Ms. Walhberg도 전혀 상관없으시대요. **(166)**
모두 도와줘서 고마워요.

Allison Costello [오후 1시 19분]
별 말씀을요. 이따 봐요, Jessica.

164 작성자들은 어디에서 근무하는가?
(A) 극장
(B) 병원
(C) 식당
(D) 호텔

165 모든 작성자들에 관해 무엇이 사실이겠는가?
(A) 같은 상사 밑에서 일한다.
(B) 함께 저녁을 먹을 것이다.
(C) 정기적으로 영화를 본다.
(D) 모두 Haverford에 산다.

166 오후 1시 18분에, Mr. Villa가 "Ms. Walhberg도 전혀 상관없으시대요"라고 할 때 무엇을 의미하는가?
(A) 계획이 맘에 들지 않는다.
(B) 그를 데리러 올 수 있다.
(C) 일주일 동안 그를 대신해 근무할 것이다.
(D) 일정 변경에 개의치 않는다.

167 오늘 저녁에 누가 원래 계획보다 늦게 근무를 마치겠는가?
(A) David Villa
(B) Lamar Jackson
(C) Allison Costello
(D) Jessica Choi

168-171번은 다음 이메일에 관한 문제입니다.

수신: 영업팀 관리자
발신: Peter Bristow
날짜: 5월 21일
제목: 정보

영업팀 관리자께,

올해 최고 성과를 낸 직원들에게 영업 우수상으로 공로를 인정해주는 시기가 돌아왔습니다. **(168)** — [1] —. 이 상은 Prion Energy의 가치를 가장 잘 보여주고 그 이상에 도달하려는 자세를 지닌 직원에게 수여됩니다. 따라서 팀원을 추천하실 때에는 **(168)** 판매 수치와 더불어 공동체에의 기여도를 고려해 주시기 바랍니다. — [2] —.

팀원 추천 양식은 www.prionenergy.com/awards에 있습니다. **(171)** — [3] —. 양식은 6월 16일까지 인사부 앞으로 이메일로 발송해주시기 바랍니다. 정규직 직원이 모두 대상이지만, 지금까지 한번도 수상한 적 없는 직원을 추천해 주시길 권장 드립니다 **(168)**. 수상자는 7월 3일 연중 만찬 행사에서 공개합니다. **(169)/(170)** — [4] —. Chevalier Room을 예약해 놓았으며, 다과도 제공됩니다. **(170)**

의견 주셔서 감사드립니다.

Peter Bristow 드림
Prion Energy, 인사부

168 이메일의 목적은 무엇인가?
(A) 계획 변경을 발표하기 위해
(B) 직원의 추천을 요청하기 위해
(C) 행사 장소 투표를 실시하기 위해
(D) 새로운 정책을 강조하기 위해

169 7월 3일에 무슨 일이 일어날 것인가?
(A) 일부 티켓이 주문될 것이다.
(B) 몇 가지 요구 사항에 대해 설명될 것이다.
(C) 일부 후보가 취합될 것이다.
(D) 일부 수상자가 발표될 것이다.

170 행사에 관하여 언급된 것은 무엇인가?
(A) 초청 연사가 포함될 것이다.
(B) 음식과 음료가 제공될 것이다.
(C) 날짜가 확정되지 않았다.
(D) 야외에서 열릴 것이다.

171 [1], [2], [3], [4]로 표시된 곳 중 다음 문장이 들어가기에 가장 적절한 곳은 어디인가?

"문서 사본도 제공해 드렸습니다."

(A) [1]
(B) [2]
(C) [3]
(D) [4]

172-175번은 다음 기사에 관한 문제입니다.

복원 프로젝트, 다시 궤도에 오르다

Garo (10월 21일) — 상징적인 Sigil Building을 복원하는 프로젝트가 순조롭게 진행되지 않으면서 Garo 주민들은 격동의 시간을 보냈다. 다행히도, 프로젝트를 맡고 있는 기업인 Cashera Builders에서 프로젝트를 예정대로 진행한다고 발표했다.

Cashera Builders에서 건물 복원안을 처음 공개했을 때, 엇갈린 평가를 받았다. 주민들은 기간을 비현실적이라 여겼고 비용이 명시된 것보다 상당히 더 높아질 것이라 생각했다. **(172)** — [1] —. Cashera Builders의 CEO인 Armanda Way는 "Cashera에서는 가용 자원을 최대한으로 활용할 수 있다고 봅니다. 사람들은 불가능한 약속이라고 봤지만, 저희는 지킬 수 있다고 확신합니다."라고 말했다. Ms. Way는 자사가 언제나 건설업계의 선두주자로 인정받아왔다고 언급했다. — [2] —.

Cashera Builders에서 제안한 기간과 비용은 지난 1월 전문가들로 구성된 패널의 필수 정밀 검토를 받았다. **(173)** 전문가들은 논의하는데 많은 시간을 보냈지만, 제안서는 최종적으로 통과되었다. 투표에서 Cashera의 손을 들어준 중요한 요인은 포트폴리오였다. **(175)** — [3] —.

프로젝트는 처음에 Cashera에서 통제할 수 없는 요인들로 인해 상당한 지연에 부딪혔다. 악천후가 길어지면서 작업은 지연되어야 했다. 다행스럽게도, 건설팀의 끈질긴 노력 덕분에 프로젝트는 이제 재개되었다. — [4] —.

프로젝트의 현재 상황은 일반인이 열람하도록 공개되어 있다. 누구나 추가 정보를 요청하거나 의견을 제시할 수 있다. 관련 링크를 확인하려면 www.garocouncil.gov.au/sigil을 방문하면 된다. **(174)**

172 기사에 따르면, Sigil Building을 복원하는 데 관한 초기 우려는 무엇이었는가?
(A) 짧은 소요시간
(B) 도로 혼잡 증가
(C) 손상 가능성
(D) 의회 승인 필요성

173 Cashera Builders에서 제출한 제안서에 관하여 알 수 있는 것은 무엇인가?

    (A) 여러 번 수정되어야 했다.

    (B) 마감기한을 지나 제출됐다.

    (C) 만장일치로 승인 받았다.

    (D) 많은 전문가의 검토를 받았다.

174 온라인으로 무엇을 이용할 수 있는가?

    (A) Cashera의 포트폴리오

    (B) 예산 품의서

    (C) 제안서 원본

    (D) 프로젝트 진행상황

175 [1], [2], [3], [4]로 표시된 곳 중 다음 문장이 들어가기에 가장 적절한 곳은 어디인가?

    "과거 복구 프로젝트가 상당한 부분을 차지했다."

    (A) [1]

    (B) [2]

    (C) [3]

    (D) [4]

176-180번은 다음 전단지와 이메일에 관한 문제입니다.

Idalou 도시 마켓에서
모든 공예가들을 초대합니다

Idalou 도시 마켓이 6월 12일부터 15일까지 Skyline 공원으로 돌아옵니다. 공예가는 자신의 재능과 제품을 뽐낼 기회를 갖게 됩니다. 매년 방문객의 수가 증가해왔고, 올해도 마찬가지일 것이라 예상합니다. **전년도에는 Texas에 사는 장인들만 참여할 수 있었지만,**(179) 저희는 거주하는 주에 상관없이 모두 수용하는 걸로 규칙을 바꿨습니다.

지원하시려면, 다음을 따라주세요.

1. www.idaloumarket.com/register로 가서 양식을 작성해 주세요. **가판대를 공유할 예정인 분들의 경우, 양측이 하나의 양식을 사용할 수 있습니다. 하지만, 등록비 35달러는 여전히 두 판매자에게 모두 적용됩니다.**(178)

2. 마켓에서 전시할 예정인 품목의 사진을 10장 이하로 업로드해 주세요. 파일이름을 다음과 같이 지정해 주세요: 품목 설명_판매자 이름.

필수 서류 제출 마감일은 4월 20일입니다. **승인되면, 5월 2일까지 이메일이 전송될 것입니다.**(176) 해당자는 5월 16일까지 나머지 525달러의 가판대 관리비를 지불하셔야 합니다. 이 요금에는 원하는 대로 사용하실 수 있는 5피트 길이의 테이블 4개가 포함됩니다. 제공해주신 사진은 귀하의 홈페이지 링크와 함께 저희 웹사이트 "출품자" 탭에 게재될 것입니다.(177)

수신: e.orville@idaloumarket.com

발신: rin.takai@takaisupply.com

참조: henry.reiss@reissphotos.net

날짜: 5월 9일

제목: 도시 마켓

안녕하세요.

저의 가판 파트너인 Henry Reiss와 저는 승인 이메일을 받았고, 저희는 올해 축제에 참여하게 되어 매우 기쁩니다. 저희는 웹사이트에 있는 계좌번호로 계좌 이체를 통해 공유 가판대에 대한 비용을 지불했습니다.(178) 올해 행사에 관해 더 많이 듣고 싶습니다.

저는 작년에 행사에 참여할 기회가 있었고,(179) 몇몇 장인들이 제공한 개별 지도 시간이 정말 좋았어요. 올해도 그와 유사한 무언가가 있을까요? 저는 관객에게 저희의 공예품을 어떻게 만드는지 보여주고 싶어서 만

약 있다면 저에게 알려주세요.(180)

Rin Takai

---

176 승인 이메일은 언제 발송되는가?

    (A) 4월 20일

    (B) 5월 2일

    (C) 5월 16일

    (D) 6월 12일

177 전단지에서는 Idalou 도시 마켓에 관해 무엇을 언급하는가?

    (A) 모든 참가자들에게 무료 주차를 제공한다.

    (B) 온라인 페이지에서 참여하는 공예가들을 홍보한다.

    (C) 처음으로 개최될 것이다.

    (D) 입장료를 받지 않는다.

178 Ms. Takai와 Mr. Reiss에 관하여 알 수 있는 것은 무엇인가?

    (A) 서로 다른 양식을 작성했다.

    (B) 테이블이 더 필요할 것이다.

    (C) 둘 다 35달러의 요금을 지불했다.

    (D) 비디오 사용 지침서를 제공한다.

179 Ms. Takai에 관하여 사실인 것은 무엇이겠는가?

    (A) 그녀의 공예품이 작년에 인기 있었다.

    (B) 그녀의 작품이 잡지에 실렸다.

    (C) 온라인 페이지를 갖고 있지 않다.

    (D) Texas에 거주한다.

180 이메일에서, Ms. Takai는 무엇에 관해 물어보는가?

    (A) 기술을 보여줄 가능성

    (B) 가판 규격

    (C) 다른 예술가들의 연락처

    (D) 허용되는 결제 수단

181-185번은 다음 이메일들에 관한 문제입니다.

수신: ASG 콘퍼런스 참석자

발신: Conrad Waters

날짜: 4월 23일

제목: ASG 콘퍼런스 업데이트

ASG 콘퍼런스 참석자께,

ASG 콘퍼런스가 5월 20일부터 5월 23일까지 Cloverfield 호텔에서 열리게 됐음을 알려드립니다.(181) 호텔은 다양한 교통수단을 이용할 수 있는 Ashburton의 중심부에 위치합니다.

귀하의 입장권과 함께 객실을 예약하셨으면, Cloverfield 호텔에서 보내는 확인 메일을 받으셨을 겁니다. **아직 객실이 일부 남아 있습니다. 마음이 바뀌어 객실을 원하시는 경우, 최대한 빨리 저에게 알려주시기 바랍니다.**(184) 또한, 일부 참석자는 교통수단 지원이 필요하신 걸로 알고 있습니다. **도착 시간을 이 이메일에 회신해 주시면, 귀하의 요청을 수용해 드릴 수 있습니다.**(183)

콘퍼런스는 5월 20일 오후 12시에 올해 주최자의 연설로 시작합니다. 그 **이후 시간에는 동료들과 자유롭게 도시를 둘러보셔도 됩니다.**(182) 강연과 프레젠테이션은 5월 21일 오전 9시에 아침 일찍 시작합니다. 일정이 확정되면, 웹사이트에 게시하겠습니다.

감사합니다.

Conrad Waters

행사 담당자

S&P Food Group

수신: Conrad Waters
발신: Ethel Elliott
날짜: 4월 24일
제목: 회신: ASG 콘퍼런스 업데이트

Mr. Waters께:

확인 메일 감사합니다. 당신과 전화로 여러 번 통화했더니 직접 만나뵐 일이 기대됩니다. 저는 금요일 오전 11시에 Ashburton에 도착합니다.

객실을 예약하기엔 너무 늦었나요? 예전 동료와 함께 머물려던 계획이 틀어져서, 갑자기 필요한 상황입니다. **(184)** 또한, 제가 강연에 쓸 제 작품 샘플 몇 개를 가져갈 예정인데요, 그래야 훨씬 더 편리할 거거든요. **(185)** 그렇지 않더라도, 문제되지는 않습니다. 제가 방법을 마련할 수 있을 거에요.

도와주셔서 감사합니다.

Ethel Elliott 드림
수석 제품 디자이너
Magnum Opus Inc.

181 첫 번째 이메일의 목적은 무엇인가?
(A) 일정을 변경하기 위해
(B) 여행객에게 지불을 요청하기 위해
(C) 행사장 목록을 발송하기 위해
(D) 행사 세부사항을 확정하기 위해

182 Mr. Waters가 5월 20일에 관해 무엇을 언급하는가?
(A) 행사가 오전에 시작할 것이다.
(B) 도시 투어가 제공될 것이다.
(C) 오직 한 개의 행사만 계획됐다.
(D) 차량 이용이 필요하다.

183 첫 번째 이메일에서 두 번째 단락, 다섯 번째 줄의 단어, "accommodate"와 의미상 가장 가까운 것은?
(A) 처리하다
(B) 만족시키다
(C) 포함하다
(D) 결정하다

184 Mr. Waters는 Ms. Elliott을 위해 무엇을 하겠는가?
(A) 그녀를 동료에게 소개할 것이다.
(B) 숙박을 확보하려고 시도할 것이다.
(C) 세부 일정을 마련할 것이다.
(D) 자가용 서비스를 고용할 것이다.

185 두 번째 이메일에서 Ms. Elliott에 관해 알 수 있는 것은 무엇인가?
(A) 행사 준비를 도왔다.
(B) 첫 번째로 초대받았다.
(C) 최근 승진했다.
(D) 연사 중 한 명이 될 것이다.

186-190번은 다음 공지, 기사, 이메일에 관한 문제입니다.

Bradbury 미술관 관람객 여러분께:

Pioneer시에서 41번가에 보수작업을 하는 동안 때때로 미술관 출입구가 폐쇄됩니다. 안타깝게도, 이는 미술관이 가끔 폐관해야 함을 의미합니다. **(186)** 이 일정에 관한 가장 최신 정보를 보시려면 미술관 웹사이트를 방문해 주세요.

시내에는 현대사 박물관이나 우표 박물관 같은 다른 박물관들이 있음을 기억해주시기 바랍니다. **보수작업은 7월 31일까지 완료될 예정입니다.** **(187)** 이 일로 인해 발생할 혼란에 대해 사과 드립니다.

Pioneer시 Observer

(9월 2일) ― 8월말까지 이어진 거의 두 달에 걸친 보수작업 끝에, **41번가 공사가 드디어 완료되었다.** **(187)** Bradbury 미술관이 이 기간 동안 방문객 수의 상당한 감소를 겪었기에, 마침내 한숨 돌릴 수 있게 되었다. 미술관은 정상 일정을 재개하는 것 외에, 새로 추가된 시설은 곧 공개될 것이다. 시의회의 자금 지원 덕분에, **미술관은 마침내 라이브 콘서트 및 공연용 무대를 갖춘, 경치가 좋은 안뜰을 제작하는 자체 공사 프로젝트를 마무리 지을 수 있었다.** **(188)**

Bradbury 미술관은 축하행사로 10월 20일에 새 뜰에서 무료 음악 축제를 주최한다. 출연이 예정된 공연그룹에는 Charles Liou의 재즈 메신저와 색소폰 연주자 Ann Sandman이 포함된다. **모든 참석자는 경품추첨 행사에 응모한다.** **(189)**

날씨가 좋지 않을 경우, 행사는 10월 22일로 옮겨질 수 있다. **(190)** 추가 세부사항은 www.bradburymuseum.org/events에서 확인할 수 있다.

수신: charlesliou@messengers.net
발신: terrygreen@bradburymuseum.org
날짜: 10월 23일 **(190)**
제목: 축하합니다.

Mr. Liou께,

어제 오후의 공연에 대해 감사 드리고 싶었어요. **(190)** 날씨가 개어서 시민들이 당신 밴드의 훌륭한 공연을 들을 수 있어 다행입니다. 그렇게 열광적인 관객들을 볼 수 있어 너무 좋았습니다. 제가 아는 사람들은 모두 아직도 그 공연 얘기를 하고 있어요!

곧 Pioneer시에 다시 와주세요.

Terry Green

186 공지는 주로 무엇에 관한 것인가?
(A) 곧 있을 건물 폐쇄
(B) 인상된 회비
(C) 박물관 일자리
(D) 고객 서비스 정책

187 도로 보수 프로젝트에 관하여 알 수 있는 것은 무엇인가?
(A) 8월에 시작되었다.
(B) 추가 자금이 필요했다.
(C) Mr. Green이 감독했다.
(D) 예상보다 오래 걸렸다.

188 기사에 따르면, 박물관에 무엇이 건설되었는가?
(A) 주차장
(B) 오락 공간
(C) 기념품점
(D) 실내 극장

189 기사에서 축제의 한 가지 특징으로 무엇을 언급하는가?
(A) 시식 행사
(B) 신규 미술 전시회
(C) 경품 추첨
(D) 경매

190 축제에 관하여 알 수 있는 것은 무엇인가?
(A) 연기되어야 했다.
(B) 지역 주민들에게만 개방되었다.
(C) 매년 열릴 것이다.
(D) 많은 참석자들을 유치하지 못했다.

191-195번은 다음 광고와 이메일들에 관한 문제입니다.

Satoru Suite
지금 관람을 예약하세요!

Eden 공원 중심에 위치한, 최근 개조된 건물인 Satoru Suite는 Hamilton에 사무 공간을 만들고자 하는 신생 기업에 이상적인 장소입니다. 귀 사업체가 성장하는 데 필요한 모든 것을 갖출 수 있도록 수많은 추가 시설을 마련했습니다. **(191)** 모든 가구에는 공유 카페테리아 뿐만 아니라, 공동 회의실, 콘퍼런스 홀 이용이 포함됩니다. 맨 위층에는 고급 시설이 있는데, 동일한 시설을 포함하나 전용 체육관이 추가되어 있습니다. **(193)**

중심에 위치하여 지하철 또는 버스로 접근이 용이합니다. Satoru Suite 인근에는 추가 식사 선택지로 음식점 및 카페도 위치해 있습니다. 건물에 가장 최근에 추가된 시설에는 근무 전후 편리하게 쇼핑을 하실 수 있는 슈퍼마켓이 포함되어 있습니다. **(192)**

저희 웹사이트에서 관람을 예약하실 수 있을 뿐만 아니라 사진도 보실 수 있습니다. 공간이 빠르게 나가고 있으니, 오늘 귀하의 공간을 예약하세요!

수신: Tracy Cowell <tcowell@satorusuite.com>
발신: Mindy Howard <mhoward@dratmostpartners.com>
날짜: 9월 17일
제목: 관리비

Ms. Cowell, 안녕하세요.

Satoru Suite에 공간을 마련하는 문제로 연락 드렸습니다. 제 인테리어 디자인 사업에 신규 고객이 필요한 상황인데, 현재 사무실이 너무 외진 곳에 있는게 큰 문제인 것 같습니다. **(194)** 저는 Satoru Suite의 위치가 너무 마음에 들고, 최상층 세입자에게 제공되는 추가 기능이 저에게는 큰 장점이 됩니다. **(193)** 월 임대료 3,000달러에 청소 및 물품 관리비가 포함되나요? **(195)**

Mindy Howard

수신: Mindy Howard <mhoward@dratmostpartners.com>
발신: Tracy Cowell <tcowell@satorusuite.com>
날짜: 9월 17일
제목: 회신: 관리비

Ms. Howard께,

Satoru Suite에 관심을 가져 주셔서 감사드립니다. 저희 가격에는 공과금 뿐만 아니라 모든 관리비가 포함됩니다. 이렇게 할 경우 보통 대부분은 임대료에 300달러 정도 추가되겠지만, 저희 가격에는 이미 모든 것이 포함되어 있습니다.

또한 지금이 입주를 고려하기에 아주 좋은 시기라고 말씀드리고 싶습니다. 시설 재개관을 기념하기 위해 앞으로 두 달 안에 계약하는 모든 입주민을 대상으로 첫 달 임대료를 면제해 드립니다. **(195)** 저희가 신청을 승인하기 전에 귀하에 대한 신원 조회를 진행한다는 점에 유념해 주시기 바라며, 비용은 100달러입니다.

Tracy Cowell
임대 대리인, Satoru Suites

---

191 누가 광고된 공간을 이용하겠는가?
(A) 창고 직원
(B) 공무원
(C) 공장 노동자
(D) 사무 근로자

192 광고에 따르면, Satoru Suite 내에서 무엇이 이용 가능한가?
(A) 식료품점
(B) 도서관
(C) 우체국
(D) 카페

193 Ms. Howard는 어떤 특별한 추가 시설에 관심 있다고 암시하는가?
(A) 코너 사무실
(B) 운동 시설
(C) 공유 주방
(D) 콘퍼런스 홀

194 Ms. Howard는 왜 사업체를 현재 위치에서 옮기고 싶어 하겠는가?
(A) 직원을 더 추가했다.
(B) 최근 임대료가 올랐다.
(C) 사무실이 공사 중이다.
(D) 장소가 다른 사업체들과 너무 멀리 떨어져 있다.

195 Ms. Howard에게 할인이 얼마 제공되는가?
(A) 300달러
(B) 400달러
(C) 2,700달러
(D) 3,000달러

196-200번은 다음 언론 보도자료, 이메일, 초대장에 관한 문제입니다.

즉시 배포용
2월 7일

연락처: Wesley Mcguire
wmcguire@wyndhaminn.com

(Du Bois) — Thames Terrace에 위치한 The Wyndham 여관이 기나긴 정비 기간을 마치고 다시 한번 정식으로 방문객을 맞이한다. **(196)** 11월에 정비가 마무리될 예정이었으나, 열악한 기상 상황으로 호텔의 연회장 확장 프로젝트가 연기됐다. **2월 16일부터 30명 이상의 대규모 인원을 수용하는 새로운 연회장을 예약할 수 있다. (198)** 인근 식당 Canopy Plaza에서 콘퍼런스나 행사용 음식 및 케이터링 서비스를 예약할 수 있다.

The Wyndham 여관의 매니저인 Olga Hampton은 "저희가 이곳에 만든 변화를 대중에게 보여주게 되어 설렙니다. 호텔의 많은 부분을 개조했고 객실에는 최신 기술을 도입했습니다"라고 말했다. The Wyndham 여관은 객실 60개와 회의실, 이그제큐티브 라운지, 무료 와이파이를 제공한다. **(197)**

수신: Olga Hampton
발신: Gordon Wallace
날짜: 2월 12일
제목: 예약 요청

Olga, 안녕하세요.

The Wyndham 여관 연회장에서의 연례 시상식 주최 건에 관한 Du Bois 엔지니어 협회(DEA)의 요청을 전해 주셔서 감사합니다. 3월 첫째 주에 개최하는 것을 고려하고 있다고 들었는데, **(198)** 가능할지 모르겠습니다. **(200)** 가능하다면 미루고자 합니다. 우선, 저희 식당의 케이터링 파트가 생긴지 얼마 안 된 편이고, 이렇게나 급하게 그러한 대규모 행사를 저희가 감당할 수 있을지 자신이 없습니다. 둘째, 저희가 현재 새로운 수석 요리사를 찾는 중입니다. 이상적으로는, 행사를 한 달 늦췄으면 합니다. 어쨌든, 날짜가 확정되면 알려주세요. 날짜를 바탕으로 예상되는 문제가 있으면 알려드리겠습니다.

감사합니다.

Gordon

Du Bois 엔지니어 협회(DEA)에서 올해의 엔지니어 공로상 수상자로 **Ms. Caldwell**에게 표창하게 된 것을 자랑스럽게 생각합니다.(199) 부디 함께 하셔서 이러한 성과를 축하해 주시고 작년 한 해 동안 새롭게 알게 된 내용들을 공유하는 시간을 가지시기 바랍니다.

4월 15일 금요일 오후 6시(200)
Saddleback House, Lionel Road 콘퍼런스 센터
174 Cairn Square, Du Bois

작년 수상자이신 Martin Ross께서 개회사를 맡고, DEA의 Beverly Graves 사장님이 상을 수여할 예정입니다.

행사 담당자 Derek Kim에게 참석 여부를 dkim@deadubois.com으로 이메일을 보내서 알려주시기 바랍니다.

196 보도 자료에서 무엇을 발표하는가?
(A) 여관 재개관
(B) 수상
(C) 신규 서비스 출시
(D) 신임 관리자 채용

197 보도자료에 따르면, The Wyndham 여관에서 무엇을 제공하는가?
(A) 정원 투어
(B) 운동 시설
(C) 인터넷 연결
(D) 수영장

198 Mr. Wallace가 받은 예약 요청에 관하여 알 수 있는 것은 무엇인가?
(A) 30명 이상이 참석하는 행사용이다.
(B) 이미 확정됐다.
(C) 케이터링 서비스가 필요하지 않을 것이다.
(D) 특별 장비가 필요할 것이다.

199 초대장에 따르면, 누가 상을 받는가?
(A) Mr. Kim
(B) Mr. Ross
(C) Ms. Caldwell
(D) Ms. Graves

200 DEA 행사에 관하여 알 수 있는 것은 무엇인가?
(A) 오후 6시에 끝날 것이다.
(B) 다른 날짜로 옮겨졌다.
(C) 추가 연사를 초청했다.
(D) 텔레비전으로 방송될 것이다.

TEST 07

PART 5　　　　　　　　　　　　　　　P. 202

101 전문 패션 디자이너들은 종종 미적 특성을 높이기 위해 색상 선택에 변화를 준다.

102 Mr. Maxwell은 회사 이전에 관한 추가 정보를 자신의 관리자에게 메시지로 보냈다.

103 콘서트 주최자들은 원래 Dartmoor 대학에서 행사를 주최하려고 계획했지만, 그곳은 너무 외진 곳으로 여겨졌다.

104 영양소 섭취 권장량은 나이와 성별에 따라 다양하다.

105 Sultan 금융 그룹의 웹사이트는 오전 2시에서 4시 사이에는 접속할 수 없을 것이다.

106 입학을 희망하는 학생은 다른 필수 서류 외에 추천서를 제출해야 한다.

107 프로젝트 제안서 준비 지침의 경우, 이 요청에 첨부된 유용한 문서를 참조해 주세요.

108 SKG 회계에서의 10년의 경력 덕분에, Mrs. Ho는 기업 세무 컨설팅에 대한 완벽한 지식을 갖고 있다.

109 Ms. Clark는 소비자 보고서가 거의 마무리됐다고 마케팅 쪽에 확인해줬다.

110 신규 우주 탐사용 엔진에 대한 진척이 더디게 진행되고 있지만, 그럼에도 불구하고 내년에는 발사 준비가 갖춰질 것이다.

111 출장 중인 Mr. Ponchartrain은 Ms. Hyun이 계속 Carter 사 계정을 담당하게 했다.

112 Ms. Guelph는 최신 마케팅 설문조사 결과로 세미나를 마칠 것이다.

113 Randit사의 30년에 걸친 신뢰할만한 서비스 역사는 업계에서 유일무이하다.

114 계약서 최종본이 서명된 후, Ms. Cheng은 교섭자들에게 그들이 들인 시간과 노력에 대한 감사를 표했다.

115 공익기업들은 절차를 더 편리하게 하기 위해 온라인 요금납부 서비스를 점점 더 많이 제공해오고 있다.

116 건설자재가 늦게 배송됐음에도 불구하고, 공사직원들은 신속히 작업했고, 프로젝트 일정을 지켰다.

117 감사역은 예술 작품의 가격을 50,000달러로 평가하기는 했지만, 당신이 온라인으로 송금할 수 있다면 소유주가 기꺼이 협상해 줄 수도 있다.

118 표본 그룹이 Route 1 Shoes의 현재 광고를 기억에 남기지 않는다고 묘사한 후, 회사는 새로운 버전을 촬영하기로 결정했다.

119 Zahir 미술관 후원자들은 소식지에 등록하면 다음 번 구매한 것에 5퍼센트 할인을 받을 기회를 얻는다.

120 기자 회견에서 시 관계자는 기자들의 질문에 종종 유머 있게 대답한다.

121 Papillion 사는 일단 문서의 세부 내용들 일부를 재조정한 후 Lunae기업과 비즈니스 계약에 들어갈 것이다.

122 시장 점유율을 확대하려는 목표로 Hazel's Boutique에서는 연말까지 신규 지점을 34개 개장하고 싶어 한다.

123 Ms. Fontaine은 이미 그 날에 회의에 참석해야 했기에 학회와 일정이 겹쳤다.

124 전 직원은 계약상 변경을 요청하기 전 Ms. Lee와 상의해야 한다.

125 새로운 회사 본사에 관한 직원 의견이 이사회에 의해 추구됐다.

126 신규 노트북 판매 수치가 지난 6개월간 크게 증가했다.

127 후원자들의 관대한 기부 덕분에 우리는 전시공간을 추가로 지을 예정이다.

128 Meadowlark 호텔 리조트 그룹의 입사 지원 절차는 복잡하기에, 가급적 빨리 시작하시길 권장 드립니다.

129 많은 사람들이 정기 검진을 위해 치과 의사를 기다리는 시간을 거의 참을 수 없어 한다.

130 더 엄격해진 정부 규정의 결과로 많은 제조업체들이 에너지 효율이 좋은 에어컨을 더 많이 생산하고 있다.

PART 6　　　　　　　　　　　　　　　P. 205

131-134번은 다음 메모에 관한 문제입니다.

수신: drivers@canberratransport.gov.au
발신: Harold Strahan
날짜: 5월 7일
제목: 차량 평가

기사 여러분,

지난 주 말씀 드린 것처럼, 시장실에서 나온 대표단이 저희 버스에 대해 평가를 **131. 실시할 예정입니다.** 그들은 내년에 **132. 어떤** 장거리버스와 운송용 화물차가 교체되어야 하는지 결정할 계획입니다.

이 **133. 사안**에 대해 저희를 도와주시면, 도움이 될 것입니다. 시간 있으실 때, 차량을 운행하면서 지속적으로 발생했던 문제들을 저희에게 알려주세요. 이 정보를 관리팀에 mgmt@canberratransport.gov.au로 이메일을 보내주세요. **134. 정확한 기술적 설명은 필요하지 않습니다.** 저희는 단지 차량 등록번호, 모델연도, 문제에 대한 간략한 요약만 있으면 됩니다.

여러분의 헌신에 항상 감사 드립니다.

134 (A) 저희는 보고된 피해 수준에 깜짝 놀랐습니다.
(B) 정확한 기술적 설명은 필요하지 않습니다.
(C) 수리는 가능한 한 빨리 실시될 것입니다.
(D) 여러분이 추천한 사람이 채용되면, 100달러의 보너스를 받게 됩니다.

135-138번은 다음 이메일에 관한 문제입니다.

수신: team@algermuseum.com
발신: qat@algermuseum.com
날짜: 3월 17일
제목: 전시품 글

큐레이터 여러분께,

이전 메일에서 말씀드린 것처럼, Alger 박물관에서는 방문객을 늘리기 위해 많은 노력을 기울이고 있습니다. 저희가 몇몇 유명 박물관과 이야기를 나눠본 결과, 흥미로운 **135. 제안**을 따를 것을 제안합니다. 많은 박물관에서 시사하기를, 방문객은 글이 많은 전시품에 집중하지 않습니다. **136. 사실, 방해물이나 다름 없습니다.**

우리에게 시사하는 바는, 우리 전시품은 상당수 글이 너무 길고 읽기 힘든 설명을 담고 있다는 점입니다. 제가 일부 살펴봤는데, 전부 **137. 최소** 200자는 담겨 있더군요. 게다가, 아주 전문적인 용어를 자주 사용합니다. 다른 박물관에서는 설명에 50단어 정도만 포함하도록 개편했어요. 그렇게 거둔 성공을 감안해, 우리가 글을 짧고 **138. 간결하게** 써야 할 것 같습니다. 그렇게 하면, 전시품마다 부담스럽게 느끼지 않게 될 겁니다.

136 (A) 방문객들은 단체로 오는 경향이 있습니다.
(B) 사실, 방해물이나 다름 없습니다.
(C) 박물관은 주말에 가장 붐빕니다.
(D) 저는 그 변경안을 승인하지 않았습니다.

139-142번은 다음 공지에 관한 문제입니다.

실험실 장비: 유리 비커 프로토콜

뛰어난 재사용성으로 인해, 저희 실험실 장비 대부분은 플라스틱 보다는 유리로 만들어집니다. **139. 반면,** 플라스틱과 달리, 유리는 깨지기 쉽습니다. 그 결과, 유리로 된 도구를 사용하여 실험을 할 때는 특별한 주의가 필요합니다. 특히, 유리용기를 원심분리기에 싣거나 내릴 때는 용기에 이가 나가거나 긁히거나, 아니면 손상되지 않았는지 간단히 점검해 주세요. **140. 이를 수행하기 전, 모든 안전 지침을 먼저 읽어주시기 바랍니다.** 저희가 소다 석회 유리 **141. 만들어진** 플라스크를 포함해 최고 내성 기준에 미치지 않는 모든 장비를 없애고 있지만, 일부는 남아서 쓰이고 있습니다. 혹시 발견하시게 되면, 사용하지 마시기 바랍니다. 제대로 측정되지 않을 수 있습니다. 종이에 잘 싸서 일반 **142. 쓰레기통** 대신, 초록색 재활용 통에 넣어 주시는 것만 기억하시면 됩니다.

140 (A) 이것은 플라스틱 용기가 유리보다 우수한 한가지 장점입니다.
(B) 유리 비커는 사용 전 완전히 건조시켜야 합니다.
(C) 그것들은 앞으로 따로 보관되어야 합니다.
(D) 이를 수행하기 전, 모든 안전 지침을 먼저 읽어주시기 바랍니다.

143-146번은 다음 광고에 관한 문제입니다.

사업체가 지역 시장의 범위를 넘어서서 진출할 준비를 갖췄다면, The Pacific Times의 광고란에 광고를 게재하는 것이 아시아 태평양 전역의 구매자와 **143. 연결되는** 최고의 방법이 됩니다. **144. 출판물**은 그 지역에서 10년 넘게 최고의 독자 층을 보유해 왔습니다. 관심 있으시면, pacifictimes.com/advertise를 방문하셔서 다양한 옵션을 선택하세요. **145. 크기, 색상, 광고 위치**를 정할 수 있습니다. 그런 다음 신청서를 제출하시면, 친절한 저희 팀원이 전체 견적을 제공해 드립니다. **146. 또한,** 저희는 다양한 국가의 여러 지역 신문사와 제휴를 맺고 있는데, 국제 면에도 귀하의 광고를 게재해 드립니다. 투자하신 돈에 대비해 최고의 가치를 제공해 드립니다.

145 (A) 크기, 색상, 광고 위치를 정할 수 있습니다.
(B) 온라인 버전에도 액세스할 수 있습니다.
(C) 저희 편집자들은 때때로 각자의 의견을 기고합니다.
(D) 광고비가 꾸준히 인상되었습니다.

PART 7
P. 209

147-148번은 다음 온라인 기사에 관한 문제입니다.

http://www.yeoviltribune.co.uk/local

우승자 선발을 도와주세요:
연례 Yeovil 최우수업체 여론조사

3년 연속, 저희는 주민 여러분께 지역 내 최우수 업체 선정을 도와주시길 부탁드리는 바입니다.(147) 올해에는 구독자뿐만 아니라, 모든 Yeovil 주민들이 참여할 수 있습니다.

저희 직원들이 최우수 소매점, 카페, 식당, 및 숙박업소에 대한 후보목록을 만들었습니다. 고객만족도 설문조사를 근거로, 부문별 6개의 우수업체가 후보로 선정되었습니다. 설문조사 결과를 보시려면, **여기**를 클릭해 주세요.

가장 좋아하는 후보를 우승자로 만들어주시려면, 이번 달에 참가업체들 중 한 곳을 방문하셔서 투표용지를 작성해주세요.(148) 참여하시면, 우리 지역을 특별하게 만들어주는 기관들의 홍보를 돕게 됩니다. 너무 오래 지체하지 마세요. 투표는 5월 9일 오전 11시에 종료됩니다.

147 이 기사의 주요 목적은 무엇인가?
(A) 업체들에게 돈을 기부해달라고 요청하기 위해
(B) 독자들에게 선택을 하도록 격려하기 위해
(C) 신규 잡지구독을 홍보하기 위해
(D) 대회 우승자를 거론하기 위해

148 Yeovil 최우수업체 여론조사에 관하여 알 수 있는 것은?
(A) 온라인으로 할 수 있다.
(B) 참가자들에게 현금 인센티브를 제공한다.
(C) 6개 부문이 있다.
(D) 여러 장소에서 실시된다.

149-150번은 다음 광고에 관한 문제입니다.

다음 프로젝트를 생각 중이신가요?
비용을 절약하시려면 Mike's Supply Shed를 둘러보세요!

저희는 지역 여기저기서 나무 자재, 각종 금속, 오래된 가구를 받습니다.(149) 이곳에 들어오면, 어떤 물건이든, 철저한 세척 및 수리 과정을 거칩니다. 저희는 모든 물건에 대해 가격을 대폭 낮출 뿐만 아니라,(150) 모든 수익금은 도시를 청소하는데 사용됩니다. 돈을 절감하면서 좋은 일에 동참해 보세요!

149 Mike's Supply Shed에 관해서 언급된 것은?
(A) 기부를 통해 재료를 받는다.
(B) 고객별 구입할 수 있는 양을 제한한다.
(C) 지방 의회에서 자금을 지원받는다.
(D) 작년에 설립되었다.

150 Mike's Supply Shed의 물품에 관해서 사실인 것은?
(A) 온라인으로 구입할 수 있다.
(B) 추가 요금을 내면 배송 받을 수 있다.
(C) 품질이 철저하게 점검된다.
(D) 가격이 낮아진다.

151-152번은 다음 광고에 관한 문제입니다.

The Supreme 만능공구 – 필요한 모든 것을 주머니 속에 50달러

공구

바늘코 펜치 – 좁은 공간에 넣거나 작은 물체를 잡기에 알맞음(151)

와이어 스트리퍼 – 모든 유형의 전선 둘레의 플라스틱 피복을 안전하게 벗겨냄

나이프 – 단단한 재료를 자를 수 있는 고탄소 스테인리스강으로 제작

스프링 가위 – 스프링이 자르는 동작을 도와 손의 부담을 덜어줌

캔 및 병따개 – 통조림 제품과 병 음료를 쉽게 열어줌

중간크기 드라이버 – 어떤 접지 나사든 풀거나 조여줌

쉽게 주머니에 넣고 다닐 수 있게 해주는 가죽 케이스 포함(152)

---

151 바늘코 펜치에 관하여 언급된 것은?
(A) 좁은 공간에서 사용할 수 있다.
(B) 다양한 종류의 재료를 자른다.
(C) 헐거워진 나사를 조인다.
(D) 금속용기를 연다.

152 The Supreme 만능도구에 관하여 언급된 것은?
(A) 여러 색상으로 출시된다.
(B) 부대용품이 딸려 온다.
(C) 평생 품질보증을 받는다.
(D) 읽기 쉬운 설명서가 들어있다.

153-155번은 다음 블로그 게시물에 관한 문제입니다.

제품을 팔려면 고객부터 파악해야 한다

사업체로서 주된 목적은 매출을 늘리는 것이다. 이는 주로 무언가 요구를 충족하는 제품을 만들면서 행해진다. 따라서 성공적인 사업체가 되려면, 고객이 누구고, 고객이 원하는 바부터 파악해야 한다.(153) — [1] —. 바로 그렇게 하는 방법은 다음과 같다.

1단계: 고객 확인하기
자신의 사업을 이해하는 첫 번째 단계는 제품을 구입하는 사람들이 누군지 알아내는 것이다. 매장을 관찰하고 누가 문을 열고 들어오는지 보는 것처럼 간단할 수 있다. 고객의 성비뿐만 아니라 어느 인구계층에 속하는지 또한 파악할 수 있어야 한다. — [2] —. 고객이 누구인지 알면 회사의 전략을 구체화하고 집중하는데 도움이 된다.

2단계: 이유 물어보기
고객이 왜 우리 제품을 구입하는가? 최저가 제품을 제공해서인가, 아니면 다른 이유가 있는가? 고객이 제품의 어떤 면을 좋아하는지 알면 향후 제품을 개선하거나 만드는데 도움이 된다. 설문조사는 필요한 정보를 수집하는데 엄청나게 유용할 수 있다.(154) 고객에게 설문 작성을 요청하는 방

법으로 약간의 할인으로 사례할 수도 있다. 이를 통해 방대한 정보를 이용할 수 있다. — [3] —.

3단계: 제품 개선하기
이제 고객에 대해 수집한 정보를 이용해 사업체를 개선할 준비를 갖췄다. 고객이 가격에 신경을 쓴다는 것을 알았다면, 제품에서 비용을 절감할 수 있는 방법을 살펴라. 또한, 고객이 누구인지에 대해 알고 있는 내용을 활용해 해당 특정 집단에 맞춘 광고 캠페인을 설계해라.(155) — [4] —.

---

153 블로그 게시물은 누구를 대상으로 하는가?
(A) 신규 사업 발굴을 물색하는 고객
(B) 새로운 지역으로 진출하고 싶은 기업
(C) 간접비를 낮춰야 하는 제조업체
(D) 수익 증대를 원하는 사업체

154 블로그 게시물에 따르면, 실문조사는 왜 권장되는가?
(A) 고객이 요구할 수 있는 통로를 제공한다.
(B) 회사가 고객의 생각에 관심을 가진다는 것을 보여준다.
(C) 고객이 브랜드의 어떤 점을 가치 있게 여기는지에 대한 통찰력을 제공한다.
(D) 다른 자료 수집 기법에 비해 상대적으로 간단하다.

155 [1], [2], [3], [4]로 표시된 곳 중 다음 문장이 들어가기에 가장 적절한 곳은 어디인가?

"연구 결과에 따르면, 고객은 자신을 잘 파악하는 브랜드를 좋아한다."

(A) [1]
(B) [2]
(C) [3]
(D) [4]

156-157번은 다음 문자 메시지 대화에 관한 문제입니다.

Pam Graham (오전 9시 05분)
안녕하세요, Lewis. 저한테 다소 긴급한 문제가 생겼어요. 제 차가 고장 났어요.(156)

Lewis Holt (오전 9시 06분)
제가 대신 회의를 진행할까요?

Pam Graham (오전 9시 08분)
네, 그렇게 해주세요. 고객들이 아래층에 계실 거예요.

Pam Graham (오전 9시 09분)
로비에서 만나서 회의실로 모시고 가면 돼요.

Lewis Holt (오전 9시 11분)
서명할 계약서는 준비됐어요?

Pam Graham (오전 9시 14분)
맞아요. 제가 말하는 걸 깜박했네요. 그쪽에서 계약서를 대신 가져올 거예요. 계약서를 받아주시겠어요?(157)

Lewis Holt (오전 9시 15분)
알았어요.(157) 다른 건요?

Pam Graham (오전 9시 17분)
그게 다예요. 고마워요. 나머진 제가 처리할 게요.

Lewis Holt (오전 9시 18분)
네.

---

156 Ms. Graham은 왜 Mr. Holt에게 연락하는가?
(A) 그에게 서류를 보내달라고 요청하려고
(B) 제안 일정을 보내주려고
(C) 회의 장소를 확인하려고
(D) 그에게 곤란한 상황을 알리려고

157 오전 9시 15분에, Mr. Holt가 "알았어요"라고 할 때 무엇을 의미하겠는가?

    (A) Ms. Graham이 지시한 내용을 이해했다.
    (B) 관리자를 회의에 참석하도록 초대했다.
    (C) 고객과 주고받은 최근 이메일을 읽을 것이다.
    (D) 회의 전에 서류를 받았다.

158-160번은 다음 회람에 관한 문제입니다.

수신: Camcom 전직원
발신: Katie Comstock 부사장
날짜: 9월 1일
제목: Rhonda Hanna

Rhonda Hanna가 영업 이사직을 맡게 되었음을 모두에게 알리게 되어 기쁩니다. **(158)** Ms. Hanna는 Pennsylvania 주립 대학교 졸업생이며, Boston의 Ernst and Sawyer에서 6년 동안 근무한 후 우리 회사에 입사했습니다.

지난 여름, Ms. Hanna는 외부 영업팀에 합류했습니다. 그녀는 판매 수치를 거의 두 배로 만들면서 바로 영향을 주었는데, 이전까지는 수치가 저조했습니다. 그녀의 리더십으로 저희는 GloboTech와의 계약을 수주할 수 있었고, 그녀의 부서는 사내 최고 매출 부서 중 한 곳이 되었습니다. **(159)**

Ms. Hanna의 새 직위는 월요일에 공식 발표될 것입니다. 그리고 그녀의 승진을 축하하기 위해, **(158)** 저는 이번 주 목요일 Dorsia에 사적 연회장을 예약했습니다. 많은 분들께 그 식당의 유명한 랍스터 스튜에 대해 듣고 나니, 어서 먹어보고 싶네요. **(160)** 자리가 한정되어 있으므로, 오실 계획이라면 꼭 오늘 오후까지 Terry Wright에게 이메일을 보내주시기 바랍니다.

---

158 회람은 왜 게시되었는가?
    (A) 계약 체결을 알리려고
    (B) 구인광고를 하려고
    (C) 새로운 동료를 소개하려고
    (D) 직원의 승진을 알리려고

159 외부 영업팀에 관하여 언급된 것은?
    (A) 팀원들에게 급여를 인상해주었다.
    (B) 직원들이 정기적으로 교육에 참석할 것이다.
    (C) 수익이 상당히 증가했다.
    (D) Boston 지점으로 이전할 것이다.

160 Dorsia에 관하여 알 수 있는 것은?
    (A) Camcom 직원들 사이에서 인기 있다.
    (B) 영업시간이 매우 한정되어 있다.
    (C) 전용 좌석은 없다.
    (D) 해산물만을 제공한다.

161-164번은 다음 이메일에 관한 문제입니다.

수신: Alexa Ramirez <ramrez@gibbs.com>
발신: Jesse Auerbach <auerbach@gibbs.com>
제목: 도움 요청
참조: Beth Park <part@gibbs.com>
날짜: 7월 8일

Ms. Ramirez께,

중요한 프로젝트에 당신의 도움이 필요합니다. —[1]—. 저희 팀은 Colbert Medical이 환자 기록 추적에 사용할 신규 시스템 개발을 담당하고 있습니다. **(161)** 업무를 수행할 수 있는 경험 많은 직원이 부족해, 예정보다 진행이 늦어지고 있습니다. —[2]—. 일이 원활히 진행되도록, 당분간 당신이 데이터 이동용 소프트웨어를 맡아주셨으면 합니다. **(161)**

당신의 부서장 Beth Park에게 저희 상황에 관해 얘기했더니, 몇 주 동안은 당신의 도움을 받아도 된다고 하더군요. **(162)/(164)** —[3]—.

이 업무를 하는 동안 민감한 정보를 많이 접할 것이라서, **저와 함께 비공개 서약서를 검토하셔야 합니다.** 오늘 오후에 40층에 있는 제 사무실에 들러주실래요? **(163)** —[4]—. 그리고 팀원들에게 당신을 소개할 수 있게 다음주 월요일 저희 회의에도 와주셨으면 좋겠습니다.

Jesse Auerbach 드림

---

161 Ms. Ramirez의 직업은 무엇이겠는가?
    (A) 공사 감독자
    (B) 의사
    (C) 채용 담당자
    (D) 컴퓨터 프로그래머

162 Mr. Auerbach는 무엇을 요청했는가?
    (A) 프로젝트를 위한 추가 자금
    (B) 환자기록 모음
    (C) 직원의 일시적인 도움
    (D) 빈 사무실의 평면도

163 Mr. Auerbach는 왜 Ms. Ramirez와 만나고 싶어 하는가?
    (A) 교육을 제공하려고
    (B) 양식을 논의하려고
    (C) 신제품을 소개하려고
    (D) 평가회를 열려고

164 [1], [2], [3], [4]로 표시된 곳 중 다음 문장이 들어가기에 가장 적절한 곳은 어디인가?

    "그녀가 며칠 날에는 부서에 당신이 없어도 괜찮을 거라고 했습니다."

    (A) [1]
    (B) [2]
    (C) [3]
    (D) [4]

165-167번은 다음 편지에 관한 문제입니다.

Sirius International

Stafford 주민 여러분께,

Sirius International은 모두에게 전세계의 식품을 저렴한 가격으로 제공한다는 사명을 가지고 있습니다. 그러한 목적을 위해 저희는 바로 이곳 Stafford에 매장을 열 계획입니다. 그 전에, 시 정부에서 매장 개장을 허가하도록 설득하는 데 여러분의 도움이 필요합니다.

이 지역 주민에게 받은 수많은 요청으로 인해 저희는 Stafford를 선택했습니다. 외국 식품을 구입하러 다른 지방으로 가야 하는 일은 아주 성가실 수 있습니다. **(165)/(166)** 또한, 이곳에 매장을 여는 것은 지역사회에 많은 일자리를 창출하면서 동시에 지역 내 교통량을 늘려줄 것입니다. 저희의 목표는 Stafford 지역사회에서 커다란 부분을 차지하는 것입니다.

www.siriusintl.com/projects에 로그인하셔서 저희의 임무를 달성하는 것을 도와주실 수 있습니다. Stafford 신규 매장을 위한 제안서 전체를 보실 수 있습니다. 저희를 지지하고 싶으시다면, 제안서에 성함만 서명만 하시면 됩니다. **(167)**

대단히 감사합니다.

Ellen Robbins, Sirius International

---

165 편지에 따르면, Stafford 주민은 Sirius International의 신규 매장으로 어떻게 혜택을 보겠는가?
(A) 매장 내 모든 상품에 대해 할인을 받게 된다.
(B) 웹사이트에서 온라인 쇼핑을 할 수 있게 된다.
(C) 시 정부로부터 매주 지급금을 받게 된다.
(D) 해외 상품을 구입하러 멀리 이동할 필요가 없어진다.

166 Stafford에 관하여 알 수 있는 것은?
(A) 외국 제품을 판매하는 상점이 없다.
(B) 관광객을 유치할 축제나 행사를 주최하지 않는다.
(C) 항구 옆에 편리하게 위치한다.
(D) 주민 일자리 부족현상을 겪고 있다.

167 편지에 따르면, 독자는 왜 웹사이트를 방문해야 하는가?
(A) 매장에 입사지원하기 위해
(B) 제안서에 지지를 표하기 위해
(C) Ms. Robbins에게 연락하기 위해
(D) 전체 제품 목록을 보기 위해

168-171번은 다음 이메일에 관한 문제입니다.

수신: b.obafemi@lwmail.com
발신: sandra.lukacs@renosmith.com
날짜: 5월 29일
제목: 회신: 설계도

Ms. Obafemi께,

설계도와 관련해 빠른 답변 주셔서 감사 드립니다. 저는 우리가 지난 금요일에 만났을 때 많은 진전이 있었다고 생각합니다. 귀하의 주거용품점은 곧 현실이 될 것입니다.

제안된 상점의 규격과 저희가 논의한 사양에 따라, 저희가 이제 일을 진행하는 데 취해야 할 조치가 더 명확해지고 있습니다.(168) 귀하께서 말씀하셨던 자금 문제에 주목했습니다. 하지만 저는 적당히 비용 효율적인 부품들로 화강암 외관과 타일 작업을 하기에 충분하다고 생각합니다.(169) 제가 다음주 화요일까지 전체 항목별 견적서를 보내드리겠습니다. 하나하나 검토해 보신 후 저에게 알려주세요. 그리고 나서 저희는 회의를 잡아서 필요한 수정사항들을 반영할 수 있고, 귀하께서 전체 내용에 대해 승인해 주시면 됩니다.(170)

그리고 굴착 중장비(171)를 7월 1일부터 7일까지 대여하기로 일정을 잡았습니다. 제가 사전에 작업 허가증을 받아야 해서 이 날짜들이 곤란하시면 저에게 바로 연락주세요. **시 규정 때문에, 주거지역에서 그렇게 소음이 큰 기계를 가동하려면 특별 허가를 받아야 합니다.**(171)

함께 일하게 되어 기쁘고, 이렇게 중요한 프로젝트에 Reno-Smith를 파트너로 선택해 주셔서 다시 한번 감사드립니다.

Sandra Lukacs 드림

168 이메일의 목적은 무엇인가?
(A) 문서의 승인을 요청하려고
(B) 프로젝트의 다음 단계를 상세히 설명하려고
(C) 계획에 추가된 내용을 설명하려고
(D) 프로젝트의 총 비용을 설명하려고

169 Ms. Obafemi에 관하여 알 수 있는 것은?
(A) 성공적인 점포를 소유하고 있다.
(B) 한정된 예산을 가지고 있다.
(C) 허가증을 신청해야 한다.
(D) 자신의 사업체를 이전하고 싶어한다.

170 이메일에 따르면, Ms. Obafemi는 다음 회의를 위해 무엇을 준비해야 하는가?
(A) 설계도를 만들어야 한다.
(B) 일부 수치를 검토해야 한다.
(C) 일부 자재를 구입해야 한다.
(D) 계약서에 서명해야 한다.

171 Ms. Lukacs는 왜 중장비를 언급하는가?
(A) 요청 날짜에 이용 가능함을 확인하려고
(B) 그녀에게 충분히 대규모의 공사 작업반이 있음을 확실히 하려고
(C) 규정이 준수되고 있는지 확실히 하려고
(D) 중장비가 건물 규격에 맞을지 확인하려고

172-175번은 다음 온라인 채팅 대화문에 관한 문제입니다.

Charlie Stokes (오전 11시 07분)
자선 점심 일정은 웹 사이트에서 볼 수 있어요. 내부용이라서 비밀번호가 걸려 있어요.(172) 이게 비밀번호예요: clunch07

Jamie Wade (오전 11시 18분)
잠깐 봤어요. The Fortune Group에서는 보통 전직원용 티켓을 구입해요. 항상 저희 최대 기여자예요.(173)

Sheldon Padilla (오전 11시 22분)
올해도 사람을 더 채용했어요. Earnest 룸으로 공간이 충분하지 않을 것 같아요. Reverence 룸으로 옮겨야겠어요.(173)

Charlie Stokes (오전 11시 25분)
알았어요. 제가 지금 바로 변경할게요. Sheldon, 제가 확정 참석자 명단 취합해 달라고 부탁했었죠. 그거 지금 저한테 보내줄래요?(174)

Jamie Wade (오전 11시 27분)
룸이 확정되면 제가 일정이랑 티켓을 발송할게요. 알려만 주세요.

Charlie Stokes (오전 11시 31분)
대형 추첨행사에서는 당첨자를 어떻게 발표할까요? 모두 로비로 불러놓고 마이크로 당첨자를 발표해야 할까요?(175)

Sheldon Padilla (오전 11시 35분)
기술팀에 요청해서 각 방에 텔레비전을 설치할 수 있어요. 그렇게 하면, 우리 손님들이 경품 행사에 참여하면서 식사를 할 수 있어요.(175)

Jamie Wade (오전 11시 39분)
저는 왜 그 생각을 못했죠?(175)

172 Mr. Stokes는 일정에 관해 무엇을 언급하는가?
(A) Mr. Wade의 확인을 받아야 한다.
(B) 이미 발송되었다.
(C) 일반에 공유되면 안 된다.
(D) 이미지를 일부 포함한다.

173 Mr. Padilla는 왜 The Fortune Group을 다른 방으로 옮기는 것을 제안하는가?
(A) 참석자가 많을 예정이다.
(B) 다른 손님들보다 더 일찍 도착할 것이다.
(C) 추가 요금을 지불했다.
(D) 특수 장비를 요한다.

174 Mr. Stokes는 Mr. Padilla에게 무엇을 해달라고 요청하는가?
(A) 메뉴를 확정해 달라고
(B) 행사담당자를 지명해 달라고
(C) 예약을 해달라고
(D) 손님 목록을 보내달라고

175 오전 11시 39분에, Ms. Wade가 "저는 왜 그 생각을 못했죠?"라고 할 때 무엇을 의미하겠는가?
(A) Mr. Padilla의 제안을 선호한다.
(B) 행사가 연기돼야 한다고 생각한다.
(C) 높은 비용을 염려한다.
(D) 경품행사를 변경하고 싶어한다.

176-180번은 다음 도서 리뷰 및 이메일에 관한 문제입니다.

<The Enigmatic Floor> Willis Nguyen 지음
Kristina Bryan 리뷰 작성

<The Enigmatic Floor>는 3년의 공백을 깬 Willis Nguyen의 최신작이다. **자신의 조부가 살던 마을에서 일어난 사건에서 영감을 받아,**(176) 이 책에서는 세상에 자신의 능력을 숨기고 살아가는 지역 화가인 Andre Vasquez에 관한 이야기를 들려준다. Andre는 어느 날 흔적 하나 없이 마을에서 자취를 감춘다. 경위가 수사를 하러 Andre가 사라진 장소를 방문하자, 이내 Andre가 그림 속에 자신의 행방에 관한 단서를 남긴 것을 발견한다. 마을 전체가 Andre의 메시지를 풀어 그가 있는 장소를 알아내려고 합심한다. 중간중간 늘어지는 부분도 있긴 하지만, 충분히 결말까지 읽을 만하다. **Nguyen은 서스펜스와 드라마적 요소를 능수능란하게 결부시켜 매력적이면서도 감동적인 이야기를 전달한다.**(177)

수신: Willis Nguyen <wnguyen@comostudios.com>
발신: Leigh Oliver <l.oliver@fletcher.edu>
날짜: 7월 8일
회신: 초대

Mr. Nguyen께,

8월 2일 화요일에 Fletcher 대학교에서 제 현대 작문 강의 수강생들에게 초청 강연을 하기로 수락해 주셔서 다시 한번 감사드립니다.(178)/(179)/(180) 상당수 학생이 작가가 되고 싶어 하기에, 선생님께서 오시는 것에 대한 반응이 열광적입니다. 학생들은 선생님의 구상 과정 및 마음을 사로잡는 줄거리를 이끌어내는 방법에 대해 많은 질문들을 할 것입니다. **화가의 실종에서 어느 정도가 실제인지도 모두가 궁금해하고 있습니다!**(178)

캠퍼스까지 9번 버스를 타고 오실 거라고 하셨죠.(180) 정문 바로 앞에서 하차하시게 될 것입니다. 제가 1시에 밖에서 기다렸다가, 함께 Elberta 홀까지 걸어가면 될 것 같습니다.

Leigh Oliver 드림

---

176 Mr. Nguyen 의 소설에 관하여 언급된 것은?
(A) 실화를 바탕으로 한다.
(B) Mr. Nguyen의 첫 번째 책이다.
(C) 권위 있는 상을 받았다.
(D) 두 가지 언어로 출간됐다.

177 도서 리뷰에서 첫 번째 단락, 여덟 번째 줄의 단어, 'ties'와 의미상 가장 가까운 것은?
(A) 어울리다
(B) 고정하다
(C) 혼합하다
(D) 덧붙이다

178 현대 작문 수업 학생들에 관하여 알 수 있는 것은?
(A) 올해 말에 졸업할 것이다.
(B) <The Enigmatic Floor>를 읽었다.
(C) Elberta Hall 인근에 산다.
(D) 저녁 수업을 듣는다.

179 Ms. Oliver는 누구겠는가?
(A) 대학 교수
(B) 변호사
(C) 버스 기사
(D) 편집자

180 이메일에서 Mr. Nguyen에 관하여 알 수 있는 것은?
(A) 전에 Ms. Oliver를 만난 적이 있다.
(B) Fletcher 대학교를 다녔다.
(C) 사전 약속을 취소해야 할 것이다.
(D) 8월 2일에 대중 교통을 탈 것이다.

181-185번은 다음 기사와 이메일에 관한 문제입니다.

HYDESVILLE (10월 13일) — 몇 달 간 진행된 지연 끝에 Echo Rock Isles (ERI)가 11월 1일에 정식으로 개관한다. 쇼핑센터에는 20개의 상점과 다수의 레스토랑, 카페, 수많은 오락거리가 갖춰진다.(181) **모든 상점에는 공통점이 한 가지 있는데, 모두 뉴질랜드로 진출한 국제 기업이라는 것이다.**(182)

말레이시아에 본사를 둔 Big Turtle Clothiers는 ERI에 지점을 확보한 최초 매장 중 한 곳이다.(182) "저희는 아시아에서 큰 성공을 거둬, 대 아시아 태평양 지역으로 진출하기를 기대하고 있습니다. ERI는 저희가 그것을 실행할 완벽한 기회처럼 들렸습니다."라고 Big Turtle Clothiers의 창립자인 Alyssa Cohen이 말했다.

ERI는 월요일부터 금요일에는 오전 9시부터 오후 6시까지, 주말에는 오전 10시부터 오후 8시까지 영업한다.(184) 주차는 지하 1층과 지하 2층에서 이용할 수 있다.

수신: Leonard Austin <l.austin@neutronmail.com>
발신: Jane Phillips <jphillips@btclothers.com.my>
날짜: 11월 5일
제목: Big Turtle Clothiers의 입사 교육
첨부: 계약서

Mr. Austin께,

Big Turtle Clothiers에 입사 제안을 받게 되셔서 진심으로 축하 드립니다. 합류하시게 되어 기쁩니다.

귀하는 브랜드를 대표하는 인물로서, 주로 고객에게 우리 브랜드 및 제품라인을 설명하게 됩니다. **첫 근무일은 매장 문을 여는 11월 8일 토요일입니다.**(184) 우선 저를 만나면, 제가 시설을 견학시켜드릴 겁니다. 오후 12시에 간단히 점심시간을 가진 후, **Mr. Carson과 만나시게 됩니다.**(185) 그분이 우리 브랜드의 정체성과 우리가 고객에게 판매하고자 하는 것에 대해 설명해주실 것입니다.

살펴보시고 서명하실 수 있도록 고용 계약서를 첨부해 드렸습니다.(183) 첫 날에 서명본을 가져오시면 제가 처리해 드리겠습니다.

다시 한번 축하 드리며, 만나게 되길 기대하겠습니다.

Jane Phillips 드림
매장 관리자

---

181 기사의 한 가지 목적에 해당하는 것은?
(A) 공사로 야기된 혼란을 강조하려고
(B) 신규 복합건물의 개장을 알리려고
(C) Big Turtle Clothiers의 제품을 광고하려고
(D) 신규 건물의 역사를 열거하려고

182 Big Turtle Clothiers에 관하여 알 수 있는 것은?
(A) 작년에 문을 열었다.
(B) 몇몇 자선 단체에 수익금을 기부한다.
(C) 새 매장 관리자를 채용하고 있다.
(D) 뉴질랜드 시장에는 처음이다.

183 Ms. Phillips는 Mr. Austin에게 무엇을 보냈는가?
(A) 회의 안건 목록
(B) 업무 문서
(C) 제품 카탈로그
(D) 시설 지도

184 Mr. Austin은 매장에 언제 도착해야 하는가?
(A) 오전 9시
(B) 오전 10시
(C) 오후 12시
(D) 오후 6시

185 Mr. Austin은 토요일 오후에 무엇을 할 것인가?
(A) Mr. Carson을 만날 것이다.
(B) Echo Rock Isles를 둘러볼 것이다.
(C) 계약서에 서명할 것이다.
(D) 고객과 만날 것이다.

186-190번은 다음 이메일, 양식, 기사에 관한 문제입니다.

수신: 전원
발신: 인사팀
날짜: 2월 13일
제목: 신흥 지도자 계획
첨부: 신청서

JTB Motors에서 근무한지 2년 미만인 직원은 새로운 리더십 계획에 신청하실 수 있는데,**(188)** 이는 선발된 20명의 주니어 직원들을 사내 가장 경력 있는 직원과 짝을 맺어 줍니다.**(186)** 프로그램은 주니어 직원들에게 다양한 능력을 가다듬고 네트워크를 만들 기회를 제공하는 것을 목표로 하는데, 이는 그들이 경력상 다음 단계로 나아갈 수 있도록 준비시켜 줍니다. **참여자들은 오로지 전문분야와 업무를 기반으로 멘토들과 매칭됩니다.(189)** 4월부터 각 팀은 매주 최소 1시간 동안 정기적으로 만나게 됩니다.

이 프로그램에 선발되려면, 첨부 문서를 작성하셔서 <신흥 지도자 계획> 담당자 Daria Donnelly에게 2월 25일까지 이메일을 보내주세요. 선발된 지원자는 3월 3일에 Ms. Donnelly에게 수락 이메일을 받게 됩니다. **(187)**

신흥 지도자
신청서

이름: Ned Griffin**(188)**
부서: 상품개발
직원 ID: N_Griffin

경력 목표 및 직업적 포커스
저는 해외시장에 국한된 상품을 디자인하는 과정과 그러한 아이디어를 보다 설득력 있는 방식으로 상사에게 더 잘 제시하는 방법에 대해 더 배우고 싶습니다.**(189)** 모든 커리어 관련 조언을 환영합니다

가능 시간
수요일에서 금요일 오후

JTB Motors Quarterly

<신흥 지도자 계획, 결실을 맺다>

베테랑 크리에이티브 디렉터 Phillip Jackson은 지난 봄 인사팀에서 연락해 그가 사내 젊은 직원들 중 한 명을 멘토링해줄 수 있는지 물었을 때 어떨지 궁금했다. 그는 희망적이긴 했지만, 이렇게 보람 있을 거라고는 예상하지 못했다. "Mr. Griffin과 함께 일한 후로,**(189)** 저는 제가 유망한 직원에게 도움이 되고 있다고 느끼게 되서 매일 출근하는 게 더 즐겁습니다.**(190)** 다만 유일하게 아쉬운 점은 제가 오래 전에 여기서 근무를 시작했을 당시 저에게는 조언을 해준 사람이 없었다는 점이에요"라고 Jackson은 말했다.

Mr. Griffin은 자신의 입장에 대해, "저는 제 디자인 아이디어를 설득하는 법을 저에게 알려줄 사람을 찾고 있었어요."라고 말한다. 프로그램에 참여한 후로, 그는 전기 엔진의 필수 부분을 포함해서, 자신의 디자인 몇 개가 사용되었다고 말한다. 그는 보다 자신감이 생겼고, 이제는 JTB Motors에서 성공하는데 필요한 것이 무엇인지 안다. "저는 이보다 더 명확한 목표를 가진 적도, 직장에서 이보다 더 성취감을 느낀 적도 없었어요. 그리고 이건 모두 Mr. Jackson 덕분입니다."**(190)**

프로그램은 확대될 예정이다. 참여하고 싶으면, 인사팀의 Daria Donnelly에게 연락하면 된다.

---

186 이메일에서는 계획에 관해 무엇을 암시하는가?
(A) 참가자 수가 한정될 것이다.
(B) 제품 개발 직원들을 위한 것이다.
(C) 회사의 신입직원들이 요청했다.
(D) 참가자들은 친목교류 행사에 참석해야 할 것이다.

187 주니어 직원들은 어떻게 선발되겠는가?
(A) 상사들의 추천을 받을 것이다.
(B) 잠재 멘토들과 면접을 볼 것이다.
(C) 학력에 기반하여 선발될 것이다.
(D) Ms. Donnelly의 평가를 받을 것이다.

188 Mr. Griffin에 관하여 알 수 있는 것은?
(A) Mr. Jackson의 부서로 이동했다.
(B) 해외 고객들에게 디자인 제안서를 제출했다.
(C) JTB Motors에서 근무한 지 2년 미만이다.
(D) 최근 승진을 했다.

189 Mr. Jackson에 관하여 무엇이 사실이겠는가?
(A) 여러 직원들의 멘토였다.
(B) 인사팀에서 근무한다.
(C) 회사의 최장 근속 직원 중 한 명이다.
(D) 해외 상품 개발 경험이 있다.

190 Mr. Griffin과 Mr. Jackson 둘 다 계획으로부터 어떻게 이익을 얻었는가?
(A) 보다 명확한 목표
(B) 급여 인상
(C) 향상된 직무 성취감
(D) 더 나은 고용 안정

191-195번은 다음 이메일들과 행사정보에 관한 문제입니다.

수신: Joseph Lucchese
발신: XiaoHui Huang
날짜: 7월 12일
제목: 8월 12일 포스터
첨부파일: 포스터 내용

안녕하세요, Joseph

말씀 나눴던 대로, 포스터에 실릴 내용 보내드립니다. 각 지점의 다양한 곳에 게시하려면 최소 100부는 필요합니다. 제공해주신 템플릿을 검토해보니, 배경은 '핫핑크', 글자 대부분은 '연하늘색'으로 해야 할 것 같습니다. 그리고 연사들의 이름은 사람들의 시선을 끌 수 있게 화려한 폰트를 쓰는 걸로 합시다.**(191)**

경영진도 이 부분에 대해 이해할 수 있도록, **반드시 기념행사보다 훨씬 전에 샘플을 보여드릴 수 있도록 해요.(192)** 다음 주까지 한 부 준비해줄 수 있겠어요?

고맙습니다.

XiaoHui Huang,
프로그램 준비위원

ErgoBuff 연구소
35회 공로표창

8월 12일, 오후 7시-10시, Overlook 호텔**(193)**

오후 7시 – 오후 7시 15분 – CEO Tony Bibbo의 개회사
오후 7시 15분 – 오후 8시 15분 – 만찬 및 Juan Talavera의 음악 공연
오후 8시 15분 – 오후 8시 45분 – 특별 강연 1: <생활양식으로서의 체육관> (Silver 체육관, 마케팅 담당 부사장 Roger Severen)
오후 8시 45분 – 오후 9시 15분 - 특별 강연 2: <영양제 산업의 미래> (Tamaulipas 대학교, Ernest Jung 교수)**(191)**
오후 9시 15분 – 오후 9시 45분 – 시상
오후 9시 45분 – 오후 10시 – 폐회사

수상자:**(193)**

Philip Bain – 우수 사업모델 개발**(193)**
Shruti Chandrashekar – 최우수 영업**(193)**
Rebecca Wilson – 25년 근무**(193)/(194)**
Eileen Vogel – 최우수 신규 아이디어**(193)**

수신: XiaoHui Huang
발신: Eric Eilenberger
날짜: 7월 19일
제목: 8월 12일 포스터 내용

안녕하세요, XiaoHui

제안하신 포스터 디자인을 검토했는데, 전체적으로 좋습니다. 배경과 폰트 색상이 밝아서, 확실히 전년도에 내걸었던 포스터들보다 더 발랄한 느낌입니다! 연사들도 직함에서부터 확실히 인상적이네요.

한 가지만 참고해 주세요. 25년 근속상 수상자는 회사에서 25년 이상 근무한 사람입니다.(194) 대부분의 경우, 고위 관리직에 있죠. 그 부분을 제외하면, 현재의 순서가 좋습니다. **하지만 뭐든지 마무리하기 전에는, 반드시 Mr. Bibbo의 승인을 받으세요. 그리고 포스터에 있는 모든 이름이 제대로 적혀 있는지도 확인하세요. 특별 행사이니까요.(195)**

우리가 이용하는 인쇄소는 보통 일 년 중 이맘때 아주 바쁩니다. 그래서 자주 연락을 취하는 것이 중요합니다. 2년 전에는 프로그램 준비자가 주문을 너무 늦게 해서, 포스터가 행사 당일에 나왔답니다.

Eric Eilenberger
인사부장

---

191 누구의 이름이 포스터에 특별한 스타일로 나오겠는가?
(A) Tony Bibbo
(B) Ernest Jung
(C) Juan Talavera
(D) Eileen Vogel

192 첫 번째 이메일에서 두 번째 단락, 첫 번째 줄의 단어 "far"와 의미상 가장 가까운 것은?
(A) 거리가 먼
(B) 오래
(C) 깊이
(D) 늘어진

193 8월 12일에 어떤 행사가 열릴 것인가?
(A) 시상식
(B) 관리자 회의
(C) 지점 개업
(D) 상품 출시

194 Ms. Wilson에 관하여 알 수 있는 것은?
(A) 8월 12일 행사에서 엔터테인먼트를 제공할 것이다.
(B) ErgoBuff에서 25년 이상 근무했다.
(C) 행사 준비자로 일했었다.
(D) 인사부를 감독한다.

195 Mr. Eilenberger는 Ms. Huang에게 무엇을 하라고 요청하는가?
(A) 다른 판매업체를 선택하라고
(B) 용품을 더 주문하라고
(C) 정보가 맞는지 확인하라고
(D) 배경색을 변경하라고

196-200번은 다음 공지와 이메일들에 관한 문제입니다.

미술 전시회가 6월 15일부터 6월 19일까지 Colorado의 Bee Spring Plaza에서 열립니다. **이 연례 행사는 현지인과 여행객 모두에게 큰 인기를 끌며, 매년 2만 5천명이 찾습니다.(196)**

저희는 전국 각지의 예술가를 초청해 그들의 예술을 전세계에 선보입니다. **심사위원단이 선정한 최고의 예술가 80명이 전시회에 출품합니다. 작년에는 1천 명이 넘는 예술가가 전시회 자리를 두고 경쟁했으니, 오늘 지원서를 받으세요.(197)** www.beespringplaza.org로 가셔서 지원서 양식을 다운받으세요. 지원서의 일부로 지원비 50달러와 함께 미술품 원본 다섯 작품의 사진을 첨부해야 합니다. 작성된 지원서는 웹사이트에 업로드하거나 이메일로 제출해야 합니다. 모든 지원서는 3월 10일까지 접수 되어야 심사됩니다. 전시회에 선발될 경우, 늦어도 4월 5일까지는 통보를 받게 됩니다.

부스 크기 및 요금은 다음과 같습니다:
· 8피트x8피트 부스 300달러
· **8피트x12피트 부스 450달러(199)**
· 12피트x12피트 부스 525달러
· 16피트x16피트 부스 700달러

참조: 모든 예술가는 행사장까지의 미술품 운송 수단을 각자 마련해야 합니다. 저희는 미술품 파손에 책임지지 않습니다.

수신: Ray Dawson <rdawson@dawsonworks.com>
발신: Veronica Murphy <vmurphy@beespringplaza.org>
제목: Bee Spring Plaza 미술 전시회
날짜: 4월 1일
첨부: 계약서

Mr. Dawson께,

축하드립니다! 올해 Bee Spring Plaza 미술 전시회에 귀하의 미술품 출품을 초청하게 되어 기쁩니다. **Colorado의 다채로운 풍경을 포착한 귀하의 회화는 심사위원들에게 큰 감동을 주어, 수많은 현지인의 마음을 울릴 것이라 생각합니다.** (198) 이 이메일에 계약서를 첨부해 드렸습니다. 초대를 수락하시려면 계약서에 서명하셔서 4월 30일까지 저희에게 제출해 주세요. 계약서와 더불어, 귀하의 간단한 약력과 함께 부스비도 포함해 주시기 바랍니다. 약력은 200자 이하여야 합니다.

또한 저희는 만남의 장 세션을 개최할 예정인데, 손님들과 만나 질문에 답하는 자리를 가질 수 있습니다. **6월 15일 수요일부터 6월 18일 토요일까지 오후 4시에 피크닉 구역에서 세션을 열 예정입니다.** (200) 참가에 관심 있으시면, 어느 날짜가 좋은지 명시해 주시기 바랍니다. 전시회에서 뵙게 되길 바랍니다.

Veronica Murphy 드림, 책임자
Bee Spring Plaza

수신: Veronica Murphy <vmurphy@beespringplaza.org>
발신: Ray Dawson <rdawson@dawsonworks.com>
제목: 회신: Bee Spring Plaza 미술 전시회
날짜: 4월 3일
첨부: 계약서, Dawson_약력

Ms. Murphy께,

Bee Spring Plaza에 제 작품을 전시할 기회를 주셔서 감사합니다. 초대를 수락하게 되어 매우 기쁩니다. 간략한 제 약력과 서명한 계약서를 송부해 드립니다. **부스비 450달러도 보내드립니다.** (199)

저는 만남의 장 세션 참석에도 관심이 많습니다. **이상적이게는 제가 토요일에는 시간이 안 될 것 같아서 금요일 세션에 참석하고 싶습니다.** (200)

Ray Dawson 드림

196 공지에서 Bee Spring Plaza 미술 전시회에 관하여 언급된 것은?
(A) 실내 행사다.
(B) 전세계 예술가를 초청한다.
(C) 입장료를 부과한다.
(D) 일년에 한 번 개최된다.

197 공지에서는 행사에 관해 무엇을 암시하는가?
(A) 행사 기간에 미술품이 판매될 수 있다.
(B) 날짜가 변동될 수 있다.
(C) 지원자는 부스 요금을 할인 받는다.
(D) 심사 과정에 경쟁이 있다.

198 첫 번째 이메일에서 Mr. Dawson에 관하여 언급한 것은?
(A) 풍경을 그린다.
(B) 전시회 준비를 도왔다.
(C) Colorado에서 자랐다.
(D) 사진작가이다.

199 Mr. Dawson은 어떤 크기의 부스를 사용하겠는가?
(A) 8피트x8피트 부스
(B) 8피트x12피트 부스
(C) 12피트x12피트 부스
(D) 16피트x16피트 부스

200 Mr. Dawson은 어느 날짜에 만남의 장 세션에 참여하겠는가?
(A) 6월 15일
(B) 6월 16일
(C) 6월 17일
(D) 6월 18일

TEST 08

PART 5 P. 232

101 십 년 동안 Margate 대학은 연례 기금 마련 행사를 통해 지역의 청소년 단체들을 후원하는 데 적극적이었다.

102 Feder 사의 새 가전제품군의 시연은 기술 박람회에서 많은 관심을 불러일으켰다.

103 인사팀원들은 그들의 것이 수리되는 동안 마케팅 부서의 복사기를 사용할 수 있다.

104 Mr. Coulson은 새 본부의 개관을 위한 의식과 기자 회견을 준비할 것이다.

105 어제 5,000명 이상의 사람들이 Kowloon 금융의 웹사이트를 방문했다.

106 경영진은 직장 내 직원 사기를 높이는 방안에 적극적으로 주력한다.

107 Rotherton 박물관을 개조하겠다는 Calumet 건설의 제안서가 오늘 오전 경영진의 승인을 받았다.

108 거의 100달러의 가격이 붙은 모든 제품은 할인 쿠폰이 함께 제공된다.

109 매달 20일 이후 청구된 어느 금액이든 그 다음 달 명세서에 반영될 것이다.

110 최고의 품질을 보장하기 위해, Mason 전자는 자사 스마트폰에 철저한 내구성 및 온도 테스트를 실시한다.

111 방문객들은 Montcrew 박물관의 새로 개관한 고대 그리스-로마관을 관람하도록 안내 받는다.

112 Dr. Rangit은 짧은 상담을 위해 목요일 오후 1시부터 6시까지 사무실에 있을 것이다.

113 판촉 행사 이후에 판매량이 급증해서, 매장 관리자는 특가 상품을 더 제공하는 것을 고려할 것이다.

114 Deerfield 대학교의 전자 도서관에서 학생들은 전자책 수천 권과 데이터베이스를 가상으로 이용할 수 있다.

115 스코틀랜드 작가 Giles Fitzpatrick의 초기 소설 초고는 오늘 개인 수집가에게 알려지지 않은 금액에 판매되었다.

116 역사적으로 중요한 Van Tassel 빌딩에 있는 정원은 주말마다 방문객에게 개방된다.

117 Guangzhou에서 Shenzhen까지 운행하는 시외 버스는 30분 간격으로 터미널에서 출발한다.

118 Costa Sol 농산물 회사는 대단히 습한 봄과 여름으로 인한 사상 최고의 아보카도 작물 수확량을 발표했다.

119 이용자는 장기 요금제에 가입하기로 결정하기 전에 저희 스마트폰 애플리케이션을 7일간 무료로 시험 사용해 볼 수 있습니다.

120 저희가 환불을 처리해 드리길 원하시면 손상된 제품의 사진과 설명을 제출해 주시기 바랍니다.

121 창고 관리자는 선적부에 더 많은 직원들이 재배치될 때까지 그들이 추가 근무를 해야 할 것이라고 말했다.

122 운송회사에서 예측한 배송 날짜와 시간은 예상대로였고 정확했다.

123 우리의 새로운 노트북을 위해 ABM 컴퓨터를 선택한 것에는 신뢰도와 단가가 동등하게 고려되었다.

124 고대 이집트 미술에 관한 세미나 시리즈에 대한 관심이 기대에 미치지 못했기 때문에, 신속히 취소되었다.

125 매일 2리터의 물을 마시는 것보다 충분한 영양 섭취를 유지하는 데 더 필수적인 것은 없다.

126 시각 효과 팀은 영상 편집 소프트웨어의 최신 업데이트 없이는 제대로 된 그래픽을 제공할 수 없다.

127 모든 고객 통화는 제공되는 서비스의 품질을 보장하기 위해 녹음된다.

128 구Mr. Briggs의 경력에서 앞으로 무슨 일이 일어나든지 간에, 그는 DK 엔지니어링에서 감독관으로 일하며 많은 경험을 쌓았다.

129 Wonder Grow 튤립 구근은 여름 성수기에서 적어도 8주 후에 심어져야 한다.

130 퇴사하는 직원들은 청구하지 않은 의료 혜택을 포기하지만 미사용 유급 병가에 대해서 환급을 받는다.

PART 6 P. 235

131-134번은 다음 광고에 관한 문제입니다.

최신 유행 스타일을 찾고 계신가요?

여러분의 선택이 환경에 미치는 영향이 신경 쓰이시나요?

그러시다면, Eka 부티크를 방문하세요. **131.** 저희는 환경을 파괴하지 않는 직물로 만들어진 드레스와 재킷 및 기타 유행 제품을 취급합니다. 여기에는 재활용된 면, 모, 그리고 3가지 종류의 실크가 포함됩니다. 보시면 만족하실 거라고 보장합니다!

저희 Eka 부티크는 언제나 제품의 원산지 **132.** 에 관심을 가집니다. 이것이 저희가 검증된 제조 시설에서 제작된 의류만을 제공 **133.** 하는 이유입니다. 더 자세한 내용을 알아보시고 **134.** 전체 카탈로그를 보시려면, 저희 웹사이트 www.ekasboutique.co.uk를 방문해 주세요.

131 (A) 저희 부티크는 최근 지역의 방직 공장과 계약을 체결했습니다.
(B) 저희는 환경을 파괴하지 않는 직물로 만들어진 드레스와 재킷 및 기타 유행 제품을 취급합니다.
(C) 저희 부티크는 Fashion Valley에 편리하게 위치해 있습니다.
(D) 저희는 오전 10시부터 오후 8시까지, 주 7일 영업합니다.

135-138번은 다음 회람에 관한 문제입니다.

발신: Fred Dixon, 인사부
수신: 전 직원
날짜: 7월 12일
제목: 사무실 폐쇄

7월 29일 토요일에 있을 연중 직원 **135.** 행사 준비 차, 7월 28일 금요일 오후 3시에 사무실을 폐쇄할 예정입니다. 따라서, 회의가 있으신 게 **136.** 아니라면 그날은 재택근무를 계획해 주시길 요청드립니다. 있으시다면, 저희가 요청을 수용해 드릴 수 있도록 저희에게 이메일을 보내주세요. 행사와 관련해서는, 모든 분께 초대장을 발송해 드렸습니다. 아직 받지 못하셨다면, **137.** 즉시 저희에게 알려주시기 바랍니다. 마지막으로, 저희가 지역 내 출장 연회 업체의 추천을 아직 받고 있습니다. **138.** 아는 곳이 있으신 경우, 저희에게 알려주세요.

138 (A) 물품은 보관함에 있습니다.
(B) 제안 목록을 획득했습니다.
(C) 7월은 종종 사업장에게 바쁜 시기입니다.
(D) 아는 곳이 있으신 경우, 저희에게 알려주세요.

139-142번은 다음 이메일에 관한 문제입니다.

수신: board@regrowthfoundation.org
발신: ian@regrowthfoundation.org
날짜: 12월 8일
제목: 재무 보고서
첨부: 재무보고서_12_8.pdf

이사진 여러분께,

연례 재무 보고서 준비를 마무리해, 모든 분께 공유해 드립니다. 살펴보시고 궁금한 점이 있으시면, 다음 주에 있을 연말 이사회에서 말씀하시면 됩니다. **139.** 참석이 어려우신 경우, 문의 사항을 저에게 이메일로 보내 주시기 바랍니다.

가장 중요한 요점은 저희 재정 상태가 **140.** 나빠지고 있다는 것입니다. 다양한 행사를 통해 훨씬 더 많은 돈을 벌었지만, 지출을 자세히 살펴봐 주세요. 지난 5년간 매년 증가해 왔습니다. 이에 비용 절감 **141.** 방안을 마련해야 합니다. 마지막으로, 올해 기업 기부금으로 받게 될 예상액을 추산해야 할 것입니다. 저희가 내년도 예산을 수립하는 데 필요합니다. 작년에는 기부금 목표액을 초과 달성했지만, 여러분께서 신중을 기해 주셨으면 합니다. **142.** 야심 찬 목표를 세우는 것은 대개 좋지만, 비현실적인 기대를 양산할 수도 있습니다.

139 (A) 참석이 어려우신 경우, 문의 사항을 저에게 이메일로 보내 주시기 바랍니다.
(B) 저는 이전 이메일에서 그 우려를 언급했습니다.
(C) 변경 사항은 공식 절차를 거쳐야 할 것입니다.
(D) 참석률은 매년 상당히 저조했습니다.

143-146번은 다음 기사에 관한 문제입니다.

PIERCE (6월 17일) — Primord Fitness에서 **143.** 기술 거래 기업인 Lifegate와 제휴해 새로운 시계를 출시할 예정이다. **144.** 개인용 체력 단련 프로그램을 제작하는 데 전문 기술을 보유한 것으로 유명한 Primord에서 이제 고객이 자신의 체력 단련 목표에 보다 빠르게 도달하도록 돕고자 한다. 그리하여 Primord에서는 Lifegate의 프로그래밍 팀과 협업한 후, 사용자의 운동 중 데이터를 기록하는 신규 소프트웨어를 자사 시계에 **145.** 포함했다. **146.** 운동 시간과 소모 열량 같은 주요 정보가 저장된다.

일부 운 좋은 고객들은 이달 초 시계를 시험 사용하는 기회를 누렸다. "시험 사용은 순조롭게 진행되었고, 저희가 많이 배웠습니다."라고 회사 대변인 Mr. Jeff Jensen이 말했다. "이제 보다 정교한 세부 사항을 해결했기에, 시장에 진입할 준비가 되었다고 확신합니다."라고 덧붙였다.

146 (A) 운동 시간과 소모 열량 같은 주요 정보가 저장된다.
(B) 결과를 확인하기 위해 추가 테스트가 필요할 것이다.
(C) 일반적으로 날씨가 더 추운 달에는 이용 가능성이 낮다.
(D) 회사 웹사이트에서 설명서를 구할 수 있다.

PART 7
P. 239

147-148번은 다음 정보에 관한 문제입니다.

모든 Electric Avenue 청취자 여러분께!

이제, 저희 청취자 여러분은 모든 주요 온라인 스트리밍 플랫폼에서 프로그램에 접속하실 수 있습니다. (147)

• **언제든지 저희 콘텐츠를 스트리밍하세요** (148)
• 전 목록을 무료로 재생하세요

귀하의 음악 구독 서비스에서 'Electric Avenue'를 검색하세요. 아니면 WCCRB에 채널 고정하셔서 오후 8시부터 자정까지 생방송으로 청취하세요.

147 정보의 주요 목적은 무엇인가?
(A) 새로운 스트리밍 플랫폼을 알리기 위해
(B) 특별 생방송 행사를 홍보하기 위해
(C) 팬들을 위한 새로운 선택 사항을 광고하기 위해
(D) 라디오 방송에 신규 청취자를 유치하기 위해

148 스트리밍 서비스에 관하여 언급된 것은 무엇인가?
(A) 청취자는 하루 24시간 프로그램에 접속할 수 있다.
(B) 청취자는 월 이용료를 지불해야 한다.
(C) 일부 청취자만 이용할 수 있다.
(D) 청취자는 이메일을 통해 계정을 활성화해야 한다.

149-150번은 다음 문자 메시지 대화문에 관한 문제입니다.

Andre Wiseau [16:58]
저기, Dana. 오늘 피자가 충분하지 않은 것 같아요. 8상자를 주문했는데, 7상자밖에 없네요.

Dana Blanc [16:59]

그러면 안 되는데. 주문을 확인하지 않아서 죄송해요. 지금 피자 가게에 연락해 볼게요.

Andre Wiseau [17:16]

한국에서 오는 관광 단체가 곧 도착해요. ⁽¹⁴⁹⁾ 지금 돌아오는 길이세요?

Dana Blanc [17:18]

10분 후에 도착할 거예요. 가게에서 피자를 새로 만들어야 하는 것 같아요. 바로 시작했어요. ⁽¹⁵⁰⁾

Andre Wiseau [17:19]

알겠어요. 방금 Will에게 서관도 들르라고 했어요. 그들에게 고대 중국 유물들을 짧게 견학시켜 줄 거예요. ⁽¹⁴⁹⁾

Dana Blanc [17:28]

다행이에요. 여기는 지연된 것 때문에 음료를 무료로 주신대요.

Andre Wiseau [17:28]

네. 계속 상황을 알려 주세요.

149 Mr. Wiseau에 관하여 무엇이 사실이겠는가?
(A) 관광 단체를 인솔하고 있다.
(B) 피자 만드는 것에 능숙하다.
(C) 역사 박물관에서 근무한다.
(D) 음료수를 구입할 것이다.

150 17시 18분에, Ms. Blanc이 "바로 시작했어요"라고 쓸 때 무엇을 의미하는가?
(A) 음료수가 리필되고 있다.
(B) 새로운 관광 단체가 방금 도착했다.
(C) 몇몇 손님들이 식사를 하기 시작했다.
(D) 주문이 빠르게 처리되고 있다.

151-154번은 다음 안내 책자에 관한 문제입니다.

저희와 함께 중장비 조작법을 배워보세요!

저희 Sunbelt 교육은 지게차나 크레인 같은 중장비 조작 교육을 전문으로 하고 있으며, 놀라운 속도로 성장하고 있습니다. 현재 중장비 기사들의 수요가 그 어느 때보다 높습니다. 저희와 함께하시면, 취업이 보장되며, 그렇지 않으면 수업료를 환불해 드리겠습니다. ⁽¹⁵¹⁾

저희 6개월 과정은 여러분을 자립시켜 중장비 기사로 일할 수 있도록 준비해 드릴 것입니다. 저희가 제공하는 놀라운 패키지가 여기 있습니다:

◆ 여러분이 선택할 수 있는 3일 일정은 다음과 같습니다:
 - 아침 수업: 월요일/수요일/금요일, 오전 8시~오후 12시
 - 저녁 수업: 화요일/목요일/토요일, 오후 6시~오후 10시
◆ 교육 센터 통학 무료 교통편
◆ 6개월 이상 실업 상태인 경우 수업료 인하 ⁽¹⁵²⁾
◆ 경험이 풍부한 기사와 연결시켜 드리는 수상 경력에 빛나는 개인 지도 시스템. 여러분의 코치가 모든 학습 내용을 안내하고 시험 준비를 도와드립니다. ⁽¹⁵³⁾
◆ 지속적인 전문적 도움의 손길로, 본 과정을 수료하는 즉시 일자리를 찾아 드릴 뿐만 아니라 업계에서 출세하는 법에 대해 조언해 드릴 것입니다. ⁽¹⁵⁴⁾

저희와 함께 여러분의 인생의 새로운 장을 시작할 준비가 되셨나요?

저희 정보의 밤 행사에 오시면 더 많은 것을 얻으실 수 있습니다!

| 세션 1 | 9월 8일, 화요일 |
| 세션 2 | 9월 12일, 토요일 |

더 많은 정보를 원하시면, www.sunbelttraining.com을 방문하시거나 간단히 425-555-4685로 전화 주시면 됩니다.

151 안내 책자에 따르면, 중장비 기사로 일하는 혜택은 무엇인가?
(A) 주말 교대 근무가 없음
(B) 높은 해외 수요
(C) 취업의 용이성
(D) 저렴한 진입 비용

152 수업료의 인하 대상은 누구인가?
(A) 미취업자
(B) 지역 주민
(C) 35세 미만인 사람
(D) 학사 학위 보유자

153 안내 책자에 따르면, 수업에 관하여 강조되는 것은 무엇인가?
(A) 업계에서 수업료가 가장 낮다.
(B) 자율 학습 요소가 포함되어 있다.
(C) 수상 경력이 있는 강사에게 수업을 받는다.
(D) 멘토링 프로그램이 포함되어 있다.

154 Sunbelt 교육에서 제공하는 것은 무엇인가?
(A) 취업 면접 연습
(B) 경력 발전 조언
(C) 수업료 대출 제도
(D) 이력서 견본

155-157번은 다음 안내문에 관한 문제입니다.

산호를 구해 주세요

호주 환경 에너지청(ADEE)이 Great Barrier Reef를 구하기 위한 전 세계적 기금 마련 행사를 진행하고 있습니다. —[1]—. 월말까지 1,000만 호주 달러라는 목표가 설정되었으며, 전 세계의 친구 여러분이 세계의 위대한 자연계 불가사의 중 하나의 보존을 돕는 데 기여해 주시기 바랍니다. ⁽¹⁵⁵⁾ —[2]—. 모금액은 상승하는 해수 온도나 증가한 악천후의 빈도와 같은 위협으로부터 산호를 더 잘 보호할 방법에 대한 연구에 사용될 것입니다. ^{(156)/(157)} —[3]—.

산호를 구하기 위해 할 수 있는 일에 관해 더 자세히 알아보시려면, www.environment.gov.au/savethereef/info를 방문해 주세요. —[4]—.

오늘 여러분의 도움을 보여 주세요!

155 안내문은 왜 작성되었는가?
(A) 새로운 에너지 계획을 설명하기 위해
(B) 월간 혜택을 광고하기 위해
(C) 기부를 요청하기 위해
(D) 새로운 연구 결과를 보고하기 위해

156 Great Barrier Reef에 관하여 알 수 있는 것은 무엇인가?
(A) 다양한 해양 생물들의 서식지이다.
(B) 기후 변화의 영향을 받고 있다.
(C) 호주 최대의 관광 명소이다.
(D) 대중에게 공개되어 있지 않다.

157 [1], [2], [3], [4]로 표시된 곳 중 다음 문장이 들어가기에 가장 적절한 곳은 어디인가?

"또한, 일부는 주변 지역의 수질 개선을 돕는 데 사용될 것입니다."

(A) [1]
(B) [2]
(C) [3]
(D) [4]

158-160번은 다음 구인 광고에 관한 문제입니다.

미술관 큐레이터 채용 공고

직책

Montreal 국립 미술관은 고대 미술 부서에 경력자를 필요로 하고 있습니다. 큐레이터의 책무에는 방문객들을 교육하고 전시에 관해 알려주는 일뿐만 아니라 유물 수집, 소장품 관리 및 전시가 포함됩니다.

자격 조건

지원자는 박물관이나 미술관에서 최소 2년의 근무 경험이 있어야 합니다. 또한, 성공적인 지원자는 프랑스어의 유창한 구사 능력을 갖출 것입니다.**(158)** 지원자는 또한 미술 또는 미술사 같은 학과의 학사 학위나 그에 상응하는 자격을 갖춰야 합니다. **석사 학위는 필수 사항이 아니나, 추가 이점이 됩니다.(159)**

지원 방법

지원서를 작성하시려면 웹사이트 www.montrealart.com/jobs/ancientart를 방문해 주십시오.

연락

문의 사항이 있거나 직책에 관해 더 자세히 알아보시려면, 인사부장에게 janlopez@montrealart.com으로 이메일을 보내 주시기 바랍니다.**(160)**

---

158 해당 직책에 필요한 자격 조건은 무엇인가?
(A) 석사 학위
(B) 탄탄한 의사소통 능력
(C) 특정 언어에의 유창함
(D) 미술을 가르쳐본 경험

159 두 번째 단락, 네 번째 줄의 단어 "bonus"와 의미상 가장 가까운 것은
(A) 상
(B) 장점
(C) 수수료
(D) 보상금

160 직무에 대한 추가 정보는 어떻게 얻을 수 있는가?
(A) 취업 박람회에 참석해서
(B) 직원에게 연락해서
(C) 박물관에 가서
(D) 홈페이지를 방문해서

161-164번은 다음 온라인 채팅 대화문에 관한 문제입니다.

Manuel Aguilar [오전 9시 32분]
안녕하세요, Thelma. 인쇄소로 보내기 전에 1면을 살펴보고 있는데요.**(161)** 사진은 아주 잘 나왔는데, 표지 특집 기사에 지역 시민들의 의견이 충분히 담기지 않았어요.**(161)/(162)** 기사에 개인 이야기가 더 많이 담기면 정말 좋을 것 같아요.

Thelma Lambert [오전 9시 34분]
안녕하세요, Manuel. 기사가 너무 길어질까 봐 걱정됐어요. 제가 인터뷰를 몇 건 한 게 있어서, 그것을 넣는 선택지가 있어요. 아마 글을 더 실으려면 사진을 작게 줄이면 될 거예요.**(162)**

Manuel Aguilar [오전 9시 36분]
그렇군요. 당신은 어떻게 생각하세요?**(162)**

Thelma Lambert [오전 9시 39분]
기사에 인터뷰를 추가할게요. 그리고 나서, 사진 크기를 조정할게요. 그리고 우리는 우리가 쓰는 종이 종류를 바꾸는 것도 생각해 봐야 할 것 같아요. 신문 용지가 더 좋아지면 사진이 정말 돋보일 거예요.**(163)**

Manuel Aguilar [오전 9시 42분]
그건 예전에 우리가 고려한 적이 있어요. 비용에 어떻게 영향을 미칠까요?**(164)**

Thelma Lambert [오전 9시 45분]
신문 바깥 면에만 사용하는 걸 생각해 봤어요. **우리가 부과하는 신문 요금에 많은 영향을 미치지 않을 거예요.(164)**

Manuel Aguilar [오전 9시 47분]
아주 좋은데요. 인쇄소에서 견적을 받고 다시 연락할게요.

---

161 Ms. Lambert의 직업은 무엇이겠는가?
(A) 프로젝트 책임자
(B) 상법 변호사
(C) 부동산 중개인
(D) 뉴스 리포터

162 오전 9시 36분에, Mr. Aguilar가 "당신은 어떻게 생각하세요?"라고 쓸 때 무엇을 알고 싶어 하겠는가?
(A) 인터뷰 실시 건수
(B) 프로젝트 마감일 시점
(C) 추가 내용의 포함 여부
(D) 고객에게 연락해야 하는지 여부

163 Ms. Lambert는 왜 더 좋은 신문 용지를 사용하고 싶어 하는가?
(A) 사진을 더 좋게 만든다.
(B) 환경 친화적이다.
(C) 더 보호된다.
(D) 비용 효율이 더 좋다.

164 Ms. Lambert는 비용에 관하여 무엇을 제안하는가?
(A) 장차 개정되어야 한다.
(B) 고객의 의견이 필요할지도 모른다.
(C) 이미 너무 높다.
(D) 큰 금액은 아닐 것이다.

165-166번은 다음 공지에 관한 문제입니다.

Elkton Community 작업 공간 이용 규칙

George Park 102번지에 있는 저희 작업 공간을 이용하고자 하는 Elkton 신생 기업은 반드시 다음 규칙에 동의해야 합니다:

· 작업 공간은 선착순으로 선점됩니다. 요금이 없는 반면, 미리 자리를 맡아 놓는 것은 허용되지 않습니다.

· **작업 공간을 사용하는 참여 업체는 제공되는 종이를 사용해 출입 기록을 해야 합니다.(165)** 공부와 같은 다른 목적으로 작업 공간을 사용할 수 없습니다. 작업 공간은 신생 기업이 서로 어울리고 협력하는 공간이어야 합니다. 따라서, 이 구역을 오로지 업무 목적으로만 지정합니다.

· 작업 공간은 사용 후 청소되어야 합니다. 이 서비스를 이용하는 업체는 다른 업체가 그 구역을 사용할 수 있도록 뒷정리를 해 줄 것을 요청드립니다. **청소를 하지 않아 적발된 사용자는 경고를 받을 수 있으며, 벌금이 부과될 수 있습니다.(166)**

---

165 참여자는 무엇을 하도록 기대되는가?
(A) 다른 업체를 돕도록
(B) 자리를 예약하도록
(C) 종이를 작성하도록
(D) 사업을 등록하도록

166 공지에 따르면, 참여자는 왜 경고를 받겠는가?
(A) 작업 공간에서 공부를 해서
(B) 구역을 청소하지 않아서
(C) 과도한 소음을 내서
(D) 외부 재정 지원을 받아서

167-168번은 다음 기사에 관한 문제입니다.

유망 광고 회사인 Affinity Views는 논란의 여지가 있는 광고 전략으로 인해 최근 몇 달간 철저한 조사를 받았다. **상업 위원회는 회사가 계속 공정 거래법을 위반할 시 그에 대한 조치가 취해질 것임을 분명히 밝혔다.** 이를 염두에 두고 Affinity Views에서는 회사가 규칙을 지키는 데 도움을 줄 Mr. Gordon을 고용했다.⁽¹⁶⁷⁾ Affinity Views의 최근 캠페인에는 바이럴 광고 캠페인으로 헬리콥터에서 위조 지폐를 떨어뜨리는 것이 포함되었다. 캠페인은 비난을 받았는데, 대중은 이목을 끌려는 그러한 행동이 근시안적이며 위험하다고 논평했다. Mr. Gordon은 자신의 방대한 경험을 살려 회사가 좋은 홍보 효과만 낼 수 있게 할 생각이다. 그는 내년에 회사의 새로운 이미지를 제시할 것이라고 넌지시 알렸다. 논란에도 불구하고, Affinity Views는 사상 최고 수치를 발표했다. **작년 수익은 총 1천 5백만 달러로, 이 중에서 5백만 달러를 해외에서 벌어들였다.**⁽¹⁶⁸⁾ 회사는 내년에 해외 고객이 상당히 증가할 것으로 예상하고 있다.

167 Affinity Views는 왜 Mr. Gordon을 고용했는가?
(A) 회사의 해외 진출을 관리하려고
(B) 회사가 규정을 준수하도록 하려고
(C) 회사의 재정을 체계화하려고
(D) 회사의 홍보 효과를 늘리려고

168 Affinity Views는 작년에 얼마를 벌었는가?
(A) 5백만 달러
(B) 1천만 달러
(C) 1천 2백 5십만 달러
(D) 1천 5백만 달러

169-171번은 다음 설명서에 관한 문제입니다.

Sparkle Again

우선, 쏟은 액체의 넘치는 잔여물을 종이 타월로 흡수시켜 닦아내세요. 그 다음에, 소량의 용액을 직물에 발라 주세요. **Sparkle Again 용액을 원을 그리며 부드럽게 문질러 줍니다. 얼룩이 옅어지면서 사라지기 시작할 것입니다. 여전히 얼룩이 보인다면 덧발라 주세요.**⁽¹⁶⁹⁾

Sparkle Again은 천연 원료만을 사용하여 옷이 변색되지 않게 보호합니다. 최상의 효과를 위해서는, 쏟은 직후에 발라 주세요. **Sparkle Again은 세심한 주의를 요하는 재료로 만들어진 옷감을 손상시킬 수 있기 때문에 그렇지 않은 직물에만 바르실 것을 강력히 권장합니다.**⁽¹⁷⁰⁾

추가 정보를 얻거나 Sparkle Again 사용법에 관한 동영상을 보시려면, **웹사이트 www.sparkleagain.com/howto를 방문해 주세요.**⁽¹⁷¹⁾ 저희 친절한 고객 지원 서비스 상담원과 직접 대화하고 싶으시면, +(41) 555-8274로 전화하시거나 cs@sparkleagain.com으로 이메일을 보내 주세요.

169 Sparkle Again의 용도는 무엇인가?
(A) 표면에 광을 내기 위해
(B) 색상을 밝게 하기 위해
(C) 얼룩을 제거하기 위해
(D) 악취를 방지하기 위해

170 설명서에 따르면, 제품 사용 시 무엇을 하는 것이 중요한가?
(A) 세심한 주의가 필요한 직물에 사용을 피하는 것
(B) 여러 번 바르는 것을 피하는 것
(C) 옷에 바른 후 말리는 것
(D) 액체를 모두 흡수시키는 것

171 Sparkle Again에 관하여 알 수 있는 것은 무엇인가?
(A) 제품이 합성 원료를 함유하고 있다.
(B) 회사 웹사이트에서 사용 지침서를 제공한다.
(C) 제품을 온라인이나 매장에서 구매할 수 있다.
(D) 손상된 옷에 대해서는 고객에게 변상해 준다.

172-175번은 다음 웹 페이지에 관한 문제입니다.

www.lsw.net

잡지	조언	회사 소개	기회

<Logan Square Weekly>는 이곳 Logan Square와 Palmer Square, Humboldt Park 지역 주민들에 의해 제작됩니다. 매주 화요일 저녁에 온라인으로 게재됩니다.⁽¹⁷²⁾ **여름 SLAM 음악 축제를 위한 <최고의 LSW 수집가 호>도 출간됩니다.**⁽¹⁷⁵⁾ —[1]—.

<Logan Square Weekly>는 지역 관점의 뉴스와 지역 내 최고 상점 정보, 다가오는 지역 행사 정보를 소개합니다.⁽¹⁷²⁾ —[2]—. Peter Moorman과 Anna Kim을 비롯하여 유능한 칼럼니스트들이 식당 추천부터 부동산 조언까지 모든 걸 제공합니다.

올가을, <Logan Square Weekly>에서 지역 상인을 표창하는 기획을 시작할 것입니다.⁽¹⁷³⁾ 이를 위해, 독자 여러분께 지역 사회에 상당한 기여를 한 우수 사업주 추천을 해 주실 것을 요청드립니다. —[3]—. 후보를 추천하려면, RyanS@LSW.net으로 이메일을 보내 주시기 바랍니다. 여러분의 선택을 검토한 후, 올해의 최우수 상인 2명을 선발할 것입니다. **수상자들은 10월 15일 지역 공로자 연회에서 상을 수여받게 됩니다.**⁽¹⁷⁴⁾ —[4]—. 또한 두 수상자 모두 <LSW> 10월 12일 호 첫 페이지에 프로필이 실리게 됩니다.

172 웹 페이지의 목적은 무엇인가?
(A) 지역 출판물을 광고하기 위해
(B) 식당 개업을 보도하기 위해
(C) 지역 선거에 관해 설명하기 위해
(D) 콘서트 일정을 발표하기 위해

173 어떤 새로운 특징이 발표되고 있는가?
(A) 재무 조언을 위한 신규 칼럼
(B) 웹 채팅 서비스
(C) 상인들을 표창하려는 계획
(D) 부동산 목록 페이지

174 10월 15일에는 어떤 일이 있을 것인가?
(A) 출판물에 기사가 실릴 것이다.
(B) 시 공무원들이 임명될 것이다.
(C) 새 상점이 문을 열 것이다.
(D) 상이 수여될 것이다.

175 [1], [2], [3], [4]로 표시된 곳 중 다음 문장이 들어가기에 가장 적절한 곳은 어디인가?

"늘 그렇듯, 행사 기간 내내 1달러에 구매하실 수 있습니다."

(A) [1]
(B) [2]
(C) [3]
(D) [4]

176-180번은 다음 이메일과 청구서에 관한 문제입니다.

발신: Janae Meeks <j.meeks@parallelhotel.com>
수신: Taisha Chen <t.chen@outermail.cn>
전송: 7월 3일, 금요일, 오전 9시 07분[176]
첨부: @객실 예약

Ms. Chen께,

머무르시는 동안 Parallel 호텔에서 투숙하시기로 선택해 주신 데 감사의 말씀 드립니다. 이것은 귀하의 7월 19일과 20일 디럭스 싱글 룸 예약 확인 메시지입니다.[178] 귀하의 예약을 완료하기 위해, 제가 보증금 지불 청구를 할 것이며, 오늘 오후에 있을 예정입니다.[176] 호텔에 체크인하실 때, 잔액이 청구된다는 점에 유념해 주시기 바랍니다.

요청하신 사항과 관련하여, 만찬 회동에 대한 식단 제한 사항을 기꺼이 수용해 드리겠습니다.[179] 하지만, 의사소통상 단절이 발생하는 경우에 대비해, 서빙 직원에게 재차 알려주시는 게 좋을 것 같습니다. 그 외에, 다른 필요하신 사항이 있으시면 저에게 알려주세요. 어떤 문제든 기쁘게 해결해 드리겠습니다.[177]

귀하를 이곳에 다시 모시게 되길 바랍니다.

Janae Meeks 드림
호텔 서비스

Parallel 호텔 · 15 Ryecroft Field · Pennsylvania 15057

투숙객: Taisha Chen
주소: 293 Bradford Manor, Elma, New York

객실 번호	516	객실 요금	375달러/박
도착	7월 17일[178]	출발	7월 20일

날짜	내용	요금
7월 17-20일[178]	객실료	1,125달러
7월 17일	룸 서비스	30달러
7월 18일[179]	레스토랑 저녁 식사[179]	250달러
7월 18일	룸 서비스	25달러
7월 19일	레스토랑 점심식사	50달러
7월 20일	공항 배웅[180]	30달러
	총	1,510달러

---

176 Ms. Meeks는 7월 3일에 무엇을 했겠는가?
(A) 약속을 취소했다.
(B) Ms. Chen의 사무실로 전화했다.
(C) Ms. Chen의 신용카드에 청구했다.
(D) 광고 공간을 구매했다.

177 이메일에서 두 번째 단락, 네 번째 줄의 구, "iron out"과 의미상 가장 가까운 것은
(A) 실행하다
(B) 처리하다
(C) 개발하다
(D) 관념화하다

178 Ms. Chen의 Parallel 호텔 투숙에 관하여 암시되는 것은 무엇인가?
(A) Parallel 호텔에 처음 투숙했다.
(B) 예상보다 더 비쌌다.
(C) 비상 상황으로 인해 일찍 떠났다.
(D) 애초에 계획한 것보다 더 빨랐다.

179 Ms. Chen은 언제 회의에 참석했겠는가?
(A) 7월 17일
(B) 7월 18일
(C) 7월 19일
(D) 7월 20일

180 Parallel 호텔에 관하여 알 수 있는 것은 무엇인가?
(A) 공항 기사 서비스를 제공한다.
(B) Pennsylvania에서 가장 오래된 호텔이다.
(C) Ms. Meeks가 소유하고 운영한다.
(D) 최근 가격을 인상했다.

181-185번은 다음 웹 페이지와 이메일에 관한 문제입니다.

---

https://www.looper.com/packages

왜 Looper인가?	**패키지**	이용 약관	연락처

Looper는 신생 기업과 대기업 모두에게 안성맞춤인 온라인 플랫폼입니다. 저희 프로젝트 관리 소프트웨어는 직원들이 서로 교류하고 사내 일상 업무에 대해 잘 알 수 있게 해 줘서 귀사의 효율성과 생산성을 극대화해 줄 것입니다.[181]

신생 기업 패키지
직원 수 100명 이하인 신생 기업에 적합합니다. 내장된 메시지 발송과 파일 공유 기능 및 단체 일정표, 팀원당 10GB의 클라우드 저장 공간을 제공하는 모바일 및 데스크톱 버전을 이용해 보세요.

프리미엄 패키지
직원 수 500명 이하의 사업체에 추천합니다. 신생 기업 패키지의 모든 기능 외에도, 토론 게시판과 포트폴리오 관리, 프로젝트 진행 상태 추적, 팀원당 20GB의 클라우드 저장 공간을 이용하실 수 있습니다.

기업 패키지
직원 수 800명까지의 기업에 안성맞춤입니다. 프리미엄 패키지의 기능 외에도 팀당 35GB의 클라우드 저장 공간과 더불어 활동 피드와 설문 조사 및 피드백 발송 기능, 일대일 화상 회의를 누려 보세요.

다국적 패키지
이 패키지는 직원 수 1,000명 이상인 기업을 위한 것입니다. 기업 패키지의 모든 기능 외에도, 양방향 화면 공유 기능으로 최대 20명까지 참여할 수 있는 음성 및 화상 회의와 연중무휴 고객 지원, 동기화된 문서 편집, 직원당 50GB의 저장 공간을 누려 보세요.[184]

한 달 무료 체험을 신청하세요. 무료 체험이 끝날 때쯤에는 왜 세계에서 가장 크고 성공한 기업들이 경쟁업체가 아닌 저희 소프트웨어를 선택하는지 알게 되실 것입니다.[182] 귀사에 적합한 패키지를 더 알아보시려면, '연락처' 탭을 클릭하셔서 저희 영업 사원과 상담하시기 바랍니다.

발신: p.malkin@capsun.ca
수신: a.crosby@looper.com
날짜: 5월 19일
제목: Looper 패키지

Ms. Crosby께,

제 이름은 Paul Malkin이고, 저는 Capsun 산업의 최고 전략 책임자입니다. 저희는 지난 5년 동안 Looper를 사용해 왔으며, 저희의 성장에 있어 귀사의 소프트웨어 중요도는 아무리 강조해도 지나치지 않습니다.[185] 저희는 최근 확장 계획을 마무리 지어, 조만간 캐나다 전역에 1,300명 이상의 직원을 보유할 것입니다. 귀사에서 제공하는 클라우드 저장 공간을 잘 활용해 왔습니다만, 이제는 업무 진행 상황을 추적할 더 좋은 방법뿐만 아니라, 직원당 35GB 이상이 필요할 것입니다.[183]/[184] 여기에 맞는 것이 있으신가요?[183]

답장 기다리겠습니다.

Paul Malkin
최고 전략 책임자
Capsun 산업

---

181 Looper 소프트웨어는 어떻게 사용되겠는가?
(A) 신입 사원을 모집하기 위해
(B) 온라인에 상품을 광고하기 위해
(C) 고객에게 도움을 제공하기 위해
(D) 직원 생산성을 향상하기 위해

182 Looper에 관하여 사실인 것은 무엇인가?
(A) 제품들이 주요 기업들에 의해 사용된다.
(B) Capsun 산업과 합병했다.
(C) 첫 소프트웨어 제품군이 5년 전에 출시되었다.
(D) 200명 이상의 직원이 있다.

183 이메일의 목적은 무엇인가?
(A) 제품 구매를 확정하기 위해
(B) 제품 선택에 대한 조언을 구하기 위해
(C) 프로그램 문제에 대해 불만을 제기하기 위해
(D) 최신 사용자 설명서를 요청하기 위해

184 Ms. Crosby는 어느 제품을 추천하겠는가?
(A) 신생 기업 패키지
(B) 프리미엄 패키지
(C) 기업 패키지
(D) 다국적 패키지

185 이메일에서 첫 번째 단락, 두 번째 줄의 단어 "stress"와 의미상 가장 가까운 것은
(A) 예상하다
(B) 걱정하다
(C) 강조하다
(D) 압력을 가하다

186-190번은 다음 이메일, 광고, 메모에 관한 문제입니다.

발신: Lew Burns (영국 Flotech)
수신: Ashraf Bhagat (파키스탄 Flotech)
날짜: 12월 5일
제목: Awad 엔지니어링

안녕하세요, Ashraf.

Awad 엔지니어링의 방문을 맞이할 준비를 하고 계시다고 들었어요.(186)/(189) Flotech 컨설팅 영국 지사가 이곳 London에서 수년째 Awad 엔지니어링과 협력해 와서, 그들은 Flotech 파키스탄 팀과도 좋은 관계를 맺을 거라 매우 기대하고 있어요.(186) 제 생각에 당신도 그들이 상대하기 매우 편한 사람들이라는걸 알게 될 거예요.

1월 12일로 준비하고 계신 식사에 관해서는,(187)/(189) 엔지니어들 중 몇 명이 다소 엄격한 음식 제한 사항이 있다는 걸 말씀드려야겠네요.(187) 준비하실 때 이 점을 염두에 두는 게 좋을 거예요.

궁금한 점이 있으시면 전화해 주세요.

고맙습니다.
Lew

Darbar 출장 뷔페
Karachi

완벽한 행사를 계획하고 싶으실 때는, Darbar 출장 뷔페를 찾아 주세요. 당사는 1955년부터 Karachi에서 고객분들께 많은 기쁨을 드려 왔는데, 기업과 가족 모임 모두에 최상의 음식과 음료를 제공해 오고 있습니다.

왜 Darbar여야 할까요? 자, 저희를 돋보이게 하는 점은 다음과 같습니다:
*귀사 로고를 포함한 맞춤 제작 장식물
*서양식, 남아시아식 및 중식 인기 품목을 포함하는 국제적인 메뉴
*다양한 음식 기호에 맞춰 만들어 드리는 특별 메뉴(187)
*요청 시 이용 가능한 무도장 설치 및 음악 오락 서비스

저희 서비스는 매일 정오부터 오후 10시까지 이용하실 수 있습니다.(188)

더 자세한 내용은 (92) 0213-555-1212로 전화해 주세요.

Bilal 리조트
Avaricor 그룹 호텔(190)

1월 12일(189)

Mr. Opfel께,(189)

파키스탄에 오신 걸 환영합니다! London에서부터 즐거운 여행이셨길 바랍니다! 오후 12시 30분에 이 리조트 2층 Rainbow 홀에서 있을 특별 오찬에 저희와 함께 해 주신다면 저희 팀과 저에게는 영광이겠습니다.(189)/(190) 공사 현장으로 가기 전에, 좋은 음식을 먹으면서 귀하에 대해 조금 알게 되길 기대하고 있습니다.

그 동안, 제가 도와 드릴 일이 있다면 (92) 0304-551-2522로 저에게 전화해 주세요.

이만 줄이겠습니다.
Ashraf Bhagat

---

186 이메일은 왜 발송되었는가?
(A) 신규 계약 조항을 논의하기 위해
(B) 고객에 관하여 다른 지점과 협력하기 위해
(C) 엔지니어 자리의 후보자를 추천하기 위해
(D) 고객과의 오찬 회의 일정을 다시 잡기 위해

187 Darbar 출장 뷔페의 어떤 특징이 행사에 가장 적합한 업체로 만들어주는가?
(A) 저렴한 서비스
(B) 넓은 장소
(C) 주문 맞춤 제작 메뉴
(D) 오락 선택

188 광고에 따르면, Darbar 출장 뷔페는 어떤 유형의 행사에 도움이 되지 않겠는가?
(A) 시상식 만찬
(B) 기업 조찬
(C) 연휴 기념 행사
(D) 졸업 파티

189 Mr. Opfel은 어디서 근무하겠는가?
(A) Awad 엔지니어링에서
(B) Darbar 출장 뷔페에서
(C) Flotech 컨설팅에서
(D) Avaricor 그룹에서

190 Mr. Opfel은 어디에서 메모를 전달받았겠는가?
(A) 리조트 안내 데스크에서
(B) Flotech에서 주최하는 사교 모임에서
(C) London 공항의 출발 탑승구에서
(D) Awad 엔지니어링 본사에서

191-195번은 다음 웹 페이지와 이메일들에 관한 문제입니다.

www.maroteateries.com/news

Marot 식당은 길고 긴 공사 기간을 거쳐 이제 다시 문을 열었습니다. 새로운 식당은 개별 행사를 할 수 있도록 재설계되었습니다. [191] 아래층 구역은 최대 50명까지 수용할 수 있으며, 위층 구역에는 최대 30명이 수용 가능합니다. [193] 단체는 두 구역 모두 또는 한 구역을 예약할 수 있습니다. 현재 저희는 점심과 저녁 행사를 모두 받고 있습니다.

두 구역은 모두 무드 조명, 마이크, 프로젝터를 비롯해 귀하의 요구 사항에 맞게 만들어 드립니다. 요청하시면 노트북뿐만 아니라 인터넷 이용도 제공합니다. 하지만, 사전에 알려주실 것을 요청드립니다.

저희는 네 가지 식사 패키지를 제공합니다:
· 패키지 A: 애피타이저와 주 요리가 포함된 기본 점심 메뉴
· 패키지 B: 애피타이저, 주 요리, 디저트가 포함된 3코스 점심 메뉴
· 패키지 C: 애피타이저, 샐러드, 주 요리가 포함된 3코스 저녁 메뉴
· **패키지 D: 애피타이저, 샐러드, 주 요리, 디저트, 커피/차가 포함된 디럭스 저녁 메뉴** [194]

예약하시려면 reservations@maroteateries.com으로 연락하시기 바랍니다.

수신: Rosa Logan <rlogan@bubulina.com>
발신: Lester Murphy <lmurphy@maroteateries.com>
날짜: 7월 30일
제목: 예약

Ms. Logan께,

8월 3일 저녁 **Marot** 식당에서의 **Bubulina** 저녁 행사에 관한 세부 내용을 확인드립니다. [192] 귀하의 일행은 23명입니다. 같은 시간에 48명이 참석하는 다른 행사도 진행되오니, 이에 불편함이 없으시길 바랍니다. [193] 귀하께선 전원 바닷가재 비스크로 애피타이저를 요청해 주셨고, 주 요리로 소고기 14인분, 생선 9인분을 선택해 주셨습니다. 샐러드는 오늘의 샐러드로 나갈 예정입니다. [194]

특수 장비나 요청 사항 관련해서는 제가 아직 아무런 연락을 받지 못했습니다. 요청 사항을 이행하려면 하루 전에 알려주셔야 한다는 점에 유의해 주시기 바랍니다.

문의 사항이 있으시거나 계획이 변경되면, 가능한 한 빨리 저에게 알려 주세요.

Lester Murphy 드림
행사 진행자, Marot 식당

수신: Lester Murphy <lmurphy@maroteateries.com>
발신: Rosa Logan <rlogan@bubulina.com>
날짜: 7월 31일
제목: 회신: 예약

Mr. Murphy께:

확인해 주셔서 감사합니다. 우선, 다른 행사가 있을 거라는 점 이해합니다. 소음이 크게 문제 되지 않길 바랍니다. 또한, 요청드릴 일부 변경 사항이 있습니다. 다행히도 환상적인 분기를 보낸 덕에 저희가 보너스를 받았습니다. 그래서, 근사한 식사를 하며 축하하려고 합니다. 전원에 초콜릿 무스와 커피 및 차를 추가할 수 있나요? [194] 그리고, 제가 직원들에게 상을 나눠 주려고 합니다. 마이크로 충분하니 프로젝터 같은 건 필요하지 않습니다. [195]

도와주셔서 감사합니다.

Rosa Logan
마케팅 책임자
Bubulina

---

191 웹 페이지에서 Marot 식당에 관해 언급하는 것은?
(A) 채식 메뉴를 제공한다.
(B) 개조되었다.
(C) 경영진이 새로 바뀌었다.
(D) 지역에 새로 생겼다.

192 첫 번째 이메일의 목적은 무엇인가?
(A) 다가올 행사의 세부 정보를 확인하기 위해
(B) 새로운 메뉴 구성을 변경하기 위해
(C) 서비스에 대한 사전 결제를 요청하기 위해
(D) 경영진과의 약속 일정을 잡기 위해

193 Bubulina 행사에 관하여 암시되는 것은 무엇인가?
(A) 예정보다 참석자가 더 많아질 수 있다.
(B) 매년 같은 식당에서 열린다.
(C) 위층 구역에서 열릴 것이다.
(D) Mr. Murphy가 연설을 할 것이다.

194 시상식 만찬에서 어떤 식사 메뉴가 제공되겠는가?
(A) 패키지 A
(B) 패키지 B
(C) 패키지 C
(D) 패키지 D

195 Ms. Logan은 어떤 장비를 요청하는가?
(A) 특수 조명
(B) 프로젝터
(C) 마이크
(D) 노트북

196-200번은 다음 온라인 포럼 게시물들과 이메일에 관한 문제입니다.

http://www.picturefresh.net

제목: 사이트 조언
날짜: 3월 21일
작성: hiljacobs

안녕하세요!

제가 제 사진을 광고 및 판매할 플랫폼을 찾는 중인데, 어느 사이트가 저에게 가장 좋을지 잘 모르겠습니다. **제 사진 대부분은 제가 업무상 참석하는 패션쇼 사진입니다.** [197] 저는 계속 일을 할 예정이라, 이것은 제 정규 수입에 보너스 정도 될 것입니다. 그래서, 저는 부업으로 제 사진을 최대한 쉽게 판매할 수 있는 사이트를 찾고 있습니다. [196] 추천해 주실 분 계신가요?

감사합니다!

Hillary Jacobs
hjacobsconcepts.com

http://www.picturefresh.net

제목: 사이트 조언
날짜: 3월 22일
작성: timfrank

안녕하세요, Ms. Jacobs.

반갑습니다! 제가 당신의 웹사이트를 빠르게 훑어봤는데, 우리가 같은 행사에 참석했던 것 같아요. 우리가 전에 만나봤을지도 모르겠네요! 우리 둘 다 같은 분야에서 활동하는 사진작가인 것 같아요. (197) 당신의 질문에 답변을 드리자면, 찾고 계신 것을 제공해 줄 주요 사이트가 3군데 있어요.

Desiree — 무료지만, 거래당 1달러 사이트 수수료 있음. 한 번에 사진 최대 30장 가능.

Temerit — 매년 50달러에 사진 최대 30장. 30장 초과 시, 100장 제한으로 늘리려면 비용이 50달러입니다.

Moiyam Lite — 매달 12달러, 무제한 용량, 모든 수익은 당신이 가져갑니다.

Moiyam Pro — 매달 20달러에, (199) 무제한 용량, 모든 수익은 당신이 가져가고, 전문 편집 도구 및 홈페이지 광고 포함됩니다.

그런데, 사진 서비스만 선택하면 수익이 많이 나지 않을 거예요. 사람들이 당신을 알아야 높은 매출을 올릴 수 있어요. **따라서, 제 추천은 소셜 미디어 플랫폼에 작품 샘플을 올려서 팬을 만드는 거예요.** (198)

Tim Franklin

수신: hjacobs@hjacobsconcepts.com
발신: helpdesk@moiyam.com
날짜: 3월 25일
제목: 환영 인사

Ms. Jacobs께,

Moiyam Pro에 가입해 주셔서 감사합니다! (199) 귀하의 페이지가 생성되어, 이제 업로드를 시작하실 수 있습니다. URL은 www.moiyam.com/hillary_jacobs입니다. 사용자 이름은 'hillary_jacobs'이고, 비밀번호는 'pl2&f9Vm$a'입니다. 로그인하시면, 비밀번호를 변경하라는 안내를 받게 될 것입니다. 반드시 숫자, 문자, 기호를 조합하여 강력한 비밀번호를 사용해 주세요.

고객이 귀하의 페이지를 볼 수 있기 전에, 먼저 프로필을 설정해야 합니다. 이때 귀하의 사진을 업로드하고 간략한 개인 이력을 제공해 주셔야 합니다. (200) 프로필을 설정하려면, 귀하의 계정에 로그인하셔서 상단에 'Profile'이라고 적힌 링크를 클릭해 주세요. 사이트 이용이 어려우신 경우, 저희에게 알려 주시기 바랍니다.

Moiyam팀 드림

---

196 Ms. Jacobs는 첫 번째 포럼 게시물을 왜 작성했는가?
(A) 사진 편집 안내서를 찾고 있다.
(B) 사진 수업을 가르칠 계획이다.
(C) 자신의 업무상 인맥을 넓히고 싶어 한다.
(D) 수입을 늘리고 싶어 한다.

197 Mr. Franklin은 어떤 종류의 사진에 주력하는가?
(A) 패션
(B) 자연
(C) 건축
(D) 동물

198 Mr. Franklin은 Ms. Jacobs에게 무엇을 하라고 제안하는가?
(A) 광고비를 내라고
(B) 작품을 온라인에 공유하라고
(C) 대규모 행사에 참석하라고
(D) 지역 사업체와 제휴를 맺으라고

199 Ms. Jacobs는 연간 얼마를 지불할 것인가?
(A) 0달러
(B) 50달러
(C) 144달러
(D) 240달러

200 이메일에 따르면, Ms. Jacobs가 자신의 포트폴리오 페이지를 공개하려면 무엇을 해야 하는가?
(A) 비밀번호를 변경해야 한다
(B) 정보를 채워 넣어야 한다
(C) 자신의 계정을 인증해야 한다
(D) 고객 서비스 직원에게 말해야 한다

TEST 09

PART 5   P. 262

101 공항 셔틀버스는 승객을 호텔로 곧장 데려다 줄 것이다.

102 Duoyi의 가장 인기 있는 건강 추적기는 최신 GPS 시스템이 특징이다.

103 주택 보험에서 돈을 절약하는 방법에 대해 더 알아보시려면, 지금 전화 주세요.

104 Ms. Pangchom은 수요일에 출장에서 돌아와서 이메일에 답장할 것이다.

105 모든 고객에게 피드백 요청서를 발송했지만, 다수가 답변하기를 거부했다.

106 그래픽 디자이너는 광고 캠페인을 위해 회사 로고를 수정했다.

107 출판사에 최종본을 보내기 전에, 편집자들의 승인을 받았는지 확인하세요.

108 Ball 주방용품점은 지구 온난화에 주의를 끌려는 시도로 재활용 플라스틱과 유리의 용도를 변경하여 샹들리에로 만들었다.

109 이사회에서 후임자를 선택할 수 있을 때까지, Pete Watkins가 부회장 직무 대행 역할을 할 것이다.

110 Shamrock 마라톤은 이번 주 지나치게 높은 기온으로 인해 취소되었다.

111 Cornwall Barriers는 안전 점검을 받을 수 있도록 생산 시설의 일주일간 폐쇄를 시행할 것이다.

112 시간 부족으로 인해, 회사 프로그래머들이 최근에 모바일 애플리케이션을 업데이트하지 못했다.

113 계약서를 판매상에게 이메일로 보내기 전, 공급업자는 일부 최종 수정이 필요하다는 것을 알아챘다.

114 주인인 Mr. Walsh가 휴가를 떠나기에, 다음 주 월요일부터 커피숍은 임시로 문을 닫을 것이다.

115 인사과 면담을 통해 직원들 대부분이 경영진을 신뢰하고 있다고 드러났다.

116 마케팅 담당자 직책의 최종 후보자 5명은 선발되자마자 연락을 받을 것이다.

117 내부 문의는 운영 부서로 보내져야 한다.

118 상점에 판자를 대서 막는 일을 도와준 소수 인원을 제외하고 악천후로 인해 West Oak 가구점 직원 대부분은 일찍 퇴근했다.

119 Mr. Valdez는 새로운 레이저 절단기가 설치되면 작동법을 보여 줄 것이다.

120 프로젝트 책임자들은 모든 절차가 확실히 제대로 진행되도록 작업 흐름 내내 전 단계를 감독한다.

121 최근 고무업계의 불확실성에도 불구하고, 자동차 타이어에 대한 수요는 꽤 안정적으로 유지되어 오고 있다.

122 생일 케이크를 가지러 올 남자는 그의 것이 냉장고에 있다는 안내를 받을 것이다.

123 면접관들은 잠재 판매업체와 각각 만남의 시간을 가진 후, 자신들의 생각을 논의할 시간을 따로 마련해 두어야 한다.

124 Ms. Chu는 행정 직원들의 도움을 받아 새로운 문서 정리 시스템을 시행할 것이다.

125 엄격한 공부 일정이 최고이긴 하지만, Lahp의 개인 지도 서비스는 귀하에게 부족할 수 있는 지혜를 제공해 드립니다.

126 기말 과제의 잠정 마감일이 5월 첫째 주로 정해졌지만, 상급 학년 주간 일정에 따라 달라질 것이다.

127 재정적 지원으로 새로운 시립 공원 건립을 가능하게 했던 Hiroko Mifune이 준공식에서 연설을 할 것이다.

128 직원 상여금에 영향을 주는 예산 변경 안은 즉시 CEO에게 제출되어야 한다.

129 Monique's 하이패션의 의류는 때때로 제조사의 권장 소매 가격보다 훨씬 더 비쌀 때가 있다.

130 젊은 고객층에 도달하는 데 있어 보다 큰 주안점은 광범위한 시장 조사에서 기인한다.

PART 6   P. 265

131-134번은 다음 기사에 관한 문제입니다.

> **TRA 사, 신규 임원 임명**
>
> Tokyo (3월 10일) — 오늘 오전 기자 회견에서, TRA의 대변인은 Hiro Musashi가 고객 관리 이사직을 맡게 될 것이라고 발표했다. Mr. Musashi는 국내외 기업들과 사업 관계를 **131. 구축하는** 부서를 관리하게 될 것이다.
>
> TRA 회장 Aiko Ogawa는 "저희는 Mr. Musashi와 함께 일하게 되어 기대되며, 그는 저희가 다른 지역들에 진출하여 새로운 협력 관계를 구축 **132. 할 수 있게 할** 것이라 생각합니다."라고 말했다. **133.** Mr. Musashi

는 거의 20년의 업계 경력을 갖고 TRA에 합류하게 된다. 그는 Wango Solutions에서 기업 관계 책임자로 있을 때, 매년 연간 매출을 평균 5퍼센트씩 증가시키는 데 도움을 주었다.

TRA는 일본 전역의 주요 도시들에서 상업용 컴퓨터 네트워크에 대한 **134. 지원**을 제공한다. 아시아와 유럽의 다른 지역에도 서비스를 제공하고 있다.

133 (A) Mr. Musashi는 Tokyo에 있는 본사로 전근 갈 것이다.
(B) Mr. Musashi는 Wango Solutions의 전 회장이었다.
(C) Mr. Musashi를 환영하는 회사 파티가 있을 것이다.
(D) **Mr. Musashi는 거의 20년의 업계 경력을 갖고 TRA에 합류하게 된다.**

135-138번은 다음 회람에 관한 문제입니다.

수신: 전 직원
발신: 총무부
날짜: 4월 8일
제목: 새로운 분리수거함

올해에는 사무실 내 지속 가능성을 향해 보다 큰 도약을 할 것이라고 약속드린 바 있습니다. 사무실에 있는 여러 가지 색상의 쓰레기통을 **135. 보셨을지도 모릅니다.** 저희는 이 사무실에서 사용되는 모든 것을 재활용해서 처리 공장으로 보낼 것입니다. 파란 통은 유리, 노란 통은 캔, 빨간 통은 플라스틱용입니다. 각 색상에 관련된 **136. 종류**를 잊으신 경우, 통의 측면에 도움이 되는 기호가 있습니다. 모든 물품이 재활용될 수는 없다는 점을 유의해 주세요. **137. 여기에는 음식 잔여물이 아직 남아 있는 물품이 포함됩니다.** 확실하지 않을 때는, 쓰레기통에 넣는 것이 낫습니다. 저희의 친환경 행보에 도움이 되도록 **138. 동참**해 주심에 감사합니다.

137 (A) 추가 쓰레기통은 연말에 설치될 것입니다.
(B) 직원들은 하루 중 시간에 주의를 기울여야 합니다.
(C) 그 계획은 우리의 지속 가능성 점수를 올릴 것입니다.
(D) **여기에는 음식 잔여물이 아직 남아 있는 물품이 포함됩니다.**

139-142번은 다음 광고에 관한 문제입니다.

TBD 금융의 새로운 Endeavor 카드는 귀하가 자신에게 투자하는 것에 대한 보상을 제공합니다.

TBD 금융은 재고 주문에서 신규 사무용 가구 구입에 이르기까지 일일 사업 경비로 포인트를 적립할 수 있는 사업용 보상 신용카드를 제공해 드리게 되어 기쁩니다. 이제, 일하면서 다음 휴가를 위한 저축을 시작하실 수 있습니다. 왜 식당에서 식사를 하거나 영화를 보는 데만 보상을 주는 카드에 **139. 만족하시나요?** Endeavor 카드는 매 구매의 1.5%를 포인트로 전환해주 **140. 지만,** 사무용품, 가스, 모바일 서비스와 같은 주요 사업 경비에 대해서는 두 배로 제공해 드립니다. 이는 자신의 사업을 최우선 순위에 놓는 **141. 개인들**에게 최고의 선택입니다. 오늘 TBD 금융에 가입하시고 500달러의 특별 선지급 보너스 기회를 누리세요. **142. 이 굉장한 혜택은 3월 1일에 끝나니, 지체하지 마세요.**

142 (A) **이 굉장한 혜택은 3월 1일에 끝나니, 지체하지 마세요.**
(B) Endeavor 카드는 식당 사용액에 대해 보너스 포인트를 제공하지 않습니다.
(C) 교통 관련 비용에는 포인트가 발생하지 않습니다.
(D) 추천해 주시는 분들도 각각 가입 선물을 받게 됩니다.

143-146번은 다음 광고에 관한 문제입니다.

저희 ShapeShift 고급 매트리스에서 매일 밤 완벽한 휴식을 취하세요. 특허 받은 저희 메모리 폼은 최고의 편안함을 선사하기 위해 끊임없이 여러분의 자세에 맞춰질 것입니다. **143. 열**을 발산하는 기능이 있어 여러분을 확실하게 쾌적하고 편안하게 유지시켜 드립니다. 어떤 크기의 매트리스를 찾으시든, 여러분께 딱 맞는 사이즈를 구비하고 있습니다. **144. 맞춤 사이즈도 제공해 드립니다.** ShapeShift 고급 매트리스는 Pocopson에서 제조되며, 10년 품질 보증이 함께 제공됩니다. 눕는 순간 저희 매트리스를 **145. 아주 마음에 들어 하실** 거라 확신합니다. 이유 불문하고 30일 환불 보장을 제공할 정도로 매우 자신 있습니다. 구입하신 물건이 마음에 들지 않는다고 알려만 주시면, 매트리스를 수거할 **146. 사람**을 보내 드립니다.

144 (A) 배송료도 여러분이 계신 곳에 따라 다를 수 있습니다.
(B) 이 프로모션은 연말까지 계속됩니다.
(C) **맞춤 크기도 제공해 드립니다.**
(D) 당사 매트리스의 판매가 호조를 보였습니다.

PART 7
P. 269

147-148번은 다음 정보에 관한 문제입니다.

저희 점심 및 저녁 식사 선택의 전체 목록이 제공되었습니다. **객실에 제공된 양식을 이용하셔서 주문하려는 항목에 체크표를 해 주십시오.**[147] 마치시면, 문밖에 양식을 놓고 프런트에 알려 주시기만 하면 됩니다. 저희 서비스는 오전 7시에 시작해 오후 8시에 종료된다는 점을 주의해 주십시오.[148] 이 시간 이외에 행하신 주문서는 처리해 드릴 수 없습니다. 지불 금액은 숙박이 끝날 때 정산됩니다. 최종 청구서에는 숙박 기간 동안 주문하신 서비스의 항목별 목록을 포함해 드립니다.[147]

147 정보는 누구를 대상으로 하겠는가?
(A) 호텔 접수 직원
(B) 주방 직원
(C) 여행사 직원
(D) **호텔 손님**

148 서비스에 관하여 언급된 것은 무엇인가?
(A) 현금으로 지불해야 한다.
(B) **특정 시간에만 이용 가능하다.**
(C) 할인 금액에 이용할 수 있다.
(D) 배송에 대한 추가 요금을 포함한다.

149-150번은 다음 웹 페이지에 관한 문제입니다.

www.kilkennyperformingartscentre.ie

<Street Wildlife> 공개 오디션
Kilkenny 음악원

저희는 Saoirse Kilpatrick이 연출하는 **클래식 뮤지컬 <Street Wildlife>**[150] 작품의 코러스에서 노래할 재능 있는 지역 청년들(12세에서 16세 사이)을 찾고 있습니다.[149]

공연 일정:
Waterford의 Avalon 극장, 10월 12-18일[150]

예선:
3가지 선택지가 있습니다: 2월 25일, 26일, 그리고 28일 오후 4-6시, Church가 174번지 Kilkenny 음악원 스튜디오. 최고의 참가자들을 위한 재통보 오디션은 3월 2일 토요일에 있을 것입니다. 다과가 제공됩니다. "Streetlight People (반복 부분)"을 부를 준비를 해 주세요.

149 웹 페이지에 따르면, 누가 Ms. Murphy에게 연락해야 하는가?
(A) 가수
(B) 모델
(C) 감독
(D) 예술가

150 <Street Wildlife>에 관하여 암시된 것은 무엇인가?
(A) Ms. Kilpatrick이 썼다.
(B) 원래 Waterford에서 공연되었다.
(C) 10월에 공연될 것이다.
(D) 3회 공연될 것이다.

151-152번은 다음 이메일에 관한 문제입니다.

수신: ugrant@baltor.com
발신: jingram@hae.com
날짜: 9월 5일
제목: Milton 호텔 숙박 시설

무역 박람회 판매업체께,

무엇보다도 먼저, 저희 가전제품 박람회(HAE)팀(151)은 올해 귀하의 참가에 감사드리고 싶습니다. 저희는 인근 Milton 호텔과 협의하여 모든 판매업체에 숙박 요금 할인 혜택을 드리게 되었음을 알려드리게 되어 기쁩니다. 모든 HAE 판매업체는 Milton에서 투숙하시는 동안 20퍼센트 할인을 받게 됩니다. HAE 판매업체 공식 확인서에 귀사의 고유 식별 번호가 있습니다. 할인을 적용하시려면, 호텔 웹사이트로 객실을 예약하실 때 판촉 코드란에 이 번호를 입력하시면 됩니다.(152) 이 호텔은 만실이 될 것이 확실하므로 조속히 이 혜택을 이용하시길 권장드립니다.

Janette Ingram(151)

151 Janette Ingram은 누구겠는가?
(A) 호텔 지배인
(B) 여행사 직원
(C) 행사 진행자
(D) 사업주

152 식별 번호는 어떻게 사용될 수 있는가?
(A) 시설에 입장하기 위해
(B) 가격 할인을 받기 위해
(C) 기기를 구매하기 위해
(D) 회원 계정에 접속하기 위해

153-154번은 다음 문자메시지 대화문에 관한 문제입니다.

Michelle Ingles (오전 8시 05분)
안녕하세요, 저는 Ingles and Company의 Michelle입니다. 저희에게 오전 8시 Belmont와 1번가에 있는 귀하의 신규 점포에 싱크대 수리를 예약해 주셨는데요.(153) 저희에게 알려주신 사무실 번호로 전화 드리고 문을 두드렸는데, 아무런 대답이 없었습니다.(154)

Monte Derwin (오전 8시 07분)
죄송해요!(154) 제가 방금 도착한 재고를 확인하느라 창고에 있어서요. 그리고 내일은 지나야 초인종이 설치될 거에요. 제가 가려면 10분 정도 더 걸리겠지만, 저희 직원에게 문을 열어드리라고 할게요.

Michelle Ingles (오전 8시 08분)
알겠습니다.

Monte Derwin (오전 8시 10분)
기다리시게 해서 정말 죄송합니다. 다음번에는 비밀번호 '56813'을 이용하셔서, 필요하실 때 출입하세요.

153 오전 8시에 무엇이 예정되어 있었는가?
(A) 재고 회의
(B) 초인종 설치
(C) 배관 수리
(D) 상품 배달

154 오전 8시 07분에, Mr. Derwin은 왜 "죄송해요!"라고 썼겠는가?
(A) 그는 점포에 들어갈 수 없다는 것을 깜박했다.
(B) 그는 Ms. Ingles를 언제 도울 수 있는지 확신하지 못한다.
(C) 그는 Ms. Ingles가 다음 날 올 거라고 생각했다.
(D) 그는 직원이 비밀번호를 공유할 거라고 예상했다.

155-157번은 다음 이메일에 관한 문제입니다.

수신: Jane Shepheard <jshepheard@bibbomail.com>
발신: Tad Maynor <tad83@destinationstore.com>
제목: 인사
날짜: 1월 2일
첨부문서: j_shepheard

Ms. Shepheard께,

같은 팀에서 일하게 되어 반갑습니다. 만나서 이야기 나눈 것처럼, 귀하는 Barksdale Road 1774번지에 있는 Oaklands 공원 지점에서 부점장직을 맡게 됩니다. 교육은 1월 22일에 시작할 예정입니다. 그날 오전 8시에 본사 21층으로 가시기 바랍니다.(155) 그곳에서 일주일간 새로운 동료 몇 명과 함께 Destination 매장 필수 교육을 받게 됩니다. 이 수업으로 회사 제품군 및 핵심 철학을 익히게 됩니다. 이 기간 동안, 귀하의 근무 시간은 오전 9시부터 오후 6시까지입니다. 오리엔테이션이 끝난 후에는 매장 정규 교대 근무조로 배정되고, 퇴직 연금을 비롯한 회사 복리 후생을 신청할 수 있습니다.(156)

우선, 첨부해 드린 서류를 작성해 주세요. 거기에 작성 및 서명하시면, 새로운 직위 및 업무를 이해하고 수락함을 인정하게 됩니다.(157) 문의 사항이 있으시면, 저에게 바로 이메일을 보내 주세요.

행운을 빕니다.

Tad Maynor
인사부장

155 Mr. Maynor는 왜 이메일을 썼는가?
(A) 매장 홍보 계획을 의논하려고
(B) 퇴직 정책을 설명하려고
(C) 직책에 대한 세부 사항을 알려주려고
(D) 회의 일정을 다시 잡으려고

156 Mr. Maynor에 따르면, 일주일 후에 무슨 일이 있겠는가?
(A) Ms. Shepheard가 기념 행사에 참석할 것이다.
(B) Ms. Shepheard의 임금이 인상될 것이다.
(C) Ms. Shepheard가 다른 도시로 이주할 것이다.
(D) Ms. Shepheard의 근무 시간이 조정될 것이다.

157 Mr. Maynor는 이메일에 무엇을 포함했는가?
(A) 동의서
(B) 보험 안내서
(C) 오리엔테이션 일정표
(D) 제품 목록

158-160번은 다음 이메일에 관한 문제입니다.

수신: emacpherson@naismith.org
발신: Carl@customizedcookwarehouse.com
제목: 주문 번호 234-19887
날짜: 4월 2일

Mr. Macpherson께,

이 이메일은 귀하의 최근 주문에 관한 것입니다. —[1]—. **안타깝게도, 아래 나열된 상품이 이미 품절되었습니다:**(158)

"맞춤형 주방" 전문가용 세라믹 들러붙지 않는 프라이팬 세트, 150달러

이로 인해 발생할 수 있는 혼란에 사과드립니다. —[2]—. **저희는 완벽한 사용자 경험을 제공해 드리기 위해 노력하지만, 가끔 문제가 발생합니다.**(160) —[3]—. 마지막 남은 세트를 몇 시간 전 다른 고객이 구매했습니다. 결제 처리가 지연되어, 저희 재고 시스템에 해당 상품이 품절임을 반영하는 업데이트가 제대로 이루어지지 않았습니다. 이는 드물지만 당혹스러운 오류로, 저희는 이를 해결하기 위해 노력하고 있습니다.

저희는 귀하의 Cookwarehouse.com 계정으로 구매에 사용하신 포인트를 환불해 드렸습니다. 저희 웹사이트에서 포인트가 보이는지 확인해 주시되,(159) 환불이 처리되는 데 2시간에서 6시간 정도 걸린다는 것을 감안해 주시기 바랍니다. —[4]—.

Carl Weizen 드림
Customized Cookwarehouse 고객 관리부

158 이 이메일의 주요 목적은 무엇인가?
(A) 상품을 구매할 수 없다는 것을 말하기 위해
(B) 주문이 지연될 것임을 알리기 위해
(C) 특정 상품에 대한 판매를 촉진하기 위해
(D) 물품이 배송되었는지 확인하기 위해

159 Mr. Macpherson은 무엇을 하라고 요청받는가?
(A) 새로운 결제 방식을 제공하라고
(B) 온라인 계정을 확인하라고
(C) 고객 관리팀에 이메일을 보내라고
(D) 특별 할인 쿠폰을 사용하라고

160 [1], [2], [3], [4]로 표시된 곳 중 다음 문장이 들어가기에 가장 적절한 곳은 어디인가?

"이것이 귀하의 사례에서 발생했습니다."

(A) [1]
(B) [2]
(C) [3]
(D) [4]

161-163번은 다음 회람에 관한 문제입니다.

회람

수신: BrightSide 마케팅팀 전 직원
발신: Candice Harris, 총 관리자
날짜: 8월 19일
제목: 회신: 후원

올해 BrightSide 마케팅은 Severn 시에 엄청난 자선 공헌을 하고 있습니다. Woodlawn 고등학교와의 제휴를 통해, 저희 직원들은 일부 학생의 멘토 역할을 할 기회를 얻게 됩니다.(161)

이 프로그램의 요지는 학생들이 저희 직원과 한 명씩 연결을 맺어, 직장에서의 하루를 함께 보내게 됩니다. 학생들에게 사무실에서 일하는 것이 어떤 것인지 볼 기회가 되면서, 동시에 소중한 직장 체험을 얻을 수 있는 기회가 될 것입니다. 나중에는, 여러분의 멘티와 연락하고 지내며 지원을 해 줄 수 있습니다. 행사는 9월 내내 진행되니, 그때 너무 바쁘시다면, Ms. Henry에게 이메일을 보내 주세요. 그렇게 하면, 그분이 귀하를 부적격자로 표기해 드릴 수 있습니다.(162) 이 프로그램은 조만간 Woodlawn 고등학교에서 발표될 예정이며, 제가 향후 이메일로 관련 신문 기사를 전달해 드리도록 하겠습니다.(163)

161 회람의 목적은 무엇인가?
(A) 직원들에게 자선 프로그램에 대해 알려 주기 위해
(B) 경쟁사와의 합병 가능성을 알려 주기 위해
(C) 보다 생산적인 업무 회의를 장려하기 위해
(D) 직원들에게 정기적으로 휴식을 취하라고 권고하기 위해

162 어떤 집단의 직원들이 Ms. Henry에게 연락해야 하는가?
(A) 부서 변경을 원하는 사람들
(B) 회사 신입 사원들
(C) Woodlawn 고등학교를 나온 사람들
(D) 참여할 수 없는 사람들

163 회람에 따르면, 어떤 후속 정보가 발송될 것인가?
(A) 세부 일정
(B) 참가 신청서
(C) 공식 발표
(D) 학생 명단

164-167번은 다음 온라인 채팅 대화문에 관한 문제입니다.

Edith Crawley [오후 12시 38분]
안녕하세요, Joan, Dave. 여러분 중에 저희가 곧 출시할 FPX-2220 에어컨에 대한 최신 자료를 보신 분 있나요?

Joan Mitchell [오후 12시 39분]
방금 전에 봤어요. 저는 그게 에너지 효율이 더 좋으면서도, 더 빠르게 냉각될 수 있다는 점에 놀랐어요.

Dave Edison [오후 12시 40분]
맞아요! 제가 Baez Systems와 회의할 때 그 점을 보여줄 수 없다는 게 아쉬워요.(165)

Joan Mitchell [오후 12시 40분]
제가 사본을 부서 전원에게 이메일로 보냈어요.

Edith Crawley [오후 12시 42분]
그런데 그건 3시 30분으로 예정되어 있잖아요.(165) 가장 적당한 그래프를 골라서 슬라이드쇼에 넣을 시간이 충분할 거예요.

Dave Edison [오후 12시 44분]
문제는 제가 1시에 교육 세미나를 하고, 끝나면 바로 Baez 새 본사로 운전해서 가야 하거든요. 그곳이 이제 거의 30마일 떨어진 거리에 있어요.(166)

Edith Crawley [오후 12시 45분]
제가 대신 처리해 드릴 텐데, 전 이미 공항으로 가는 길이에요.

Joan Mitchell [오후 12시 46분]
제가 할게요. 제가 제일 좋은 표로 파일을 만들어서 플래시 드라이브에 넣어 놓을게요.(167) 가시기 전에 제 자리에 꼭 챙겨 가세요.

Edith Crawley [오후 12시 48분]
회의가 성공하길 바래요. Baez가 주요 구매에 협의하면, 분명 축하할 일이 될 거예요.(164)

Dave Edison [오후 12시 51분]
응원 감사해요!

164 Mr. Edison의 직업은 무엇이겠는가?
(A) 컴퓨터 프로그래머
(B) 프로젝트 책임자
(C) 판매 대리인
(D) 수리공

165 오후 3시 30분에 무슨 일이 일어날 것인가?
(A) 비행기가 이륙할 것이다.
(B) 지원서가 제출될 것이다.
(C) 회의가 열릴 것이다.
(D) 상이 수여될 것이다.

166 Baez Systems에 관하여 암시되는 것은 무엇인가?
(A) 곧 신상품을 출시할 것이다.
(B) Ms. Crawley는 그곳에 고객이 많다.
(C) Mr. Edison은 한 때 거기서 근무했었다.
(D) 본사가 최근 이전했다.

167 오후 12시 46분에, Ms. Mitchell이 "제가 할게요"라고 쓸 때 무엇을 의미하겠는가?
(A) 그녀가 교육을 실시할 것이다.
(B) 그녀가 이메일을 보낼 것이다.
(C) 그녀가 자료를 모을 것이다.
(D) 그녀가 시각 자료를 만들 것이다.

168-171번은 다음 기사에 관한 문제입니다.

Suzanne Shore의 부상

5년 전, Suzanne Shore는 소규모 회사의 안내원이었다. 현재 **Ms. Shore는 New York에 본사를 둔 사업체인 Shore's Delights의 창립자이자 소유주이다.**[171] — [1] —. 회사는 작년에만 밀키트 5백만 개를 판매했고, 올해에는 훨씬 더 많이 판매할 예정이다.

— [2] —. 회사에서 그녀를 내보내야 했을 때, Ms. Shore는 Steuben에 작은 아파트를 임대했다. **요리에 대한 열정으로, 그녀는 식사를 준비할 시간이 없는 자신의 바쁜 친구들을 위해 밀키트를 준비해 주기 시작했다.**[168]/[169C] — [3] —.

우연히도, 그녀의 옆집에 새로운 이웃이 이사 왔다. 알고 보니 이웃은 Wharton 금융의 상무이사인 Justin Rice였다.[169B] "제가 만들어 온 밀키트에 대해 그에게 말해 주자, 그의 눈에서 정말 빛이 났어요."라고 Ms. Shore가 말했다. — [4] —. 그만의 사업이 정세로 유명한 Mr. Rice는 Ms. Shore에게서 엄청난 기회를 보았다.[170] 업무용 주방을 임대하고, 직원을 고용하며, 웹사이트를 마련하자, 주문이 물밀듯 쏟아졌다.[169D]

"이제 시작입니다. 미국 전역에 저희 제품을 유통할 계획을 마련하고 있어요."라고 Ms. Shore가 말했다.

---

168 Ms. Shore에 관하여 암시되는 것은 무엇인가?
(A) 가족과 함께 산다.
(B) 사업을 시작할 의도가 없었다.
(C) New York으로 최근 이사했다.
(D) 과거 서비스 산업에 종사한 적이 있다.

169 Ms. Shore의 성공 이유로 언급되지 않은 것은 무엇인가?
(A) 대학 학위
(B) 운 좋은 만남
(C) 취미
(D) 인터넷

170 Mr. Rice에 관하여 암시되는 것은 무엇인가?
(A) 집에서 요리하지 않는다.
(B) 과거에 부동산 분야에 종사했다.
(C) 타 주로 출장을 자주 간다.
(D) Ms. Shore의 사업체 출시를 도왔다.

171 [1], [2], [3], [4]로 표시된 곳 중 다음 문장이 들어가기에 가장 적절한 곳은 어디인가?

"소액의 월 비용을 내면, 회사는 New York 전역으로 밀키트를 보내준다."

(A) [1]
(B) [2]
(C) [3]
(D) [4]

172-175번은 다음 기사에 관한 문제입니다.

전 세계 음식
Jack Bowman 작성

SYDNEY (3월 30일) — 지난달에, Sydney 버킷 리스트, 즉 식사하기 가장 좋은 곳의 명단을 만들기 위해, 시내에서 식사하는 장소에 대한 의견을 내 달라고 구독자에게 요청했다.[172] 결과가 들어오자, 한 가지는 명백히 드러났다: Sydney 시민들이 지역을 지탱해 온 다양한 전 세계 요리를 받아들이고 있다는 것이다. **가장 인기 있으면서 흥미로운 식당을 종합해, 도시의 최고 식당들에 상이 수여되었다.**[172]

최고 인기 식당 대상의 영예는 Chada Thai에게 돌아갔는데, 1위 표를 가장 많이 받았다. **외식업에 새로 합류한 Chada Thai는 주인인 Mr. Sukkasem의 정통 조리법으로 유명해졌다.**[173] "제 부모님이 태국에서 식당을 운영하셨죠. 제가 Sydney에 정통 요리를 소개할 수 있도록 제가 알고 있는 모든 것을 가르쳐 주셨어요."라고 Mr. Sukkasem은 인터뷰에서 말했다.

Min-Hee Lee는 자신의 식당 Nolbune으로 특별상을 받았다. **대한민국에서 태어난 Ms. Lee는 신문에 언급된다는 것만으로도 엄청난 성취를 이룬 것 같다고 말했다.**[174] Ms. Lee는 20살 때 호주로 이주했고, 그녀의 식당은 15년 넘게 Sydney의 외식업계에서 주요한 역할을 해 왔다. Nolbune은 닭튀김에서 각종 국에 이르기까지 정통 한국 음식을 제공한다.

명단에 이름을 올린 특이한 한 곳은 The Melting Pot인데, 독특한 컨셉 덕분에 표를 받았다. 고정 메뉴 대신, **식당 주인인 Oliver Carroll**[174]이 매달 Sydney 전역에서 초빙한 게스트 요리사를 교체해 가며 활용한다. **"호주 시민권을 받기 전에는, 이민자 사회에서 시간을 많이 보냈어요.**[174] 덕분에 세계 전역의 요리와 인연을 맺게 됐죠." Mr. Carroll은 Melbourne에 2호점을 개장할 계획인데, 8월에 문을 열 예정이다.

수상자 전원의 인터뷰를 포함해 전체 명단은 <The Sydney Times> 웹사이트 www.sydneytimes.com.au에서 확인할 수 있다.[175]

---

172 기사의 목적은 무엇인가?
(A) 식당에서 외식하는 비용을 조사하기 위해
(B) Sydney 내 유명 식당을 비교하기 위해
(C) 좋은 영양의 가치를 주제로 요리사를 인터뷰하기 위해
(D) 지역 사회 식당 투표의 우승자에 주목하기 위해

173 Chada Thai에 관하여 알 수 있는 것은 무엇인가?
(A) 출장 요리 서비스로 유명하다.
(B) 비교적 새로 생긴 식당이다.
(C) 고객은 미리 예약해야 한다.
(D) 어린이에게 할인을 제공한다.

174 Ms. Lee와 Mr. Carroll은 어떤 공통점을 가지고 있는가?
(A) 전문 요리사 교육을 받았다.
(B) 둘 다 해외 출신이다.
(C) 도시에 사업체를 여러 개 소유하고 있다.
(D) 같은 지역에 식당을 열었다.

175 <The Sydney Times>에 관하여 암시되는 것은 무엇인가?

(A) 온라인에 수상자 명단을 게재한다.
(B) 매달 지역 사회 투표를 연다.
(C) Sydney에서 가장 오래된 신문사다.
(D) 구독자가 감소했다.

176-180번은 다음 웹 페이지와 후기에 관한 문제입니다.

http://www.starshotcameras.com/products

사진이 취미든, 열정이든, 직업이든, Starshot 카메라에는 귀하가 필요로 하는 것이 있습니다. 저희는 아주 다양한 종류의 카메라를 제공합니다. 하지만 저희 카메라는 모두 귀하의 정확한 필요 사항에 맞춰 주문 제작 가능합니다.(176)

H2C—기본 카메라로, 사진을 처음 시작한 사람들에게 특히 적합합니다. 사용하기에 매우 직관적이고, 많은 기기와 호환됩니다. 1600만 화소 카메라로 무장하면, 아름답게 나오는 사진을 촬영하실 수 있을 겁니다.(178) H2C는 사진 세계로 입문하는 완벽한 디딤돌이 됩니다.

42C—H2C보다 한 단계 높은 42C에는 H2C의 전 기능에 더해, 수동으로 카메라의 초점을 맞추는 기능뿐만 아니라 더 많은 저장 공간을 제공합니다.(177)/(179) 이러한 작은 세부 사항 덕분에 카메라의 자동 초점 기능에 의존하기보다는 귀하가 원하는 정확한 장면을 포착하실 수 있게 됩니다.

K2P— K2P는 상업용 카메라 중 첫 단계에 해당합니다. 3000만 화소 카메라에, 서로 다른 줌 설정을 위한 호환 가능한 렌즈 3개, 긴 배터리 수명을 특징으로 합니다. K2P는 자신의 사진을 한 단계 끌어올리려는 신예 사진작가에게 안성맞춤입니다. 하드웨어 및 소프트웨어 설치가 필요합니다.

P4X—P4X는 상업용 고급 카메라입니다. 4500만이라는 최고 화소 카메라를 특징으로 하며, 이 카메라는 견고하게 제작되었습니다. 방수 기능이 들어 있으며, 일상생활 마모에 내구성이 강합니다. 휴대가 편리한 주머니에 모두 포장된 렌즈 및 케이스 다수도 포함됩니다.

가까운 Starshot 카메라 매장에 오늘 방문해 보세요. 귀하에게 완벽한 카메라를 구입하실 수 있도록 저희 영업 사원이 기쁜 마음으로 도와 드리겠습니다.(180)

저는 최근에서야 진지하게 사진을 찍기 시작해서, 값비싼 장비를 구입해야 한다는 게 신경이 쓰였어요. 전문 사진작가인 이웃의 추천을 받았습니다. Starshot의 기본 카메라가 출발점으로는 훌륭할 거라고 알려 줬어요. Velma Potter의 도움 덕분에, 매장 내 경험은 아주 수월했습니다.(180) 저는 오토 줌 기능에 답답할 때가 종종 있어서 결국은 제가 사진에 통제권을 조금 더 가질 수 있는 카메라로 선택했습니다.(179) 게다가, 기본 카메라와의 가격 차이가 제 생각보다 크지 않았어요. 제가 구입한 것에 아주 만족해요!

—Jim Frank

176 웹 페이지에서는 Starshot 카메라에 관해 무엇을 언급하는가?

(A) 상업용으로 설계된 카메라만 판매한다.
(B) 정확한 사양에 맞출 수 있다.
(C) Starshot 카메라 매장에서만 구입할 수 있다.
(D) 품질로 유명하다.

177 H2C에는 없는 42C의 기능은 무엇인가?

(A) 조절식 렌즈
(B) 수동 초점
(C) 탈착식 배터리
(D) 방수

178 웹 페이지에서 두 번째 단락, 두 번째 줄의 단어, "Armed"와 의미상 가장 가까운 것은

(A) 운반된
(B) 전문화된
(C) 갖춘
(D) 디자인된

179 Mr. Frank는 어떤 제품을 구입했겠는가?

(A) H2C
(B) 42C
(C) K2P
(D) P4X

180 Ms. Potter는 누구겠는가?

(A) Starshot 카메라 영업 사원
(B) Starshot 카메라 주인
(C) Mr. Frank의 이웃
(D) 야생 동물 사진작가

181-185번은 다음 이메일과 전단에 관한 문제입니다.

수신: 품질 보증 팀 <qc@techquest.com>
발신: Barry Walker <b.walker@techquest.com>
날짜: 11월 2일 화요일
제목: 곧 있을 워크숍
첨부: 전단

팀원 여러분께,

다음 주에 열리는 일일 워크숍에 대해 설명하는 전단을 보내드립니다.(181) 이번 일일 워크숍은 CEO의 신규 계획의 일환으로 진행하는 행사가 될 겁니다. 아쉽게도, 두 번째 세션은 우리 팀 주간 회의와 일정이 겹칩니다.(182) 하지만, 여전히 다른 시간대 중 하나에 참석하실 수 있을 겁니다. 워크숍을 진행하는 분은 해당 주제에 대해 저서를 여러 권 집필했고, 그 분야에서 가장 존경 받는 인물 중 한 분입니다.(183) 워크숍이 필수는 아니지만, 참석하면 모든 분에게 크게 도움이 될 것 같습니다.(181)

감사합니다.

Barry Walker
품질 보증 팀장

11월 전문성 개발 워크숍

이번 달 워크숍에서는 직원들이 예측의 개념 및 과거의 매출 자료를 이용해 직접 예측하는 법에 대한 이해를 높여줍니다. 진행자는 워크숍에서 스프레드시트 소프트웨어를 이용해 이러한 자료를 준비하는 법을 살펴봅니다.(184)

진행자: Emma Drake는 ITO 기업 소속 데이터 과학자입니다.(183) 국제 콘퍼런스에서 정기적으로 강연하며, 다수의 대기업에서 컨설턴트로 활동하고 있습니다.

곧 있을 세션 (오전 10시 30분부터 오후 3시 30분까지):(185)
11월 8일 월요일
11월 10일 수요일(182)
11월 11일 목요일

세션별 등록자 수에 제한이 있습니다. 등록하시려면, 인사부 Alfred Ballard(내선 번호 792)에게 연락해 주세요. 등록되면, 시작 시간 한 시간 전에 업무 수신함으로 워크숍 자료가 발송될 것입니다.(185)

181 이메일의 목적은 무엇인가?
(A) 워크숍 참석을 독려하기 위해
(B) 회의에 관한 세부 정보를 요청하기 위해
(C) 최근의 결정을 다루기 위해
(D) 팀원들에게 변경 사항을 알리기 위해

182 Mr. Walker의 팀은 언제 다음번 팀 회의를 할 것인가?
(A) 11월 2일에
(B) 11월 8일에
(C) 11월 10일에
(D) 11월 11일에

183 Mr. Walker는 Ms. Drake에 관하여 무엇을 언급하는가?
(A) 자신의 분야에 대해 아주 박식하다.
(B) 같은 대학교를 다녔다.
(C) 품질 보증팀에 자문을 했다.
(D) 최근에 새로운 역할을 시작했다.

184 11월 워크숍의 목적은 무엇인가?
(A) 직원들에게 새로운 기술을 가르치기 위해
(B) 업무 안전 보건 기준을 개정하기 위해
(C) 직원 간 소통을 향상시키기 위해
(D) 직원들에게 중요한 트렌드에 대해 알려 주기 위해

185 워크숍 참가자들은 언제 자신의 자료를 받는가?
(A) 오전 9시 30분에
(B) 오전 10시 30분에
(C) 오후 2시 30분에
(D) 오후 3시 30분에

186-190번은 다음 이메일, 명함, 온라인 후기에 관한 문제입니다.

수신: Ruth Bryant <rbryant@palumork.com>
발신: Webb Physiotherapy <help@webbphys.com>
날짜: 2월 12일
제목: 예약

Ms. Bryant께,

귀하의 보증금을 저희가 수령했다는 것을 확인해 드리기 위해 이 메시지를 드립니다. 현재 귀하의 Webb 물리 치료실 예약이 2월 15일 오전 10시로 확정되었습니다. [187]

병원에서 의뢰를 받으셨기에, 병원 의뢰서와 정밀 검사 자료를 가져오시기 바랍니다. 이는 귀하의 다친 발목을 진단하는 데 도움이 됩니다. 제대로 된 진단을 받을 때까지, 치료실을 오갈 때 도와줄 사람과 함께 오시길 권해 드립니다. [186] Dr. Erica Moore께서 부상 정도를 진찰하기 위해 몇 가지 검사를 할 예정입니다. [189]

곧 뵙게 되길 바랍니다.

Melinda Russell 드림
접수 담당자, Webb 물리 치료실

Webb 물리 치료실

12 Eider Drive, Lost River
Custer, Idaho, 83255
info@webbphys.com

운영 시간:
월 ~ 금요일, 오전 11시 ~ 오후 6시
토요일, 오후 12시 ~ 3시
일요일, 오전 9시 ~ 오후 1시 [187]

저희 물리 치료실에 대해 궁금하시면, www.webbphys.com에서 연혁을 읽어 보세요.

치료나 진료를 예약하려면, www.webbphys.com/form에서 온라인 양식을 작성해 주세요. [188]

저희는 주요 신용카드를 받으며, 할부 결제 방식도 제공합니다.

---

www.webbphys.com/testimonials

제가 다른 물리 치료사 두 명을 찾아가 봤는데, 둘 다 제 발목이 괜찮다고 했어요. 저는 Webb 물리 치료실을 가 보기로 했고, Dr. Henry Wallace께서 드디어 제 문제를 진단해 주실 수 있었죠. [189] 저는 Montana로 간 수학여행에서 발목을 다친 후 학교를 쉬고 있습니다. [190] 우연히도, Dr. Wallace께서 저와 같은 Montana 출신인데다, 실제로 저랑 같은 동네에서 자라셨더라고요! 하지만 그분은 물리 치료를 공부하러 해외로 갔고 스페인에서 실무 경험을 많이 쌓으셨습니다. 작년에야 돌아와 Webb 물리 치료실에 새로운 진단과 방법을 많이 도입하셨습니다. 그분께서 제가 발목에 느끼는 통증을 일부 가라앉혀 주셨습니다. 저는 이제야 다시 제 직장인 학교로 돌아갈 준비가 되었습니다. [190]

제가 Webb 물리 치료실에서 겪은 경험은 훌륭했고, 모두에게 전적으로 추천하고 싶습니다.

—Ruth Bryant, 2월 18일

---

186 이메일에서 Ms. Bryant는 무엇을 하라고 당부받는가?
(A) 문서에 서명해 달라고
(B) 도와줄 사람을 데려오라고
(C) 결제를 해달라고
(D) 친구를 소개해 달라고

187 Ms. Bryant의 예약은 언제인가?
(A) 월요일에
(B) 수요일에
(C) 토요일에
(D) 일요일에

188 명함에 따르면, 환자들은 Webb 물리 치료실에 어떻게 예약해야 하는가?
(A) 이메일을 작성해서
(B) 사무실에 전화해서
(C) 앱을 다운로드받아서
(D) 양식을 작성해서

189 Dr. Wallace에 관하여 암시되는 것은 무엇인가?
(A) 원래 Ms. Bryant의 진료를 볼 예정이 아니었다.
(B) 일하면서 대학교도 다니고 있다.
(C) Montana 지역 출신이 아니다.
(D) 2년 넘게 Webb 물리 치료실에서 근무했다.

190 온라인 후기에서는 Ms. Bryant에 관하여 무엇을 언급하는가?
(A) Dr. Wallace의 유년 시절을 알고 있었다.
(B) 학교에서 일한다.
(C) 운동을 하다가 부상당했다.
(D) 최근 해외에서 돌아왔다.

191-195번은 다음 기사, 웹 페이지, 온라인 주문서에 관한 문제입니다.

BROOKLYN (9월 25일) — 최근 출시된 앱이 Williamsburg 지역에서 사람들의 식습관을 변화시키고 있다. Thrive Fresh는 현지인 Jason Vernon이 시작한 음식 배달 앱이다. 앱은 사용자에게 다양한 현지 식당의 수백 가지 메뉴에 대한 상세한 영양 및 원산지 정보를 이용할 수 있게 한다. 월 요금으로, 사용자의 주문 내역을 추적할 수도 있고 필요 및 선호 사항을 기반으로 식단 추천 또한 해 준다.

Mr. Vernon은 전통적인 배달 서비스 음식이 기름진 경향이 있음을 알아차렸을 때 이런 생각을 하게 되었다. (191) "제가 예전 직장 동료들과 꽤 자주 야근을 하여, 그때마다 음식을 주문하곤 했는데, 신선한 재료는 거의 없었어요. 저희 대부분은 먹는 것에 신경쓰려고 노력했지만, 배달 음식에 관해서라면 저희는 아무것도 몰랐죠."

이에 대응하여, Mr. Vernon은 투명성과 건강을 촉진하는 시스템을 개발했다. Thrive Fresh는 유기농 음식만을 판매하는 현지 식품 제공업체들과 협력한다. (194) 매우 다양한 건강에 좋은 선택 사항들과 저렴한 가격 덕분에 이 서비스는 거대한 단골 고객층을 구축할 수 있었다. (192) 앱은 아직 Williamsburg 지역 내 이용자들에게만 배달해 주지만 12월에는 New York 시의 나머지 지역으로 확대될 것이다. (195)

---

http://www.squawk.com/chakra

소개	후기	연락	예약

Chakra Indian Cuisine이 Thrive Fresh와 제휴한 새로운 서비스를 자랑스럽게 알려드립니다. (193)/(194) 거의 20년 간, 최첨단과 전통 조리법 모두를 활용한 고급 요리를 제공해 드리는 것이 저희의 사명이었습니다. 저희는 Thrive Fresh를 통해 더 많은 사람들에게 저희의 요리를 제공해 드리게 되어 기쁩니다.

물론, Broadway와 Leonard 근처에 위치한 Chakra Indian Cuisine의 새로 개조된 공간은 변함없이 매일 오전 11시부터 오후 9시까지 영업합니다. 그리고 언제나처럼, 저희의 대표적인 맛을 내주는 허브와 향신료를 판매하는 Chakra 수입품 시장은 화요일부터 토요일까지 옆 건물에서 영업할 것입니다.

Thrive Fresh 주문 확인서

주문:

Manpasand 퀴노아 샐러드 7.00달러
시금치 코프타 카레 12.00달러
달 마카니 13.00달러

음식 32.00달러
회원 할인 -3.20달러
세금 1.06달러
총액 29.86달러
(신용카드로 문 앞 결제)

이름: Jill Klein (195)
주소: 169 Lynch St., Apartment 3B
전화번호: 718-555-9922
배달 시간: 9월 29일, 14:35-14:50 사이 (195)

---

191 기사는 주로 무엇에 관한 것인가?
(A) 독자들을 건강한 생활 방식으로 이끌 식단 종류
(B) 저렴한 가격대의 식료품을 살 수 있는 장소
(C) 음식 서비스 앱이 생겨난 배경
(D) 식당이 성공한 이유

192 기사에 따르면, Thrive Fresh가 인기 있는 이유는 무엇인가?
(A) 빠른 배송 시간
(B) 고품질 사용자 인터페이스
(C) 24시간 이용 가능성
(D) 합리적인 가격

193 Chakra Indian Cuisine 웹 페이지에 발표되는 것은 무엇인가?
(A) 신규 지점
(B) 사업 제휴
(C) 구인 공고
(D) 곧 있을 보수 작업

194 Chakra Indian Cuisine에 관하여 무엇이 사실이겠는가?
(A) 유기농 음식만 판매한다.
(B) Thrive Fresh를 통해서만 이용할 수 있다.
(C) 20년 동안 영업해 왔다.
(D) 여러 지점이 있다.

195 Ms. Klein에 관하여 암시되는 것은 무엇인가?
(A) 엄격한 영양 식단을 따른다.
(B) Mr. Vernon의 동료이다.
(C) Williamsburg에 산다.
(D) 9월 29일에 행사를 열 것이다.

196-200번은 다음 안내 책자와 이메일들에 관한 문제입니다.

Nevardo's

Palm Springs 바로 외곽의 Cathedral 시의 사막 지역에 있는 Nevardo's는 그 어떤 종류의 세미나, 파티, 또는 예식에도 완벽한 장소를 제공합니다. (196) 매우 아름다운 Indian Canyon 자연 보호 구역의 끝자락에 위치한 이곳은 널찍한 파티오 라운지에서 바라보면 숨막히는 전망이 특징입니다.

내부에는, Coachella Room이 150명까지 수용할 수 있고, Agua Caliente 홀은 250명을 거뜬히 수용할 수 있습니다. (198) 콘퍼런스의 경우, Joshua Tree Room이 최대 75명의 단체까지 소화하며, 혹은 그 이상의 참여 인원은 새롭게 복원된 Lucille Ball 강당에 수용될 수 있는데, 이곳은 100석이 마련되어 있습니다. 뒤의 두 곳에는 성공적인 프레젠테이션이 가능하도록 최고급 시청각 장비가 완비되어 있습니다.

저희의 수상 경력에 빛나는 뷔페인 Nopalitos Grill에서는 환상적이고 다양한 멕시코 및 남서부 지역 요리를 제공합니다. 5월 5일에 저희의 특별 Cinco de Mayo 메뉴를 꼭 확인해 주세요!

자세한 내용은 저희 웹사이트 www.nevardos.com을 참조해 주시기 바랍니다.

저희는 일부 날짜에 Coachella Valley 업체들에게 30퍼센트 지역 협력 업체 특별 할인을 제공합니다. 자세한 내용은 760-555-1212로 전화해 주세요.

수신: Dan Chan <dchan@ charpentierfinancial.com>
발신: Fadila Boumaza <fboumaza@charpentierfinancial.com>
날짜: 1월 4일
제목: 합병 축하 행사 계획

Mr. Chan께,

저는 당신이 월요일 회의 때 언급한 장소인 Nevardo's를 확인해 봤습니다. 저희 기업 합병 파티 장소로 안성맞춤인 것 같습니다. 그 장소의 경치가 너무 좋고, 타지에서 참석하시는 분들까지 현재 200명이 넘는 많은 참석자가 있어, (198) 방문하시는 분들께 사막의 아름다움을 보여드릴 수 있는 좋은 기회입니다. 그곳에는 5월 11일, 5월 25일, 5월 27일에 이용 가능한 적당한 공간이 있습니다. 첫 번째 날짜는 저희 같은 지역 업체들에게 상당한 할인을 제공하는 날입니다. (200)

회계팀에 확인해 주시고, 그쪽에서 예약을 해도 좋다고 하면 저에게 알려 주세요. (197) 하지만 너무 지체하지 않는 게 좋을 것 같아요. 그곳은 이미 4월까지 예약이 찼고, 5월 빈자리들도 곧 마감될 거예요. (199)

감사합니다.

Fadila

수신: Fadila Boumaza <fboumaza@charpentierfinancial>
발신: Dan Chan <dchan@ charpentierfinancial>
날짜: 1월 4일
제목: 회신: 합병 축하 행사 계획

Fadila께,

Nevardo's에 관한 세부 내용들을 보내 주셔서 감사합니다. **회계 담당자와 논의한 후, 저희는 할인 금액을 적용받을 수 있는 날짜로 하는 걸로 결정했습니다.** (200) 이는 저희 예산에 도움이 될 거예요. Nevardo's에 전화해서 장소를 예약해 주세요.

Dan Chan
인사 총괄 임원, Charpentier 금융

---

196 안내 책자에 따르면, Nevardo's에 관하여 무엇이 사실인가?
　　(A) 강당을 리모델링할 계획이다.
　　(B) 식당 메뉴를 최근 업데이트했다.
　　(C) Palm Springs 시내에 위치한다.
　　(D) 다양한 종류의 행사에 적합하다.

197 Ms. Boumaza는 기업 합병 파티에 관하여 무엇을 언급하는가?
　　(A) 여러 날짜에 열릴 것이다.
　　(B) 다른 사람들의 승인을 필요로 한다.
　　(C) 비디오 프레젠테이션을 포함할 것이다.
　　(D) 연기될지도 모른다.

198 기업 합병 파티는 어디서 열리겠는가?
　　(A) Coachella Room에서
　　(B) Agua Caliente 홀에서
　　(C) Joshua Tree Room에서
　　(D) Lucille Ball 강당에서

199 Ms. Boumaza는 왜 걱정하는가?
　　(A) 행사장 비용이 인상될 수 있다.
　　(B) 장소가 너무 불편할 수 있다.
　　(C) 다수의 손님들이 참석을 확정하지 않았다.
　　(D) 가장 알맞은 공간을 이용할 수 없을 수도 있다.

200 Charpentier 금융의 파티는 언제 열리겠는가?
　　(A) 5월 5일에
　　(B) 5월 11일에
　　(C) 5월 25일에
　　(D) 5월 27일에

TEST 10

PART 5
P. 292

101 Mr. McKinney는 회의에서 기조연설을 하도록 선발됐지만, 그는 그 제안을 거절해야 했다.

102 Mr. Klein은 아주 사소하더라도 문법 오류를 포함한 입사 지원서에 대해 비판적이다.

103 Kraven 로스쿨에서는, 대학원생으로서의 자격 취득을 위해 6개월 간의 법률 관련 인턴십이 요구된다.

104 식당 손님들은 새로 문을 연 Merchant 식당에서 일년 내내 특별한 요리를 경험해 볼 수 있다.

105 Ms. Silva는 <Viewer Digest>에 실린 평론이 자신의 제작사의 최신 프로젝트에 긍정적인 홍보를 야기할 것이라고 생각한다.

106 이제 연례 점검이 완료되었으므로, 창고 작업반은 추가 선반의 설치를 시작할 수 있다.

107 Ms. Clarke는 인기 있는 선거 운동을 성공적으로 펼쳐서 시장으로 선출됐다.

108 Ms. Kim은 <Design Monthly>의 최신호에 새로운 광고 캠페인을 포함했다.

109 10월 3일부로, 모든 골드 레벨 승객은 무료로 항공편을 취소할 수 있다.

110 Mr. Zhukov는 자동차 리모콘이 제대로 작동하지 않아서 교체했다.

111 Ms. Romanov는 유통망을 늘림으로써 Robertson 사에서 소중한 재원이 되었다.

112 Ms. Park의 영화가 끝난 후, 관객들은 짧은 토론을 위해 남아 있도록 권장된다.

113 사무실 공간은 작업자들이 가구를 치우는 대로 청소될 것이다.

114 갑작스러운 배관 파열로 인해, 반경 200미터 이내 사업체들은 미처리 하수가 거리로 흘러 들어왔을 때 문을 닫아야만 했다.

115 Helvetica 사의 연구 개발 부서에서는 직원 혁신에 대해 보상을 제공한다.

116 SAC의 상주 예술가 프로그램은 다양한 분야의 예술가들을 하나로 모으기에, 서로 아이디어를 교환할 기회를 제공한다.

117 저희 최신 스마트폰 뱅킹 앱으로 예금 계좌를 개설할 수 있습니다.

118 모든 지역 사회 수영장은 운영되려면 공인 인명 구조원의 감시를 받아야 한다.

119 수석 연구 분석가는 최근 몇 년간 반도체 산업의 낮은 성장률에 대해 타당한 근거를 들어 우려를 표한다.

120 안전상의 이유로, Militech 공장의 방문객들은 현장에 있는 동안 에스코트를 받아야 한다.

121 음식 공급업체들은 모든 농산물 공급업자들의 호가를 평가하고 자신들의 메뉴에 맞는 것을 선택할 것이다.

122 새 Strom 스마트폰은 작은 디자인 덕분에 사용자의 주머니에 쉽게 들어갈 수 있다.

123 Ms. Denali는 업계에 대한 귀중한 통찰을 얻을 수 있도록 미디어 콘퍼런스에 참석할 예정이다.

124 자연사 박물관의 방문자 수는 신규 공룡 전시 개장 이후 급속히 증가했다.

125 손님들은 그들이 선호하는 7가지 각기 다른 종류의 과일이나 치즈가 포함된 무료 선물 바구니를 제공받는다.

126 Barrow Road 사는 자사 난방기가 업계 내 가장 에너지 효율이 좋다고 주장한다.

127 Kayleigh Traylor의 주문 제작 가구는 견고한 마호가니로 만들어진 후, 천연 광택을 위해 광택제로 코팅된다.

128 모든 관계자가 달리 합의하지 않았다면, 공휴일에 일하는 행상인들에게 금전적 보상이 제공될 것이다.

129 Wasson 사는 Huvier 주(州) 비즈니스 네트워크의 신임 받는 회원으로 공식 인정받게 되어 영광입니다.

130 채널 8의 '9시 뉴스'와의 방송 인터뷰에서 올해 최고 인기를 끈 스마트폰 애플리케이션의 개발자가 어떻게 'Cent Saver'의 아이디어를 제안해 내게 되었는지에 관해 이야기를 나눌 것이다.

PART 6
P. 295

131-134번은 다음 공지에 관한 문제입니다.

저희 온라인 영화 스트리밍 서비스 구독자로 **131. 계속 남아 있기**를 원하시면, 개인 정보를 업데이트해 주실 것을 요청드립니다. 진행하시려면, 저희 웹사이트로 가셔서 귀하의 인증 정보로 로그인하시고 **132. 계정** 페이지에 접속해 주세요. 페이지 상단에서, '내 정보' 탭을 선택하세요. '내 정보 업데이트' **133. 링크**를 클릭하셔서 양식을 작성해 주세요. **134. 허용 가능한 유형의 신분증을 이용해 개인 정보를 인증해 주셔야 할 것입니다.**

134 (A) 쾌적한 시청 경험을 위해 안정적인 인터넷 연결을 권장합니다.
(B) 새 공개물이 홈페이지에 표시될 것입니다.
(C) 휴가 기간은 고객 서비스 팀의 가용한 기간에 영향을 미칠 것입니다.
(D) 허용 가능한 신분증을 이용해 개인 정보를 인증해 주셔야 할 것입니다.

135-138번은 다음 이메일에 관한 문제입니다.

수신: Eric Bollman <ebollman@leihouma.com>
발신: Nancy Jensen <njensen@leihouma.com>
제목: 수도 문제
날짜: 9월 10일 월요일

Leihouma San Francisco 지점에 오신 것을 환영합니다. 저는 당신이 새로운 이곳 지점에 잘 적응하시도록 책임지고 있습니다.

135. 배관공을 부르셔야 한다는 메시지를 받았습니다. 욕실 개수대가 작동하지 않고 있다니 유감입니다. 수리 기사가 내일 오전 7시에 댁에 들르도록 일정을 잡아 놓았습니다만, 만약 **136.** 그 전에 문제가 해결된다면 취소될 수 있습니다. 이런 경우에는, 알려 주시기 바랍니다. 그리고, 기사가 댁에 방문하면, 반드시 **137.** 사원증을 보여 주시기 바랍니다.

사후 조치로 모든 것이 제대로 진행되고 있는지 확인하기 위해 내일 오전에 다시 **138.** 이메일로 연락드리겠습니다.

Nancy Jensen 드림
인사담당자

135 (A) Ichiro 배관사 직원이 다음 주 금요일 오후 3시에 당신과 만날 수 있습니다.
(B) 이 생수 배송 서비스는 첫 달 동안만 무료입니다.
(C) 식수의 품질은 크게 향상되었습니다.
(D) 배관공을 부르셔야 한다는 메시지를 받았습니다.

139-142번은 다음 기사에 관한 문제입니다.

DRG, 최고 지점 표창

Dawson Restaurant Group (DRG)에서 4월 한 달 동안 최고 실적을 기록한 지점을 표창했다. 4개월 **139.** 연속해서, 최우수상은 Appling 지점으로 돌아갔는데, 최고 매출을 달성하는 동시에 고객 만족도 조사에서 최고 점수를 기록했다. "이는 그곳의 **140.** 모두에 의해 이룬 대단한 성취입니다."라고 DRG 회장인 Colleen Payne이 말했다.

다른 두 지점 역시 주목받았다. Stewardson 지점은 이번 달 최대 매출 증가를 기록했고, Damascus 지점에서는 지역 사회 기금 모금 행사를 마련했다. **141.** 기금은 시청 건립에 사용됐다. "저희는 항상 지점들에 지역 사회를 돕도록 장려합니다."라고 Ms. Payne은 말했다. "지역 사회에 새로운 존재임 **142.** 에도 불구하고, Damascus 지점은 Rockbridge 시 개선을 위해 노력하고 있습니다."

141 (A) 내년에 새로운 지점이 문을 열 것이다.
(B) 기금은 시청 건립에 사용됐다.
(C) 직원 유지가 새로 주력해야 하는 부분이어야 한다.
(D) 고객들은 매력적인 디자인에 가장 이끌린다.

143-146번은 다음 이메일에 관한 문제입니다.

수신: staff@hbcentertainment.com
발신: Amanda Nguyen
제목: Jakob Bernal의 새로운 일자리
날짜: 11월 21일

안녕하세요.

저는 여러분께 Jakob Bernal이 HBC 엔터테인먼트를 떠나 Etten 미디어에 운영 담당 부사장으로 합류한다는 소식을 전하게 되어 매우 자랑스러우면서도 조금은 아쉽습니다. 이곳에서의 그의 **143.** 마지막 날은 1월 31일 목요일입니다.

Jakob은 우리 회사에서 근무하는 동안, 생산 부서에서 큰 역할을 해 왔습니다. 특히 지난 2년 동안, 그는 가장 크고 성공적인 프로젝트 몇 건을 이끌었습니다. 그 당시, 그는 HBC 엔터테인먼트의 많은 사람들과 돈독하고 지속적인 우정을 **144.** 쌓았습니다. 그의 열정과 리더십은 우리가 의지할 만한 것이었습니다. **145.** 저는 우리 모두가 그의 뛰어난 재치와 유머, 헌신을 그리워할 것이라고 확신합니다.

앞으로 며칠간 시간 나시면, Jakob에게 연락해 주세요. 우리 모두 그의 새로운 직책에 행운과 **146.** 지속적인 성공을 빌어 줬으면 합니다.

Amanda Nguyen 드림
CEO

145 (A) 그는 Khepri Faried와 협력하여 프로그램을 개발했습니다.
(B) 인사팀은 자격을 갖춘 후보자를 광범위하게 조사했습니다.
(C) 그는 이전에 DeBrunye 사의 미디어 디자인팀에서 근무했습니다.
(D) 저는 우리 모두가 그의 뛰어난 재치와 유머, 헌신을 그리워할 것이라고 확신합니다.

PART 7

P. 299

147-148번은 다음 공지에 관한 문제입니다.

Lend-a-Device 단체

집에 방치된 오래된 컴퓨터나 노트북이 있다면, 지금이 바로 변화를 만들 기회입니다. 저희는 사용하지 않는 전자 기기를 어려운 사람들에게 보내 새 생명을 얻도록 도와주는 자선 단체입니다. 당신의 먼지 쌓인 컴퓨터는 한 아이에게 귀중한 컴퓨터 기술을 배울 기회를 선사해 그야말로 인생을 바꿔줄 수도 있습니다. **(147)** 저희에게 555-1977로 전화해 주시면, 더 이상 필요하지 않는 기기를 가져가도록 조치해 드립니다. 날짜와 시간이 정해지면, 기기를 라벨을 붙인 상자에 넣어 집 밖에 놓아만 주시면, 저희 기사가 방문해 수거할 것입니다. **(148)** 변화도 일으키면서 집에 있는 잡동사니도 치워 보세요!

147 공지의 목적은 무엇인가?
(A) 제공된 서비스에 할인을 요청하기 위해
(B) 사람들에게 전자기기 기부를 독려하기 위해
(C) 새로운 정책 추가를 제안하기 위해
(D) 새로운 학습 형태를 광고하기 위해

148 사람들은 기기로 무엇을 하라고 요청받는가?
(A) 아직 작동하는지 확인해 달라고
(B) 참여 매장에 제출해 달라고
(C) 사양을 적어 달라고
(D) 상자에 넣어 달라고

149-150번은 다음 광고에 관한 문제입니다.

Belinda의 배니싱 크림

Belinda의 배니싱 크림의 공식 출시는 저희에게 엄청난 충격이었습니다. 연휴철이라 높은 수요를 예상하긴 했지만, 이렇게 빨리 매진될 줄은 예상하지 못했습니다. 좋은 소식은 저희가 내달 크림의 다음번 일괄 양을 받을 예정이며, **사전 주문하시는 모든 분께 특별 할인가로 제공해 드립니다.**(150)

크림은 알로에처럼 천연 원료에서만 추출했습니다. **다른 어떤 제품보다도 당신의 피부를 촉촉하게 하고 보호해 줄 것이라 보장합니다.**(149) 오늘 주문하셔서 직접 경험해 보세요!

---

149 어떤 종류의 제품이 홍보되고 있는가?
(A) 다이어트 보조제
(B) 헤어 제품
(C) 얼굴 제거제
(D) 피부 보습제

150 제품 가격에 관하여 언급된 것은 무엇인가?
(A) 조기 구매자에게 할인되었다.
(B) 다음 연휴철까지 변동되지 않을 것이다.
(C) 높은 수요로 인해 인상되었다.
(D) 일괄 양에 따라 달라질 것이다.

151-153번은 다음 광고에 관한 문제입니다.

Converge TravelFree를 이용하셔서 출장 시 간소하면서도 멋지게 여행하세요.

얇은 디자인의 Converge TravelFree에는 노트북과 회의록을 넣을 공간이 많습니다.(151) — [1] —. 내부는 널찍한 반면, 17 X 22 X 42cm 크기라서, 비행기 좌석 아래에 쉽게 들어갑니다. 바깥 층은 소지품을 보호하도록 완충 기능을 제공합니다. — [2] —. 게다가, 방수되는 재질로 만들어졌습니다. 이는 폭우가 쏟아져도 배낭과 소지품은 젖지 않는다는 뜻입니다.(152) 내부에는 비밀 공간도 있습니다.(153) — [3] —.

Converge 전 제품은 2년의 품질 보증서가 함께 제공됩니다. — [4] —. 결함을 발견하거나 가방이 파손된 경우, 구입 증명서를 지참하시고 가까운 Converge 매장을 방문하시면 제품을 교체해 드립니다.

---

151 Converge는 어떤 종류의 회사인가?
(A) 보안 제품 회사
(B) 배낭 제조사
(C) 가구 회사
(D) 헬스 기구 제조업체

152 Converge TravelFree에 관하여 언급된 것은 무엇인가?
(A) 비 오는 날씨에 사용하기 적합하다.
(B) 다양한 색상으로 나온다.
(C) 매년 할인을 자주 한다.
(D) 온라인으로 주문할 수 있다.

153 [1], [2], [3], [4]로 표시된 곳 중 다음 문장이 들어가기에 가장 적절한 곳은 어디인가?

"신용카드와 여권을 보관하기에 완벽한 공간이 됩니다."

(A) [1]
(B) [2]
(C) [3]
(D) [4]

154-156번은 다음 웹 페이지에 관한 문제입니다.

---

www.eonarmight.com

홈	소개	갤러리	소식 & 행사

EonarMight가 공개 상장 기업으로서 5주년을 맞이합니다. 지역 내 업계 1위 공유 오피스 제공업체임을 자랑스럽게 생각합니다. 기념 행사의 일환으로, 입주민 전원을 특별 행사에 초대합니다.(155D)

행사는 4월 23일 오후 6시 30분에 열립니다. 저희는 여러분이 내년에 보셨으면 하는 기대 사항을 공개할 예정입니다.(156) 또한 행사는 다른 입주민과 만나 인맥을 쌓는 기회가 될 것입니다. 이 행사는 입주민만을 대상으로 하기에, 저희는 깜짝 특별 선물을 계획해 놓았습니다.(155A) 게다가, 행사에 참석하는 입주민은 다음 달 임차료를 면제받게 됩니다.(155B) 이는 수년간 보내 주신 지속적인 성원에 대한 감사의 표시입니다.

행사 장소는 Arundel Banks 42번지에 있는 저희 본사가 될 것입니다. 주차는 길 건너 General 식료품점에 시간당 3달러의 특별 할인가로 이용하실 수 있습니다.(154)

---

154 EonarMight에 관하여 알 수 있는 것은 무엇인가?
(A) 슈퍼마켓 근처에 위치한다.
(B) 요금을 경쟁사보다 높게 책정한다.
(C) 매년 기념 행사를 개최한다.
(D) 최근 경영진에 변화가 있었다.

155 광고되고 있는 행사에 관하여 사실이 아닌 것은 무엇인가?
(A) 초대 전용 행사이다.
(B) 참석자에게 혜택을 제공할 것이다.
(C) 입장료 지불을 요한다.
(D) 중요한 날을 기념할 것이다.

156 두 번째 단락, 첫 번째 줄의 단어, "hope"와 의미상 가장 가까운 것은
(A) 탐내다
(B) 선호하다
(C) 바라다
(D) 기대하다

157-158번은 다음 문자메시지 대화문에 관한 문제입니다.

Owen Garcia [오후 3시 23분]
안녕하세요, Rosie. 다음 주 표지 기사에 대한 당신의 승인을 받으려고 했어요.(157)

Rosie Hunter [오후 3시 25분]
늦어서 정말 미안해요, Owen. 눈코 뜰 새 없이 바빴네요. 어젯밤에 겨우 봤는데, 아주 좋은 것 같아요! Byrd 사건에 대한 우리의 보도가 피드백을 아주 잘 받았어요.(157) 이번 사건은 전 국민의 관심을 끄는 것 같아요.

Owen Garcia [오후 3시 27분]
그럼요. 우리가 한 취재에 대한 감사 메일을 지금까지 그 어느 때보다 더 이 받고 있어요.

Rosie Hunter [오후 3시 31분]
그건 그 분석 정보에 대한 상승세를 설명하는 것이기도 하죠, 특히 젊은 사람들을 대상으로요.(158)

Owen Garcia [오후 3시 34분]
저도 그렇게 들었어요.(158) 제가 직접 그 자료를 검토하기를 고대하고 있어요.

Rosie Hunter [오후 3시 38분]
디지털 형식에 더 많은 이야기를 담으려고 바꿨던 게 정말 결실을 맺은 것 같습니다.(157)

---

157 작성자들은 어떤 업종에 종사하겠는가?
(A) 회계 법인
(B) 온라인 상점
(C) 식당
(D) 신문사

158 오후 3시 34분에, Mr. Garcia가 "저도 그렇게 들었습니다"라고 쓸 때, 그가 의미한 것은 무엇이겠는가?
(A) 그도 최근의 인기에 대해 알고 있다.
(B) 그는 방금 들은 정보를 확인하고 싶어 한다.
(C) 그는 상승세에 다른 이유가 있을지도 모른다고 생각한다.
(D) 그는 관리자들이 무언가를 잘못 이해했다고 생각한다.

159-160번은 다음 기사에 관한 문제입니다.

KAISER, 성공을 기리다

TOLEDO (9월 3일) — 국내 법률 서비스 회사인 Kaiser 파트너스는 회사 이력에 중요한 이정표를 기념하고 있다. Kaiser 파트너스는 올해 일하고 싶은 100대 기업을 선정했다. **Kaiser 파트너스는 원래 50여 년 전 Bill Chandler에 의해 설립되었는데, Bill Chandler는 이 회사를 이곳 Toledo에서 1인 운영 체제로 운영했다.** 20년 동안, Mr. Chandler는 기업 인수 전문가로 명성을 떨쳤다. [159]

그의 딸 Charlotte Chandler가 1980년에 그 회사에 들어갔을 때 비로소 회사는 기하급수적으로 성장하기 시작했다. **오늘날, 회사는 여전히 Chandler 가의 전유물이다.** [160] 그러나, 바로 작년, 회사는 처음으로 가족이 아닌 Tonya Bowen을 CEO로 임명했고, Ms. Chandler는 자신의 건강을 돌보기 위해 물러났다.

Kaiser 파트너스는 여전히 국내 기업 인수를 주력으로 하는 회사이지만, Ms. Bowen에 따르면, 법률 서비스의 모든 면에서 누구나 아는 기업이 될 계획이라고 한다.

159 기사의 주요 목적은 무엇인가?
(A) 회사 이력을 제공하기 위해
(B) 회사의 전망에 대해 예상하기 위해
(C) 법률 서비스의 영향에 대해 논의하기 위해
(D) 회사의 소유 구조를 비판하기 위해

160 현재 Kaiser 파트너스에 관하여 무엇이 사실인가?
(A) 가족이 운영하는 업체이다.
(B) Toledo에서는 법률 서비스만 제공했다.
(C) 해외에 본사를 두고 있다.
(D) 기업 인수를 하는 유일한 기업이다.

161-163번은 다음 이메일에 관한 문제입니다.

수신: mailinglist@topmall.com
발신: Top Mall
날짜: 10월 12일
제목: 공지

Top Mall은 온라인 소매업의 선두주자로, 전 세계 국가에 광범위한 제품을 제공합니다. **사이트의 높은 접속량으로 인해, 즐거운 쇼핑경험을 보장해 드릴 수 있도록 저희는 지속적으로 서버를 업그레이드해야 합니다.** [161]

따라서, 10월 15일 그리니치 표준시 기준 오전 3시부터 11시까지 이 업그레이드 작업을 수행하기 위해 웹사이트가 접속이 차단됩니다. [161] 이 시간 동안, 이용자는 상품 둘러보기, 장바구니 접속, 주문 변경 등을 하실 수 없습니다. 그러나, 저희 고객 서비스 직원이 문의 및 궁금한 사항들에 대해 영어와 중국어, 스페인어로 답변해 드릴 것입니다. [162] 유감스럽게도 이 과정을 진행하는 동안 일부 계정정보는 이용하지 못하실 수도 있습니다. 여러분의 이해에 감사드립니다.

10월 15일 이후에는, 고객 여러분의 쇼핑에 필요한 모든 것들을 훨씬 더 잘 도와드릴 수 있게 됩니다. **또한 Top Mall은 고객들에게 특가품과 판촉 행사에 관한 정보를 담은 주간 회보 제공을 시작합니다. 이메일로 바로 받아보시도록 온라인으로 신청하시면, 다음 구매 시 15퍼센트 할인받을 수 있는 할인 쿠폰도 보내 드립니다.** [163]

161 이메일은 왜 발송되었는가?
(A) 주문을 확인하기 위해
(B) 신제품을 소개하기 위해
(C) 시스템 업그레이드를 공지하기 위해
(D) 최신 배송 정보를 제공하기 위해

162 Top Mall에 관하여 알 수 있는 것은 무엇인가?
(A) 웹사이트 이용이 편리하다.
(B) 직원들이 여러 언어를 구사할 수 있다.
(C) 여러 국가에 지점이 있다.
(D) 고객들로부터 높은 평가를 받았다.

163 독자들은 어떻게 쿠폰을 받을 수 있는가?
(A) 온라인 서비스를 업그레이드해서
(B) 회보를 구독해서
(C) 일정 금액 이상을 써서
(D) 고객 서비스 직원과 통화해서

164-167번은 다음 온라인 채팅 대화문에 관한 문제입니다.

Rosemary Patton 오전 9시 12분
아시다시피, 지난주는 여러 가지 이유로 이례적이었어요. Perry에게 상황을 설명해 주자면, 사무실에 정체를 알 수 없는 병이 돌아, 직원 몇몇이 결근했어요. [165] 이게 무슨 의미인가 하면, 우리가 중요한 단계를 일부 놓치게 됐다는 겁니다. 특히, 소프트웨어 쪽은 진행이 상당히 더뎠어요. [164]

Santiago Morrison 오전 9시 14분
고객한테 연락을 받기까지 시간이 너무 오래 걸려서 뒤쳐졌어요. 저희가 작업을 시작하기 전에 일부 사양에 대해 확인을 받아야 해요. 일주일 넘게 답변을 기다리는 중이에요.

Rosemary Patton 오전 9시 16분
알았어요. 대화 내역 사본을 최대한 빨리 저에게 주세요. [166] 그렇게 하면, 답변을 더 빨리 안 주면 프로젝트가 위태로워진다고 제가 고객에게 알릴게요. [167]

Perry Frazier 오전 9시 18분
잠시 후에 수신함을 확인해 보세요, Rosemary. [166]/[167] 그리고, 저는 이 프로젝트에 동원 가능한 인력에 대해 우려를 표하려고 해요. 저희에게 일손이 부족한 것 같아요.

Faith Morris 오전 9시 20분
동의해요. 제가 인사부에 연락해서 개발자를 더 구해 달라고 했어요.

Santiago Morrison 오전 9시 22분
면접이 몇 건 잡혀 있어요. 후보자들이 아주 유망해 보여서, 희망적이에요.

Rosemary Patton 오전 9시 23분
잘됐네요. 채용 건이 어떻게 진행되고 있는지 제가 계속 알아볼게요. Santiago, 면접이 언젠지 알려 줄래요?

164 Ms. Patton의 직업은 무엇이겠는가?
(A) 고객 서비스 담당자
(B) 프로젝트 책임자
(C) 잡지 작가
(D) 상품 디자이너

165 Mr. Frazier에 관하여 암시되는 것은 무엇인가?

(A) 최근 직장을 바꿨다.

(B) 병에 걸렸다.

(C) 자리를 비웠었다.

(D) 다음 주에 휴가를 간다.

166 오전 9시 18분에, Mr. Frazier가 "잠시 후에 수신함을 확인해 보세요"라고 쓸 때 무엇을 의미하겠는가?

(A) Ms. Patton과의 회의 일정을 잡았다.

(B) 자신의 이메일에 접속할 수 없다.

(C) 오늘 회의에 늦을 예정이다.

(D) 요청받은 정보를 Ms. Patton에게 보내 줬다.

167 Ms. Patton은 업무를 마치기 전에 무엇을 하겠는가?

(A) 동료와 면접을 준비할 것이다.

(B) 일부 업무 규정을 개정할 것이다.

(C) 지연 가능성에 대해 고객에게 알릴 것이다.

(D) 기존 일정을 업데이트할 것이다.

168-171번은 다음 이메일에 관한 문제입니다.

수신: Dobob Punt 수신자 명단
발신: Sylvia Barton
제목: 최신 정보
날짜: 8월 24일

회원 여러분께,

Dobob Punt 복합 건물 보수 공사가 아직 진행 중입니다. **많은 구역이 공사 중이긴 하지만, 건물 일부 구역은 회원에게 개방되어 있습니다.**(168)

북 주차장은 다시 이용 가능하며, 경기장은 북쪽 문을 통해 입장 가능합니다.(168)/(169) 이렇게 하면 새로운 식당 구역으로 들어가게 됩니다. — [1] —. 현재 개방된 구역 명단은 입구에 있는 공지를 확인해 주세요.(170B)

— [2] —. **남쪽에 있는 실내 농구장도 완공되었습니다.**(171) 하지만, 다른 출입구가 공사 중인 관계로 북쪽 문을 통해서만 입장 가능합니다.(169)

드디어, 저희는 다음 달부터는 새로운 엔터테인먼트 층 작업을 시작합니다. 현재 계획으로는 영화관과 오락실을 짓는 것입니다. — [3] —. **추가할 시설 종류에 대해 아직 투표를 진행하는 중입니다. dobobpunt.com/newyear에서 투표해 주시기 바랍니다.**(170C)

월간 최신 정보가 웹사이트에 게시되어 있습니다. 저희 최신 계획을 읽어 보실 수 있고 진행 상황의 사진도 보실 수 있습니다. — [4] —. **추가 문의 사항이 있으신 경우, 저에게 알려 주시면 연락드리겠습니다.**(170A) Dobob Punt를 오래도록 이용해 주셔서 감사합니다.

Sylvia Barton 드림
커뮤니케이션 수석 고문

168 이메일의 목적은 무엇인가?

(A) 건물에서 일할 직원을 채용하기 위해

(B) 프로젝트의 최신 상황을 제공하기 위해

(C) 신규 시설의 승인을 발표하기 위해

(D) 예산 요청에 관한 의견을 조사하기 위해

169 Dobob Punt Complex에 관하여 알 수 있는 것은 무엇인가?

(A) 입구가 두 개 있다.

(B) 지역 내 최대 규모 건물이다.

(C) 비회원에게 입장료를 부과한다.

(D) 두 번째 복합 건물을 열 계획이다.

170 다음 중 이메일에서 회원들에게 해 달라고 요청하지 않은 것은 무엇인가?

(A) 질문해 달라고

(B) 공지를 확인해 달라고

(C) 결정에 대해 투표해 달라고

(D) 사진을 제출해 달라고

171 [1], [2], [3], [4]로 표시된 곳 중 다음 문장이 들어가기에 가장 적절한 곳은 어디인가?

"예상치 못한 지연에도 불구하고, 체육관이 완공되었습니다."

(A) [1]

(B) [2]

(C) [3]

(D) [4]

172-175번은 다음 웹 페이지에 관한 문제입니다.

Screech.com/il/italian

Italia Soleggiata
509 E Main
Libertyville, IL 60049
219-999-2218
영업시간: 매일 오후 12시 – 오후 11시 (일부 공휴일 제외)

추천 86%

테이블을 예약하시려면, 식당 웹사이트(www.italiasoleggiata/reservations)를 방문하십시오. 특별 행사나 준비가 필요하시면, 정규 영업시간에 전화해 주세요. **대규모 인원(최대 30명)의 경우, East 다이닝 룸을 예약할 수 있지만, 보증금을 지불하셔야 합니다.**(173)

| 평가 | 메뉴 | 지도에서 찾기 |

Barry Evans 추천
이 식당에 관해 많이 들었는데, 정말 기대했던 대로였습니다. 긴 테이블 대기 시간을 제외하면, 정말 좋은 식사 경험이었습니다. **뭘 주문할지 고민했는데, 담당 웨이터가 매우 사려 깊었고 도움이 되는 추천을 해 줬습니다.**(172) 그리스식 샐러드는 최고였고,(175) 식사와 함께 올리브 한 접시가 무료로 나왔습니다. 정말 따뜻한 곳입니다!

Kim Gordon 추천
음식이 맛있었고,(175) 의외로 채식주의 메뉴가 많았습니다. 하지만 실내 장식은 정말 좀 바꿔야겠어요. 너무 구식입니다.

Sheila Rajneesh Jr. *비추천*
음식의 품질이 훌륭했지만,(175) 모든 사람들이 말하는 것만큼 특별하지는 않았습니다. 위치가 시내에서 멀고, 대부분 메뉴는 독창적이지 않습니다. 멀리까지 간 보람도 없고, 물론 돈을 쓴 보람도 없었습니다.

Dave Lynch 강력 추천
최고 수준의 식당입니다. 싸지는 않지만, **제 생일 파티를 하기에 완벽한 곳이었어요. 모두 East 다이닝 룸의 아름다운 수준을 보고 감동하였습니다.**(173) 무엇을 주문하든 후회하지 않을 겁니다. **메뉴 전체가 환상적입니다.**(175)

Paul Mulhouse 추천
멋진 식사였어요. 이 식당에서 사무실 크리스마스 파티 음식을 공급받았습니다. **직원들이 여기 와 있는 동안 정말 많이 신경 써 주어서,**(174) 빠르게 모두에게 서비스해 주었고 **이 지역 최고의 이탈리아 요리**(175)도 먹을 수 있었습니다.

172 Barry Evans는 Italia Soleggiata의 무엇을 가장 좋아했는가?
(A) 식당의 인테리어
(B) 채식주의 선택 사항의 다양함
(C) 훌륭한 고객 서비스
(D) 할인 쿠폰

173 Dave Lynch가 한 예약에 관하여 무엇이 사실이겠는가?
(A) 보증금이 필요했다.
(B) 웹사이트에서 이루어졌다.
(C) 밤 11시 이후에 이루어졌다.
(D) 할인을 받을 수 있었다.

174 Italia Soleggiata에 관하여 알 수 있는 것은 무엇인가?
(A) 출장 뷔페 서비스를 제공한다.
(B) 시내 지점을 열 것이다.
(C) 연중 무휴로 운영된다.
(D) 이탈리아 음식만 제공한다.

175 모든 평가자들은 식당의 어떤 면에 동의하는가?
(A) 요리의 맛
(B) 장식의 우수함
(C) 널찍한 주차장
(D) 저렴한 메뉴

176-180번은 다음 이메일과 공지에 관한 문제입니다.

수신: employees@bellingercorp.com
발신: Petra Stojakovic <petras@bellingercorp.com>
제목: 주차 공간 재배정
날짜: 4월 22일 **(179)**

직원 여러분께 알려 드립니다.

이 이메일로 Bellinger 사의 신규 R&D 시설 공사가 4월 29일에 시작됨을 다시 알려드립니다. **(176)**

4월 27일부터, J와 K 주차장은 완공 예정일인 7월 9일까지 이용하실 수 없습니다. **(176)/(179)** J와 K 주차장에 배정된 직원 여러분은 방문자 주차장에 주차할 수 있는 임시 '방문자' 주차증을 받게 됩니다. **(177)** 시설 관리부에서 내일 정오까지 이 주차증을 자리로 가져다 드릴 것입니다. 주차증을 차량 조수석 앞 유리에 놓아 주십시오.

J와 K 주차장으로 이어지는 도로는 공사장 출입로 제작으로 인해 폐쇄될 것입니다. 또한, 보안 사무실과 회원의 주 출입구도 폐쇄됩니다. 두 장소에 모두 대체 출입구를 사용하실 수 있을 것입니다. **(178)**

유입되는 차량 수를 줄일 수 있도록, 급한 용무가 아니면 이들 구역을 피해 줄 것을 요청드립니다. **(178)** 잊지 마세요, 임시 출입구를 사용하실 때는 페인트로 표시된 통로만을 이용해 주시기 바랍니다.

협조해 주셔서 감사합니다.

Petra Stojakovic 드림
시설 관리부

BELLINGER 사 빌딩 안내 데스크에 오신 것을 환영합니다.

중요 공지:
J와 K 주차장은 8월 1일까지 폐쇄됩니다. (179)

이들 주차장으로 배정되었는데 임시 주차증을 받지 못한 직원들은 가급적 조속히 보안 사무실을 방문해야 합니다. 사원증과 자동차 등록증이 필요합니다.

공사 현장이나 적하 구역과 같은 지정 작업 구역 근처에 주차된 차량은 견인 대상입니다. **(180)** 정당한 허가증 없이 주차장에 세워진 차량에는 하루 30달러의 벌금이 부과될 것입니다.

직원들이 여러분을 도와 드립니다.

176 일부 주차장이 왜 폐쇄되어 있는가?
(A) 방문자만 이용할 수 있게 된다.
(B) 청소 및 다시 페인트칠하는 작업이 진행 중이다.
(C) 곧 공사가 시작된다.
(D) 회사가 그곳을 행사에 사용할 것이다.

177 이메일에 따르면, 누가 임시 주차증을 받을 것인가?
(A) 평소 J와 K 주차장에 주차하는 사람들
(B) R&D 시설을 견학하는 사람들
(C) Bellinger 사 입사 면접을 보는 사람들
(D) 시설 관리부에 신청한 사람들

178 직원들은 왜 보안 사무실 방문을 피하려고 해야 하는가?
(A) 방문객이 안내 데스크를 이용할 수 있도록
(B) 보안 직원들이 점검을 실시할 수 있도록
(C) 정원을 즐길 수 있도록
(D) 교통량을 줄일 수 있도록

179 4월 22일에 이메일이 발송된 이후 무엇이 바뀌었는가?
(A) 이용할 수 없는 주차장 종류
(B) 일부 주차장을 이용할 수 없는 기간
(C) 직원들이 주차증을 받는 시점
(D) 주차증이 놓여야 하는 위치

180 공지에 따르면, 직원 차량은 왜 견인될 수 있는가?
(A) 7월 9일 이후에 주차장에 세워진 경우
(B) 적하 구역 옆에 주차된 경우
(C) 주차증이 없는 경우
(D) 방문자 주차장에 주차된 경우

181-185번은 다음 보도 자료와 이메일에 관한 문제입니다.

보도 자료
연락처: media@ropavieja.com

Phoenix, 3월 15일 – Ropavieja Retailers는 6월 1일까지 80개 지점에 700명의 신입 직원을 배치하기를 희망하며 다음 주에 춘계 신입 채용을 시작한다고 밝혔다. **(181)** Ropavieja는 전 지점에 판매 사원과 계산 직원을 증원하려고 한다. 이 소매 체인은 교육비 지원이나 보육 같은 복리 후생과 더불어 보수가 좋기로 유명하다.

일부 도시의 Ropavieja 지점에서는 4월 매주 수요일 저녁 지역 관리자들이 진행하는 설명회도 개최할 것이다. **(183)/(185)** 참석자들은 개별 면접을 통해 회사에 관해 질문하고 채용 기회에 대해 이야기할 기회를 얻게 된다. 설명회 자리를 예약하려면, 3월 22일까지 recruit@ropavieja.com으로 이메일을 보내야 한다. **(183)** 전체 구인 목록을 보려면, www.ropavieja.com을 방문하면 된다.

Ropavieja는 20년 전 Tucson 시내에 작은 상점으로 시작했다. 현재는 북미 전역에 지점이 있으며 앞으로 몇 주 이내 California의 El Centro에 하나를 더 오픈할 예정이다. **(182)**

수신: Steve Henry <shenry@bkmail.com>
발신: Brad Narukawa <narukawa@ropavieja.com>
제목: 세부 사항
날짜: 4월 10일

Mr. Henry께,

지난주 수요일 저녁에 만나서 반가웠습니다.(185) 그날의 만남을 토대로, 다시 만나서 남부 California에서 영업 부장으로 일할 가능성에 관해 논의하고 싶습니다. 저희 영업 담당 이사인 Letty Cantu도 면접에 참석하실 겁니다.

4월 12일 오후에 시간 괜찮으신가요?(184) (505) 555-1212로 저에게 전화주셔서 확인 부탁드립니다.

Brad Narukawa 드림(185)

---

181 보도 자료에 따르면, Ropavieja Retailers는 곧 무엇을 시작할 것인가?
(A) 신제품 홍보
(B) 대규모 채용 활동
(C) 회사 합병
(D) 이사회 선거

182 Ropavieja Retailers에 관하여 암시되는 것은 무엇인가?
(A) 회장이 사임할 것이다.
(B) 예산이 삭감될 것이다.
(C) 최초 매장이 California에 있다.
(D) 사업이 성장하고 있다.

183 수요일 저녁 행사에 관심 있는 사람들은 무엇을 해야 하는가?
(A) 예약을 해야 한다
(B) 양식을 다운로드해야 한다
(C) 회사 본사를 방문해야 한다
(D) 교육에 관한 정보를 조사해야 한다

184 이메일의 목적은 무엇인가?
(A) 신규 서비스를 홍보하기 위해
(B) 프로젝트 일정을 논의하기 위해
(C) 곧 있을 할인 행사를 알리기 위해
(D) 시간 약속을 잡기 위해

185 Brad Narukawa에 관하여 암시되는 것은 무엇인가?
(A) El Centro에서 태어났다.
(B) 최근에 Ropavieja Retailers에 채용되었다.
(C) 지역 관리자다.
(D) 신규 지점으로 옮겨갈 것이다.

186-190번은 다음 이메일, 웹 페이지, 기사에 관한 문제입니다.

수신: Mildred Roberson
발신: Perry Barrett
날짜: 3월 21일
제목: 사무실 변경

Mildred, 당신이 이메일에서 아주 흥미로운 포인트를 제기해 주셨어요. 제가 이 일대 임대료가 계속 오르는 게 걱정이었거든요. 그렇게 높은 요금을 계속 지불하는 게 정말 말이 안 돼요, 특히나 우리가 재택근무로 방향을 전환하는 추세잖아요. (186) 우리는 고급 지역에 사무실이 필요하지 않아요. **차라리 Renburton 시내에 머무르면서 임대료를 최저가로 내는 편이 낫겠어요.**(187) 더 많은 인재를 영입하려면 높은 급여로 지불할 돈을 저축해야 해요.

이주에 대해 우려되는 게 있긴 해요. 현재 위치에서 벗어난다면, 그게 우리 회사의 위신에 영향을 미치게 될지 궁금해요. Renburton 내 최고층 타워에 사무실이 있었던 게 과거에 저희에게 큰 효과를 발휘했잖아요. 임대료에 경비를 절감하는 것이 평판에 손해보게 될 가능성을 감당할 만한 가치가 있는지 제가 가늠해 봐야 해요. 이때 만나서 이 문제에 대해 자세히 논의합시다.

Perry

---

http://www.ozair.com/betterliving
이용 가능한 사무실 건물

Argosy Close 385번지
Penrose 내 가장 오래된 건물에 머무르면서 역사의 일부가 되는 경험을 누리세요. 인근 고속도로 이용이 용이하고 대중교통을 이용할 수 있습니다.

Wessex Courtyard 16번지
한 층을 이용 가능. 대규모 사업체에 적합. 임대 계약을 하시면 경영진에 전용 주차 공간이 제공됩니다.

Stonefield Road 97번지
빈 공간이 많은 신축 건물. 1층에 카페테리아가 생길 계획입니다. **수많은 신규 업체들과 교류할 최고의 기회입니다.**(189)

Crescent Street 45번지
Renburton의 중심가에 위치.(187) 도심 전망이 돋보이는 5층입니다. 쇼핑몰 바로 맞은편에 위치합니다. 지하철까지 도보 이용 가능 거리입니다.

Grigg Lane 879번지
시 경계 바로 옆에 위치. 수많은 교외 지역에 인접해 통근하기에 아주 좋습니다. 버스 정류장뿐만 아니라 이용 가능한 인근 주차장도 많습니다.

잘나가는 Renburton

RENBURTON (9월 25일) — **지역 내 사업 급증으로 계속 늘어만 가는 임대료에도 불구하고, 시에서는 계속해서 사업을 유치 및 유지해 오고 있다.** 지역 내 머무르며 얻는 이득이 막대한 비용보다 더 큰 것은 분명해 보인다.(188)

지난 5년간 Renburton 지역에 머물러 온 사업체인 Fizdale Designs의 사업주와 이야기를 나눴다. 사업주 Perry Barrett은 지역 내 머무르기로 한 결정에 대해 이야기했다.

"임대료가 감당할 수 없게 되자, 사무실을 다른 곳으로 옮기려고 논의했습니다."라고 Barrett은 말했다. "결국에는 눈부신 경제 성장이 한창인 Renburton에 머무르는 비용으로는 적은 액수라고 결정했습니다. 게다가, 저희 직원을 상당수가 이곳에서 자라서, 떠나는 것은 꿈도 꾸지 않을 것입니다."

Fizdale Designs는 최근 Renburton 내에서 사무실을 옮기기로 결정했다. Barrett에 따르면, 이는 전략적인 결정이었다.

"**저희가 새로운 고객을 유치해야 한다는 것을 깨달았어요. 엄청 많은 새로운 사업체들이 생겨나고 있고, 그들과 가까워지고 싶어요.**(189)"라고 Barrett이 말했다. "**저희는 처음부터 같은 고객과 쭉 함께했어요.**(190) 이들 고객은 규모가 크고 확실히 자리 잡은 기업들이에요. 그들은 아주 좋지만, 저희는 다양한 고객들과 일하고 싶기도 합니다."

---

186 이메일의 목적은 무엇인가?
(A) 보류 중인 변경 사항에 대한 긴급성을 전하기 위해
(B) 이전 가능성에 대해 논의하기 위해
(C) 신규 프로젝트에 대한 피드백을 요청하기 위해
(D) 신규 관리 시스템에 대해 문의하기 위해

187 Crescent Street 45번지의 어떤 특징이 Mr. Barrett의 요건을 충족하겠는가?
(A) 고속도로 접근성
(B) 시설
(C) 비용
(D) 위치

188 기사는 Renburton에 관하여 무엇을 언급하는가?
(A) 최근 몇 년간 경제가 번영하고 있다.
(B) 신규 사업체에 대한 세금 혜택이 후하다.
(C) 건물들의 보수 기한이 지났다.
(D) 경제 잡지에 실렸었다.

189 Fizdale Designs에서 어느 지역을 선택했겠는가?
(A) Argosy Close 385번지
(B) Wessex Courtyard 16번지
(C) Stonefield Road 97번지
(D) Crescent Street 45번지

190 기사는 Fizdale Designs의 고객에 관하여 무엇을 암시하는가?
(A) 다른 회사보다 더 높은 금액을 지불하는 편이다.
(B) Fizdale Designs의 사무실을 자주 방문하지 않는다.
(C) Fizdale Designs와 오래도록 함께해 왔다.
(D) Renburton 지역에 위치한다.

191-195번은 다음 웹 페이지, 이메일, 회람에 관한 문제입니다.

---

http://www.hepsonmattresses.com
Elysian 연구소 지식 포럼

4월 22일: 인터넷을 기반으로 한 마케팅 캠페인으로 얻는 통찰[191]
— 수석 마케팅 분석가 Gladys Chandler와 함께합니다

5월 8일: 소비자에게 울림을 주는 것은 메시지인가, 색상인가?[191]
— Borgen Limited의 총괄 책임자 Lynette Hopkins와 함께합니다

5월 17일: 목표 인구층 관찰하기: 효과적으로 조사하는 법[191]/[194]
— 제품 출시 전문가 Elisa Wheeler와 함께합니다.[194]

6월 2일: 기억하기 쉬운 광고 음악의 비결[191]
— Ingram Associates의 대표이사 Franklin Guerrero와 함께합니다

한 쌍 또는 한 팀으로 등록하시면 모두에게 등록비 할인을 제공해 드립니다.[192] 더 자세한 내용은 오늘 저희 웹사이트를 방문해 주세요.

수신: ewheeler@launchpad.com
발신: Calm Waves Air
날짜: 5월 28일
제목: 항공편 확정 및 여행 일정

Ms. Wheeler께,

Calm Waves Air를 선택해 주셔서 감사합니다. 현재 항공편이 확정되었으며, 세부내용은 아래와 같습니다.

출발: 6월 21일

항공편	출발	도착[195]
185	Baltimore, 오전 8시 50분	Denver, 오후 12시 43분
760	Denver, 오후 2시 10분	**Seattle,[195]** 오후 4시 46분

출발: 6월 24일

항공편	출발[195]	도착
241	**Seattle,[195]** 오전 7시 25분	Oklahoma City, 오전 11시 13분
697	Oklahoma City, 오후 1시 08분	Baltimore, 오후 6시 02분

회람

수신: Kavelock 전 직원
발신: Marjorie Ellis, 전략 실장
날짜: 6월 19일
제목: 회신: 보고서

얼마 전 Elysian 지식 포럼에서 훌륭한 프레젠테이션을 해 주셨던 Elisa Wheeler가 이번 주에 방문할 예정입니다. 그녀는 처음에 했던 강연을 바탕으로 그 개념들이 Kavelock에 어떻게 적용될 수 있는지 설명해 줄 것입니다.[194]/[195] 이를 고려해, 우리가 Cataria에 계획했던 모든 일을 Ms. Wheeler의 방문 이후로 유예했으면 합니다. 대신에, 한 명도 빠짐없이 온라인으로 제공되는 그녀의 강연을 시청해 주세요.[193] 그렇게 하면, 우리가 할 질문 내용을 미리 생각해 놓을 수 있습니다.

191 모든 웨비나에서 다루는 보편적인 주제는 무엇인가?
(A) 자료 수집
(B) 제품 설계
(C) 효율적인 실무
(D) 광고 전략

192 웹 페이지에 따르면, 참가자는 할인을 받기 위해 무엇을 할 수 있는가?
(A) 단체로 등록할 수 있다
(B) 연사를 지정할 수 있다
(C) 행사에 일찍 등록할 수 있다
(D) 웨비나를 여러 개 구입할 수 있다

193 회람의 한 가지 목적은 무엇인가?
(A) 자원 연사를 요청하기 위해
(B) 기념 행사 일정을 정하기 위해
(C) 일부 업무 순위를 다시 정하기 위해
(D) 제품에 대한 피드백을 수집하기 위해

194 Kavelock의 다가올 행사의 주제는 무엇이겠는가?
(A) 조사 실시하기
(B) 비용 구조 최적화하기
(C) 부동산 확보하기
(D) 인터넷 광고

195 Kavelock는 어디에 위치하겠는가?
(A) Baltimore에
(B) Denver에
(C) Seattle에
(D) Oklahoma City에

196-200번은 다음 이메일, 전단지, 일정표에 관한 문제입니다.

발신: Julian Kojima <julian@maddux.com>
수신: Christine Walters <christine@maddux.com>
날짜: 4월 30일 (197)
제목: 팀워크 행사

Christine께,

잘하고 계시리라 믿습니다. 처음에는 모든 걸 다 따라가는 게 다소 힘들 수 있지만, 곧 익숙해지실 거라 믿습니다. **매년 이맘때, 저희 관리팀 직원이 전사 차원의 행사를 준비합니다.(196)** 2월 면접 때 이 이야기를 나눈 걸로 알고 있어요.(196)/(197) 지난 몇 년간, 저희는 여러 가지 중에서도 축구 경기를 보러 갔고, 국립 공원에서 등산을 한 적이 있어요. 업무 외적으로 서로 알게 되는 좋은 기회입니다.

올해는, 콘서트에 가면 좋을 것 같습니다. 많은 직원들이 음악 광팬이고 Leeper Pavilion에서 열리는 야외 콘서트 시리즈에 관해 이야기해 왔어요. 평일에 하는 콘서트여야 할 거고, 재즈 공연이어야 해요.(200) 우리는 올해 예산으로 400달러가 있어요. 그리고 가격을 훑어보니, 전 직원에게 티켓을 제공하기에 충분할 거 같아요.(199)

도움이 필요하면, Scott이 당신을 도와줄 수 있어요. 그가 예전에 행사 준비하는 걸 도왔었거든요.(196)

Julian Kojima 드림
사장, Maddux 산업

---

*Leeper Pavilion*에서 기억에 남을 저녁 시간을 함께하세요

대규모 단체의 경우 콘서트 티켓을 할인가에 구입할 수 있습니다. 12장 이상 구입 시 할인이 시작되고, 많으면 많을수록 좋습니다!(198) 보너스로, 귀하의 단체에게는 조기 입장과 무료 다과가 제공되며, 무대 뒤에서 연주자들을 만날 수 있는 VIP 입장권을 받을 수 있는 경연에 응모됩니다.

단체 요금
- 12매 240달러
- **25매 375달러(199)**
- 50매 650달러
- 100매 1,200달러

문의 사항이 있으시면, 219-555-5040으로 전화나 문자 주세요.

Leeper Pavilion의 봄
5월 콘서트 일정표

연주자	날짜	요일	장르	시간
Merrion-Clark 앙상블	5월 11일	토요일	재즈	오후 4시 30분
Hill Street Seven	5월 16일 (200)	목요일(200)	재즈(200)	오후 7시
Marcia Barton 5중주	5월 26일	일요일	클래식	오후 2시
Elkhart 교향악단	5월 29일	수요일	클래식	오후 8시

티켓은 현재 www.leeperpavilion.gov/concertseries에서 구입할 수 있습니다.

---

196 Mr. Kojima가 Ms. Walters에게 이메일을 보낸 주된 이유는 무엇인가?
(A) 그녀를 팀워크 하이킹에 초대하기 위해
(B) 새로운 파일링 프로토콜을 소개하기 위해
(C) 그녀에게 행사 준비를 지시하기 위해
(D) 그녀에게 자신의 곧 있을 휴가를 알려 주기 위해

197 이메일은 Ms. Walters에 관하여 무엇을 암시하는가?
(A) Maddux에 최근 고용되었다.
(B) 신규 프로젝트 착수를 위해 재배치될 것이다.
(C) Leeper Pavilion에서 하는 공연에 참석했었다.
(D) 재즈 음악 팬이다.

198 전단지에 따르면, 티켓 대량 구입의 장점은 무엇인가?
(A) 더 낮은 티켓 가격
(B) VIP석
(C) 매점 할인
(D) 선물 가방

199 Maddux 산업의 직원 수는 몇 명이겠는가?
(A) 12명
(B) 25명
(C) 50명
(D) 100명

200 Maddux 산업은 어떤 날짜에 행사를 개최할 것인가?
(A) 5월 11일
(B) 5월 16일
(C) 5월 26일
(D) 5월 29일